An Introduction to Positive Political Theory

Prentice-Hall Contemporary Political Theory Series
David Easton, *Editor*

An Introduction to Positive Political Theory

WILLIAM H. RIKER and PETER C. ORDESHOOK

University of Rochester   *Carnegie-Mellon University*

PRENTICE-HALL, INC., Englewood Cliffs, New Jersey

Library of Congress Cataloging in Publication Data

RIKER, WILLIAM H.
  An introduction to positive politcal theory.

  Includes bibliographies.
  1. Political science—Methodology. 2. Political
science—Mathematical models. I. ORDESHOOK, PETER C.,
joint author. II. Title.
JA73.R48   320'01'8   72–2512
ISBN 0-13-493064-9

© 1973 by Prentice-Hall, Inc., Englewood Cliffs, New Jersey

10 9 8 7 6 5 4 3 2 1

Printed in the United States of America

PRENTICE-HALL INTERNATIONAL, INC., *London*
PRENTICE-HALL OF AUSTRALIA, PTY. LTD., *Sydney*
PRENTICE-HALL OF CANADA LTD., *Toronto*
PRENTICE-HALL OF INDIA PRIVATE LIMITED, *New Delhi*
PRENTICE-HALL OF JAPAN, INC., *Tokyo*

*To our parents
who led us to learn*

Contents

Preface

Most science starts out as investigation of the properties of obviously important features of the real world. It is wholly empirical in tone, inductive in method, and commonsensical in organization. As the knowledge of properties increases, however, it becomes increasingly difficult both to organize knowledge and to plan further investigation. The sheer bulk of the sentences and the relationships among them discourage further inductive work and make it hard to evaluate the significance of new discoveries. At this point in the history of science, scholars begin to theorize, subsuming much empirical detail under abstract sentences, and generating models as simplifications of the complexity of the real world—simplifications that presumably explain the most significant features. The scientific method changes from the purely inductive to include the deductive as well. It then becomes just as important to generate and test out new theories as to investigate obvious phenomena. And the organization of the science now is based on the arcane knowledge of the scientist, not on the appreciation of the common reader.

Political science is now entering this stage. It is beginning to proliferate new theories, new bases for empirical investigation, and new forms of organization of knowledge. It is even beginning to be deductive in method.

This book is intended to introduce some of this development for students at the junior-senior and graduate levels. Its emphasis is on recently developed theory and, as the adjective "positive" indicates, on theory of an axiomatic, deductive type. So far as we know it is the first attempt to systematize such theory and we know that, as a first attempt, it is not sufficient. In a field as rapidly developing as this one, surely many revisions of ideas in this book will follow. We hope mainly that our work will encourage others to participate in this development.

This book was written during time provided by a grant from the National Science Foundation. We thank the Foundation and its officers very much for their financial and moral support of this enterprise.

We have had the help of many colleagues and students in developing the ideas of this book. Unfortunately, we cannot name them all, but the following have helped especially with comments and criticism, although we have not always accepted their suggestions: Kenneth Shepsle, Steven Brams, Otto Davis, Mancur Olson, Jr., E. Wood Kelley, William T. Bluhm, Howard Rosenthal, and Jan Siccama. We have had the help also of many secretaries who have cheerfully retyped successive drafts: Nancy Henley, Harriet Levinson, Marjorie Grabek, Janice Brown, and, especially, Marguerite Gross. And finally each of us thanks his wife for her understanding of our long preoccupation with this volume.

WILLIAM H. RIKER
PETER C. ORDESHOOK

1

Introduction:
The Meaning of Politics

Here we begin to build a positive theory of politics, and so it seems appropriate to offer first an explanation of what we think politics is. We do not have the temerity to utter a formal definition; but we can indicate the kinds of things we intend to talk about, without, of course, claiming that these are all of politics or even that we have arranged them in proper order of importance.

We start with people, who, for our purposes, are bundles of opinions about nature and of preferences about the alternatives nature offers them. We assume that these people behave as if they sort out and logically arrange the preferences in their bundles. Furthermore, we assume that they are able to use the sorted bundles for decisions so that, when faced with a choice, they can choose as directed by their preferences. Thus, the people in our model have will and reason and use these abilities to make decisions.

Some of the preferences in each bundle concern essentially private things, such as the dishes to be chosen from a given menu. Such private preferences are typically of small relevance to politics, though of primary relevance to economics. (Indeed, one of the main differences between the activity of politics and the activity of economics is the kind of preferences each involves.) Other preferences in the bundles, however, are essentially public in the sense that the realization of them concerns not only their holders but also other people. In this event, the realization of one person's preference may depend crucially on the denial of another's chance to realize his. For example, if our neighbor wants to live in a theocracy, he cannot be satisfied unless we also live in a theocracy—and we may not want to do so. Or again, our neighbor may, for the sake of breathing pure air, wish to require that every car owner eliminate hydrocarbons from his car's exhaust, but the realization of our neighbor's wish is not possible without our expenditure of money, which we may be unwilling to undertake.

The preferences that involve other people in their realization, and especially the preferences that are realized only by cooperating with others or by denying the chances of others to achieve their preferences, are the raw material of politics. The activity of politics is the selection of the preference of some person (or the potential preference of some person) to be the choice of society. And of course, the interest in choosing preferences for society is to exploit the authority and force of society in realizing these choices over the objections of those whose preferences must remain unrealized. So, if our neighbor's preferences are selected, we may be forced, in spite of our initial resistance, to live in a theocracy and breathe pure air.

We have thus at least three central processes in politics: the selection of society's preferences, the enforcement of the choices that revealed them, and, finally, the production of goals or outputs that embody the choices. The art of politics is the actual selection, enforcement, and production. And this is the mystery in the art: that we start with the contradictory preferences of many and end up with a single bundle of more or less realized choices for the whole. Admittedly, this singularity is somewhat spurious, because citizens may differ in their perception of the bundle. Nevertheless, in a legal sense and for most practical purposes, there is just one bundle of social choices, which is the mystery of politics. How this bundle comes to be, what it can be, and what it is—these are the unknowns which the science of politics is intended to reveal.

In speaking of the choices for society we have been careful to avoid suggesting that the preferences of individuals are somehow aggregated to reveal a preference for society. True, this is one possible method of selection, but it is far from the only one. And at this initial stage we wish to keep the discussion as general as possible. Consequently, we leave it undecided whether the selection is autocratic so that the preference of one prominent person becomes the social choice or whether the selection is democratic in the sense that, by some process of aggregation, individual preferences are amalgamated into a social preference. We exclude only this possibility: that social choice is wholly independent of individual preference.[1] With Rousseau, we can imagine the circumstance where everybody desires one alternative (which is, when aggregated, "the will of all") and yet the alternative adopted or normatively suggested for society ("the general will") is quite different, perhaps contradictory, and thus independent of individual desires. Unlike Rousseau, we cannot conceive of this imaginary event occurring, simply because we cannot conceive of any institutions that might bring it about. So we exclude the possibility that social choices are independent of individual preferences. Note, however, that this does not exclude the possibility that the revealed preference of society is different from

[1]We do not, of course, exclude the case where a preferred mechanism of choice (e.g., a market) produces one particular result (among many) that no one likes.

all preferences of individuals, just as a mean may be different from all the numbers averaged. Similarly, we do not exclude the possibility that social preferences are established by natural or divine law. For such to occur there must be an interpreter—judge or bishop, philosopher or monarch—and of course the social choice is his preference as expressed in his interpretation. (These interpreters, said Hobbes, wish "as . . . in play after trump is turned, to use for trump on every occasion, that suite whereof they have most in their hand.")

In our understanding of politics we impose, however, no other restrictions on the process of revealing social preferences aside from the one just mentioned, that they depend on at least one individual. In particular, we do not require that the political process be consciously directed toward the goal of generating social choices. Of course, it often is conscious—and indeed the study of politics has often been restricted to such consciously legislative processes as:

(a) elections and representative lawmaking, in which social choice is aggregated from the individual preferences (indistinctly) revealed in election;
(b) autocratic fiat, in which social choice is discovered by the autocrat's introspection;
(c) common-law judgment, in which social choice is arrived at by the judges in their marginal adjustments of past social choices to suit present circumstances;
(d) oligarchic agreement, in which social choice is the common interest of some subgroup (e.g., a party) in the society.

As against these processes, which are consciously intended to arrive at a social choice, is the market, which operates ostensibly to realize individual preferences (i.e., by means of facilitating exchange) but which in the large also arrives at a social choice or total allocation of goods and services. It has been common for political scientists to regard the market process and market-generated social preferences as peculiarly the domain of economics. But this restriction we do not admit, because much of the work of the consciously legislative institutions is directed to the revision of allocations made unconsciously by the market. Left to itself and in the absence of effects on non-participating persons, the perfectly competitive market is invariably efficient in that it produces Pareto-optimal allocations of resources. (This means that, for a given allocation in comparison with all possible allocations, none of the other possible ones is at least as good for everybody and better for some. Thus, if an allocation is Pareto-optimal, no alternative allocation can improve things for everybody. Any improvement for one must come at the expense of another.) Pareto-optimal allocations are thus minimally unanimous, but they may, however, be highly undesirable in the preferences of individuals, even though economically efficient.

Thus, for example, if the initial distribution of income is "unfair" in the judgment of someone, the market optimum does not disturb the unfairness; typically it magnifies it. Thus, if person 1 has $1000 and person 2 has $100 and if jointly they gain $10 through trade, then, given certain special rules, a Pareto-optimal allocation may be such that 1 gets $9.50 and 2 gets $0.50 of the gain. Thus, while 2 is better off absolutely, he has lost relatively. Or, for another example, the market might yield a social choice regarded by everyone as inferior to a choice that could be produced by some alternative allocative mechanism. Such inferior outcomes are commonly associated with the presence of external effects (e.g., where a third party is hurt by a transaction between two others). For example, if, in distributing autos, it is cheaper for both buyer and seller to attach inefficient mufflers, an externality occurs because the air is polluted by seventy million poor exhaust systems, even though it is to the long-run advantage of the owners of every one of the seventy million cars to eliminate air pollution. The market thus fails to account adequately for this external effect (that is, air pollution), and a social preference for bad air is revealed. The conscious legislative institutions are then employed, as they may also be in the case of "unfair" distributions of income, to modify these market-generated and individually undesired social preferences.

In general, the market weights participants according to the initial distribution of resources and encourages accounting for individual outlays only. Hence in the institutions of conscious reevaluation, one can weight people as one wishes and take account of joint costs, which is what these institutions are for. Inasmuch as the generation of social preferences thus begins in the market and ends in the legislative institutions where market outcomes may be modified, it seems reasonable to include both kinds of social allocation devices in the realm of politics.

By discussing first social choice and revealed social preference, we do not mean to relegate enforcement to a secondary position. It is true that American political science has tended to lay great stress on the formation of opinion, the construction of constitutions, the operation of representative institutions, the selection of rulers, the formation of policy and the social allocation of resources, and a variety of other processes having to do with the selection of social preferences. This is, however, simply an accident of taste, one which, in our opinion, much deserves to be redressed.

It means little to society to select a preference that, however definitively chosen, is nevertheless unenforceable. Suppose, for example, in a democratic society, a large majority individually prefers high employment to low employment. Suppose further this same majority prefers the state of affairs where every employed person receives at least a minimum wage to the state of affairs where some do not. Then, the enforcement of the preference in the second pair (i.e., a minimum wage) clearly denies the realization of the preference in the first pair (i.e., high employment), provided that there is more than one employer and that either employers can easily move to another jurisdiction or goods can easily be imported. If either provision occurs, then, to enforce a minimum wage is to invite employers to move or to import, thus lowering employment. In such circumstances, if one assumes that high employment is preferred to a minimum wage, then a minimum wage is a strictly unenforceable social preference, however strong the affirmation by which it was chosen. And if it is unenforceable, there is not much point to choosing it.

It is, we believe, typical, as in the case just alluded to, that considerations of enforcement are necessarily evaluated in the process of selection. Thus, for example, a majority of individuals in a society might be willing to adopt a social preference for prohibiting the use of alcohol, if the cost of enforcement were at most a million dollars annually. But if the cost is in fact a billion dollars annually, this same majority might be totally unwilling to prefer prohibition. It seems quite likely that the revelation of actual costs between 1920 and 1933 was what brought a reversal of judgment on prohibition in the United States.

Of course, enforcement is no problem if the society is unanimous in its selection of social preference. As we indicate, however, it is just exactly those individual preferences that can be satisfied only by the denial of the realization of the preferences of other individuals which are the essential raw material of politics. Consequently, it is typical of politics that men disagree. And when men disagree, whatever the social preference chosen, there is a defeated minority that can be expected to continue to seek to realize its defeated preferences in spite of the social decision. Hence, also, enforcement of a social preference is typically essential if the preference is to be realized. Without continued enforcement, the reconstruction amendments were evaded in the South for nearly a hundred years. And so it is quite generally: enforcement is the necessary companion of selection. In our analysis, we hope to place it as a theory of regulation alongside a theory of social choice.

In the discussion so far we have emphasized the processes of choice and regulation rather than their outputs. This is not particularly strange, since quite a bit of twentieth-century social science has the same tone. We deplore this tone, however, and point out that it cannot be maintained. No serious study of processes can ignore their culminations, whether we call them outputs or products, effects, social choices, revealed social preferences, outcomes, values, imputations, or whatever.

Indeed, the main social justification for studying processes is that we thereby learn how the processes shape and restrict the outputs. As in all studies of the causes of things, an apparent interest in the cause is an ultimate interest in the effect. Typically in science, knowledge of a cause permits us to produce an effect—that is, to predict and manipulate. In the science of politics this is somewhat less frequently the case because the idiosyncratic element in the cause of the gross social events of politics is much more significant than in the cause of the minute physical events of particle interaction. In both kinds of science, one generalizes about the process, fully aware, of course, that specific effects result both from the general features of the process and from the particular interaction of particular movers and actors within the general framework.

Even though the unique element in social causation renders prediction and manipulation difficult, still we generalize about political processes for the same reasons we generalize about any natural processes: to produce, insofar as we can, particular effects. In Aristotelian terms, politics is a practical science, aimed at using knowledge to manipulate the world. And since it is effects or outputs that we are interested in, any description of politics that fails to highlight them is profoundly mistaken.

In the same way that the problems of enforcement enter into the selection of social preferences, so also do problems of producing outputs. Thus, for example, in choosing a preference for national defense against external attack, many people might be influenced by the nature of the production function for defense, by the mix of nuclear and conventional weapons, by the efficiency of the military organization, and so on. Furthermore, the problem of production is invariably present in the selection of preference. Even if a society is unanimous about a goal, so that no problem of enforcement exists, the problem of production is still present. Consequently, we again emphasize that descriptions of politics must highlight outputs.

Two interrelated questions arise about social choice, the outputs of politics. First we need to know, for a given process, what choices can occur—the class of the possible. Second we need to know what choices ought to be made—the class of the desirable. So long as politics is a practical science, neither question can be neglected. Suppose we seek to select the desirable while neglecting the possible. Then we run the risk, if the desired outcome is not also possible, of opting for utopia, i.e., nowhere. This is the error committed, for example, by communists, who expect that the individual will, when group and individual goals are in conflict, support group goals. Suppose, conversely, we seek to select the possible while neglecting the desirable. Then we run the risk, if the possible outcome is not also desired, of confusing ideology with science. This is the error committed, for example, by social Darwinists, who, finding that a particular economy produces a particular distribution of income, identify that outcome as inevitable and desirable, without comprehending that the economy may be made to produce quite different results with different ground rules. In a science, however, one wishes to avoid both ideology and utopia; hence it is important to look for outcomes that are both desirable and possible.

Currently there is much controversy over whether the science of politics has room for "ought" sentences. Some wish to concentrate exclusively on normative imperatives, others to banish them altogether. Both sides err, for in a practical science the moral and the descriptive go, as we have shown, hand in hand.

To summarize, we believe that politics at least includes the selection, enforcement, realization (or production), and evaluation of social choice. The science of politics thus explains the mystery of how social choice evolves out of individual preference. We are not certain, however, how we should treat individual preference, whether as part of the system or as the undefined elementary particle. Our uncertainty is based on the uncertainty of the facts. Some features of individual preference can be explained in terms of feedback from social choice. Children are trained to prefer the institutions of their society because those people who accept the existing social choice also provide the civic education. Such individual preferences are in a loop with social choice and as such are surely a part of politics. Other individual preferences, however, are independent of preexisting social choice and hence are truly unexplainable in terms of a political science. So we conclude that sometimes politics involves the development of individual preference and sometimes not. But it always involves at least the selection, enforcement, and evaluation of social choice.

SUGGESTIONS FOR FURTHER READING

These suggestions, which are appended to each chapter, are intended to help those whose first acquaintance with formal theory comes with this book. Hence they are not complete bibliographies, nor are they even listings of the research materials on which we have relied. (For those who want to go to those materials, we have indicated directions in our footnotes.) Rather these suggestions are intended to direct readers to other explanatory works which may complement the explanations we offer.

Though brief, Chapter 1 has the ambitious intent of defining politics and hence political science in order to lay the basis for a theory of politics. It owes a good deal, in inspiration though not in content, to DAVID EASTON, *The Political System* (New York: Knopf, 1953). Except for DUNCAN BLACK, *The Theory of Committees and Elections* (Cambridge: Cambridge University Press, 1958) and ANTHONY DOWNS, *An Economic Theory of Democracy* (New York: Harper & Brothers, 1957), very few other writers have interpreted politics as the selection and enforcement of preferences for society. Consequently, there is little other literature to which to refer the readers. They may, however, find it instructive to compare our approach with the very different approach of recent writers in the behavioral tradition: HEINZ EULAU, *The Behavioral Persuasion* (New York: Random House, Inc., 1962) and KARL DEUTSCH, *The Nerves of Government* (New York: Free Press, 1963).

2

The Assumption of Rationality

THE FUNCTION OF THE ASSUMPTION

Previously we started with the assumption that people behave as if they arranged their preferences in some logical pattern. Such behavior we describe as *rational*, and the assumption of rational behavior thus becomes an essential prerequisite to our theory. Because it is so important, we begin with an analysis and explication of the notion of rationality.

By way of introduction we note that, for a political science and a political theory, we need general sentences—that is, sentences describing the properties of classes of events as distinct from particular sentences describing unique events. General sentences, especially those about classes that will have new members in the future, are the form in which we utter descriptive laws of nature and scientific predictions. So at the beginning of the discussion of a science it is important to identify the kind of grammar we shall be using. There are some observers of man and society who, however, refuse to use it and who are content to assemble information only in particular sentences. Poets, of course, are specialists at describing single significant moments and persons in precise and affectionate detail. Insofar as these moments and persons are like many others, particular sentences about them are quasi-generalizations. But since these sentences are presented as particulars, it is always unclear to what degree they are general. Similarly, some historians are collectors of gossip about the past. They occasionally attempt to dignify chronicles with the explanation that, since all events are unique, they cannot be classified and described in general sentences. But the implication that all members of a class must be identical in every respect is an elementary mistake in logic. A class includes

8

those things that have at least one common feature, and this fact in no way implies that its members are alike in all respects. Since the historicist position, by reason of its mistake in logic, denies the possibility of abstract thought, a theoretical and scientific understanding must reject it clearly at the outset. Instead we seek to describe and predict by classifying and by relating classes to each other, which is to say that we speak in general sentences.[1]

We can get to general sentences in two distinct ways: empirically, by observed regularity, and theoretically, by postulated regularity. Assume that, for the observer, the world is initially an undifferentiated mass. Then the process of abstraction by observation is simply the use of the (seemingly innate) ability of humans to abstract. One notices a common factor in otherwise dissimilar objects or events and then one classifies these objects or events together and uses the classes in descriptive or predictive sentences. Proverbs of all kinds, such as weather wisdom, fall into this category of general sentences. Generalizations about voting behavior and campaign strategy are typically of this empirical sort. Distinct from this simple, almost reflexive, kind of abstraction is the complicated process of abstraction based on postulated regularity. In this case there is assumed to be some reason for the regularity involved in a classification or a relation. Given an observed regularity, one accepts it as nonaccidental only if there is some sentence describing the motion or action of the regularity such that the sentence is a logically necessary deduction from a set of postulates. Indeed, theoretical descriptions or explanations amount to an assertion and, hopefully, a demonstration that an observed event cannot logically occur in any other way than the way it actually does occur.

To illustrate the difference between observed and postulated regularity, consider the observation of tosses of nine fair coins all of which show heads. By the empirical standard, this is a regularity and one is justified in the generalization that fair coins fall heads. From this, one would predict empirically that heads would show from the toss of a tenth fair coin. In a postulated regularity, however, there must be a reason for regularity or there is none. Since, in the now-conventional postulate of Western science, a coin is a mechanism without human or divine preference, there is no reason for it to fall heads more than tails. By the theoretical standard, the observed regularity of nine heads is simply the occurrence of one chance in 512—that is, simply fortuitous—and one really cannot generalize about these nine coins (unless, of course, we question the initial assumption of fairness and examine the possibility that the coins are biased). Contrasting with the empirical prediction, the best theoretical prediction is that the tenth coin will fall heads with a probability of one-half. These are quite different predictions, even though they concern the same (imaginary) experience. In the one case, regularity comes directly from the

---

[1]Lest it be thought that the extreme historicism described in this paragraph is a straw man, we call the reader's attention to Peter Winch, *The Idea of a Social Science* (New York: Humanities Press, Inc., 1958), where it is seriously argued that the mere fact of differences in the cultural context of words and institutions renders a general and objective social science impossible.

observation, which is taken at its face value; in the other case there is no regularity—even though one is in fact observed—because there is no reason for it.

When one is generalizing about the physical world, the conventional postulate is the mechanistic one; that is, we rule out vitalism, divine intervention, luck, witchcraft, and so on. When one is generalizing about the social world, however, where, clearly, the actors are vital, one can hardly rule out vitalism. Hence the postulate for regularity changes to a notion of the pursuit of goals; that is, we assume actors in society seek to attain their purposes. Persistence in this search, or "goal-directed behavior" to use the current jargon, is the substance of rationality. This is what we postulate to obtain that regularity which is desired for theory and hence for general sentences.

The postulate of rationality admits of regularity thus: At the beginning of observation, the world is—we assume as before—an undifferentiated mass of behavior. Because it is unexplained it is also universally random, so far as anyone knows. Vital agents are seen to behave, of course, but, in the absence of the postulate, any kind of behavior at all is to be anticipated. If one observes a man walking in a northerly direction, there is no more reason to suppose that a minute later he will still be walking north than there is to suppose he will be walking east, south, or west, just as in a table of random numbers there is no reason to expect any particular succession of digits. Once we postulate that agents seek goals, however, there is a rationale for behavior, and it is possible to say that an observed regularity is a necessary one because it involves the pursuit of a purpose, rather than random movement. Then, when we observe the man walking north and when we assume there is some purpose in his action, we can, in the absence of some event that might change his goal, predict with some assurance that he will continue to walk north.

To illustrate the effect of the assumption of rationality, consider the observation that in three specific elections people who believed the outcome would be close were more likely to vote than people who believed the outcome would not be close. So stated, there is nothing necessary about the relation, although it is an observed regularity over a fairly large number of observations. It may, however, be no more than random behavior and have the same standing in science as nine heads on nine tossed coins. On the basis of these observations alone, we would be as loath to predict that believers in a close outcome are especially likely to vote in the fourth election as to predict a head on the tenth toss. And we would be loath in each case for the same reason, viz., the absence of a rationale for the observed regularity.

Let us now, however, make the assumption that behavior is rational—an assumption which entails an attempt to gain a benefit. Since, in the case of voting, it turns out on close analysis that getting a benefit is logically related to breaking a tie, it follows that the closer an outcome appears to be, the greater the chance of benefit also appears. And the greater the chance of benefit, the greater also, by reason of the assumption of goal-directed behavior, the likelihood of voting. The relation between anticipated closeness and voting is, therefore, more than an accident; indeed, if people are rational, the relation must necessarily occur.[2] In this example the assumption of rationality promotes an observed regularity to a postulated regularity.

We can, however, offer an example of the opposite sort, where the assumption of rationality demotes an observed regularity to an accident. In the nineteen-forties in the United States it was commonly believed on the basis of repeated observation that increases in the proportion of citizens voting in an election favored the Democratic party or, stated another way, marginal voters tended to prefer Democrats. The reasons offered for this did not have to do with the pursuit of goals; rather they were simply assertions of further intuitively discovered (and hence not logically necessary) class inclusions, e.g., that marginal voters are poor and poor people tend to favor Democrats, and so on. The 1952 election, however, was both a great Democratic debacle and an election with very high turnout. This observation revealed the accidental nature of the previous empirical regularity. But it could have been as easily revealed by an analysis of goals that there was no good reason to associate marginality with Democratic preference. Instead such analysis would reveal that marginality is associated with very weak preference and hence with a tendency to accept the currently dominant preference whether it be Democratic or Republican.[3] Thus the assumption of rationality would demote an observed regularity to a chance event, as in the case of nine tosses and nine heads.

In any case, however, it is clear that the assumption of rationality and the assumption of mechanism play comparable roles in the explanation of the social and physical worlds. The mechanical assumption asserts that there is something about things that assures us they will (usually) move regularly, and the rationality assumption asserts that there is something about people that makes them behave (usually) in a regular way. In each case the function of science is to generalize about the regularities, although the task of social science is perhaps more difficult. Mechanical relationships are fairly straightforward—at least as they appear to us in contemporary science—and, so far as we have yet discovered, universal; purposeful behavior, however, is more difficult to understand and, furthermore, a larger proportion of social than of physical behavior may appear to be simply random.

It can thus be seen that the notion of rationality plays a fundamental role in social science. It is one of the ways by which we arrive at the regularity necessary for generalization. Whether or not it is better than simple observation is currently the subject of some discussion in political science, being a particular form of the old debate between inductive and deductive methods or between

[2]William H. Riker and Peter C. Ordeshook, "A Theory of the Calculus of Voting," *American Political Science Review,* vol. 62 (1968), pp. 25–42.

[3]Angus Campbell, Philip Converse, Warren Miller, and Donald Stokes, *Elections and the Political Order* (New York: Wiley, 1967), pp. 40–62.

radical empiricism and theoretical science.[4] As is apparent, we side with deductive methods and postulated regularity, largely because we believe them more efficient than their alternative. By the method of postulated regularity one can at least hope to avoid erroneous generalizations based on accident, like nine heads on nine tosses or marginal voters preferring Democrats, although one cannot avoid errors of observation that occur with either method. At the same time the method of postulated regularity is positively more efficient, because it permits the easy generation of hypotheses and offers a single parsimonious explanation of behavior. As against this efficiency, the method of observed regularity is *ad hoc*. No hypothesis can be derived without a set of prior observations, and every hypothesis is another kind of explanation. This often results in a myriad of noncontradictory hypotheses that need theory to bring them together.[5] Even if catalogued into hypotheses, behavior appears extraordinarily complex, when, with a simplifying and coordinating theory, much of the complexity disappears. On the practical grounds of efficiency, therefore, we prefer postulated regularity. Hence the notion of rationality must play an extremely important role in our theory of politics.

RATIONALITY AND GOALS

Rationality is the something we postulate in people that makes them behave in a regular way. And the essence of that something is that people relate their actions to their goals. The first step, then, in an explication of rationality is an explication of goal-related behavior.

To say that behavior is related to goals is to say it is purposeful. In the field of cybernetics, where the notion of purpose is also all-important, Rosenbluth, Wiener, and Bigelow define purposeful behavior thus:

> *Active behavior may be subdivided into two classes: purposeless (or random) and purposeful. The term purposeful is meant to denote that the act or behavior may be interpreted as directed to the attainment of a goal—i.e., to a final condition in which the behaving object reaches a definite correlation to another object or event. Purposeless behavior then is that which is not interpreted as directed to a goal.*[6]

We identify rational behavior as a subset of purposeful behavior, a subset which satisfies other properties which we will discuss a few paragraphs hence.

To say that rational behavior is purposeful is not, however, to specify the

---

[4]The debate is, unfortunately, poorly conducted. At a recent professional meeting there were many papers on "empirical theory," which phrase makes no more sense than, for example, "incorporeal body."

[5]As an example see Lester Milbrath, *Political Participation* (Skokie, Ill.: Rand McNally, 1965), where many unrelated hypotheses about political participation are proved by the method of observed regularity. We do not criticize this careful work, but rather point to the confusion to which multiple hypotheses lead.

[6]A. Rosenbluth, N. Wiener, and V. Bigelow, "Behavior, Purpose and Teleology," *Philosophy of Science*, vol. 10 (1943), p. 18.

goals. And in this respect our analysis of rationality differs from the tradition of political rationalism. In the nineteenth and twentieth centuries most writers have been so preoccupied with discussions à la Nietzsche and Freud of whether or not men are rational that it is easy to forget how rarely this question had been raised in the earlier tradition. Almost all writers on society up to that time had assumed that men are rational and goal-pursuing. The questions they then debated about were what the goals ought to be. The goals of a whole political order we call justice, and under that name it is, traditionally, the main subject of political philosophy. Some writers, like Plato and Rousseau, have sought to prescribe a general goal for the whole society—in the one case, hierarchical order; and in the other, a general will. Other writers, such as Machiavelli and the other advisors to princes, have sought to prescribe goals for rulers—in the one case, the unification of Italy by fair means or foul; and in most other cases, the imposition of a Christian polity. Still others, such as Hobbes and natural-law theorists, have sought to prescribe a goal for individuals—in the one case to obey in order to receive protection, and in the others to obey in order to do right. As even these three foregoing sentences are perhaps enough to indicate, the main problem of traditional political rationalism has been to prescribe goals for everybody in the social order.

This is, however, not our intention. As socially participant humans, we of course have prescriptions for goals for ourselves and others; and our feelings about these goals may occasionally creep into these pages. But description is antecedent to prescription, at least in logic if not in fact. Our interest is initially in good description, and so we ignore prescription until we know what might be prescribed for.

In the beginning of observation, the social world is, for the observer, an undifferentiated mass of random action. In order to understand and explain this world, we separate out portions of the action in a variety of ways. One way is to separate out a regularity and its temporal and spatial antecedent, i.e., a cause. Another way, which is probably the scientifically more useful, is to separate out a regularity and give it a theoretical explanation, i.e., a logically necessary and sufficient reason.[7] In the case of human action, to give a reason is to demonstrate that the actors acted *as if* they were seeking to achieve a parti-

---

[7] In strict usage causes are, of course, necessary and sufficient conditions, so that there is no distinction between these methods. [See William H. Riker, "Events and Situations," *Journal of Philosophy*, vol. 54 (1957), pp. 57–70, and "Causes of Events," *ibid.*, vol. 55 (1959), pp. 281–292).] But today, when social scientists often speak of multiple causes of an event and even identify cause with a beta-weight in a regression equation, the equivalence is not readily apparent in scientific usage. If a cause is a necessary and sufficient condition, there is at most one cause of anything. (Viz.: Suppose two conditions are each shown to be sufficient. Then, at least one of them is not necessary. So if a cause exists, it is unique.) In proper usage, the partial causes of contemporary social science are no more than marginal influences on outcomes. So long as the notion of cause is confused by social scientists, it is probably worthwhile to distinguish between, on the one side, causal explanations (that is, marginal influences popularly and crudely construed as cause), and on the other side, theoretical explanations (which are causal in the strict sense).

cular goal. For each such reason, we eliminate some of the apparent randomness in human behavior.[8]

The social scientist has two available procedures to discover reasons and eliminate randomness. We call them revealed preference or posited preference.[9] In the procedure of revealed preference, we assume initially that persons behave in accord with logical rules, e.g., transitivity in ordering. Applying these rules to choices, we then discover what goals must have existed in order to lead logically to these choices. Goals are therefore inferred from (a) actual choices and (b) assumptions about behavior. In this procedure rationality is assumed to be universal, and the question for research is the nature of the goals.

In the procedure of posited preference, we assume initially that an actor has a given goal (e.g., to win an election, to maximize profit) and we infer that behaving in accordance with rules of logic and this goal leads to particular choices. If such choices actually occur, then we further infer both that the actor actually does have the assumed goal and that he behaves in accord with rules of logic. If such choices do not occur, then we are at a loss to discover whether the fault lies in our attribution of logic or our attribution of goals.

We call the first method *revealed preference* (because we discover the goals from the choices) or *procedural rationality* (because the essential assumption is the universality of logical behavior, a procedural assumption). We call the second method *posited preference* (because we test out an assumed goal) or *substantive rationality* (because the goal itself is the essential assumption). Both procedures are devices to discover human goals; and the procedure of substantive rationality is, in addition, a method to discover whether or not goals and choices are logically related.

Which approach, revealed or posited preference, one uses is largely determined by the particular problem one is trying to solve. Indeed, all social science works back and forth between the two methods. In the study of behavior

---

[8]Perhaps we can clarify the whole process by putting the argument in semiformal terms. For a given universe of behavior, U, all behavior is initially described as random in an error term, ε. So, $U = \varepsilon_0$. Once a utility function, $u_i(x)$—which is a measure on preference—is fitted to some behavior, x, we have $U = u_1^1(x) + \varepsilon_1$. To achieve as complete an explanation as possible, additional or refined functions are fitted until ε is as small as is feasible, thus

$$U = u_1^n(x) + u_2^n(x) + \ldots + u_n^n(x) + \varepsilon_n.$$

One should note, however that there are some occasions in which random behavior is a part of rational behavior and cannot (and should not) be eliminated by the method of successive refinements of explanations. In some conflict situations an appropriate strategy is to behave in a truly random fashion, thereby completely hiding one's plans from an opponent by hiding them from oneself. When one is matching pennies, for example, or playing Stone, Paper, and Scissors, the best strategy is, as von Neumann and Morgenstern have so elegantly demonstrated, a randomized one [John von Neumann and Oskar Morgenstern, *The Theory of Games and Economic Behavior* (Princeton, N.J.: Princeton University Press, 1947).] It is probably also best in more serious and complex affairs of life such as fighting battles. In such circumstances, of course, the genuinely random behavior is nevertheless closely related to goals; indeed, such randomness is adopted as a means to a goal and as such is wholly rational.

[9]In another connection we have called them procedural and substantive rationality. See Peter C. Ordeshook, *Theory of the Electoral Process* (University of Rochester dissertation, 1969) chap. 1; and William H. Riker and William Zavoina, "Rational Behavior in Politics: Evidence from a Three Person Game," *American Political Science Review*, vol. 64(1970), pp. 48–60.

in organizations, for example, one posits for individuals the goal officially adopted for the organization and discovers that some behavior is well explained. In complicated decision problems of the sort now studied by such methods of systems analysis as game theory or linear programming, the goal posited is, of course, the official goal, such as making a profit, winning, and so on. The analyst then says to the decision maker, "If your goal is the official one, then your best choice of alternative actions is . . ." Turning game theory or systems analysis from a normative to a descriptive use, one posits that the decision maker in fact has the official goals, and then looks to see how much behavior is described by that assumption. If, as is often the case in microeconomics but seldom the case in the study of nonprofit organizations, it turns out that a large enough proportion of behavior is explained by this method to permit accurate predictions, then one can cease the description. That is, one has learned that the official goal is the operative goal. If not, however, one proceeds by means of revealed preference, in which one assumes only that behavior follows logically from goals and asks what structure of goals could have produced these choices. Then one discovers other goals motivating behavior—even, perhaps, private goals quite at odds with official ones. In either case, however, one has discovered goals.

In nineteenth-century economics it was common to assume an economic man who wished as a producer to maximize income and as a consumer to minimize cost. While most writers were probably aware that such a queer man as this never existed, still to suppose producers behaved in this way has turned out to be an adequate assumption for prediction. But as numerous economists from Veblen onwards have pointed out, it is not an adequate assumption with respect to consumers, where, besides cost minimization, many other goals (e.g., conspicuous consumption) may be involved. It has, therefore, turned out to be necessary to study consumption by the method of revealed preference. In the study of behavior in organizations, the famous Hawthorne experiment and its consequences display the same kind of change in methods. In that experiment the original assumption was that individual workers would work hard to achieve conventional goals such as higher pay and better working conditions. Since it turned out that the subjects worked just as hard when deprived of the stimulus of these goals, the researchers were no longer able to posit the conventional goals. Instead they assumed that subjects were maximizing something else and determined by a kind of elimination that the thing maximized was individual satisfaction with the group. They then constructed a new theory positing this satisfaction as a goal. Thus they moved from posited preference to revealed preference and back again.[10]

Although it is often thus necessary to move back and forth between methods, researchers often themselves become confused in the process. They posit a particular goal and then, if subjects do not maximize with respect to it, research-

[10]F. S. Roethlisberger and William J. Dickson, *Management and the Worker* (Cambridge, Mass.: Harvard University Press, 1939).

ers often infer that the behavior is irrational. It may, of course, be irrational—that is, purposeless. It usually turns out, however, that the subjects have merely not adopted the goal the researcher thinks they ought to.

It is thus that a kind of dictation about goals often slips back into the descriptive process. The researcher, having made a bad guess about subjects' goals, refuses to recognize his own failure and instead blames the subjects, calling them irrational. Our impression is that many attributions of irrationality are of this nature—i.e., a dispute about goals. Since we have no objective method to determine what goals are right or proper for a particular situation, we will avoid speaking of any person as irrational unless it seems clear that his behavior is indeed purposeless.

LOGICAL PROPERTIES OF RATIONAL BEHAVIOR

Purposeful action is the main element of the notion of rationality, but the way we comprehend the existence of purpose is from the existence of preference. That is, it is the preferential ordering of goals and outcomes that reveals the existence of purpose. Orderings are logical forms and have logical properties, and it is to an explanation of these properties that we now turn.

The relation of preference, call it P, among objects of the set N: $\{a, b, \ldots, n\}$ is:

(1) connected, i.e., either aPb or bPa, and
(2) transitive, i.e., if aPb and bPc, then aPc.

To say that preference is a connected relation is to say that, with respect to the persons who do the ordering, there is something to order. Suppose, to the contrary, there is no connection among objects in the minds of the subjects; then the objects are simply not comparable and there is no point to an attempted ordering. One would expect "inconsistent orderings" simply because subjects would have neither rationale nor motive to order properly. To avoid this difficulty, we must insist that N is not an arbitrary set but one among the members of which there is some subjective connection.

Many of the instances of apparently irrational behavior in the world arise because an observer believes a set is connected while the actors do not. Suppose there are two referenda propositions on a ballot, along with many others, and that informed persons agree these two are contradictory. If voters simultaneously approve both, are we to conclude that, for those who voted both yes or both no, the inconsistency is irrational? Not at all, for it seems likely that the voters simply do not care.[11] For them the set of these two referenda is not connected. While the constitution makers and proposition writers

[11]For a particularly good discussion of such a circumstance see John Mueller, "Voting on the Propositions: Ballot Patterns and Historical Trends in California," *American Political Science Review*, vol. 63 (1969), pp. 1197–1212.

probably expect voters to treat the set as connected, the voters are, of course, under no compulsion to do so and probably often do not.

Analogous to and probably derived from the distinction between a posited and a revealed goal is a distinction between posited and revealed connectedness. If observers posit connectedness, then, if subjects choose contradictorily, they are irrational; but if observers do not posit connectedness, then, if subjects choose contradictorily, they have simply revealed that the set of choices is not, for them, connected. On the other hand, if subjects choose consistently—in the example of referenda just discussed, either no-yes or yes-no—then they are rational by either the posited or revealed standard of connectedness.

The notion of transitivity is as acceptable intuitively as the notion of connectedness. Both are indispensable ingredients of the notion of an ordering. To say that preference is transitive is to say that the persons who arrange the members of a connected set can do so in at least an ordinal sequence: first, second, . . . , nth. And such an ordinal sequence is the essence of the idea of an ordering. To see the necessity of transitivity for an ordering, assume connectedness: then it is the case either that aPb or that bPa. Assume the former so that a stands unambiguously ahead of b in the ordering of a and b. Now, from the similar pair bPc and cPb, also assume the former so that b stands unambiguously ahead of c in the ordering. On this basis of assuming connectedness, we can write an order: first a, second b, third c; but this is ambiguous, for we have not determined the relation of a and c. Is aPc or cPa? If cPa, the ordinal sequence is destroyed, because c is ahead of a in first place. But c is also in fourth place thus: first c, second a, third b, fourth c. We do not know unambiguously which location c is in. Since cPa leads to a lack of order, we insist on aPc, which unambiguously orders c third in the sequence. Thus, having assumed connectedness, we have shown that, if we assume aPb and bPc, then the assumption of cPa renders ordering impossible. If ordering is to occur, we must assume aPc—and this is precisely the assumption of transitivity, i.e., if aPb and bPc, then aPc.

The assumption of transitivity is thus our guarantee that persons in the political model can arrange objects in order. Without this guarantee the notion of purpose would be itself in doubt, for it is difficult to imagine a choice among objects when it is uncertain that there is an ordinal sequence of preference among them.

As in the case of connectedness, many cases of apparently irrational behavior arise because an observer believes a set is preferentially ordered, while the actors do not. For example, in an often-cited experiment by Kenneth May, college freshman male math students, when asked their preferences among brides who had one property from each of the pairs: beautiful-ugly, smart-dumb, and rich-poor, replied in such a way that a large minority revealed intransitivities.[12] That is, they preferred, for example, a (a beautiful-smart-

[12]Kenneth May, "Intransitivity, Utility, and the Aggregation of Preference Patterns," *Econometrica*, vol. 22 (1953), pp. 1–13.

poor wife) to *b* (a beautiful-dumb-rich wife) and *b* to *c* (an ugly-smart-rich wife) and then perversely preferred *c* to *a*. Presumably some choosers were unable to order the set because they were confused about which criteria of desirability should dominate. Given the temporal and psychological distance of these subjects from the actual problem of choosing a wife, one should not be surprised at their failure to achieve transitivity even though they apparently believed that the set was connected.

Clyde Coombs has offered a persuasive explanation of the failure to attain transitivity in situations such as this.[13] Let a chooser have an ideal point for an attribute such as a shade of grey (as in Coombs' data) or properties of a wife (as in May's data). Set this ideal point on a unidimensional scale, thus dividing the scale into two parts. Then offer the chooser some choices between pairs of stimuli also on this scale. If both stimuli lie on the same side of the ideal point, call the pair unilateral. If they lie on opposite sides, call the pair bilateral. For triples of stimuli, there are three categories:

1. unilateral triples, in which all three are on the same side of the scale from the chooser's ideal;
2. bilateral adjacent triples, in which two adjacent stimuli in the ordered triple are on one side of the scale from the ideal and the third (either the first or last) is on the other side;
3. bilateral split triples, in which the first and last stimuli in the ordered triple are on one side of the scale from the ideal and the middle one is on the other.

Coombs argued (and his data supported his assertion) that most choosers would achieve transitivity with unilateral triples and bilateral split triples. In these cases, the location of the stimuli facilitates the recognition of distances from the ideal. But with bilateral adjacent triples, it is easy enough to compare the unilateral pair in them, but difficult to estimate the relative distances from the ideal of the members of this pair and the stimulus on the other side of the ideal. Hence one would expect intransitivity when the stimuli involve bilateral adjacent triples. The best one can say about such cases, it seems to us, is that they undoubtedly occur, so that surely some irrationality occurs in nature. On the other hand, Coombs' data concerns judgments of color. One wonders if he would have found as much error as he did if the data had concerned something important.

Again analogous to and logically derived from the distinction between posited and revealed goals is a distinction between posited and revealed transitivity. If one posits transitivity, then the ability of humans to order preferences is assumed to be absolute. If, on the other hand, one does not

[13]Clyde H. Coombs, *The Theory of Data* (New York: Wiley, 1964), pp. 80–121. See also his essay "On the Use of Inconsistency of Preferences in Psychological Measurement," *Journal of Experimental Psychology*, vol. 55 (1958), pp. 1–7.

posit transitivity, then what is revealed is the proportion of times that choosers actually do order preferences.

In any investigation of choice, it seems necessary either to posit goals or to posit transitivity. Indeed there is necessary reciprocation between them. If the experimenter assumes a goal for his subjects, then he discovers in the experiment whether or not they choose among alternatives consistently with respect to the given goal. If, on the other hand, the experimenter assumes that subjects are able to order transitively, then he discovers in the experiment what goals the subjects reveal in their choices among alternatives. Thus posited goals reveal transitive orderings and posited transitivity reveals preference. One cannot test both for goals and consistency at once. Research on rational behavior must move back and forth between these two approaches.

RATIONALITY AND CARDINAL ORDERING

It is an elementary requirement of rational behavior that one be able to order alternatives transitively. Often, indeed, rationality is defined as this simple ability.[14] Yet in many circumstances this is not an adequate definition. Consider the following problem of choice: Let the chooser have transitively ordered three outcomes, O_1, O_2, O_3, so that O_1 is preferred to O_2 and O_2 to O_3. Let the chooser have two alternatives of action, a_1 and a_2, such that a_1 gives him a chance p of obtaining O_1 and a chance $(1 - p)$ of obtaining O_3, while a_2 gives him O_2 for certain. Thus, alternative a_1 gives him a lottery on his best and worst outcome, while a_2 surely gives him his middling outcome. In this case the fact that the chooser has ordered his outcomes transitively is simply not enough basis for him to choose between a_1 and a_2. Even if he knows what p is, he still cannot choose unless he knows about how much he prefers O_1 to O_2.

Such circumstances of choice are common enough in the everyday world. For an example, consider the problem of the chairman of a political party which has a small majority of seats on a city council and which can be expected to lose its majority in the upcoming election. Suppose further that by appropriate redistricting (gerrymandering) it is possible to restructure the situation. Suppose further that the chairman has ordered the outcomes thus: O_1, to win a majority of seats; O_2, to win a large minority, sufficient to prevent the other party from passing by themselves (with a two-thirds vote) bond issues requiring an extraordinary (two-thirds) majority; and O_3, to win less than one-third of the seats. And suppose, finally, the chairman's judgment is that the possible gerrymanders, which would be aimed at his party's winning in each of a majority of districts by a small majority, may fail so that his party would lose in most districts. Thus a gerrymander, a_1, gives him O_1 with some probability p and O_3 with $(1 - p)$, while leaving the districts as they are gives him O_2

---

[14]Kenneth Arrow, *Social Choice and Individual Values*, 2d ed. (New York: Wiley, 1963), pp. 19–21.

almost for certain. The fact that the chairman prefers O_1 to O_2 and O_2 to O_3 is not enough to help him solve his problem rationally.

What he needs for the solution is some measure on his preferences, to be able to speak quantitatively and to say how much he prefers O_1 to O_2. So we assume that a measure on preference exists. Then, the chairman can order his preferences cardinally and he can say that the numerical value or utility of O_1 is an amount $U(O_1)$. The determination of his choice between a_1 and a_2 is then simple. He can calculate an expected value for the two alternatives and then choose that one with the higher expected value. Specifically, he can calculate expected values $E(a_i)$, thus:

$$E(a_1) = pU(O_1) + (1 - p)U(O_3),$$
$$E(a_2) = pU(O_2).$$

If $E(a_1) > E(a_2)$, the chairman chooses to gerrymander; if $E(a_2) > E(a_1)$, he does nothing; and if $E(a_1) = E(a_2)$, he flips a coin to choose between a_1 and a_2.

Whether or not it is possible to use a decision rule to choose that alternative which maximizes expected utility depends on whether or not people act as if it is possible to arrive at cardinal utility numbers, $U(O_i)$. Since the publication and scholarly acceptance of the second edition of von Neumann and Morgenstern's *The Theory of Games and Economic Behavior* (1947), the notion of cardinal measurement of utility has been generally accepted by economists. In an appendix to this chapter we point to some reasons for believing such measurement is not as fully applicable to political problems as economic ones. Nevertheless, we believe that in the range of everyday political judgment—involving problems such as that facing the chairman who may or may not gerrymander—cardinal utility is just as applicable in politics as in economics. For that reason we believe it is usually possible to define rationality in terms of expected utility: rational behavior is, then, the choice of that alternative which maximizes expected utility.

CRITICISM OF EXPECTED UTILITY

It is an open question whether or not enough people actually behave frequently enough in accordance with the principle of maximizing expected utility to render this principle a parsimonious description of nature. That economic theories based on the principle work as descriptions in at least the economic department of life is presumptive evidence of the usefulness generally of the principle. Nevertheless, the debate about expected utility continues. One widespread criticism of the principle comes from the psychoanalytic tradition in which the guilt-sprung desire for self-punishment and ultimately for death is supposed to drive persons to do self-frustrating things. Hence, it is said to follow that actions taken do not maximize and may even minimize expected utility. This is a somewhat befuddled position, which we will try to straighten out by considering the following cases:

1. *People do desire to frustrate themselves and do.* Presumably self-frustration is the main goal as indicated by their action. Hence, to frustrate and even to kill themselves is utility-maximizing with respect to the goal. Such behavior may be bizarre, but it does not violate the principle of maximizing expected utility.
2. *People do not desire to frustrate themselves and do not.* Here there is no problem because no apparent nonmaximizing behavior occurs.
3. *People do desire to frustrate themselves but do not.* This is the case wherein people wish simultaneously to maximize and to minimize. In the confusion, maximizing occurs and there is again no problem.
4. *People do not desire to frustrate themselves but nevertheless do so.* When there is a dispute about goals, the only external evidence of what people want is what people do. We assume therefore that this is really case 1, with the difference that people say they do not want to do what they are in fact doing. How much credence can be given to their protestations? If these can be believed, then a true paradox occurs; but if they cannot be believed, then we have case 1 without question. So the problem is: when words and actions differ, which is to be given credence? The behaviorist position is to believe the inferences from action. Psychoanalysts appear to believe the words, although they—most acutely of all scholars—ought to be accustomed to lies.

Since this criticism of the principle of maximizing expected utility occurs only in the fourth case and since it seems to be based on no more than undue gullibility, we can dismiss this particular doubt about the principle as unwarranted.

A more plausible criticism of the principle is that offered in support of the notion of satisficing.[15] It is said that in the complex environment of decision making in the real world, choosers are not aware of all possible alternatives, so that they choose not the best alternative but rather a satisfactory one. They do not maximize, but satisfy. This argument does not deny—and indeed assumes—that people calculate in the manner postulated in the expected-utility principle. Rather it raises a question about the set of alternatives over which the calculation takes place. The possible sets over which one might maximize or satisfy are:

   A: in a given situation, the set of alternatives consciously evaluated by the decision maker, and

   B: in the same situation, the set of alternatives, probably infinite in number, noticed by any observer (i.e., including God).

Note that *A* is a subset of *B;* i.e., some alternatives in *B* may not be in *A.* We may call these sets the decision maker's set and God's set, respectively. With reference to the decision maker's set, the maximizing and satisficing rules for decision are identical. While some enthusiasts have misinterpreted his argument

---

[15]Herbert Simon, *Models of Man* (New York: Wiley, 1957), pp. 241 ff.

as antirational, in fact Professor Simon does not suppose that, when better and worse alternatives are clearly available to the chooser, he may reject the better for the worse just because the worse is satisfactory. Hence, over set A, the maximizing agent and the satisficing one make the same choice. The problem concerns the choice over God's set. Here the rule of satisficing leads to the choice of the same alternative as in the decision maker's set. But what happens with the rule of maximizing? If this rule is interpreted as if the chooser had perfect information, then the choice may differ from that in A; but if the rule is interpreted as if the chooser were merely human, then again the choice in the two sets is the same for both rules. It is apparent, therefore, that the principle of satisficing is distinguishable from the principle of maximizing only if, under the latter, perfect information is assumed. Otherwise the principles are identical.

The question is, therefore, whether or not one ought to include perfect information in the rule of maximizing expected utility. We think not. Here are two quite distinct axioms: (i) that choosers seek to maximize expected utility and (ii) that choosers have perfect information. Except in the writings of the theorists of "satisficing," these two axioms have not been put together. There is no apparent reason to do so. Not only does putting them together occasion ambiguity in the sense that sets A and B are confused, but also the attribution of perfect information sets an unreasonably high standard for rational behavior. Indeed, if we require perfect information for rationality, then only God is or can be rational.

This is to say that humans are restricted to choice over the set A, in which the satisficing and maximizing standard lead to exactly the same result. Furthermore, and we stress the point firmly, it is wholly reasonable that people should be thus restricted. One might, of course, require as part of the definition of rationality that choosers always expand set A into set B. But, then, what if such expansion is itself counterproductive and lowers utility? Surely, if this occurs, choosers can be expected to search only over the set A, where maximizing and satisficing mean the same. And expansion of A into B can be counterproductive because information is not costless. To ascertain and evaluate additional alternatives in B but not in A is to develop information, and it is reasonable to ask people to develop information only if the anticipated benefits of informed action exceed the benefits of uninformed action. Often they do not.

Furthermore, when considerations of anticipated cost enter the calculus, it becomes clear that, for all human decision makers, maximizing and satisficing must be the same standard of behavior. We may examine the situation heuristically by imagining a decision maker confronted with alternative procedures:

α_1: select the optimal alternative from the set $A = \{a_1, a_2, \ldots a_n\}$.

α_2: search for an additional alternative, a_{n+1}, evaluate it, and select the optimal alternative from the set $A' = \{a_1, a_2, \ldots, a_n, a_{n+1}\}$.

Assume that, if the decision maker adopts procedure α_1, he chooses alternative a_i and receives utility $U(a_i)$. If, however, he adopts α_2, he incurs the cost, C, of searching for and evaluating a_{n+1}. Of course, he cannot know the result of his search ahead of time. But he can have some expectation (based on learning and inference from previous experience) about how his search will turn out. And this expectation is the subjective probability, p, of finding an alternative which is better than a_i. Thus the expected utility of procedure α_1 is $U(a_i)$, while the expected utility of α_2 is the utility of a_i times the probability of selecting it, plus the anticipated utility of a_{n+1} times the probability of selecting it minus the cost, C:

$$U(\alpha_2) = pU(a_{n+1}) + (1 - p)U(a_i) - C.$$

It is reasonable to suppose that the decision maker chooses procedure α_1 (i.e., maximizes over the set A, or, equivalently, satisfices)—and thereby rejects any proposal to attempt to use α_2 and to expand A into B—if $U(\alpha_1) > U(\alpha_2)$, or if

$$U(a_i) > pU(a_{n+1}) + (1 - p)U(a_i) - C.$$

With some algebraic manipulation this condition reduces to:

$$[U(a_{n+1}) - U(a_i)] < \frac{C}{p}.$$

Suppose this condition holds, that the gain in utility from a_{n+1} over a_i is less than the cost of information divided by the probability of a successful search. Then it is reasonable to choose from A and it is counter-productive to expand the alternatives. This is what we mean by satisficing. So, if the cost is large enough for the condition to hold, it is rational to satisfice. By satisficing, one is in fact maximizing expected utility. The two standards are identical.

Suppose, on the other hand, $[U(a_{n+1}) - U(a_i)] > C/p$. Then one knows that one will gain expected utility from the search. To refuse to search (that is, merely to satisfy) would be to reject what is known to be better for what is known to be worse. Certainly Professor Simon is not asking for this, because even in his terms it is irrational to reject better for worse. As an irrationality, satisficing cannot then be expected to occur. Hence we are back to our original point: unless we ask decision makers to play God, maximizing and satisficing are the same thing.

RATIONALITY AND ERROR

Having rejected these two theoretical criticisms of the principle of maximizing, we turn to the practical criticisms. The most important is that, by erring, people fail to maximize expected utility. There is in this case no dispute, as in the case of the psychoanalytic criticism, about what the goals are, or about the fact that people try to maximize with respect to them. It is merely asserted that people often fail to maximize expected utility with respect to goals that all agree they have. Observing the frailty of human wit, it is foolish to deny the possibility of error. The question is not, however, about the existence of error and hence of a kind of irrationality by default—for that existence no one doubts. Rather the question concerns the frequency of error. Is it so general and pervasive that the concept of rationality is useless as description because it is not parsimonious?

The answer doubtless varies according to the complexity of circumstances. When there are only two alternatives and when the consequences of each for the chooser's goals are completely apparent, it seems probable that very little error occurs. When, on the other hand, the range of alternatives is infinite and when the consequences of choosing each alternative are uncertain, it is likely that most choices involve errors. We offer an example of each extreme, leaving it to the reader to judge the degree of error likely to occur in the median cases.

At the extreme of complexity and uncertainty about the effect of alternatives, recall the response to the several rulings of the Supreme Court (in *Baker* v. *Carr* and *Reynolds* v. *Sims*) that representative districts should be such that the votes of all citizens in all districts have about the same effect. The reason for this decision was, of course, that the Court sought to eliminate the large number of rotten boroughs and to realize the ideal of "one person, one vote." The Court was especially concerned to reduce the great overrepresentation of rural areas where, in spite of declining population over several decades, districts had retained the same boundaries.

Given a set of districts, some overpopulated and others underpopulated, there appear to be two ways in which one might achieve the kind of equality the Court required: (1) the districts might be equal in population and each representative might have the same number of votes (usually, one)—a system we will call "equal voting." (2) Alternatively, the districts might be unequal in population and the number of votes for each representative might be proportional to the population of his district, so that, if the district had k percent of the total population, the representative would have k percent of the votes in the legislature. This system we will call "weighted voting."

In some overrepresented rural areas the representatives foresaw that, if the system of equal voting were used to comply with the ruling, many rural districts would be combined and some rural representatives would lose their seats. In an effort to keep their seats (and salaries) if not their significance, these representatives proposed weighted voting systems in which rural areas would continue to have about the same number of representatives as previously but each such representative would have a diminished vote. Thus the scene was set for a political conflict in which the citizens of rural areas, who would be in low-weight districts, favored weighted voting, while the citizens of cities and suburbs, who would be in high-weight districts, opposed it.

Both sides assumed, of course, that the legislative strength or significance of a representative would be directly proportional to his weight, so that each citizen would have, through his representative, an equal influence on outcomes. Rural citizens would thus not be overrepresented even though they had more representatives. It turns out, however, that on careful analysis legislative strength is not proportional to weight. Using the Shapley-Shubik power index (see Chapter 6), which increases with a representative's chance to pivot (i.e., to be the last added member of a minimal winning coalition), it turns out that usually the greater a representative's weight the greater still is his chance to pivot. Hence, under a system of weighted voting, the relative strength of a representative increases faster than his weight. Thus, rural citizens, with more representatives, would be underrepresented.

Assuming that, in the controversy over weighted voting, the voters wanted to assure that through their representatives they had as much influence as possible in the legislature, then in view of our wider knowledge the positions of both sides of the controversy were irrational. Rural citizens, who would be in low-weight districts and thereby lose influence relatively from weighted voting, nevertheless favored it. Urban citizens who would be in high-weight districts and thereby gain influence relatively from weighted voting, nevertheless opposed it.[16]

This is about the extreme of error—that nearly everyone involved favors an alternative inimical to his supposed goals. In this case only the rural representatives themselves, who would gain by saving jobs for themselves, chose efficiently. And in so doing, they misled both their own constituents and urban voters. Yet even here, where the calculation of one's best interests is very difficult, relatively little erroneous action occurred. Some courts rejected weighted voting, not for the major defect just described but rather for difficulties involved in voice votes, committee votes, and so on. Regardless of reasons, however, they did reject the proposals. Furthermore, during the course of the controversy calculations of the effect of weighted voting on relative influence did appear and may have influenced the choices. Pointless as the controversy was, therefore, it produced relatively little irrational behavior.

And this may be the general case. Since irrational behavior is by definition self-defeating, one can suppose that most of the time some energy is spent on erasing it. And certainly, when the effect of alternatives is unclear, one can expect some caution—as displayed by the judges' action on weighted voting. Although there are massive "irrationalities" in the world, such as, perhaps, excessive population and the nation-state system, it is still the case that the species survives and prospers, which suggests that errors are also avoided and corrected.

At the extreme of simplicity of judgment, our second example concerns the behavior of players in a quasi-political game. Here we find much less error, largely, we suppose, because there are only two alternatives and the

[16]William H. Riker and Lloyd S. Shapley, "Weighted Voting: A Mathematical Analysis for Instrumental Judgments," in Roland Pennock, ed., *Nomos X: Representation* (New York: Atherton Press, 1968), pp. 199–216.

consequence of choice is much less uncertain.[17] In this three-person game the object is for two of the players to form a coalition, which the experimenter pays according to the following schedule:

if (1, 2) forms, it receives $4;
if (1, 3) forms, it receives $5;
if (2, 3) forms, it receives $6;
if (1), (2), (3) and (1, 2, 3) form, they receive nothing.

This game captures something of the political situation in that the central activity is coalition-formation and the motive called forth is the desire to win, both of which are central features of politics.[18] Players, who are mostly college students, negotiate in pairs (with the third person in another room) for five-minute sessions in the sequence (1,2), (1,3), (2,3), which is repeated twice or more so that negotiations continue for at least a half or three quarters of an hour. These negotiations, which concern whom to ally with and how to divide the prize, have been long enough and spirited enough that players begin to grasp some of the very considerable complexities of the game. After negotiations, players vote privately on the coalition and the division of the spoils. If two players agree, they are paid off by the experimenter.

There is a solution to this game in the sense that there is a division of spoils that should be achieved by accurate and efficient judgment given that the players' goals are to get more money rather than less and that, in the range of $1 to $4, players' utility is linear with money. Setting x_i as the gain of the ith player, a solution consists of a set, V, of divisions, $\mathbf{x}$, where $\mathbf{x} = (x_1, x_2, x_3)$. For this game,

$$V = \begin{cases} (1.50,\ 2.50,\ 0), \\ (1.50,\ 0,\ 3.50), \\ (0,\ 2.50,\ 3.50), \\ (1.50 \le x_1 \le 3.50, 2.50 \le x_2 \le 4.50, 0 \le x_3 \le 2.00), \\ \text{where } \sum_{i=1}^{3} x_i = 6.00, \\ (1.50 \le x_1 \le 2.50, 0 \le x_2 \le 1.00, 3.50 \le x_3 \le 4.50), \\ \text{where } \sum_{i=1}^{3} x_1 = 5.00, \end{cases}$$

where the first three divisions are the so-called "principal points" of the solution.

In a number of ways laboratory experiments with this game indicate that subjects choose efficiently or rationally. We assume initially that subjects want to win—and indeed they stated that this was their goal and behaved as if they were quite disappointed when they lost. We assume further that they

[17]Riker and Zavoina, "Rational Behavior in Politics."
[18]William H. Riker, *The Theory of Political Coalitions* (New Haven: Yale University Press, 1962), chap. 1.

preferred more money to less and that the amounts offered were significant to them. Again they acted pleased when they won and were paid off. Assuming these goals, the worst thing that could happen is that no coalition formed so that no player received anything. Out of 227 matches, some coalition formed 211 times. About 93 percent of the time, therefore, the players were efficient in avoiding disaster. (Note that at least two players not only must choose wisely but also must coordinate their efforts in order to assure some winning.) Furthermore, out of the 206 times that two-person coalitions formed, the players in the winning coalition received amounts that averaged very close to the quotas for the players of $1.50, $2.50, and $3.50, with statistically insignificant variations. This clearly indicates that the players reached in practice, without (usually) understanding in theory, the mathematically derived rational outcome. Even more remarkable, the outcomes in the five matches with three-person coalitions were also within the limits specified in the solution—a result that ought to surprise even game theorists.[19]

Looking solely at the outcomes, then, the subjects in these 227 matches appear to have been highly rational almost all the time. If one looks at the intentions of individuals, this conclusion is strongly reinforced. In the last 100 matches, subjects were asked to estimate how they believed the other players in the match would vote. Let p_{ij} be i's estimate of the chance that j will vote for i and let x_{ij} be the amount i believes he will get in a coalition of i and j. Assuming that the players' main goal is to win, the first rule of rational behavior for player i then is: if $p_{ij} > p_{ik}$, then i votes for j. Assuming that the players' second goal is to get more money rather than less, then, if $p_{ij} = p_{ik}$, the decision rule for i should be: if $x_{ij} > x_{ik}$, then i votes for j; and if $x_{ij} = x_{ik}$, then i votes for j with a probability of 0.5. As it turned out, subjects followed these rules quite well. Of the 300 times i voted for j, on 197 of them $p_{ij} > p_{ik}$; furthermore, on 77 others $p_{ij} = p_{ik}$ and of these $x_{ij} > x_{ik}$ for 59 times. Hence, if the subjects can be believed about their own perceptions, they behaved efficiently and rationally 256 out of 300 times or about 85 percent. Most of the 44 instances of apparent irrationality were genuine errors due to confusion, although in possibly ten of these instances subjects were probably trying to maximize with respect to some other goals, such as to satisfy a sense of honor or to gamble.

This seems to us a remarkably high degree of rational behavior, especially since the players must learn that they cannot maximize rewards simply by seeking the largest amount of money. (Indeed, the structure of the game is such that greediness is almost always penalized.) Nevertheless, this high degree of rationality (in the sense of consistency) may be more apparent than real if the subjects are trying not so much to behave rationally as to reduce cognitive

[19]William H. Riker, "Three-Person Coalitions in Three-Person Games," *Mathematical Applications in Political Science,* vol. 6 (1972), pp. 125–42. For evidence of rational choice in an even more complex situation, see James D. Laing and Richard V. Morrison, "Coalitions and Payoffs in Three-Person Sequential Games" (Carnegie-Mellon University, SUPA, 1972).

dissonance. If player i has decided for quite extraneous reasons having nothing to do with the relative sizes of p_{ij}, p_{ik}, x_{ij}, and x_{ik} to ally with player j—if, for example, i has decided to vote for j because j is friendly or handsome—then i might be expected to report that $p_{ij} > p_{ik}$ simply in order to reduce cognitive dissonance. That is, at the time of the player i's decision the probability is only 0.5 that $p_{ij} > p_{ik}$; but subsequent to the decision, this probability is falsely reported to have been 1.0. There are thus two possibilities about the causal sequence:

(1) i votes for j because $p_{ij} > p_{ik}$,
(2) $p_{ij} > p_{ik}$ because i votes for j.

If the subjects behave rationally, then (1) holds and our evidence is valid. If, however, (2) holds, then our evidence is irrelevant because the sizes of p_{ij} and p_{ik} are not the standard of behavior but rather the consequences of behavior. Whether the evidence just cited of rational behavior is reliable or not thus depends on whether (1) or (2) holds. It is probably not possible to prove that (1) holds, but it is possible, we think, to show that (2) is almost certainly false.

If (2) were true, then the p's (which are i's estimate of the chances j and k will vote for him) would be unrelated to the actual votes by j and k. That is, the p's would be manipulated to satisfy i's previous decision and not to fit the real world. If, therefore, the p's are accurate and do fit reality, we have evidence that (2) is not true. By default, therefore, it would appear likely that (1) holds. Figure 2.1 presents the evidence that the p's are accurate. On the horizontal axis are five categories of player i's judgment of the size of p for players j and k. On the vertical axis is the percent of times that j and k voted for i. Perfect accuracy for the judgments in the whole group would occur if for each category the j's and k's actually voted for i in the ratio of the midpoint of the category. Thus, if, for all judgments that the probability of j or k voting for i is between 0.0 and 0.2, the percent of times j or k did actually vote for i was 10 percent, one would conclude that the group as a whole was quite accurate, even though individuals cannot be this accurate when uttering probabilistic predictions about dichotomous events. As is apparent from Figure 2.1, the group as a whole is much closer to accuracy than inaccuracy.[20] It seems reasonable to conclude, therefore, that sentence (2) is false and that the true relationship probably is that i votes for j because $p_{ij} > p_{ik}$.

In this section thus far we have attempted to indicate the degree of error, first, in an exceedingly complex situation and, second, in a situation of less complex but still uncertain choice. Between these extremes error varies from almost one hundred percent to about ten or fifteen percent. We asked, then, whether or not this rate of error renders the concept of rationality useless for research. We are now able to begin to answer this question. We start by point-

[20]Riker and Zavoina, "Rational Behavior in Politics."

ing out that error may occur either because of confusion or because of faulty calculation and faulty information or because of both. Whether or not error renders the concept of rationality useless depends, we believe, on its causes: If all the error results from confusion so that erroneous behavior is random behavior, then, if error is frequent, it is difficult to explain behavior in terms of the pursuit goals. If, on the other hand, error results mostly from miscalculation and misinformation, then randomness is not implied by such error. Hence, in this case, after due allowance for error, it is possible to use the concept of rationality to explain behavior. To answer our question about the significance of error, therefore, it is necessary to assess its causes.

THE CAUSES OF ERROR

Most obviously, error derives from inadequate technology. In the example of weighted voting, nearly everybody erred because the choosers lacked a method of calculation that brought all the important considerations into play. Since probably none of them had heard of the Shapley-Shubik power index or of the notion of pivoting and since probably few of them were accustomed to making

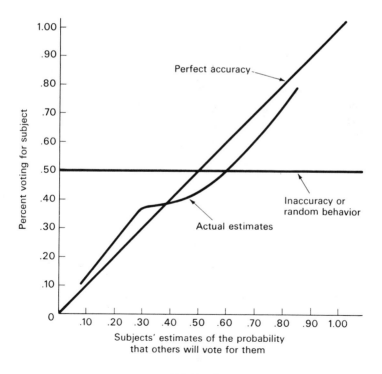

FIGURE 2.1
Accuracy of subjects' estimates of the state of the external world

probabilistic calculations, it follows that they could hardly be expected to discover the full consequences of weighted voting. Hence they erred, but their actions were not random. They proceeded in a logical way from their (false) premises to an (erroneous) conclusion. So it is with all technological error. Typically it is fully consistent and, given the false premises, entirely explicable in terms of goals.

Second, error sometimes derives from choosers' rejection of further calculation on the ground of excessive cost. Consider, for example, citizens who are uninformed about the policies candidates for public office advocate. Undoubtedly, such citizens frequently make choices which we, as political scientists, do not interpret as being in their best interests. A voter, however, is unlikely to affect materially the outcome of most elections, and the outcome, moreover, may be of little consequence to him. Thus, the benefits anticipated from casting an informed vote differ infinitesimally from the benefits of an uninformed choice. Conversely, the costs of becoming informed are probably substantial. Hence the citizen, faced with the low benefit and high cost of information, may well prefer to remain uninformed and risk an erroneous choice. This should not be construed as an argument that the avoidance of error in voting is irrational. The benefits from voting and the cost of information are continuous measures, and their point of equalization varies from citizen to citizen. Thus, rationality dictates that some citizens become informed while others vote for candidates about whom they know little. And, if they do so vote, they may well err but in a way induced by a maximizing calculation. Note that this kind of error is no more than satisficing (or maximizing over the set A).

Third, we cannot ignore the possibility that some people cannot calculate expected utilities and thus cannot clearly ascertain the logical consequences of actions. Undoubtedly, these circumstances often occasion error, so we must consider whether or not such error must be regarded as irrational. Initially, we emphasize that a facility with mathematics or academic excellence are not prerequisites for rational action. We postulate goals for people and infer a mathematical calculus from their actions not because people in fact have such goals or perform such calculations, but because they act as if they had the postulated goals and used a calculus.[21] For example, so-called satisficing behavior can be understood by the rather involved calculus described previously—not because people necessarily perform such calculations consciously, but because this calculus satisfactorily accounts for observed behavior.[22] Thus,

[21]For an excellent review of the as if principle as interpreted in economic theory see Milton Friedman, Essays in Positive Economics (Chicago: University of Chicago Press, 1953), chap. 1.

[22]Friedman constructs the example of the expert billiard player where, to explain and predict such a player's actions, we infer that he employs theorems of trigonometry and geometry. The billiard player is not consciously familiar with such theorems, and, if asked about them, replies that his actions are determined by experience and a "feel" for the game rather than by a theory. Still, in examining his behavior we may find no empirical evidence contrary to the inference that he uses a theoretical calculus. Thus, we would assert that such a player calculates his shots as if he used trigonometry and geometry (Essays in Positive Economics, p. 21).

many people are unable to comprehend our descriptions of them, but we infer that these descriptions are satisfactory to the extent that they satisfy the scientific canons of prediction and parsimonious explanation. Consequently, error which is attributed to the human condition of ignorance is not assigned necessarily to the realm of irrational action.

On the other hand, some error is occasioned by confusion—by a total inability to trace the implications of one's actions for one's goals. This error does not result from a mere inability to calculate, but it reflects an inability to act as if one had calculated. In our example of choice in a three-person game, one of the subjects who failed to maximize his probability of winning wrote in explication of his decision: "Total confusion, total insecurity, complete distrust." So it is with at least some error—and, of course, error from this source is irrational or random behavior.

Finally, error is occasioned by the fact that, in calculating about events involving the future and involving other people, events may not turn out as we expect. In anticipating physical events we may have insufficient knowledge of nature to predict with assurance, as, for example, in the well-known difficulties about predicting the weather. And in anticipating events involving actions by other people, we must take into account the choices of others. And sometimes the error of one is occasioned by the irrationality of the other. We try to minimize both these kinds of errors, however, by introducing some adjustments into calculations of value and utility. In response to our ignorance about the exact future we estimate the state of nature probabilistically so that, while we may not be accurate about a particular prediction, we are accurate in our expectations of the several possibilities. (In Chapter 3 some techniques for dealing with the future are introduced as part of the conceptual equipment.) The more difficult problem, which we defer to Chapter 8, is that involving interdependence of choice, the fact that one person's decision depends on what a second person's decision is going to be. To respond to this kind of ignorance, we must not only estimate the future probabilistically but also estimate it with the alternatives of rational choices available to others. Altogether it is possible by appropriate probabilistic calculations to compensate for a large amount of the error emanating from these two kinds of ignorance. Nevertheless, some error arising from ignorance about others' choices is ineradicable, because some such situations lack an equilibrium.

After this brief survey of the occasions for error, we revert to our original question: is the amount of error sufficient to render the notion of rationality useless? And we conclude in the negative. Much, if not most, error results from misinformation and reasoned rejection of the cost of correction, not from simple stupidity. And if we are right in these conjectures, then error, if properly accounted for, does not interfere with explication by means of the notion of rationality.

Some may dispute our judgment, however, on the ground that the pervasiveness of error precludes parsimonious explanation with our individualist assumptions. And it is true that, when we go into this cluttered world which we barely understand, we find it harder to isolate the causes of error. Yet even here it is possible to isolate evidence of behavior in accord with the principle of maximization of expected utility. V. O. Key, in his posthumously published study of voting over the last generation, not only argued that "the electorate behaves about as rationally and responsibly as we should expect" (p. 7) but furthermore offered detailed evidence that voters "who shift to the winning side resemble (on major policy issues . . .) the standpatters of that side. This should be regarded as at least a modicum of evidence for the view that those who switch do so to support governmental policies or outlooks with which they agree, not because of subtle psychological or sociological peculiarities" (p. 104).[23] An even more impressive study of switchers, in this case children who switch from their parents' party identification, comes from Arthur S. Goldberg.[24] Goldberg noted that the children most likely to switch were those who were well educated and whose parents were deviant in identification with respect to the usual sociological indicators. Those who were least likely to defect were the well-educated children of the normally identified parents. In between were the poorly educated children of the deviant, then of the normal. In seeking to explain the difference, Goldberg argued that the well-educated children of the misidentified were most likely to change simply because they could most easily see the "error" in parental identification. What Goldberg thus did was to successfully posit a goal for that part of those in the class whose behavior had previously been ascribed wholly to sociological determinism. In other words, the half who switched presumably behaved as if they had carried through a rational calculus.

But what about the other part, the nonswitching, well-educated children of the deviantly identified parents? Did their error imply irrationality? Or was their calculus simply different? Goldberg's analysis cannot tell us. But this should not be particularly disturbing. As we remarked in beginning this discussion of rationality, scientific explanation of society amounts to the successful ascription of a rational calculus as the basis of behavior. Each step in science is difficult, especially when, as in Goldberg's case, one is trying to make sense out of behavior which is known only through the intercession of a questionnaire, and which must be analyzed with aggregate statistical methods. That a portion of hitherto unexplained behavior was explained is itself a significant achievement which should suggest that, in general, behavior can be explained by ascribing a rational calculus, even though error and irrationality exist. That so little is explained is more a reproach than a barrier to social science.

---

[23]V.O. Key, Jr., *The Responsible Electorate* (Cambridge, Mass.: Harvard University Press, 1966).
[24]Arthur S. Goldberg, "Social Determinism and Rationality as Bases of Party Identification," *American Political Science Review,* vol. 63 (1969), pp. 5–25.

THE ASSUMPTION OF INDIVIDUALISM

A commonly reiterated criticism of our rationalistic approach is that politics concerns the activities of collectivities such as interest groups, legislatures, and nations—in addition to people. Consequently, it is said, a theory of politics which interprets social action in terms of the postulate of individual rationality is incapable of adequately describing events.[25] Intuition and direct observation ostensibly support this criticism: social processes appear to differ *qualitatively* from individual actions, and frequently social choice is seemingly independent of people's idiosyncratic goals. Notions such as the public interest or social values, moreover, suggest the existence of utility functions of a higher order than those posited to exist for people—thereby supporting the conclusion that the individualistic approach is not entirely appropriate for the study of politics.

Consider, however, the economist who, like his colleagues in political science, is concerned also with social choice and the processes that govern social institutions. Focusing on choices and organizations associated with market activity, he examines the preferences and choices of people, and seeks to derive the patterns of interaction that emerge from them. Thus, Buchanan writes, "The organization that comes into being as a result of individuals participating variously in exchange processes is called 'the economy.' This organization, this economy, as such, has no independent existence apart from the interaction of individual participants in it."[26] We thereby attribute purposive action to markets only as such action can be derived from the actions of many persons, each pursuing his own goals.

The contrary (and erroneous) notion that the rationalist, individualist assumptions of economic theory are inadequate for fully understanding social processes arises from a failure to appreciate the relationships between individual action and its social context. Individual preference and the choices that reveal them have social consequences. Indeed, these consequences together make up the social environment and are in fact social institutions. As such

---

[25]See, for example, Kenneth Prewitt and Heinz Eulau, "Political Matrix and Political Representation: Prolegomenon to a New Departure from an Old Problem," *American Political Science Review*, vol. 63 (June 1969), pp. 427–441. Professors Prewitt and Eulau assert that "A viable theory of representation . . . cannot be constructed from individualistic assumptions alone. It must be constructed out of an understanding of representation as a relationship between two collectives . . . ." (p. 428). Of course, it is easily possible—and indeed usual—for an individual legislator to desire to be a delegate and thus to subordinate what would otherwise be his goals to the goals of those whom he believes dominate his constituency. By similar assumptions about the whole system, an individualistic theory of representation can follow. But see Frank A. Pinner, "On the Utility of Utility: Policy, Decision Makers and Individual Choice," paper presented at the Annual Meeting of the American Political Science Association, September 1969.

[26]James M. Buchanan, "An Individualistic Theory of Political Process," in David Easton, ed., *Varieties of Political Theory*, (Englewood Cliffs, N.J.: Prentice-Hall, Inc., 1966), p. 25.

they stand behind all individual action. Hence individual choice is not independent of prior social choice, which itself originated in individual choice. Certain selected and enforced social choices are, therefore, the causes as well as the effects of individual persons' acts. Even private acts, such as those in a market which are typically of little relevance to politics, are public in the sense that they are contingent on the publically available technology.

This inexorable relationship between individual and social choice dispels any possibility of a satisfactory distinction between individual and collective decision making. Faced, therefore, with Whitehead's observation that everything is related to everything else, which impels us to the impossible task of saying everything at once, we surmount the problem by initially isolating individual behavior. This we do, in part, for convenience, but also because we cannot find a principle to explain the preferences and choices of society other than to derive them from people's preferences and choices. (Such derivation, nevertheless, does not exclude the possibility that social preferences are established by natural or divine law—perhaps designated as the public interest or general will. For such to occur we require only that there minimally be one interpreter who internalizes the public interest as his preference. And because the assumption of rational action does not preclude altruistic motives, the interpreter's choices may be regarded by all as good.)

If we construct a theory of collective decision making without individualistic assumptions, then we must assume collective rationality in order to exclude randomness from our theory. Because rationality implies utility maximization of some sort, we must specify a group preference to understand collective decisions. (Otherwise we must relegate collective decision making to the inexplicable world of the irrational.) We note, however, that such functions can be defined only if preferences are transitively ordered, and Arrow and Black demonstrate that collective preferences cannot generally be transitive.

So simple an example demonstrates this impossibility that it bears repeating. In Table 2.1 we present the preference orderings of three citizens, 1, 2, and 3, for three alternatives, A, B, and C. Assuming that the collective preference is determined by a majority vote—although such an assumption is not essential— we easily see that A defeats B, B defeats C, and C defeats A. Thus, the social summation of individual preference, $A \longrightarrow B \longrightarrow C \longrightarrow A$, is intransitive. This situation, referred to as the paradox of voting, demonstrates that, although the assumptions pertaining to rationality are satisfied for all three voters, one assumption is not satisfied by their collective preference. So the concept of a collective utility function cannot be defined; and, consequently, we cannot construct a rational calculus for a collective citizen such as an interest group, a legislature, a political party, or a nation.[27]

---

[27]In Karl W. Deutsch's criticism of the relevance of game theory to politics he questions the generality of the transitivity assumption for individual preferences. The examples he cites in which this assumption apparently is not satisfied, however, concern only collective situations. Table 2.1 demonstrates that intransitive collective preference is consistent with transitive individual preferences. *The Nerves of Government* (New York: Free Press, 1963), pp. 54–55.

TABLE 2.1

CITIZEN	CITIZEN'S PREFERENCE
1	A ⟶ B ⟶ C
2	B ⟶ C ⟶ A
3	C ⟶ A ⟶ B

As against our assumption that the essential logic of collective action is deduced from individual persons' preferences and choices, there is a contrary theoretical principle: the intuitive idea that there is a "ghost in the machine"— that the behavior of collectivities differs qualitatively from the simple additive properties of individual choice. This intuition, commonly embodied in organic social theories, plausibly asserts that collectivities are somehow "greater than the sum of their parts." While we reject the necessity for organic concepts, we do not exclude the (seemingly qualitative) differences between collective and individual action; these differences are real. But they are real only in the sense that the character of water is distinct from that of its constituent parts— hydrogen and oxygen.[28] To utter general sentences about the chemical properties of this compound—such as its ability to react with other substances and the products of these reactions— requires only that we know that it is composed of two parts hydrogen to one part oxygen. Similarly, to utter general sentences about collective preference and choice requires only our individualistic assumptions.

Consider, for example, a legislature consisting of three members whose preferences for three alternatives are those described in Table 2.1. The collective preference is intransitive, so the postulate of utility maximization is inadequate for ascertaining the choice of the group. But assume that the paired sequential order of voting on the alternatives is predetermined, perhaps by law or custom. Specifically, assume that the motions A and B are first paired for a vote, with the undefeated measure paired against C, and the surviving measure being the social choice. Hence, A defeats B, and C defeats A, so C is the social choice. Thus, if we adopt an organic theory of collective action we should assert that the legislature's preference is C ⟶ A ⟶ B. Assume now that the legislature votes on an identical set of measures at some later date by the same procedure and the preference B ⟶ C is revealed. We might conclude, then, that this choice is random and that the laws of probability determine social outcomes; alternatively we might refrain from uttering any general sentences about social preference. Nevertheless, this apparently random behavior in which first C, then B, is the social choice is readily explained if we consider once again

---

[28]We do not exclude the possibility, of course, that it may be efficient to speak of social choice in organic terms. Ultimately, however, such discourse must be reducible to individualistic terms.

individual preference and choice. Realizing that C wins under the given sequence of voting with the given preferences of each member, citizen 1 strategically misrepresents his preferences on the second attempt to pass B or A over C. Specifically, he behaves as if his true preference is B $\longrightarrow$ A $\longrightarrow$ C, so that B defeats A, and B defeats C. Now B is the social choice; and this is a more preferred outcome than is C for citizen 1. Thus, if we grant citizen 1 the ability to learn and to calculate, social choice is not random, and, in fact, is quite understandable.

Of course, citizens 2 and 3 might perceive similar opportunities for strategic maneuver, so that the preferences citizens reveal might best be predicted by some game-theoretic analysis. The point of this simple example, however, is that the legal structure of the collectivity—specifically, the order in which motions are presented for a vote—determines social choice only as it affects individual preferences. If we know only the intransitive preference of the group and the temporal sequence of voting, we cannot explain a revealed social preference for B. We might, therefore, be tempted to say that, in some organic sense, the group as a group prefers something other than the sum of individual preferences. But we would be wrong, for here the outcome occurs because each person's choices are contingent on the choices of others, and because collective choice is derived from individual choice.

The inseparability of individual and collective choice, moreover, suggests that a person's actions can be interpreted as rational only if some collectivity is posited to be an element of his environment. This, perhaps, is what some critics of the individualistic approach to politics regard as absent from those individualistic assumptions that constitute the foundation of our theory. But if we regard collective behavior as the product of individual action, and if we assume that individuals perceive and respond to the actions of others, then the collectivity necessarily becomes an element of the environment. Consider our previous example: citizen 1 might consistently reveal the preference A $\longrightarrow$ B $\longrightarrow$ C for a class of motions, but vote B $\longrightarrow$ A $\longrightarrow$ C on the final motion. Without ascertaining the implications of his vote for the collectivity—specifically, without ascertaining the strategic potential of misrepresenting one's true preferences—his vote might appear to be little more than the tenth toss of a fair coin which falls tails after a string of heads. But his vote is explicable theoretically if the collectivity is included in the reckoning. Thus, the individualistic approach implicitly requires consideration of the collective context of individual decision making.

The political scientist, however, must examine not only the patterns of individual action that emerge from specific organization environments, but also the determinants of the structure, function, and evolution of collectivities. Consider a legislature and its procedural rules. Previously we demonstrated that such rules—specifically, the order of paired comparisons—affect social choice and citizen 1's potential response to them. Our example also demonstrates that these rules are subject to rational manipulation and thereby to rational explanation.[29] Instead of misrepresenting his preferences, citizen 1 might attempt to reverse the order of voting to, say, B against C, and then the winner against A. If the citizen is successful, his most preferred outcome, A, is the social choice. Thus, any such manipulation of the legislature's rules is readily explained in terms of a goal and is, thereby, rational.

Of course manipulation of these rules may be impractical where, for example, they are widely accepted; without any significant promise of success in such a venture the citizen perhaps should adopt the less costly strategy of misrepresenting his preferences. Thus, a willingness to abide by a predetermined procedure is explained by comparing the anticipated rewards and costs of alternative actions, so that the stability of a particular organizational structure is dependent on the benefits people derive from such structures, the costs of maintaining them, and the probable benefits and costs of seeking change. Conversely, new structures emerge to supplant old ones, or preexisting structures are employed to alter the choices made by others, when those capable of initiating change anticipate benefits from doing so. Hence, the collective environment is effect as well as cause, and "explaining social institutions essentially amounts to explaining changes in these institutions . . . [and] these changes themselves must be ultimately explained in terms of personal incentives for some people to change their behavior."[30]

In summary, we do not deny that collectivities exist and that it is the business of political science to study them. Furthermore, we insist that people in collectivities often—indeed typically—display regularities of behavior. These regularities are in one aspect what we call institutions. Sometimes these regularities reveal a common interest or goal or value that is socialized into all individuals in the group so that each desires and acts to obtain what he or she conceives of as a common good. What we insist upon, however, is that collectivities, regularities about people in them, and the common goals and values of collectivities can be understood only by understanding the individual persons who make up the collectives. And in that sense our method is individualistic.

APPENDIX
Political Life and the Theory of Cardinal Utility

In Chapter 2 the question is raised of whether or not the notion of cardinal utility, developed in the setting of economic theory, is applicable to the subject

---

[29]On the strategic manipulation of procedural rules see Duncan Black, *The Theory of Committees and Elections* (Cambridge: Cambridge University Press, 1958). James M. Buchanan and Gordon Tullock extend this line of thought to a consideration of the rationale for alternative constitutional structures in *The Calculus of Consent* (Ann Arbor: University of Michigan Press, 1962).

[30]John C. Harsanyi, "Rational Choice Models of Political Behavior vs. Functionalist and Conformist Theories," *World Politics*, vol. 21 (1969), p. 532.

matter of politics. This appendix is an attempt to answer that question in some detail.

In the theory of cardinal utility what one wants is a measure on a set of ordinally ordered outcomes. That is, if a set of outcomes is transitively ordered so that O_1 is preferred to O_2 and O_2 to O_3, one wishes to say how distant numerically in some psychological space O_1 is from O_2 and O_2 from O_3.

If by invoking the principle of insufficient reason one could say that the distances between the ordinal ranks tend to be equal, there would be no problem.[1] We could then treat each rank as a unit of distance. But as is both obvious to common sense and easily demonstrable by means of paradox, there is sufficient reason to believe that, typically, the distances between ranks are not equal. Surely the distances between the adjacent members of the ordered set: {(1) twenty million dollars; (2) nineteen million dollars; (3) one penny}, are equal for very few, if any, persons.

The insight that permits one to arrive at a numerical distance is embodied in the following experiment: After a subject has transitively ordered a set of outcomes, $\{O_1, O_2, \ldots, O_r\}$, place the ordinally first, say O_1, equal to some arbitrary maximum number, say 1, and the ordinally last, say O_r, equal to some arbitrary minimum number, say 0. Thus are created the bounds for utility numbers for all outcomes in the ordered set:

$$U(O_1) = 1, \ldots, U(O_r) = 0.$$

To find the numerical value of $U(O_i)$, where O_i is ordinally between O_1 and O_r, offer the subject a series of choices between a lottery option and a certain option. The lottery always consists of a chance, p, of obtaining O_1 and a chance $(1 - p)$ of obtaining O_r. Hence, given p, the value of the lottery option can always be readily calculated from the maximum and minimum numbers already assumed. That is, for the lottery L,

$$U(L) = pU(O_1) + (1 - p)U(O_r).$$

The certain option consists of the certain gain of O_i, which is the outcome other than O_1 or O_r for which one wishes to find a utility number. Offering the subject repeatedly a choice between the lottery option and the certain option, one will (presumably) find the following behavior: when p is large, the subject chooses the lottery simply because its calculated value is larger than the value to him of the certain option. This lottery value is larger because it consists of a high probability of obtaining his most preferred outcome. When p is small, he chooses the certain option because the calculated value of the lottery is smaller than the value to him of the certain option. The lottery value is smaller because it consists of a high probability of obtaining his least

---

[1]In this application, the principle of insufficient reason amounts to this argument: that the distances in the psychological space are much like probability numbers, that these numbers are completely unknown to us, and that, in our ignorance, we are compelled to regard them as equiprobable so that, in terms of expected values, the distances between adjacent ranks are equal.

preferred outcome. But at some in-between value of p, the subject will be unable to decide between the lottery and O_i—that is, he will be indifferent.

This experiment leads to a definition of a cardinal value of the utility for O_i thus: the utility of O_i is the utility of the lottery option for that value of p for which the subject is indifferent between O_i for certain and the lottery on O_1 and O_r. Thus, for an experimentally chosen chance, p^0:

$$U(O_i) = p^0 U(O_1) + (1 - p^0) U(O_r).$$

By appropriate repetition of the experiment one can find numerical values for all outcomes ordered between the best and the worst.

This method of assigning cardinal utilities depends on a set of assumptions, not all of which seem to apply perfectly to the circumstances of politics.

We must first assume that an ordinal ordering is possible. Hence:

Assumption 1. The relation of preference, P, and indifference, I, and preference and indifference combined, R, are

(a) connected, i.e., either aRb or bRa;
(b) transitive, i.e., if aRb and bRc, then aRc;

and, for any set of objects ordered by them, at least one pair must be ordered by P.

(The latter clause of the assumption is simply to avoid the trivial circumstance that indifference holds among all objects of the set.) While we know from many experiments that not all people at all times satisfy this assumption in actual behavior, it seems reasonable to accept it as a statement of an ideal for behavior which almost everybody accepts in the abstract.

Second, we must assume that the experiment just described has as an outcome an indifference point:

Assumption 2. For an outcome O_i in the ordered set $\{O_1, O_2, \ldots, O_r\}$, where O_i differs from O_1 and O_r, there is a number p such that a chooser is indifferent between $U(O_i)$ and $[pU(O_1) + (1 - p)U(O_r)]$.

This assumption, which is often called the Axiom of Archimedes, is the crucial one and, as we will presently show, is not always acceptable even as an ideal for behavior.

Third, we must assume that the range in which O_i is valued is a continuous one. As a matter of terminology, for that value of the lottery to which O_i is indifferent, we can write $O_i I \tilde{O}_i$, where $U(\tilde{O}_i) = pU(O_1) + (1 - p)U(O_r)$. Since in the experiment we assumed that the utility of O_1 was maximum [write: $U(O_1) = U_{\max}$] and that the utility of O_r was minimum [write: $U(O_r) = U_{\min}$], we can now write that the utility of $\tilde{O}_i$ is equivalent to the utility of the lottery option:

$$U(\tilde{O}_i) = pU_{\max} + (1 - p)U_{\min}.$$

We now want to assume that the range from U_{max} to U_{min} is continuous, which is to say:

Assumption 3.   For $x = U(\tilde{O}_i)$, as p increases from 0 to 1, x increases from U_{min} to U_{max}.

This continuity assumption assures us that, if O_i is ordinally between O_1 and O_r, there will be a number on the scale to which the utility of O_i corresponds. As in the case of Assumption 1, despite practical 'difficulties of measurement, Assumption 3 seems quite acceptable as an ideal.

Fourth, we must assume that $\tilde{O}_i$ is fully substitutable for O_i in the necessary applications:

Assumption 4.   In any outcome, $\tilde{O}_i$ is substitutable for O_i. That is, in a choice between alternatives, A and A', which consist of lotteries over outcomes, such that $A = (p_1O_1, \ldots, p_iO_i, \ldots, p_rO_r)$ and $A' = (p_1O_1, \ldots, p_i\tilde{O}_i, \ldots, p_rO_r)$, where $p_1 + p_2 + \ldots + p_r = 1$, it is the case that A is indifferent to A'.

This assumption assures us that the chooser appreciates and acts upon the elementary notion of probability theory that, if two lotteries are equivalent, the chooser is indifferent between them. Again, this may not always describe behavior but it is a readily acceptable ideal for behavior.

Von Neumann and Morgenstern have shown that a preference ordering satisfying these assumptions can be represented by a cardinal utility function which is unique up to a positive linear transformation.[2] [That is, for any constants a and b such that $a > 0$, if $U'(A) = aU(A) + b$, then $U'(A)$ is a transformation of $U(A)$ and we refer to U' as a positive linear transformation of U.] Such numbers are, of course, what is needed to talk about a psychological distance between O_i and O_j in an ordinal ordering. That these numbers are unique up to a linear transformation assures us that the experiment just described will result in a higher value for $U(O_i)$ than $U(O_j)$ if O_iPO_j.

As we indicated, the crucial question concerns the validity of assumption 2, the Axiom of Archimedes. Since the other assumptions seem intuitively acceptable ideals for behavior, whether or not cardinal utility is appropriate depends on whether or not Assumption 2 is an acceptable ideal. The difficulty with the axiom is that the imaginary experiment we have described may never result in an indifference point.

Consider the following possibility: A voter must choose between two candidates who differ only on four issues. Candidate 1 proposes to abolish the draft, increase tariffs, end foreign aid, and reduce military appropriations, while candidate 2 proposes to maintain the status quo on all four items. The voter himself wishes most of all to abolish the draft, O_1, and secondarily to

---

[2]John von Neumann and Oskar Morgenstern, *The Theory of Games and Economic Behavior*, 2d ed. (Princeton, N.J.: Princeton University Press, 1947), pp. 617–632. An excellent brief presentation is in Karl Borch, *The Economics of Uncertainty* (Princeton, N.J.: Princeton University Press, 1968), pp. 25–30.

maintain the status quo on tariffs first, O_2, on foreign aid second, O_3, and on military appropriations third, O_4. Thus relative to the draft he prefers candidate 1, while relative to the economic issues he prefers candidate 2. Suppose that the voter says that, on balance, he prefers candidate 1 and that we, as researchers, wish to ascertain the depth of his preference—perhaps in order to advise candidate 2 on how to win the voter's support or candidate 1 on how to keep it.

For the voter to say that he prefers candidate 1 is to say that the voter's utility from candidate 1's positions,

$$U(O_1) - U(O_2) - U(O_3) - U(O_4),$$

is greater than his utility from candidate 2's positions,

$$- U(O_1) + U(O_2) + U(O_3) + U(O_4),$$

which is to say

$$U(O_1) - U(O_2) - U(O_3) - U(O_4) > -U(O_1) + U(O_2) + U(O_3) + U(O_4),$$

$$2U(O_1) > 2U(O_2) + 2U(O_3) + 2U(O_4),$$

$$U(O_1) > U(O_2) + U(O_3) + U(O_4).$$

To ascertain the depth of the voter's preference, we must discover precisely what the utility numbers are in the previous sentence. We can assign the values

$$U(O_1) = 1 \quad \text{and} \quad U(O_4) = 0,$$

but we need to know also the values of $U(O_2)$ and $U(O_3)$. For that latter purpose we must conduct a von Neumann experiment. We therefore offer the voter a lottery on O_1 and O_4, i.e.,

$$[pO_1 + (1 - p)O_4],$$

as against O_2 for certain—all for several values of p. If we find a point of indifference, we then have a value for $U(O_2)$; and similarly we can get a value for $U(O_3)$. With these values we can then discover *how much* this voter prefers candidate 1 to candidate 2; and, if we wish, we can advise candidates 1 or 2 accordingly. But suppose we never can find a point of indifference. Suppose that, no matter how small p becomes, the voter always prefers the lottery on O_1 and O_4 to the certainty of O_2. This means that, for him, any chance at all, however minute, of abolition of the draft is more important than the sum of maintaining low tariffs, and so on, which nevertheless he rates as having some importance. (Surely, there were in 1971 in the United States at least some voters for whom this is a true statement.) It appears, therefore, that the voter's attitude on O_1 is just not on the same scale as his attitude toward O_2, O_3, and O_4. That is, O_1 is incommensurate with the others and the Axiom of Archimedes fails. Because it does fail, we as researchers cannot use an expected-utility calculation to estimate the depth of the voter's preferences, although we know that he must choose candidate 1 who satisfies the immeasurably greater O_1 over candidate 2 who merely satisfies the immeasurably less O_2, O_3, and O_4.

Why, in this imaginary case, does the Axiom of Archimedes fail to hold? We offer some possible reasons. The most obvious is a technical one, which probably should not justify rejection of the axiom. The subject whose cardinal utility an experimenter is trying to evaluate may be quite unable to think about probability numbers in a precise way. When offered a lottery on his best and worst goals, he is offered, of course, an objective chance, p and $(1 - p)$. But when he actually chooses, he chooses on the basis of a subjective chance, q, which is the internalized meaning of the objective chance. It may be that the relation between p and q is not perfectly linear for some choosers, especially for people inexperienced with gambling choices, and more generally for people who are asked to order what are for them quite disparate objects. Thus it may be, when p is small, that q is always larger than p. For example, in Figure 2.2, the solid diagonal line is the linear relation one might expect

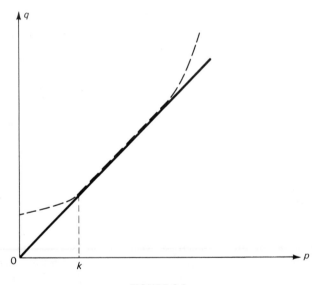

FIGURE 2.2

for expert choosers and the dotted line is the relation one might expect for difficult choices and for inexperienced choosers. The relation depicted by the dotted line is such that, when $p < k$, $q > p$, so that no matter how small p gets, q is larger. Thus, in the range beneath k, p is consistently overestimated when transformed into q. Hence, if the best goal is greatly preferred to the one being measured, so that measurement occurs in the range beneath k, it may easily happen that there is no indifference point (as happened in the case of the draft-hating voter). Furthermore, it is quite conceivable that, were the subject able to transform p into q linearly (call the result "Lq") he would be able to find an indifference point, while with a nonlinear transformation (call the result "non-Lq") he is not able to find one. That is, for a given chooser, for a given p equivalent to an Lq and to a non-Lq, and for the choice offered between the lottery $[pO_1 + (1 - p)O_r]$ and the certainty (O_i), it may be the case that

$$[LqO_1 + (1 - Lq)O_r] \, I \, [O_i]$$

while

$$[\text{non-}LqO_1 + (1 - \text{non-}Lq)O_r] \, P \, [O_i]$$

If the experiment fails for the foregoing reason, it does not seem compelling to abandon the axiom. Its inapplicability is no more disconcerting than the occasional inapplicability of transitivity. But there may be a deeper reason for the failure of the experiment—namely, that O_1 is truly incommensurate with O_i. In such case, the subject uses $q = p$ in the entire range of p and yet invariably chooses the lottery option, no matter how small q is. The circumstance in which O_1 and O_i are incommensurate is, typically, when O_1 is passionately and intensely desired and O_i is not. Then even a tiny chance of O_1 is better than O_i.

Reverting now to the question raised at the beginning of this Appendix, we ask if the possible inapplicability of the Axiom of Archimedes is sufficient to render the notion of cardinal utility useless for political science. Our answer is somewhat equivocal.

Probably almost all comparisons of objects in the economic sphere are governed by the axiom. Commodities and factors of production are everyday things about which most people have enough experience in thinking that they usually achieve the state where relevant objects are fully commensurable. But many of the objects ordered in the political sphere are so passionately desired or hated or so seldom judged that true incommensurability· may occur. Thus, we conclude that choices involving only "ordinary" political goals, such as election victory, economic policy, and so on, can usually be ordered cardinally. Sometimes there may be difficulty because people are not so accustomed to comparing, e.g., election outcomes, as they are to comparing, e.g., investments. This difficulty aside, cardinal utility with ordinary goals is possible. It may not be possible, however, with extraordinary goals, such as those involving questions of peace and war, personal safety, race, caste, and the like.

SUGGESTIONS FOR FURTHER READING

Very few writers have attempted to use rationalism (in the sense of the expected-utility hypothesis) as a basis for political theory. In the absence of more extensive literature, therefore, we cite ANTHONY DOWNS, *An Economic Theory of Democracy* (New York: Harper & Row, 1957), WILLIAM H. RIKER, *The Theory of Political Coalitions* (New Haven: Yale University Press, 1963), and JAMES BUCHANAN and GORDON TULLOCK, *The Calculus of Consent* (Ann Arbor: University of Michigan Press, 1962). The first chapter of each of these books gives a brief discussion of the premise of rationality in its political context. A discussion of this premise in the context of social science generally is to be found in chaps. 2 and 3 of R. DUNCAN LUCE and HOWARD RAIFFA, *Games and Decisions* (New York: Wiley, 1957).

The notion of utility on which current ideas of rationalism are based is most frequently studied by economists. An excellent collection of essays and chapters, both classic and recent, on the development of the idea is ALFRED N. PAGE, *Utility Theory: A Book of Readings* (New York: Wiley, 1968). The principles of utility theory are well analyzed in WILLIAM FELLNER, *Probability and Profit* (Homewood, Ill.: Irwin, 1965), chap. 3; and an excellent elementary discussion of probability notions involved in decision theory is HOWARD RAIFFA, *Decision Analysis* (Reading, Mass.: Addison-Wesley, 1968).

3

Participation

We note in Chapter 1 that the realization of preferences involving other people is the raw material of politics, which is to say that the study of politics involves initially the analysis of individual choice in a social context. Because we wish to present theoretical primitives first, we focus our discussion in the previous chapter primarily on the abstract properties of the postulate of rational action. Now we seek to add some substantive detail to this postulate so as to make it a more useful tool for studying politics. Specifically, we examine the (somewhat ambiguous) concept of participation—a concept that focuses on the reciprocal relationships between individual choice and the social context of choice—and we offer a general decision-theoretic analysis of participation. In subsequent sections of this chapter we consider two substantive applications of this analysis. The first, which concerns a citizen's decision to vote in democratic elections, illustrates the application of the postulate of rational action to instances in which the choices by others are fixed parameters of a person's calculus. The second, which concerns the formation and maintenance of groups in politics, illustrates the generality of an analysis that treats participation as rational decision making and introduces the analysis of rational choice in instances in which the interaction among individual choices is more apparent than in our first example.

THE CONCEPT OF PARTICIPATION

Participation consists of many things, such as voting, conducting revolutions, forming parties and leading them, managing bureaucracies, and rioting.

Despite this diversity, however, all forms of participation consist of action and therefore involve that kind of decision-making which is the selection of one action out of a set of alternative actions. And because we seek a theory that *explains* individual political activity rather than relegating it to the inexplicable realm of the irrational, we assume that participation is rational in the sense that it consists of the examination of alternative actions and the selection of that alternative which yields the greatest expected utility. With this framework we exclude then the possibility that some manifestations of political activity differ theoretically from other manifestations. Instead, we assume that the theoretical primitives necessary to understand one activity, say, voting, are equally appropriate for understanding such things as leadership.

We are not, of course, asserting that the parameters affecting a citizen's decision to seek public office, for example, are necessarily identical to those affecting his decision to vote. On the contrary, the structural content of a rational calculus requires redescription in various social processes. Thus, the notion of a rational calculus provides only the base upon which complex theories of political action are constructed. But a common and unifying calculus of participation is essential, because frequently we must explain not only why a person participates or fails to participate, but also why he selects a particular mode of participation. That is, we wish to explain not only why a person votes, but also why he does or does not simultaneously seek public office, form a neighborhood action committee, or even attempt to overthrow a regime by force. Most forms of political activity and their combinations are alternatives to each other, and if we eventually hope to understand why one alternative is selected rather than another, we require a common theoretical perspective for examining people's choices.

We begin by restating a commonsense criterion that activities must satisfy before they are undertaken. From our discussion of rationality and utility maximization in Chapter 2 we know that a person adopts one alternative rather than another if he believes that the net benefits of the chosen activity exceed the net benefits of any alternative activity. Thus, if we let B denote the benefits of an activity and C its costs, and if we identify alternatives by subscripts, then alternative i is preferred to alternative k if

$$B_i - C_i > B_k - C_k, \tag{3.1}$$

and alternative i is chosen if this inequality is satisfied for all perceived alternatives to i. [We note parenthetically that the condition in expression (3.1) is frequently simplified incorrectly by asserting that an activity is chosen if the chooser believes that the benefits of the activity exceed its costs—or, equivalently, that net benefits exceed zero—or,[1]

$$B_i > C_i. \tag{3.2}$$

[1]This simplified choice rule, however, is correct and, in fact, is equivalent to (3.1) if we include *opportunity costs* in our calculation of C_i. Briefly, the opportunity cost of an alternative i

Observe, however, that there may be other activities for which the discrepancy between costs and benefits is greater, in which case these alternative activities are preferred and i is not chosen. Observe also that alternative i may be selected even though expression (3.2) is not satisfied. This situation arises when no action—including doing nothing—yields a positive net benefit, in which case the person simply performs the least objectionable alternative. Hence, it is expression (3.1) and not expression (3.2) that expresses the condition for the adoption of an alternative.]

Despite the simplicity of expression (3.1) we infer from it that our analysis of participation begins within the theoretical framework of decision theory, although from that point it must proceed by means of a careful examination of relative costs and rewards in the substantive context of choice. Of course, the literature of decision theory is extensive and spans such diverse topics as measurement theory, statistical inference, learning theory, sequential analysis, and cost-benefit analysis. Hence, we can present here only the very rudiments of this theory, which are essential for developing the logical foundations of our approach and for applying the more esoteric elements of decision theory to politics. Furthermore, we do not in this chapter consider in detail the complexities of choice occasioned by the fact that choosers choose independently. We consider such detail later, while here we focus on a chooser who takes as a given (perhaps only probabilistically) the choices of others.

We begin by observing that the symbolic representation of the condition for rational choice—expression (3.1)—is poorly suited for analyzing particular kinds of participation. It is misleading because it conceals the infinite variety of benefits and costs and the seemingly boundless difficulties one faces when calculating these terms. As we show later, naivety about these difficulties leads many researchers to draw incomplete and incorrect inference about choice. We are not interested in knowing simply that a person selects an alternative because benefits exceed costs and then in attempting to make intelligent guesses as to the nature of B and C. Rather we wish to be able to deduce contextually appropriate behavioral assumptions about how a person calculates B and C, about how these calculations are affected by his environment, and about how his calculations and, therefore, his choices change as his environment changes.

---

is the net benefits of the next best alternative that must be forgone if alternative i is selected. Thus, if k is the next best alternative to i, we can rewrite (3.2) thus;

$$B_i > C_i',$$

where

$$C_i' = C_i + (B_k - C_k).$$

Hence, the condition becomes

$$B_i > C_i + (B_k - C_k)$$

or simply

$$B_i - C_i > B_k - C_k.$$

which is equivalent to (3.1) since k is the best alternative to i (i.e., the net benefits of k are greater than the net benefits of any other alternative except, perhaps, i). For a more complete and general discussion of the concept of cost see James M. Buchanan, *Cost and Choice* (Chicago: Markham, 1969).

We want to avoid the simplistic method of assuming that a person's decisions are rational and then seeking *post hoc* evidence to demonstrate that these decisions conform to expression (3.1). Instead, we wish to construct, *a priori*, methods of calculating B and C for rather specialized classes of political actions like voting. Our hope is that for such specialized classes we can find empirical evidence to verify our *a priori* calculus.

THE FORMAL NOTION OF PARTICIPATION

Expression (3.1) must be reformulated, therefore, so as to be more amenable to the development of the kind of theory we require. The first stage of reformulation consists of denoting a person's alternative actions by the set:

$$A = \{a_0, a_1, \ldots, a_n\}.$$

(Our notation supposes that alternatives are discrete and finite; but it may be the case, such as when we choose a time, that A is a continuous variable and therefore infinite. Our discussion need not be constrained to the discrete case, but to simplify exposition we adopt the notation of the discrete.)

We do not now assume any substantive specification of the content of A. Action, like participation, consists of simple things such as voting for a preferred candidate and complex things such as the adoption of a strategic plan for national defense. Hence, so long as we discuss decision-making generally, the members of A must remain unspecified. Furthermore, even when we become more particular, we will have difficulty in specifying the a_i because there is a potential ambiguity inherent in the conceptualization of A in even the most simple choice situations. Consider electoral behavior, where voting and abstaining appear to be unambiguously identifiable alternatives. But voting is not a self-contained act for many citizens and it is frequently accompanied by other political activities such as canvassing, soliciting funds, and political debate, so that each alternative denoted by a_i is a package of political activity. Whether or not we interpret voting as a self-contained act or as an element of a package depends on the objectives of our inquiry. If, for example, our investigation concerns the effects of nationwide media coverage of presidential election returns on voting patterns in California, a simple characterization of alternatives is satisfactory. But if our investigation concerns the interaction of citizens during a campaign, a more complex characterization is necessary.

Our objective, however, is not simply to propose alternative conceptualizations for A, but to explain the alternatives people select. We assume, therefore, that each action, if selected, yields some outcome, and we assume that the desirability of each element of A is a function of the desirability of the outcomes that can occur if that alternative is chosen. Hence, we must identify outcomes: we denote the universe of possible outcomes by the following set, which again for convenience we present as discrete:

$$O = \{O_1, O_2, \ldots, O_m\}$$

where O is exhaustive (i.e., some member of O must occur) and the members of O are exclusive (i.e., if O_i occurs, then O_j, $j \neq i$, cannot occur). As is the case with A, there are inherent ambiguities in our substantive interpretation of O. Outcomes, like actions, may be either simple (such as the identification of a victorious candidate) or complex (such as the statement by precinct of the total vote received by each candidate). Any conceptualization of outcomes can in fact be elaborated further to include all foreseeable events even remotely related to a person's choices.

The ambiguities inherent in defining alternatives and outcomes can lead to "a universal theory of choice where each decision is effectively a choice among total life histories."[2] Of course, such a theory is neither practical nor a likely prospect. We restrict our focus, therefore, and assume that certain actions and outcomes are independent of others—while simultaneously constructing and testing alternative theoretical structures based on alternative specifications of actions and outcomes.

A delineation of actions and outcomes does not complete this structure, however, for now we must specify the relationships among them. As we note in Chapter 2, to specify this relation in terms of the postulate of rationality requires that we be able to assign utilities to outcomes and that we be able to relate outcomes and alternatives by means of probabilities. Specifically, we let $U_i(O_j)$ be the utility a person receives if alternative a_i is selected and outcome O_j occurs, and we let $P_i(O_j)$ be the probability that outcome O_j occurs if alternative a_i is selected.

These numbers, $U_i(O_j)$ and $P_i(O_j)$, are of course simple representations of very complicated reality. Because this reality is so complicated, we leave the substantive interpretation of these numbers to appear in our later examples. We do note, however, that $U_i(O_j)$ is the satisfaction a person receives from an outcome O_j, and it can in theory be measured by the kind of utility experiment described in Chapter 2 and justified in its Appendix. The number $P_i(O_j)$ derives from a person's uncertainty about the world around him. Among the things that the chooser may not know for certain are:

1. The states of social and physical nature. (For example, a farmer may not know what is in the soil on his farm or a soldier may not know the state of the enemy's morale.)
2. The choices of others. (Whether or not the choice of a_i leads to O_j depends in part on what some other person chooses. Whether or not my bluff at the poker table leads my opponent to fold depends on whether he chooses his action as if he believed me.)

Here we assume that the chooser takes both these uncertainties as given; and this given is incorporated in $P_i(O_j)$.

[2]Kenneth Arrow, "Utilities, Attitudes, Choices: A Review Note," *Econometrica*, vol. 26 (1958), pp. 1–23.

Using $U_i(O_j)$ and $P_i(O_j)$, we find the expected value of a_i, $E(a_i)$, to be

$$E(a_i) = P_i(O_1)U_i(O_1) + \ldots + P_i(O_m)U_i(O_m) \qquad (3.3)$$

$$= \sum_{j=1}^{m} P_i(O_j)U_i(O_j),$$

and the condition for adopting a_i is

$$E(a_i) > E(a_k) \qquad \text{for all } a_k \neq a_i. \qquad (3.4)$$

Observe that in expressions (3.3) and (3.4) we subscript the utility for an outcome with an i, which denotes the alternative selected. This subscript is necessary because no two outcomes, broadly conceived, are identical if they are preceded by the selection of different actions. Specifically, one outcome contains the history of the selection of one act, whereas the other outcome contains the history of the selection of some other act. Each alternative yields, therefore, a different and unique universe. Doubtless this observation is trivial and uninteresting in many choice situations—situations in which the means to some objective are regarded as irrelevant. But our observation is interesting and important if the means are relevant—if, for example, differential costs are incurred from alternatives so that outcomes can be distinguished at least by the costs incurred to achieve them. We might incorporate such possibilities into our analysis in either of two ways. First, we could assume that no two outcomes are equivalent when preceded by the selection of different alternatives—in which case we subscript outcomes with the same identifying number as we subscript alternatives. This approach, however, is usually intractable; a proliferation of alternatives *necessarily* yields a proliferation of possible outcomes and utility indexes for outcomes. We adopt, therefore, a second approach: we subscript with i the utility index for an outcome to show that the utility is dependent on the alternative selected.

Identifying utilities and not outcomes with the subscript for alternatives carries with it the assumption that the utility one associates with an outcome has two (presumably additive) components. The first component, denoted by $U(O_j)$, is that utility which the person associates directly with outcome O_j. The second component, denoted by U_i, is the utility the person associates with alternative a_i, and which is not dependent on the resultant outcome. Symbolically, therefore, we assume that,

$$U_i(O_j) = U(O_j) + U_i. \qquad (3.5)$$

To illustrate the calculation of expected utilities as well as the meaning of (3.5) assume that the a_i's are alternative means of securing money. Alternative a_1, then, can denote "gainful employment" while alternative a_2 denotes "murder and theft of the victim's wallet." There are two ways, now, in which we can conceptualize outcomes. In addition to specifying the state of a person's wealth, the first conceptualization includes in the description of outcomes the means by which such wealth is obtained. Thus, we can denote outcomes as

O_1: fabulous wealth via employment
O_2: subsistence wealth via employment
O_3: poverty via employment
O_4: fabulous wealth via murder and theft
O_5: subsistence wealth via murder and theft
O_6: poverty via murder and theft

Clearly, then, if a person selects alternative a_1, outcomes O_4, O_5, and O_6 cannot occur, whereas if he selects a_2, outcomes O_1, O_2, and O_3 cannot occur, i.e.,

$$P_1(O_4) = P_1(O_5) = P_1(O_6) = P_2(O_1) = P_2(O_2) = P_2(O_3) = 0.$$

Furthermore, since our description of outcomes contains the history of the act that led to them, there is no reason to subscript utility with the index i. Thus, the expected values of a_1 and a_2 are

$$E(a_1) = P_1(O_1)U(O_1) + P_1(O_2)U(O_2) + P_1(O_3)U(O_3),$$
$$E(a_2) = P_2(O_4)U(O_4) + P_2(O_5)U(O_5) + P_2(O_6)U(O_6).$$

Consider, however, an alternative conceptualization of outcomes:

O_1': fabulous wealth
O_2': subsistence wealth
O_3': poverty

Since our description of outcomes no longer contains the history of the act that led to them, and recognizing that the utility a person associates with each of these outcomes is likely to be a function of the means he chooses to obtain it, we now write $E(a_1)$ and $E(a_2)$ in accordance with (3.3);

$$E(a_1) = P_1(O_1')U_1(O_1') + P_1(O_2')U_1(O_2') + P_1(O_3')U_1(O_3'),$$
$$E(a_2) = P_2(O_1')U_2(O_1') + P_2(O_2')U_2(O_2') + P_2(O_3')U_2(O_3').$$

We have not, of course, gained much with this conceptualization of outcomes over our original conceptualization. Both yield a calculation of expected values containing six probabilities and six utility numbers. To this point, then, the two conceptualizations serve only as an excuse for different notations. Suppose, however, that we adopt expression (3.5). That is, suppose that we can separate the utility a person associates with an act (employment or murder and theft) from the consequences of the act (fabulous wealth, subsistence wealth, or poverty). Assuming that the consequences (i.e., degree of wealth) are exhaustively categorized so that

$$\sum_{j=1}^{m} P_i(O_j) = 1,$$

then the expected value $E(a_1)$ is

$$E(a_1) = P_1(O_1')[U(O_1') + U_1] + P_1(O_2')[U(O_2') + U_1]$$
$$+ P_1(O_3')[U(O_3') + U_1]$$

$$= P_1(O_1')U(O_1') + P_1(O_2')U(O_2') + P_1(O_3')U(O_3') + U_1$$

[since $P_1(O_1') + P_1(O_2') + P_1(O_3') = 1$], where the symbol U_1 denotes the utility the citizen associates with gainful employment—regardless of the wealth it brings. Similarly, for $E(a_2)$ we obtain with (3.5),

$$E(a_2) = P_2(O_1')U(O_1') + P_2(O_2')U(O_2') + P_2(O_3')U(O_3') + U_2,$$

where U_2 denotes the utility of committing murder and theft—regardless of the wealth it secures.

The assumption that utility is separable yields a slight notational efficiency—while we still have six distinct probabilities in our calculation of $E(a_1)$ and $E(a_2)$, our example now contains five rather than six utility numbers [in general, if there are n alternatives and m outcomes, our expected utility calculations involve mn distinct utility numbers without (3.5), but with (3.5) they involve only $m + n$ utility numbers]. More importantly, however, expression (3.5) is a useful assumption for uncovering the factors that affect participation in politics. Specifically, it directs our attention to the fact that people value means as well as ends and it permits us to draw out fully the implication of this fact. Thus, while we realize that (3.5) is not an assumption that we can always satisfy, we use it here. Substituting (3.5) into (3.3), then, we obtain:[3]

$$E(a_i) = \sum_{j=1}^{m} P_i(O_j)U(O_j) + U_i. \tag{3.6}$$

Using expression (3.6), we rewrite expression (3.4) to restate more elaborately the condition for choosing a_i, viz., that its net benefits must exceed the net benefits of every other alternative in A:

$$\sum_{j=1}^{m} P_i(O_j)U(O_j) + U_i > \sum_{j=1}^{m} P_k(O_j)U(O_j) + U_k \qquad \text{for } k \neq i$$

or, carrying all terms to one side of the inequality,

$$\sum_{j=1}^{m} P_i(O_j)U(O_j) - \sum_{j=1}^{m} P_k(O_j)U(O_j) + U_i - U_k > 0,$$

which, by placing all terms indexed by j under the same summation, can be rewritten as

$$\sum_{j=1}^{m} [P_i(O_j) - P_k(O_j)]U(O_j) + (U_i - U_k) > 0 \qquad \text{for } k \neq i. \tag{3.7}$$

---

[3]Rewriting (3.3) with the substitution of (3.5),
$$E(a_i) = \sum_{j} P_i(O_j)[U(O_j) + U_i]$$
$$= \sum_{j} P_i(O_j)U(O_j) + U_i \sum_{j} P_i(O_j),$$
which reduces to (3.6) if we assume that $\sum_{j} P_i(O_j) = 1$. If we assume that the $P_i(O_j)$'s are truly subjective so that they do not add to 1 like objective probabilities, we can assume simply that $U_i \sum_{j} P_i(O_j)$ is some new constant.

SOCIAL AND PRIVATE CONSEQUENCES OF THE CHOICE ABOUT PARTICIPATION

The mere complexity of expression (3.7) relative to the simplicity of expressions (3.1) and (3.4) should not be construed to mean that (3.7) constitutes a substantively meaningful theory of participation. As in the earlier expressions, some additional structure must be furnished before we can generate reasonably interesting inferences about choice. But while (3.7) is simply a more elaborate abstract condition for rational choice, it is nevertheless very useful. Unlike (3.1) and (3.4), it indicates one way to proceed in constructing substantively valuable theories about individual political action.

Specifically, expression (3.7) reveals that a chooser's comparative evaluation of alternatives consists of two kinds of calculations. The first kind, which, for reasons discussed presently, we term the *comparative evaluation of social consequences*, is represented by the terms containing the probability differences $P_i(O_j) - P_k(O_j)$. These calculations are concerned with the relative efficacy of an alternative for realizing certain outcomes. The second kind of calculation, which we term *comparative evaluation of private consequences*, is represented by the utility difference $U_i - U_k$. It concerns the relative benefits that are inherent in the action itself and are not dependent on the efficacy of the actions for outcomes. In terms of our earlier illustration, the calculations involving $P_i(O_j) - P_k(O_j)$ are concerned with the state of one's wealth, while the calculation of $U_i - U_k$ is concerned with the morality of employment and theft.

The careful examination of the properties of these calculations of social and private consequences in concrete choice situations constitutes the primary task of theorizing about political action. Therefore, we offer some remarks about them.

THE COMPARATIVE EVALUATION OF SOCIAL CONSEQUENCES

Recall from Chapter 1 that we distinguish between two kinds of preferences: private and public. Preferences are said to be public when their realization concerns other people besides their holders, whereas private preferences involve only the holder's affairs. Elaborating this distinction, we say that some actions are private in that they only casually affect other people and are without relevance to politics. Other actions, however, are public in that they significantly concern others besides the actor himself. Admittedly this distinction is arbitrary, because few, if any, actions are so self-contained that they affect no one else—other than perhaps the actions of a Robinson Crusoe. Conversely, not all actions affecting other people are of immediate relevance to politics. We do not usually consider arguments between husbands and wives as politically interesting, except perhaps when the husband is a president. The intent of our distinction—if not its operationalization—should nevertheless be clear. Some distinction between public and private action is necessary in order to identify the kinds of outcomes we are concerned with when analyzing the substantive content of expression (3.7). Specifically, we are interested only in outcomes consequent from public acts. If such acts lead to outcomes which affect a sufficiently interesting range of people, we call the outcomes socially relevant. [4,5] And, of course, if the alternatives in the set A are forms of political participation, the outcomes are invariably socially relevant.

Because the acts (i.e., elements of A) are public and the outcomes (i.e., elements of O) are socially relevant, the proportion of the benefits and costs accruing to the actor and others is variable. Typically, as the scope and efficacy of actions vary, so do the costs and benefits. By scope, we mean the number of people affected by an act. Some acts (such as discussing current events with one's friends) affect only a few people, whereas other acts (such as a formal discussion between diplomats) affect whole nations and relations among them. Sometimes the scope of an act is limited by intent, such as when we merely petition for a variance from a local zoning ordinance instead of seeking to have the ordinance repealed. Sometimes, also, scope is limited by constitutional arrangement, such as when we cast only a personal vote, constitutionally prohibited as we are from buying up the proxies of others. It is clear that the number of people affected by a person's choice is variable. And this potential for variation partially accounts for the ambiguity in our definition of public and private action: there is no certain threshold at which a private act becomes public.

A concomitant source of ambiguity is the efficacy of actions—that is, the extent to which an act, a_i, affects the probabilities of outcomes, and, therefore, the environment of other actors. Like scope, efficacy can assume an infinity of values. Voting in national democratic elections, for example, exhibits little efficacy because a single vote does not affect greatly the result of the election. Some other activities, however, such as the contribution by the members of a labor union of the services of their paid business agent as the campaign manager for a mayoralty candidate, exhibit a greater degree of efficacy because they increase the opportunity for the members to influence politically relevant outcomes through their agent (if the candidate is successful). Despite such diversity in degree, however, we can define efficacy generally in terms of expression (3.7). Specifically, by the efficacy of an act, a_i, to produce an outcome,

---

[4]It is possible, even when the act is public, that $P_i(O_j) = P_k(O_j)$ for all i, k, and j, which is to say that the person cannot affect the occurrence of outcomes. We exclude such degenerate possibilities from our discussion.

[5]If one outcome in O is socially relevant, all outcomes in O are socially relevant. To prove this somewhat surprising feature of relevance, recall that the elements of O are disjoint; i.e., if O_j occurs, some other outcome O_i in O cannot occur. Assume then that O_i is socially relevant. If O_j occurs, then O_i cannot occur. Hence, the occurrence of O_j affects the utilities of other people because it denies them O_i. The outcome O_j then is socially relevant.

O_j, we mean $[P_i(O_j) - P_k(O_j)]$.[6] From this definition we can now illustrate one important consequence of variations in efficacy, namely that such variations directly affect the attractiveness of the alternative. For expository purposes assume that A and O each consist of only two elements, a_0, a_1, O_1, and O_2, and that O_1 is preferred to O_2 [i.e., $U(O_1) > U(O_2)$]. Additionally, assume that a_0 represents doing nothing (e.g., abstaining from voting) and that $U_0 = 0$ (i.e., there are no direct benefits or costs associated with a_0). From expression (3.7), then, alternative a_1 is preferred to a_0 if[7]

$$[P_1(O_1) - P_0(O_1)][U(O_1) - U(O_2)] + U_1 > 0. \tag{3.8}$$

Finally, let us assume that a_1 is efficacious for attaining the more desired outcome, O_1 [i.e., $P_1(O_1) > P_0(O_1)$], but that $U_1 = -C < 0$ (i.e., a direct cost must be incurred to adopt a_1). Thus, we get

$$[P_1(O_1) - P_0(O_1)][U(O_1) - U(O_2)] - C > 0. \tag{3.9}$$

Observe now that both terms in the brackets are positive, whereas $-C$ is a negative quantity. Hence, a_1 is preferred to doing nothing, a_0, only if the product of the bracketed terms exceeds the direct cost of a_1. Obviously, it is possible to set C sufficiently high so that a_1 is never chosen. But the magnitude of C necessary to accomplish this depends on $[P_1(O_1) - P_0(O_1)]$—the efficacy of a_1 in our choice situation. Loosely speaking, then, we can say that, with respect to this example, the greater the efficacy of a_1 the greater is the likelihood that it will be preferred to inaction, a_0.

Although it contains a number of arbitrary assumptions, our example does illustrate in what way efficacy can significantly affect participation. And from this illustration we infer that the study of participation should include an examination of the reasons for variations in efficacy. We survey these reasons by constructing a typology. First, we categorize differences in efficacy as involving either differences among people in equivalent choice situations, or differences among social choice situations for one person. Second,

---

[6]From this definition we can see that efficacy is relative to an outcome and to two alternatives.

[7]That is, $E(a_1) > E(a)$ if, from (3.7),

$$\sum_{j=1}^{2} [P_1(O_j) - P_0(O_j)]U(O_j) + U_1 - U_0 > 0.$$

Expanding, deleting $U_0 = 0$, we get

$$[P_1(O_1) - P_0(O_1)]U(O_1) + [P_1(O_2) - P_0(O_2)]U(O_2) + U_1 > 0.$$

Noting that

$$P_1(O_2) = 1 - P_1(O_1) \quad \text{and} \quad P_0(O_2) = 1 - P_0(O_1),$$

we can rewrite

$$[P_1(O_1) - P_0(O_1)]U(O_1) + [(1 - P_1(O_1)) - (1 - P_0(O_1))]U(O_2) + U_1 > 0$$

and expand:

$$P_1(O_1)U(O_1) - P_0(O_1)U(O_1) + U(O_2) - P_1(O_1)U(O_2) - U(O_2) + P_0(O_1)U(O_2) + U_1 > 0.$$

Simplifying,

$$[P_1(O_1) - P_0(O_1)][U(O_1) - U(O_2)] + U_1 > 0,$$

which is expression (3.8).

we categorize these differences as either objective or subjective relative to the judgment of the actors. Hence, we get Table 3.1.

TABLE 3.1

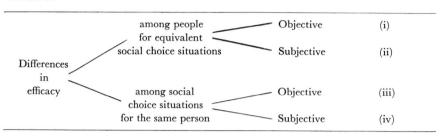

Categories (i) and (ii) concern situations in which the efficacy of one person's act differs from that of another's, even though the acts in question are otherwise identical, are chosen from the same set of alternatives, and are aimed at affecting the probabilities of the same outcomes. Such differences are objective—category (i)—when they are attributed by persons outside the scene of action. Thus, for example, if A consists of two alternatives—seeking public office and not seeking public office—and if one decision maker has initially a higher level of public prestige, he is then more likely to affect favorably the choices of voters, and, therefore, is more likely to seek public office because, *ceteris paribus*, he is more likely to win.[8] The variation in efficacy between the person of high prestige and others does not depend on his (or even their) judgment but on the prestige system in the whole society. The variations in efficacy identified by (ii), however, depend on the judgment of the actor himself and are, therefore, probably common in the world. Specifically, if people estimate the probability that some event will occur, variations in opinion are likely to be observed. Naturally, the magnitude of these variations is a function of such factors as the subjects' familiarity with the context of the event and the amount of information available. Nevertheless, even when people are confronted with identical decision-making situations in which objective probabilities might be calculated precisely, people's subjective estimates of these probabilities vary. Such variations then yield variations on people's estimates of efficacy. As a consequence, one citizen might regard some particular form of participation (say, voting) as efficacious and hence rational, while another citizen in equivalent circumstances might regard it as less efficacious and hence irrational.

Although the efficacy of political activity can vary because of variations among the attributes and judgments of people, efficacy can also vary because

---

[8]We must carefully distinguish, however, between situations in category (i) and those in which efficacy varies because the decision makers are concerned with different sets of alternatives. A person can have, for example, a greater effect on probabilities because for him A includes different and more effective alternatives.

of features of the context of social choice. Hence we get categories (iii) and (iv), where (iii) involves objective variations in the environment and (iv) involves variations in the subjective interpretation of the environment. Since (iv) is a relatively straightforward extension into the subjective world of category (ii), we concern ourselves only with (iii). In order to understand this category and the reasons for variations in efficacy, recall that, while we define efficacy in terms of some parameters of expression (3.7), the definition of scope is in terms of variables currently exogenous to this expression. But frequently, *although not necessarily,* these two concepts are closely related. In markets or in national elections the scope of a consumer or a voter's choice is large but its efficacy is small. Conversely, the scope of a person's activities in neighborhood action committees is confined to his local community, but the efficacy of these activities can be substantial. Thus we find in such instances an inverse relationship between scope and efficacy. The explanation for this inverse relationship lies, of course, in the mechanisms which aggregate individual choices into a social outcome. Typically, the greater the scope of a person's acts—the greater the number of people concerned with outcomes in O—the greater the number of people required to insure the occurrence of a particular outcome and the smaller the efficacy, *ceteris paribus,* of any single person's choice. Frequently, therefore, the efficacy of an action is inversely related to its scope, as either objectively (iii) or subjectively (iv) assessed. (A counterexample to this relationship is the assassination of a president, where both scope and efficacy are large. Clearly, then, we must scrutinize carefully the particular context of choice in order to ascertain the relationship between scope and efficacy in that context.)

The Paradox of Participation

To this point in our examination of equation (3.7) we have concentrated on the social consequences (i.e., on the term, "$[P_i(O_j) - P_k(O_j)]U(O_j)$" and on the notion of efficacy which this term expresses). Our main theme is that the efficacy of an act varies not only according to the chooser's taste and judgment but also with respect to the objective conditions in which the act is presumed to occur.

This feature of the calculus, this variation, has a profound effect on human society. It leads to what we call the paradox of participation. As society complicates, efficacy tends to diminish, not only because scope increases, but also because the individual is subjectively submerged in the mass. Hence, one incentive to participate, viz., high efficacy, tends to disappear in the large and complicated world. And as the incentives to participate diminish, so do the consequences of failing to participate. Thus, a citizen evaluates his opportunities for political action and concludes that, because his acts are of little consequence, a failure to participate does not greatly diminish his welfare. This then is the paradox of participation: while people differentially affect the probabilities that outcomes occur by participating, still the consequences of action frequently are infinitesimal for the individual person. Hence, while social outcomes necessarily occur and are made by the decisions of men, many men may not have incentives to participate to influence them.

This paradox, the absence of incentives for men to engage themselves in the life of the polity which nevertheless they value, is simply a generalization of the so-called free-rider problem. Social outcomes such as peace and an orderly society are what economists call public goods; indeed they are the primary examples of public goods. And the main feature of such goods is that, if they are supplied to and consumed by any person in a class (e.g., one citizen among all citizens), they are equally supplied to and consumed by all. Thus, once supplied, men perceive few adverse consequences if they individually avoid the costs of participation. If the lighthouse works, why should the ship captain pay for it, especially when there is no practical way to collect from him? But when everybody avoids the costs of participation, how then can society be maintained and anarchy avoided? This, of course, is the great practical question of politics. Mostly, practical men have solved the problem by use of force and use of persuasion. The great discovery of Hobbes was that men grant force to society in order to maintain peace. Men have done this from time immemorial, of course, and Hobbes saw that this was one solution to the problem of the paradox of participation. But it is not the only solution —and in thinking so, Hobbes erred—for it is possible also to solve the paradox by other means. These means are what we wish to explore next.

THE COMPARATIVE EVALUATION OF PRIVATE CONSEQUENCES

Hobbes recognized the role of force in preserving an orderly society, and with this insight he identified one means by which people can be made individually to find that their part in collective action is rational. But even if Hobbes is correct, force is a sufficient and not a necessary condition for the preservation of order.

To see how the threat of force works out, consider its consequences in terms of expression (3.7). Assume that all citizens believe it is morally right to select a common alternative, say a_1, such as dutifully paying one's income taxes, as against income tax evasion, a_0. Will they in fact do so? Since the relative contribution of each one to the financial solvency of the government is quite negligible, each potential taxpayer finds the efficacy of a_1 nearly zero. For most people, the consequence to them of adopting a_1 is indistinguishable from that of adopting a_0. Hence, whether or not they pay depends on the U_i terms. But every citizen considers his contribution to be personally costly, so that

$U_1 < 0$. In the absence of other considerations tax evasion would be universal.[9] It can be the case that a_1 is preferred to a_0 only if $U_1 > U_0$. Since U_1 is a negative number, tax paying is preferable to tax evasion only if U_0 assumes a more negative value than U_1. And that is exactly what the threat of force is designed to bring about. By threatening imprisonment, the government raises the cost of noncompliance so that private costs of paying taxes are exceeded by the private costs of evasion. Hence, it is not the threat of force, per se, that renders the solution of a_1 as against a_0 rational. Rather it is the fact that U_1 exceeds U_0. Force is simply an instrumental means for insuring this inequality, and it is possible that other equally effective means can be imagined. It is in this sense, then, that force is sufficient but not necessary for public order.

We are not concerned, however, with contriving alternative means for insuring the payment of taxes—the possibilities we might propose are limited only by our imagination. Instead, we offer this illustration as an instance of a general phenomenon involved in participation, that is, the augumentation of public benefits (or costs) by private ones—benefits that can be received by some people and denied others— so that desired public outcomes are realized. The public consequence of one individual's paying or not paying taxes are so modest that the calculus involved in $[P_1(O_j) - P_0(O_j)]$ is probably impractical to make. Furthermore, paying taxes involves a private cost. Hence, it is to the individual person's benefit to avoid payment. But every person is faced with a similar calculus, and everyone has an incentive to be a "free rider." Thus, the system is threatened with anarchy. Since nearly everyone values the survival of the government while recognizing the absence of natural incentives for compliance, nearly everyone therefore welcomes laws that increase the private incentives for compliance.

Once such laws are passed, forms of participation such as paying taxes are rational because they yield purely private benefits of the proper magnitude. Thus, the incentives to participate are not simply functions of a citizen's effect on the probabilities of events—the public consequence of action embodied in the term "$[P_i(O_j) - P_k(O_j)]U(O_j)$." Additional incentives such as legal sanctions may exist, and the existence of these selective incentives motivates our inclusion of the term $(U_i - U_k)$ in expression (3.7). Unlike the effects on expected utility of the public consequences of choice, private benefits (or costs) are not associated in (3.7) with the occurrence of any particular event. Rather, they are associated with alternatives, and whether or not a person derives these benefits is solely a function of the alternative he selects.

Our illustration of tax paying is, however, a special case of more diverse possibilities for private incentives. These incentives need not always be costs, which is to say that they need not be derived from sanctions. Sometimes we transform a socially desirable but individually undesirable action into an indi-

---

[9]It is this situation that leads to regulation. See Chapter 10.

vidually desirable one by granting a subsidy for doing it rather than exacting a penalty for not doing it. Instead of fining the owner of the cheese factory that pollutes the stream, we pay him to install waste removal equipment. Furthermore, the incentives need not always be contrived by law. If keeping public peace depended wholly on the force of law, à la Hobbes, and not at all on the sense of community, it is doubtful if peace could ever be kept.

The utility, U_i, consists, therefore, of many things. To identify some of these things we distinguish first between incentives that are benefits (e.g., subsidies) and incentives that are costs (e.g., sanctions). Thus we reexpress U_i as

$$U_i = U_i^+ - U_i^-. \tag{3.10}$$

Both U_i^+ and U_i^- also include many things. For example, U_i^- is the private monetary cost of paying one's taxes, and it is the cost incurred from legal sanctions if taxes are not properly paid. Similarly, the benefits term, U_i^+, can represent simple monetary rewards such as tax rebates, and it can include more complex rewards such as the joys of friendships made in the course of political participation. Finally, U_i^- can represent the cost of time spent participating— which suggests that this cost is universal, since all action consumes time—and the costs of securing information about alternatives and evaluating them.

It is clear, then, that U_i consists of both positive and negative elements. For many forms of participation, however, only the private costs, U_i^-, are obvious and easily identified, such as when costs are measured in terms of money and of time spent participating. The observability and universality of these costs of participation, when combined with a low degree of efficacy, leads many researchers to conclude that the net benefits of some common forms of political activity (e.g., voting) are exceeded by the net benefits of other less common acts (e.g., abstaining). Hence, they interpret a mass political activity as irrational. Their error is, of course, that they overlook those private benefits of participation and those private costs of failing to participate that are less tangible than economic factors such as time and money. Typically, upon closer inspection, one finds intangible incentives that exceed the economic costs of participation.

Stated differently, the benefits men seek from political participation frequently are not measured in terms of the effects of their actions on outcomes or in terms of such things as money. From participation, men also get prestige, friendship, the fun of playing the game, the satisfaction of indentifying with some cause, and so on. There are no laws forcing a man to become a precinct leader, to vote, to contribute to a campaign, to write a letter to one's congressman; and the possibility that social outcomes are affected by such action is frequently negligible. Nevertheless, people engage in such activities, so we must explain their actions. One essential element of our explanation is that the paradox of participation is solved by the construction of an ideology of obligation. The obligation is that men, starting from childhood, learn to value many things such as friendship, status, and self-esteem. And the solution to the paradox is that many of these things are obtained through political action. Thus, the obligation augments the relative public rewards of participation (i.e., the outcomes which are often individually insignificant) with private rewards which are dependent solely on the person's choices.

The ideology of obligation may exist by design, constructed to induce specified choices. Or it may evolve as a quite broad support for the maintenance of social order. This, for example, is where Hobbes' analysis is incomplete—it identifies force as the necessary solution to the paradox of participation. But instead of force, men can create the ideology of obligation that leads men to participate by reason of private incentives such as prestige, status, and duty. Thus, we learn that voting is an element of good citizenship, and the desire to be a good citizen leads many to vote even though the public consequence of this act (that is, its efficacy) is thought to be small. One result of political socialization, then, is the augmentation of the public consequences of one's acts with private consequences.

Finally, there are elements of U_i^+ that we label altruism and egoism, and philanthropy and misanthropy. For an explanation of why men have these sets of desires to help or hurt other people, one must turn to the science of psychology, not the science of politics. Nevertheless, the science of politics must incorporate these incentives in its theories. The biographies and autobiographies of public personages are replete with examples of men driven to public action by such private wants as these. These wants can manifest themselves as a desire for some better order for self and society together, or simply as a selfish desire without regard for any definition of the common good. They can appear as socially admirable (e.g., the obligation and self-restraint of a Cincinnatus) or as socially abhorrent (e.g., the paranoid sadism of a Hitler). Despite this diversity, such motivations must be understood as comprising an essential element of a theory of rational political action, and we summarize them as part of the term, U_i^+.[10]

We began our discussion of expression (3.7) by noting the existence of two kinds of terms in it, and by suggesting that they involve two distinct kinds of calculations. We continued with an analysis of some of the variety of phenomena that properly characterize real instances of these calculations. To conclude, however, we believe this fact is demonstrated: expression (3.7) is not in itself a substantively meaningful theory capable of explaining and predicting choice. For such a theory we must ascertain how people calculate utilities and probabilities in concrete decision-making situations. Thus, if we seek to un-

---

[10]Our analysis does not mean, however, that we cannot incorporate these motivations in $U(O_j)$ with a proper conceptualization of outcomes. And for the true philanthropist this might be the most fruitful approach. Thus, as we emphasize in our example on pp. 51–52, we can move back and forth between conceptualizations. For a treatment of philanthropy in terms of a rational calculus, see Thomas R. Ireland, "The Calculus of Philanthropy," *Public Choice,* vol. 7 (1969), pp. 23–31, and with David B. Johnson, *The Economics of Charity* (Blacksburg, Va.: Center for the Study of Public Choice, 1971).

derstand the logic of a particular form of participation, or if we seek to learn which form will manifest itself in a specific situation, our theory will at least consist of the logical relationships stated or implied by expression (3.7) and hypotheses (assumptions) about:

(a) the conceptualization and exhaustive delineation of alternative actions, A;
(b) the conceptualization and exhaustive delineation of alternative public outcomes, O;
(c) a utility function $U(O_j)$ defined over the set O;
(d) a utility function U_i corresponding to the private consequences of choice;
(e) a probability function $P_i(O_j)$ which relates alternative actions to outcomes.

In the subsequent sections of this chapter we illustrate the application of expression (3.7) to two concrete decision-making situations that concern political participation.

THE CALCULUS OF VOTING

Our first illustration concerns a citizen's decision to vote in democratic elections. We begin with the observation that much theorizing about the utility of voting concludes that voting is an irrational act in that it usually costs more to vote than one can expect to get in return.[11] The writers who constructed these analyses were engaged in an endeavor to explain political behavior with a calculus of rational choice; yet they were led by their argument to the conclusion that voting, the fundamental political act, is typically irrational. We find this conflict between purpose and conclusion bizarre, but not nearly so bizarre as a nonexplanatory theory. The function of the theory is to explain behavior, and certainly it is no explanation to assign a sizable part of politics to the mysterious and inexplicable world of the irrational. Elsewhere, we reanalyze the citizen's decision-making problem so as to develop a calculus of voting from which one infers that it is reasonable for those who vote to do so, and also that it is equally reasonable for those who do not vote not to do so.[12]

Briefly, the conclusion that voting is an irrational act follows from an incomplete and misleading specification of a citizen's calculus. Tullock, for example,

[11]See, for example, Gordon Tullock, *Toward a Mathematics of Politics* (Ann Arbor: University of Michigan Press, 1968), chap. 7. Tullock, however, should not bear the sole responsibility for this conclusion: it is one we have heard uttered countless times by colleagues in conversation.

[12]William H. Riker and Peter C. Ordeshook, "A Theory of the Calculus of Voting," *American Political Science Review*, vol. 63 (1968), pp. 25–43, and Richard D. McKelvey and Peter C. Ordeshook, "A General Theory of the Calculus of Voting," in J. F. Herndon and J. L. Bernd, eds., *Mathematical Applications in Political Science*, vol. 6 (Charlottesville: University Press of Virginia, 1972). For additional empirical research based on this analysis see Howard Rosenthal and Subrata Sen, "Electoral Participation in the French Fifth Republic: The FY Vote," *American Political Science Review* (forthcoming); and H. Rosenthal, "Coalitions and Spatial Models of Elections: An Empirical Analysis for the French Election of 1951" (GSIA Working Paper, Carnegie–Mellon University, 1970).

defines R, which is the expected utility of voting less the expected utility of abstaining, thus:

$$R = PB - C,$$

where C is the cost of voting, B is the differential benefit that an individual voter receives from the success of his more preferred candidate over his less preferred one, and P is the probability that the citizen will, by voting, materially affect the outcome. Since P is assumed to equal one divided by the number of voters, it is asserted that PB must be a very small number, so that C outweighs PB, leaving R negative. Thus the expected utility of abstaining is greater than the expected utility of voting, in which case it is irrational to vote. Unfortunately, this analysis is entirely *ad hoc*; there is no reason to suppose that P equals one over the number of voters, or that $PB - C$ is an adequate representation of the voter's decision calculus.

Consider first the utility, U_i, in expression (3.7). We know that this utility can have both negative and positive components. But the structure of the term $PB - C$ implies that U_i consists only of the negative component, $-C$. Of course, the costs, C, are universal—consisting, for example, of the time and energy it takes to get to the polls. Nevertheless, the private benefit component of U_i, namely, U_i^+ (which we refer to as D in our original analysis), is substantial, and its omission from the representation of a citizen's calculus seriously impairs the adequacy of the description. Among the factors that contribute to U_i^+ are the following satisfactions:

1. The satisfaction of complying with the ethic of voting, which if the citizen is at all socialized into the democratic tradition, is significant.
2. The satisfaction from affirming allegiance to the political system: for many people this is the main rationale for voting.
3. The satisfaction from affirming a partisan preference.
4. The satisfaction of deciding, going to the polls, and so on. These items are usually regarded as costs, but for those who enjoy the act of informing themselves for the decision, these supposed costs are actually benefits.
5. The satisfaction of affirming one's efficacy in the political system: the theory of democracy asserts that individuals and the act of voting are meaningful, and for most people the only chance to show that they and their actions are in fact meaningful is in the voting booth.

Doubtless, there are other satisfactions that have not occurred to us; but this list is sufficient to indicate the nature of U_i^+ in elections.

With the addition of U_i^+ to the equation for the expected utility of voting, we provide an excuse to render R positive for voters. But we say nothing to alter the intuitively persuasive supposition the PB term typically is very close to zero because P equals one divided by the number of voters. And if this intuitive supposition is correct, the addition of U_i^+ then makes voting rational only to the extent that we say the decision to vote by those who have been socialized to vote is a rational decision. Thus, P and B must be examined more carefully to see if more interesting inferences can be derived from this analysis.

First, let O_j be the outcome "candidate j wins," let $P_i(O_j)$ be the probability that candidate j wins if the citizen votes for i, and let $P_0(O_j)$ be the probability that j wins if the citizen abstains. Finally, let O_{ij} be the outcome "candidates i and j tie for first place," and so on. In a parallel fashion we can define the probabilities $P_i(O_{ij})$, and so on. Hence, the expected value of voting for candidate i, $E(a_i)$, is

$$E(a_i) = \sum P_i(O)U(O) + U_i^+ - U_i^-,$$

where the summation is taken over all possible outcomes. For example, if only two candidates compete, the expression for $E(a_i)$ becomes

$$E(a_i) = P_i(O_1)U(O_1) + P_i(O_2)U(O_2) + P_i(O_{12})U(O_{12}) + U_i^+ - U_i^-.$$

Similarly, the expected value of abstaining is[13]

$$E(a_0) = \sum P_0(O)U(O).$$

A citizen votes now if at least one $E(a_i)$ exceeds $E(a_0)$, and, if he votes, he votes for candidate i if $E(a_i)$ exceeds all alternative expected values.

To simplify our discussion, assume that if the citizen votes, he votes for candidate 1.[14] Hence, the necessary and sufficient condition for voting is

$$E(a_1) - E(a_0) = \sum_j [P_1(O_j) - P_0(O_j)]U(O_j) + U_1^+ - U_1^- > 0,$$

which is simply the restatement of expression (3.7).

If we now supply two additional assumptions, this expression can be reduced further to more meaningful terms. The first assumption is simply that the utility of a tie is the average of the utilities associated with the candidates involved in a tie. For example, we assume that the utility of a first-place tie between candidates 1 and 2, $U(O_{12})$, equals $[U(O_1) + U(O_2)]/2$.

The second assumption is more fundamental to this analysis. We assume that the choices by other members of the electorate are unaffected when one person chooses to vote rather than abstain. This is probably a realistic assumption when there are hundreds or millions of voters, but it may not be totally realistic in, say, small committees. In such committees, one person's decision can significantly affect the probabilities that particular outcomes occur; and

---

[13]We assume that $U_0^+ = U_0^- = 0$. If for some reason they are not equal to zero, we can include them in the values for U_0^- and U_0^+ by normalizing our equations.

[14]This does not imply, however, that candidate 1 is his preferred candidate, i.e., that $U(O_1) > U(O_j)$ for all alternatives j. It may be that his most preferred candidate has little or no chance of winning, in which case the voter selects his best viable candidate. On this point see the debate between Gerald Kramer and Thomas Casstevens [letters to the editor, *American Political Science Review*, vol. 62 (1968), pp. 955–956, and vol. 65 (1971), pp. 187–189] concerning Casstevens's essay "A Theorem about Voting," *American Political Science Review*, vol. 62 (1968), pp. 205–207. For two-candidate contests, however, if a citizen votes, he votes for his preferred candidate (see note 31, Chapter 12). Thus, our assumption is equivalent to the assumption that the citizen prefers candidate 1 if candidate 2 is the only opponent.

since this effect is likely to be perceived by everyone, everyone is likely to attempt to adjust his choice accordingly. In large electorates, however, such effects are small objectively and, while a person's subjective estimate of his effects on probabilities may be larger than our objective calculation of them, others will probably disregard the implication of another person's decision. Consequently, if we restrict the interpretation of our analysis to large electorates, we may assume that one person's choice does not affect the choices by others.

With these assumptions and with some extensive formal manipulations which are not reproduced here, the expression for $E(a_1) - E(a_0)$ can be reduced to a manageable form, and meaningful empirical inferences can be made. In lieu of this reduced form, the derivation of which involves some complex notation, we present here an analysis of two-candidate contests, since a cost-benefit analysis of voting is well illustrated by this simple case.[15]

For two-candidate contests we get

$$E(a_1) - E(a_0) = [P_0(O_{12}) + P_1(O_{12})]\left[\frac{U(O_1) - U(O_2)}{2}\right] + U_1^+ - U_1^-,$$

where $P_1(O_{12})$ is the probability that the candidates tie if the citizen votes for candidate 1, and $P_0(O_{12})$ is the probability that the candidates tie if the citizen abstains. Hence, in terms of the notation introduced earlier,

$$P = [P_0(O_{12}) + P_1(O_{12})] \text{ and } B = \tfrac{1}{2}[U(O_1) - U(O_2)].$$

P, then, is simply the probability that by voting the citizen either creates a tie or breaks a tie.[16] Thus, the closer the anticipated outcome, the higher is P, which is to say that P is a function not simply of the number of voters, but also of the estimated closeness of the vote.

[15]For three-candidate contests, for example, $E(a_1) - E(a_0)$ reduces to the sum of two terms (disregarding U_1^+ and U_1^-, which are also present). The first term consists of the calculation that candidates 1 and 2 tie for first place (which we can call the relative competitiveness of candidates 1 and 2) times the utility differential between them. The second term involves a similar calculation for candidates 1 and 3. In fact, we can show that for the addition of each new candidate we get one such new term, where each term involves a comparison between the candidate for whom the citizen intends to vote and some other candidate. And we can observe from these results that if the number of candidates exceeds two, we cannot simultaneously combine and factor all of these terms so that we get one term with two factors, where the first factor involves only probabilities and the second factor involves only utilities. Hence, if we wish to construct indices to predict turnout, our examination of costs and benefits reveals that
  (a) a single subjective index of competitiveness for multicandidate contests is unsatisfactory—the empirical referents of competitiveness are a series of measures involving pairs of candidates;
  (b) a single subjective index of the importance of an election is unsatisfactory—the empirical referents of importances or degrees of caring are a series of paired utility comparisons.
Hence, a rigorous analysis of the benefits and costs citizens derive from voting reveals a mechanism for constructing indices that quite possibly have a wider application.

[16]Clearly, if the number of voters, say v, is even, the citizen can break a tie but he cannot create one. Thus, if v is even, $P_1(O_{12}) = 0$, and $P_0(O_{12})$ equals the probability that candidate 1 receives $v/2$ votes. Similarly, if v is odd, the citizen can create a tie by voting, but he cannot break one. Hence, if v is odd, $P_0(O_{12}) = 0$, and $P_1(O_{12})$ equals the probability that candidate 1 receives $(v+1)/2$ votes.

Illustrations of the Calculus of Voting

This fact can be visualized as in Figure 3.1. There are two distributions in this figure, f_1 and f_2, with approximate equivalent forms and variances but with different means, μ_1 and μ_2. These two distributions represent the citizen's estimate that alternative outcomes occur (say, the probability that candidate 1 receives x votes), and are drawn so that f_1 represents a closer election (i.e., μ_1 is closer to the point representing a tie than is μ_2). Clearly, P is greater for f_1 than for f_2.

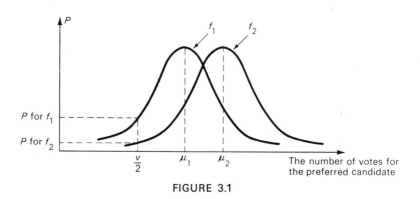

FIGURE 3.1

In the foregoing illustration we assume, however, that the variances of f_1 and f_2 are equal. This need not be so. Indeed, the probability function for a particular citizen is a function of certainty. Thus, a citizen who is very uncertain about how the election will turn out can be said to have a density function with a greater variance than a citizen who is quite certain about the outcome. Typically, certainty is a complicated function of information such that increases in information may either increase or decrease certainty. For example, information from opinion surveys taken successively closer to the election and showing a large and sustained majority for one candidate might increase certainty, while information from opinion surveys showing an increase in undecided voters as the election approached might decrease certainty. Observe now that the value of P for a citizen who believes the outcome is not close but is uncertain about his estimate can be greater than the value of P for a citizen who believes the outcome will be close but who is quite certain about his estimate. This situation is depicted in Figure 3.2, where f_1 is the density for the more certain citizen and f_2 the density for the less certain citizen. Clearly, then, P is a very complicated number, since it is a function of estimated closeness and certainty.

But P is also a function of the number of voters. In the derivation of the identity for P we suppose that probabilities are discrete, while in the arguments of the preceding paragraphs we imply that they are continuous (i.e., we represent f_1 and f_2 as continuous). In small electorates the use of discrete probabilities is probably descriptively accurate, whereas in large societies like ours it may not be, for it is hard to imagine a citizen estimating, e.g., the probability that candidate 1 gets exactly 37,492,303 votes. But if a voter assumes a continuous density function, then $P=0$ because, in general, the probability is zero that any specific outcome occurs when probability densities are continuous. Stated differently, the objective probability of a tie decreases, *ceteris paribus,* as the number of voters increases. Doubtless, it was this fact about large electorates that led to the use of $P = 1/v$, and the belief that PB is typically zero.

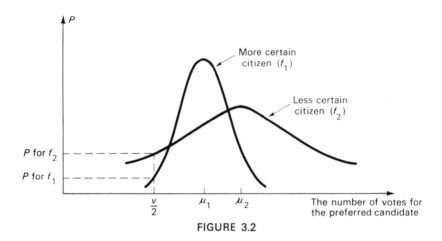

FIGURE 3.2

Clearly, an objective calculation of P in most instances reveals that it is indeed small, but we must recall that P is a subjective variable. And it is likely that, for many people, their subjective estimate of P is higher than is reasonable, given objective circumstances. Subjected as we are to constant reminders that a few hundred carefully selected votes by nonvoters could reverse the results of a very close election, such as the presidential election of 1960, the subjectively estimated chance of a tie may be as high as the propaganda urges it to be. We can hypothesize, however, that the subjective value of P is related monotonically to its objective calculation. Specifically, this theory should be taken to mean that as v increases or as perceived closeness decreases, the subjective value of P decreases, *ceteris paribus.*

To this point we assume that the citizen conceptualizes outcomes in terms of who wins or loses; but people can also conceptualize outcomes in terms of how many votes each candidate receives. For example, some citizens may place additional value on a landslide victory, such as some who voted for Johnson in 1964. We account for this possibility by assuming that a citizen's utility function, $U(x)$, increases continuously as the vote for his preferred candidate,

x, increases. Hence, even if his preferred candidate is certain to win or certain to lose, the citizen derives some benefit from adding to this candidate's total vote. We may assume also that the maximum rate of change in $U(x)$ occurs at $v/2$, which is to say that the citizen derives the most significant change in utility when his preferred candidate becomes a winning candidate, and that he receives somewhat smaller increments in utility as his favored candidate's vote increases thereafter. Assuming now that the most likely outcome is μ, we wish to consider the citizen's marginal rate of change of expected utility for various values of μ.[17] We know that the citizen is more likely to participate if this rate is large than if it is small. This rate is maximized when $\mu = v/2$, i.e., when the most likely outcome occurs at the inflection point of $U(x)$.[18] Thus, as before, PB is maximized if the most likely outcome is a tie.

But this result can be interpreted more broadly so that it reveals one effect of leadership on followers. Assume, for example, that x measures the cleanliness of the air. It is not unreasonable to suppose that a person's utility function for clean air resembles $U(x)$, which is to say that small improvements when the air is very dirty or very clean do not add greatly to a person's welfare, but similar increments when the air is on the borderline of being toxic can be

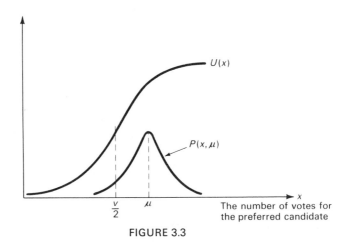

FIGURE 3.3

[17]Assume as in Figures 3.1 and 3.2 that the probabilities of electoral outcomes are represented by a continuous density, $P(x, \mu)$, and if the citizen abstains, let the mean of $P(x, \mu)$ be μ. Such a density is represented in Figure 3.3. The citizen's expected utility of abstaining is simply $U(x)$ times $P(x, \mu)$ summed over all possible values of x, i.e., for all x in the interval $[0, v]$. For the case of continuous functions, we represent this summation as

$$E = \int_0^v U(x)P(x, \mu)dx.$$

By voting for his preferred candidate, the citizen effectively increases the value of μ. If we let $dE/d\mu$ denote the rate at which E changes as μ changes (i.e., the marginal rate of change of expected utility), $dE/d\mu$ equals the citizen's marginal expected utility of voting less the expected utility of abstaining (ignoring, of course, U^+ and U^-, which are not functions of x and μ).

[18]See the appendix to Riker and Ordeshook, "A Theory of the Calculus of Voting."

regarded as significant. Hence, a person is more likely, *ceteris paribus*, to participate in antipollution programs if the most likely situation is that the air is on this borderline. Suppose now that a leader organizes those that seek clean air, either by private sanctions or other private inducements, so that the mean, μ, shifts to the inflection point of $U(x)$—i.e., the leader increases the likelihood that some critical supply of clean air is attained.[19] As this occurs, everyone's marginal benefits increase, and possibly they can be made to exceed marginal cost, in which case people contribute to the supply of clean air without the private incentives that the leader supplied originally. The initial organizational expenses of a candidate serve as another example of shifting μ so that, soon, additional electoral support sustains itself. Consequently, we frequently observe candidates seeking to convince supporters that they are in the running, and we can well imagine that the logic of their pleas is similar to the one just described.

This analysis of a citizen's decision to vote demonstrates how an act that some regard as irrational and that others study with a seemingly endless series of empirical generalizations can be understood with a simple cost-benefit calculus. This is not to say, however, that this calculus is complete or that prior empirical research is irrelevant and useless. While we seek with this calculus to offer a more complete delineation of the costs and benefits of voting and while we offer several hypotheses that relate these costs and benefits to the size of the electorate, the closeness of the election, and the state of a citizen's information, this analysis does not fully explain how citizens arrive at their subjective estimates of P, $U(O_j)$, U_1^+, and U_1^- or how we might assign values to these variables. It seems to us, however, that many empirical generalizations concerning participation in general and voting in particular—generalizations that commonly consist of correlations between some measure of participation and variables such as socioeconomic status, race, religion, region, and so on—can be reinterpreted as generalizations about the properties of these probabilities and utilities. Thus, as we seek to reinterpret empirical research as the attempt to measure and to account for the values of the parameters of this calculus, we supply a focus to research that currently lacks a rigorous theoretical perspective.

THE LOGIC OF COLLECTIVE ACTION

We cannot here pursue the foregoing suggestion more deeply. Instead, we explore further the content and implications of our theoretical analysis of participation with a second example. Our analysis of voting focuses on the choice by a single citizen, and so we assume that the choices of other citizens

---

[19]The leader may not, of course, actually change μ, but rather he may be successful in changing peoples' subjective estimates of μ.

are fixed. Our second example is taken from Olson's *The Logic of Collective Action*, which examines more closely the implications of the interdependencies of decisions in politics.[20] The fundamental question Olson addresses is: when does a person find it in his interest to initiate or to participate in collective action? Stated differently, what are the necessary and sufficient conditions for people to coordinate their activites in collective action so as to achieve a mutually beneficial result? Contrary to the belief that groups form whenever some common, collective interest can be served by collective action, we find that even though the net benefits of collective action are positive for every potential member of the group, this is not a sufficient condition for such action. "Unless the number of individuals in a group is quite small, or unless there is coercion . . . rational, self-interested individuals will not act to achieve their common or group interests."[21]

The key to this conclusion is the definition of a collective good, the group interest: "A common, collective, or public good is . . . any good such that, if any person . . . consumes it, it cannot feasibly be withheld from others in that group."[22] Thus, if one person purchases, say, tariff protection for his private consumption, he cannot prohibit others in the industry from also consuming this protection. For another example, if one person acts to increase the likelihood that a candidate wins an election, he cannot prohibit others from "consuming" the benefit (if they also prefer the candidate) of any such increase in probabilities. For yet a third example, public peace and order are public goods, perhaps the primary examples of things in this category.

Following this definition and these examples, the property of collective goods that accounts for Olson's conclusion is that in producing them people do not necessarily act optimally. A person supplies (produces) a collective good up to the point that his marginal costs equal his marginal benefits. Assuming that everybody desires the good, this typically occurs at a level of supply less than that which everybody would agree is desirable if their actions could be coordinated (i.e., if the costs of production could be shared by all who benefit from the provision of the good). The problem with coordinated or collective action, however, is that once the good is optimally supplied, the person then has an incentive to become a free rider—to stop producing his share so as not

[20]Mancur Olson, *The Logic of Collective Action* (Cambridge, Mass.: Harvard University Press, 1965). See also Mancur Olson and Richard Zeckhauser, "An Economic Theory of Alliances," *The Review of Economics and Statistics*, vol. 43 (August 1966), pp. 266–279; Philip M. Burgess and James A. Robinson, "Alliances and the Theory of Collective Action," *Midwest Journal of Political Science*, vol. 13 (1969), pp. 194–218, and Robert H. Salisbury, "An Exchange Theory of Interest Groups," *Midwest Journal of Political Science*, vol. 13 (1969), pp. 1–32.

[21]Olson, *The Logic of Collective Action*, p. 2. For a presentation of the "group theory," which assumes that groups form wherever there is an interest, see Arthur F. Bentley, *The Process of Government* (Chicago: University of Chicago Press, 1907), and David B. Truman, *The Governmental Process* (New York: Knopf, 1958).

[22]*Ibid.*, p. 14. An extensive literature exists concerning definitions of public or collective goods (and the related concept of externalities). We return in Chapter 9 to a consideration and elaboration of Olson's definition.

to incur any costs—unless he is somehow coerced into fulfilling his obligation.[23] Since every person is faced with similar incentives, the supply of the public good stabilizes at a nonoptimal level.

Turning then to the question of the magnitude of deviations from optimality, Olson argues that "there is a tendency in small groups towards a suboptimal provision of goods . . . [but] the more individuals in the group, the more serious the suboptimality will be."[24]

Two factors are identified to account for his conclusion concerning the relations between size and optimality. The first is organizational cost, which is typically greater in larger groups. The second is the magnitude of the impact of an action on one's welfare and on the welfare of the group. Since this impact is likely to grow relatively smaller as the size of the group increases, the incentives for participation in a collective effort are less in larger groups. The effect of size, moreover, suggests a typology where groups are characterized by their members' incentives. The first type, privileged groups, are those in which one or more persons are willing to supply an optimal provision of the collective good even if they must bear the entire cost of provision. Groups of the second type, intermediate groups, consist of people who are unwilling to act alone and bear the entire cost but who are not so numerous so as to preclude any possibility that they can be organized to supply the collective good. The final type, latent groups, typically are large groups in which a person "cannot make a noticeable contribution to any group effort, and since no one in the group will react if he makes no contribution, he has no incentive to contribute."[25] The problem for members of a latent group, then, is to alter people's preferences so that the provision of a collective good is rational. And Olson states that "only a *separate and selective incentive* will stimulate a rational individual in a latent group to act in a group-oriented way."[26] Specifically, a latent group can be mobilized to supply a collective good either by raising the private benefits of participation or by increasing the cost of nonparticipation.

These selective incentives are, of course, the elements of U_i—the private consequences of choice—appropriately defined. This aspect of Olson's theory, then, is readily related to our discussion of expression (3.7), so that we know that these selective incentives include such things as status, prestige, altruism, and

---

[23]To show this, it is necessary to prove that the person gains more by not incurring the cost than he does by decreasing the amount of the collective good he supplies. This can be shown to follow from the earlier assumption that he is not willing to supply an optimal amount by himself.

[24]Olson, *The Logic of Collective Action*, p. 28. We assume, of course, that optimality is Pareto optimality, and by "group" we mean all persons, consciously organized or not, who might benefit from a collective good. To define, now, "degree of suboptimality," suppose that T^* is an optimal level of supply of a public good and let $T(S_g)$ denote the level of supply in a group of size S_g. Assuming that the good is a good that everyone desires, $T(S_g)$ is not optimal if $T(S_g) < T^*$; and a group of size S' produces a less optimal supply than a group of size S'' if $T(S'_g) < T(S''_g)$. Olson's hypothesis can be restated, then, as $T(S'_g) < T(S''_g)$ if $S''_g < S'_g$.

[25]*Ibid.*, p. 50.

[26]*Ibid.*, p. 51.

legal sanction. More importantly, however, we can now identify the correspondence between Olson's analysis and the several terms of expression (3.7).

The Logic of Collective Action and the Theory of Participation

We begin by recalling the definition of outcomes of political consequence. An outcome is socially and therefore politically relevant if it enters the utility calculations of several people. Hence, outcomes in the set O must exhibit at least one feature of a collective good (or "bad"), namely that if a person "purchases" an outcome in this set, then other people also "consume" this outcome in the sense that it affects their welfare also. Correspondingly, alternatives in the set A can represent the decision to supply a specific level of a collective good.[27] Thus, the decision to participate is equivalent to the decision to supply or to assist in supplying a collective good.

One difference, nevertheless, does distinguish Olson's calculus from ours. Specifically, Olson assumes that all decision-making occurs in an environment of complete information. Thus, a decision-maker is assumed to know precisely the amount of the collective good being supplied and the amount that will be supplied if he acts. We assume, however, that outcomes can occur probabilistically.[28] Thus, a person "purchases" either a specific amount of a collective good, if certainty prevails, or he "purchases" a probability distribution which is defined over the outcome set O if decision-making involves risk.

With this equivalence of structure we can now reconstruct the logical basis of Olson's analysis of participation. Specifically, we consider the effects of the

---

[27]Observe that we represent alternatives and outcomes as discrete, whereas Olson assumes that they are continuous (i.e., a person can decide to supply any amount of a collective good from zero to infinity). This difference is readily bridged if we simply assume that the sets A and O are continuous, where $a \in A$ represents the decision to supply an amount a of the collective good and O represents the outcome O of the collective good supplied. (We can let $a \equiv O$). Additionally, the probabilities $P_i(O_j)$ are now represented by the continuous density function $P(a, O)$. Assuming that all utilities are positive, the expected value of choosing $a \in A$ is

$$E(a) = \int_0^\infty P(a, O)U(O)dO + \bar{U}(a),$$

where $U(O)$ is the utility the person receives from O, and $\bar{U}(a)$ is the private utility he receives simply by selecting a. Since a is continuous, the person "purchases" the amount of the collective good that maximizes $E(a)$. This amount is readily found by differentiating the above expression with respect to a, setting it equal to zero, and, if the functional forms of P, U and $\bar{U}$ are known, solving for a [and, of course, carefully confirming that we have found a maximum rather than a minimum value for $E(a)$].

[28]All $P_i(O_j)$'s equal either zero or one on Olson's analysis. Thus, for the continuous calculus (see previous footnote), $P(a, O)$ collapses about one point, and the expression for $E(a)$ becomes

$$E(a) = U(O) + \bar{U}(a),$$

where there is a one-to-one correspondence between values of A and values of O (i.e., $a \equiv O$). Hence, we can write

$$E(O) = U(O) + \bar{U}(O).$$

characteristics of the group—the most notable characteristic being size.[29] First, if we define group size as the number of people directly affected by the supply of the collective good, the notion of size and the notion of scope introduced earlier are synonymous.[30] Recalling that, typically, scope and efficacy are inversely related, we can readily see that the incentives to participate and group size are typically related inversely. Hence, we can restate Olson's conclusion concerning optimality and the effect of size as: the larger the group, the smaller, *ceteris paribus*, are the incentives for participation.

Among these *ceteris paribus* conditions, of course, is cost. Cost in this instance is the person's private cost of collective action. The relationship of such costs to size is generally a function of the content of the act of participation. If participation includes the formation or the maintenance of an organization, cost typically increases as the size of the organization increases. Thus, as size increases, increasing costs complement the effects of declining efficacy by decreasing the likelihood of participation. Conversely, costs may actually decline in some instances. Consider air pollution, where the number of automobiles purchased every year permits significant economies of scale. Thus, antipollution devices can be installed on cars at relatively little additional cost to the consumer. As in this example, however, decreased cost typically is offset by decreased efficacy, so Olson's conclusions concerning size and participation remain a valid generalization.[31]

Turning now to the matter of private incentives, we have shown in earlier

[29]We postpone for future chapters topics such as efficiency (optimality) of collective action, bargaining, and alternative allocation mechanisms.

[30]We exclude, then, situations in which some people regard the collective good as a collective "bad." Such situations are more properly the subject of interpersonal conflict and, therefore, are examined in subsequent chapters.

[31]Olson attempts to prove deductively that the incentives to participate necessarily decrease as the size of the group increases; but his analysis appears to us to be incomplete. First, we note that there are two quite distinct questions to be answered with Olson's analysis:

(1) As the size of the group increases, do individuals necessarily alter their private choices so as to decrease their supply of the public good (i.e., do their incentives to participate decrease)?

(2) As the size of the group increases, does the group necessarily tend towards a more suboptimal provision?

The first question is the more important, since we are not presently interested in normative concerns but rather in questions of choice. Considering, however, *only* the factors that Olson uses in his analysis, our answer to this question is *No*. To see this, note that he defines S_g as the size of the group and T as the amount of the collective good supplied. Defining V_g as the group benefit, he sets $V_g = S_g T$. Defining V_i as the gain to individual i, and F_i as the proportion of the group gain consumed by individual i, he sets $F_i = V_i/V_g$. The amount of the collective good that an individual buys if he acts alone is that amount which satisfies

$$dV_i/dT - dC/dT = 0,$$

where C is his cost of supplying T. That is, one buys additional quantities of the collective good until the marginal gain less the marginal cost is zero. Since $V_i = F_i V_g$, this condition becomes

$$F_i(dV_g/dT) - dC/dT = 0.$$

From this form of the condition it appears that the person with the largest F_i purchases the sections of this chapter that the private consequence of choice can augment the public incentives to participate. Olson's valuable observation is that large groups cannot "support themselves without providing some [private] sanction, or some [private] attraction distinct from the public good itself." Hence, private incentives are frequently established consciously by such organizations as labor unions, lobbies, and society to insure participation. Thus, labor unions sell insurance, lobbies also collect and sell market data, and society at large provides status, privilege, and other private benefits. For another example, observe that public officials, their programs, and the legitimacy of a government are collective goods, in which case voting in democratic elections is collective action because it chooses officials and programs and because it renders them legitimate. Perhaps in recognition of this fact and the fact that PB is typically too small to offset the private cost of voting, a private incentive to vote, U_1^+, is supplied through socialization.

Conversely, Olson argues, the collective goods of large (latent) groups are not supplied if these private incentives do not exist, because these groups are not organized into functioning bodies for meaningful collective action. Richard

---

most of the good; and, since the good is public, the amount he purchases is exactly the amount made available to the group. Olson concludes that, since the F_i for the largest participant typically decreases as S_g increases, the amount supplied also decreases as S_g increases. Thus, the suboptimality by supply is greater in larger groups. But this conclusion does not seem to us to follow. To see why not, consider the example of a pure public good. For such goods we note that everyone must consume an identical amount of the good (i.e., $V_i = V_j$ for all i and j) and that each person's consumption equals the total supply of the good (i.e., $V_i = T$). Thus, for a pure public good, $dV_i/dT = 1$, in which case the condition for what the individual, acting alone, will buy becomes

$$1 - \frac{dC}{dT} = 0,$$

which, without additional assumptions about C, has nothing to do with S_g. We can see where the misunderstanding occurred by recalling the definition of V_g, which is $V_g = S_g T$, so that $dV_g/dT = S_g$. But, in the special case of the pure public good, $F_i = V_i/V_g = T/S_g T = 1/S_g$. Hence, $F_i(dV_g/dT) = 1$. Thus, for pure public goods at least, Olson's conclusions about size follow from assumptions about C (and efficacy) and not F_i. [For an analysis of the relationship between efficacy, group size, and the optimality of collective decisions, see Norman Frohlich and Joe A. Oppenheimer, "I Get By With a Little Help from My Friends," *World Politics*, vol. 23 (October 1970), pp. 104–120.]

Consider now the second question. If "optimality" and "degree of suboptimality" are defined as in footnote 24, page 71, our answer to this question also is *No*. Since, as we have just shown, as size increases in Olson's model, individual choices do not change if the good is public, $T(S_g') = T(S_g'')$ for all values of S_g, where $T(S_g)$ is the level of supply in a group of size S_g. There is, however, one definition of optimality and suboptimality that changes our answer from No to Yes. Specifically, let T^* denote the optimal level of provision, and let $T^* - T(S_g)$ denote the degree of suboptimality to the *individual*. Finally, let $S_g[T^* - T(S_g)]$ denote the degree of suboptimality to the *group* (i.e., we add up the degree of suboptimality of all individuals in the group). Clearly, then, while $T^* - T(S_g)$ is a constant for all S_g, $S_g[T^* - T(S_g)]$ increases as S_g increases. Thus, the degree of suboptimality to the group increases as S_g increases. This, however, is all very unsatisfactory. First, an interpersonal comparison of utilities is necessarily made by summing the losses of individuals in order to obtain a group loss. Second, it obscures the answer to the first question that, in Olson's analysis, individual choices do not vary as size of the group increases.

E. Wagner, however, offers an illuminating extension of the argument.[32] He observes that, while consumers and the elderly surely satisfy the criteria for being latent groups, each has benefited from much recent legislation. And, for the elderly at least, there is no significant pressure group that organizes them in order to supply collective benefits. What, then, accounts for the beneficial legislation? The answer is the actions of a political entrepreneur—the person who seeks political profits by championing collective interests. The entrepreneur as envisioned by Wagner carries through that function we commonly attribute to leadership, for a leader is one who inspires goals and leads a collectivity towards their realization. Wagner sought only to specify one mechanism by which latent groups can have their interests organized, but in doing so he introduced a missing element into Olson's analysis—leadership.

The leader's calculus is readily explained, requiring no new theoretical primitives in the calculus of participation. First, we might suppose that the leader's acts are predicated on the attainment of some private benefit such as election to office. His interest in the collective good can be marginal, with the private good as his central quest. Or, the reward may derive from ethical considerations concerning the collective good, and the obligation of leadership may provide the incentive. Hence, altruism and philanthropy enter as legitimate justification for acts of leadership. Additionally, the leader as well as the led can benefit from the collective good. Perhaps this possibility strays from Wagner's notion of the political entrepreneur, but certainly some leaders also share the collective goal.

The benefits for leaders can be both private and public, which is to say that, unlike the rewards for members of the latent group, they are not preponderantly public. But in addition to the special private incentive, some other factors that distinguish a leader from his followers come immediately to mind: his attitudes toward risk, his future orientation, and his relative freedom from constraints on resources. First, some people are more likely to select risky alternatives than are others and clearly the benefits of leadership frequently involve risky prospects. Leaders, therefore, may have a higher propensity to seek these risky prospects than do followers, who prefer the costless alternative of doing nothing. To see how we might represent the preferences of risk takers and risk averters, consider Figure 3.4, where we illustrate two utility curves, one for a risk taker and the other for a risk averter. Utility (or disutility if it is negative) is indicated on the vertical axis, and outcomes are arranged on the horizontal axis at three points: the status quo, an unsuccessful outcome the value of which we normalize for both persons at -1, and a successful outcome the value of which we normalize at 1. (This particular normalization is, of course, simply illustrative and is of no consequence for our example.) Assume now that these two persons

[32]Richard E. Wagner, "Pressure Groups and Political Entrepreneurs: A Review Article," *Papers on Non-Market Decision Making*, vol. 1 (1966), pp. 161–170. For the leader's calculus of participation, see Norman Frohlich, Joe A. Oppenheimer, and Oran R. Young, *Political Leadership and Collective Goods* (Princeton, N. J.: Princeton University Press, 1971).

face two alternatives: a_0, which is to do nothing, and a_1, which is to participate. Assume, furthermore, that, if a_0 is selected, the status quo prevails with certainty, whereas if a_1 is selected, a favorable outcome and an unfavorable outcome each occur with a probability of one-half. For both persons, then, the expected value of a_1, $E(a_1)$, equals zero [that is, $1/2(1) + 1/2(-1) = 0$]. But the value of the status quo for the risk averter is greater than zero, and for the risk taker it is less than zero. Thus, $E(a_1) > E(a_0)$ for the risk taker, and $E(a_1) < E(a_0)$ for the risk averter. The risk taker thus has a rational motive to participate, and possibly to assume the role of leader, while the risk averter has a rational motive to reject participation.

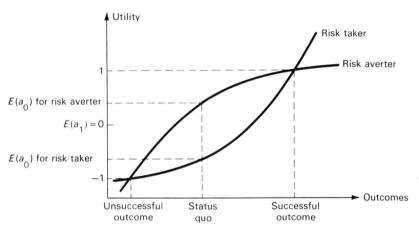

FIGURE 3.4

A second possible distinction between leaders and followers (or between participators and nonparticipators) is that leaders may be more future-oriented than others. Typically, the rewards of collective action are realized in the future, whereas costs must be borne immediately. If a person discounts heavily for time, benefits are diminished, but costs are not. Hence, the smaller the discount for time, the greater the likelihood that a person participates, and the greater the likelihood that he seeks to persuade others to join his effort.

Finally, our third factor—relative freedom from constraints on resources—embodies the observation that leaders generally hold some advantage of resources. They often have more information; they are more likely than others to hold public office; they are likely to have more financial resources and more access to the public media. For people with such resources, the initial cost of organization and provision of the collective good is less of a constraint on choice than it is for others. Hence, the greater the resources the greater the likelihood that a person is willing to bear the cost of collective action.

These three features of leadership—risk taking, future orientation, and abundance of resources—are, of course, interdependent. Thus, the greater the resources the smaller the likelihood that a person is risk-averse—if only because he can survive the cost of misfortune. Again, abundant resources encourage a future orientation thus: if a person has resources sufficient to bear the initial costs of organization but not to sustain them, he might reasonably invest in organizing a latent group in the hope that, as other members participated, eventually benefits would exceed costs. Of course, such calculations are similar to those made when calculating, say, the benefits of a public works project. Our point is that the decision to supply leadership can represent a similar investment.

An essential element of leadership, nevertheless, is the ability to get others to make choices they otherwise would not make. Hence, a leader must also change the benefits people derive from collective action. We suggest in the previous section, for example, that leaders can change a person's estimate of the likelihood of outcomes and thereby increase the marginal benefits of participation. Also, leaders can seek to increase the private incentive U_1^+. In the case of voting, where U_1^+ is typically a product of socialization, we observe political entrepreneurs—candidates and party chairmen—contributing to the maintenance of this private benefit within their constituency or party. Finally, leaders can seek to affect the utility that people associate with outcomes. We examine in Chapters 11 and 12 the logic of a candidate's attempt to affect the electorate's evaluation of the outcome of his winning the election.

SUGGESTIONS FOR FURTHER READING

The literature on political participation is, of course, vast, and we have neither the time nor the space for an adequate bibliography on the subject. Few writers, however, approach participation from the perspective of decision theory. Work that nevertheless contributes to this approach includes Downs' *An Economic Theory of Democracy* (New York: Harper & Row, 1957), Gordon Tullock, *Toward a Mathematics of Politics* (Ann Arbor: University of Michigan Press, 1967), Mancur Olson, *The Logic of Collective Action* (Cambridge, Mass: Harvard University Press, 1965), and Norman Frohlich, Joe A. Oppenheimer, and Oran R. Young, *Political Leadership and Collective Goods* (Princeton, N.J.: Princeton University Press, 1971).

Like participation in general, the literature of decision theory is extensive, given that it encompasses such diverse topics as measurement, statistical inference, learning theory, sequential analysis, and cost-benefit analysis. Howard Raiffa's *Decision Analysis* (Reading, Mass.: Addison-Wesley, 1968) is an excellent introduction to the subject and it requires only an elementary knowledge of mathematics. Ward Edwards and Amos Tversky, eds., *Decision-Making* (Baltimore: Penguin, 1967) is an excellent collection of essays that treat the topics of this chapter more broadly and in greater detail. A more mathematically advanced introduction that examines the decision-theoretic nature of statistical inference is M. H. DeGroot, *Optimal Statistical Decisions* (New York: McGraw-Hill, 1970). Two relatively nontechnical expositions whose focus is primarily the methodology and philosophy of inquiry are R. Ackoff, *Scientific Method: Optimizing Applied Research Decisions* (New York: Wiley, 1962), and C. W. Churchman, *Prediction and Optimal Decision: Philosophical Issues of a Science of Values* (Englewood Cliffs, N. J.: Prentice-Hall, Inc., 1961).

4

The Paradox of Voting
and Majority Rule

In the previous chapter we analyze a kind of personal and individual decision with special importance for politics: the decision about whether or not to participate. This decision stands at the threshhold of politics, and without it politics cannot exist. Nevertheless, this individual decision is not the substance of politics; it is only the preface. We turn, therefore, in this chapter from the preliminary decisions to the actual decisions of politics themselves.

Political choices are assignments of preferences or allocations of values for members of society. It is with such events that we will be concerned throughout the rest of this book. In the beginning we note, however, that the phrase "social decision" is itself something of a contradiction in terms. As we point out in the first chapter, only people can decide. Since a society is not itself human, it cannot properly be said to make a decision. How then can one have a supposed decision by society? Before proceeding further with our discussion of politics, we must determine whether societies can be said to behave as if they made decisions, and if so, what the properties of a social decision are.

Society, not being human, cannot have preferences in any proper sense of "have," nor indeed can it order the preferences that it does not have. Furthermore, society cannot choose that alternative which maximizes its utility, simply because society, not being human, does not have a preference order over which a utility measure can be constructed. Suppose, by some mechanism of adding up votes on alternatives, we come to a so-called social preference structure (really, a summation) such that aPb, bPc, cPa—which, as will be recalled from the discussion at the end of Chapter 2, is quite possible. How then can one construct a utility measure, or even know which alternative is first? Any method of measuring utility, whether ordinally or cardinally, depends on knowing the order in which alternatives are arranged. But in this example of intransitivity, it is just exactly this information that we do not have, and indeed can never get, because it does not exist. It seems strange, therefore, to speak of a social decision about either preferences or alternatives.

Nevertheless, we often anthropomorphize the collectivity and speak of "social decisions," "social orderings," and "social choice" as if they really occurred in the supposed mind of society just as decisions and orderings actually do occur in the minds of human beings. For example, we speak of electoral decisions in which the decider is, presumably, the political unit wherein the election was held or of market decisions in which the decider is, again presumably, the social mechanism of the market. The problem is that these events of "electoral decision" and "market decision" are clearly not decisions in the human sense of wilful preference, yet they are enough like real decisions that the analogy is repeatedly and thoughtlessly made. Our problem is: in what sense are these social events like and unlike human decisions? To what degree is it possible for society to appear to act as if it were maximizing utility?

INDIVIDUAL BASES OF SOCIAL OUTCOMES

In Chapters 1 and 2 we rule out as inconceivable any so-called social decisions that are historically unrelated to some individual decisions. Our reason for this elimination is that we cannot conceive of any institutions by which a general will unrelated to individual wills might come into existence. We are thus required now to begin our analysis of social choice with people. Specifically, we assume the existence of individual preference orderings and individual choices among alternatives. That is, for matters on which so-called social decisions occur, there exists in at least some people an individual preference ordering, and these people can and do choose among alternatives so as to maximize their individual utility. Having assumed this much, we now ask: how does one get from individual preference and decision to social choice?

The short answer is that, in every social situation in which social choice is said to occur, there is some device to pick out individual decisions and render them the social choice. As a prelude to more detailed examination of these devices, we sketch out two of them:

Committee Decision

In most legislatures and committees the device for selection consists of (1) a solicitation by the chairman of individual members' opinions about and choice among alternatives, and (2) an announcement by the chairman of that alternative which, on the basis of some generally approved rule of decision, he has picked out to be the choice of the collectivity. One can describe an abstract committee in which a motion is formulated by some member; the other members carry through private calculations to determine whether or not they wish this motion to be the social choice; they vote yes if their calculations lead them to favor the motion, otherwise they vote no; and finally the chairman uses some rule of decision which combines the individual yeas and nays to decide whether or not the motion is to be the social choice.

Clearly, the degree to which the individual choices expressed in the solicitation are related to the social choice ultimately announced depends on the rule the chairman uses. For purposes of illustration we list some of the rules, which we can call the *Chairman's Rules of Social Choice*:

1. *Dictatorship*. Under this rule, the chairman simply announces his own choice or the choice of some other single member as the social choice, regardless of the preferences or choices of others. Of course, when a majority of others agree, it may not be apparent that this rule is being applied. But if less than a majority (and especially if no one else) agrees with his announced choice, and yet this announced choice is said to be the social choice, then it may be assumed that the rule of dictatorship is being applied. Typically, one finds this rule in collegial bodies whose function is primarily advisory. There is a story (probably apocryphal) about Lincoln's announcing the result of a Cabinet vote in which his was the only affirmative: "One aye, seven nays," he is reported to have announced, "The ayes have it."

2. *The sense of the meeting*. Under this rule, the presiding officer directs discussion until he senses agreement among the members. Then he formulates this agreement as the sense of the meeting. If the officer is successful and the members are in fact reconcilable, the announced sense stands as the social decision. To the extent that this procedure works as it is expected to, the discussion leads to unanimity, and so the social choice is the same as each individual choice as finally expressed in the chairman's formulation. We think this is different from the kind of unanimity that results from unanimous votes aye on a prior motion, however, because the statement announced as the social choice is one devised subsequent to discussion and may be the original preference of no one (including the chairman). This rule is, as the name implies, the procedure of the Quaker meeting and probably works well only when all members have a strong sense of compromise in the interests of community solidarity.

3. *Vote-counting*. Under this rule, the chairman counts the yeas and nays and, if the yeas reach some predetermined number, the chairman announces that the motion is the social choice. Naturally, the rule about the number required to adopt varies widely according to the nature of the body and the motion. It is as low as 4/9 (in the United States Supreme Court on motions to grant *certiorari*, where it is believed that it should be the social choice to hear any case that a substantial minority wants heard). It is as high as unanimity (in the seventeenth-century Polish Diet where under the so-called librum veto every member present was required to assent in order to pass a motion, a rule which recognized the equality of peers but which also led to some ingenious methods of excluding anticipated dissenters). Of course, the typical rule is that "more than one-half of those present" assent, although on motions of special importance extraordinary majorities may be required. Thus, two-thirds of those present in each House of Congress must assent to motions to override Presidential vetoes, and in some jurisdictions 80 percent of the adjacent landowners must assent to motions to close a public street.

For our present concerns, the important point about the rule of counting votes is not the variation in the number of assenting votes, but rather the fact that the rule depends on the chairman's count of the House. The essential notion involved in vote-counting is, of course, that the chairman is thus given an easily followed rule which, superficially, at least, allows him no exercise of judgment. It forces him to state a social choice that relates in some predetermined numerical way to the whole group of individual choices. Of course, chairmen do not always easily give up their chance to have greater-than-average influence, so there are many procedural rules on vote-counting in common use. Because, when many vote simultaneously, chairmen often have heard badly on purpose, there are many ways to appeal from a chairman's ruling on the outcome of a vote viva voce, such as calling for a tally or a full-scale roll call. All the variations in these procedural rules, however, simply emphasize the basic theme of the rule on decision, which is to eliminate as much as possible the chairman's subjective judgment.[1] Thereby, the social choice depends only on the set of individual choices.

The common theme in all three of these Chairmen's Rules of Social Choice—and doubtless there are others with the same theme—is that some individual formulation of choice, a motion, is selected to be the social choice. Much of the history of republican government can be written in terms of the development of particular Chairman's Rules, especially of those which completely eliminate the Chairman's discretion in formulating motions and counting votes. By reason of this development, we have somewhat obscured the essential process involved in these Rules of picking out some individual choice and making it the social choice. The system of committee decision commonly used today seems utterly mechanical. But it is not.[2] Some individual member proposes a motion, which is presumably his preference either on its merits or for strategic reasons. Then the chairman carries through a decision procedure; and the individual choice proposed becomes the social choice, if and when the chairman, having applied his accepted rule, announces so. We emphasize, therefore, that what comes out of a committee as a social choice started out as an individual decision and became social by the chairman's use of a Chairman's Rule.

Market Decisions

Committee decisions sometimes appear by reason of contemporary procedure to be wholly social, the product of a "group mind," although we have shown that they always start as individual decisions and are transformed by the Chairman's procedure into social decisions. In the case of market decisions,

---

[1] Of course, the very best method of eliminating the chairman's judgment is to make the committee so large that the counting be bureaucratized. This is one side consequence of, for example, making social choices by referenda. And, of course, the elaborate election law to prevent fraud in counting votes in elections for presidents and parliaments is just a complicated version of the elimination of chairman's judgment.

[2] The rules are themselves social outcomes. This is well demonstrated in James Buchanan and Gordon Tullock, *The Calculus of Consent* (Ann Arbor: University of Michigan Press, 1962).

however, the situation is even more deceptive. Individual decisions on goods and services are the things that occur. Furthermore, they are transformed by the market into social choices on price, quantity, and the allocation of scarce resources. But aside from professional economists, no one is watching the transformation as a general process. Hence, it is easy for even the participating individual decision makers to believe that the social choices were made by the market mechanism itself. So we sometimes speak of market decisions as if they were totally nonhuman, the product of a mechanical society and not of the people who compose it. In committees, even in very large electorates, there is much give and take of discussion and negotiation among participants. The casting of individual votes is often accompanied by an elaborate and personal rationale. Hence, it is hard to forget the individual basis of so-called social decisions. But in a market, when sellers offer, buyers come forth at a specific rate; and that simple information is about all the sellers know. By experimentation, they can perhaps generate a demand schedule and calculate elasticity; but they are probably foreclosed forever from knowing with certainty such obviously relevant detail as buyers' budgets and tastes. Buyers are equally ignorant of sellers, knowing only a portion of the supply schedule and something about elasticity. Truly, the cash nexus and it alone holds the market system together. In this abstract society, the people in it appear less-than-human. Hence, we often do not attribute decisions to these shadowy participants, and say instead that some mechanism, an unseen hand, a trading god from the market machine, made a particular allocation of resources.

But this is, of course, metaphor. Market decisions are always individual. The market consists of transactions, agreements between buyers and sellers, and these are always matters of individual decision on price and quantity by individual buyers and individual sellers. It is true that some sellers may set an inflexible price, but this is a matter of convenience for them and does not affect the uniqueness of each transaction.

Apart from their anonymity, the way that market decisions come to appear mechanical is that their consequences are often interpreted by observers in summary terms. The observers say, for example, that, by reason of the market, the production of automobiles declined by 5 percent. What this means is that in a long series of decisions, some buyers decided not to buy (perhaps because of changes in their budgets) and some sellers, observing the state of inventories and turnover, decided not to produce. One can summarize all these decisions by noting the 5 percent decrease. One should remember, however, that this is a summary, an abstract decision consisting of the cumulative constraints of thousands of concrete decisions. The market did not reduce production and sales; people did. So-called market forces are no more than a summary statement by observers about specific transactions and perhaps also about tastes, budgets, and costs of production.

It is easy to see that the observer's summary is closely analogous to the chairman's vote-counting. In both cases, the interpreter (i.e., economist, presiding officer) constructs a "social decision" by using a rule to declare that some individual decisions have a social result. The main difference between them is that in the committee procedure, the participants are consciously constructing a social choice, while in the market the participants are usually not conscious of the social effects of their actions, though of course the interpreter is. This difference in consciousness is, however, of very little moment. It does result in some apparent difference in authority; the committee decision has authority because the participants will it, while the market decision has authority because of the physical constraints it places on other individual decisions and social outcomes. But this difference in authority is more apparent than real, for typically market constraints, coming as they do from individual budgets and cost calculations, are inferentially willed, while the decision to legislate in committee imposes a quasi-market constraint on society. Thus, although there is a marked difference in consciousness between committees and markets, their effects are substantially the same.

Social choices take on a life of their own because of their complex structure. A building does not appear to be energy and atoms, but simply, for most of us, a building and nothing more. So a social choice appears to be a product of society. Just as the physical scientist examines components in order to understand the whole, so the social scientist attempts to get around the anthropomorphism of ordinary speech. This is what we have attempted with our emphasis: people make decisions; their decisions agglomerated and interpreted as decisions by society are called social outcomes.

FUNDAMENTAL DIFFERENCE BETWEEN INDIVIDUAL DECISION AND SOCIAL OUTCOME

The foregoing examination of markets and committees was undertaken to show that they both work with the same basic material, i.e., individual decisions on how to vote or what to buy or sell. From this material, both produce social outcomes. But though the building blocks of social outcomes are individual decisions, social outcomes are not the same kind of thing as their raw materials. There is a profound difference between them, a difference which must be understood if one is to comprehend the true nature of human society.

The difference is that a series or a related set of individual decisions can always be made to display an underlying coherence, while it may be the case that social outcomes can not. Individual decisions are the consequence of ordered preference in the individual. Social outcomes are the consequence of the interaction of individual decision makers in the context of a particular rule of summation. Individual decision is the choice of an alternative (e.g., yea or nay, to buy or not) selected as if to maximize the individual's utility. Since utility is a measure on his underlying preferences, it follows that there is consistency in a series or set of individual decisions. There is no reason to expect consistency in social outcomes, however, for they are not selected to maximize anything, merely to reflect the views of majorities or of groups selected by other rules of summation. Since in any series of social choice, the set of those deciders who determine the outcome (always a subset of society) may vary from choice to choice, there is no reason to suppose that individual consistency among decisions will carry over to the group. Indeed, the expectation is that it does not.

From this feature of social outcomes, we note certain profoundly important consequences:

1. Unlike individual decisions, which are always ordered arrangements of preference, social choices are not. In that sense, social outcomes may lack coherence.
2. To the degree they lack coherence, social outcomes can appear arbitrary.

THE CONDITIONS OF ARROW'S THEOREM

Much of the rest of this volume will be devoted to elaborating the foregoing propositions. We start with a demonstration that we cannot assure coherence in social outcomes.

The fundamental demonstration that social choices are not generally ordered is made by means of Arrow's generalization of the paradox of voting. This paradox, which was described at the end of Chapter 2, is simply the fact that, sometimes, when three or more choosers whose preferences are ordered over three or more alternatives actually choose between pairs, they may choose in such a way that the winning alternatives cannot be ordered. For example, if person 1 orders alternatives (from best to worst) ABC, if 2 orders BCA, and 3 orders CAB, then alternative A defeats alternative B (because of persons 1 and 3), B defeats C (because of 1 and 2), and—in a fully disordered and circular way—C defeats A (because of 2 and 3).[3] Thus, in a society composed

---

[3]*Historical note.* This paradox, which now looms so large in political theory, has for all practical purposes been in the storehouse of theoretical ideas for only twenty-five years or so. It was first noted, so far as is known, by Condorcet and then by Borda in the late eighteenth century. Appropriately, it was discovered at a time when chairmen's rules on vote-counting were becoming socially important. But the general scholarly public was sufficiently enamoured with the supposed simplicity of majority rule to forget Condorcet's discovery. It was noted again in the nineteenth century by Lewis Carroll, presumably when he was planning his strategy for a college meeting, and yet again by a theorist of proportional representation, E. J. Nanson. It remained for Duncan Black, however, to realize the theoretical significance of the paradox. His essays of the late 1940's, which are summarized in his *The Theory of Committees and Elections* (Cambridge: Cambridge University Press, 1958) and his book with R. A. Newing, *Committee Decisions with Complementary Valuation* (Glasgow: William Hodge, 1951), brought the subject into the center of political thought; and, of course, Kenneth Arrow's great work, *Social Choice and Individual Value* (Chicago: 1951; New York: Wiley, 2d ed., 1965) guaranteed it would stay there. The history of the study of the paradox, up to the 1940's, is contained in Black, *The Theory of Committees and Elections,* pp. 156–240; up to 1961, in William H. Riker, "Voting and the Summation of Preferences," *American Political Science Review,* vol. 55 (1962), pp. 900–911; and up to 1965 in the Appendix to the second edition of *Social Choice and Individual Value.*

of individuals who are able to organize their preferences coherently, the society itself is incoherent.

The great question about the paradox is: under what conditions can it be expected to occur? If these conditions are politically irrelevant, then it is socially trivial, merely a clever mathematical puzzle important only to the degree that constitution-writers do not take the trouble to prevent it. But if the conditions are relevant to political decision, then the paradox is a fact of fundamental importance for all social life. To the degree that it occurs, social outcomes are essentially incoherent simply because they cannot be arranged in order. Since Arrow has shown that the paradox cannot be avoided, at least provided that the system of decision satisfies certain standards of equity, it follows that to some degree at least a fundamental disorder is always possible in society.

In the remainder of this chapter we examine the conditions under which the paradox does and does not occur and we analyze some of the efforts that have been made to estimate generally the nature of the incoherence thus imposed.

If we were to examine, one by one, various systems of choice, such as majority rule, markets, or proportional representation, and to ask about each whether or not it contains the conditions of the paradox, we would find in every case that it does. But because we had not looked at every conceivable system—an impossible task—we would not be sure that the possibility of the paradox was in fact universal. In order to be completely certain, therefore, we examine, not particular systems, but a fully general, abstract system. When we find that the possibility of the paradox exists in it, we will then know, *for certain,* that it is possible in all systems having the same properties as the abstract system. So, following Arrow, we begin with the construction and examination of an abstract system of choice.

Since we are concerned with human preferences among alternatives, we first postulate the existence of a set of choosers, $M: \{1, 2, \ldots, m\}$, and a set of alternatives, $A: \{a_1, a_2, \ldots, a_n\}$, where, for technical reasons soon to be obvious, $m \geq 2$ and $n \geq 3$. We further postulate that the choosers are able to impose an ordering relation, R, on the alternatives. This means that a chooser is able to say that he likes a_i better than a_j or that he is indifferent between them.[4] The relation, R, may be thought of as preference and indifference combined. In the area of choice it is the analogue of the relation of greater than or equal to in the area of numerical comparison. (Breaking R into its components, the relation of preference, P, is the analogue of *greater than* and the relation of indifference, I, is the analogue of *equal to.)*

---

[4]Formally, we say R is (i) connected and (ii) transitive:
(i) $a_i R a_j$, for all i, j, and
(ii) if $a_i R a_k$ and $a_k R a_j$, then $a_i R a_j$.
As we showed in Chapter 2, properties (i) and (ii) are both essential to an ordering.

The essence of the paradox is, of course, that the transitive ordering of three alternatives is not necessarily preserved when the operation of vote-counting is carried through only on *pairs* of alternatives. Since we start with transitively ordered triplets and add parts of these orderings by pairs, we may, when we put the added-up pairs back together again, fail to have a transitively ordered triplet. This failure is what we want to investigate; and so we must also postulate the ordering properties (axioms) of R in relation to the alternatives:

Axiom I. *Either $a_i R a_j$ or $a_j R a_i$.*

This is the axiom of connectivity that guarantees comparability between members of every pair of alternatives. While there is no postulated restriction on the alternatives—they may be, for example, candidates for an office, dishes on a menu, colors to paint a house, or indeed anything that humans might wish to choose among—still the connectivity of R requires that A not be *any* arbitrary set. Its members must be things that are reasonable to compare. Thus, A might be a set of several candidates for governor, but it could not be a set of one candidate for governor, one for senator, and one for mayor.

Axiom II. *If $a_i R a_j$ and if $a_j R a_k$, then $a_i R a_k$.*

This is the axiom of transitivity. Together Axioms I and II guarantee that the individual choosers are able to rank the members of A in complete order. Thus we are assured that the individuals will not be confused about their preferences. If, therefore, confusion shows up in a social outcome, we will know that it derives from the methods of picking a social outcome out of the set of individual preferences themselves.

Having postulated what is necessary and sufficient for the choosers to order alternatives, we must now postulate the existence of a method of constructing a social outcome from the individual preference orders. The social outcome may be either a preference order or something like a preference order that satisfies Axiom I but not Axiom II. We may think of the thing that produces the outcome as a vote-counting method like a chairman's rule or summarizing machine or a selection device. Arrow, who wrote within the tradition of welfare economies, called it a social welfare function. Furthermore, we must postulate certain conditions for the summarizing machine to assure that its operation is fully general and satisfies some elementary notions of justice. These conditions, which are the heart of the problem, are:

Condition I: Universal admissibility of individual orderings. *All logically possible R-orders of A are admissible as choices by members of M.*

There are $n!$ (read: "n-factorial"—that is, $1 \times 2 \times \ldots \times n$) ways in which the n elements of A can be R-ordered. (This is the number of permutations of n things.) For example, if A consists of a_1, a_2, and a_3, then there are 3! possible R-orders of A:

(1) a_1Ra_2, a_2Ra_3, and a_1Ra_3; or $a_1a_2a_3$;
(2) a_1Ra_3, a_3Ra_2, and a_1Ra_2; or $a_1a_3a_2$;
(3) a_2Ra_1, a_1Ra_3, and a_2Ra_3; or $a_2a_1a_3$;
(4) a_2Ra_3, a_3Ra_1, and a_2Ra_1; or $a_2a_3a_1$;
(5) a_3Ra_1, a_1Ra_2, and a_3Ra_2; or $a_3a_1a_2$;
(6) a_3Ra_2, a_2Ra_1, and a_3Ra_1; or $a_3a_2a_1$.

The sense of this condition is that a member of M may choose any one of these six orders.

The purpose of this condition is to assure that the method of constructing a social outcome is fully general. This condition is necessary for the possibility of the paradox. Its justification is that one would not wish, presumably, to restrict individual freedom of choice simply in order to avoid paradoxes in the summation. Actually, as we show later in more detail, many of the effective institutions to avoid the paradox exploit a violation of this condition, e.g., the two-party system and run-off election. The main effect of these institutions is to impose severe restrictions on individual freedom of choice by forcing social conflict into a binary mold. When there are n candidates, $n \geq 3$, each voter in M is required by these systems to express an R-order of one of the following two types,

$$a_1, \ldots, a_2, \ldots \quad \text{or} \quad a_2, \ldots, a_1, \ldots.$$

Specifically, R-orders of the following types cannot effectively occur simply because there is no institutional means for a voter to express them:

$$a_i, \ldots, a_1, \ldots, a_2, \ldots, \quad \text{or} \quad a_i, \ldots, a_2, \ldots, a_1, \ldots.$$

Thus, in a two-party system, if a_1 is Jones, the Democratic candidate, and a_2 is Smith, the Republican candidate, it is difficult, even impossible, for a voter to express a first preference for a_i, say Brown, a potential third-party candidate. As will be shown later, when preference-orders are limited to those in which some a_i cannot be in first place, paradoxes cannot occur. It can thus be seen that this condition of freedom is necessary for paradoxes.

Condition II: Nonperversity or positive association of individual and social values. *Given a set of R-orders of A by members of M such that the method of summation produces the social outcome a_iRa_j, then, if members of M either raise a_i in their preference order or do not change its position, the social outcome is a_iRa_j.*

The effect of this condition, which is Benthamite in spirit, is to assure some positive connection between individual preference and social outcomes. Arrow remarks in justification of this condition: "Since we are trying to describe social welfare and not some sort of illfare, we must assume that the social welfare function [i.e., method of summation] is such that the social ordering responds positively to alterations in individual values or at least not negatively."[5] Although they are probably not common in nature, it is easy to

---

[5]Arrow, *Social Choice and Individual Value*, p. 25.

imagine a method of summation that violates this condition—for example, a method in which some voters' votes are counted negatively. Let a leader with an advisory body believe that some of his advisors are loyal and others disloyal, and let him discount the votes of the latter by counting them negatively. Let the advisory body recommend candidates a_1, a_2, and a_3 for an office according to the following schedule:

	a_1	a_2	a_3
Loyal	6	7	3
Disloyal	0	1	4
Net	6	6	-1

so that a_1 and a_2 are tied with 6 votes each and a_3 has -1 vote. Let the leader call for a new vote to break the tie and let all of the disloyal supporters of a_3 change to support of a_1 so that the new totals are:

	a_1	a_2	a_3
Loyal	6	7	3
Disloyal	4	1	0
Net	2	6	3

and, clearly, a_2 is the winner. It is such bizarre arrangements as this that the condition prohibits.

Condition III: Independence from irrelevant alternatives. *Given a set of R-orders of A by members of M such that the social outcome is a_iRa_j, then if the alternative a_h is deleted from A, the social outcome remains a_iRa_j.*

The effect of this condition is to render the presence or absence of a_h irrelevant to the social summary of the relation of a_i and a_j. It requires that the social comparison of a_i and a_j be strictly pairwise, without reference to any other relationships.

This is doubtless the most controversial of Arrow's conditions because some people believe it is neither ethically nor technically justified. We therefore examine it in some detail, although in this section we merely offer an illustration. Let there be five voters $(1, \ldots, 5)$ and four candidates $(a_1, \ldots, a_4)$ and let the voters order the candidates thus:

VOTERS	RANK ORDER OF ALTERNATIVES			
	1st	2nd	3rd	4th
1	a_1	a_2	a_3	a_4
2	a_1	a_2	a_3	a_4
3	a_2	a_3	a_1	a_4
4	a_4	a_1	a_2	a_3
5	a_2	a_4	a_1	a_3

where $a_h\ a_i\ a_j\ a_k$ means a transitive order such that a_hPa_i, a_iPa_j, and a_jPa_k. We will now examine the social outcomes obtainable from this set of individual

R-orders with two different methods of summarizing—one in which Condition III is imposed and one in which it is not.

Suppose the summary is made by majority rule in a series of contests between each pair of alternatives, a method that satisfies Condition III.[6] In such a set of contests, a particular alternative might beat zero, one, two, . . . , or $n-1$ other alternatives; we will adopt the convention, however, that no alternative can be said to be a winner unless it defeats $n-1$ others. (Black refers to this as the Condorcet criterion for winning. This is a less stringent requirement than, for example, that an alternative be in the first rank order for a majority of voters; indeed it is the weakest criterion compatible with majority rule and Condition III.) In this particular case there is a Condorcet winner, a_1, as can be seen from the following table:

COMPARING a_1 WITH:	a_1 IS PREFERRED BY A MAJORITY COMPOSED OF:
a_2	1, 2, 4
a_3	1, 2, 4, 5,
a_4	1, 2, 3

Since a_1 is able to beat all of a_2, a_3, and a_4 in head-to-head contests. it is the undisputed winner. Note especially that the social outcome ranks a_1 above a_2 regardless of whether a_3 and a_4 are under consideration, simply because the method of summary did not consider them at all where a_1 and a_2 were compared. Thus Condition III is fully satisfied.

Suppose, however, that the social outcome is arrived at by adding the rank orders of alternatives in the several individual R-orders and declaring the winner to be the alternative with the largest sum. (Black calls this the Borda criterion of winning.) Continuing our illustration, we now show that the Borda method clearly violates Condition III. Since there are four candidates, let the highest rank order have four points, the next highest have three points, the next two, and the lowest one. For the four candidates we thus get:

VOTERS	CANDIDATES			
	a_1	a_2	a_3	a_4
1	4	3	2	1
2	4	3	2	1
3	2	4	3	1
4	3	2	1	4
5	2	4	1	3
Totals	15	16	9	10

[6]That majority rule in pairwise contests satisfies Condition III is apparent from the facts that (i) in a pairwise contest only the two relevant alternatives—and no irrelevant ones—are under consideration and (ii) with majority rule there must, in the absence of a tie, be a decision between these two alone. This does not mean, of course, that voters are prohibited from adopting strategies based on considerations about a third alternative.

As is apparent from the totals, a_2 stands highest and is therefore the winner by the Borda criterion. In order to create the circumstance for Condition III, suppose that candidates a_3 and a_4 are deleted, as might be done in a run-off election. Since only two candidates remain, this means that the higher ranks get two points and the lower ranks get one, with the following result:

Voters	a_1	a_2
1	2	1
2	2	1
3	1	2
4	2	1
5	1	2
Totals	8	7

where now a_1 is the winner. Thus the deletion of a_3 and a_4 changed the winner, under the Borda criterion, from a_2 to a_1, which is precisely the kind of change that Condition III forbids.[7]

The initial justification for Condition III (we discuss others at a later point) is contained in this example. It is based on the assumption that the best kind of winning is that which satisfies at least the Condorcet criterion and therefore it is sufficient to guarantee that, if a Condorcet winner exists, it is in fact chosen. Systems of summation that fail to satisfy Condition III permit the mere introduction of additional candidates to bring about the defeat of the Condorcet winner, as in the foregoing illustration where the introduction of a_3 and a_4 changes the winner from a_1 to a_2. In Arrow's analysis, it is assumed that such a change of winners is a fundamental inequity and Condition III is intended to prohibit it. (As is shown in the last section of this chapter, Condition III also prohibits interpersonal comparisons of utility and measures of intensity. While these are very important and related matters, we believe that the fundamental feature of Condition III is its insistence on Condorcet winning.)

---

[7]If, instead of deleting both a_3 and a_4, we had deleted just one of them, the social outcome would have gone through a similar but less dramatic change. Thus we get:

	WITH a_3 OUT			WITH a_4 OUT		
Voters	a_1	a_2	a_4	a_1	a_2	a_3
1	3	2	1	3	2	1
2	3	2	1	3	2	1
3	2	3	1	1	3	2
4	2	1	3	3	2	1
5	1	3	2	2	3	1
Totals	11	11	8	12	12	6

where a_1 and a_2 are tied.

Condition IV: Citizens' sovereignty. *For any pair of alternatives, a_i and a_j, there exists a set of R-orders of A such that the method of summation yields a_iPa_j as the social outcome.*

Failure to satisfy Condition IV is to prohibit the order a_iPa_j even if *all* individuals prefer a_i to a_j. If a_iPa_j is not permitted, for some pair, a_i and a_j—that is, if, at most, a_iRa_j is the social outcome for any set of individual orders—we then say that the social outcome is *imposed*. Restating Condition IV: *The method of summation is such that the social outcome is not imposed.*

The point of this condition is to outlaw the possibility of an objectively given social policy which is unrelated to the preferences of members of the society. In Rousseau's terms, the condition outlaws a general will. Rousseau distinguished between the "general will," which he seems to have defined as what was objectively right for a society, and the "will of all," which he defined as a social outcome arrived at by the amalgamation of all the individual preferences. As is well known, Rousseau wished to construct a society in which the general will would triumph over the will of all. Condition IV, however, requires a society in which the will of all is adopted whenever it conflicts with a supposed general will. The reason for this condition is, of course, the fact that the general will need not be desired by anyone; and, when this is the situation, a Benthamite democracy of the sort assumed in this discussion is not consistent with the imposition of a general will.

Condition V: Nondictatorship. Initially we define a dictated social outcome: For an individual i, i in M, we say that, if i orders a_iPa_j and if the social outcome is a_iPa_j, the social outcome is dictated. The condition then is: *The social outcome is not dictated.*

The rationale of this condition is that, again from the point of view of Benthamite democracy, one would not wish to admit a dictator. Incidentally, the difference between Conditions IV and V is that IV prohibits a dictator outside the system, while V prohibits one inside.

Arrow's Theorem. In our presentation of Arrow's argument, we started out by stating the properties of an ordering of alternatives. We have now followed this with the statement of a number of conditions that the machinery of summation of individual preferences ought to satisfy in order to meet elementary demands of social coherence and social justice. Now we are able to state Arrow's theorem: *Every method of summation satisfying Conditions I–III and producing a connected, transitive social ordering violates either Condition IV or V.* Stated another way: *The five conditions are inconsistent with the two ordering properties (axioms).* Stated still another way: *Given certain elementary requirements of fairness in summation (i.e., the conditions), it is impossible to assure that social outcomes will not be paradoxical.*

One very important feature of Arrow's work is that he proved this theorem without reference to any particular method of summation such as majority rule or markets. This is why it is possible to emphasize, as we did earlier, that Arrow's proof demonstrates, *for certain,* that the paradox cannot be avoided if his conditions are satisfied. In order to realize the full meaning of the theorem, it is desirable, therefore, to have some understanding of the proof. Consequently we have set forth a rather informal proof:[8]

To begin the proof, we define a Decisive Set: *A set, V, of choosers is said to be decisive for a_i against a_j if the social outcome is a_iPa_j for all sets of individual orderings in which the members of V have the ordering a_iPa_j.* Note that this definition of a decisive set has nothing to do with majorities or minorities but is consonant with any rule of summation including dictatorship.

We also adopt (without a proof, because a proof would be both obvious and tedious) a condition on unanimity derived from Conditions II and IV:

Condition P: Unanimous consent or Pareto optimality. *If every person in M holds a_iPa_j, then the social outcome is a_iPa_j.*

The effect of this condition is to forbid a social ordering of a pair of alternatives contrary to what everybody unanimously desires. Such a contrary result could occur only in two ways, both of which are forbidden: (1) a social outcome nobody wants could come out of the method of summation, but this is forbidden by Condition II, (nonperversity); or (2) such a social outcome could be imposed from outside the system, but this is forbidden by Condition IV (citizens' sovereignty). Hence it follows that, if everybody prefers a_i to a_j, so does society. Since Condition P embodies Conditions II and IV, it is sufficient to prove the main theorem by showing the inconsistency of I, III, V, and P.

The strategy of the proof of the main theorem is to show, first, that, if a single individual is a decisive set all by himself for any pair (a_i, a_j), he is a dictator in violation of Condition V. Then, by an adaptation of the paradox of voting, we show that a single individual can in fact be decisive for a pair under Conditions I, III, and P. It thus follows that these conditions are inconsistent with V.

Using this strategy, we first prove that the consequent follows from the antecedent in the following sentence:

(1) If a single chooser, 1, is decisive for a_1 against a_3, where $a_1 \neq a_3$, then he is decisive for an alternative in each pair drawn from the triplet (a_1, a_2, a_3).

While the proof thus appears to be limited to the case where there are only $n = 3$ alternatives, any larger set of alternatives, A, can always be broken down into triplets. If there is an inconsistency within any triplet, then of course there is an inconsistency in the larger set also.

To prove the validity of the implication in (1), it is enough to show that, if 1 is decisive for a_1 against a_3, then he is also decisive for a_i against a_1 and a_3, where a_i ranges over a_2 and a_3. Since the triplet admits of three pairs: (a_1, a_3), (a_1, a_2), and

[8]This simplified and abbreviated proof follows not only Arrow, *Social Choice and Individual Value,* but also R. Duncan Luce and Howard Raiffa, *Games and Decisions* (New York: Wiley, 1957), pp. 339–340, and William H. Riker, "Arrow's Theorem and Some Examples of the Paradox of Voting," *Mathematical Applications in Political Science,* vol. 1 (Dallas: Southern Methodist University Press, 1965), pp. 41–60.

(a_2, a_3), this amounts to proving that, if a person is decisive in the first pair, he is decisive in all pairs.

Construct two sets: V', which consists of chooser 1; and W, which consists of all other choosers, 2, 3, . . ., m. Assume the following individual orderings, which are of course admissible under Condition I:

for V': $\quad a_i P a_1$, $a_1 P a_3$, and $a_i P a_3$;

for W: $\quad a_3 P a_i$, $a_i P a_1$, and $a_3 P a_1$.

Given these preference structures, we now calculate the social outcome by means of series of pairwise comparisons, in accordance with the requirements of Condition III. Since both V' and W prefer a_i to a_1, by Condition P the social outcome is $a_i P a_1$. Furthermore, by reason of the antecedent in sentence (1), the social outcome is $a_1 P a_3$. And, by transitivity from $a_i P a_1$ and $a_1 P a_3$, we get the social outcome $a_i P a_3$. Note, however, only chooser 1 prefers a_i to a_3. Thus:

(2) V' is decisive for a_i against a_3.

It remains to be shown that 1 is decisive for a_i against a_1. For that we again assume some individual orderings admissible by reason of Condition I:

for V': $\quad a_i P a_3$, $a_3 P a_1$, and $a_i P a_1$;

for W: $\quad a_3 P a_1$, $a_1 P a_i$, and $a_3 P a_i$.

By reason of (2), the social ordering is $a_i P a_3$. By Condition P, socially, $a_3 P a_1$. And by transitivity from $a_i P a_3$ and $a_3 P a_1$, the social ordering is $a_i P a_1$. But only chooser 1 prefers a_i to a_1. Hence:

(3) V' is decisive for a_i against a_1.

Thus, having assumed the antecedent in (1), we have shown by (2) and (3) that the consequent in (1) necessarily follows. We have thus completed the first part of the proof and we now turn to the second part, which is to show that the antecedent of (1) may in fact be true.

We now show that a single chooser may be decisive for a_1 against a_3, where $a_1 \neq a_3$. First, we construct V_1, a minimally decisive set. This set is minimal in the sense that subtraction of a single member would render it indecisive for any pair. V_1 exists for, by Condition P, at least M is decisive and V_1 can be constructed from M by subtracting members until V_1 is arrived at. V_1 cannot be empty because, if it were, its complement M would be indecisive; but, by Condition P, M must be decisive. In addition to V_1 we construct the following sets:

V', a single member of V_1;

V_2, the remaining members of V_1 so that $V' \cup V_2 = V_1$ (read, "the union of V' and V_2 equals V_1");

V_3, the members of M not in V_1, so that $V_1 \cup V_3 = M$.

Note that, since $m \geq 2$, V_2 and V_3 cannot both be empty. Assume that the members of these sets have the following individual orders, all admissible under Condition I:

for V : $\quad a_1 P a_2$, $a_2 P a_3$, and $a_1 P a_3$;

for V_2: $\quad a_3 P a_1$, $a_1 P a_2$, and $a_3 P a_2$;

for V_3: $\quad a_2 P a_3$, $a_3 P a_1$, and $a_2 P a_1$.

Readers will recognize this as a set of socially paradoxical individual preference orders.

Making pairwise comparisons as required by Condition III, we note first that both V' and V_2 prefer a_1 to a_2 and that together V' and V_2 are the minimally decisive set. Hence:

(4) The social outcome is a_1Pa_2.

Suppose a_3Pa_2 is the social outcome. This is clearly impossible, for only V_2 prefers a_3 to a_2, and V_2 is by definition not a decisive set. Hence:

(5) The social outcome is: not (a_3Pa_2), which is a_2Ra_3.

[That "not (a_3Pa_2)" is equivalent to "a_2Ra_3" is easily appreciated by noting that the possible relations among a_2 and a_3 are: a_2Pa_3, a_2Ia_3, and a_3Pa_2. To say "not (a_2Pa_3)" is therefore to affirm the latter two possibilities. But a_2Ra_3 is exactly those possibilities: either a_2Ia_3 or a_2Pa_3. So "not (a_3Pa_2)" is "a_2Ra_3."]

By transitivity from (4) and (5), we have:

(6) The social outcome is a_1Pa_3.

Only the single member of V' prefers a_1 to a_3. Hence we have shown a case in which, using Conditions I, III, and P, a single chooser was decisive for one alternative in a pair. We have already shown that, if decisive for one pair, a single chooser is decisive for all pairs and thus is a dictator in violation of Condition V. This completes the proof.

EXPECTED FREQUENCY OF MAJORITY RULE

This impressive proof assures us that any method of summation (like markets or voting in legislatures) that satisfies these equitable conditions is nevertheless liable to offer paradoxical outcomes. On first confronting this uncomfortable conclusion, one asks: How important is the paradox? Does it pervade all social life, or is it simply something on the periphery of several systems? If it is pervasive, what in fact does it do to social outcomes? How much and what kind of incoherence does it introduce into society? Most important, one asks about its philosophical implications: Are we to view it as merely an amusing trick or does it tell us something of profound importance about the nature of society? These are difficult questions, in part because of the novelty of the problem. Duncan Black presented the paradox to the scholarly world only twenty-five years ago, and scholars have taken all this time to ingest it without really comprehending its significance for social theory generally. We will try, however, in the remainder of this chapter to report on the initial efforts of theorists to interpret its meaning.

One attractive way to initiate inquiry, a method Black himself suggests, is to ask what chance there is, given a particular mechanism such as majority rule, for a paradox to occur.[9] In its usual form, this question is tied directly to majority rule by another question: what is the probability that no majority winner occurs? The relation between these questions can be seen thus: An intransitive or paradoxical arrangement of three alternatives in a social outcome under majority rule is equivalent to the absence of a majority winner

[9]Black, *The Theory of Committees and Elections*, pp. 50–51.

in the Condorcet sense. A Condorcet winner, it will be recalled, is that alternative which defeats all $(n-1)$ others. Thus, for a paradox, if

$$\text{persons} \begin{Bmatrix} 1 \\ 2 \\ 3 \end{Bmatrix} \text{ have orderings } \begin{Bmatrix} a_1a_2a_3 \\ a_2a_3a_1 \\ a_3a_1a_2 \end{Bmatrix}, \text{ under majority rule,}$$

a_1 defeats a_2 $(1, 3)$, but loses to a_3 $(2, 3)$;

a_2 defeats a_3 $(1, 2)$, but loses to a_1 $(1, 3)$;

a_3 defeats a_1 $(2, 3)$, but loses to a_2 $(1, 2)$;

so that no alternative defeats $(n-1)$ others. (Sometimes this property is referred to as a cyclical majority because the winners can be arranged thus: $a_1 \to a_2 \to a_3 \to a_1$.) In this case and generally, the best any alternative in a paradox can do is to defeat $(n-2)$ others. Thus, for three alternatives, to say that a paradox occurs is to say also that there is no majority winner. For a larger number of alternatives, the relation is somewhat more complicated: It is possible for an additional alternative, a_4,

(1) to defeat all the others, thus: $a_4 \to a_1 \to a_2 \to a_3 \to a_1$;
(2) to be in the cycle, thus: $a_1 \to a_2 \to a_3 \to a_4 \to a_1$; or
(3) to be defeated by all the others, thus: $a_1 \to a_2 \to a_3 \to a_1 \to a_4$.

In the latter two cases, a paradox implies (as before) that there is no majority winner; but in the first case both a paradox (among a_1, a_2, and a_3) and a majority winner, a_4, exist.[10]

To approach in its simplest form the question of the chance of no majority winner, assume three choosers $(m=3)$ and three alternatives $(n=3)$. There are, of course, $3!=6$ transitive orders of the alternatives; and we will suppose that the chance that a chooser selects one of these orders is equal to the chance that he selects another one, i.e. $1/6$., (The assumption of equiprobability is, of course, highly restrictive, but no one has yet found an easy way to banish it because no other general assumption is available.) In general, since there are $n!$ orders and since each of the m choosers can choose any one of them, there are $(n!)^m$ possible ways that an m-person society might arrange individual preference orders. In the $m=3$, $n=3$ case, there are $(n!)^m=216$ such ways. We offer three examples:

EXAMPLE 1		EXAMPLE 2		EXAMPLE 3	
Persons	*Orders*	*Persons*	*Orders*	*Persons*	*Orders*
1	$a_1a_2a_3$	1	$a_1a_2a_3$	1	$a_1a_2a_3$
2	$a_1a_2a_3$	2	$a_1a_3a_2$	2	$a_2a_3a_1$
3	$a_1a_2a_3$	3	$a_3a_2a_1$	3	$a_3a_1a_2$
Social outcome:	$a_1a_2a_3$		$a_1a_3a_2$		$a_1a_2a_3a_1$

[10]See note 17, page 100, for a complete categorization of the relationships between paradoxes and no majority winners.

Under majority rule, example 1 (unanimity) leads to a transitive social result as does example 2, while example 3 is a paradox. Out of 216 cases, six involve unanimity and 90 involve a majority (two persons) selecting the same order of alternatives. Naturally these 96 cannot involve paradoxes. Of the remaining 120 cases where all three choosers select different orders, there are 12 that involve selection of these sets of orderings:

$$\begin{Bmatrix} a_1 a_2 a_3 \\ a_2 a_3 a_1 \\ a_3 a_1 a_2 \end{Bmatrix} \quad \text{or} \quad \begin{Bmatrix} a_1 a_3 a_2 \\ a_3 a_2 a_1 \\ a_2 a_1 a_3 \end{Bmatrix}$$

by permutation of the three choosers; and these 12 result in paradoxes, either $a_1 a_2 a_3 a_1$ or $a_1 a_3 a_2 a_1$. Thus there are 12 paradoxes (which, in the case of three alternatives, is the same as no majority winner) out of 216 equally probable cases so that the expectation is $12/216 = 0.0556$.

Niemi and Weisberg have generalized this calculation, and we set forth some of their results in Table 4.1.[11] This table deserves careful study: we point to two obvious features:

TABLE 4.1

Probabilities of No Majority Winner under Majority Rule with Equally Likely Selection of Orders by Choosers

NUMBER OF ALTERNATIVES (n)	NUMBER OF CHOOSERS (m)—ODD ONLY							
	3	5	7	11	15	29	59	∞
3	.0556	.0694	.0750	.0798	.0820	.0848	.0863	.0877
4	.1111	.14	.15					.1755
5	.16	.20	.22					.2513
6	.20	.25	.27					.3152
7								.3692
15								.6087
25								.7297
49								.8405

SOURCE: The four-decimal results are by Niemi and Weisberg. The two-decimal results they have adopted from Klahr, "A Computer Simulation of the Paradox of Voting."

[11] Richard G. Niemi and Herbert F. Weisberg, "A Mathematical Solution for the Probability of the Paradox of Voting," *Behavioral Science*, vol. 13 (1968), pp. 317–323. Similar calculations are set forth in Frank Demeyer and Charles Plott, "The Probability of a Cyclical Majority," *Econometrica*, vol. 38 (1970), pp. 345–354; and in Mark B. Garman and Morton I. Kamien, "The Paradox of Voting: Probability Calculations," *Behavioral Science*, vol. 13 (1968), pp. 306–317. Some steps toward the development of these calculations are included in David Klahr, "A Computer Simulation of the Paradox of Voting," *American Political Science Review*, vol. 60 (1966), pp. 384–390, and in William H. Riker, "Voting and the Summation of Preferences: An Interpretive Bibliographic Review of Selected Developments during the Last Decade," *American Political Science Review*, vol. 55 (1961), pp. 900–911.

1. If the number of choosers, m, is greater than ten or so, the chance of no majority is almost the same as when m approaches infinity. This suggests that even a small number (e.g., ten) of choosers is sufficient to complicate matters almost as much as they can be complicated. Any large assembly or market is therefore almost certain— given the assumption of equiprobability—to contain enough choosers for incoherence.
2. When the number of alternatives, n, is small (e.g., $n \leq 5$), as in voting on motions, the chance of no majority is relatively much less than when n is large (e.g., $n \geq 25$), as in markets with pure competition.

The overall conclusion one draws from this table is that when m or n is small, the likelihood of no majority winner is also relatively small. Hence one infers that the paradox is not particularly significant for summations by voting, though it does indicate that markets (in which, of course, n and m are large) allocate resources in nontransitive ways.

SOPHISTICATED VOTING AND CONTRIVED PARADOXES

We think, however, that such an inference about voting is not warranted. One fundamental assumption underlying the foregoing calculation is that choosers are equally likely to select any one of the $n!$ orders. For any realistic situation this is almost certainly incorrect. At this point, therefore, we delineate two kinds of forces in nature that make for deviations (in, however, opposite directions) from equiprobability. These have the effect of casting doubt on the utility of the calculations in Table 4.1.

One reason for a higher-than-expected chance of paradoxes is that there is an advantage in contriving them. We distinguish between (a) accidental paradoxes which occur when voters, each expressing his own true taste, reveal a paradoxical collection of orderings and (b) contrived paradoxes which occur when voters, some not expressing their true tastes, act to engender a paradox. The calculation in Table 4.1 refers only to accidental paradoxes; it tells us nothing about contrived ones. Each contrived paradox is, of course, constructed out of a situation that otherwise would have been nonparadoxical. So to say contrived paradoxes exist is to say Table 4.1 understates the total number of paradoxes. Furthermore, since it is laborious to contrive paradoxes, men are likely to do so only on the more important subjects; so that in a deeper sense this calculation understates the social significance of paradoxes.

All known systems of voting, especially if they do not embody Condition III (independence from irrelevant alternatives), are vulnerable to manipulation by voters.[12] We speak of *sincere* voting, which occurs when a voter acts in accord with his true tastes, and of *sophisticated* voting, which occurs when a voter acts other than in accord with his true tastes in order to achieve a larger

[12]See Robin Farquharson, *Theory of Voting* (New Haven: Yale University Press, 1969).

goal. To say that voting systems are vulnerable to manipulation is to say that sophisticated voting can change the outcome. To offer a simple illustration from plurality voting, a system that does not conform to Condition III, we imagine an election with three candidates (a_1, a_2, a_3) and three parties (I, with 45 percent of the electorate, II with 30 percent, III with 25 percent) having these preferences:

$$I \ (45\%): \quad a_1a_3a_2$$

$$II \ (30\%): \quad a_2a_3a_1$$

$$III \ (25\%): \quad a_3a_2a_1$$

In plurality voting, if all the voters are sincere, a_1 wins with a plurality of 45 percent. If the voters in parties II and III are sophisticated, however, they can combine on one of their first preferences, say a_2, so that a_2 beats a_1 55 percent to 45 percent.

In this example, the shocking feature is not just the possibility of manipulation—many writers would doubtless condone or even justify that— but rather the fact that given plurality voting, neither the winner under sincerity (a_1) nor another winner under sophistication (a_2) satisfies reasonable requirements for winning. By the Condorcet criterion (i.e., that the winning alternative defeat each of the other in pairwise contests), the winner is a_3! It beats a_2 by 70 percent to 30 percent and a_1 by 55 percent to 45 percent. Plurality systems are in general subject to both this kind of manipulation and this kind of distortion.[13]

Such distortion and indeed quite a bit of manipulation by sophisticated voting can be avoided in any system that embodies Condition III. Voting by pairwise comparison, thus:

step 1: a_1 vs. a_2
step 2:   survivor of step 1 vs. a_3
⋮   ⋮
step $n - 1$: survivor of step $n - 2$ vs. a_n
step n: survivor of step $n - 1$ vs. all other motions

effectively eliminates much of the manipulation and distortion that can be eliminated. If there is a winner by the Condorcet criterion, it wins under this procedure if voting is sincere.[14] Suppose a Condorcet winner exists: It must enter the voting at some step and because it defeats all others it survives through the last step. Thus distortion is eliminated. Manipulation can still occur by sophisticated voting; but the adoption of round-robin voting, wherein each motion is pitted against each other, eliminates manipulation if there is a Condorcet winner.

---

[13]Readers may find the example in the text more interesting if they think of it as an approximation of the election of 1912, where I is the Democratic Party, II is the Progressive, and III is the Republican, a_1 is Wilson, a_2 is Roosevelt, and a_3 is Taft. Evidently, voting was then sincere, although the presumed Condorcet winner (Theodore Roosevelt) actually came in second, while the lowest in the social ordering (Wilson) was, historically, the winner.

[14]Black, *Theory of Committees*, pp. 21, 43–44; Farquharson, *Theory of Voting*, pp. 61–67.

Nevertheless, voting under Condition III does not eliminate all manipulation, although it renders the opportunities fewer. Indeed, one way to interpret Arrow's theorem is to say that manipulation can never be entirely eliminated. If no Condorcet winner exists—which is exactly when the paradox exists—then all voting, even under Condition III, is vulnerable to manipulation. If, on the other hand, a Condorcet winner exists, then, under Condition III, the only kind of sophisticated voting possible is to create a paradox, a process such as follows:

There is an alternative, a_1, supported by a majority; to take a historical example of some importance, let a_1 be the proposal of the Seventeenth Amendment for the direct election of senators. The minority supporting a_0, the status quo, are certain to lose unless they can introduce another alternative, a_2, which will generate a paradox. Under Anglo-American procedure, when a paradox occurs, the status quo then wins. So the minority (conservative Republican) introduces the DePew amendment, which provides for federal supervision of direct elections of senators. Of course, in 1900, as perhaps still today, such supervision is detested by white Southerners, most of whom otherwise support a_1. On the other hand, all non-Southern Republican supporters of a_1 also profoundly favor a_2, the one kind of measure then uniting the Republican party. The minority (3) thus split the majority into two parts (1 and 2), resulting in factions with these preference orders:

1. Republican supporters of a_1: $a_2 a_1 a_0$
2. Democratic (North and South) supporters of a_1: $a_1 a_0 a_2$
3. Republican supporters of the status quo: $a_0 a_2 a_1$

These factions, approximately equal, are all less than $m/2$, so the DePew amendment (a_2) defeats (i.e., is added to) the Seventeenth Amendment as originally proposed (a_1) and then a_2 (i.e., the amended Amendment) loses to a_0 (the status quo). That brilliant parliamentary maneuver delayed the Amendment by nearly ten years.[15]

To manipulate outcomes in plurality systems is relatively easy: supporters of second, third, . . . alternatives can combine against the first, or, alternatively, opponents of the leading alternative can introduce others likely to split its support. Such manipulation is an almost constant feature of all systems lacking Condition III. But manipulation is more difficult when Condition III is satisfied, for then the only possible maneuver is to contrive a paradox. Nevertheless this does occur and this is why the calculation in Table 4.1 is mislead-

[15]For a detailed account of this event, see William H. Riker "Arrow's Theorem and Some Examples of the Paradox of Voting," *Mathematical Applications in Political Science*, vol. 1 (Dallas: Southern Methodist University Press, 1965), pp. 41–60. In the same paper is a description of a paradox over federal aid to education and desegregation. For an account of other contrived paradoxes, see William H. Riker, "The Paradox of Voting and Congressional Rules for Voting on Amendments," *American Political Science Review*, vol. 52 (1958), pp. 349–366, on appropriations for soil conservation; Farquharson, *Theory of Voting*, pp. 52–53, on highway appropriation; and Arrow, *Social Choice and Individual Value*, p. 3, on federal aid to education and churches.

ing: it does not take notice that all attempts at manipulation are of necessity attempts to contrive paradoxes. We have no empirical measure of the frequency of such attempts, although we know that they may be planned every time an amendment is offered. One cannot contrive a paradox in Anglo-American legislatures without amendments; hence, devices to prohibit amendments (such as the closed rule in the U. S. House of Representatives) should probably be interpreted in part as methods to prevent contrived paradoxes. In actual practice closed rules—which are hated by minorities, probably because they work—are imposed rarely, which suggests that paradoxes are contrived most often on highly controversial measures, which are by definition politically important. Hence we conclude that the significance of paradoxes is much greater than the calculation in Table 4.1 suggests.

CONDITIONS OF MAJORITY RULE

Since we cannot estimate the significance of failures to have a majority winner simply by an expected-frequency calculation, we must look more deeply into their nature. One way to do so is to determine what conditions are sufficient for simple majority rule. This leads us into an evaluation of the appropriateness of Arrow's conditions and into an investigation into the ways in which violations of his conditions occasion a paradox. We begin by assuming that a social outcome is constructed by simple majority voting, and we seek to ascertain under what conditions the social outcome is transitive or, failing that, under what conditions a motion exists that can defeat all *others* even if the total outcome is not transitive.[16]

[16]The categories suggested in the text can be summarized thus:

I. Transitive social outcomes, e.g.: *"abcd"* or aPb, c, d and bPc, d and cPd.
1. A majority prefers some alternative most, i.e., more than $m/2$ persons place a_i in the first place. E.g.:

$$
\begin{array}{ll}
\text{I:} & a_1a_2a_3a_4 \\
\text{II:} & a_1a_3a_2a_4 \\
\text{III:} & a_2a_1a_3a_4 \\
\hline
& a_1a_2a_3a_4
\end{array}
$$

2. Some alternative is preferred by the voters to $(n-1)$ other alternatives, but no alternative has a majority of first-place choices (a Condorcet winner or a dominant alternative). E.g.:

$$
\begin{array}{ll}
\text{I:} & a_1a_2a_3a_4 \\
\text{II:} & a_2a_1a_3a_4 \\
\text{III:} & a_3a_1a_2a_4 \\
\hline
& a_1a_2a_3a_4
\end{array}
$$

II. Nontransitive social outcomes, e.g.: *"abcdb"* or aPb, c, d and bPc, and cPd and dPb.
1. A majority prefers some alternative most, while other alternatives are in a cycle. E.g.:

$$
\begin{array}{ll}
\text{I:} & a_1a_2a_3a_4 \\
\text{II:} & a_1a_3a_4a_2 \\
\text{III:} & a_1a_4a_2a_3 \\
\hline
& a_1a_2a_3a_4a_2
\end{array}
$$

Although no one has yet been able to state a completely general necessary condition for a transitive social outcome or a Condorcet winner under majority rule, a number of alternative ways of stating sufficient conditions have been devised. Clearly, one sufficient condition is that a majority of choosers rank the same alternative highest. Failing such an obvious condition, undoubtedly the most well-known and indeed most immediately useful condition of sufficiency is Black's notion of single-peakedness. To define this geometric condition, consider a two-coordinate system with the alternatives arranged on the horizontal axis and the rank in the individual chooser's preference order on the vertical axis. Thus, if a person prefers a_2 to a_1 and a_1 to a_3, his preferences can be represented as in Figure 4.1. Note that rank 1 is highest or most preferred, rank 2 next highest, and so on. A curve is said to be single-peaked if, reading from left to right,

(a) it always slopes up or always down,
(b) it slopes up to a point and then down, changing direction at most once.

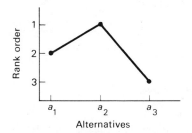

FIGURE 4.1
Geometric representation of a
preference order

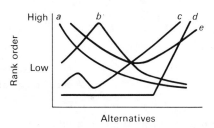

FIGURE 4.2
Single-peaked and nonsingle-
peaked curves

In Figure 4.2 we have assumed that the alternatives are numerous so that the curves are nearly continuous, and we have depicted some single-peaked curves (a, b, d) and some nonsingle-peaked curves (c, e). Black's condition of single-peakedness then is: if a set of preference orderings by individuals can by

2. Some alternative is preferred to $(n-1)$ others, while there is a cycle among the others (a Condorcet winner or a dominant alternative). E.g.:

I: $a_1a_4a_2a_3$
II: $a_2a_1a_3a_4$
III: $a_3a_4a_1a_2$
$a_1a_2a_3a_4a_2$

3. A paradox exists among all alternatives. E.g.:

I: $a_1a_2a_3a_4$
II: $a_2a_3a_4a_1$
III: $a_3a_4a_1a_2$
$a_2a_3a_4a_1a_2$

appropriate arrangement of alternatives on the horizontal axis be represented as a set of single-peaked curves, then some alternative (specifically the one at the peak of the median curve) is preferred by a majority and the social outcome is transitive.

To visualize the meaning of this condition, Figure 4.3 shows a set of single-peaked curves for three persons. (Note that these would not be single-peaked for all possible arrangements of alternatives on the horizontal axis; but it is sufficient for the condition to apply if they are single-peaked under at least one arrangement.) The fact that a curve is up-sloping from left to right, say

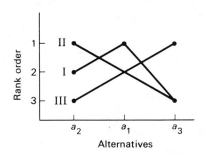

FIGURE 4.3
A set of single-peaked curves

from a_2 to a_1 as the curve for voter I is in Figure 4.3, means that, for him, $a_1 P a_2$. Conversely, the fact that a curve is down-sloping from left to right, say from a_1 to a_3 as the curve for voter II is, means that, for him, $a_1 P a_3$. Consider then in Figure 4.3 the alternative, a_1, beneath the median peak. It can defeat the alternatives to its left, a_2, because a majority of the curves are up-sloping between a_2 and a_1. Similarly, a_1 can defeat the alternative to its right, a_3, because a majority of the curves are down-sloping between a_1 and a_3. Thus, in general, if an arrangement of alternatives on the horizontal axis exists so that the curves above it are single-peaked and if the number of voters is odd, then the alternative beneath the peak of the median curve can defeat all other alternatives. This median alternative is, therefore, the majority winner by the Condorcet criterion. An equivalent analysis reveals that the social outcome is transitive.

The reason single-peakedness results *for certain* in a transitive social outcome and a majority decision is that it abandons Condition I. That is, it prohibits some possible selections of alternatives by individuals. In effect it requires that, if persons 1 to $m - 1$ have chosen a set of orderings verging on the paradoxical, then the *mth* person cannot choose an ordering that results in a paradox. Suppose, for example, that persons I and III have chosen as in

Figure 4.3; then the requirement of single-peakedness does not allow person II to choose $a_2a_3a_1$. Suppose person II did so choose, resulting in

> I: $a_1a_2a_3$
> II: $a_2a_3a_1$
> III: $a_3a_1a_2$

In Figure 4.4 we show that this set of orderings cannot be single-peaked under *any* possible arrangement of alternatives on the horizontal axis. Thus it is clear that the rule of single-peakedness guarantees majority rule by forbidding certain combinations of individual orderings.

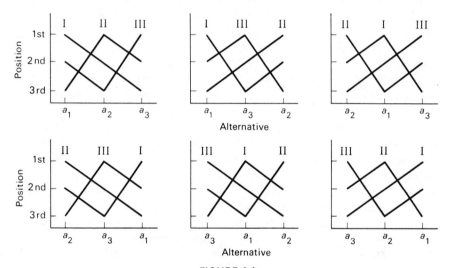

FIGURE 4.4
A nonsingle-peaked set of orderings

In the particular case of $n=3$ and $m=3$, where the possible orderings are

> 1. $a_1a_2a_3$
> 2. $a_1a_3a_2$
> 3. $a_2a_1a_3$
> 4. $a_2a_3a_1$
> 5. $a_3a_1a_2$
> 6. $a_3a_2a_1$,

the requirement of single-peakedness prohibits the joint selection of

> 1. $a_1a_2a_3$⎫
> 4. $a_2a_3a_1$⎬   or
> 5. $a_3a_1a_2$⎭

> 2. $a_1a_3a_2$⎫
> 3. $a_2a_1a_3$⎬
> 6. $a_3a_2a_1$⎭

each of which results in a cyclical majority.

If one examines the two cyclical majorities displayed in the previous sentence, it is immediately apparent that, in each set of three orderings (i.e., [1, 4, 5] and [2, 3, 6]), each alternative appears, for at least one individual, in every rank order. Sen exploits this fact to state a fully general sufficient condition for majority rule.[17] For a triplet of alternatives, he defines the "value" of an alternative as "best" for an individual if it appears first in his rank ordering, "worst" if it appears last, and "medium" if it is in between. Then he defines the notion of value-restrictedness, which is comparable to, but more general than, single-peakedness. A set of individual preference orders is said to be *value-restricted* if there is *some alternative that, in all the individual orders, is never best or never worst or never medium.* Thus the set in Figure 4.3 is value-restricted because a_1 is never worst. Sen proves that majority rule satisfies Conditions II–V and transitivity, provided the set of alternatives is value-restricted. His proof amounts to showing that value-restrictedness forbids, for the examples in the previous paragraph, the choosing of at least one ordering from the set of orderings [1, 4, 5] and at least one from the set [2, 3, 6] and thus does not permit either of the two possible kinds of paradoxes to appear.

This theorem is particularly enlightening, for it shows that coherence in social outcomes under majority rule is possible with only the violation of Condition I. As we point out in our explanation of this condition, many of the commonly used devices for narrowing choice do no more than this; and yet we know by Sen's theorem that they impose coherence. In a world with many alternatives, the two-party system in well-disciplined legislatures requires that there be at most two alternatives appearing first in any legislator's ordering. This is precisely value-restrictedness, for some third, fourth, etc., alternatives that are not approved by one of the two parties cannot be best for any individual. The same effect is produced by run-off elections, where at the run-off no third candidate from the original election can be best for anyone. Even in apparently less restricted situations, we often find quasi-value-restrictive rules that guarantee Condorcet winners. Constitutional prohibitions, for example, have this effect. When

a_1 is aid to no schools,
a_2 is aid to public schools only, and
a_3 is aid to all schools including private religious ones,

the First Amendment prohibition on establishment of religion has the effect of preventing the revelation of any preference order in which a_3 stands first. Only a_1 and a_2 are Constitutional motions. And a_3 can never be set against a_1 or a_2. Hence a_3 cannot be revealed as best in an individual preference order. The only possible votes, therefore, are those in which a_1 is set against a_2. From

[17]Amartya K. Sen, "A Possibility Theorem on Majority Decisions," *Econometrica*, vol. 34 (1966), pp. 491–499.

such a vote there must certainly be a Condorcet winner. The Constitutional rule thus eliminates the possibility of an occurrence of the paradox by preventing the revelation (in a vote) that a_3 is in first place.

In an even broader way, the conventions and ideals of a culture are value-restrictive. Rousseau—who was surely the most conscious of any of the classic political philosophers of the problem of coherence, even though he did not know about the paradox—emphasized that, in practice, the only sure way to have a coherent public policy was to have in the cultural background a great Legislator who imposed a set of ideals. Sparta had Lycurgus, Athens had Solon, Geneva had Calvin—and all these men imposed a set of ideals on their cities. Since the imposed ideals effectively prevented other ideals from being best in any individual ordering, the great Legislator provided, in our terms, for value-restrictedness.[18] Even in larger societies we find similar conventions: North American culture strongly discourages any orderings of states of society in which a life of religious contemplation is best. Medieval culture, however, encouraged men to put the contemplative life first.

The epitome of Black's and Sen's conditions is that social outcomes are ordered if some sort of inner harmony exists among choosers. Some writers suggest that this inner harmony is in fact a kind of scalability.[19] And Coombs shows that single-peakedness can be understood in terms of his general method of scaling, the unfolding technique. Specifically the existence of single-peaked preference curves is equivalent to the existence of a common *qualitative* dimension along which individual preferences (and the social outcome) can be ordered. (It appears likely that this relation also exists for value-restrictedness.) On account of this relation between curves and scale, the single-peaked curves reflect a cultural uniformity about the standard of judgment, even though people differ about what ought to be chosen under that standard.

The fact of cultural uniformity suggests two extensions of our previous inquiry. Continuing the investigation of the probability of the paradox under the assumption of equiprobability of preference orders, we can ask: Suppose that a proportion less than one of the choosers subscribes to a common standard of judgment, what is the chance of the paradox as that proportion varies? Or, continuing the investigation by means of the study of sufficient conditions, we can ask: Suppose several standards of judgment—all universally accepted—are employed simultaneously. What then are the sufficient conditions of a transitive social outcome under majority rule?

The first question is explored by Niemi, who starts out by observing that complete unidimensionality (or perfect single-peakedness) is unlikely to occur in nature. He therefore asks: How likely is a paradox that precludes a majority

[18]Rousseau, *Social Contract*, chap. 7.

[19]G. Th. Guilbaud, "Les théories de l'intérêt général et le problème logique de l'aggrégation," *Economie Appliquée*, vol. 5 (1952), pp. 501–584; Clyde Coombs, *The Theory of Data* (New York: Wiley, 1964), pp. 383–402. But see Herbert Weisberg and Richard Niemi, "The Relationship between Single-Peaked Preferences and Guttman Scales," forthcoming.

winner when less than complete unidimensionality exists? Specifically, he considers the situation where there are three alternatives and where some but not all of the voters have rank orders satisfying the single-peakedness condition.[20] Assuming rank orders are equally probable among both those with and those without single-peaked curves, the probability that the paradox occurs can be calculated. This calculation reveals that:

> for three alternatives ... even a moderate degree of unidimensionality makes it unlikely that the paradox will prevent a transitive majority decision. Depending on the size of the [voting population] paradoxes will infrequently occur if only 75% or 70% or even fewer of the individuals adopt a common standard of judgment.

Since it must be the case with three alternatives that $66\frac{2}{3}$ percent adopt a common standard, the fact that so little additional unidimensionality is sufficient to make the paradox unlikely suggests that, when the social situation is well structured by institutions such as political parties, paradoxes are rare things.

This conclusion holds when the society uses at most one standard of judgment. Suppose, however, that society employs several standards simultaneously, with everyone agreeing on the relevance of these standards. School budgets, for example, can be evaluated both by the criterion of the quality of education and by the criterion of the size of the tax rate. Even in "homogeneous groups," such as legislative committees, we commonly find several criteria being used by *all* members for evaluating issues before them.[21] Another way of determining the significance of the paradox is, then, to identify sufficient conditions for transitive social outcomes or majority rule when alternatives are evaluated on several dimensions.

As we move from a one-dimensional world of judgment to a multidimensional world, we must generally seek a less loftier objective than a sufficient condition for a completely transitive social ordering.[22] Instead we can formulate conditions for the existence of a dominant alternative, which is one that can defeat $(n-1)$ others even if a cycle exists among defeated alternatives. (These are the categories of winners mentioned in I-2 and II-2 of note 16.) Since much of the interest in avoiding the paradox lies not in achieving a completely transitive

---

[20]Richard G. Niemi, "Majority Decision-Making with Partial Unidimensionality," *American Political Science Review*, vol. 63 (1969), pp. 488–497.

[21]Robert Samberg, *Conceptualization and Measurement of Political System Output: Decisions within Issue Contexts* (Ph.D. Dissertation, University of Rochester, 1971).

[22]At least one condition for a perfectly transitive ordering, albeit a restrictive one, is formulated in Otto A. Davis, M. DeGroot, and M. J. Hinich, "Social Preference Orderings and Majority Rule," *Econometrica* (forthcoming). Another sufficient condition, which requires the assumption that choice is made probabilistically and that some choosers abstain, is set forth in Melvin J. Hinich and Peter C. Ordeshook, "Transitive Social Preference and Majority Rule Equilibrium with Separable Probabilistic Choice Functions" (forthcoming).

social ordering (categories I-1 and I-2 of note 16) but in achieving simply a Condorcet winner or dominant alternative, we will be content when we discover sufficient conditions for this less rigorous case.

One sufficient condition for the existence of a Condorcet winner has been developed by Charles Plott, who shows that an alternative exists which is preferred to all others if (1) the distribution of most preferred points is radially symmetric "so that individuals [whose most preferred points are not the majority choice] can be divided into pairs whose interests are diametrically opposed"; and (2) both individuals in a pair weight the relative salience of dimensions in an identical fashion.[23] An example of a distribution satisfying Plott's condition is a normal density function.

Conditions such as Plott's are, however, restrictive. To see this we consider in Figure 4.5 a situation that fails to satisfy these conditions. The two axes of this illustration, C_1 and C_2, represent the two criteria three citizens employ to evaluate alternatives. Hence, we assume that an alternative can be identified by a value for C_1 and a value for C_2. Representing the most preferred alternatives of these three citizens by X_1, X_2, and X_3, we assume that the closer an

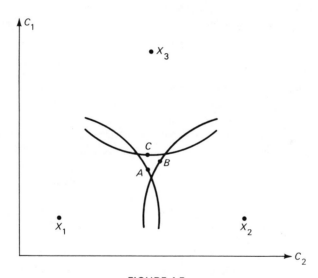

FIGURE 4.5

[23]Charles R. Plott, "A Notion of Equilibrium and its Possibility under Majority Rule," *American Economic Review,* vol. 57 (1967), pp. 787–806. Plott states his conditions in somewhat different and, of course, more precise form. Unfortunately a detailed statement of his conditions would necessitate some fairly complex mathematics, so we offer instead a loose reformulation. For an alternative formulation of this condition see Gordon Tullock, "The General Irrelevance of the General Impossibility Theorem," *The Quarterly Journal of Economics,* vol. 81 (1967), pp. 256–270; Paul B. Simpson, "On Defining Areas of Voter Choice," *The Quarterly Journal of Economics,* vol. 83 (1969), pp. 478–490. These approaches generally are all sophisticated elaborations of Black, *The Theory of Committees and Elections,* and Black and Newing, *Committee Decisions with Complementary Valuation.*

alternative is to X_i the more citizen i prefers that alternative. Observe now that although in Figure 4.5 we have a "well-behaved" situation in the sense that it is easily characterized mathematically, it fails to satisfy Plott's conditions: the individuals cannot be paired into those that prefer diametrically opposed positions. Assuming that the curves in Figure 4.5 are arcs of circles of constant distances from the ideal points X_1, X_2, and X_3, then for three typical alternatives, A, B, and C, individuals 1 and 2 prefer A to C, individuals 1 and 3 prefer C to B, and individuals 2 and 3 prefer B to A, and the social preference is intransitive.

We might suppose, therefore, that, if a dominant position does not exist for such simple situations as this, a dominant position is unlikely whenever alternatives are evaluated by several standards. Such a pessimistic conclusion, however, is not entirely warranted; Condorcet winners always exist if people abstain from voting in a particular way.

Two unrealistic assumptions in Plott's analysis are often violated in the real world, so that Condorcet winners are probably more common than Plott's analysis suggests. First, Plott, as well as Arrow and Black, implicitly assumes that all eligible voters vote. No matter how disinterested the voters, no matter how similar the alternatives, everyone must vote. Similarly Sen limits his argument to those "concerned citizens" who actually do vote. Second, Plott and most other writers assume that voter's choices are deterministic, i.e., if a voter prefers a_1 to a_2, then he votes for a_1 with a probability of one. The lack of realism in these assumptions is clear: often eligible participants do not in fact participate and it is possible that people often choose probabilistically, i.e., they choose an alternative with some probability between zero and one. In an effort to approach the problem with alternative assumptions, therefore, Hinich, Ledyard, and Ordeshook assume that voters may abstain and that

(a) the probability that a person votes for a motion increases as the utility he associates with that motion increases; and

(b) the probability that a person votes for a motion remains constant or decreases as the utility increases of the motion to which it is compared.

Then they prove that, if persons vote sincerely, there exists a unique motion that defeats all alternatives (i.e., a Condorcet winner exists, though not necessarily a transitive ordering of alternatives), regardless of the distribution of preferences, the number of dimensions necessary to characterize preferences and motions, or the patterns of relative saliency.[24] This result demonstrates that the use of several standards for evaluating alternatives does not preclude necessarily the existence of a Condorcet winner. Hence, while the evaluation of alternatives by several standards acts to increase the likelihood that a paradox

[24]Melvin J. Hinich, John O. Ledyard, and Peter C. Ordeshook, "The Existence of Equilibrium under Majority Rule," *Journal of Economic Theory*, vol. 4 (1972), pp. 144–153, and Hinich and Ordeshook, "Transitive Social Preference."

exists, the possibility that people choose probabilistically and that they can abstain from revealing a preference decreases this likelihood.

We have been trying in the last several sections to estimate the degree of coherence in social outcomes. We found initially that the possibility of contrived paradoxes suggested more incoherence than might be supposed from an equiprobable calculation. Turning to a study of the conditions for majority rule (i.e., Condorcet winners), we found that some conditions (e.g., Black's, Sen's, and Plott's) are very difficult to satisfy, requiring as they do an inner harmony. From them one would expect very little majority rule, although some institutions, e.g., two-party systems, force more single-peakedness and value-restrictedness than might occur by chance. On the other hand, Hinich, Ledyard, and Ordeshook's conditions that incorporate nonvoting and probabilistic choice and thus permit the voter to express a strength of preferences render majority rule certain in these restricted circumstances.

THE CONDITION OF INDEPENDENCE FROM IRRELEVANT ALTERNATIVES

Another way of judging the significance of the paradox is to reevaluate Condition III (independence from irrelevant alternatives). Suppose that we do not impose this condition on the device for summation. Then it is possible for many kinds of devices to guarantee transitive social outcomes.[25] The paradox disappears and we have an apparently coherent social order. This is an attractive result, and one immediately asks: Why not forget Condition III entirely? Unfortunately, the attraction of this result is illusory. To assure transitivity by ignoring Condition III is to admit another—and much worse— kind of incoherence, namely, the adoption of outcomes opposed by a majority. In our description of Condition III we show that the method of complete pairwise comparison using the Condorcet criterion (thereby embodying Condition III) guarantees that, if a Condorcet winner exists, it is selected. If it does not exist, nothing is selected. On the other hand, the method of adding rank orders using the Borda criterion (one of the innumerable methods not satisfying Condition III) permits Condorcet winners to lose. Thus, transitivity, which is one kind of coherence, is achieved at the cost of allowing a loser to win, which is another kind of incoherence.

Nevertheless, in spite of the fact that methods of summation not satisfying Condition III admit this (possibly worse) kind of incoherence, many people have argued both that we ought not to impose Condition III and that institutions do not in fact impose it. Let us examine each assertion.

Methods of summation not satisfying Condition III allow relative intensities of preferences to influence the outcome. Referring back to our discussion of the

[25]John G. Kemeny, "Mathematics Without Numbers," *Daedalus*, vol. 88 (1959), pp. 577–591.

Borda criterion on pages 89–90, the Borda method in effect counts rank orders as degrees of intensity and weighs the degrees of the several voters together. In the example discussed, a_1 is the Condorcet winner; but using the Borda method, a_1 loses and a_2 wins when there are four ranks. This occurs because a_2 is relatively high on four of the five individual preference orders while a_1 is relatively high on only three orders. When we reduce the number of ranks from four to two, however, the relative intensity is invisible and a_1 clearly beats a_2. The sensitivity of the outcome to the number of ranks provided is surprisingly great: Voter 1 is depicted in the Borda method as believing a_1 is twice as good as a_2 when there are two ranks. But when there are four ranks, he apparently believes a_1 is only $1\frac{1}{3}$ times as good as a_2, a decline of fully one-third in relative valuation occasioned only by the small increase in the number of alternatives.

In contrast, all systems of summation that require independence from irrelevant alternatives do not admit measures on intensity of feeling. Whether a person ranks a_1 ahead of a_2 by one rank or by many ranks makes no difference in a pairwise comparison. All occasions on which a_1 is ahead of a_2, regardless of emotional distance, are regarded as equivalent because only the fact of being ahead is counted in the comparison. So we see that the initial effect of the independence condition is to deny consideration of intensity. Conversely, all methods of summarizing that take intensity into account violate Condition III.

Stating the matter in this way, it is easy to understand why some people argue that Condition III should not be imposed. They are thereby arguing for the social relevance of the fact of differences in intensity of preference. If, in a society of two people, person 1 wants a_1 very much more than a_2 while person 2 wants a_2 only a little bit more than a_1, is it not just, they ask, for person 1 to get his way? Furthermore, they apparently believe that, if 1 can pay 2 some compensation so that both are better off than were a draw to occur, then the justice of the outcome is beyond question. Indeed, it is even said that systems of summation that ignore the fact of differences in intensity omit one important kind of information in the calculus of winning and are, to that degree, unfair.[26]

On the other hand, other writers have argued just as determinedly that intensity of preferences should be ignored. Their rationale is that, in summarizing, any consideration of the intensity of taste necessarily involves interpersonal comparison of utility, which is always arbitrary and hence potentially unfair. To consider a standard counterexample against the relevance of intensity, suppose there is a society of two people having a choice simply between both drinking coffee and both drinking milk, where each have the following preferences:

[26]Leo Goodman and Harry Markowitz, "Social Welfare Functions Based on Individual Rankings," *American Journal of Sociology*, vol. 58 (1952), pp. 257–262. See also Robert Dahl, *A Preface to Democratic Theory* (Chicago: University of Chicago Press, 1956), pp. 90–123.

RANK ORDER OF ALTERNATIVES

PERSON	1	2
1	coffee	milk
2	milk	coffee

Ignoring intensity, there is a tie. But intensity can be compared by introducing irrelevant alternatives (e.g., other beverages), so that we get:

RANK ORDER OF ALTERNATIVES

PERSON	1	2	3	4	5
1	coffee	milk	cola	beer	tea
2	milk	beer	cola	tea	coffee

If we score by rank orders as before (i.e., five points for rank 1, four points for rank 2, and so on), coffee gets six points and milk nine, so that milk clearly wins. The equity of this outcome can be said to follow from the fact that person 1 doesn't care much which he gets—or so one infers from rank orders—while person 2 vastly prefers milk to coffee. Presumably the intensity of person 2 outweighs—and morally should outweigh—the indifference of 1.

But note that we achieve this result only by assuming that the ranks are about the same psychological distance apart from each other in each person. If the ranks were not similar for the two, we might possibly have something like this:

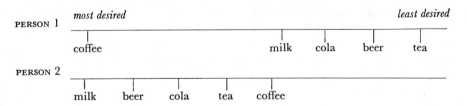

And if the world were in fact so arranged, it would appear proper to choose coffee, because even the coffee-hater (2) likes coffee more than the milk-hater likes milk.

If we make one assumption about the comparison of degrees of intensity, we choose milk; if we make another assumption, we choose coffee. Which is right? To answer we must measure the intensities of preference on the same scale. And there the problem is to select the one scale we will use. To calibrate measures of intensity in two persons, we need an absolute zero, a universally accepted point of least happiness. But this we cannot have, owing to the fundamental subjectivity of taste and preference. The reader will recall that, in the discussion of measures of utility in Chapter 2, we stress that the origin and unit of the measure of utility are unique for each person. Hence it is probably always true that measures of intensity of preference are made on different scales for different persons.

It follows therefore that interpersonal comparisons of utility are comparisons of noncomparable things. Such comparisons are thus nonsense. To admit such comparisons is to admit completely arbitrary social outcomes, which many writers believe is an even worse social result than intransitivity.

We started this discussion by suggesting that it might be reasonable to ignore the independence condition in order to account for intensity of preference. Now we see, however, that to count intensity is to compare interpersonally. And to admit interpersonal comparison is to admit arbitrary outcomes. In this way we run the risk of an incoherence even worse than might come from the paradox itself. It seems unreasonable, therefore, to try to escape from the paradox by not imposing Condition III. If we can possibly embody it in real-world institutions, we should try to do so.

But it is not always possible. Many important institutions of summations, such as cumulative voting or proportional representation, do not admit Condition III. And other institutions, such as legislative voting, that are supposed to admit it, in fact allow it to be circumvented. The Anglo-American procedure of voting in committees, for example, guarantees there will be no departure from the status quo unless there is a winner by the Condorcet criterion. Suppose there are a motion (a_1) and an amendment (a_2) on the floor—as well as the alternative of the status quo (a_3). The formal rules provide that a_1 be tested against a_2 and that the survivor (call it a_s) be tested against a_3. If a_s beats a_3, we know it can beat the other motion and is in fact the Condorcet winner, so a_s is adopted. If, however, a_3 beats a_s, we conventionally adopt a_3, not because we know it is a Condorcet winner (we don't), but because we know for certain that alternatives to the status quo $(a_1$ or $a_2)$ are not Condorcet winners. We don't change the status quo for a loser. In its abstract form this procedure thus provides that the substance of Condition III be imposed on the search for a winner.

But what happens in reality? People can evade the sense of these rules by logrolling. The idea of logrolling is that a legislator who favors a_1 *very much* persuades others (who are hostile to it) to vote for it nonetheless by promising to vote for other bills or motions, $a_2, \ldots, a_n$, that they favor. Thus some degree of intensity is introduced into the judgment over the whole set of bills or motions. The legislator reveals his very great preference for a_1 by buying the votes of some others. And they of course reveal that their hostility to a_1 is relatively mild by the very fact that he is able in some way to purchase their votes. If a perfect market exists, then each legislator's interest over a set of bills is expressed in the utility prices paid by him to get support and to him for his support. Several writers have extolled logrolling as a quasi-market in which intensity of preference is partly revealed and counted in the method of summation.[27]

Logrolling can thus be said to eliminate the independence condition legally embodied in parliamentary procedure. To visualize this fact, consider a situation in which members of a legislature have conducted a vote-market on a_1, . . ., a_n bills and exchanged votes until everyone is maximally satisfied by the way bills pass and fail. Condition III requires that, if some bill, a_k, which failed, had never been proposed, then the same outcomes would occur on every other bill. But in a logrolling market this need not be so.[28] Some resources were devoted to votes for a_k—either by individuals who voted for it because they favored it themselves or by individuals whose votes for it were purchased. So also were resources devoted to votes against it. In its absence, these resources must be reallocated. And, unless everybody has the same degree of intensity on a_k, the allocation of resources on the other bills will not be the same as when a_k was present. Indeed, a bill that could pass when a_k was present might fail in its absence and vice versa. Consequently, it may well be that the mere proposal of an irrelevant alternative, here a_k, is sufficient to change the outcomes of summation on other bills. This is, of course, exactly what Condition III forbids.[29] It thus appears that it is not always possible to embody Condition III in viable institutions.

It is possible to argue, however, that we should try to enforce Condition III whenever possible. Many writers (including Kemeny, Buchanan and Tullock, and Coleman) have seen the avoidance of this condition as a means of evading the paradox. But we see that, in the attempt to avoid the paradox, one can fall into the selection of a nonmajority winner or the arbitrariness of interpersonal comparison. It may well be a case of jumping from frying pan to fire.

This conclusion leads us also to a different estimate of the degree of coherence in society from many other writers. Those who condemn the independence condition and praise logrolling also usually believe that logrolling is endemic and pervasive. If they are correct, society tends toward the kind of incoherence implied in the absence of the condition. But it seems likely that logrolling is

---

[27]See, for example, James Buchanan and Gordon Tullock, *The Calculus of Consent* (Ann Arbor: University of Michigan Press, 1962) and James Coleman, "The Possibility of a Social Welfare Function," *American Economic Review*, vol. 56 (1966), pp. 1105–1122.

[28]The following argument is drawn from Robert Wilson, "An Axiomatic Model of Logrolling," *American Economic Review*, vol. 59 (1969), pp. 331–341. It should be noted, however, that the fact that logrolling violates Condition III does not mean that it provides a measure of relative intensity. Like a market it merely records the consequences of intensity without measuring it.

[29]That logrolling inevitably involves violations of the Condition of Independence from Irrelevant Alternatives is shown in R. E. Park, "Comment [on Coleman, 'The Possibility of a Social Welfare Function']," *American Economic Review*, vol. 57 (1967), pp. 1300–1304, and in D. C. Mueller, "Comment [on Coleman, *op. cit.*]," *American Economic Review*, vol. 57 (1967), pp. 1304–1311, as well as in Wilson, "An Axiomatic Model of Logrolling."

less common than they believe. The purpose of party discipline in legislatures is to avoid it. And in the case of large legislatures, the market for votes is doubtless highly imperfect.[30] Insofar as market mechanisms fail and parliamentary procedures are imposed, Condition III is also imposed and we have no more social incoherence than is implied by the inevitability of the paradox itself.

CONCLUSION

We started this investigation of coherence in social outcomes with the discovery that the incoherence involved in the paradox is logically ineradicable, given the conditions of Arrow's theorem. We investigated somewhat the chances of the occurrence of the paradox in order to estimate the seriousness of the ineradicability in a world of complete participation. Our results were equivocal, however, and we have no adequate estimate of the seriousness. We then looked for a possible way to avoid the paradox and discovered that, while such ways exist, there are other difficulties involved with them. We are led to conclude, therefore, that some kind of difficulty in arriving at social outcomes inevitably exists and that there is probably nothing we can do about it.

We can, however, reassess our attitude toward it. When the paradox was rediscovered a generation ago, some writers asked: Why should social outcomes have the transitive property that individual preference orders have? Society, they pointed out, cannot have preferences and cannot order them. We should expect intransitivities, they therefore suggested, and we should not be alarmed when they are brought to our attention. Surely we should not expect society to be coherent in exactly the same way an individual is.[31]

In the same way, we are not deeply disturbed by the paradox, for it serves mainly to remind us that society is not the same as the people who compose it. People are not invariably disturbed by the inconsistencies and incoherencies of market outcomes—such as the oft-discovered fact that society spends more on liquor than education though surely a majority would wish otherwise. Markets have been churning out such inconsistencies for centuries without leading us to reject them as useful tools. Similarly there is no reason to reject other institutions of summation simply because they also are incoherent by human (i.e., individual) standards.

We conclude this chapter with an observation made at the beginning. Social decisions are not the same kind of thing as individual decisions, even though the former are constructed from the latter. As a consequence of that

---

[30]See James Murphy, *The Empty Pork Barrel* (forthcoming), where it is shown that even in the provision of public works—traditionally the center of logrolling activity—relatively little logrolling occurs.

[31]I. D. M. Little, "Social Choice and Individual Values," *Journal of Political Economy*, vol. 60 (1952), pp. 422–432. But see also William Vickery, "Utility, Strategy, and Social Decision Rules," *Quarterly Journal of Economics*, vol. 74 (1960), pp. 507–535.

difference, social decisions are sometimes arbitrary in a way personal decisions are not: personal decisions follow from persons' tastes, but social decisions do not follow from the taste of society simply because it is never clear what the taste of society is.

SUGGESTIONS FOR FURTHER READING

The best introduction to the problems of collective choice is DUNCAN BLACK, *The Theory of Committees and Elections* (Cambridge: Cambridge University Press, 1958); and, of course, KENNETH ARROW, *Social Choice and Individual Value*, 2nd ed.(New York: Wiley,1963), is the classic exposition of the problem. The most elaborate statement, in alternating nonmathematical and mathematical chapters, is AMARTYA K. SEN, *Collective Choice and Social Welfare* (San Francisco: Holden-Day, 1970) and the beginner would do well to use Sen's book as a guide through the literature. Incidentally it contains a good but not exhaustive bibliography. Another good elementary exposition is JEROME ROTHENBURG, *The Measurement of Social Welfare* (Englewood Cliffs, N. J.: Prentice-Hall, Inc., 1961). A most careful and formal discussion is to be found in PETER C. FISHBURN, *Social Choice Theory* (forthcoming).

5

N-Person Games

We have discussed in the previous chapter one kind of social disequilibrium, namely that the outcomes of summations of preferences may not be transitively ordered. Ordering is a characteristic of individual arrangements of alternatives. Summation of the arrangements over several persons may not, however, preserve order. Hence a fundamental disequilibrium is possible in social choice.

That is, if there is no unambiguous first choice (which is the most extreme form of the paradox), then the alternative that happens to stand first in the arrangement has no good reason to be there in the sense that it is socially preferred, but stands first only because of a particular history. Presumably, given another history, it can be displaced. Suppose we have the social outcome *abca*, where there is no first choice or Condorcet winner. Conventionally we say that *a* is in first place, and institutionally it may be so. But the arrangement might as easily have *b* first (i.e., *bcab*) or *c* first (*cabc*). That one rather than others is first is not wholly a matter of the structure of individual preferences, but rather is a consequence of the form and operation of institutions, social interactions (e.g., bargains or strategic maneuvers), and events outside the models of voting discussed in the previous chapter. Thus *a* might be first simply because the motion for *a* was put last. Had the supporters of *c* been clever, the motion for *c* might have been put last and it might be the "winner." Or again *a* might be first because, using the market to summarize, individuals spent more money on *a* than *c*, although had ballots been used to summarize opinion, the group of individuals might prefer *c* to *a*. In these ways, therefore, a profound social disequilibrium is always possible.

Furthermore, assuming voters are certain of their preferences, then, even if an equilibrium exists, it is based on the fact of value restrictedness—that is, the agreement of people on standards of judgment in ordering alternatives. Such agreement is, from the point of view of the structure of the system of choice, purely arbitrary. So even in the case of a majority choice, equilibrium is, in a sense, partly and possibly accidental, a matter of adoption of one standard of judgment rather than two or more standards. Thus, not only are some outcomes in disequilibrium, but, when we look behind the fragile equilibrium we have found, we discover that it too is almost as arbitrary as disequilibrium.

This discovery of disequilibrium is based on one kind of social outcome, namely the effect of a summary on preferences. But it is also possible to look at the output of society in another way as the choice of some winner's preference. This is what we intend for this chapter. Naturally, having discovered the profound disequilibrium in summarizing, we are led to ask of this alternative view of output: is it in disequilibrium as well? Unfortunately, as the example in the next paragraph illustrates, the response is substantially affirmative.

Each of the alternatives ordered by a single person in a situation of choice may be thought of as a state of society for that part of society under discussion. Suppose the problem of choice is a family budget; then it might be that:

an alternative yields the outcome consisting of a state of society (or budget)

$$a_1 \quad \longrightarrow \quad O_1 \qquad \begin{cases} w_1 \text{ for food} \\ w_2 \text{ for clothing} \\ w_3 \text{ for housing} \end{cases}$$

$$a_2 \quad \longrightarrow \quad O_2 \qquad \begin{cases} w_1 - \varepsilon \text{ for food} \\ w_2 \text{ for clothing} \\ w_3 + \varepsilon \text{ for housing} \end{cases}$$

$$a_3 \quad \longrightarrow \quad O_3 \qquad \begin{cases} w_1 - \delta \text{ for food} \\ w_2 + \delta \text{ for clothing} \\ w_3 \text{ for housing} \end{cases}$$

Each of the alternatives, a_1, a_2, or a_3, and consequent outcomes, O_1, O_2, or O_3, is a complete budget or complete state of society. To order the alternatives is to order the states of society. So our question is: suppose the states of society are ordered by the participants so that we have a Condorcet winner in the terms used in the previous chapter—is it still possible that the internal structure of the first-choice alternative is itself unstable? For example, if we say that, conventionally, father prefers an evenly distributed budget (i.e., he orders $a_1a_2a_3$), mother prefers an emphasis on housing (i.e., she orders $a_2a_3a_1$), and daughter prefers an emphasis on clothes (i.e., she orders $a_3a_2a_1$), then the social ordering $a_2a_3a_1$ occurs under majority (and matriarchial) rule. Is then the structure of the ordering $a_2a_3a_1$ stable and is its Condorcet winner, a_2, a stable first choice? Or is the structure unstable because the very content of a_2 is itself in doubt? Although father prefers a_1, might he not realize that this is unobtainable since both mother and daughter—for different reasons—put it in the lowest priority? Failing any chance for a_1, might he not then try to make his second choice, a_2 or an emphasis on housing, more attractive to himself by threatening or bribing his wife to change a_2 itself into something closer to a_1? Might he not influence her to change the content of a_2 by threatening to vote for a_3 over a_2? Might he not point out that the victory of a_2, her first choice, depends, *inter alia*, on his vote and that he could just as easily support clothing over housing unless she makes ε smaller? Thus we move from allocation by simple voting to allocation by the more complex procedure of bargaining in which the outcomes of voting can be changed. If, in the bargaining situation, the father's threat works, then the very shape of the winning alternative is itself unstable. This is the kind of possible instability we wish to discuss in this chapter.

To put the question as precisely as possible, we need a general form for objects like a_1, a_2, and a_3. These are states of society and as such are actual allocations of the things men divide up: goods, services, standards of behavior. A particular state of society might include an allocation of quite different kinds of things, as, in a legislature, passage of a budget (w_1) and a pork barrel bill (w_2), rejection of a declaration of war (w_3), elimination of capital punishment (w_4), and so on. To the people in the legislature and the society, this particular distribution of resources and standards of behavior has value, so that it is possible to discuss this melange of quite different things in terms of the rewards that people receive. Thus we can transform person 1's judgment on the package $(w_1, w_2, w_3, w_4, \ldots)$ into a utility number x_1 which is the summary value that person 1 gets out of the actual allocations. Similary, person 2's judgment on $(w_1, w_2, w_3, w_4, \ldots)$ can be summarized as x_2; $\ldots$; and person n's as x_n. Thus a vector **x**, where $\mathbf{x} = (x_1, x_2, \ldots, x_n)$, is a statement of the valuation of $(w_1, w_2, w_3, w_4, \ldots)$ by all the members of the legislature. Since x_i may be person i's utility for many possible combinations of goods and standards, naturally the vector **x** does not refer to a unique physical state of society. Rather **x** is a class of physical states where the class has the property that, for each person i, the utility of all the w's in the package is x_i.

For the time being we will call these vectors, **x**, *payoff configurations* because they are simply summary statements in terms of cardinal utility of what everybody gets out of a particular state of society.[1] (Later, as we impose conditions

[1] In order to compare one configuration with another, we assume that utility is "unrestrictedly transferable." Of course, what men actually transfer are the objects, w_i, which utility numbers represent. So in assuming transferability we are in effect assuming, as Luce and Raiffa say, that utility is a commodity that "for all the world behaves like money." We could avoid this possibly unrealistic assumption by talking always about concrete payoffs, but our discourse would be so complicated as to render theorizing difficult. Of course, it may be that utility is like money, in which case the assumption is unobjectionable. If in fact two utility scales are linear in money, then direct transferability with money and utility is easily possible. If they are not so transformable, however, the assumption is unrealistic. The lack of realism need not bother us, however, nor lead us into interpersonal comparisons, because we can be careful to limit our comparisons to single individuals. Thus we can compare, for person i, his payoffs in two configurations, x_i and y_i; but we cannot compare, for one configuration **x**, payoffs to

on the **x**'s, we will change their name.) The question about stability can now be stated with respect to a payoff configuration: is there anything in the internal structure of a payoff configuration that renders it stable so that, if adopted as a first choice, it will be adhered to? If there is, we will regard it as being in equilibrium.

Note how this question of equilibrium goes beyond the one we previously discussed. In Chapter 4 we analyze the stability of a choice among three or more alternatives, which may, of course, be vectors **x**, **y**, and **z**. Now we turn to an analysis of the internal stability of **x** in order to discover whether or not the same problems arise here as arose in Chapter 4.

THE THEORY OF GAMES

There is available a branch of mathematics, the theory of games, in which the central questions concern the existence and the nature of the stability we are investigating. The name of the theory, although historically understandable, is unfortunately delusive. It suggests that the theory is about only the playful affairs of life. Actually, of course, it is about interactions among people; whether these things are ludicrous or serious depends on one's point of view. Parlor games are highly stylized, involve limited interactions, and have often been interpreted—because of the limitations—as a kind of abstraction from more complicated social life, especially as abstractions having to do with interpersonal conflict. Kings, for example, once studied chess because they thought it an informative abstraction from war. Using the word "game" as a generic term for all abstractions from (conflictual) social interactions, the theory of games is a theory of abstract social interaction. John von Neumann and Oskar Morgenstern, the main developers of the theory, describe a game as the totality of rules that describe it. Thus a game is the abstract features of a social event, and a theory of games is a theory about what goes on in such abstract events. The main activity is, of course, the adoption of states of society, which can be summarized as vectors **x**, which are in turn individual evaluations of concrete outcomes, w. The main product of the theory about this activity is, therefore, an explanation of payoff configurations. This is, of course, precisely what we want to study, so we turn now to a relatively informal development of n-person game theory.[2]

---

two persons, x_i and x_j. It is necessary to assume, however, that each person's utility scales can be constructed such that utility can be transferred, in the sense that, if one person in a game gains some utility on his scale, another person (or persons) loses some utility on his (or theirs). It is not required, of course, that the amounts gained and lost in transfers be equal, because there may be gains and losses from the trade itself.

[2]John von Neumann and Oskar Morgenstern, *The Theory of Games and Economic Behavior*, 2d ed. (Princeton, N. J.: Princeton University Press, 1947); R. Duncan Luce and Howard Raiffa, *Games and Decisions* (New York: Wiley, 1957); Anatol Rapoport, *N-Person Game Theory* (Ann Arbor: University of Michigan Press, 1970).

Consider a social situation with n persons ($n \geq 2$), all of whom have individual interests about something they all value, namely, significant outcomes of social interaction. We do not initially specify how the individual interests are related, whether they are parallel or contradictory.[3] We simply assume that the interests are individual without specifying whether or not they are complementary. We do, however, insist that the interests are about something and that everyone regards the stakes as worthwhile. If, for example, one person does not regard the stakes as worthwhile, then the situation is not n-person, but ($n-1$)-person.

While ultimately, of course, the intention (and performance) of persons in this idealized situation (or game) is to generate a state of the world which can be evaluated as a payoff configuration, this is not what occurs immediately. Rather the participants take actions which consist of choosing alternatives. These choices in turn modify or determine the state of the world. The problem of game theory is to relate the interim actions of choice to the payoff configuration that measure the states of the world.

COALITIONS

We assume initially that each of the n persons can act alone to achieve something of what he wants. But we also assume that those with complementary interests may join together and that they in fact do so if such joining is advantageous. Such an alliance we call a coalition.

The idea of a coalition is a primitive notion in the theory of games. It comprehends a wide variety of joint action to exploit a complementarity of interest. Thus, any of the following kinds of joint action constitutes a coalition:

1. Players negotiate an agreement to act together, and this contract is enforceable in the courts and by police. In effect players form a corporate body.
2. Players organize an only slightly less tight organization in which participants are forced to act together by effective threats of punishments from inside the association. An example is the strictly disciplined political party.
3. Players agree to act together so long as it is to their individual advantage, as in alliances in the international system. An instance of this kind of coalition is the one, already discussed in the example of family budgets, where one member succumbs to threats from another and modifies her budget preference in order to assure his vote.
4. Players, without directly communicating, act so as to establish a habit of moving

---

[3]At one extreme is direct conflict as in duels. We call such conflict zero-sum, for the positive gains of one plus the negative gains (losses) of the other add up to zero. Again, the conflict may be somewhat attenuated, so that interests are partly parallel and partly opposed. Thus, in a market, if a buyer is eager to buy and a seller to sell, their interests are to some degree parallel even though they may haggle over price. To complete the categorization, at the other extreme interests may be wholly parallel, as when two people are trying to find each other in a crowded place. We call the latter two situations nonzero-sum. At this point, however, we do not limit our attention to any one of these categories.

together, just as regulated entrepreneurs rely on regulating bureaucrats to maintain the conditions of advantage for the regulated—an unspoken alliance of regulator and regulated.

Coalitions of one sort or another are possible in most games larger than one person, and they are desirable, even inevitable, in most cases. When coalitions are desirable or inevitable, the main initial action to determine the payoff is to form them. The main initial problem of game theory is, therefore, to characterize and specify the possible coalitions in a game. There are certain special situations in which coalitions are pointless, and for these the game theoretic problem is somewhat different:

1. *Two-person, zero-sum games.* In these the interests of the two participants are exactly opposed, so that there is no point to any kind of coalition. In this situation, therefore, one studies the advantages one player can have over another from an appropriate choice of moves. If there are three persons in a zero-sum game, the payoffs of course sum to zero, but the interests of members of any pair are not entirely opposed— because their payoffs do not sum to zero. Hence coalitions are possible. Similarly, if there are two persons in a nonzero-sum game, the overlap in interests admits of cooperation and hence coalition. So it is only in the very special case when a game is both two-person and zero-sum that coalitions are out of the question.
2. *Games in which nothing is gained by forming coalitions.* These are typically games in which the participants have no information about each other and cannot communicate in any way. Indeed, there is nothing at all to do in them.

Aside from these two special and quite restricted cases, however, most kinds of games involve some type of joint action or coalition formation as a prelude to imposing a payoff.

To characterize and describe the possibilities of coalitions, von Neumann and Morgenstern identified coalitions with the mathematical objects known as sets or collections of (unspecified) discrete things. This identification placed the whole mathematics of the theory of sets at the disposal of the theory of games, especially the elementary ideas listed in the footnote to this paragraph.[4]

CHARACTERISTIC FUNCTIONS

Once having identified coalitions with sets, von Neumann and Morgenstern offered the notion of a *characteristic function* as a measure on sets (coalitions) and

[4]Interpreting the set of all players (the grand coalition) as the identity or unit set, I, all coalitions including the individual players are subsets of I. We will reserve capital letters, S, T, etc., to name such coalitions, although to identify a coalition of a single player i, $i \in I$, we will use the symbolism: "$\{i\}$." If there are n members of I, then—following a well-known result in set theory—there are 2^n subsets including, *inter alia*, the empty set, single-member sets, and the identity set, I, itself. Of particular importance are two operations on sets:

thus a specification of the limits of action in a game. In accord with their usual cautious conservatism in all problems of valuation, they defined the value of a coalition as what it could assure itself, even in the worst strategic situation—such as when everybody else combined against it. Some writers have criticized this approach as unduly pessimistic because it makes the value of a coalition a minimum security level, an amount which it can assure itself by itself. Of course, the worst does not always happen. If S forms, it does not follow that its complement, $-S$, forms to oppose it. The mere existence of the American Iron and Steel Institute to lobby for steel producers does not call forth some Institute of Steel Users to protect the ultimate consumer. Such action could only result from a group theory of the sort which, as we report in Chapter 3, Olson has shown to be inconsistent with individual rationality. If the characteristic function were intended as a description of the play of a game or as the prediction of the outcome, then this extreme pessimism would be inappropriate. But such is not the intention. The characteristic function is like the value in a two-person zero-sum game:[5] it represents the strategic possibilities, not the likely occurences. One can thus think of it as useful information for players who are thinking of forming coalitions—a statement of the worst that each of the alternatives before them can do.

Formally, a characteristic function, v, is a real-valued function satisfying the following restrictions:

$$v(\phi) = 0, \quad \text{where } \phi \text{ is the empty set.} \tag{5.1}$$

This is a technical restriction embodying the reasonable intuition that an empty coalition cannot gain a reward.

$$v(S \cup T) \geq v(S) + v(T), \quad \text{where } S \text{ and } T \text{ are disjoint.} \tag{5.2}$$

This is the crucial feature and is known as superadditivity. In effect (5.2) permits coalitions by prohibiting punishments for forming them. In a system in which coalitions are treated as conspiracies and appropriately punished, it would be the case that, for some S and T,

$$v(S \cup T) < v(S) + v(T), \tag{5.3}$$

which is precisely what (5.2) prohibits.[6]

(i) the union of sets, symbolized "$S \cup T$," where $S \cup T$ is the set of all the members of either S or T or both.

(ii) the intersection of sets, symbolized "$S \cap T$," where $S \cap T$ is the set of all members simultaneously in S and T.

Where the intersection of S and T is empty, we speak of S and T as disjoint; i.e., they have no members in common.

[5]Indeed, this is its mathematical source. See Chapter 8.

[6]Indeed (5.3) carries the definition of a characteristic function to absurd results. Accepting the value of a coalition as its security level, to affirm (5.3) is to deny the existence of $(S \cup T)$. Yet (5.3) was intended not to abolish $(S \cup T)$ but merely to place a measure on it. Recall that $v(R)$ is defined as the amount that R as a unit can assure itself by itself, regardless of opposition. Specifically, then, S should be able to guarantee $v(S)$ and T able to guarantee $v(T)$. But if $(S \cup T)$ forms, one or both cannot so guarantee, because of the inequality in (5.3). Hence,

We offer several examples of characteristic functions:

1. Couples.

This is the basic example of a three-person game used by von Neumann and Morgenstern to exhibit the central problem of all n-person games. They describe it:

---

if (5.3) is true, $(S \cup T)$ should not exist, because its existence denies that S and T assure themselves of at least $v(S)$ and $v(T)$.

It is, of course, conceivable that real-world circumstances exist in which (5.3) holds. For example, two banks might, when independent, be unnoticed by regulatory authorities, but, when merged, be subject to intense harrassment by these same authorities because the combined size of the banks makes them appear monopolistic. Thus the merged firm may be worth less than the sum of the value of two independent firms. Nevertheless, despite such real-world possibilities, we reject (5.3). The whole point of a characteristic function is to impose a measure on the value of coalitions; it seems paradoxical to define the function so as to guarantee that reasonable people would not form them. Since (5.3) renders coalitions worthless and since we want to study situations in which they are worthwhile, we reject (5.3) in favor of (5.2).

It would be interesting to know if a characteristic function in the sense of a security level could be other than superadditive. That is, may a game exist in which (5.3) is true for some S and T, while (5.2) holds otherwise?

In the real world it is true that, owing to frictions, some coalitions $(S \cup T)$ are not worth enough to exist. This occurs when there is some cost, C, of organizing the coalition so that:

$$v(S \cup T) = v(S) + v(T) - C,$$
$$\text{so that } v(S \cup T) < v(S) + v(T).$$

Since in this section we are concerned only with the formation of coalitions, the occurrence of frictions and imperfections that prevent coalitions need not delay us here. If, however, we were to use a characteristic function to analyze a particular political situation, the existence of high costs might lead us to assume the nonexistence of $(S \cup T)$.

Leaving aside simple frictions, Rapoport offers the characteristic function of a three-person prisoners'-dilemma game which, he asserts, fails to satisfy superadditivity. His example is, however, based mainly on an ambiguity derived from alternative verbal definitions of a characteristic function. These alternative definitions are:

(1) the minimum amount that a coalition, S, can assure itself (i.e., the security level of S);
(2) the minimum amount S receives when $-S$ forms.

Rapoport uses the second and chooses as an illustration a characteristic function:

$$\text{if } S \text{ has } \begin{Bmatrix} 0 \\ 1 \\ 2 \\ 3 \end{Bmatrix} \text{ members,} \qquad v(S) = \begin{Bmatrix} 0 \\ 2 \\ 0 \\ 3 \end{Bmatrix}$$

which is not superadditive because by themselves $v(1) + v(2) = 2 + 2 = 4$, which is more than their value together, $v(1, 2) = 0$. That is, he offers a case where the amount S receives when $-S$ forms (definition 2) is higher than the security level (definition 1). Of course, he overlooks that $-S$ has no motive to form and so his argument is confused: if S has one member and $-S$ has two, each of the two loses by forming $-S$. It is hardly likely that $-S$ will form in this circumstance. Using, as we do here and as is more customary, definition 1, in Rapoport's illustration the characteristic function is:

$$\text{if } S \text{ has } \begin{Bmatrix} 0 \\ 1 \\ 2 \\ 3 \end{Bmatrix} \text{ members,} \qquad v(S) = \begin{Bmatrix} 0 \\ -1 \\ 0 \\ 3 \end{Bmatrix}$$

which is superadditive because by themselves $v(1) + v(2) = (-1) + (-1) = -2$, which is

Each player, by a personal move, chooses the number of one of the two other players. Each one makes his choice uninformed about the choice of the two other players.

After this the payments will be made as follows: If two players have chosen each other's numbers we say they form a *couple*. Clearly, there will be precisely one couple, or none at all. If there is precisely one couple, then the two players who belong to it get one-half unit each, while the third (excluded) player correspondingly loses one unit. If there is no couple, then no one gets anything.[7]

For this game the characteristic function is:

$$\text{if } S \text{ has } \left\{ \begin{array}{c} 0 \\ 1 \\ 2 \\ 3 \end{array} \right\} \text{ members,} \quad v(S) = \left\{ \begin{array}{c} 0 \\ -1 \\ 1 \\ 0 \end{array} \right\}.$$

Note that there is no institutional way for a three-person coalition to exist, so we infer its value is zero, in which case the game is zero-sum in the sense that each coalition receives exactly what its complement loses. For such games we may add the following properties of the characteristic function:

$$v(S) = -v(-S), \quad \text{where } -S \text{ is the complement of } S; \quad (5.4)$$

$$v(I_n) = 0. \quad (5.5)$$

Sentence (5.4) is the zero-sum property, and (5.5) is a direct inference from (5.1) and (5.4) thus:

$$v(I_n) = -v(-I_n) = -v(\phi) = 0.$$

Parenthetically, but nevertheless emphatically, we point out that Couples (or its larger form Talleyrand, or its constant-sum form Division) is the quintessence of politics. The similarity of Couples to the human political condition is so close that it in itself justifies intense study of game theory by anyone interested in political analysis. The heart of politics is people choosing each other either implicitly or explicitly—that is, forming groups, parties, factions, coalitions, alliances, ententes, and so on, every one of which involves choosing up sides. All the bargaining, negotiating, maneuvering, wheeling and dealing, ideologizing, philosophizing, persuading, rhetoricizing, and the like that characterize politics—all this is the preface to choosing, the artistic elaboration on the fundamental political action. Couples, as the abstract form of choosing up sides, is therefore the most elementary model of politics.

---

less than their value together, $v(1, 2) = 0$. Hence Rapoport's counterexample depends on a special definition, which he abandons a few pages later. Can counterexamples be found that are not dependent on this odd definition? [See A. Rapoport, *N-Person Game Theory* (Ann Arbor: University of Michigan Press, 1970), pp. 79–81, 90.]

[7]Von Neumann and Morgenstern, *The Theory of Games and Economic Behavior*, pp. 222–223.

2. Talleyrand

This is a five-person game very much like Couples. Players negotiate until a firm coalition is formed, and it then takes its value from the remaining players for division among its members. The characteristic function is:

$$\text{if } S \text{ has } \begin{Bmatrix} 0 \\ 1 \\ 2 \\ 3 \\ 4 \\ 5 \end{Bmatrix} \text{ members,} \qquad v(S) = \begin{Bmatrix} 0 \\ -2 \\ -4 \\ +4 \\ +2 \\ 0 \end{Bmatrix}.$$

Note that this game is zero-sum also because, e.g., the three-person coalition wins precisely what its complement loses.

Returning to the discussion of superadditivity, it is apparent that for some coalitions the equality of (5.2) holds and for some the inequality. Thus, if S is a coalition of one member, player 1, and T is another coalition of one member, player 3, then

$$v(1, 3) = v(1) + v(3) = (-2) + (-2) = -4,$$

while, if S is a coalition of two members, players 1 and 3, and T is a coalition of one member, player 4, then

$$v(1, 3, 4) = 4 > v(1, 3) + v(4) = (-4) + (-2) = -6.$$

It is apparent from this example what superadditivity accomplishes. One can easily see a motive for the formation of three-person coalitions, but it is difficult to see the motive for two-person coalitions except as stepping stones to or unintended complements of three-person coalitions. Superadditivity is what makes the formation of coalitions worthwhile. It is possible, however, to imagine a game without superadditivity, i.e., in which only the equality of (5.2) holds.

3. Time Out

This is an n-person game in which as many as wish stop work for ten minutes and drink coffee. For those who do so there is a satisfaction of one unit, which does not occur if the player does not take time out. The characteristic function is:

$$\text{if } S \text{ has } \begin{Bmatrix} 0 \\ 1 \\ 2 \\ \cdot \\ \cdot \\ \cdot \\ n \end{Bmatrix} \text{ members,} \qquad v(S) = \begin{Bmatrix} 0 \\ 1 \\ 2 \\ \cdot \\ \cdot \\ \cdot \\ n \end{Bmatrix} \text{ units.}$$

Since each person in this game can accomplish by himself all that can conceivably be accomplished, there is no point to a coalition. Since there is nothing to do socially, such games are called *inessential* (see page 121, item 2). By contrast, all games in which the inequality of (5.2) holds for some S and T are *essential*.

While Couples and Talleyrand are zero-sum, not all essential games share this feature. Some are, for example, constant-sum.

4. Division of Plunder

Three people divide up one unit (supplied from outside the game) among any pair or the trio as a whole. The characteristic function is:

$$\text{if } S \text{ has } \left\{ \begin{array}{c} 0 \\ 1 \\ 2 \\ 3 \end{array} \right\} \text{ members,} \quad v(S) = \left\{ \begin{array}{c} 0 \\ 0 \\ 1 \\ 1 \end{array} \right\}.$$

In abstract form, this is very like Couples and Talleyrand, differing only in the definitions comparable to (5.4) and (5.5):

$$v(S) = k - v(-S) \qquad \text{[in lieu of (5.4)]}, \tag{5.6}$$
$$v(I_n) = k \qquad \qquad \text{[in lieu of (5.5)]}.$$

where k is a constant. Constant-sum games may be transformed into zero-sum games and vice versa merely by the subtraction (or addition) of an appropriate constant. Hence characteristic functions of constant-sum games have essentially the same properties as those of zero-sum games. Many games, however, are neither constant- nor zero-sum:

5. The Three-Person Market

This game, like Couples, is a basic example from von Neumann and Morgenstern:[8]

> The three participants are 1,2,3—the seller 1, the prospective buyers 2,3, ... The transaction. . . is the sale of one (indivisible) unit A of a certain commodity by 1 to either 2 or 3. Denote the value of the possession of A for 1 by u, for 2 by v, and for 3 by w.
>
> In order that these transactions should make sense for all participants, the value of A for each buyer must exceed that for the seller. Also, unless the two buyers, 2,3, happen to be in exactly equal positions, one of them must be stronger than the other—i.e., able to derive a greater utility from the possession of A. We may assume that. . . the stronger buyer is 3 . . . . We have
>
> $$u < v \leq w.$$

Expanding on the detail, it is not difficult to imagine such a market, say in

---

[8] *The Theory of Games and Economic Behavior,* p. 565. See Luce and Raiffa, *Games and Decisions,* pp. 206, 231, where this example is elaborated.

a village where the demand for houses is slow, where A is a large house, where 1 is an old couple who have raised their family and are tired of a big house, where 2 is a young couple with a large family and a great need for a big house but a limited budget, and where 3 is a nursing-home operator. For the sake of specifics, we can assume utility is linear with money and thus put dollar prices on the utilities of the participants:

$$(u = \$10,000) < (v = \$20,000) < (w = \$30,000).$$

If we set the store of wealth other than the house equal to zero, then the characteristic function of the game to dispose of the house in the market is:

$$v(1) = \$10,000, \quad v(2) = v(3) = 0;$$
$$v(1,2) = \$20,000, \quad v(1,3) = \$30,000, \quad v(2,3) = 0;$$
$$v(1,2,3) = \$30,000.$$

This means that a coalition of, e.g., 1 and 3 can guarantee themselves at least $30,000. If 1 sells the house to 3 for $25,000, then 1 has the money and 3 has the house, which is worth $30,000 to him, less the money paid out, for a net of $5,000. Thus, the sum of what 1 and 3 have is $30,000. If $(1,3)$ forms, it can certainly guarantee its members that much.

This game cannot be constant-sum. Considering the requirement

$$v(S) = k - v(-S), \quad \text{where } k \text{ is a constant,}$$

if S is 1, then

$$10,000 = k - 0, \quad k = 10,000;$$

while if S is 2, then

$$0 = k - 30,000, \quad k = 30,000.$$

So k is not in fact a constant.

One final technical point about characteristic functions: it is customary in most discussions to normalize them—that is, to transform the values into a specified interval in the real-number system. There is an infinity of games (i.e., sets of rules) called Talleyrand, for example, which differ from each other only in the size of the stakes measured in terms of utility. Assuming that these games all offer the same strategic possibilities—which is probably not true among nonprofessional players—then it is reasonable to pick out just one of these games for comparison with other games with different rules. The game we pick out is that one which occurs in the interval of normalization. We can define such an interval in terms of what one player by himself receives and what all the players together receive. Thus, if $v(\{i\}) = 0$ and $v(I_n) = 1$, we speak of "$(0, 1)$-normalization;" or if $v(\{i\}) = -1$ and $v(I_n) = 0$, we speak of "$(-1,0)$-normalization." Both kinds are common in the literature, but we will use the "$(-1, 0)$-normalization" because we think it makes more intuitive sense to speak of the grand coalition as winning nothing. So normalized, the characteristic function of Talleyrand is:

$$\text{if } S \text{ has } \left\{ \begin{array}{c} 0 \\ 1 \\ 2 \\ 3 \\ 4 \\ 5 \end{array} \right\} \text{ members,} \quad v(S) = \left\{ \begin{array}{c} 0 \\ -1 \\ -2 \\ 2 \\ 1 \\ 0 \end{array} \right\}.$$

A characteristic function reveals the strategic possibilities of a game, namely, what coalitions, if they form, can do—minimally—for themselves (and against each other). This information is necessary for any further analysis, and in that sense the characteristic function is fundamental. But there is much to know that the characteristic function does not tell us. It says nothing, for example, about the payoff configuration or the way an individual player is likely to fare. And usually it does not even tell us anything about which coalition is likely to form. Thus, for the three-person coalitions in a symmetric five-person game (such as Talleyrand) the characteristic function tells us only that these coalitions are worth an amount $v(S)$. It does not tell us which of the ten possible three-person coalitions might form—or even if these might be preferred by the members to four- and five-person coalitions. Most deficiently of all, it does not tell us about the division of v among the players; yet this is the thing we would in most circumstances most like to know. Given this interest in the payoff to individuals, therefore, we now lay aside the characteristic function and return to the study of payoff configurations.

IMPUTATIONS

Initially we can put some limits on the payoff configuration—that is, on the vector $\mathbf{x}$, where $\mathbf{x} = (x_1, x_2, \ldots, x_n)$. We define the worst a player can do when he is by himself in a coalition of one person as an amount, $-\gamma$. [In the $(-1, 0)$-normalization, $\gamma = 1$.] If the player is rational, then it must be the case that the loss of $-\gamma$ is the worst that can ever happen to him regardless of what coalition he is in. Suppose that in some coalition of more than one member, a particular player, i, is asked to accept less than $-\gamma$. One can visualize such a request in a two-person coalition, (i, j), with a normalized value of -2, where j tries to force i to bear more than half the cost of (i, j), say $-1\frac{1}{2}$. No matter how weak i may be, however, he can always evade such pressure by resigning from (i, j). Then i is in a coalition by himself and receives at worst $-\gamma = -1$. Assuming that no person can ever be forced to take less than $-\gamma$, we may then place the restriction of individual rationality that no one ever does take less than he can make in a coalition with himself:

$$x_i \geq v(\{i\}) = -\gamma. \tag{5.7}$$

Similarly we may place a restriction of "group" rationality on the payoff to the entire set of players. Suppose that, in some coalitional structure, the sum of the payments to players is less than the value of the game for the grand coalition—that is,

$$\sum_{i \in I_n} x_i < v(I_n).$$

Then it is possible for the payoff to some or all persons to be improved without any loss or cost to other players. For example, each player might get $[v(I_n) - \sum x_i]/n$. That is, the excess of value over payoffs might be divided up equally. Or again, one person might observe the excess and grab it for himself—on the principle that nature abhors a vacuum. In any event, we assume that there is enough intelligence in the group as a whole not to allow the excess to exist, regardless of whether it is wiped out by joint or individual action. In short, we assume that some at least are not stupid.[9] We can thus require that the effect of the sum of individually maximizing decisions is

$$\sum_{i \in I_n} x_i \geq v(I_n). \tag{5.8}$$

It is apparent, however, that (5.8) permits too much. Clearly it is not feasible to pay players more than the game is worth. So we arrive at

$$\sum_{i \in I_n} x_i \leq v(I_n). \tag{5.9}$$

Restrictions (5.8) and (5.9) combine:

$$\sum_{i \in I_n} x_i = v(I_n). \tag{5.10}$$

That is, the sum of payoffs to all players exactly exhausts the value of the grand coalition.

Any payoff configuration satisfying (5.7) and (5.10) is what von Neumann and Morgenstern defined as an *imputation,* meaning thereby a distribution of winnings possible among reasonable people. The set of imputations is thus a proper subset of payoff configurations or vectors **x**.

All imputations are Pareto-optimal which means that, in some quite weak sense, they are minimum expectations among a group of rational actors. The notion of Pareto optimality originated in an attempt to answer the question: by what standard can one state of society, S_1, be objectively preferred to another, S_2? The answer supplied by this notion is that if, in S_1 as compared to S_2, at least one person is better off and no one else worse off, then S_1 is preferred to S_2. A payoff vector, **x**, for a state, S_i, is then Pareto-optimal if:

(i) it is feasible—that is, if there is enough value in the whole state to give each person what he is assigned in the vector of payoffs;

(ii) it cannot be improved upon for anyone without hurting someone else.

[9]The trouble with this assumption is less likely to arise from stupidity than from confusion growing out of the complexity of a game. Sometimes (5.8) may not be satisfied in the real world simply because the search for a satisfactory configuration is too expensive. In the abstract, however, we think it is a proper assumption to make.

These properties of Pareto optimality are clearly properties of imputations. Restriction (5.10) guarantees that imputations have property (i) because (5.10) does not permit the value of the situation (i.e., the whole group, I_n) to be less than enough to pay each and every person what he is assigned in the vector of payoffs. And restriction (5.10) also guarantees that imputations have property (ii) because, by exhausting the value of the situation in the payoffs to the players, it is impossible to add to the payment for one without subtracting from the payment(s) to other(s). Thus the set of imputations is exactly the set of Pareto-optimal payoff configurations.

To equate the restriction, (5.10), that defines imputations with Pareto optimality indicates how bold are the assumptions involved in the notion of imputations. Many social systems have been described in which Pareto-optimal allocations simply do not occur. For example, Olson's analysis of membership in groups reveals that it is unlikely that people in large groups will communicate well enough to arrive at Pareto-optimal allocations. Indeed, it may be that these can be achieved only when there is extensive bargaining (as in markets or, alternatively, in small groups). It is well to remember, therefore, that in addition to the formal requirements for imputations there are probably also some sociological ones which we do not examine in detail here.

It is helpful to display geometrically the effect of the formal requirements for imputations, (5.7) and (5.10), for a three-person game such as Couples. In Figure 5.1 there is a system of three axes making angles of 60 degrees with each other. For a payoff vector $\mathbf{x} = (x_1, x_2, x_3)$, the values of $x_1, x_2,$ and x_3 are measured by the length of the perpendicular line from x_i to the appropriate axis, i. [For a normalized zero-sum game such as Couples we may set the axes at zero so that their intersection is $\mathbf{x} = (0, 0, 0)$; but for more general classes of games we may set them where appropriate.] If, as in Figure 5.1, the origin is at $(0, 0, 0)$, then the sum of perpendicular distances from the axes is zero.

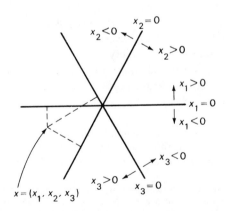

FIGURE 5.1

If the origin is at some other point O such that $k = O_1 + O_2 + O_3$, then generally $x_1 + x_2 + x_3 = k$. Hence every point in the plane satisfies (5.10). [To display payoff vectors not satisfying (5.10) we can imbed this plane in 3-space so that each parallel plane contains all points for payoff vectors with some unique sum, k, of x_i.]

While every point in the plane is a payoff vector satisfying (5.10), only those points contained within and on the sides of the triangle in Figure 5.2 are imputations also satisfying (5.7). Each side of the triangle represents the minimum value for x_i. That is, along the base (labeled $x_1 = -1$) are all the payoff vectors in which $x_1 = -1$. Since this is the worst that player 1 can do in Couples, no payoff vectors below $x_1 = -1$ can be an imputation. Similarly, no imputations can be outside the triangle in any direction, so that the entire set of vectors satisfying (5.7) and (5.10) are included in the triangle in Figure 5.2. Von Neumann and Morgenstern call this the "fundamental triangle"; it may be thought of as the space of all imputations.

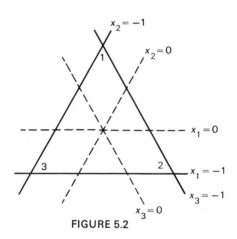

FIGURE 5.2

As a consequence of this construction, a vertex represents the imputation in which the player whose worst payoffs are on the opposite side does his very best, and in which the players whose minimum values intersect do their very worst. Thus in Figure 5.2, the vertex labeled 1 is the imputation $(2, -1, -1)$, which is the best possible for player 1 and the worst possible for players 2 and 3. The vertex labeled 2 is the imputation $(-1, 2, -1)$ and 3 is $(-1, -1, 2)$.

SOLUTIONS AND IMPUTATIONS

This chapter is devoted to a search for internal stability in payoffs. Since the definition of imputations is based so directly on the axioms of individual rationality, we can confidently limit our search to at most the members of the class of imputations. Restating our question about stability, we ask: is there any imputation so obviously stable that it will be sought and retained by society? Assuming that the game model catches something of the spirit of social life, it is likely that a unique preferred imputation almost never exists. Social life exhibits great variety, and it is to be expected, therefore, that a model of social life also exhibit variety. Hence, even when social situations are relatively stable, there usually are viable alternative outcomes. In the theory, therefore, one should not expect a single imputation as the predicted outcome of a game. Rather one should expect the prediction of a set of possible outcomes. Such is in fact the case. So the question recurs, more realistically: is there any set of imputations so obviously stable that one among them will be sought and retained by society?

To answer this question, game theorists have offered a number of concepts of solutions—of, that is, sets of imputations some one of which is highly likely to be chosen as the outcome in the actual play of a game. We will not consider all these concepts here, since they differ more in detail then in spirit; rather we will confine our attention to two main notions, the *core* and the *von Neumann-Morgenstern solution*, using them as illustrations of the kind of equilibrium concepts encountered in *n*-person game theory.

Domination

Inherent in these concepts is the notion that one imputation is better than another. This notion is formalized as the idea of *domination*. We say one imputation, **x**, dominates another imputation **y**, with respect to some nonempty coalition, S, if

(i) **x** is feasible, i.e., $\sum_{i \in S} x_i \leq v(S)$, and

(ii) $x_i > y_i$, for all i in S.

So that our definition will not depend on specific subsets of players, we say that **x** dominates **y** if there exists a feasible, nonempty coalition, S, that satisfies property (ii). Property (i) is the requirement that the "better" imputation, **x**, be technically possible and not merely an unachievable pipe dream. (Some writers have here wished to add the requirement that S itself be achievable; but this is a sociological condition that we do not wish to insert in the formal analysis.) Note that property (ii) is a strict inequality. This means that, in order to call **x** "better than" **y**, *every* member of the relevant coalition must find his payoff in **x** better than (not just as good as) his payoff in **y**. Thus, if **x** dominates **y** and if imputation **y** is in effect, every member of S has a positive reason to move from **y** to **x**. Note, however, that domination is not, in general, a transitive relation, because it is quite possible for **x** to dominate **y** with respect to R, for **y** to dominate **z** with respect to S, and for **z** to dominate **x** with respect to T.

This situation is, of course, reminiscent of voting paradoxes, and we will consider it in greater detail later.

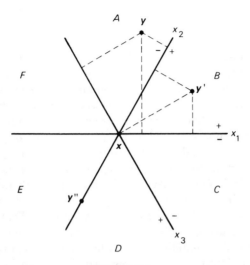

FIGURE 5.3

The notion of domination may be expressed geometrically using the system of axes of Figure 5.1. Through any point, $\mathbf{x}$, in the plane we may draw similar axes as in Figure 5.3. It is clear that the point $\mathbf{x}$ dominates the point $\mathbf{y}$ with respect to the coalition (2, 3) because

$$x_1 < y_1, \qquad x_2 > y_2, \qquad x_3 > y_3.$$

On the other hand, point $\mathbf{x}$ is dominated by $\mathbf{y}'$ with respect to coalition (1,2) because

$$x_1 < y_1', \qquad x_2 < y_2', \qquad x_3 > y_3'.$$

In general point $\mathbf{x}$ in Figure 5.3 dominates any $\mathbf{y}$ in sextants A, C, and E, not including their edges. In turn $\mathbf{x}$ is dominated by all imputations (such as $\mathbf{y}'$) in sextants B, D, and F, again not counting the edges. The relation between $\mathbf{x}$ and $\mathbf{y}''$, which has one axis in common with $\mathbf{x}$, is

$$x_1 > y_1'', \qquad x_2 = y_2'', \qquad x_3 < y_3''.$$

Hence there is no domination between the pair. In general, all points lying on the axes of point $\mathbf{x}$ are undominated and undominant with respect to each other.

Every notion of a solution—that is, a set of imputations preferred for some reason by rational players—ought to involve some kind of selection of imputations that are in some way superior from the point of view of the dominance relation. To say the imputations in a set are preferred to imputations outside it is simply to say that the rational players of the game find the imputations in the set better than those outside. The sense in which the chosen imputations are better is what the notion of dominance is all about.

THE CORE

We turn now to one main kind of solution concept, the core. As we will ultimately show in detail, *the core is the set of undominated imputations*. To be undominated means that there is no imputation that is clearly better from the point of view of any coalition, S. Thus the set of undominated imputations is the set of imputations that are at least as good as any others possible in the game. Presumably, undominated imputations, if they occur, should under any circumstances be included in the solution. The advantage of the notion of the core is that it does pick them out for inclusion. The disadvantage of the notion, however, is that in a great many games—especially in those that model the typical situations of politics—there is no core; that is, there are no undominated imputations. This is why there is so much difficulty in the abstract world of theorizing about stability and, very likely, so much difficulty in the real world of achieving stability. Even when the core exists, however, some dominated imputation may, as we show later, be chosen by rational players. Consequently, even though the core is an attractive notion, it is not wholly adequate—which is the case with all the alternative solution concepts.

One usual way to formalize the definition of the core as the set of undominated imputations is to add another restriction about payoff configurations to (5.7) and (5.10). By (5.7) configurations are required to satisfy the security level of individuals. By (5.10) they are required to satisfy the group as a whole. Additionally, once the configurations satisfy (5.7) and (5.10), thus qualifying as imputations, they may be required to satisfy the security level of all coalitions. That is, for an imputation $\mathbf{x}$, if

$$\sum_{i \in S} x_i \geq v(S), \qquad \text{for all } S \text{ in } I_n, \tag{5.11}$$

then $\mathbf{x}$ is in the core. This is the requirement that, for any possible coalition, its members together receive at least as much in the imputation, $\mathbf{x}$, as that coalition is worth according to the characteristic function.

The core is then the set of imputations, if any, satisfying (5.11). One may think of (5.11) as a test applied to an imputation. Suppose an imputation $\mathbf{x}$ is offered as a candidate for the core. Then one asks for each of the 2^n coalitions in I_n: do the members of S, where S is any coalition, make at least as much in $\mathbf{x}$ as in $v(S)$? If the answer to every one of these 2^n questions is affirmative, then $\mathbf{x}$ is in the core; otherwise not. Thus, every imputation in the core is one in which every coalition makes at least as much as its security level or what it can guarantee itself by itself.

It is easy to see that in some games there may not be any imputations satisfying (5.11). Consider the game of Couples (p.123) and suppose $\mathbf{x}$ is a candidate for the core. Consider further all the two-person coalitions, which are the point of the game. By reason of (5.11) players 1 and 2, who in (1, 2) have $v(1, 2) = 1$, can insist that, in **x**, the sum of the payments to 1 and 2 also equal one. By similar arguments, we get for all three of the two-person coalitions

$$x_1 + x_2 = 1,$$
$$x_1 + x_3 = 1,$$
$$x_2 + x_3 = 1.$$

Summing, we get

$$2x_1 + 2x_2 + 2x_3 = 3$$

or

$$x_1 + x_2 + x_3 = 3/2;$$

but, by reason of (5. 10):

$$x_1 + x_2 + x_3 = v(1, 2, 3) = 0.$$

Hence **x** cannot be in the core. That is, **x** cannot simultaneously satisfy the security levels of all three coalitions. In general, essential constant-sum games (and, therefore, zero-sum games) do not have any imputations satisfying (5.11) and thus lack cores.[10] For these important of games the categories concept of the core is, therefore, irrelevant.

Not even all nonconstant-sum games have cores. Shapley and Shubik offer an example of a pair of similar games, one with and the other without a core.[11] "Suppose," they say, "a donor promises to distribute $3.00 among three contestants, but only if they agree unanimously on the shares [i.e., form a

---

[10]To prove this statement, assume $\mathbf{x} = (x_1, x_2, ...,x_n)$ is in the core. Then, by (5.11),

$$\sum_{i \in S} x_i \geq v(S) \quad \text{and} \quad \sum_{i \in -S} x_i \geq v(-S)$$

for all $S \subseteq I_n$. Since $(S \cup -S) = I_n$,

$$\sum_{i \in I_n} x_i \geq v(S) + v(-S).$$

For constant-sum games

$$v(I_n) = v(S) + v(-S),$$

so that

$$\sum_{i \in I_n} x_i \geq v(I_n).$$

But this inequality directly violates (5.10)—that is, **x** is not feasible. The contradiction arose from our assumption that **x**, being in the core, satisfied (5.11). To extricate ourselves from the contradiction, we must instead assume:

$$\sum_{i \in S} x_i = v(S) \qquad \text{for all } S \subseteq I_n.$$

In particular, if S has one member, this implies $x_i = v(i)$. So we obtain

$$\sum_{i \in S} v(i) = v(S),$$

which is to say that the game is inessential. Thus no essential constant-sum games have cores.

[11]Lloyd Shapley and Martin Shubik, "On the Core of an Economic System with Externalities," *American Economic Review*, vol. 59 (1969), pp. 678–684.

three-person coalition]. However, if only two can agree [i.e., form a two-person coalition], he will distribute a smaller prize between them with nothing to the third." They then offer two versions, one in which the smaller prize is $1.50 and the other in which it is $2.50.

In the first game, the characteristic function is

$$v(1) = v(2) = v(3) = 0,$$
$$v(1, 2) = v(1, 3) = v(2, 3) = \$1.50,$$
$$v(1, 2, 3) = \$3.00.$$

Stating the payments in two-person coalitions, we have

$$x_1 + x_2 = \$1.50,$$
$$x_1 + x_3 = \$1.50,$$
$$x_2 + x_3 = \$1.50;$$

and summing, we get

$$2x_1 + 2x_2 + 2x_3 = \$4.50.$$

Since the sum of the payments individual players can get in two-person coalitions is less than they can make in a three-person coalition, i.e.,

$$x_1 + x_2 + x_3 = \$2.25 < v(1, 2, 3) = \$3.00,$$

no two-person coalition is preferable, among rational players, to the three-person coalition. Hence, some imputations appropriate for the three-person coalition (e.g., $\mathbf{x} = (1.00, 1.00, 1.00)$) are undominated and a core exists.

To see that $\mathbf{x} = (1.00, 1.00, 1.00)$ is undominated, note that other imputations, $\mathbf{y}$, such that $\sum y_i = 3.00$, cannot dominate $\mathbf{x}$ with respect to $(1, 2, 3)$. Thus if $\mathbf{y} = (1.00 + \epsilon, 1.00, 1.00 - \epsilon)$, no domination occurs because, while $y_1 > x_1$, still $y_3 < x_3$ and $y_2 = x_2$. Furthermore, no imputation for a two-person coalition, say (i, j), can upset $\mathbf{x}$. Since $x_i + x_j = 2.00$, players i and j have no reason to desert $\mathbf{x}$ for a coalition (i, j) where, at most, they can together make $1.50.

In the second game, on the other hand, the characteristic function is

$$v(1) = v(2) = v(3) = 0,$$
$$v(1, 2) = v(1, 3) = v(2, 3) = \$2.50,$$
$$v(1, 2, 3) = \$3.00;$$

and the payments to two-person coalitions are

$$x_1 + x_2 = \$2.50,$$
$$x_1 + x_3 = \$2.50,$$
$$x_2 + x_3 = \$2.50,$$

which sum to

$$x_1 + x_2 + x_3 = \$3.75.$$

In this game there is no core, because any pair of players can make more in a two-person coalition than in the three-person one. Hence, with respect to two-person coalitions, many imputations, $\mathbf{y}$, dominate imputations, $\mathbf{x}$, appropriate for three-person coalitions. Thus, if $\mathbf{x} = (1.00, 1.00, 1.00)$ and $\mathbf{y} = (1.25, 1.25, 0)$, then $\mathbf{y}$ dominates $\mathbf{x}$ with respect to coalition $(1, 2)$. But $\mathbf{y}$ also is dominated by, for example, $\mathbf{z} = (0, 1.30, 1.20)$ with respect to coalition $(2, 3)$. Generally, there are no undominated imputations, and this game has no core.

While the notion of the core assumes a game involving cardinal utility, we can perhaps understand it a little better if we consider an analogous situation in the voting problem of Chapter 4, where, typically, ordinal utilities are involved. In a simple majority voting system with m voters and n alternatives, it is clear that, if a majority of voters place alternative a_i first, then surely the imputation, $\mathbf{x}(a_i)$, associated with the adoption of a_i, is undominated because each member of the majority coalition obtains more from $\mathbf{x}(a_i)$ than from any alternative imputation $\mathbf{x}(a_j)$. On the other hand, a situation in which a paradox exists is a game without a core. For three alternatives a paradox is a case in which no alternative can beat every other. Assume that S, a majority coalition, can bring the victory of a_i over a_j, with the resultant $\mathbf{x}(a_i)$, and that S', another (overlapping) majority coalition, can bring victory for a_j over a_h, with the resultant $\mathbf{x}(a_j)$, and that S'', still a third (overlapping) majority coalition, can bring victory for a_h over a_i, with the resultant $\mathbf{x}(a_h)$. Then $\mathbf{x}(a_i)$ dominates $\mathbf{x}(a_j)$ with respect to S, $\mathbf{x}(a_j)$ dominates $\mathbf{x}(a_h)$ with respect to S', and $\mathbf{x}(a_h)$ dominates $\mathbf{x}(a_i)$ with respect to S''. Since the system is fully circular, no imputation is undominated. Hence voting paradoxes lack cores.

But what about situations in between these two extremes of a majority of first place votes for a_i and a paradox? For example, does a core exist when there is no majority of first-place votes for a_i but a_i is a Condorcet winner? To see that a core does exist, consider the following three-person, three-alternative case:

PERSON	ALTERNATIVES		
	BEST	MEDIUM	WORST
1	a_1	a_2	a_3
2	a_2	a_1	a_3
3	a_3	a_1	a_2

Assuming no logrolling or other violation of the independence-from-irrelevant-alternatives condition, and assuming that voting is *sincere* (see Chapter 4, p. 108) the characteristic function for this game is

$$v(1, 2, 3) = \mathbf{x}(a_1),$$

because, if the coalition agrees to vote and if each voter votes his own preference—as by assumption he is required to do—then a_1 is, indisputably and unblockably, the Condorcet winner;

$$v(1) = v(2) = v(3) = \min [\mathbf{x}(a_1), \mathbf{x}(a_2), \mathbf{x}(a_3)],$$

because if each voter acts entirely on his own, the loner cannot prevent the imposition of anything, including his least desired outcome;

$$v(1, 2) = \min [\mathbf{x}(a_1), \mathbf{x}(a_2)],$$

because 1 and 2 can block a_3, leaving a tie between a_1 and a_2;

$$v(1, 3) = \min [\mathbf{x}(a_1), \mathbf{x}(a_3)],$$

because 1 and 3 can block a_2, leaving a_1 and a_3 in a tie; and

$$v(2, 3) = \min [\mathbf{x}(a_1), \mathbf{x}(a_2), \mathbf{x}(a_3)],$$

because 2 and 3 cannot block anything, leaving thus a three-way tie. The adoption of a_1 gives every coalition at least its value because no coalition can block $\mathbf{x}(a_1)$. Hence the imputation associated with a_1 (i.e., best for 1, medium for 2 and 3) is the core. If, however, there is no Condorcet winner, there is no core. To say there is no core is to say there is no imputation that cannot be upset; similarly, to say there is no Condorcet winner is to say that there is no first choice that cannot be upset by sophisticated voting. Equating alternatives with imputations establishes the correspondence between the absence of a core and the absence of a Condorcet winner.[12]

There are many nonconstant-sum games that do have cores, especially those that model economic situations. Consider the three-person market game (p.126), which is not constant-sum. In Figure 5.4 we depict the imputation space for that game in which the house is worth at least $10,000 to its owners who have raised their family, $20,000 to the young family as a prospective buyer, and $30,000 to the nursing-home operator as a buyer. Setting the store of wealth other than the house equal to zero, then the characteristic function of the game to dispose of the house in the market is, as noted on page 127:

$$v(1) = 10,000, \qquad v(2) = v(3) = 0;$$
$$v(1, 2) = 20,000, \quad v(1, 3) = 30,000, \quad v(2, 3) = 0;$$
$$v(1, 2, 3) = 30,000.$$

In Figure 5.4 the effect of (5.11), the requirement for a core, is depicted by dashed lines. The line pq excludes all imputations to its left because in them the sum of the payments to 1 and 2 is less than v (1, 2) = $20,000. The line rs excludes all imputations to its right (i.e., all except those on the side itself) because in them the sum of the payments to 1 and 3 is less than $v(1, 3)$ = $30,000. The line tv excludes all imputations above it (i.e., none) because in them (if they were to exist) the sum of payments to 2 and 3 would be less than $v(2, 3) = 0$. This leaves as the core the thickened portion of the left side from point (30, 0, 0) to point (20, 0, 10). These are the imputations in which

---

[12]See Robert Wilson, "An Axiomatization of Voting Games," Working Paper 181, Stanford Business School, February 1971, in which it is shown that Arrow's theorem is "essentially the observation that the core of a voting game is ordinarily empty."

$$20,000 \leq x_1 \leq 30,000,$$

$$x_2 = 0,$$

$$0 \leq x_3 \leq 10,000,$$

$$x_1 + x_3 = 30,000.$$

Thus the core consists of those imputations that reflect the sale of the house by 1 to 3 at some price between \$20,000 and \$30,000, so that 1 gets the price w and 3, who values the house at \$30,000, gets (\$30,000 $- w$). It is easy to see that these are the undominated imputations. Every imputation inside the triangle and on its right and bottom sides is dominated by some imputation on the left side via its sextant C. (See Figure 5.3.) One might expect in turn that imputations on the left side would be dominated by interior imputations via their sextants A and E. Domination via E, however, involves coalition (1, 2), which is meaningless when 1 gets \$20,000 or more as he does in all imputations on the upper half of the left side. When 1 gets this much from 3, he has no motive to go with 2. Consequently, domination of the upper half of the right side via E is impossible. Similarly domination of the core via A is impossible because A involves coalition (2, 3). Since (2, 3) is valueless alone, it can have meaning only in (1, 2, 3) where 3 pays 2 not to bid so that 3 can buy the house from 1 at some price between \$10,000 and \$20,000. Thus, it is the same case as (1, 2) where domination via A of the upper half of the right side is impossible. Hence the core is undominated.

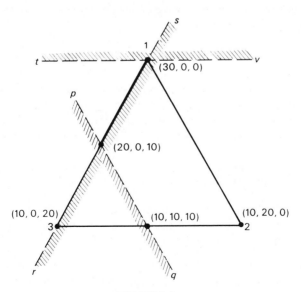

FIGURE 5.4

Knowing only the rules of the game and the utility structure of the players, one would certainly wish to include all the points in the core as reasonable possibilities for outcomes. To reduce further the number of points one would need to know a great deal about the personalities and experience of the players in an actual match. Which imputation in the core is chosen in a real-world application of, for example, the game in Figure 5.4 depends on the relative bargaining ability, emotional state (e.g., degree of desperation), and so on of players 1 and 3. For all abstract games, therefore, it seems impossible to reduce the set of possible outcomes to anything smaller than the core.

The real question, however, is whether or not the core contains all the reasonable possibilities. We think not. Of course when the core doesn't exist, it contains no possibilities, reasonable or unreasonable. Since the core doesn't exist for all constant-sum games and many nonconstant-sum ones, this is a fundamental defect of the concept. Even when the core does exist, however, some dominated imputations may be even more likely to occur than the undominated imputations of the core. Thus, in Figure 5.4, the imputation (15, 2, 13), which is dominated with respect to players 1· and 3 by, *inter alia*, (16, 0, 14), might nevertheless occur thus: player 3 pays player 2 the amount of $2,000 for 2 not to bid on the house; then 3 offers player 1 the amount of $15,000, which, in the absence of an alternative bid, 1 is constrained to take; thus, for an outlay of $17,000, player 3 gets a house worth $30,000 to him, a clear gain of $13,000. Every point on the inside of the small triangle with vertices (20, 0, 10), (10, 10, 10), and (10, 0, 20) can be considered possible by the same rationale. Thus even when the core exists, it does not describe all the reasonable possibilities. This, coupled with the fact that the core often does not exist, means that we must look elsewhere for an adequate concept of a solution for n-person games.

THE V-SOLUTION

We turn therefore to the notion of a *solution* as set forth by von Neumann and Morgenstern, which, to distinguish it from other solution concepts, we call the *V-solution*, following in part their nomenclature. The complexities of this concept reveal, we believe, the essence of the problem of stability in human society.

Looking back at the notion of the core, we note that it involves three kinds of vetoes of possible payoff vectors:

(5.7) — by individuals for failure to achieve individual security levels,
(5.10)—by the group as a whole for failure to achieve the value of the game,
(5.11)—by each coalition for failure to achieve its value.

The problem of cutting out too many vectors arose only with (5.11). So we retain (5.7) and (5.10), which define imputations, and start over again looking for stability among imputations.

We revert also to the notion of dominance. That is, we seek again to use this notion to define a set of stable imputations. From our experience with the notion of the core we know, however, that it is not enough that the set be undominated: it must also dominate. Von Neumann and Morgenstern offer the following standards for the set, V, of stable imputations:

(I) Every imputation y not in V is dominated by some x in V.
(II) No y in V is dominated by an x in V.

These together define the set of imputations that, while not dominating each other, together dominate all other imputations in the game.

To illustrate this definition consider the (zero-sum) game of Couples, where the characteristic function is:

$$\text{if } S \text{ has } \begin{Bmatrix} 0 \\ 1 \\ 2 \\ 3 \end{Bmatrix} \text{ members,} \qquad v(S) = \begin{Bmatrix} 0 \\ -1 \\ 1 \\ 0 \end{Bmatrix}.$$

One set of imputations that satisfies the definition of V is

$$\{x = (\tfrac{1}{2}, \tfrac{1}{2}, -1); \; y = (\tfrac{1}{2}, -1, \tfrac{1}{2}); \; z = (-1, \tfrac{1}{2}, \tfrac{1}{2})\}.$$

It is easy to see that no one of these dominates another. Testing x against y, with respect to the several coalitions, we find:

(1, 2): while 2 prefers x to y because $x_2 > y_2$, still 1 is indifferent because $x_1 = y_1$;
(1, 3): while 3 prefers y to x because $y_3 > x_3$, again 1 is indifferent because $x_1 = y_1$;
(2, 3): while 3 again prefers y to x because $y_3 > x_3$, still 2 prefers x to y because $x_2 > y_2$.

Thus it is never the case that both members of a coalition prefer x to y or y to x. Hence neither x dominates y nor y dominates x. By a similar analysis it is clear that within the pair y and z and within the pair x and z neither imputation dominates the other. Thus the entire set of imputations possesses property (II), that no y in V be dominated by an x in V.

To see that this set also possesses property (I), that every imputation y outside V be dominated by an x in V, consider an imputation $x' = (\tfrac{1}{2} + \varepsilon, \tfrac{1}{2} - \varepsilon, -1)$, which is constructed from x by a redistribution within the coalition $(1, 2)$ but which retains the basic feature of x that $x_1 \geq 0$, $x_2 \geq 0$, $x_3 \leq 0$. Conceivably x' might be generated from x if, in $(1, 2)$, player 1 is stronger and greedier than player 2. Comparing x' with z, it is clear that 2 and 3 prefer z because $z_2 > x_2'$ and $z_3 > x_3'$. Hence z dominates x'. In general, z dominates any imputation x' that shares the basic character of x but that departs from x by favoring 1, i.e., $\tfrac{1}{2} < x_1' \leq 1$. Similarly, y dominates any imputation x'' that departs from x by favoring 2. For example, y dominates $x'' = (\tfrac{1}{2} - \varepsilon,$

$\frac{1}{2} + \epsilon, -1)$ with respect to $(1, 3)$ because $y_1 > x_1''$ and $y_3 > x_3''$. Finally, any imputation $\mathbf{x}'''$ that departs from $\mathbf{x}$ by favoring 3 (i.e., $-1 < x_3 \leq 0$) is dominated by some imputation in V:

$(\frac{1}{2}, \frac{1}{2} - \epsilon, -1 + \varepsilon)$ is dominated by $\mathbf{z} = (-1, \frac{1}{2}, \frac{1}{2})$ with respect to $(2, 3)$;
$(\frac{1}{2} - \epsilon, \frac{1}{2}, -1 + \varepsilon)$ is dominated by $\mathbf{y} = (\frac{1}{2}, -1, \frac{1}{2})$ with respect to $(1, 3)$;
$(\frac{1}{2} - \varepsilon/2, \frac{1}{2} - \varepsilon/2, -1 + \varepsilon)$ is dominated by $\mathbf{x}$ itself.

In a similar way it can be shown that any imputation sharing the basic characteristic of $\mathbf{y}$ (i.e., $y_1 \geq 0, y_2 \leq 0, y_3 \geq 0$) but departing from it to favor some player is dominated by $\mathbf{x}$, $\mathbf{z}$, or $\mathbf{y}$ itself. So also for $\mathbf{z}$. These exhaust the possibilities, for there are only three cases (represented by the three members of V) where the payoff to one player is less than zero. (Of course if the payoff to two players is less than zero, some imputation in V dominates. The zero-sum condition precludes that either none or three players be paid less than zero.) Hence *any* imputation not in V is dominated by one in it, and thus V possesses property (I).

With this illustration in mind, it is possible to see some of the fundamental reasons for the stability of V.

Suppose the players in Couples negotiate for an unlimited amount of time prior to the actual play of the game, i.e., the voting. There is nothing in the rules to prohibit such negotiation. And it is advantageous because it helps players reduce uncertainty in two ways: First, players can try to form pairwise coalitions in which members promise to vote for each other, thus raising for that pair the probability of being in a couple. Second, the probability of the outcome $(0, 0, 0)$, which occurs where no couple is formed—that is, when 1 votes for 2, 2 for 3, and 3 for 1; or when 1 votes for 3, 3 for 2, and 2 for 1—may be reduced from 0.25 to almost zero. Since negotiations to form coalitions and reduce uncertainty are not prohibited and are definitely advantageous, they may be expected to occur.

Suppose, in such negotiations, players arrive at some imputation $\mathbf{w}$ outside of V. The fact of property (I) that every outside imputation is dominated by an inside one means that $\mathbf{w}$ will be found unsatisfactory by a majority of the players. They will, therefore, abandon it and move, presumably to something in V or closer to it. Thus the dominating imputations in V render every outside imputation unlikely.

At the same time, the fact of property (II) that the imputations in V do not dominate each other means that there is no reason to abandon an $\mathbf{x}$ in V for a $\mathbf{y}$ in V, once an $\mathbf{x}$ is arrived at. Thus, if $(1, 2)$ has formed so that $\mathbf{x} = (\frac{1}{2}, \frac{1}{2}, -1)$ is temporarily agreed upon and if 3 (the loser in $\mathbf{x}$) proposes to, e.g., 1 that together they form $(1, 3)$ and adopt $\mathbf{y} = (\frac{1}{2}, -1, \frac{1}{2})$, 1 has no motive to abandon $\mathbf{x}$ for $\mathbf{y}$ because $x_1 = y_1$. In general, the fact of property (II) means that any proposal to move from one imputation in V to another is likely to fail because there is at least one crucial player who has no reason to change.

Of course the real threat against the stability of an imputation in V does not come from another one in V. If there is no domination—as within V there is not—then there is no threat. Instead, the threat comes from outside, from some dominating imputation. Suppose in the negotiations players have arrived at coalition (1, 2) with imputation $\mathbf{x} = (\frac{1}{2}, \frac{1}{2}, -1)$. Naturally, 3, who is disadvantaged in $\mathbf{x}$, would like to break up (1, 2). He can attempt to do so by offering 1 the chance to form (1, 3) with an imputation of, say, $\mathbf{w} = (\frac{3}{4}, -1, \frac{1}{4})$. Since $\mathbf{w}$ dominates $\mathbf{x}$ with respect to (1, 3), it might be expected that players abandon $\mathbf{x}$ readily. Yet there is some reason not to do so. Suppose 1 actually accepts 3's offer and $\mathbf{w}$ displaces $\mathbf{x}$. Then it is possible for 2, who is the disadvantaged player in $\mathbf{w}$, to disrupt (1, 3) with an offer to 3 to form (2, 3) with the imputation $\mathbf{z} = (-1, \frac{1}{2}, \frac{1}{2})$. Since $z_3 > w_3$, and $z_2 > w_2$, $\mathbf{z}$ dominates $\mathbf{w}$ with respect to (2, 3). Hence 3 has good reason to accept 2's offer, and negotiations have settled again on an imputation, $\mathbf{z}$, in V. Thus, while outside imputations are superficially attractive alternatives to inside imputations, the fact that the outside ones are in turn dominated from inside renders the outsiders unstable. It may be that, in course of protracted negotiations, outside imputations are arrived at, but the expectation is that players will revert to inside ones—all because of property (I).

In the illustration in the previous paragraph, the player (1) who first departed from a two-person coalition ultimately wound up in a coalition by himself. In Couples, at least, nature apparently punishes greed. Imputations outside the solution are attractive, but they are "unsound" in that, while a player may initially get more from them, he risks ultimately getting less. It is this danger that makes the solution, V, so attractive and relatively stable.

Some readers may regard the kind of considerations set forth in the previous paragraph as abstractly reasonable but unlikely to occur in practice. We have much evidence, however, from actual experiments with a nonconstant-sum version of Couples that after a little bit of experience (e.g., three to five matches each with a half-hour negotiation) players tend to seek imputations in or very close to V and to reject initially advantageous departures from it as unsound.[13] One can see similar situations in everyday life: Typically producers of, e.g., copper refuse to raise prices "excessively" in a period of shortage for fear of driving users to permanent substitution of aluminum for copper. Or typically, professors refuse to gain immediate popularity by giving all students "A"

[13]See William H. Riker, "Bargaining in a Three-Person Game," *American Political Science Review*, vol. 61 (1967), pp. 642–656; William H. Riker, "Experimental Verification of Two Theories about Three-Person Games," *Mathematical Applications in Political Science*, vol. 3 (Charlottesville: University Press of Virginia, 1968), pp. 52–62; William H. Riker and William Zavoina, "Rational Behavior in Politics: Evidence from a Three-Person Game," *American Political Science Review*, vol. 64 (1970), pp. 48–60. In these experiments, even though the players knew nothing about the theory of solutions, they regarded the amount assigned to them in imputations in the solution as a quota. The typical experienced players then refused to take more than the quota and regarded an offer of more than the quota as a set-up for the development of a situation in which the greedy player would lose.

grades for fear of being permanently regarded as unintellectual. There seems to be, therefore, little question that, in the laboratory and in real life as well as in the theory, the V-solution possesses a kind of stability that makes feasible and attractive imputations outside of it seem unsound.

Given that stability, it may well seem that our search for a stable payoff configuration is over. If we have not found a unique vector, at least we have found a stable *set* of vectors, a set that is defined for wide classes of games.[14] We started our search by eliminating all payoff vectors that were not imputations. Within the set of imputations we first selected the core but ultimately rejected it as unduly restrictive, though recognizing it to be often useful. Now the V-solution appears satisfactory: it is larger than the core, but smaller than the set of imputations.

Unfortunately, the appearance is deceptive. If there were a unique V-solution to each game, perhaps our search would be over. But in fact there is an infinity of such solutions. And *every* imputation is in some V-solution. Thus the concept of a V-solution does not narrow the set of potentially stable imputations because there is an infinity of V-solutions.

A Geometry of V-Solutions

The fact of an infinity of V-solutions can be illustrated, for the case of the three-person game, by a geometric analysis of Couples. First we interpret the requirements for V geometrically for the three-person game:

(I) *Every imputation* **y** *not in V is dominated by some* **x** *in V.* Geometrically, domination is expressed thus: A point representing an imputation **x** dominates a point representing **y** if, for a set of three axes through **x** dividing the plane into sextants (as in Figure 5.3), **y** falls in sextants A, C, or E. Recall that the set of all imputations in the three-person game is, geometrically, all the points in and on the fundamental triangle. Then, to satisfy (I), it must be the case that, except for those points in the V-solution, all points in the fundamental triangle lie in some sextant, A, C, or E, with respect to at least one imputation point in the V-solution. If any imputation points in the fundamental triangle are not in V and are not in some sextant A, C, or E of a point in V, then those points are both not in V and not dominated from V, thereby violating requirement (I).

(II) *No* **y** *in V is dominated by an* **x** *in V.* Nondomination between a pair of imputations, **x** and **y**, implies, in the three-person case, that, for some i, $x_i = y_i$. Geometrically, $x_i = y_i$ when x_i and y_i lie on a straight line parallel to the ith edge of the fundamental triangle. Thus **x** and **y** are equidistant and in the same direction from the axis through the origin for payments to player i. To satisfy (II), therefore, it must be that, for every pair of imputations in V, the pair lies on a line parallel to some side of the fundamental triangle.

[14]But see W. F. Lucas, *A Game with No Solution*, Memorandum RM 5518-PR (Santa Monica: The Rand Corporation, 1967), and W. F. Lucas, *The Proof That a Game May Not Have a Solution*, Memorandum 5543-PR (Santa Monica: The Rand Corporation, 1968), where it is shown that a core, but no solution, exists for a rather strange ten-person game.

The V-solution of Couples already discussed, viz.,

$$V = \left[\left(\frac{1}{2}, \frac{1}{2}, -1\right), \left(\frac{1}{2}, -1, \frac{1}{2}\right), \left(-1, \frac{1}{2}, \frac{1}{2}\right)\right],$$

is depicted geometrically in Figure 5.5, where the solid lines form the fundamental triangle. Imputations $\mathbf{x}$, $\mathbf{y}$ and $\mathbf{z}$ of V are at points x, y, and z, the

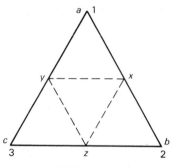

$$\mathbf{x} = \left(\frac{1}{2}, \frac{1}{2}, -1\right)$$

$$\mathbf{y} = \left(\frac{1}{2}, -1, \frac{1}{2}\right)$$

$$\mathbf{z} = \left(-1, \frac{1}{2}, \frac{1}{2}\right)$$

FIGURE 5.5

midpoints of the sides. Line bc represents the worst player 1 can do (here -1) so that $z_1 = -1$. Similarly line ac is the worst 2 can do and $y_2 = -1$; and ab is 3's worst and $x_3 = -1$. Point a represents the best 1 can do (here $a_1 = +2$, when $a_2 = a_3 = -1$). Since line yx is midway between -1 and $+2$, all points on it have, for 1, a value of $\frac{1}{2}$. Thus, $x_1 = y_1 = \frac{1}{2}$. Similarly for xz, $x_2 = z_2 = \frac{1}{2}$ and for yz, $y_3 = z_3 = \frac{1}{2}$.

It is easy to see geometrically that points x, y, and z satisfy requirements (I) and (II). Requirement (I) is satisfied because;

> all points inside $axzy$ and on lines ya and ax (except points x and y) are in sextant A of axes through point z;
> all points inside $bzyx$ and on lines zb and xb (except points x and z) are in sextant C of axes through point y;
> all points inside $cyxz$ and on lines cy and cz (except points y and z) are in sextant E of axes through point x;
> so that x, y, and z together dominate all other points in the triangle.

Requirement (II) is satisfied because

> x and y lie on line xy which is parallel to the cb edge;
> x and z lie on line xz which is parallel to the ac edge;
> y and z lie on line yz which is parallel to the ab edge;
> so that x, y, and z do not dominate each other.

Thus we have a geometric interpretation of one V-solution of Couples. We undertook this geometry, however, because we wished to show that many other V-solutions exist:

$$V' = [\text{all points on the line } pq \text{ of Figure 5.6}]$$

These are all the points $\mathbf{w} = (w_1, w_2, w_3)$ such that $w_1 = c$, where c is a fixed amount, and $w_2 + w_3 = -c$, where $(-c)$ is divided in all possible ways between 2 and 3. It is easy to see that V' also satisfies both requirements: (I) Any point, a, above pq is dominated by at least one point, say w^*, on pq, because a lies in sextant A (as in Figure 5.3) of point w^*. Any point, b, in the area below pq is

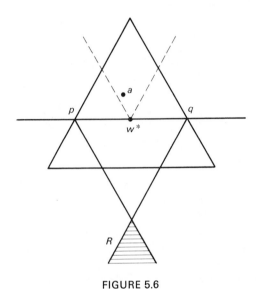

FIGURE 5.6

dominated by at least one point on pq because b lies in either sextant C or E of some point w^* on pq. Note, however, that points in the shaded area marked R are *not* dominated from pq because p dominates only to the right of R and q dominates only to the left of R. Since, as we have drawn pq, R is outside the fundamental triangle, however, all points on pq together dominate the rest of the triangle. (II) Since all the points on pq are on a line parallel to one of the sides of the fundamental triangle, points on pq do not dominate each other.

The line pq is determined by the payoff $w_1 = c$. The maximum value of c is limited by the need to keep the shaded area, R, in Figure 5.6 outside the fundamental triangle, because the points in this area are undominated from line pq. If $c \geq \frac{1}{2}$, line pq is far enough above the base so that part of area R in Figure 5.6 is inside the fundamental triangle, which violates the definition of a solution. Hence it must be that $c < \frac{1}{2}$. Since it also must be that $c \geq -1$ to be in the triangle at all, we have

$$-1 \le c < \frac{1}{2}.$$

Some of the V-solutions with $w_1 = c$ are indicated by horizontal lines in Figure 5.7 for various values of c such as c, c', c'', and c_2'''. The whole triangle can, of course, be rotated so that $w_2 = c$ and $w_3 = c$. The entire infinity of V-solutions is schematically indicated in Figure 5.8. Note that *every* point in the fundamental triangle is in some V-solution. Many points are in several solutions.

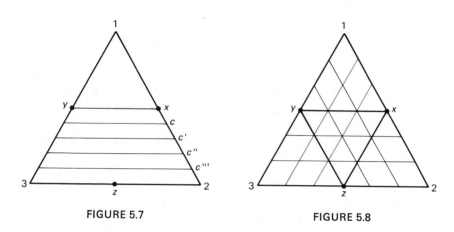

FIGURE 5.7   FIGURE 5.8

Von Neumann and Morgenstern distinguish between two kinds of V-solutions:

nondiscriminatory, which are the sets of imputations in which, if each imputation in the set is equally likely, the expected value of the individual payoffs is equal—in the three-person case, this is the set: $(\mathbf{x}, \mathbf{y}, \mathbf{z})$;
discriminatory, which are all the rest of the V-solutions.

In the nondiscriminatory V-solution every player is treated equally. In the discriminatory ones, however, the payoffs to some players are fixed (either advantageously or disadvantageously), and the remaining players then bargain for the rest of the value of the game.

In the natural world, which one of the infinity of V-solutions actually occurs is determined by local standards of behavior. Some institutions, such as the perfectly competitive market and pure democracy, encourage nondiscriminatory solutions. Others, such as monopoly and slavery, encourage discriminatory solutions.

We may think of a household with a slave, for example, as a constant-sum game in which the slave receives an amount, c, for subsistence, and the remainder of the household net income is divided by bargaining between master and mistress. Whether c is large or small depends on the kindness of the owners, the productivity of the slave, and so on. In this way cultural standards do make a difference. Depending on the commonly held attitude on personal failure, one may, for example, reject nondiscriminatory solutions with their emphasis on exact equality and symmetry that implies utter failure for someone. This accounts for the widely held preferences for discriminatory solutions in which, even if $c < 0$, at least $c > -1$. Thus, in the nineteenth century the free market seemed attractive because of its equality of opportunity. But in the twentieth it has been widely supplanted by regulated markets in which, if there is less opportunity, there is also less extreme failure.

REFLECTIONS ON SOLUTION CONCEPTS

The multiplicity of V-solutions defies further analysis. Society can choose—or arrive at—*any* standard of behavior compatible with the notion of imputations. There is no *a priori* way to determine which V-solution will prevail, hence no way in the abstract to select a stable imputation.

Nevertheless, society does have standards of behavior, and it thus selects a set—or perhaps, with several standards, several sets—of imputations that are stable within the set. Hence our search for stability has led to a curious kind of minimal equilibrium: there is no unique stable imputation, but rather a stable set of imputations, which is, however, embarrassingly large, especially if $n > 3$. Noting that solutions may be discriminatory and nondiscriminatory, there are infinitely many stable sets of imputations.

Furthermore, within each set the stability depends on what von Neumann and Morgenstern call "soundness." A particular standard of behavior specifies a particular V-solution and its imputations, which are considered "sound." These sound imputations are consistent in that they do not dominate each other [requirement (II)] and yet together dominate all others [requirement (I)]. Nevertheless, unsound imputations may dominate sound ones, a fundamental weakness of the V-solution. What then renders sound imputations stable? The answer is that an unsound imputation, "although preferable to an effective set of players, will fail to attract them, because it is 'unsound.' "[15] It is unsound because it is not sanctioned by the standard of behavior, while of course the standard of behavior is ultimately determined by what is "sound." Von Neumann and Morgenstern observe that the argument is circular, but they also comment that "this sort of circularity is not unfamiliar in everyday considerations dealing with soundness." Perhaps we could add that the soundness of a solution is related to its self-policing property. Given a cultural standard leading to a set V, imputations outside of V are unattractive because of the enforcement involved in requirement (I). Hence, a standard of behavior is reinforced by a solution and a solution is adopted because of a standard of behavior. Such circularity seems both universal and inevitable.

[15]Von Neumann and Morgenstern, *The Theory of Games and Economic Behavior*, p. 265.

Given the multiplicity of V-solutions and the essentially arbitrary basis for selection among all these, there is no way to predict in the abstract which V-solution will socially prevail. It is all a matter of standards of behavior. And given the choice of a solution, so fragile is the stability that there is no way to predict which of the (often many) imputations in the stable set will actually be arrived at in society. The usual scientific reason for searching for an equilibrium is to permit prediction. Here, however, we have found an equilibrium that is so slight and tenuous that no prediction is possible.

For all practical purposes our search for a solution—during which we examined the core and the V-solution—is ended here. We could elaborate on the V-solution, showing that as it is extended to the nonconstant-sum game, its stable set becomes unmanageably large and complicated.[16] But aside from the illustration in the marginal notes, we think the detail of theory about V-solutions will not bring us closer to an understanding of equilibrium. We could also develop in some detail alternative solution concepts, such as Aumann and Maschler's notion of the bargaining set.[17] But alternative solution concepts that do not admit of extensive inclusion of cultural and institutional detail do

[16]As a glimpse into that theory, we offer for comparison a nonconstant-sum version of Couples, where the characteristic function is:
$$v(1) = v(2) = v(3) = 0; \quad v(1, 2) = \tfrac{2}{3}; \quad v(1, 3) = \tfrac{5}{6}; \quad v(2, 3) = 1; \quad v(1, 2, 3) = 1.$$
The principal points of the nondiscriminatory V-solution are:
$$\mathbf{x} = (\tfrac{3}{12}, \tfrac{5}{12}, -\tfrac{2}{3}), \quad \mathbf{y} = (\tfrac{3}{12}, -\tfrac{5}{6}, \tfrac{7}{12}), \quad \mathbf{z} = (-1, \tfrac{5}{12}, \tfrac{7}{12}).$$
In Figure 5.9, these dominate all the points on the inside of the inner dashed triangle as well

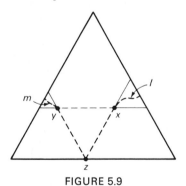

FIGURE 5.9

as all the rest of the fundamental triangle except the two small triangles originating at x and y. To assure that enough and the right kind of those undominated points are incorporated into the solution, we draw a curve from x and y through the small triangles to the sides of the fundamental triangle, a curve that never deviates from the perpendicular from the point to the side by more than 30 degrees. The V-solution is then the three principal points and all the points on lines l and m. Since l and m can be drawn arbitrarily, all the points in these two triangles are eligible for various nondiscriminatory V-solutions. Discriminatory solutions are achieved by lines through the triangle xyz along with similar and appopriate curves in the triangles at the sides.

[17]Aumann and Maschler impose less severe restrictions on payoff configurations than do von Neumann and Morgenstern. Aumann and Maschler apply individual rationality (5.7) but not Pareto optimality (5.10) and thus get, in place of the imputation, the individually rational

not lead to strikingly different theoretical results.[18] So it appears that we have gone as far in our search as we can, even though our results are highly inconclusive.

SOCIAL EQUILIBRIA

In the last two chapters we have been searching for a social equilibrium. We think of an equilibrium as a property of the society as a whole, of all the people together in a collectivity. But it is just as much a property of individuals separately because it is achieved when men, acting rationally in pursuit of personal goals, move society to a particular outcome. It is understood, of course, that the outcome chosen is not necessarily identical with any personal goals, but is rather some composite of what the several persons want and are able to get. Thus, a price is a composite of the preferences of buyers and sellers, each weighted for elasticities.

The advantage of identifying an equilibrium position is that, with a known equilibrium, it is possible to predict collective results by assuming no more than individual rationality. It is appropriate at this point, we think, to ask just what we have so far discovered about the pervasiveness of equilibria.

To begin our retrospective survey, we note that at least three types of equilibria can be distinguished. In all cases equilibria are social outcomes which are arrived at because each (or some) individuals have a motive under individual rationality to move toward these outcomes. Equilibria differ, however, according to the following categorization:

I. *Strong, unique equilibrium.* A social outcome that is the product of interaction so precise and goals so specific that society will certainly arrive at it. If this social outcome is displaced by some adventitious circumstance, society will return to it as soon as possible. Prices in a competitive market are, of course, the standard example; and this equilibrium is, in the limit as the number of traders becomes very large, equivalent to the core of an *n*-person game.[19]

---

payoff configuration. The bargaining set is a set of individually rational payoff configurations essentially similar to the *V*-solution of imputations, although the bargaining set is arrived at by means of considerations somewhat more realistic and *ad hoc* than the *V*-solution. See R. J. Aumann and M. Maschler, "The Bargaining Set for Cooperative Games," in M. Dresher, L. S. Shapley, and A. W. Tucker, eds., *Advances in Games Theory*, Annals of Mathematics Studies, no. 52 (Princeton, N.J.: Princeton University Press, 1964).

[18]There are solution concepts that allow for the incorporation of much institutional detail. The most useful of these is Shapley's notion of a value for *n*-person games, which is discussed in the next chapter. In addition Luce's notion of ψ-stability [see Luce and Raiffa, *Games and Decisions*, pp. 220–231 and the literature there cited, especially R. Duncan Luce and Arnold Rogow, "A Game Theoretic Analysis of Congressional Power Distributions for a Stable Two-Party System," *Behavioral Science*, vol. 1 (1956), pp. 83–95] admits much institutional detail but has not been particularly useful in analyzing social situations.

[19]Gerald Debreu and H. Scarf, "A Limit Theorem on the Core of an Economy," *International Economic Review*, vol. 4 (1963), pp. 235–236; H. Scarf, "The Core of an *N*-Person Game," *Econometrica*, vol. 35 (1967), pp. 50–69. For the most recent comprehensive analysis, see Lester G. Telser, *Competition, Collusion, and Game Theory* (Chicago: Aldine-Atherton, 1972).

II. *Weak, unique equilibrium.* A social outcome that is the product of (usually) more complicated interaction toward (usually) more complicated goals such that society tends toward it. If movement toward this outcome is accidentally deflected, society will resume movement toward it as soon as possible. The tendency of the economy toward a specific degree of inflation with a specific increase in the quantity of money is an example of this weaker kind of equilibrium.

III. *Nonunique equilibrium* (unstable equilibrium). A social outcome that is a member of a set of outcomes, where the set is such that the interaction of goal-seeking persons will lead them to some unspecified outcome in the set, not necessarily that one toward which the society originally began to move. If deflected from its course, the society will as soon as possible return to a course toward some member of the set, not necessarily the one toward which it was moving earlier. The concentration of production in a few (but unspecified number of) firms in an industry characterized by large economies of scale is a strong example of this kind of equilibrium, while the location of a price in a range (possibly quite wide) among two bargainers is a weak example.

In our examination of the process of socially summing preferences, we found either Type I equilibrium or complete disequilibrium. When people in a collectivity or, failing that, when each person's calculus of voting conforms to the conditions set forth on pages 100 and 101, then Type I equilibrium occurs. But in the absence of such conditions the system is in disequilibrium and all outcomes are dependent on idiosyncratic circumstances. Such equilibrium as exists, therefore, depends, not on the nature of social processes nor on the structure of society, but rather on cultural agreement.

When we turned to an examination of payoff configurations we discovered the same kind of arbitrary cultural agreement underlying whatever equilibrium exists. An examination of payoff configurations in the abstract revealed at best a Type III kind of equilibrium. Since the sets of outcomes in equilibrium are typically very large, often infinite, and since the range in variation among outcomes in the sets is often as wide as the commonsense possibilities, the Type III equilibria found here (e.g., cores, V-solutions) are not typically of much use for prediction. Indeed, equilibria among members of an infinite set may not differ much from general disequilibria. Furthermore, it turns out that, in the case of the V-solution at least, the kind of equilibrium in existence depends entirely on an arbitrary cultural and institutional setting. As in the case of summing preferences, equilibria in payoffs is based on human will, not on social processes or structures.

We thus discover that the heart of social equilibrium lies not in the abstracted structure of society but rather in the cultural and institutional arrangements that happen to pertain. One is reminded of Rousseau's observation that a society could discover its general will only if its essential unanimity had been impressed by some Great Legislator of the past, a Solon, a Lycurgus, or a Calvin. What Rousseau dimly (and inaccurately) perceived, we are now able to perceive in its full complexity. The predictability of social outcomes derives not from their nature as society's output, but from the particular content in the particular outcome. It is the particular, not the general, that we can most fruitfully interpret.

For this reason we turn in the next and following chapters to less abstract models of society. By adding institutions and cultural settings to the wholly abstract models heretofore discussed we hope to be able to find particular equilibria, even if a general equilibrium is a will-o'-the-wisp.

POLITICS AND ECONOMICS

Another—and perhaps more compelling—reason for turning to the study of the particular is inherent in the nature of politics itself. In this chapter we have identified two kinds of nonunique equilibria, the core and V-solutions. Although the core is probably the more stable by far, we found it unsatisfactory because it so often does not exist. We might have rejected it just as easily, however, on disciplinary grounds—on the basis that it is irrelevant to politics. It seems to us that the core does not exist in exactly those games that are most typical of politics. The economic abstraction from social life often displays a quite general equilibrium as in the case of a free competitive market. The core is one such typical economic equilibrium. But the political abstraction from social life seldom has a core. Politics is, we believe, often constant-sum in form and even sometimes zero-sum—and these features render the core nonexistent. But even when politics is not constant-sum, it typically involves a conflict between proponents of two noncomplementary moral values. In such case the institutionalization of one value precludes the institutionalization of the other. And this too is just exactly the kind of social situation in which the core is undefined. Hence, politics has fewer general equilibria than economics. If we are to find equilibria in politics at all, it must be in the particular situations to the analysis of which we now turn.

SUGGESTIONS FOR FURTHER READING

Two good elementary introductions to the theory of n-person games are in MORTON DAVIS, *Game Theory* (New York: Basic Books, 1970), chap. 6, and in R. DUNCAN LUCE and HOWARD RAIFFA, *Games and Decisions* (New York: Wiley, 1957), chaps. 7–12. A slightly more extensive treatment is found in ANATOL RAPOPORT *N-Person Game Theory* (Ann Arbor: University of Michigan Press, 1970). Unfortunately, most of the discussion of n-person games is extremely formal. A good introduction to this formalism is GUILLERMO OWEN, *Game Theory* (Philadelphia: Saunders, 1968), chaps. 8–9. The enthusiastic reader may want to study the main work: JOHN VON NEUMANN and OSKAR MORGENSTERN, *The Theory of Games and Economic Behavior*, 2d ed. (Princeton, N. J.: Princeton University Press, 1947). Many of the subsequent mathematical contributions are contained in M. DRESHER, L. S. SHAPLEY, and A. W. TUCKER, eds., *Advances in Game Theory*, Annals of Mathematics Studies, no. 52 (Princeton, N. J.: Princeton University Press,

1964); A. W. Tucker and R. D. Luce, eds., *Contributions to the Theory of Games*, vol. 4, Annals of Mathematics Studies, no. 40 (Princeton, N. J.: Princeton University Press, 1959); M. Dresher, A. W. Tucker, and P. Wolfe, eds., *Contributions to the Theory of Games*, vol. 3, Annals of Mathematics Studies, no. 39 (Princeton, N. J.: Princeton University Press, 1957); and H. W. Kuhn and A. W. Tucker, eds., *Contributions to the Theory of Games*, vols. 1 and 2, Annals of Mathematics Studies, nos. 24, 28 (Princeton, N. J.: Princeton University Press, 1950, 1953).

6

The Power Index

The conclusion of the previous chapter is that a general political equilibrium is not necessarily a consequence of individual rationality, but that equilibria are to be found as a result of particular institutions and cultural arrangements. In this chapter and the next we therefore introduce both some methods for analyzing the more restricted situations and some more particular models of political life.

THE SHAPLEY VALUE

The two solution concepts discussed in the last chapter (the core and the V-solution) both involve (typically) what we called Type III or nonunique equilibria, namely several imputations, even an infinity of them. Hence, the expectation for any particular player, i, is quite indefinite: Suppose $\mathbf{x}$ and $\mathbf{y}$ are both in the core or the V-solution. Then if $\mathbf{x}$ prevails, i receives x_i; if $\mathbf{y}$ prevails, i receives y_i; and so on, where, of course, x_i and y_i may vary through a wide range. Solution theories of this type do not, of course, predict whether $\mathbf{x}$ or $\mathbf{y}$ occur. In short, from the point of view of player i, the equilibria are not very interesting because they tell him only that many things might happen. Most players are already aware of this before they begin to study the game. As against this indefinite prediction of the core and the V-solution, the individual player would doubtless like to have some expectation of what he is likely to receive from a game, i.e., a kind of average of his part in the outcomes, if only to determine whether or not the game at hand is worth playing.

Shapley attempts to provide such a computation with his notion of a value for n-person games, often also called the "power index" in the literature of political science.[1] This value or index is a kind of Type II (weak, unqiue) equilibrium. In effect, Shapley offers a way to pass from a Type III equilibrium, the most general result for a game that models society, to a Type II equilibrium, which is less general but in some respects more useful. The requisites for passing from a Type III to Type II equilibrium are, as we repeatedly indicate, a set of particular institutions and cultural arrangements. Thus the Shapley value involves many notions, wholly absent from the theory of the core or the V-solution, that serve to restrict the Shapley value to a Type II equilibrium. There are, for example, the associated notions of winning and losing and of majority and minority. Or again, the Shapley value relies heavily on a notion of marginal contribution of a player to a coalition, which is absent from the more general theory of V-solutions.

Since the Shapley value or power index is a Type II equilibrium (i.e., a unique prediction), it is especially useful in situations in which:

(a) a player wishes to decide whether or not to play a game. Heretofore, we have implicitly supposed that all must play. But in some kinds of social situations, such as at the adoption of a constitution, the actual subject for decision is not an allocation of values but rather a determination of whether or not to participate. In such a case, one wants detailed information about one's own expected position in order to decide whether or not to support a constitution or to join a group or to play a game. The core and V-solution, however, typically tell one only what principle of division of payoff will be used in the game, not how much each individual can expect. The Shapley value, on the other hand, does tell what each player can expect in the long run, and therefore admits of individual judgments about whether or not to participate.

(b) it is desirable to compare the positions of several players. If for example, when thinking of a legislature with n-parties as an n-person game, a legislator faces a choice between joining party i and party j, his choice is easy when there is a single value for each party. But if there is one payoff when this coalition forms and another when that coalition forms, and so on, the choice among parties is difficult. In general, the existence of a unique equilibrium with specific values for each player, as provided by the Shapley value, admits of such comparisons, while nonunique equilibria such as the core and the V-solution do not.

Thus, the Shapley value is really another kind of solution couched in terms of an expected value, v_i, for each player. It builds on the characteristic function, which divides up the value of the game among coalitions; then it divides up the coalition values among all the individual players, regardless of which coalition forms. In effect, the Shapley value involves a distribution among the players of the values from the characteristic function.

Since there exist an infinity of methods of splitting the values of coalitions

[1]L. S. Shapley, "A Value for N-Person Games," in H. W. Kuhn and A.W. Tucker, eds., *Contributions to the Theory of Games,* Annals of Mathematics Studies, no. 28 (Princeton, N. J.: Princeton University Press, 1953), pp. 307–317; L. S. Shapley and Martin Shubik, "A Method for Evaluating the Distribution of Power in a Committee System," *American Political Science Review,* vol. 48 (1954), pp. 787–792.

among their members, the choice of any particular one involves some initial judgment on what kind of procedures are intuitively justifiable. At least the three following assumptions are made for the Shapley value:

1. Relationship among values of coalitions

We begin with the problem that, from the characteristic function by itself, we do not know how to assess the relation among the values of the several coalitions, especially if they are overlapping. In Couples, for example, we have eight possible coalitions of zero, one, two, and three persons. Of course, the larger coalitions sometimes contain the smaller; when this happens, surely some of the value of the larger is assignable to the smaller which it subsumes. Suppose, for two-member coalitions, S_2,

$$w \leq v(S_2) \leq w + \varepsilon$$

and for three-member coalitions, S_3,

$$v(S_3) = w + \varepsilon.$$

Then, in dividing up $v(S_3)$ among its members, $i, j, \ldots$, some of $v(S_3)$ must go to them in their capacities as members of S_3 and some in their capacities as members of S_2. But in what proportions? And until we have a practical way of deciding these proportions we cannot break down the values of the characteristic function by assigning parts of these values to individuals.

The practical problem of computation is obvious: For the value of a coalition, $v(S: \{i, j\})$, assign some portion, $q^i{}_{ij}$, to player i as part of his Shapley value, v_i; for $v(S: \{i, j, k\})$, also some portion, $q^i{}_{ijk}$, to v_i, and so on. Then the Shapley value for the individual, v_i, is the sum of these assignments over all the coalitions of various sizes to which i can belong,

$$v_i = \sum_{S \in I_n} q^i{}_S.$$

At the end it must be that the sum of the values of all the players is equal to the value of the grand coalition; that is,

$$\sum_{i=1}^{n} v_i = v(I_n).$$

But unless careful accounts are kept, it may well be that

$$\sum_{i=1}^{n} v_i \lessgtr v(I_n),$$

either of which is impossible. Suppose it is the case that some of $v(S: \{i, j, k\})$, is accounted for by $v(S: \{i, j\})$, yet suppose that, in dividing up the values of the characteristic function to individuals, assignments are made so that all the value of both $\{i, j, k\}$ and $\{i, j\}$ go to individuals thus:

$$q^i_{ijk} + q^j_{ijk} + q^k_{ijk} = v(S: \{i, j, k\})$$

and

$$q^i_{ij} + q^j_{ij} = v(S: \{i, j\}).$$

Then surely

$$\sum_{i=1}^{n} v_i > v(I_n)$$

because, when $v(S: \{i, j, k\}) = v(I_n)$, to add $v(S: \{i, j\})$ simply inflates $\sum v_i$. One might compensate for such double counting in some completely arbitrary way. For example, one might substract from each player's value, v_i, an equal share of the excess of $\sum_{i=1}^{n} v_i$ over $v(I_n)$. That is, one might calculate a revised value, v_i',

$$v_i' = v_i - \frac{1}{n} [\sum_{i=1}^{n} v_i - v(I_n)].$$

Such a procedure would distort the meaning of v_i, however, by hurting those players who were members of many coalitions less than those who were members of few. Rather than compensate in this highly arbitrary way, therefore, the Shapley value counts only the *increments* that a player brings to a coalition.

Consider the build-up of a grand coalition by a sequence of additions of one player, thus: $(1) \longrightarrow (1, 2) \longrightarrow \cdots \longrightarrow (1, 2, \ldots, n)$. Assuming a coalition, S, has s members, each addition to it [e.g., from s to $(s + 1)$] occasions some increment (positive or negative) to its value, $v(S)$; that is, $v(S)$ becomes $v(S + \{i\})$. Thus, as one adds members and adds (or subtracts) increments, one gets to $v(I_n)$. These increments are the amounts $[v(S) - v(S - \{i\})]$; and, for any coalition S, the amount divided among its members is just exactly this increment. Thus, for any S,

$$\sum_{i \in S} q^i s = [v(S) - v(S - \{i\})].$$

Since the sum of the increment is $v(I_n)$, if the shares, q, are the only values assigned to players, then we can assure ourselves that

$$\sum_{i=1}^{n} v_i = v(I_n).$$

2. Principle of division

While the previous procedure keeps track of overlapping values, it tells us nothing about the fractions q or how the increments are divided among players. In the sequence of all players, $h, j, \ldots, i, \ldots, k$, how is $[v(S) - v(S - \{i\})]$ to be divided among the members of S, who are the players $h, j, \ldots i$? Some obvious possibilities for rules of division are:

A. Some player gets the entire increment:
1. The last member, sequentially and chronologically, gets the increment, as might happen if each person were able to insist on receiving his marginal contribution to the value of the coalition. Where players are able to withhold membership—and hence contributions—this is a common rule.
2. The first player gets it all, as might happen if one rewarded the first person in a coalition, its originator, with all that it subsequently earned. This may be interpreted as a high payment for entrepreneurship.
3. A member, j, who is neither first nor last, gets it all, as might happen in a dictatorial system where j is dictator.
B. Members of the coalition $(h, j, \ldots, i)$ share the increment:
1. All members share equally, as might happen in a determinedly equalitarian society. This is the world of the commune and the monastery.
2. The last member, i, gets: $k[v(S) - v(S - \{i\})]$, where $0 < k < 1$, and each other member gets $[v(S) - v(S - \{i\})](1-k)/(s-1)$, as might happen when old members are able to force a new one to share some of his marginal contribution.
3. All the members, except the most recent addition, share equally the increment which that addition generates, as might happen were there a requirement that all players be in a coalition larger than one person. The institutions of apprenticeship in the world of trade and of seniority (as on congressional committees) embody something like this rule.

Clearly, many such arrangements are possible.

It makes a considerable difference which principle of division is used. In Table 6.1 we show values for individual players in the nonconstant-sum version of Couples. The calculations were made by the Shapley method except that a variety of principles of division were used. (The calculation is set forth in detail below, pp. 161–62 for the rule A.1, and in footnote 2 for the rule B.2.[2] Readers will recall from note 16, Chapter 5 (p. 149), that this

---

[2]In order to illustrate Table 6.1 in more detail, we also set forth in this note the calculation of v_1 according to Rule B.2, where the marginal member of a coalition gets k proportion of his contribution and other members get $(1 - k)$ proportion divided equally among them. Assuming $k = \frac{1}{2}$ and defining, for the last added member, i, of a coalition, S, of size s,

$$\alpha_i{}^S = (s - 1)! \, (n - s)!$$

then

$$
\begin{aligned}
v_1 &= k\left[\frac{1}{n!} \alpha_1^{S:\,(1)}(v(1) - v(\phi))\right] + k\left[\frac{1}{n!} \alpha_1^{S:\,(1,2)}(v(1,2) - v(2))\right] \\
&\quad + k\left[\frac{1}{n!} \alpha_1^{S:\,(1,3)}(v(1,3) - v(3))\right] + k\left[\frac{1}{n!} \alpha_1^{S:\,(1,2,3)}(v(1,2,3,) - v(2,3))\right] \\
&\quad + \frac{1-k}{s-1}\left[\frac{1}{n!} \alpha_2^{S:\,(1,2)}(v(1,2) - v(1))\right] + \frac{1-k}{s-1}\left[\frac{1}{n!} \alpha_2^{S:\,(1,2,3)}(v(1,2,3) - v(1,3))\right] \\
&\quad + \frac{1-k}{s-1}\left[\frac{1}{n!} \alpha_3^{S:\,(1,3)}(v(1,3) - v(1))\right] + \frac{1-k}{s-1}\left[\frac{1}{n!} \alpha_3^{S:\,(1,2,3)}(v(1,2,3) - v(1,2))\right] \\
&= \frac{1}{2} \cdot \frac{1}{6}(0!2!)(0 - 0) + \frac{1}{2} \cdot \frac{1}{6}(1!1!)(4 - 0) \\
&\quad + \frac{1}{2} \cdot \frac{1}{6}(1!1!)(5 - 0) + \frac{1}{2} \cdot \frac{1}{6}(2!0!)(6 - 6) \\
&\quad + \frac{1}{2} \cdot \frac{1}{6}(1!1!)(4 - 0) + \frac{1}{4} \cdot \frac{1}{6}(2!0!)(6 - 5) \\
&\quad + \frac{1}{2} \cdot \frac{1}{6}(1!1!)(5 - 0) + \frac{1}{4} \cdot \frac{1}{6}(2!0!)(6 - 4) \\
&= 1.75.
\end{aligned}
$$

game has the characteristic function:

$v(1) = v(2) = v(3) = 0;\ v(1,2) = 4;\ v(1,3) = 5;\ v(2,3) = 6;\ v(1,2,3) = 6.$

TABLE 6.1

Individual Values Under Different Principles of Division

PRINCIPLES OF DIVISION

		A.1	A.2	B.1	B.2 ($k = \frac{1}{2}$)	B.3
VALUES	v_1	1.5	2	1.833	1.75	1.583
FOR	v_2	2	2	2	2	2.417
PLAYERS	v_3	2.5	2	2.167	2.25	2

Since, as Table 6.1 clearly indicates, it makes a considerable difference which principle of division is used, it is desirable, we think, to offer some *a priori* reasons for choosing, as Shapley does, principle A.1, or the principle of marginal contribution. (To choose and defend A.1 in this way does not, of course, rule out the possibility of developing another individual value, v_i*, using some other principle of division such as A.2, A.3, B.1, B.2, B.3, etc.) In those games most typical of social life, in which the actors are self-directing, a player can be expected to join a coalition only if he gets something out of it. This is the rationale for the superadditive property of the characteristic function and indeed it seems almost universal, except for such circumstances as those envisioned by rule B.3. Furthermore, if $v(S) > v(S - \{i\})$, player i when in S can get some portion of the increment, $[v(S) - v(S - \{i\})]$, without cost to other members of S. Indeed, they can costlessly offer him the entire value of his marginal contribution. If there are two coalitions, $(S - \{i\})$ and $(T - \{i\})$ that are bidding against each other for i, then i should be able to exact his full marginal worth. The extreme example of such competition occurs when i makes the difference between two evenly matched coalitions:

$v(S - \{i\}) = v(T - \{i\}) = -1$ and $v(S) = v(T) = v(I_n) = 1.$

In this case, of course, i could reasonably expect to get the entire value of the game. This is the situation in, for example, a legislature where, on a hotly contested motion, its supporters and opponents are each just less than one half the body and there is one undecided member.

It is, of course, possible that competition runs the other way. To take a similarly extreme instance, there is just one coalition, $(S - \{i\})$, with more than one member and $v(S) = 1$, while $v(S - \{i\}) = 0$. All the remaining players are in valueless single-member coalitions. In this case, the isolated players may compete to get into $S,$ especially if there is some reason that they cannot form a coalition to compete with S. Then a player i might be willing to give up "almost all" of his marginal contribution just to be admitted. This is the situation in, for example, a market where a monopolistic seller faces an atomistic set of buyers.

The question then is: which circumstance is the more likely? Do leaders compete to lead or do followers compete to be led? Both surely occur in nature, but the common perception is that the leaders are the ones who most often compete. Thus, they are the ones who pay out. And if so, then the socially appropriate principle of division is A.1, the principle of marginal contribution, or something very like it.

3. Relative frequency of coalitions

Even if we assume that each new member of a coalition receives the increment his addition generates, we still cannot calculate a player's expected value, v_i, because we do not know how often the various coalitions can be expected to occur. In thinking of the Shapley value as the expectation for an individual under a constitution where a very large number of coalitions will occur in daily politics over many years, what is the expected frequency of coalition S as against coalition T? As often in such cases of complete ignorance, we invoke the principle of insufficient reason. Knowing nothing about the social circumstances or the players, we simply assume that any one way of forming a coalition is as likely as another. Since we have already assumed that coalitions are formed in a sequence, $(1) \rightarrow (1, 2) \rightarrow \ldots \rightarrow (1, 2, \ldots, n)$, this means that there are $n!$ ways in which coalitions might be formed. This is the $n!$ sequences of permutations of n things and we assume that each of the sequences is equiprobable.

CALCULATION OF THE SHAPLEY VALUE

With this final assumption the calculation of the Shapley value becomes quite easy. What we want to know is i's expected marginal value. To find this, (1) we count the number of sequences in which i is the last added member of coalition S of size s; (2) we multiply this number by i's marginal contribution to the value of the coalition S; (3) we sum this product for all S to which i belongs; and finally (4) we divide the sum by $n!$ to get an average marginal value.

Taking this procedure step by step, we start by counting, for each S to which i belongs, the number of sequences in which i is the last added member of S. We do this by fixing i in the sth position, by permuting the $(s - 1)$ predecessors in the sequence and $(n - s)$ successors, and taking the product of the two permutations. Then

$$\alpha_i^S = (s - 1)!(n - s)!$$

where α_i^S is the number of sequences for coalition S where i is in the sth position. Graphically:

$$\underbrace{h, j, \ldots, i-1, i,}_{s-1} \overbrace{}^{s} \quad \underbrace{i+1, \ldots, k}_{n-s}$$

Turning to the next step (2), we recall that i's marginal contribution, v_i^S, to the value of S is

$$v_i^S = [v(S) - v(S - \{i\})].$$

To give each of the sequences counted by α_i^S its proportionate weight in terms of i's contribution, we multiply: $\alpha_i^S v_i^S$. Then, in step (3), we sum all these weighted values over all S to which i belongs; and finally (4), to get an average we divide by $n!$. Thus, for i belonging to S:

$$v_i = \frac{1}{n!} \sum_{S \subset I_n} \alpha_i^S v_i^S.$$

Since v_i is an average,

$$\sum_{i=1}^{n} v_i = v(I_n).$$

As an example of the computation of the Shapley value, we calculate it for the nonconstant-sum version of Couples with the characteristic function:

$v(1) = v(2) = v(3) = 0$; $v(1, 2) = 4$; $v(1, 3) = 5$; $v(2, 3) = v(1, 2, 3) = 6$.

Bearing in mind the six distinct sequences (a through f) of the three players,

a:	123,	d:	231,
b:	132,	e:	312,
c:	213,	f:	321,

we note that, for player 1,

$$v_1 = \frac{0!2!}{3!}(0-0) + \frac{1!1!}{3!}(4-0) + \frac{1!1!}{3!}(5-0) + \frac{2!0!}{3!}(6-6).$$

$$\text{(term 1)} \qquad \text{(term 2)} \qquad \text{(term 3)} \qquad \text{(term 4)}$$

Term 1: There is one one-member coalition of which 1 is the marginal member. This coalition appears in $(s-1)!\,(n-s)!$ or $(0!2!)$ sequences (that is, a and b) out of 3! total sequences. (Note: Conventionally, $0! = 1$.) Player 1's marginal contribution in the one-member coalition of himself $v_1^{(1)}$ is

$$v_1^{(1)} = [v(1) - v(\phi)] = 0 - 0,$$

where ϕ is the empty set.

Term 2: There is one two-member coalition of 1 with 2 in $(1!1!)$ sequences (that is, c) and player 1 contributes

$$v_1^{(1,2)} = [v(1, 2) - v(2)] = 4 - 0.$$

Term 3: There is one two-member coalition of 1 with 3 in (1!1!) sequences (that is, e) and player 1 contributes

$$v_1^{(1,3)} = [v(1,3) - v(3)] = 5 - 0.$$

Term 4: There is one three-member coalition of 1 with 2 and 3 in (2!0!) sequences (that is, d and f) and player 1 contributes

$$v_1^{(1,2,3)} = [v(1,2,3) - v(2,3)] = 6 - 6.$$

Simplifying,

$$v_1 = \frac{2}{6}(0) + \frac{1}{6}(4) + \frac{1}{6}(5) + \frac{2}{6}(0) = \frac{9}{6} = 1\frac{1}{2}.$$

Similarly:

$$v_2 = \frac{0!2!}{3!}(0-0) + \frac{1!1!}{3!}(4-0) + \frac{1!1!}{3!}(6-0) + \frac{2!0!}{3!}(6-5)$$

$$= \frac{2}{6}(0) + \frac{1}{6}(4) + \frac{1}{6}(6) + \frac{2}{6}(1) = \frac{12}{6} = 2,$$

$$v_3 = \frac{0!2!}{3!}(0-0) + \frac{1!1!}{3!}(5-0) + \frac{1!1!}{3!}(6-0) + \frac{2!0!}{3!}(6-4)$$

$$= \frac{2}{6}(0) + \frac{1}{6}(5) + \frac{1}{6}(6) + \frac{2}{6}(2) = \frac{15}{6} = 2\frac{1}{2}$$

Hence the Shapley values, (v_1, v_2, v_3), are (1.50, 2.00, 2.50).

Some of the complexities of the Shapley procedure are revealed by comparing these individual expected values with the principal imputations in the V-solution of the same game:

$$V = \begin{cases} (1.50, 2.50, 0) \\ (1.50, 0, 3.50) \\ (0, 2.50, 3.50) \\ \quad . \\ \quad . \\ \quad . \end{cases}$$

Since the V-solution is intended to express an inner stability in bargaining, it cannot simultaneously say how much individual players can expect to win. Certainly, it does not lend itself to direct transformation into individual expected values. Speaking of the positive x_i's in the imputations of V as quotas, w_i, it is clear that the w_i are not individual expected values because $\sum w = 7.50$, which is greater than the value of the game, $v(I_n) = 6.00$. Nor are the average, m_i, of the quotas (in the principal imputations) individual expected values because $m_1 = 1.00$, $m_2 = 1.67$, and $m_3 = 2.33$, and $\sum m_i = 5.00$, which is less than the value of the game.

Since one cannot, in these simpleminded ways, transform a V-solution into expected values, a better procedure to find them is to go back to the beginning—back, that is, to the characteristic function. This is what the Shapley value does. The V-solution is inferred from the characteristic function in answer to the question: how might players in each coalition be expected to divide its value? On the other hand, the Shapley value is inferred from the characteristic function in answer to the question: how much might players expect to win, given various possibilities of coalitions?

THE POWER INDEX

The power index is a version of the Shapley value fitted to legislative circumstances. Because we are modeling a legislature, we assume that only winning coalitions (i.e., those which have as many votes as—or more than—are required to pass a motion) have positive value. Losing and blocking coalitions have no value, which accords with the intuitive perception that one cannot achieve a legislative goal unless one can put through a motion. This is a bold simplification, of course, to ignore the negative value of losing and the possible gains in delaying tactics. Further, we assume that minimal winning coalitions have as much or more value than any larger coalition, where minimum winning means a coalition that would cease to be winning if one vote were subtracted. The rationale for this assumption is that, after a coalition has won, additional members are unnecessary and cannot therefore add value.[3] Thus we get a characteristic function [in the $(0, 1)$-normalization], where m is the minimal winning size:

$$v(S) = 0 \quad \text{if } s < m,$$
$$v(S) = 1 \quad \text{if } s \geq m.$$

(Of course, m and s may be votes as well as persons.) Finally, in the spirit of the Shapley value, we assume that the uniquely significant position is that of the chronologically last-added member of a minimal winning coalition. This position is known conventionally as the pivot, p. We then define a power index, ϕ, for a player, i:

$$\phi_i = \frac{p_i}{n!} \, ,$$

where "p_i" is the number of sequences in which i pivots. Thus the index is a ratio of, on the one hand, the number of sequences in which i makes the marginal contribution to winning and, on the other hand, the total number of sequences.

The power index is supposed to be a measure of a single legislator's chance to influence. To political scientists of an empirical bent it often seems far too abstract to capture the variety and nuances of legislative situations. Nevertheless, it embodies, as one of us has shown elsewhere, a quite defensible model

---

[3]In Chapter 7 we analyze the situation in which additional members weaken a coalition and thus decrease its value; here, however, we ignore that feature of the world.

of a legislature, where there are supporters and opponents of a motion, as well as some members who are undecided.[4]

> Let the manager of a bill persuade by various inducements (such as rewriting the bill, promising votes on another bill, etc.) enough of the undecided to support the bill so that the supporters become a minimal majority. In such circumstances, when the vote occurs, some of the undecided who were not approached by the bill's manager may nevertheless vote for the bill, perhaps because they have concluded that their vote will make a good impression on their constituents. One can say that the original supporters and especially those undecideds who became supporters for a consideration have influenced the outcome. But it is very hard to say the same thing about the undecideds who became supporters without solicitation, i.e., those who joined after the pivot. These latter have not influenced the form of the bill which passes, nor have they traded influence on this bill for influence on another one . . . So we shall assume that their support is without significance. . . .
>
> Similarly, we may discount the influence of the supporters who preceded the pivot. Typically, the main inducement the manager of a bill offers to the undecideds is a modification of the bill into something they can support. Presumably, the original supporters were satisfied with the bill as originally introduced, so that each modification lessens the desirability of the bill for them. Hence the undecideds who have become supporters after modification are more satisfied with the modified form of the bill, while the original supporters are less satisfied. Carrying this argument to extremes, the single legislator most satisfied is the last one added to the minimal winning coalition, that is, the pivot.
>
> . . . Arrange the undecideds on a scale of hostility to the bill as originally introduced and consider the problem of the manager of a bill who is soliciting their support. . . . Presumably the least hostile will become a supporter for the lowest price (i.e., the smallest promise), the next least hostile for the next higher price, and so forth. Since we can assume the manager of the bill has limited resources, we can assume also that he will buy the least hostile undecided first, the next least hostile second, and so forth. Thus clearly the highest price he must pay goes to the legislator in the pivot position.

Although the power index thus makes intuitive sense, it is not intended to be a description of nature, except in a very broad stroke. On the contrary, it is intended as a means of evaluating all possibilities of coalition-formation, even though one knows almost certainly that some possible coalitions will not occur. The problem is that one does not know which will occur and which will not. It is certain, however, that only some will occur; and, to the extent that the nonoccurring are reflected in the index, it is of course inaccurate. Probability calculations provide a precise description of, say, roulette only after much play, although before the play they are an excellent description of one's chances. Likewise the power index is probably not accurate about any one constitution until the experience with it is longer than the careers of men.

---

[4]William H. Riker and Lloyd S. Shapley, "Weighted Voting: A Mathematical Analysis for Instrumental Judgments," in Roland Pennock and John W. Chapman, eds., *Nomos X: Representation* (New York: Atherton Press, 1968), pp. 199–216.

And very few constitutions last that long without significant modification—certainly, at least, very few or none in the modern world. And in that sense the index is an inaccurate prediction, even though it is a good description of one's chances.

For that reason, one may use the index to evaluate one's prospects in a legislature under a proposed constitution. Suppose one does so and finds that one has an advantage in the sense that one's power index is greater than one's equal weight in the proposed system, that is, $\phi_i > 1/n$. And on the basis of this evaluation alone, one might decide to support the proposal, even though one knows that the advantage showed by the index may be forthcoming only occasionally. Accidents of events (e.g., long-term changes in partisan habits of voters) may destroy the advantage so that it subsequently turns out that i never pivots. But this does not mean i was ill-advised to use the index for his decision. Nothing can tell him the future for certain, and the failure of the index as a prediction is nothing more than the failure of men to take *all* relevant detail into consideration. What makes the index attractive is that it captures the several possibilities more reasonably than any intuitive judgment.

The index is an expected value. The statement "i's chance of pivoting is ϕ_i" is of exactly the same kind as "i's chance of tossing heads is $\frac{1}{2}$." As an expected value or probability statement, its validity for the real world depends on whether or not the feature extracted in the calculation is in fact crucial in the real world. We have indicated that it makes sense to us, but we cannot be sure that it makes sense to everybody. One of us has therefore endeavored to find out whether or not real politicians behave as if they coveted the chance to be pivotal. While the investigation was inconclusive, it did, we believe, unearth some evidence that politicians want to pivot.[5]

In the Third and Fourth French Republics, with ten to twenty parliamentary parties and many more electoral ones, party loyalty in the legislature was relatively weak. But, while legislators often changed parties, internal party discipline was fairly tight on roll calls. Hence the party, despite changes in size, tended to act as a unit. This was especially true of extremist parties on the right and left, which in the Fourth Republic were a majority. Hence, ignoring the fact that moderate parties were poorly disciplined, one could interpret the legislature as frequently changing games with ten to twenty differently weighted players, that is, players with different numbers of votes. Since in a weighted majority game the power index for each player can vary remarkably, it may have been that legislators migrated from one party to another to gain chances to pivot. If legislators indeed behaved as if they were trying so to gain, it would perhaps indicate that real people desired to pivot.

To test for this possibility, all migrations in 1953–54 were examined. There were 34 such migrations involving 61 changes of party affiliation by 46 mem-

[5]William H. Riker, "A Test of the Adequacy of the Power Index," *Behavioral Science*, vol. 4 (1959), pp. 120–131.

bers. For each party, A, with a members, a power index was calculated for the party, when the party was interpreted as a unified voter. For each individual i in party A, a power index was calculated on the assumption that each shared equally in the party's earnings:

$$\phi_i = \frac{\phi_A}{a}.$$

Furthermore, ϕ_i was calculated in game G_α, which existed before a migration, and in game G_β, which existed after the migration. Thus, for each migration j, where j is a member of the set M of migrations, it is possible to calculate a value, R, for the migrator, i:

$$R_{ij} = (\phi_i; G_\beta) - (\phi_i; G_\alpha).$$

The test then was: if for all i, $\sum_{j \in M} R_{ij}$ is positive, then legislators were acting to increase the chance to pivot. Unless this result was unconscious, one could then infer they desired to do so. As it turned out, however, $\sum R_{ij}$ was a tiny negative number, so that one could easily conclude that legislators were not noticing their chances to pivot.

On the other hand, another circumstance suggested that the chance to pivot provided a strong motive for migration. In most weighted majority games, some players have an advantage (i.e., $\phi_i > 1/n$, where n is the number of players) and others a disadvantage. In this case one would expect migrations to occur when players were disadvantaged, which is mostly what happened: ". . . of the 61 individual changes of party affiliation, 45 occurred when the member was in a disadvantageous position . . . . Some of these were in an exceptionally bad position: Seven suffered a disadvantage of 15% or more and one was 43%. Furthermore, in no instance in which an advantageously situated member migrated was the advantage more than 5% . . . . Advantages of this order are surely not perceptible in day-to-day bargaining."[6]

The conclusion of this study is that in large assemblies such as the 1953–54 French one (627 members), variations in the index are hard to observe unless they are large. But, when large, they may occasion efforts to increase the chance to pivot.

Features of the Power Index

We now examine some of the features of the power index. When voters have equal votes and are for all practical purposes interchangeable, the power index reflects this symmetry:

$$\phi_i = 1/n,$$

where there are n voters in the system. Thus, in a three-person system where

[6]Riker, "A Test of the Adequacy of the Power Index," p. 130.

it takes two to win, we have six sequences:

$$\text{(a) } 123 \quad \text{(b) } 132 \quad \text{(c) } 213$$
$$\text{(d) } 231 \quad \text{(e) } 312 \quad \text{(f) } 321$$

Voter 1 is in the pivot (i.e., second) position in sequences (c) and (e), so: $\phi_1 = \frac{2}{6} = \frac{1}{3}$. Voter 2 pivots twice [in (a) and (f)] as does voter 3 [in (b) and (d)], so: $\phi_2 = \phi_3 = \frac{2}{6} = \frac{1}{3}$.

But the initial position of the members need not be symmetric. One can have more votes than another; the procedure by which they vote may be different; and so on. In such cases the index is also not symmetric, but the distance from symmetry is not typically the same in the index and the initial position, at least for the small numbers of people found in legislatures. Even so small a departure from symmetry as to divide otherwise equal legislators into two houses results in a significantly different index for members. Of course, if, for example, one house always originates bills, its members cannot, in a formal sense, pivot. But, assuming that coalitions are made by managers who approach undecided members without regard to house of membership, then it would appear that members have equal chances to pivot. But this not so. Consider, for example, a two-house legislature with three members in one house and five in the other and the rule of passage that a motion must have a majority in each house. Let A: $(a_1, a_2, a_3, a_4, a_5)$ and B: (b_1, b_2, b_3) be the houses. The opportunities for a_1 to pivot are:

1. When he is preceded by two other members of A and two members of B. The number of possible combinations of a's to precede a_1 is $\binom{4}{2}$ and the number of possible combinations of b's also to precede a_1 is $\binom{3}{2}$. The four predecessors of a_1 may be permuted 4! times and the three successors 3! times. Thus the number of sequences is

$$a_i \; a_j \; b_i \; b_j \; \left| \begin{array}{c} \text{pivot} \\ a_1 \end{array} \right| \; a_k \; a_h \; b_k$$

$$\binom{4}{2} \; 4! \; \binom{3}{2} \qquad\qquad 3!$$

$$\frac{4!}{2! \, 2!} \cdot 4! \cdot \frac{3!}{2! \, 1!} \cdot 3! = 2592 \text{ sequences.}$$

2. When a_1 is preceded by two other members of A and three members of B:

$$a_i \; a_j \; b_i \; b_j \; b_k \; \left| \begin{array}{c} \text{pivot} \\ a_1 \end{array} \right| \; a_k \; a_h$$

$$\binom{4}{2} \; 5! \; \binom{3}{3} \qquad\qquad 2!$$

$$\frac{4!}{2! \, 2!} \cdot 5! \cdot \frac{3!}{3! \, 1!} \cdot 2! = 1440 \text{ sequences.}$$

Hence there are 4032 sequences in which a_1 pivots, and his index is

$$\phi_{a_1} = \frac{p(a_1)}{n!} = \frac{4032}{40,320} = \frac{1}{10} \, .$$

The members of A are in a symmetric position within A, so

$$\phi_{a_2} = \cdots = \phi_{a_5} = \frac{1}{10} \,.$$

And the index for the whole house is

$$\phi_A = \frac{1}{2} \,.$$

On the other hand, the index for the B house is also $\frac{1}{2}$, and since the positions of its members are also symmetric, we have

$$\phi_{b_i} = \frac{1}{2} \cdot \frac{1}{3} = \frac{1}{6} \,.$$

Thus the members of the smaller house have a higher index than the members of the larger house even though the eight legislators are in all other ways equal. Perhaps this is why Senators usually have more prestige than Representatives.

Possibly the most extreme variation from symmetry occurs when voters have different numbers of votes, as do the parties in France in the previous example. To give the calculation for a simpler example, consider a three person committee in which the voters have 50, 49, and 1 votes respectively, and at least 51 votes can win (as might happen in, e.g., the board of a small corporation). Then the pivots are those marked with asterisks in the six sequences:

$$1, 49, 50^*; \qquad 49, 1, 50^*; \qquad 50, 1^*, 49;$$
$$1, 50^*, 49; \qquad 49, 50^*, 1; \qquad 50, 49^*, 1.$$

The indices are

$$\phi_1 = \frac{1}{6}, \qquad \phi_{49} = \frac{1}{6}, \qquad \phi_{50} = \frac{2}{3},$$

which reflects the fact that 50 can pivot with either of the others, but 49 and 1 can pivot only with 50.

It is surprising that the player with 1 percent of the votes has $16\frac{2}{3}$ percent of the chance to pivot. This kind of divergence is common, however, so a measure of divergence, ρ, has been devised:

$$\rho_w = \phi_w / \frac{w}{W} \,,$$

where w is the number of votes or weight for a player and W is the total votes or total weight. Thus, in this case,

$$\rho_1 = \frac{1}{6} / \frac{1}{100} = 16.67,$$

$$\rho_{49} = \frac{1}{6} / \frac{49}{100} = .34,$$

$$\rho_{50} = \frac{2}{3} / \frac{50}{100} = 1.33.$$

In small bodies such as this one, ρ can be very large. But in larger bodies with no member close to one-half, no dummies, and a wide range of weights, ρ

does not vary widely. In the Electoral College in the United States, where currently weights (i.e., votes for states) range from 3 to 43, the range of ρ is:[7]

$$\rho_3 = 0.97, \qquad \rho_{43} = 1.08.$$

In this respect, at least, the distortions of the Electoral College are not so great as is commonly argued and supposed.

Applications of the Power Index

Because of the remarkable and far from obvious variations in the index, it yields some enlightening views of specific institutions. We report several:[8]

1. *Legislature of Nassau County, New York*. This body has had weighted voting since 1957, and in 1964 the six members had votes thus: 31, 31, 28, 21, 2, 2.[9] With a total of 115 votes, a minimal winning majority is 58. Hence, for some legislator, a_i, to pivot, some combination of other players must total a sum in the range from $(58 - a_i)$ to 57. It is perhaps not surprising that no subset of the others totals 56 or 57, so that the legislators with 2 votes can never pivot. But it is also the case that no subset of the others totals from $(58 - 21 = 37)$ to 57, so that the legislator with 21 votes is also a dummy. The indices in fact are: $\phi_{31} = \frac{1}{3}$; $\phi_{28} = \frac{1}{3}$; $\phi_{21} = \phi_2 = 0$. It is hard to believe that citizens of any political unit would consciously assent to a system in which their representatives can *never* win in the sense that their representatives' votes are *never* critical. Probably the bizarre defects of this legislature result entirely from a careless oversight.

2. *Weighted voting in state legislatures*. Since American experience has not included much weighted voting (except the Electoral College), American scholars have not devoted much attention to unsymmetric voting. Lacking the lore which they would have if there were active scholarship on the subject, politicians have occasionally proposed very strange things. A particularly humorous example, which we noted in Chapter 2, is the campaign that spon-

---

[7]Irwin Mann and L.S. Shapley, "The *a priori* Voting Strength of the Electoral College," in Martin Shubik, ed., *Game Theory and Related Approaches to Social Behavior* (New York: Wiley, 1964), pp. 151–165. It should be pointed out, however, that the Electoral College involves an additional distortion, namely a unit rule for voters within a state. Banzhaf has shown that, as a result of this additional weighting, a vote in New York (then the largest state) has about 3.312 times as much chance to pivot as a vote in the District of Columbia (the smallest voting unit). See John F. Banzhaf, III, "One Man, 3.312 Votes: A Mathematical Analysis of the Electoral College," *Villanova Law Review*, vol. 13 (1968), pp. 304–332. See also Lawrence D. Longley and John H. Yunker, "The Biases of the Electoral College" forthcoming in a Brookings volume, *Democracy and Presidential Selection*.

[8]In addition to the several applications reported here, see Glendon Schubert, *Quantitative Analysis of Judicial Behavior* (New York: Free Press, 1959), chap.4, on the Supreme Court, and Samuel Krislov, "The Power Index, Reapportionment and the Principle of One Man, One Vote," *Modern Uses of Logic in Law*, vol. 7 (1965), pp. 37–44, on the New York City Board of Estimate.

[9]John F. Banzhaf, III, "Weighted Voting Doesn't Work: A Mathematical Analysis," *Rutgers Law Review*, vol. 19 (1965), pp. 317–343.

taneously erupted all over the country to evade the effects of the rulings of the Supreme Court in *Baker* v. *Carr* and *Reynolds* v. *Sims*.[10] Since 1900 the political leaders of rural areas (which have been steadily losing population) have often attempted to evade the consequent decline of their influence in the legislature. Instead of accepting fewer rural legislators, they have refused to redistrict, so that they represented far fewer people than did legislators from urban districts. Indeed in the 1940's and 1950's it was not uncommon to find state legislatures where the average district size was c citizens, but rural legislators had districts with as few as $c/2$ or $c/3$. In the two decisions, the Court required that districts be redrawn so that each citizen would have the same chance as every other to influence the outcome of the legislative process. While most legislatures complied in the anticipated way by equalizing districts, some proposed to retain their unequal districts but to compensate with inversely unequal voting. In this unsymmetric system, people in rural areas would still have the same number of representatives, but each representative would have a smaller vote. Thus no rural legislator would lose his job by redistricting.

Such plans were advocated by legislators from rural places as a great benefit to rural voters; conversely they were opposed by legislators from urban places. In large legislative bodies (e.g., over twenty members) it is usually the case that members with larger weights have greater than proportional chances to pivot. Both advocates and opponents thus behaved irrationally in terms of the interests of their constituents. Urban legislators, who opposed, should have favored weighted voting; and rural legislators, who proposed it, should have kept silent.

3. *Security Council—United Nations*. State legislatures need not have weighted voting; but it is less easy to avoid in international bodies. So long as we live in a world of nation-states with wide variations in population, military strength, gross product, natural resources, and so on, it is hard to imagine national rulers agreeing to equal votes in international bodies. In 1945, when the U.N. was formed, the big nations were willing to allow the little ones equality in the Assembly, which had relatively little power. But they insisted on unequal votes in the Security Council where, it was anticipated, most business would be transacted. Assuming such insistence is typical, weighted voting seems inevitable in international voting bodies. But since political scientists and constitutional lawyers have not heretofore understood it, it is not surprising that they have produced results that they probably didn't desire.

In the voting system originally laid down for the Security Council, there were five permanent members (China, France, United Kingdom, United States, Soviet Union), and six nonpermanent members. Seven votes (including those of all five permanent members) were required to pass substantive motions. It is easy to calculate the index for some nonpermanent member. Letting P_i, $i = 1, \ldots, 5$, stand for permanent members, and T_i, $i = 1, \ldots, 6$, stand

[10]Riker and Shapley, "Weighted Voting," pp. 200, 210–216.

for nonpermanent or temporary members, it must be the case, for T_1 to pivot, that he is preceded by all five permanent members and exactly one other temporary one:

$$P_1\,P_2\,P_3\,P_4\,P_5\,T_2\;\Big|\;\underset{\text{pivot}}{T_1}\;\Big|\;T_3\,T_4\,T_5\,T_6$$

Since any one of the $\binom{5}{1}$ other temporary members may precede T_1, since the members preceding T_1 can be permuted 6! ways, since the four members succeeding T_1 can be permuted 4! ways, and since there are 11! ways of permuting all the members, we have

$$\phi_{T_1} = \binom{5}{1}\frac{6!\,4!}{11!} = \frac{1}{462}\,, \quad \text{or about } 0.002.$$

Furthermore:

$$\sum_{i=1}^{6}\phi_{T_i} = \frac{6}{462} = \frac{1}{77}\,, \quad \text{or about } 0.013,$$

$$\sum_{i=1}^{5}\phi_{P_i} \quad\;\; = \frac{76}{77}\,, \quad \text{or about } 0.987,$$

and

$$\phi_{P_i} = \frac{76}{77} \cdot \frac{1}{5} = \frac{76}{385}\,, \quad \text{or about } 0.197.$$

The ratio of the index of a permanent member to a temporary one is thus better than 98 to 1, a very large disparity.

Did the framers intend so wide a difference? We cannot know, mainly because the index was invented several years after the Charter was written. We do know, however, that in the 1930's one of the main criticisms uttered of the League of Nations was that small, unimportant governments had as loud a voice as great powers. We know also that one of the main dogmas that the framers of the U.N. brought with them to San Francisco was that the constitutional position of great powers should be strengthened. But did they wish the ratio to be 98 to 1? We doubt it. We suspect that, without a good method of measurement, they simply made an error.

In 1965, apparently to correct for the lack of influence of the small governments, the Security Council was increased in size from eleven to fifteen and a minimal majority was increased to nine (including the five permanent members). Owing, probably, to the lawyers' indifference to theory, however, the correction failed to correct. True, four more small governments got seats on the Security Council; but the indices otherwise remained almost exactly the same:

$$\phi_{T_i} = \frac{4}{2145}\,, \quad \text{or about } 0.0018,$$

so that, individually, the chance of a small government to pivot declined. Since there were more of them, however, their total chance improved slightly:

$$\sum_{i=1}^{10} \phi_{T_i} = \frac{40}{2145} = \frac{8}{429}, \quad \text{or about } 0.018$$

And the chance of a single great power therefore declined, ever so slightly:

$$\phi_{P_1} = \frac{421}{2145}, \quad \text{or about } 0.196$$

Aside from four more jobs, therefore, this reform accomplished nothing. Had the reformers calculated a few power indices, they might well have made the minimal majority eleven out of fifteen, so that

$$\phi_{T_i} = \frac{6}{715} \text{ or about } 0.008 \quad \text{and} \quad \phi_{P_i} = \frac{131}{715} \text{ or about } 0.183,$$

or even twelve, so that

$$\phi_{T_i} = \frac{1}{65} \text{ or about } 0.015 \quad \text{and} \quad \phi_{P_i} = \frac{11}{65} \text{ or about } 0.170,$$

which is, we think likely, about what was originally intended.

4. *Models of coalition formation.* All the applications so far discussed involve direct interpretation of existing constitutions. Brams and Riker have also tried to use the power index (or something like it) to explain in the abstract a kind of political behavior, namely the formation of coalitions in decision-making bodies.[11] As we point out in the next chapter, coalition-making is almost the central process of politics and yet political scientists know very little about its underlying principles. In Chapter 5 we offer several static theories about the end product of the process. These are theories about the way reasonable people might end up in coalitions, but they say nothing, of course, about the way people might get to this end. In Chapter 7 we offer a dynamic theory about the final steps of the formation of a winning coalition. But theories of neither kind have anything to say about how coalitions build up from single isolated members of the voting body to an agglomeration. It is to the analysis of this process that the Brams and Riker paper is addressed.

[11]Steven J. Brams and William Riker, "Models of Coalition Formation in Voting Bodies," *Mathematical Applications in Political Science*, vol. 6 (Charlottesville: University Press of Virginia, 1972), pp. 79–124. For subsequent elaborations of this analysis see Brams, "A Cost/Benefit Analysis of Coalition Formation in Voting Bodies," in Richard G. Niemi and Herbert F. Weisberg, eds., *Probability Models of Collective Decision-Making* (Columbus: Charles E. Merrill, 1972); Brams, "Positive Coalition Theory: The Relationship between Postulated Goals and Derived Behavior," in Cornelius P. Cotter *et al.*, eds., *Political Science Annual: Conflict, Competition, and Coalitions*, (Indianapolis: Bobbs-Merrill, 1972); Brams, "Three Equilibrium Models of Coalition Formation in Voting Bodies," in Julius Margolis and Henry Teune, eds., *Theories of Collective Behavior*, forthcoming; Brams and G. William Sensiba," The Win/Share Principle in National Party Conventions," in Donald R. Matthews, ed., *Democracy and Presidential Selection* (Washington, D.C.: Brookings Institution, forthcoming 1972); and Brams and John G. Heilman,"When to Join a Coalition, and With How Many Others, Depends On What You Expect the Outcome to Be" (forthcoming), *Public Choice*.

Their model concerns *protocoalitions*, that is, groups which seek to become winning or blocking coalitions at the end of the process but none of which is yet large enough to be either winning or blocking. Thus in a ten-member body with simple majority rule, groups of one, two, three, four, or five members are protocoalitions—provided no six-member winning coalition exists.

One can, of course, calculate values for any particular arrangement of protocoalitions as if it were a weighted voting game, so that there is a power index for each protocoalition in the arrangement. Thus, in a ten-member body, if there is one five-member protocoalition, another four-member one, and a third single-member one, then there is in effect a three-person game with weights 5, 4, and 1. It is possible, then, to treat the stages of coalition-formation as a process of going from a game with one set of weights to another with another set of weights. The weights and the power indices associated with them can be interpreted as indications of the opportunities available to the various protocoalitions in the larger game.

Brams and Riker calculate the power indices for all possible arrangements of protocoalitions in a sample ten-person majority-rule game, with the following restrictions on the action of protocoalitions:

(1) that there be two protocoalitions, *X* and *Y*, with promise of becoming winning coalitions, that *X* and *Y* have zero to six members, and that all other uncommitted protocoalitions have exactly one member each.

TABLE 6.2

Pivot Proportions of Protocoalitions

					Size of *Y*			
		0	1	2	3	4	5	6
	0 UNCOM	.10	.09	.08	.07	.06	.03	0
	X	0	0	0	0	0	0	0
	Y	0	.17	.33	.50	.66	.83	1
	1 UNCOM		.10	.11	.11	.10	.07	0
	X		.085	.07	.06	.04	0	0
	Y		.085	.17	.27	.42	.71	1
Size	2 UNCOM			.12	.13	.15	.11	0
of *X*	*X*			.15	.12	.06	0	0
	Y			.15	.23	.35	.67	1
	3 UNCOM				.17	.21	.20	0
	X				.17	.09	0	0
	Y				.17	.27	.60	1
	4 UNCOM					.33	.50	0
	X					.17	0	0
	Y					.17	.50	1
	5 UNCOM						0	
	X						0	
	Y						0	

SOURCE: Based on Brams and Riker, "Models of Coalition Formation in Voting Bodies."

(2) that there be considered in the calculation of the chance to pivot only those permutations (or combinations) containing a winning coalition of either X or Y but not both.

These calculations are set forth in Table 6.2.

This table reveals some interesting and suggestive features, expecially about the process by which uncommitted members might be expected to join X or Y. Suppose they (the uncommitted) follow the rule that, if they can make more by joining, they join, and if they can make more by remaining uncommitted, they remain uncommitted. Consider then cell $(1, 2)$ with this rule in mind and suppose that players of the ten-person game are for the moment arranged in that way. What can the uncommitted players be expected to do? If they remain uncommitted, each retains a value of 0.11. If one joins Y to go to cell $(1, 3)$, he contributes at most 0.10 to Y's value (for Y goes from .17 to .27) and hence is worth less than if he remained uncommitted. If one joins X to go to cell $(2, 2)$, he contributes at most 0.08 to X and thus has at most a value of 0.08. Clearly, in such a cell there seems to be a strong force toward uncommitment. But in the adjacent cell $(1, 3)$, each uncommitted member has a motive to join Y because, by this act, he increases Y's value from 0.27 to 0.42 and, if he gets the full marginal contribution, he increases his own value from 0.11 to 0.15. On the other hand if he stays uncommitted his value falls from 0.11 to 0.10, and if he joins X his value falls from 0.11 to 0.06.

Cells like $(1, 3)$ Brams and Riker call "take-off points." These are highly unstable in that in them the uncommitted members have a strong motive to become committed. Such a motive can be described as a bandwagon effect. An interesting feature of this effect is that it seems to occur in the model when one protocoalition (but not the other) is approaching the minimal winning majority size. Commonsense analysis has always suggested that this is where bandwagon effects occur; and in this model they appear as a significantly heightened chance to win. Brams and Riker look for "take-off points" in national party conventions and, for the few cases available, conclude that they occur in this context at about 40 percent of the vote. That they are identifiable in every relevant case, even though the cases are few, suggests that there may in fact be inflection points like this one in the real world.

No one would suggest that investigations of this sort are conclusive. They do, however, suggest interesting possibilities for the use of the power index to identify and even explain real-world phenomena as well as to evaluate constitutions.

Conclusion

The power index is a way of saying that, on the average, a particular participant, i, may expect to pivot a calculated proportion, ϕ_i, of the time. This calculated proportion is an equilibrium of Type II. It is single-valued for i, but it is likely to be achieved in nature only in the long term. As an equilibrium, it is of course also a prediction about nature, albeit a weak one. The importance of the index is not, however, as a prediction, but rather as a method of uttering normative judgments on constitutions, even though it may be used, as in the last-mentioned application, to arrive at rules of behavior.

SUGGESTIONS FOR FURTHER READING

Two good sources for the theory of this chapter are L. S. SHAPLEY, "A Value for N-Person Games," in H. W. KUHN and A. W. TUCKER, eds., *Contributions to the Theory of Games,* vol. 2 Annals of Mathematics Studies, no. 28 (Princeton, N. J.: Princeton University Press, 1953), and GUILLERMO OWEN, *Game Theory* (Philadelphia: Saunders, 1968), chap. 9. A main application is in L. S. SHAPLEY and MARTIN SHUBIK, "A Method for Evaluating the Distribution of Power in a Committee System," *American Political Science Review,* vol. 48 (1954), pp. 787–792. Other papers on applications are cited in the footnotes to the chapter.

7

The Size Principle

The theory of the V-solution and of the core, with their Type III (nonunique) equilibria, are highly informative theoretically because they help us to understand the fundamental nature of the political environment. But often they are not of much use for understanding or interpreting specific political phenomena. To get to the specifics and thence to Type II or even, hopefully, Type I equilibria, we must make more restrictive assumptions and ask more restricted questions. To get a specific content out of the theory machine we must put specific content in.

This is what is involved in, for example, the notion of the power index, which leads to a Type II (weak, unique) equilibrium. Some of the specific assumptions it uses to restrict the theory are the principle of division according to marginal contribution and the principle of insufficient reason. Probably the most significant and restrictive assumption is the inclusion in the theory of the notions of winning and losing, notions which are simply not present in solution theory and which bring a world of sociological content into the game. Not only does the Shapley value involve more specific assumptions, it also asks a different and more concrete question. While the general theory asks, "What is the range of divisions of the payoff?", the theory of value asks, "What can a particular player expect to win?" This new question, with its individualistic reference, directs the theorizing to a much more specific result.

Thus, starting from the general theory, a more specific question and more restrictive assumptions permit us to utter some interesting—even testable—sentences about the real world. This is what can be achieved when one starts with a general theory. While it is not always of much use for directly interpreting nature, it provides a model which, when expanded in relevant ways, does allow for direct study of nature.

In this chapter we turn to another and quite different expansion of the theory, one that asks a quite different question and leads to a Type II equilibrium. This is the notion of the *size principle* in zero-sum games, which was originally developed by one of us.[1] It is the assertion that "In *n*-person zero-sum games, where side payments are permitted, where players are rational, and where they have perfect information, only minimum winning coalitions occur." Minimum winning coalitions are winning coalitions that would cease to be winning if some member were subtracted. Thus the size principle asserts that winning coalitions will not be larger than they need to be.

Instead of asking, "How will the players divide the payoff?", the theory of the size principle asks a seemingly unrelated question, "What size will the winning coalition be?" These questions are not so far apart as it might first appear. They are related in purpose thus: Often the core and the V-solution contain imputations appropriate for winning coalitions of different sizes. The core, in particular, contains imputations for coalitions of the whole—maximum winning coalitions. If one can distinguish just one size of coalition as likely to occur, then the ambiguity of the solution concepts has been reduced to just those of the identified size. Hence, the size principle can be one way to throw away some of the embarrassing riches of the solution notions, especially in games with very large numbers of players.

In addition, the question of size is related to the question of division in method as well as purpose. Since the size of a coalition depends in large part on the resources available to pay the members for belonging to it, the two kinds of questions (i.e., concerning payoff and size) can be answered from the same fundamental model. We want to show that winning coalitions tend toward minimal winning size; so we begin by recalling the properties of the characteristic function of a zero-sum game, which we discuss in detail on pp. 122 to 128:

$$v(\phi) = 0, \tag{7.1}$$
$$v(S \cup T) \geq v(S) + v(T) \quad \text{(superadditivity)}, \tag{7.2}$$
$$v(S) = -v(-S) \quad \text{(zero-sum)}, \tag{7.3}$$
$$v(I_n) = 0 \quad \text{[from (7.1) and (7.3)]}. \tag{7.4}$$

If in addition we adopt the convention that the worst a player can do is to be in a coalition by himself and thereby receive the payoff of $-\gamma$, we have

$$v(\{i\}) = -\gamma. \tag{7.5}$$

The entire range of possibilities for the characteristic function may be depicted graphically as in Figure 7.1. There the size of coalitions (i.e., the number of members) is measured on the horizontal axis and the value of coalitions (i.e.,

[1] William H. Riker, *The Theory of Political Coalitions* (New Haven: Yale University Press, 1962). It is also discussed by Riker, "A New Proof of the Size Principle," in Joseph Bernd, ed., *Mathematical Applications in Political Science*, vol. 2 (Dallas: Southern Methodist University Press, 1967), pp. 167–174.

the transferable utility) is measured on the vertical axis. Some points can be ascertained directly from the properties (7.1) to (7.5): By (7.1) the value of the empty set is zero; hence (0, 0). By (7.5) the value of the set with one member is $-\gamma$; hence $(1, -\gamma)$. Since the complement of the set with $(n-1)$ members is the one-member set, condition (7.3) requires that $v(\{n-1\}) = -v(\{1\})$. We already know from (7.5) that $v(\{i\}) = -\gamma$, so $v(\{n-1\}) = --\gamma = \gamma$. Hence, we have $(n-1, \gamma)$. Finally, by (7.4) the value of the grand coalition is zero, so $(n, 0)$ is fixed. These four points are shown as large dots in Figure 7.1.

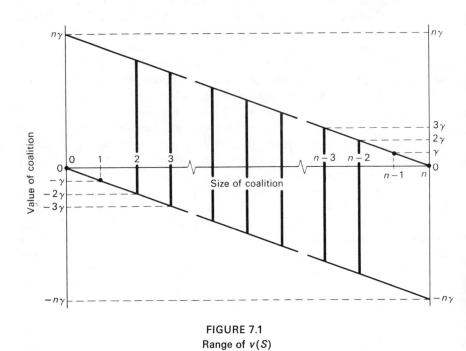

FIGURE 7.1
Range of $v(S)$

There are further constraints, however, on the values of coalitions. These constraints are derived from the assumptions of individual rationality. If the worst a single player can do is $-\gamma$, then the worst that a coalition of size s can do is $(-s\gamma)$—that is, the sum of the worst for each member. This gives a minimum value for each coalition of size s, as indicated in Figure 7.1 by the diagonal line from the point $(0, 0)$ to the point $(n, -n\gamma)$. At the other extreme, the best a coalition can do is determined by what its complement can lose, because $v(S) = -v(-S)$. If S has s members, $-S$ has $(n-s)$ members, so that $v(S) = -v(\{n-s\})$. Since $v(\{n-s\}) = -(n-s)\gamma$, it follows that $v(S) = (n-s)\gamma$. This gives a maximum value for each coalition of size s, as indicated in Figure 7.1 by the diagonal line from the point $(0, n\gamma)$ to the point $(n, 0)$. Consequently, there is a fixed range for $v(S)$ of any given size, s:

$$-s\gamma \leq v\,(S) \leq (n-s)\gamma.$$

This range is depicted in Figure 7.1 as a bold vertical line for each size s. All the possible values for any coalition are thus the four dots and the bold vertical lines on Figure 7.1.

POLITICAL CONSTRAINTS ON THE CHARACTERISTIC FUNCTION

On the basis of the characteristic function alone, we cannot further limit the range. But if we add some sociological assumptions to the mathematical ones, the range may be significantly abbreviated. In adding such assumptions we must be careful that they are reasonable in the applications we expect. If they are restrictions customarily followed in the political world, then we do no more than put some political content into von Neumann's and Morgenstern's notion of a "standard of behavior." If, however, we add a restriction that patently does not apply to politics, at best we create an unrealistic model. The assumptions described in the next paragraphs are, we believe, politically unexceptional—at least for zero-sum games—and for that reason we do not hesitate to make them here.

The political restrictions that we add to the mathematical ones are:

1. *Winning coalitions have positive value; losing or blocking coalitions have negative or zero value.* A winning coalition is defined as one that has at least m members, where m is some arbitrary majority point. Typically this point is $(n+1)/2$, if n is odd, and $(n/2)+1$, if n is even; but of course required majorities may be larger, and indeed the range of m is

   $$\frac{(n+1)}{2} \leq m \leq n \quad \text{or} \quad (\frac{n}{2})+1 \leq m \leq n.$$

   This requirement accords with our commonsense understanding that in a parliamentary body or an election, when S and $-S$ completely partition I_n, the larger coalition typically receives a positive payoff and the smaller a negative one, although if both the larger and the smaller are in the range of blocking coalitions both may receive zero. In some kinds of situations, mere numbers may not determine the recipient of value (e.g., as in a war between a small valiant army and a large indifferent one); but we can compensate for that fact by thinking of sizes of coalitions in terms of the sums of (unequal) weights of members rather than in terms merely of the sum of members themselves. In any event, we assume there is some kind of majority, either of persons or weights, and that only coalitions as large as or larger than the majority point are winning in the sense that they receive positive payoffs. We can state this assumption formally thus:

   $$\text{for } s < m, \quad -s\gamma \leq v(S) \leq 0;$$
   $$\text{for } s \geq m, \quad 0 \leq v(S) \leq (n-s)\gamma.$$

2. *The primary goal of players is to form winning coalitions.* That is, since only winning coalitions have positive value and since players are assumed to wish to obtain positive value, the formation of such coalitions is the main goal of the players.

3. *Winning coalitions are associated with imputations in which all members receive positive payoffs.*

Inconsistencies arise if the winning coalition is allowed to contain losers, and this assumption is aimed simply at eliminating these inconsistencies.

4. *Members of a winning coalition have control over its membership so that they can increase the size at will.* (Of course, only some members have this control, for ejected members obviously are without influence.) Once we have restricted the values of coalitions generally so that only winning coalitions can have positive value, it is necessary to assume that members of that kind of coalition can at least keep out the losers. If they could not do so, losers would flock into the winning coalition until they produced I_n, where at least $v(I_n) = 0$. Without the ability to restrict membership, no winning coalition with positive value could be expected to exist. On the other hand, unless coalitions have the concomitant ability to add members, blocking coalitions, for example, could not grow into winning ones and ties could never be resolved. Hence it seems necessary for realism, once having assumed the notion of a majority, also to assume that coalitions can contract or expand only by the volition of some of their members. This assumption is less restrictive than it may appear. When a bill is written or a candidate's platform is chosen, typically the content makes it difficult for some people to belong to the supporting coalition. This is a method of exclusion. For example, in current American politics, a platform emphasizing "law and order" is effectively a means of excluding blacks from the candidate's coalition.

Having made these additional sociological assumptions, we use them to restrict further the range of characteristic functions. In Figure 7.2 we depict this effect. In this figure we restrict winning coalitions to positive values and losing coalitions to negative ones. (It should be emphasized, of course, that the

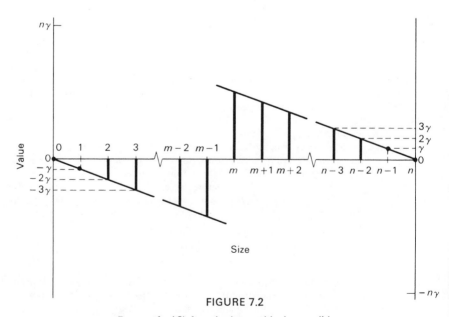

FIGURE 7.2

Range of $v(S)$ for winning and losing coalitions.

diagonal lines in the upper right and lower left of Figure 7.2 are maximum and minimum boundaries for characteristic functions, not characteristic functions themselves.

As is apparent in Figure 7.2, the range of $v(S)$ is now sufficiently restricted that it may be worthwhile to raise the question we intended from the beginning: "What size can we expect the winning coalition to be?" The values of winning and losing coalitions are, by reason of (7.3)—the zero-sum condition—and by (7.6)—the condition that only winning coalitions have positive value—rendered into mirror images of each other on the left and right sides of Figure 7.2. To know something about the winning coalitions is to know as much about losing ones. As a consequence we can confine our attention to the right side of Figure 7.2 from point $(m, 0)$ on the horizontal axis to point $(n, 0)$, as is done in Figure 7.3. From now on in this section, S will always be a winning coalition.

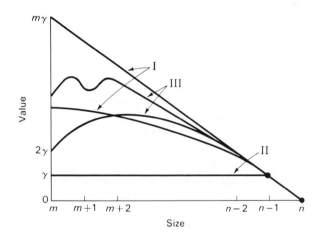

FIGURE 7.3

Since we have placed no restrictions on $v(S)$ besides those already mentioned, it is possible that the various coalitions of S in a particular game have any arbitrary selection of values within this range. Some examples are shown in Figure 7.3, where the curves are lines connecting the values of S for all S where $s \geq m$. [We will refer to this line as the line of $v(S)$, even though, strictly speaking, it is just a line connecting the discrete values of $v(S)$. Thus the line labeled "II" is a game in which all winning coalitions (except the grand coalition) have the same value regardless of size and the value of the grand coalition is zero:

$$\text{if } m \leq s < n, \quad v(S) = \Upsilon;$$
$$\text{if } s = n, \quad v(S) = 0.]$$

Although any arbitrary arrangements are possible, we may classify all the possible games in Figure 7.3 into categories according to the kind of forces working toward an equilibrium of size. We categorize the games according to the slope of the lines connecting the points of the characteristic function into those lines for which

I   the slope is always negative,
II   the slope is zero or negative,
III the slope is positive in part and negative in part.

[Note that since $v(I_n) = 0$ and $v(I_n - i) = \gamma$, where γ is positive, the slope must always be negative as one goes from the next to largest to the largest winning coalition. There can be no game with a wholly positive or wholly zero slope.]

DEVELOPMENT OF THE SIZE PRINCIPLE

The size principle is that, *assuming perfect information in zero-sum games, the equilibrium size of a winning coalition is always minimal.* (As in the discussion of the power index, we define a minimal winning coalition as one for which the subtraction of one member would render it nonwinning.) We now show that it holds for games in categories I and II of the shape of the characteristic function. We also offer some arguments to show that it holds in category III; but, since in this category we are forced to rely in part on an argument from organizational costs, we regard this demonstration as less powerful. Hence we assert that the size principle holds for certain only in categories I and II. Since, for reasons we offer subsequently, we do not believe category III applies to the real world, we do not believe this restriction is serious.

Case I: The slope of $v(S)$ is everywhere negative. It follows from this fact that $v(S) > v(S + i)$. Hence it is always advantageous, regardless of the division of $v(S + i)$ in $(S + i)$, for the s members of S to eject person i. They gain both what i was assigned and the increase in the value of S over $(S + i)$. Hence, by repeated applications of this analysis, the equilibrium size of S is m.

To clarify this argument, define $x_k{}^S$ as the payment to k when k is a member of coalition S. To analyze the gains to k from forming S by ejecting i from $(S + i)$, we note that $x_k{}^S$ is composed as follows:

$$x_k{}^S = x_k{}^{(S+i)} + \alpha_k x_i{}^{(S+i)} + \alpha_k[v(S) - v(S + i)], \qquad (7.7)$$
$$\text{(term 1)} \qquad \text{(term 2)} \qquad \text{(term 3)}$$

where α is simply an arbitrary fraction to divide the amounts in terms 2 and 3 among the members of S. (Since $\sum\limits_{k=1}^{s} \alpha_k = 1$, hereafter for convenience and simplicity we use $\alpha_k = 1/s$.) The foregoing equation says that k's earnings in S consist of

term 1—what he earned in $(S + i)$,
term 2—his share of what i earned in $(S + i)$,
term 3—his share of the gain from decreasing the size to S.

As a concrete example, consider the following characteristic function:

$$
\text{if } T \text{ has }
\begin{Bmatrix}
0 \\
1 \\
2 \\
3 \\
4 \\
5 \\
6 \\
7 \\
8 \\
9 \\
10 \\
11
\end{Bmatrix}
\text{members,}
\quad
\begin{aligned}
& \\
& \\
-(S+i) \\
-(S) \\
& \\
& \\
& \\
& \\
(S) \\
(S+i) \\
& \\
&
\end{aligned}
\quad
v(T) =
\begin{Bmatrix}
0 \\
-1 \\
-2 \\
-3 \\
-4 \\
-5 \\
5 \\
4 \\
3 \\
2 \\
1 \\
0
\end{Bmatrix}
$$

Let $(S + i)$ be a nine-member coalition and S an eight-member coalition. Assuming that, in both coalitions, members share rewards equally, we have

$$
x_k{}^S = \underbrace{\frac{1}{9}\, v(S + i)}_{\text{(term 1)}} + \underbrace{\frac{1}{8} \cdot \frac{1}{9}\, v(S + i)}_{\text{(term 2)}} + \underbrace{\frac{1}{8}\,[v(S) - v(S + i)]}_{\text{(term 3)}}
$$

$$
= \frac{1}{9} \cdot 2 + \frac{1}{8} \cdot \frac{1}{9} \cdot 2 + \frac{1}{8}(3 - 2)
$$

$$
= \frac{27}{72} = \frac{3}{8}\,.
$$

Since there are eight members of S,

$$
\sum x_k{}^S = 8 \cdot \frac{3}{8} = 3 = v(S).
$$

Thus as $(S+i)$ contracts to S, k gains from 0.22 to 0.38. Of course, when in $(S+i)$, k may not know who will be ejected and may therefore hesitate to reduce $(S + i)$, fearing that he, k, may be the one ejected. Assuming, however, that the members of S can agree, when in $(S + i)$, on who the i ejected will be, then we have identified two motives for each member of S to form S out of $(S + i)$: the gain in term 2 and the gain in term 3.

There is still a third motive. Suppose $(S + i)$ exists. Then the losing coalition is a two-member coalition, $-(S + i)$. These two members can form an alternative S, consisting of themselves and six of the nine members of $(S + i)$. We thus identify two methods of arriving at S of eight members:

1. Eject i from $(S + i)$. Then all eight members of S are former members of $(S + i)$. Identify an S with this history as simply S.
2. Two members of $-(S + i)$ and six members of $(S + i)$ join to form S. Identify an S with this history as a reconstituted coalition, S^r.

In S^r the two former members of $-(S+i)$ avoid the loss they had in their former coalition. Hence they have a powerful motive to bring S^r into existence. And, owing to this competition, eight members of $(S + i)$ who can eject the ninth have a powerful motive to bring S into existence simply to forestall S^r.

We thus identify at least three motives for the formation of S when $(S+i)$ exists:

(1) the gain of the amount $\alpha_k x_i{}^{(S+i)}$ or term 2 in (7.7);
(2) the gain of the amount $\alpha_k[v(S)-v(S+i)]$ or term 3 in (7.7);
(3) the avoidance of S^r.

Case II: The slope of $v(S)$ is zero or negative. Insofar as the slope is negative, all the considerations of Case I apply. Insofar as the slope is zero, the s members of S have, when they are in $(S + i)$, both motives (1) and (3) just listed to impel them to form S. Since at least (1) is an actual gain in which everyone can share, it is to be expected that S form. By repeated movements from $(S + i)$ to S, the equilibrium size of S is m.

Case III: The slope of $v(S)$ is sometimes positive and sometimes negative. It is doubtful if this case ever exists in the real world, at least in zero-sum situations such as we consider here. For instances of this case to occur, it must happen that players, *who know for sure they have won,* nevertheless keep on acquiring additional adherents. Of course, if players do not know they have won, they may well continue to add adherents, simply as insurance. We here assume perfect information, however, so that insurance is unnecessary. In the real world there are, of course, numerous instances in which players create coalitions larger than minimal winning size, but these are typically instances either in which players do not know *for certain* that they have won or in which they wish to demonstrate strength in some intersecting game. For example, they may be uncertain because they do not know how much it takes to win, as in warfare, or they may be uncertain because they do not know how many people have already joined, as in elections. For another example, they may want to appear to be a majority in a large unit even though the coalition is formed in a small unit, as committees try to appear unanimous in recommendations to the parent bodies. In any event, all instances of oversized coalitions we know of involve some kind of uncertainty, while this case involves deliberate expansion over a majority when players know both how much it takes to win and who has already joined them.

Such deliberate expansion over a majority involves a conflict of players' motives. We have already assumed that the motive of players is mainly to win. To say that they overexpand coalitions, however, is to attribute a motive of seeking to gain more than what comes from winning itself. Paradoxical as such behavior may seem, we nevertheless analyze it for the sake of completeness.

Of course, insofar as the slope of $v(S)$ is negative in part, all the considerations of Case I apply. The question arises about the positive portion of the slope of $v(S)$. Since a positive slope means $v(S + i) > v(S)$, there is a gain from expansion, $[v(S + i) - v(S)]$. Our question is: can we expect players to seek this gain? If the answer is affirmative, then the equilibrium size is larger than m and the size principle fails in this case. If the answer is negative, then it can be shown that the equilibrium size is m and the size principle holds.

In order to answer this question, we consider three subcases according to the relationship between the payment to person i in the coalition $(S + i)$, that is, $x_i^{(S+i)}$, and the gain to the whole coalition $(S + i)$ from being in $(S + i)$ rather than S, that is, the amount $[v(S + i) - v(S)]$. Precisely, the differentiation of the subcases is over whether or not i is paid his marginal contribution.

Case III.1: $x_i^{(S+i)} > v(S + i) - v(S)$. Here the payment in the larger coalition to the member who is not in the smaller is greater than the difference in value between the larger and the smaller. That is, i earns more than his marginal contribution. Hence, if players are in S, the s members of S lose by expansion to $(S + i)$, because they must pay i more than his marginal contribution to the new coalition. Conversely, if players are in $(S + i)$, the s members of S gain by contraction from $(S + i)$ to S because they save more in what they pay to i than what they lose by the contraction. Hence, expansion will not occur, but contraction will; so the equilibrium size of S is m.

Case III.2: $x_i^{(S+i)} = v(S + i) - v(S)$. If players are at S, there is no motive for the s members of S to expand to $(S + i)$ because i receives exactly his marginal contribution— that is, the entire gain from the expansion. Similarly, if players are at $(S + i)$, there is no motive to contract, for the s members of S receive the same amount in $(S + i)$ as in S. It would appear, therefore, that there is no motive for expansion or contraction and every size s, $m \leq s \leq n$, is an equilibrium position. There is, however, a cost of organization, which presumably increases with each member. That cost can be saved by contraction from $(S + i)$ to S. By repeated applications of this principle, the equilibirum size of S is m.

Case III.3: $x_i^{(S+i)} < v(S+i) - v(S)$. Here i does not receive his marginal contribution, so that the s members of S gain collectively from being in $(S + i)$ rather than in S. Considering the argument by which the power index, the Shapley value, and the proportional value of the V-solution were justified, it is hard to imagine a world in which players accept less than their marginal contributions. Still, for the sake of completeness, we consider this case. We begin by identifying a net increase of payments to the s members of S for being in $(S + i)$ rather than in S:

$$b = [v(S + i) - v(S)] - [x_i^{(S+i)}]. \qquad (7.8)$$
$$\text{(term 1)} \qquad \text{(term 2)}$$

In this net increase, term 1 consists of the value added to $(S + i)$ by reason of i's joining S. Under the conditions of this case, term 1 is always positive. Term 2 consists of the payment to player i when he is in $(S + i)$. It is, of course, always larger than $x_i^{(-S)}$, which is what i gets in $-S$. If it were not true that $x_i^{(S+i)} > x_i^{(-S)}$, then i would have no motive for joining $(S+i)$. Term 2 need not be positive because i might move from $-S$ to $(S+i)$ merely to lower his loss. But if term 2 is negative, its absolute value cannot exceed the value of term 1, because that would make this a version of Case III.1.

The significance of b in (7.8) is that it defines the amount available for one side to offer i. Assuming that the members of S have formed $(S + i)$ and that the $(n-s-1)$ members of $-(S + i)$ attempt to win i back to $-S$, then the s members of S can bid up to the amount b in order to retain i in $(S + i)$.

What can the $(n-s-1)$ members of $-(S+i)$ bid to attract i back to $-S$? By reason of i's defection their costs have been increased by the amount:

$$a = -[v(-(S + i)) - v(-S)] - (x_i^{(-S)}), \qquad (7.9)$$
$$\text{(term 1)} \qquad \text{(term 2)}$$

where term 1 is the amount i's defection costs the remaining members of $-S$ in decreased payments and term 2 is the share of the costs of $-S$ which were previously borne by i and which must now be borne by the $(n - s - 1)$ members of $-(S+i)$. The amount a is, then, what the members of $-(S + i)$ can pay i to persuade him to return to $-S$.

Note, however, that i makes a gain from trade by leaving $-S$ and going to $(S + i)$. This gain is the amount:

$$c = x_i^{(S+i)} - x_i^{(-S)}.$$

No matter what else they offer i, the members of $-(S + i)$ must at least offer him c. Hence their free capital for bidding is really only $a - c$.

Since term 1 in (7.8) is equal to term 1 in (7.9)—because of the zero-sum assumption—it follows that

$$a - c = b$$

or

$$[-v(-(S + i)) + v(-S)] - [x_i^{(-S)}] - [x_i^{(S+i)} - x_i^{(-S)}] = [v(S + i) - v(S)] - [x_i^{(S+i)}].$$

(The terms in x cancel and the terms in v are equal.)

Hence, if the members of $-(S + i)$ seek to attract i back once he has defected from $-S$, they have just as much bargaining power as the members of $(S + i)$ have to retain him. This being so, in a world of rational bargainers and infinite time for bargaining, the bidding may be expected to proceed until i has all of b. But then the conditions of this case are no longer fulfilled. Instead the participants are back in Case III.2, where $x_i^{(S+i)} = v(S + i) - v(S)$. Here, of course, there is no reason to expand to $(S + i)$.

Consequently, in a world of no frictions, rational behavior causes Case III.3 to collapse to Case III.2, where the equilibrium size of S is m. When this is so, we have the following distribution of payments:

(1)   members of S receive positive payments,
(2)   some members of $- S$ receive positive payments,
(3)   some members of $- S$ receive negative payments.

This is a curious situation, though no more curious, we believe, than the conditions that brought it forth. The most curious feature is that the players in category (2) above —i.e., those who receive positive payments—are receiving more than a coalition of only them is worth. Since, however, the characteristic function is a security level, the fact that a coalition or subcoalition receives *more* than it is worth is of no concern. (Were some coalition or subcoalition to receive *less*, however, as when the kind of argument advanced for Case III.3 is advanced in Case I, then the conditions of the characteristic function are violated.[2])

In Cases I and II we have shown that the equilibrium size of S is m; and in Case III, which we believe is empirically vacuous, we have advanced organizational arguments in support of that equilibrium. Hence, we reiterate the size principle as a translation into sociological terms of the discovery made in the model: "In social situations similar to n-person, zero-sum games with side payments, participants create coalitions just as large as they believe will ensure winning and no larger."

While it is derived from an analysis of the model world of game theory, the size principle is a statement about the real world of politics. Consequently, it can be tested and presumably falsified or verified. We can ask: Do people in fact behave as if they were following this sociological law? Is there a natural movement toward minimal winning coalitions?

The answer is negative in the sense that, until recently, no one consciously ascribed to politicians an intent to minimize winning coalitions. This fact does not preclude the possibility that politicians behave as if they were seeking to minimize. They may, for example, do such concrete things as: refuse to try to get additional members of a coalition that is already winning, refuse to give rewards out of a winning supply to some members in a coalition that is currently oversized (i.e., thereby suggesting that the unrewarded members leave), construct a policy that helps some crucial members of an oversized coalition but hurts some "unnecessary" members, and so on. To say that politicians are thereby minimizing is to formulate the principle underlying these actions. (The trader in a primitive market probably never heard of the notions of supply and demand, although he is as effective as anyone else in arriving at an

---

[2]This is the error committed in Richard Butterworth, "A Research Note on the Size of Winning Coalitions," *American Political Science Review*, vol. 65 (1971), pp. 741–745. Butterworth increases the value of certain winning coalitions, like those depicted by the lower line I in Figure 7.3, above that line toward the upper line I. Since the mirror images of these values are the values of losing complementary coalitions, he in effect makes the losers take less than their security levels, which is what they can guarantee for themselves by themselves. That is, he makes the losers do worse than the minimum they can guarantee, which is inconsistent. See William H. Riker, "Comment on Butterworth," *American Political Science Review*, vol. 65 (1971), pp. 745–750.

equilibrium price. Price theory then is a formulation of the principle underlying his actions, just as the size principle is a formulation of the principle underlying the behavior of leaders of coalitions.) So the question recurs: is there a natural movement toward minimal winning coalitions, even though politicians might not have traditionally thought of their actions in this way?

INFORMATION CONDITIONS

To begin with, so that not too much be expected, we point out that this is a Type II or weak, unique equilibrium, since there may be many coalitions of minimally winning size. Furthermore, in the model world equilibrium depends on perfect information and hence on certainty. But in the real world these seldom exist, so that one can expect this world only to move toward equilibrium, not necessarily to arrive at it for sure.

With respect to coalition size, there are two kinds of relevant information: (a) how much significance or weight each participant has and hence how much weight or how many participants are required to win, and (b) who belongs to which coalition, S or $-S$. To say that information is perfect means that everyone knows the answer to all possible questions of these two sorts. Now, in parliamentary bodies one knows exactly how much each vote counts and hence how many it takes to win; but one does not know the (b) kind of information, who has joined each coalition. Conversely, in balance-of-power politics and military alliances one knows pretty well, or at least most of the time, who is on what side; but does not know the (a) kind of information, how much an ally or opponent counts in terms of war potential. Most real-world situations are like these in that one or the other kinds of information must be guessed at. Thus we can safely say that information is seldom perfect.

The effect of imperfect information is to force coalitions to enlarge themselves above minimum winning size in order to increase the likelihood of winning. In *The Theory of Political Coalitions* this is referred to as the "information effect," although it is analyzed only intuitively. Niemi and Weisberg have examined imperfect information in precise detail by analyzing a voting situation in which some, at least, of the voters are uncertain about how they will vote so that other participants do not have the (b) kind of information.[3] In the foregoing formulation of the size principle, participants are assumed to decide for certain on joining or not joining coalitions, to decide, that is, with probability of one *or* zero, which is to say that the information about membership is perfect. But in the Niemi and Weisberg model participants may decide to join (or, in their terms, to vote) with any probability *between* zero and one. Even though this may be unrealistic, because people are not in fact uncertain in their actions,

[3]Richard G. Niemi and Herbert F. Weisberg, "The Effects of Group Size on Collective Decision-Making," in Niemi and Weisberg, eds., *Probability Models of Collective Decision-Making* (Columbus: Charles E. Merrill, 1972).

still they may appear to others to be uncertain and this is exactly the situation of imperfect information about membership in coalitions.

In the Niemi and Weisberg model there are two alternatives, A and B; some voters are certain to vote for A, some for B, and some are undecided. Depending on the relative numbers of certain and undecided voters, on the decision rule (the number required to win), and, finally, on the probability that uncertain voters will prefer A to B, a high probability of victory for A is sometimes associated with minimal winning coalitions, sometimes not. Typically, in small groups, if the number of undecided is high relative to the number of decided and if the probability that the undecided vote for A is relatively high, then the likelihood of oversized winning coalitions is also fairly high. Niemi and Weisberg summarize their findings thus:

> Minimum winning coalitions are more likely to form in large than in small groups.

Presumably this is because the significance of imperfect information declines as groups increase in size. Further, they find:

> In small groups, if rational actors maximize the probability of winning (or at least make that probability very high), they do not maximize the probability of minimum winning coalitions. Conversely, the probability of a minimum winning coalition is maximized only at the cost of reducing the probability of winning.

Since information is not perfect, we cannot expect a strong equilibrium in the sense of a position that players quickly and surefootedly arrive exactly at. Instead, players try to approximate it, all the while leaving room for the errors they know they will commit because their information is imperfect. For that reason we have only a weak equilibrium. People move toward it, but do not always arrive at it.

THE SIZE PRINCIPLE AND GRAND COALITIONS

Given that we have thus only a Type II equilibrium, what evidence do we have that people behave as if they were acting upon the size principle? We offer two kinds, some that are set forth in *The Theory of Political Coalitions* and some that have accumulated since the publication of that book.

A type of situation in which the operation of the size principle is especially evident is that in which grand coalitions occur. In such case, players are at the point $(n, 0)$ in Figure 7.3, where $v(S) = 0$ and $v(S - i) > 0$. There is, consequently, an instance of Case I, where the motive to contract the size of S is especially strong. If we look at all the instances of grand coalitions, it should be true that (a) they occur in a sense accidentally—that is, through miscalculation or faulty communication or as an incidental feature of an outcome sought for other reasons—and (b) they break up very quickly into something smaller and more valuable.

Grand coalitions often form "accidentally," as a result of other considerations. We note two kinds of instances:

1. A political party, using the shorthand goal of increasing its share of the vote in place of the sounder goal of winning the election, may succeed too well and wipe out the opposition. This is what happened, for example, in the Era of Good Feeling (1820) in the United States, where Republicans effectively eliminated Federalists, of course with much assistance from the latter.
2. When a small political game is embedded in a larger one, the players in the smaller game may form a coalition of the whole in the smaller game in order to win in the larger one. This is what happens when all the political parties of a country combine to run the government in a coalition of national unity. Such coalitions often occur in war, as in Great Britain in 1941–45, but also they occur simply when a nation feels itself a pawn in world politics, as in Austria, 1946–65. The coalition for national independence (see p. 191) is a special case of this kind.

To test whether or not grand coalitions contract in size, we need some zero-sum situations in which grand coalitions occasionally recur. If they then invariable satisfy requirements (a) and (b) in the previous paragraph, we have some evidence—at least for Case I situations—of the validity of the size principle.[4]

One zero-sum situation in which grand coalitions occasionally recur is total war in the Western European nation-state system. By total war we mean a war such that all important nation-states in the system participate and such that the object of the governments on one side is to destroy the governments (not necessarily the nations) on the other side. Because of the universal goal of extinction, a total war is zero-sum; and because occasionally one side does achieve its goal, there is incidentally produced a grand coalition. (To win in such a circumstance, the other side must be destroyed, and when it is destroyed, only the winners are left and they are a coalition of everybody, even if that was not the intent of the action.) Thus, when a total war is successfully concluded we have a real-world instance of a zero-sum situation in which the grand coalition satisfies requirement (a). The question then is: does it satisfy requirement (b); does it break up quickly?

In modern European history there have been three such total wars: the Napoleonic wars and World Wars I and II. Each qualifies as a total war because ultimately each came to include almost every nation-state in Europe and a good many in America, Asia, and Africa. And each involved on at least one side, and possibly both, the intention to destroy the other. Thus the English-Austrian-Prussian-Russian allies intended—and often said so—to destroy the

[4]Note that this is much stronger than the anecdotal evidence usually adduced by appeals to history. What is sought is proof that *all* instances of a particular category of grand coalition satisfy the requirements. Hence we can say, not just that some events bear out the theory, but that some whole classes of events do.

Napoleonic government in France and depose all the Bonapartist puppets elsewhere. Whether Napoleon's goal was equally to eliminate all opposition is less clear, but certainly he gave that impression to his opponents, which, perhaps, was why they feared and hated him so much. In both the World Wars, the goal of the winning allies was to eliminate the governments on the other side. Not only did they repeatedly demand unconditional surrender, but also they actually did dismember the German, Austrian, and Turkish empires after World War I and destroy the governments and punish the officials of Germany, Italy, and even Japan after World War II. Whether the Central Powers in World War I or the Axis Powers in World War II, the losers in the two wars, had similar goals of annihilation we cannot be absolutely sure. Hitler certainly intended to wipe out the Soviet Union, but what he intended with respect to the rest of the world is unclear. The Central Powers of World War I, less involved than the Allies in a moral crusade, may have had narrower goals. In any event, it is the goals of the winners that count because they are the goals that are ultimately adopted. And in all three wars the goals of the winners were to eliminate the governments of the losers.

Each of these total wars resulted in the moment of victory in a grand coalition that substantially controlled the relevant world. And, in appropriate confirmation of the size principle, each such coalition broke up almost immediately.

The winners of the Napoleonic wars constituted themselves as the Concert of Europe, presumably to preserve the status quo indefinitely. But, if the size principle holds, the status quo is the one thing that *cannot* be preserved in a grand coalition. Over the question of whether or not Prussia would acquire Saxony and Russia would retain control of the Polish territory it had acquired in the Napoleonic era, the Congress of Vienna split into two camps. Russia and Prussia supported each other's imperial expansion while England and Austria supported a return to the prewar territorial arrangements. In an effort to restrain Russia and Prussia, Austria and England called defeated France back into the system and made a secret treaty with Talleyrand. In this instance the winners of the total war fell out even before they had divided the spoils, and indeed even before the final spasm of war at Waterloo.

After World War I the winners again attempted to preserve the status quo forever with the League of Nations and the Versailles treaty, even going so far as to exclude the governments they had just wiped out. Such a goal was impossible and was shown to be so even at Versailles: England wished to revive Germany, France to destroy it forever. As it turned out, England did bring Germany back into the European system, if not into the League, and Germany in turn, in the Locarno Pact of 1925, brought the Soviet Union, which the others at first wished to ignore, into the European system also. In these maneuvers the supposed unity of 1918 was effectively destroyed—if it had ever existed.

Again, toward the end of World War II, the victorious wartime grand coalition planned to perpetuate itself forever, or such at least was the ideal behind the United Nations. But even as the charter of the U.N. was being written to perpetuate it, the Soviet Union and the United States were carving up the world into spheres of influence. Less than a year after the end of the war in Europe, the so-called cold war, with its theme of two opposing coalitions encircling the world, was in full swing. By the time of the Korean War, the Soviet Union regarded the United Nations—with some justification—as an instrument of the foreign policy of the United States.

In *all* cases, therefore, of total war in the modern world—which are *all* cases of grand coalitions in modern world politics when there is some zero-sum feature—the grand coalitions lasted only a very short time. Indeed, it is fair to say that they were being undermined even before they were effective, which is what the size principle predicts.

Other classes of grand coalitions, such as complete triumphs by one party in national election systems, also display this feature of the almost immediate collapse of the grand coalition, except where it is preserved by the most oppressive sort of dictatorship, like Hitler's or Stalin's.[5] (Of course, the reason for dictatorial oppression is the intuitive recognition that without oppression the grand coalition will evaporate.) One kind of grand coalition that has frequently appeared in recent years and invariably broken up to the intense disappointment of its originators is the coalition for national independence. The quarter-century since 1945 has been an age of the end of colonialism. Typically, within each colony all elements of society—even intensely hostile elements—have joined to get strength enough to expel the colonial power. Once it has been expelled, however, all the intense internal hostilities of the society have destroyed the coalition for independence, often resulting in civil war, racial and religious hatred, and the like. The recent history of such nations as Indonesia, Malaysia, Ceylon, Nigeria, and above all India, display this collapse of the grand coalition and all the unrealistic hopes that went with it.[6]

THE SIZE PRINCIPLE IN SMALLER COALITIONS

The failure of grand coalitions to persist for very long is indeed so universal that we can pass it by in order to study the far more difficult case of coalitions smaller than grand coalitions. Do these smaller ones also tend to get smaller, as the size principle requires?

In seeking to answer this question we have a difficult problem of assessing evidence and separating one kind of influence from another in the real world. Not only do we have the problem of the imperfection of information, but also ideology enters into consideration. Progress toward minimizing the size of winning coalitions is impeded, on the one hand, by poor information. A

---

[5] *The Theory of Political Coalitions,* chap. 3, contains an analysis of grand coalitions in the politics of the United States.

[6] *The Theory of Political Coalitions,* chap. 3, contains an analysis of this collapse in India.

coalition maker, uncertain of just exactly whom or how many he has attracted into his coalition, may go way beyond the minimal winning size in order to be absolutely certain of victory. Or, overestimating his support among undecided, he may form a losing coalition. Normally the existence of a vigorous opposition prevents this. But if the opposition is weak and the citizens fickle, then oversized and undersized coalitions may be created out of uncertainty. On the other hand, progress toward minimizing size is impeded by ideology. The size principle, based as it is wholly on considerations of winning and payoff, has no room in it for coalition-formation based on similarity of belief. Yet it would be foolish to deny that in the short run similarities of belief are relevant for decisions on membership in coalitions. Consequently, when there is a conflict between minimizing size and keeping together a satisfactory ideological formation, it may well be that in the short run it is cheaper to save the ideology.

Nevertheless, if the size principle reflects an important consideration, it should be operating in the formation of all winning coalitions, not just those that are made out of grand ones. One place where it might be expected to appear very strongly is in the coalitions of political leadership in societies without much ideology. Two such observations exist: Martin Southwold remarks that the size principle "seems to fit the facts of political life in African kingdoms and chiefdoms like Buganda even better than it fits the data to which Riker himself applied it."[7] And Frederick Barth independently developed a simple form of the size principle to explain coalitions of tribal leadership in Pathan political life.[8] Another place the size principle might be expected to appear clearly, even in cases where ideology is relevant, is in studies of great numbers of coalition-forming events. One such study reporting strong evidence of the operation of the size principle is a study of local elections in Brazil by Phyllis Peterson.[9] And the effect of the size principle ought to be clearly seen also in the politics of elections where much is at stake. In the French elections of 1951 and 1956 the electoral law had the effect of encouraging coalitions, presumably to help defeat Communists. If a coalition won over half the votes in an electoral district, it received all the seats; while if no coalition won half the votes, the seats were divided by proportional representation. Recently, Howard Rosenthal has studied such coalitions in order to estimate the evidence of use of the size principle. Looking at election results in 49 cases of coalitions, he found only three in which a member might have benefited if some other member had been ejected. Furthermore, he found some evidence that certain parties that were in similar coalitions elsewhere "were not brought into coalitions as a result

[7]Martin Southwold, "Riker's Theory and the Analysis of Coalitions in Precolonial Africa," in Sven Groennings, E. W. Kelley, and Michael Leiserson, eds., *The Study of Coalition Behavior* (New York: Holt, Rinehart and Winston, 1970), pp. 336–350.

[8]Frederick Barth, "Segmentary Opposition and the Theory of Games: A Study of Pathan Organization," *Journal of the Royal Anthropological Society*, vol. 89 (1959), pp. 5–22.

[9]Phyllis Peterson, "Coalition-Formation in Local Elections in the State of São Paulo, Brazil," in Groennings, Kelley, and Leiserson, eds., *The Study of Coalition Behavior*, pp. 141–159.

of size considerations." Altogether, he concludes that "the available evidence contains no major counterexample to Riker's size principle and in fact broadly confirms the proposition that coalitions are limited in size once the point of winning has been reached."[10]

We turn now from situations where the influence of ideology is weak to those where it is strong, e.g., cabinet formation in modern parliamentary bodies. In these cases the evidence of the operation of the size principle is more equivocal. Even here, however, the study of the longest and most detailed evidence strongly supports the size principle. In a study of cabinet-formation in Denmark from 1906 to the present, Erik Damgaard shows, not only that grand coalitions break up immediately, but that, if we interpret the members of coalitions as parties (rather than single parliamentarians), every coalition formed from 1906 onward is a minimal winning one.[11] Since, however, these minimal winning coalitions were also invariably composed of ideologically adjacent parties, this evidence is not as strong as one might wish. Furthermore, in a study of coalition-formation in the Japanese conservative party—where, because it is inside one parliamentary party, ideological considerations are minimal—Leiserson found that the size principle fairly well explained the formation of coalitions.[12] Nevertheless, he found that a somewhat similar, though wholly *ad hoc*, generalization explained them better. His alternative was that the winning coalition was the one with the fewest factional units as against the smallest weight. This, of course, is a version of the size principle obtained by treating factions as more or less equivalent.

But when one turns to parliamentary bodies where ideological concerns are often important, the size principle is somewhat less valid a description. In a study of Italian cabinets from 1953 to the present, Robert Axelrod offered a theory of coalitions based on the notion of joining ideologically similar parties rather than of minimizing the size of the coalition. It turned out to be a better description than the size principle, even though Axelrod's theory is somewhat circular in the sense that the definition of ideological similarity is partially, though not entirely, the fact of joint cabinet membership.[13]

Similarly, Abraham De Swaan set forth a theory of forming coalitions by

[10]Howard Rosenthal, "Size of Coalition and Electoral Outcomes in the Fourth French Republic," in Groennings, Kelley, and Leiserson, eds., *The Study of Coalition Behavior*, pp. 43–59. This conclusion is all the stronger since it is part of an overall effort to investigate the ideological structure of such electoral coalitions. See Howard Rosenthal, "Elements of a Model and the Study of French Legislative Elections," *Editions du Centre National de la Recherche Scientifique*, 1968, pp. 269–282.

[11]Erik Damgaard, "The Parliamentary Basis of Danish Governments: The Patterns of Coalition Formation," *Yearbook* of the Political Science Associations in Denmark, Finland, Norway, and Sweden, vol. 4 (1969), pp. 30–57.

[12]Michael Leiserson, "Factions and Coalitions in One-Party Japan: An Interpretation Based on the Theory of Games," *American Political Science Review*, vol. 62 (1968), pp. 770–787. See also Michael Leiserson, "Coalition Government in Japan," in Groennings, Kelley, and Leiserson, eds., *The Study of Coalition Behavior*, pp. 80–102.

[13]Robert Axelrod, *Conflict of Interest* (Chicago: Markham, 1970), p. 179.

minimizing the policy distance among parties, which has the merit, he asserted, "of accounting for the occurrence of large coalitions" as well as minimal ones.[14] While his theory is also somewhat circular, and while he offers no comparative evidence of its validity, still it is intended to (and probably does) describe coalition-formation in the Netherlands better than the size principle alone. These studies indicate that where ideology is especially important—here as a means to maintain coalitions for governing—it may well overwhelm the consideration of size.

Possibly, however, the Dutch and Italian cases, with so few events about which to generalize, reflect random error. If one examines a really large number of coalitions in a situation in which ideology is present, it appears that the effect of ideology can wash out and size alone become the important consideration. David Koehler has compared the size of the majority on contested roll calls with the size of the party majority for six recent sessions of Congress.[15] The size of the party majority varied from 51 percent to 68 percent but the size of the average majority on roll calls was close to constant at 60 percent. If ideology were the dominant force, one would expect the average majority on roll calls to be high when the party majority is high and low when the party majority is low. That this did not happen indicates the low impact of ideology. In a body with perfect information, the average size of the majority on roll calls should be about 51 percent. That it was here about 60 percent is doubtless due to the lack of good information. One can say the members were minimizing toward an uncertain majority of 60 percent.

THE SIZE PRINCIPLE IN AMERICAN POLITICS: THE ELECTIONS OF 1964 AND 1968

Thus it is that the size principle reasserts itself—which is doubtless why oversized coalitions seldom last long. We conclude our review of evidence about the size principle with what we think is a most persuasive example of the principle at work: persuasive because it explains much of the course of our recent politics. In 1964 Lyndon Johnson was elected President by what was clearly an oversized majority. The large size was something of an accident occasioned by the assassination of President Kennedy. Ever since 1960, Barry Goldwater had been constructing a coalition to run against Kennedy, a coalition that emphasized the South and the West as the central elements. While this coalition might have been effective against Kennedy, who was weak in just those areas, it was inap-

[14]Abraham De Swaan, "An Empirical Model of Coalition-Formation as an *n*- Person Game of Policy Distance Minimization," in Groennings, Kelley, and Leiserson, eds., *The Study of Coalition Behavior*, pp. 424–444.

[15]Koehler's work is reported in Niemi and Weisberg, eds., *Probability Models of Collective Decision-Making*.

propriate as a Republican vehicle against Johnson, who was strong in just those areas. Since the Republican party, and Barry Goldwater, turned out to be too inflexible to change their policy when Kennedy died, they lost overwhelmingly to Johnson, who had his own personal strength in the South and West and who had inherited the Kennedy strength in the East. So Johnson had a larger coalition than he needed. In such a circumstance one would expect, if the size principle is at all correct, that the President would begin to eject people from his coalition. And this is exactly what he did, in a manner of speaking.

Of course, in the rather mild, low-key politics characteristic of the United States, ejection means merely the refusal to pay any attention to the needs of the people ejected so that they must go to other leaders of other coalitions to obtain satisfaction. Johnson neglected certain elements of his coalition in order to satisfy others, and thereby ultimately weakened himself beyond repair. First, in 1965 he took strong stands on civil rights issues, thus rewarding the most important elements he had inherited from Kennedy, but thereby repelling that portion of the deep South which had hitherto trusted him more than it had trusted Goldwater. It was this action by Johnson that made it feasible for Nixon to follow a so-called Southern strategy in 1968 and later. Having thus in a sense ejected the deep South by refusing it a reward, Johnson proceeded to eject a good portion of his liberal support which he had inherited from Kennedy. This he did by prosecuting the war in Vietnam in the face of rising protests from liberals. In short, he acted to ignore the demands of one element of his coalition, presumably to satisfy other elements (and perhaps some need of his own for a "place in history"). Thus, in effect, he abandoned first one element of his coalition (to the point that he could not win it back) and then another element, so that by 1968 he did not have enough strength to run again. In four years Johnson completely dissipated his oversized majority of 1964.

It is easy to see in this concrete circumstance why size is such a potent force. In practical calculations of whether or not to try to keep an ally, the leader who wants to win again must always try to keep at least a minimal winning coalition. If, however, the coalition is oversized, as in 1964, he can feel free to solve the problems of conflicting demands by throwing some of his allies away, which is the force that constantly brings coalitions back down to minimal winning size or smaller. Thus size is always a crucial element of the calculations of leadership, even though the leader may never have heard of the size principle. The calculations are clearly apparent in this instance. In the conflict over civil rights, Johnson solved the problem simply by quoting to Congress, "We shall overcome." In free translation, this implies to one element of the coalition: "If you don't like my policy, you are free to leave my coalition. The size of my victory in 1964 indicates that I can easily get along without you." He made no attempt at all to compromise, probably because this was his first step in cutting down the coalition. Having made this cut, he was stuck with it both in conscience and in political potential. In the conflict over the Vietnamese war,

Johnson did try to compromise—that is, he tried to present himself to the public as following a middle course between the doves and the hawks. Probably his motive was that, with his coalition already cut down by the loss of the deep South, he feared that it would drop below 50 percent —as of course it ultimately did in the public opinion polls. However much Johnson might pretend to compromise, however, he was interpreted as hawk-in-chief, and so he lost the doves. By these two actions on civil rights and Vietnam, Johnson chopped off different parts of his oversized coalition. The first amputation was doubtless deliberate; the second he could not help. Perhaps, if he had not been so overconfident because of his oversized majority of 1964, he would not have so blithely sacrificed important elements of his coalition. But the fact that he made a mistake in his calculations does not hide the fact that he made calculations about size. His problem was that, in trying to save his oversized coalition by minimizing it, he ultimately came to minimize too much and ended up a loser.

DYNAMIC REFLECTIONS OF THE SIZE PRINCIPLE

We conclude this chapter with some observations about the dynamics of coalition-building, an activity which is at the very center of the art of politics and yet about which there is very little theory or systematic information. The transformation from the static model of game theory to the dynamic model of coalition-formation can be accomplished with a model of stages of development. Let there be n persons in a game with a negatively sloping curve connecting the points of the characteristic function. The dynamic action in the game is the growth of groups which we call protocoalitions as they are developing and which ultimately grow into winning, losing, and blocking coalitions. Proto-coalitions may be thought of as groups existing only while the game is going on, for they become coalitions as the game ends. Initially, of course, there are n single-member protocoalitions, and that situation we define as stage 1. Successive stages occur as one or more persons simultaneously join others to form newer and larger protocoalitions or, alternatively, as persons separate to form smaller protocoalitions. The stages can be visualized thus:

stage 1: n one-member protocoalitions
stage 2: one two-member protocoalition
and $(n-1)$ one-member protocoalitions
or
one three-member protocoalition
and $(n-2)$ one-member protocoalitions
or
two two-member protocoalitions
and $(n-2)$ one-member protocoalitions
etc.
stage r: one winning coalition and one or more losing coalitions
or two or more blocking coalitions

Since the size principle obtains, participants prefer minimum winning coalitions to coalitions of larger size in stage r. This preference gives some direction to their action in the penultimate stage, $(r-1)$, and the antepenultimate stage, $(r-2)$. As participants try to reach a minimum winning coalition in stage r, they must put themselves in an advantageous position to do so in stage $(r-1)$. This they can do because some protocoalitions in the $(r-1)$ stage have advantages over others. By an analysis of these advantages, it is possible to construct strategies of play for the latter stages of a game.

To consider the end play, assume that in the $(r-1)$ stage there are three protocoalitions, P, Q, and R, such that P is larger than Q which is larger than R. Hence $(Q \cup R)$ is the minimum winning coalition and $(P \cup R)$ and $(P \cup Q)$ are both larger winning coalitions. Because of the size principle, the values, v, of the possible winning coalitions in the r th stage are arranged thus:

$$v(Q \cup R) > v(P \cup R) > v(P \cup Q).$$

Clearly the protocoalition R, especially, and Q, to a lesser degree, have advantages in the $(r-1)$ stage. The protocoalition R we describe as *uniquely favored* because all the winning coalitions to which it belongs are worth more than those to which it does not. One would thus expect that its managers ought to be able to exact a good price for its adherence, regardless of which coalition it ultimately joins. Note, however, that Q has some advantage because there is only one minimum winning coalition and Q is a member of it. This advantage seems weaker, we believe, than that of a uniquely favored protocoalition.

From these considerations we can define precisely three degrees of advantage (or disadvantage):

A protocoalition, X, is *uniquely favored* if:
(1) any winning coalition containing X is more valuable than one which does not contain it.
(2) more than one protocoalition satisfies (1) then if there is some winning coalition that contains X and none of the others that satisfy (1).

A protocoalition, X, is a *member of a uniquely preferred winning coalition* if that winning coalition is of greater value than all others.

A protocoalition, X, is *strategically weak* if it is not possible for it to be either a member of a uniquely preferred winning coalition or a member of any of several equally and most valuable winning coalitions.

These notions can be used to state strategies of the end play. In general the fundamental strategies are: Advantaged protocoalitions should act so as to realize the advantage. This means they should seek in the $(r-1)$ stage to move immediately to the r th stage. On the other hand, disadvantaged protocoalitions should try to prevent the r th stage. Briefly put, prospective winners should try to bring the game to a conclusion, while prospective losers should try to delay.

Returning now to an analysis of the $(r-1)$ stage with these notions in mind, if there are three protocoalitions of equal size, then there is no kind of advantage, and hence no clear strategy and no predictable consequence. If, however, one protocoalition is larger than the others or if one is smaller or both, then it is true either that R is a uniquely favored protocoalition or $(Q \cup R)$ is a uniquely preferred winning coalition or both. In any event, if the three proto- coalitions are not of equal size, then R, the smallest, is advantageously situa- ted. In this way the first shall be last and the last shall be first.[16]

The problem of the end play is fairly simple when there are only three protocoalitions in the penultimate stage. It becomes more interesting and more difficult when there are four, five, and perhaps even more protocoali- tions.[17] The most striking feature of these larger situations is that no single proto- coalition invariably has the advantage. Consider a pair of cases involving four protocoalitions in a 100-member body where it takes 51 to win. Writing "$w(X) = 1$" to mean "X has one member":

	Case 1	Case 2
	$w(P) = 40$	$w(P) = 30$
	$w(Q) = 35$	$w(Q) = 29$
	$w(R) = 15$	$w(R) = 21$
	$w(S) = 10$	$w(S) = 20$
minimum winning coalition:	$w(P \cup R) = 55$	$w(P \cup R) = 51$
other winning coalitions:	$w(Q \cup R \cup S) = 60$	$w(P \cup Q) = 59$
	$w(P \cup Q) = 75$	$w(Q \cup R \cup S) = 70$

In both cases $(P \cup R)$ is a uniquely preferred winning coalition—that is, the only possible minimum winning coalition. Some kind of special advantage thus adheres in each case in the largest protocoalition, P, and the next-to-smallest, R. (And in these cases, unlike the three protocoalition case, there is no ad- vantage at all for the smallest, S.) The degree of advantage for P and R is nevertheless strikingly different. In case 1, R is uniquely favored because it alone is in the two most valuable winning coalitions: $(P \cup R)$ and $(Q \cup R \cup S)$. In case 2, however, P is uniquely favored because it alone is in the two most valuable coalitions, $(P \cup R)$ and $(P \cup Q)$. While Q and S are not advantaged in these cases, it is possible to construct cases in which they are. And so, in the four protocoalition cases and in larger cases, no protocoalition is invariably favored.

Even though it is therefore difficult to generalize about the end play when there are more than three protocoalitions, still it is possible to analyze partic-

---

[16]Other writers who have come to a similar understanding of the three protocoalition case with a somewhat *ad hoc* theory are: Theodore Caplow, "A Theory of Coalitions in the Triad," *American Sociological Review*, vol. 21 (1956) pp. 489–493; Caplow, "Further Developments of a Theory of Coalitions in the Triad," *American Journal of Sociology*, vol. 64 (1959), pp. 488–493; William A. Gamson, "A Theory of Coalition-Formation," *American Sociological Review*, vol. 26 (1961), pp. 373–382.

[17]It seems unlikely that in the real world there are often more than five protocoalitions in stage $(r-1)$. One can easily imagine configurations of six protocoalitions in a 100- member body, either of the following: (50, 10, 10, 10, 10, 10) or (17, 17, 17, 17, 16, 16). But as these numbers suggest, one would expect some further agglomeration of protocoalitions before the end comes. Hence these six protocoalitions would be expected to exist in some earlier stage than $(r-1)$.

ular cases, looking for particular kinds of advantage. One can then interpret human action in such cases as rational endeavor to realize potential advantages inherent in the situation. As an example of such a possibility we offer an interpretation of the presidential election of 1824–25, which was thrown into the House of Representatives and settled by the so-called corrupt bargain between Adams and Clay.

In 1820 Monroe was elected President as a Republican almost unanimously —there was only one non-Monroe vote in the Electoral College. This remarkable outcome was the result of a long period of decline of the Federalist party. Originally that party had appealed, *inter alia*, to conservative elements, who became a smaller and smaller proprotion of the electorate as property qualifications for voting were removed and as new states in the West with a radical tradition entered the Union. At the same time that the pool of conservative voters grew relatively smaller, reactionary elements gradually drove moderates out of the Federalist party so that its appeal was narrowed even further. The *coup de grace* was the behavior of some New England Federalists in 1813–15 when they urged a separate peace with Britain, a position that made it possible to interpret the whole party as treasonous. Once that label was successfully attached to it, the party disappeared and Monroe was reelected almost unanimously.

As might be expected, when a grand coalition came into existence, it began to break up almost immediately. The following factions soon formed around candidacies for the election of 1824:

> John Quincy Adams, of Massachusetts, Secretary of State, was the favorite of the former Federalists, although, as a moderate, he had been driven out of the Federalist party in 1808.
> William Crawford, of Georgia, Secretary of the Treasury, was the candidate of that alliance of Jeffersonians which had produced a series of Presidents from Virginia and Vice-Presidents from New York.
> John C. Calhoun, of South Carolina, Secretary of War, was the candidate of South Carolina and himself.
> Andrew Jackson of Tennessee, the hero of New Orleans, Governor of the Florida territory, and later the Senator from Tennessee, turned out to be the most popular candidate.
> Henry Clay, of Kentucky, Representative and leader of the opposition in the House, ultimately became the founder of the Whig party.

Though initially Crawford was, perhaps, the frontrunner, he suffered a stroke in 1823 and thereafter lost much of his support. Calhoun wisely settled for the vice-presidency. This left Adams, Jackson, and Clay. As Secretary of State, Adams was Monroe's presumptive successor by the Jeffersonian tradition. Jackson was, however, the great hero of New Orleans, the candidate of the southwest, and the heir of Crawford's support. Clay, geographically and ideologically in competition with Jackson, was the weakest of the four candidates.

The outcome of the election in the electoral college was:

$$
\begin{array}{lll}
\text{Jackson:} & 99 & \text{votes and a majority in 11 states} \\
\text{Adams:} & 84 & \text{// // // // // 7 //} \\
\text{Crawford:} & 41 & \text{// // // // // 3 //} \\
\text{Clay:} & \underline{37} & \text{// // // // // } \underline{3} \text{ //} \\
& 261 \div 2 = 130\tfrac{1}{2} & \qquad 24 \div 2 = 12
\end{array}
$$

Thus no candidate had a majority, so the election went to the House of Representatives, where the representatives from each state together cast one vote. With 24 states, a minimum winning coalition was thus 13. Since the Representatives were different people from the Electors and had different political opinions, it was to be expected that the lineup of states in the House would be different from the College. But in what way? The answer is easy enough to arrive at if one examines the foregoing distribution. The unique minimal winning coalition is Adams-Crawford-Clay. Jackson is strategically weak. Not surprisingly, therefore, many Representatives from states Jackson carried deserted his cause, and the line up in the House became:

Adams:	9 votes
Jackson:	7 votes
Crawford:	4 votes
Clay:	4 votes

Since the Twelfth Amendment limited the number of candidates in the House to the three highest, Clay was eliminated. What would he do with his votes? Missouri slipped away quietly to Adams. This created the situation:

Adams:	10 votes
Jackson:	7 votes
Crawford:	4 votes
Clay:	3 votes

But what about the rest? The Kentucky legislature had instructed their Representative to vote for Jackson after Clay was eliminated. But that made very little sense to Clay, for if he had swung his votes as the Kentucky legislature wished, the result would be:

Adams:	10
Jackson:	10
Crawford:	4

and Crawford managers would be the pivot between Adams and Jackson. So out of this situation was born the so-called corrupt bargain between Adams and Clay: Adams got Clay's votes and Clay became Secretary of State and, if tradition held, the next President:

Adams:	13
Jackson:	7
Crawford:	4

and Adams won.

Many institutional forces, personal idosyncracies, and so on were doubtless involved in bringing about this outcome. It is interesting, however, that it is exactly the outcome that is the rational best advantage for Adams and Clay. The bargain of 1825 may have seemed corrupt (especially to Jackson men), and Randolph of Roanoke called it an alliance between "puritan and blackleg," between "Blifil and Black George." Nevertheless it also appears rationally best to those who have the power to bring it about, and from this perspective of history, therefore, it appears natural.

SUGGESTIONS FOR FURTHER READING

This chapter is based on WILLIAM H. RIKER, *The Theory of Political Coalitions* (New Haven: Yale University Press, 1962). Papers on applications are cited in the footnotes to the chapter.

8

Two-Person Game Theory

In the previous chapters we added restrictive detail to a general model of political society by assuming that utility is transferable or that society is engaged in a zero-sum game. Another way to add restrictive detail is to limit that society to two persons or two corporate units. Because of von Neumann's well-known theorem about solutions to zero-sum two-person games—the minimax theorem—it is sometimes popularly believed that the simple reduction in size to the two-person case is sufficient to bring about general equilibria. One of the main propositions we wish to demonstrate in this chapter, however, is that the theory of two-person games is much less complete than is often supposed. It is true that, within two-person theory, exact solutions exist for zero-sum finite games; but for nonzero-sum games and especially for those nonzero-sum cooperative games that so obviously model political situations in the real world, often no definable solution and hence no definable equilibria exist at all. Lest we proceed too rapidly, however, we turn first to a reexamination of the fundamental cause of disequilibrium in our models.

INTERDEPENDENCE OF INDIVIDUAL CHOICE

In Chapter 3 we set forth a basic framework for understanding individual choice. That framework consists of four concepts: (1) alternative acts, $A = \{a_1, a_2, \ldots, a_n\}$; (2) possible outcomes, $O = \{O_1, O_2, \ldots, O_m\}$; (3) the probability that an outcome occurs if a particular act is chosen, $P_i(O_k)$; and (4) the decision maker's evaluation (utility) of an outcome if he chooses a particular act, $U_i(O_k)$. In accordance with the postulate of rationality, we then assume that a decision maker acts as if he calculates the expected utility of each a_t in A and that he chooses the alternative that maximizes this expected utility.

In that elementary analysis of Chapter 3, if the alternatives, outcomes, subjective probability estimates, and utility functions of all relevant decision makers are known, equilibrium must prevail in the abstract model of society. Information about these four features is sufficient for predicting each person's choice; therefore it is sufficient for predicting the social choice. In subsequent chapters, however, disequilibrium is a pervasive feature of the theory. Thus, since our entire analysis is presumed to be the logical consequence of the postulate of rationality, an important question arises: if equilibrium is the consequence of the framework we present in Chapter 3, why does disequilibrium occur in the analyses we review subsequently?

The answer to this question is that in many circumstances, a simple decision-theoretic framework is inadequate. It may, for example, be unreasonable to suppose that people form any subjective estimate of $P_i(O_j)$. Such situations typically occur when a person is in direct interaction with other decision makers, in which case equilibrium is not guaranteed in theories about social interaction. And since the analyses we review in Chapters 4 through 7 concern social interaction, disequilibrium occurs.

To see this more clearly, let us reconsider the analysis in Chapter 3 of a citizen's calculus of voting. The derivation (which is not shown) of expression (3.11) assumes that the citizen estimates the probability, $P_0(n_1, n_2)$, that, when he abstains, candidate 1 receives n_1 votes and candidate 2 receives n_2 votes. We then assume that if the citizen chooses to vote, the choices of other citizens are unaffected. The consequence of this assumption is that if the citizen votes for candidate 1, the probability, $P_1(n_1 + 1, n_2)$, that candidate 1 receives $n_1 + 1$ votes while candidate 2 receives n_2 votes equals $P_0(n_1, n_2)$. Thus, our assumption, which has the effect of eliminating interdependent choices from the analysis, guarantees that all conditional probabilities for all outcomes are known so that the expected values of all alternatives can be calculated and compared.

Suppose, however, that interdependent choices are allowed. Specifically, suppose that the citizen is contemplating his vote in a small committee rather than a large electorate. Then he is more likely to act as if expectations about his decision affect the decisions of others and vice versa. It is no longer reasonable now to predict choices with an estimate of $P_1(n_1 + 1, n_2)$ that equates this probability to $P_0(n_1, n_2)$, which is to say that it is no longer reasonable to suppose that we know all conditional probabilities for all outcomes and to suppose that we can predict choices from simple expected-utility calculations. Rather, it is more reasonable to analyze a voter's decision as if it were, for example, the product of some coalition-formation process. And because no definable equilibria exist for many coalition processes, we are led to conclude that any disequilibrium is the consequence of the assumption that individual choices are interdependent.

THE GENERAL REPRESENTATION
OF A TWO-PERSON GAME

Because they are the classic and most elementary paradigms of interacting decision makers, two-person games permit us to explore further the causes and extent of disequilibrium in social choice. To begin, we denote person 1's alternatives by $\{a_1, a_2, \ldots\}$, we denote person 2's alternatives by $\{b_1, b_2, \ldots\}$, and, of course, we assume that the expected utility person 1 associates with alternative a_i, $E(a_i)$, is a function of the particular b_j selected by person 2. Since the notation $E(a_i)$ fails to represent this dependence adequately, however, we introduce the concept of a payoff function,

$$\varphi^k(a_i, b_j), \qquad \text{for } k = 1, 2,$$

so that, for example, $\varphi^1(a_i, b_j)$ denotes the utility (payoff) to person 1 if he chooses a_i and if person 2 chooses b_j. To say that person 1's utility is a function of both a_i and b_j does not, of course, mean that he is unable to calculate an expected value for each a_i. He might, for example, know the particular b_j the second person intends to select, or he might be able to assign each b_j a probability of being selected. A great deal might be known about the second decision maker's personality—including his propensity to pick a particular alternative, or his prior commitment to a choice.

To explore all possibilities completely, however, suppose that the particular a_i and b_j that maximizes φ^1 does not maximize φ^2 and what maximizes φ^2 does not maximize φ^1. Suppose further that each person knows the other's utility (payoff) function so that each knows the other's preference order over the set of alternative joint choices, $\{(a_i, b_j)\}$. Finally, assume that both decision makers are aware of these facts and each is aware that the other is aware. The problem confronting a decision maker, say player 1, now is that the context of choice can compel him to reason thus: "If I think that player 2 will choose b', I should choose a'. But if player 2 thinks that I think he will play b', he will choose b'', which is his best response to a'. Of course, if I think he will choose b'', I should choose a''," and so on. The players, then, are confronted with the "he thinks that I think" regress. That is, the interdependence of choice in this instance results in the paradoxical conclusion that a good guess as to the other player's choice cannot be good because he can anticipate it.

We might, then, seek to resolve such confusion in our theory by assuming that each person invokes the principle of insufficient reason, which is the supposition that, in the absence of any information about him, the other person is as likely to choose one alternative as another. Clearly, this is an admissible decision rule, but it cannot really be used to terminate the "he thinks . . ." regress. Person 1 can reason thus: "If I employ the principle of insufficient reason, then he should also employ this principle. But if he does so, I can calculate the probability that he selects a specific alternative, and I can choose accordingly. However, if he thinks that I am about to do this, he no longer invokes the principle," and so on.

In addition to the fact that it does not really work in this case, the principle of insufficient reason is generally undesirable. It is an assumption about the behavior of others based entirely on knowledge of one's self (that is, on knowledge of one's ignorance). It seems unreasonable to impute probabilities to others on this basis alone. And in this case it is quite unjustified objectively, for we assume earlier that the persons do possess some knowledge of each other. Specifically, each person knows the other's payoff function and each knows that the other is a utility-maximizer. If a decision maker invokes the rule of insufficient reason, he fails to use this vital information effectively.

A TYPOLOGY OF TWO-PERSON GAMES

To see how such information is used, we present a standard typology of games— a typology derived from three of their essential features: (1) the relationship between φ^1 and φ^2, (2) the properties of $\{a_i\}$ and $\{b_j\}$, and (3) the possibilities for communication between the two decision makers. With respect to the first feature, we have two possibilities:

(i) *Zero-sum games.* If a game is zero-sum, φ^1 and φ^2 satisfy

$$\varphi^1(a_i, b_j) = -\varphi^2(a_i, b_j) \qquad \text{for all } a_i \text{ and } b_j.$$

This possibility is perhaps the most familiar kind of game, inasmuch as many parlor games are zero-sum. Discussions of zero-sum games are typically used to introduce the subject of game theory. Zero-sum games correspond to situations of complete conflict—the decision makers' objectives are perfectly asymmetric. That is, we can arrange the strategy pairs (a_i, b_j) such that a plot of φ^1 against φ^2 results in a 45-degree line through the origin with a negative slope. This situation is depicted in Figure 8.1.[1]

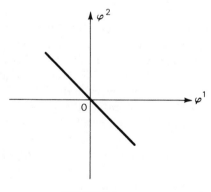

FIGURE 8.1

[1]An equivalent situation is one in which $\varphi^1 = -\varphi^2 - k$, which is the "constant-sum" game. Since utility functions are invariant with positive linear transformations, we could define $\varphi_0{}^2 = \varphi^2 + k$, which is to say that $\varphi_0{}^2$ is an equivalent utility function for person 2. Observe now that $\varphi^1 = -\varphi_0{}^2$, so that the constant-sum game is thus rendered zero-sum. The graph of a

(ii) *Nonzero-sum games.* One means of defining a nonzero-sum game is to say that at least two strategy pairs exist, say (a',b') and (a'',b'') such that

$$\varphi^1(a', b') > \varphi^1(a'', b'')$$
$$\varphi^2(a', b') > \varphi^2(a'', b'')$$

—that is, both players prefer (a', b') to (a'', b'').

The set of nonzero-sum games is, of course, simply the complement of the set of zero-sum games. Those familiar with the expository literature of game theory should recognize the names of several examples of nonzero-sum games: the Prisoners' Dilemma, Chicken, the Battle of the Sexes, and Luke and Matthew. Such a proliferation of illustrations suggests (correctly) that a great variety of interesting political situations can be modeled as nonzero-sum games.

We examine several of these situations in detail later, but for the moment we continue with our typology. The second dimension of this typology concerns the properties of $\{a_i\}$ and $\{b_j\}$. There are two general possibilities:

(I) *Both decision makers are confronted with a finite number of alternatives.* Such games are referred to as *finite* or *matrix* games because they can be represented by a matrix. The rows of such a matrix denote one person's alternatives, the columns the other person's alternatives; and the entry in each cell formed by the intersection of a row and a column denotes the payoff to both players.

Political scientists have preoccupied themselves primarily with matrix games, perhaps because of a preoccupation with the several fascinating examples of such games (e.g., the Prisoners' Dilemma). But matrix games are a special case of a potentially far more important possibility.

(II) *Both decision makers are confronted with an infinite number of alternatives.* Such games are referred to as *infinite* games.

Examples of infinite games include situations in which (1) each player must choose a time to perform a particular act, (2) the players bargain over the division of some infinitely divisible commodity, (3) each player must select a speed at which to drive his automobile, and (4) a general must decide how to allocate a large army among several battlefields. These examples illustrate the generality of the concept of an infinite game. Surprisingly, however, they receive little attention in social and political science, and so we examine them in some detail.[2]

Turning now to the third dimension of our typology—the ability of the

---

constant-sum game is just like that of a zero-sum game, namely a negatively diagonal straight line, except that for the constant-sum game this line does not run through the origin.

[2]Anatol Rapoport, for example, fails to mention infinite games entirely in *Two-Person Game Theory* (Ann Arbor: University of Michigan Press, 1966), while R. Duncan Luce and Howard Raiffa, *Games and Decisions* (New York: Wiley, 1957), relegate their discussion of them to an appendix.

decision makers to communicate before choosing their strategies—the first possibility is that:

(a)   *The game is a noncooperative game.* Noncooperative games correspond to situations in which the decision makers are unable to communicate (e.g., unable to coordinate their decisions) in any way before they choose their strategies.

The second possibility is that:

(b)   *The game is a cooperative game.* Cooperative games correspond to situations in which each decision maker can communicate noise-free with the other (e.g., the players can coordinate their decisions) before each chooses his strategy.

Clearly, (a) and (b) represent extreme possibilities. For example, it can be the case that only one decision maker is able to communicate whatever he wishes. Or, perhaps communication is imperfect, such as when a telephone conversation occurs over a faulty connection. That is, the information people transmit can contain some noise. Again, the decision makers might be able to communicate only certain things, such as the elimination of a subset of alternatives from consideration. Such situations of imperfect communication result, typically, from inadequate technology. There are other, quite different, kinds of imperfect communication—for example, the transmission of faulty information, as when one decision maker deliberately misleads the other or when he deliberately breaks off communication or any possibility of communicating. In general, games which satisfy requirement (b) allow for the possibility of discussion and coordination of action; but we do not require that any discussion or coordination actually occur.

Our typology of games is now complete. Since there are two possibilities for each of the three dimensions, we have eight types of games:

(1)   zero-sum, finite, noncooperative games [i, I, a],
(2)   zero-sum, infinite, noncooperative games [i, II, a],
(3)   zero-sum, finite, cooperative games [i, I, b],
(4)   zero-sum, infinite, cooperative games [i, II, b],
(5)   nonzero-sum, finite, noncooperative games [ii, I, a],
(6)   nonzero-sum, infinite, noncooperative games [ii, II, a],
(7)   nonzero-sum, finite, cooperative games [ii, I, b],
(8)   nonzero-sum, infinite, cooperative games [ii, II, b].

Before considering each of these combinations separately, let us first eliminate two of them—combinations (3) and (4). Zero-sum games are games of perfect conflict, so that it is irrational for one decision maker to reveal anything about his choices to the other decision maker. A person might, of course, attempt to deceive an opponent into believing something that is patently not true, but such a tactic is so trivial and obvious that we disregard (3) and (4) entirely.

We turn then to an analysis of the remaining six types of two-person games.[3]

SOLUTIONS

1. Zero-sum, finite, noncooperative games

We begin by introducing the notion of a *strategy*, which we define as a set of complete instructions for one player on how to play a game. A game consists of a series of moves, which are occasions to choose among alternatives of actions. We reduce a game to exactly one move, namely the choice of a strategy which tells one player precisely what to do at every possible move. In the game of tic-tac-toe, a move is the opportunity to choose a cell in which to put a nought or a cross, and a strategy is an instruction for each move for a particular player. For example, "At the first move, place a cross in the center cell. If at the second move the other player places a nought in a corner cell, then in the third move place a cross in another corner. If at the second move the other player places a nought in a noncorner cell, place a cross in a corner cell," and so on. Most discussion of two-person games is in terms of strategies which may be thought of as alternatives of action of the sort we have discussed as $\{a_1, a_2, \ldots\}$ and $\{b_1, b_2, \ldots\}$.

We introduce also the definition of an *equilibrium* strategy pair. Assuming that player 1 chooses a^* from A and player 2 chooses b^* from B, the chosen pair (a^*, b^*) is said to be an equilibrium pair if

$$\varphi^1(a^*, b^*) \geq \varphi^1(a_i, b^*) \qquad \text{for all } a_i \in A, \tag{8.1a}$$

---

[3]At this point it is useful to distinguish between the analyses of n-person and two-person games. In n-person theory, utility is transferable, i.e., if $v(S)$ is the value of a coalition, then v (S) can be divided up in any way among the members of S. In fact, the assumption of transferable utility is necessary to define the value of a coalition. The solution concepts of two-person games, however, do not impose this assumption. It is not imposed, first, because of its similarity to interpersonal comparability of utility and the desire to avoid such comparisons (see Chapter 4). Second, it is not imposed because with it two-person games become trivial examples of their n-person counterparts. To see this, suppose that utility is transferable, in which case a two-person game can be represented in the characteristic-function form of n-person games. The characteristic function for a zero-sum game becomes

$$v(1) = v_1, \qquad v(2) = -v_1, \qquad v(12) = 0.$$

Since $v(1) + v(2) = v(12)$, the game is inessential and of no interest. The characteristic function for nonzero-sum games in normalized form becomes

$$v(1) = 0, \qquad v(2) = 0, \qquad v(12) = 1,$$

which is to say that the task of the players is simply to agree to a division of $v(12)$. But n-person theory cannot tell us what this division will be. Clearly, the assumption of transferable utility eliminates the most interesting features of two-person games—their strategic structure. Of course, as Anatol Rapoport [*N-Person Game Theory* (Ann Arbor: University of Michigan Press, 1970), p. 169] points out, "In the context of the n-person game (n > 2), all of the information pertaining to the actual strategic structure of the game has likewise been thrown away. However, enough complexity remains when the games are presented in characteristic function form to provide material for a complex theory." To keep two-person games interesting, then, we do not assume transferable utility.

$$\varphi^2(a^*, b^*) \geq \varphi^2(a^*, b_j) \qquad \text{for all } b_j \in B, \qquad (8.1b)$$

which, since $\varphi^1 = -\varphi^2$, can be combined into a single expression thus:[4]

$$\varphi^1(a^*, b_j) \geq \varphi^1(a^*, b^*) \geq \varphi^1(a_i, b^*) \qquad \text{for all } a_i \in A, b_j \in B. \qquad (8.2)$$

Stated differently, requirement (8.1a)—or equivalently, the second inequality in (8.2)—is that, if the second player adopts b^*, the first player has no incentive to adopt any strategy other than a^* because he makes at least as much out of a^* as out of any other strategy. Requirement (8.1b)—or the first inequality in (8.2)—is that if the first player adopts a^*, then the second player has no incentive to adopt any strategy other than b^*, because he makes at least as much out of b^* as out of any other strategy. Hence, if the players are at (a^*, b^*), they are in equilibrium—neither has any incentive unilaterally to alter his strategy.

Of course, we do not yet know whether or not such an a^* and a b^* exist. First, however, we interpret (8.2) with an example. Consider the game displayed by Figure 8.2, in which the cell entries are the payoffs to the first player. (Since the game is zero-sum, the second player receives the negative of the entries.)

	b_1	b_2	b_3	b_4
a_1	10	3	-6	0
a_2	7	2	-4	-1
a_3	0	-6	-5	8
a_4	-1	9	-7	-8

FIGURE 8.2

To verify that the strategy pair (a_2, b_3) satisfies expression (8.2), note that, if the first player selects a_2, then, for $j = 1, 2, 3$, or 4,

$$\varphi^1(a_2, b_j) \geq \varphi^1(a_2, b_3) = -4.$$

Similarly, if the second player selects b_3, then, for $i = 1, 2, 3$, or 4,

$$-4 = \varphi^1(a_2, b_3) \geq \varphi^1(a_i, b_3).$$

Hence,

$$\varphi^1(a^* = a_2, b_j) \geq \varphi^1(a^* = a_2, b^* = b_3) \geq \varphi^1(a_i, b^* = b_3)$$

for all $a_i \in A$ and $b_j \in B$, so that (a_2, b_3) is indeed an equilibrium pair.

[4]Multiplying (8.1b) by -1 yields $-\varphi^2(a^*, b^*) \leq -\varphi^2(a^*, b_j)$, which is equivalent to $\varphi^1(a^*, b^*) \leq \varphi^1(a^*, b_j)$ because $\varphi^1 = -\varphi^2$. Combining this inequality with (8.1a) yields (8.2).

We can offer now an interpretation of an equilibrium pair. Suppose player 2 is omniscient, i.e., he always knows the strategy that the first player intends to play. If so, then, whatever strategy, a_i, player 1 chooses, player 2 will be able to choose a strategy, b_j, to minimize the value of φ^1. And indeed, 2 will want to minimize 1's payoff because the game is zero-sum. Player 1, then, should select the strategy that maximizes his minimum gain. In Figure 8.2, the minimum gain from a_1 is –6, from a_2 is –4, from a_3 is –5, and from a_4 is –8. Hence, confronted with an omniscient opponent, the first player selects a_2, which leads to the maximum of his several minima.[5]

Symbolically, we denote the minimum gain from a_i—the security level of a_i—as

$$\min_{j} \varphi^1(a_i, b_j).$$

Similarly, we denote the maximum of the minimum gain of the first decision-maker—his maximum security level—by

$$v_1' = \max_{i} \min_{j} \varphi^1(a_i, b_j).$$

Hence, for the game illustrated in Figure 8.1, $v_1' = -4$; that is, the important feature of the strategy is that it maximizes the minimum gain of the first decision maker: it guarantees him a payoff of at least -4. Similarly, if we define

$$v_2' = \min_{j} \max_{i} \varphi^1(a_i, b_j),$$

we find that b^* minimizes the maximum loss of the second player and that $v_2' = -4$. That is, if the second player similarly assumes that he is confronted with an omniscient opponent who is trying to make the second player lose a maximum, then player 2 tries to minimize his maximum loss by selecting his equilibrium strategy, b^*. In Figure 8.2, the second player's maximum losses are: from b_1, 10; from b_2, 9; from b_3, –4 (i.e., a gain of 4); from b_4, 8. Hence, player 2 selects b_3, which minimizes his maximum loss.

Clearly, as the example shows, equilibrium strategies sometimes exist. But is it always the case that they maximize minimum gain and minimize maximum loss? In fact, if they exist, they do indeed so maximize and minimize. To see this, observe, from the first inequality in (8.2), that the security level of a^* is $\varphi^1(a^*, b^*)$, i.e.,

[5]Sometimes a player believes that his opponents are not omniscient, indeed that they are not very smart. Acting on this assumption, he may choose, for the example of Figure 8.2, to exploit his opponents' presumed stupidity by choosing a_1. This is a dangerous policy, however, because one of the oldest and most effective tricks in the world is for smart opponents to appear dumb. (This is referred to as "badmouthing" or "leading the sucker on.") It is probably wise, therefore, for the player always to suppose that his opponents are smarter than they appear, indeed even that they are omniscient. And on this assumption, the security level of the strategy leading to an equilibrium pair is very attractive.

$$\min_{j} \varphi^1(a^*, b_j) = \varphi^1(a^*, b^*).$$

The security level of any other strategy, a_i, clearly cannot be greater than $\varphi^1(a_i, b^*)$, since from (8.1b) the second player can always keep φ^1 down to $\varphi^1(a_i, b^*)$ by adopting b^*. Hence,

$$\min_{j} \varphi^1(a_i, b_j) \leq \varphi^1(a_i, b^*).$$

But from the second inequality in (8.2), $\varphi^1(a^*, b^*) \geq \varphi^1(a_i, b^*)$. Hence,

$$\min_{j} \varphi^1(a_i, b_j) \leq \varphi^1(a_i, b^*) \leq \varphi^1(a^*, b^*) = \min_{j} \varphi^1(a^*, b_j),$$

or simply

$$\min_{j} v^1(a_i, b_j) \leq \min_{j} \varphi^1(a^*, b_j),$$

which is to say that a^* maximizes the first player's security level. That is,

$$\max_{i} \min_{j} \varphi^1(a_i, b_j) = \varphi^1(a^*, b^*),$$

so $v_1' = \varphi^1(a^*, b^*)$. In an analogous way we can show that for the second player,

$$\min_{j} \max_{i} \varphi^1(a_i, b_j) = \varphi^1(a^*, b^*) = v_2'.$$

Thus, we say that a^* is the first player's *maximin* strategy and that b^* is the second player's *minimax* strategy.

Three additional and important features of equilibrium strategies for zero-sum games follow from this analysis. First, player 1's maximin security level is equal to player 2's minimax security level. That is,

(i) $$v_1' = v_2'.$$

Second, if a game possesses more than one equilibrium pair, the players are indifferent as to which equilibrium prevails. Thus, if (a^*, b^*) and (a', b') are equilibrium pairs for the same game,

(ii) $$\varphi^k(a^*, b^*) = \varphi^k(a', b'), \qquad k = 1, 2.$$

Finally, if one or both players possesses two or more equilibrium strategies, the choice of an equilibrium strategy does not revert to the "he thinks" regress. Specifically,

(iii) $$(a^*, b') \text{ and } (a', b^*) \text{ are equilibrium pairs.}$$

Thus, a^* and a' guarantee player 1 a minimum payoff of v_1', while b^* and b' guarantee player 2 a maximum loss of v_2'. Furthermore,

$$\varphi^k(a^*, b') = \varphi^k(a', b^*) = \varphi^k(a^*, b^*) = \varphi^k(a', b'), \qquad \text{for } k = 1, 2.$$

Finally, once at (a^*, b'), (a', b^*), (a^*, b^*), or (a', b'), neither player has any incentive to alter his strategy unilaterally.

Clearly, then, equilibrium strategy pairs possess interesting characteristics—characteristics that render them powerfully attractive to the players. Given this attraction, we define the *solution* to a game as the payoffs arrived at from the selection of an equilibrium pair of strategies.

It is, of course, entirely possible that players do not choose such strategies. It might be argued, again using the example of Figure 8.2, that a_1 is a better strategy than a_2 because it maximizes the potential gain of the second player. Both persons might decide simply to take a gamble and go for broke, despite our advice in footnote 5 about assuming omniscience in the opponent. And we cannot be certain that this is not the reasoning that people sometimes use. That is, we cannot be certain that, despite the possibility of becoming trapped in the "he thinks that I think" regress, people nevertheless act as if they made probability estimates about the choices of others, in which case our task is not to ascertain equilibrium strategies but rather to understand how they arrive at their estimates of probabilities.

Other than an introspective evaluation of our own motives and psyches, there is one reason for believing that people might sometimes choose on the basis of such estimates. Specifically, the difficulty with our definition of a solution is that not all zero-sum games possess strategy pairs that satisfy (8.2). Suppose, for example, that the payoff in cell (a_3, b_3) of Figure 8.2 is increased to –3. Clearly, (a_2, b_3) is no longer an equilibrium pair, since

$$\varphi^1(a_3, b_3) = -3 > \varphi^1(a_2, b_3) = -4,$$

which is to say that player 1 prefers a_3 to a_2 if player 2 chooses b_3. But (a_3, b_3) is not an equilibrium pair either since, if the first decision maker adopts a_3, the second decision maker prefers b_2. In fact, if we examine every strategy pair, we find that this new game does not possess an equilibrium. Since we define the notion of a solution to a game in terms of the equilibrium strategies $a*$ and $b*$, the question then is: what predictions can we make about individual choice if a game does not possess strategies that satisfy (8.2)? We have already suggested one solution, namely, to assume that people act as if they make subjective probability estimates of other people's choices. To explore all possibilities with respect to the concept of equilibrium, however, we rephrase our question to: what choices *should* rational decision makers make if they cannot formulate subjective probability estimates? We can offer an answer to this slightly less demanding question.

Observe that, thus far, we require that each player select exactly one alternative. A person cannot choose two alternatives and he cannot choose alternatives probabilistically. Clearly, choosing two alternatives makes no sense and so we eliminate such an act; but there is no reason to suppose that a person cannot choose alternatives probabilistically. That is, the first player in our previous illustration might toss a coin in choosing between a_2 and a_3: if the coin falls heads, he adopts a_2, and if the coin falls tails, he adopts a_3.

To see the advantage that such a *mixed* strategy might have, suppose that the first player's mixed strategy is $p(A)$—that is, he adopts a_1 with probability $p(a_1)$, a_2 with probability $p(a_2)$, and so on, and let $q(B)$ be the second player's mixed strategy. [As an example, a mixed strategy over four pure strategies, a_1 to a_4, might be: select a_1 with the probability of $\frac{1}{12}$ or $p(a_1) = \frac{1}{12}$, $p(a_2) = \frac{1}{6}$, $p(a_3) = \frac{1}{3}$, and $p(a_4) = \frac{5}{12}$. Simply,

$$p(A) = \left(\frac{1}{12}, \frac{1}{6}, \frac{1}{3}, \frac{5}{12}\right).$$

Pure strategies may be thought of as mixed strategies where, for example, the pure strategy a_1 is denoted by $p(A) = (1, 0, 0, 0)$.] In any game the first player's expected payoff, φ^1, from the two mixed strategies $p(A)$ and $q(B)$ then is

$$\varphi^1(p(A), q(B)) = \sum_j \sum_i p(a_i)q(b_j)\varphi^1(a_i, b_j). \tag{8.3}$$

The right side indicates that the payoff is the sum of the payoffs for each possible outcome where each such payoff is multiplied by the chance that the alternatives leading to it will be chosen under $p(A)$ and $q(B)$.

The first player's maximum security level can be expressed now as[6]

$$v_1 = \max_p \min_q \varphi^1(p, q).$$

and the second player's minimax security level becomes

$$v_2 = \min_q \max_p \varphi^1(p, q).$$

Recall now that if a pure-strategy equilibrium exists, $v_1' = v_2'$ and expression (8.2) holds. In a now classic discovery—the minimax theorem—von Neumann proved that $v_1 = v_2$ for all finite zero-sum games. Stated differently, for any such game at least one strategy pair, (p^*, q^*), exists such that

$$\varphi^1(p^*, q) \geq \varphi^1(p^*, q^*) \geq \varphi^1(p, q^*). \tag{8.4}$$

Hence, if a pure-strategy equilibrium does not exist, a mixed-strategy equilibrium does. Furthermore, if a game possesses a pure-strategy equilibrium, $v_1' = v_1$, $v_2' = v_2$, and the solution to (8.4) reduces to (8.2) [i.e., $p(a^*) = 1$ and $q(b^*) = 1$]. Thus, admitting mixed strategies into a game will not upset a pure-strategy equilibrium if one exists.

Let us consider briefly now a special class of zero-sum games—*symmetric zero-sum games*. Suppose both players select their strategies from an identical set of alternatives (i.e., $a_1 = b_1$, $a_2 = b_2$, and so on) and suppose that

---

[6]The notation $\max\limits_p$ means the maximum over the set of all admissible mixed strategies for player 1, and $\min\limits_q$ means the minimum over the set of all admissible mixed strategies for player 2. A mixed strategy is admissible simply if it conforms to the two basic features of probability numbers, namely, that probabilities are nonnegative [i.e., $p(a_i)$ and $q(b_j) \geq 0$ for all a_i and b_j] and that their sum over all possible and mutually exclusive events equals 1 [i.e., $\sum\limits_A p(a_i) = \sum\limits_B q(b_j) = 1$].

$$\varphi^1(X, Y) = \varphi^2(Y, X),$$

where X and Y are any two pure or mixed strategies. That is, suppose that if the first player adopts Y and the second player adopts X, player 1's payoff is equal to player 2's payoff when they switch strategies. Such games are called symmetric games, and a symmetric zero-sum game possesses the following important properties:

(i)   if the players adopt identical strategies, the payoff to each player is zero;

(ii) if p^* is an equilibrium strategy for player 1, it is also an equilibrium strategy for player 2 [i.e., if (p^*, q^*) is an equilibrium pair, (p^*, p^*), (q^*, q^*), and (q^*, p^*) are equilibrium pairs also];

(iii) if the players are at an equilibrium, the payoff to each player is zero [i.e., $v_1' = v_2' = 0$, which is to say that $\varphi^1(p^*, q^*) = \varphi^2(p^*, q^*) = 0$].

We can illustrate the properties of a symmetric zero-sum game by modeling a two-candidate election as a game (in which the candidates' payoffs are their pluralities). If both candidates have the same opportunities to attract voters (i.e., if partisan identification does not bias a citizen's choice, and the candidates choose from indentical sets of strategies), the election game is symmetric. Thus from the properties of symmetric games, each candidate's expected plurality is zero if both choose an equilibrium strategy pair. Stated differently, the expected outcome of a symmetric election is a tie.

Before we conclude our discussion of solutions to finite, zero-sum games, we ask again whether or not it is reasonable to suppose that people actually act as if they employed mixed minimax strategies. Clearly, we cannot rule out any possibility without empirical evidence, but it is difficult, if not impossible, to imagine that they do. To assert the social reality of mixed strategies is to assert that, either by conscious calculation or by the calculations implied from learning appropriate responses to classes of situations, mixed minimax strategies are revealed and chosen. But the calculation of mixed strategies is neither easy nor costless.[7] It seems reasonable to assume that, to avoid the cost of calculation, people adopt pure "nonoptimal" strategies.

Consider, for example, the simple game illustrated in Figure 8.3. The solution to this game for the first player is the mixed strategy $p^*(a_1) = \frac{3}{4}$, $p^*(a_2) = \frac{1}{4}$; with $v_1 = \frac{1}{2}$. Suppose, however, that the cost of calculating this mixed strategy is -2. If he calculates a mixed strategy, then, his actual

[7]For some empirical evidence that strongly supports the hypothesis that people calculate and use pure equilibrium strategies but which only weakly supports the hypothesis that they calculate and use mixed minimax strategies, see Bernard Lieberman, "Human Behavior in a Strictly Determined 3×3 Matrix Game," *Behavioral Science*, vol. 5 (1960), pp. 317–22, and with D. Malcolm, "The Behavior of Responsive Individuals Playing a 2–Person Game Requiring the Use of Mixed Strategies," *Psychoanalytic Science*, vol. 2 (1965), pp. 373–74. We do not review in this book the general method for calculating the minimax solution to a finite, zero-sum game. This method is reviewed in Luce and Raiffa, *Games and Decisions*, pp. 400–446, and Guillermo Owen, *Game Theory* (Philadelphia: Saunders, 1968), pp. 25–33, 38–67.

expected payoff is $v_1 - 2 = -\frac{3}{2}$. Observe, now, that the worst he can do with either pure strategy is -1. Hence, rather than compute the mixed-strategy solution, he might (or should) prefer simply to choose (perhaps randomly) a pure strategy. We can only speculate on how such a choice is made, but it seems reasonable to assume that he reduces the game to a simple decision-making task by terminating the "he thinks that I think" regress at some point. That is, the player acts as if he knows the probability that his opponent will select a particular alternative by terminating the regress when the additional expected benefits of speculating further about the opponent's psyche are outweighted by the costs of doing so. (Of course, the regress may also be terminated by the necessity for making a choice in some fixed amount of time.)

	b_1	b_2
a_1	1	0
a_2	-1	2

FIGURE 8.3

Despite our pessimism about the relevance of the concept of mixed minimax strategies for politics, we turn now to infinite zero-sum games, where the analysis is far more exceptional than for finite games.

2. Zero-sum infinite noncooperative games

Infinite games can be divided into two categories: (1) those with an infinite but countable number of pure strategies, and (2) those with an infinite but uncountable number of strategies. An example of (1) is where A is the set of positive integers, $\{1, 2, 3, \ldots\}$, so that $a_i = i$ and i is an integer. Since the number of integers is infinite, $A = \{a_i\}$ is infinite; and each integer has a well-defined label $(1, 2, 3, \ldots)$, so A is countable. An example of (2) is $a_i = i$ and i is any number between 0 and 1. Letting the variable a denote a strategy, a can now assume an infinite number of values; but, unlike integers, not all of these values possess a clear and well-defined label (e.g., $0.80376333\ldots$), in which case the set of strategies is said to be an uncountable set.[8] Any continuous interval contains an uncountable number of numbers.

Suppose now that an infinite zero-sum game has countably many strategies—category (1) Do equilibrium strategy pairs exist for such games; that is, can we

[8]The term "uncountable" comes from the fact that all of the numbers between, say, 0 and 1 cannot be counted—they cannot all be placed in a 1-to-1 correspondence with the integers. The proof of this fact—which can be found in any introductory text on real-variable analysis—consists of showing that there are fewer integers than there are numbers between 0 and 1.

guarantee that each player possesses at least one strategy that satisfies expression (8.4) or perhaps expression (8.2)? The answer, generally, is "No." That is, infinite zero-sum games differ sharply from their finite counterparts in that they can fail to possess minimax solutions. For example, suppose that A and B are the set of integers, and that

$$\varphi^1(a_i, b_j) = \begin{cases} 1 & \text{if} \quad i > j, \\ -1 & \text{if} \quad i < j, \\ 0 & \text{if} \quad i = j. \end{cases}$$

That is, suppose that each decision maker must select an integer, and the one who selects the largest integer wins one point from the other. This game does not possess any minimax solution.[9] Another example of a game without a solution is: $\varphi^1(a_i, b_j) = i - j$. Again, each player tries to choose as large a number as possible, but, of course, for every integer there is an infinite number of larger ones. In fact, this zero-sum game is completely pathological: mixed strategies exist which yield an infinite positive expected payoff for *both* players.[10]

While countably infinite games are thus quite frustrating, games with an uncountable infinity of strategies are surprisingly tractable. One might expect to encounter at least as much difficulty in analyzing these latter games as in analyzing games with a countable infinity of strategies (if only because the integers are a subset of the real numbers). But we can simplify by imposing further restrictions on A and B, notably by imposing the assumption that each player is confronted with a continuum of pure strategies and that this continuum can be represented by the interval $[0, 1]$.[11] Such games are referred to as *games on the unit square* because if we denote a pure-strategy pair (a, b) by a point in a two-dimensional coordinate system (where one dimension measures A and the other dimension measures B), then any admissible pure-strategy pair [i.e., all (a, b) such that $a \in A$ and $b \in B$] lies in or on a square with an area equal to 1.

Assuming that A and B are the continuous, bounded interval $[0, 1]$ does not solve all our problems. We need additional restrictions. We assume also that φ^1 and φ^2 are continuous functions everywhere and that the mixed strategy $p(A)$ is a probability density function over A and that $q(B)$ is a probability density function over B.[12] If these assumptions are satisfied, then a pair,

[9]For a proof, see Owen, *Game Theory*, pp. 72–73.

[10]*Ibid.*, p. 73.

[11]The notation "[0,1]" reads "all numbers between 0 and 1, including 0 and 1." This continuum is said to be *bounded*. Alternatively, the notation "(0,1)" reads "all numbers between 0 and 1, except 0 and 1." This continuum is said to be *unbounded*. We require that the continuum for A and B be bounded. The particular interval $[0,1]$ is selected only as a convenient normalization; i.e., we could require A and B to be any bounded interval $[x, y]$ and then normalize all numbers in $[x, y]$ so that $x = 0$ and $y = 1$.

[12]Rigorous definitions of continuity can be found in any text on calculus or real-variable analysis. Roughly, we mean that φ^1 contains no instantaneous "jumps" in value (note that if φ^1 is continuous, φ^2 is continuous because $\varphi^2 = -\varphi^1$). Hence, $\varphi^1 = ab + 2a + 3b$ is continuous in a and in b whereas

$p*(A)$ and $q*(B)$, exists that satisfies (8.4).[13] That is, if φ^1 and φ^2 are continuous functions, the infinite game is much the same as a finite game.

There are, however, two problems with this solution. First, if $p*$ and $q*$ are continuous density functions (e.g., the normal density), then the probability with which a player selects any specific $a \in A$ is zero [i.e., for continuous densities, $p(a) = 0$ for each $a \in A$]. Hence, it may be somewhat difficult to interpret this result in prescriptive terms.[14] The second difficulty lies in calculating $p*$ and $q*$. For finite games, the general analytic technique of linear programming is used to compute minimax strategies. But no such general analytic device has yet been devised to calculate these strategies for continuous games. Hence, even though we know that $p*$ and $q*$ exist, it is not reasonable to suppose that people act as if they knew what they are. Even if we take on the prescriptive role of telling people what they should do, given their goals, we may have to try several alternative procedures to compute $p*$ and $q*$.[15]

As a prescriptive device, then, the general theory of infinite zero-sum games with continuous payoffs is not wholly adequate. If one is willing to impose an additional restriction on φ^k, however, then at least one result with some predictive value can be proved. Specifically, suppose that[16]

φ^1 is concave in a and convex in b,
φ^2 is concave in b and convex in a.

Thus, for any fixed value of b, φ^1 increases at a decreasing rate or decreases at an increasing rate as a increases from 0 to 1. Similarly, for any fixed value

$$\varphi^1 = \begin{cases} 1 & \text{if } a < b, \\ 0 & \text{if } a = b, \\ -1 & \text{if } a > b, \end{cases}$$

is not continuous at $a = b$.

[13]For the simplest proof of this result, see Owen, *Game Theory*, pp. 74–78.

[14]Some work, however, has been done on ascertaining conditions under which $p*$ and $q*$ are discrete functions (e.g., the binomial distribution), in which case $p*(a)$ can be positive. Unfortunately, this work is far too mathematically complex to review here. The reader is referred to Ewald Burger, *Introduction to the Theory of Games* (Englewood Cliffs, N.J.: Prentice-Hall, Inc., 1963); and Samuel Karlin, *Mathematical Methods and Theory of Games, Programming, and Economics*, vol. 2 (Reading, Mass.: Addison-Wesley, 1959).

[15]See, for example, Samuel Karlin, *Mathematical Methods*.

[16]Formally, φ^1 is said to be concave in a if, for all ξ, $0 \le \xi \le 1$,
$$\varphi^1(\xi a' + (1 - \xi)a'', b) \ge \xi \varphi^1(a', b) + (1 - \xi)\varphi^1(a'', b)$$
for all b in B and all a', a'' in A. Similarly, φ^1 is convex in b if
$$\varphi^1(a, \xi b' + (1 - \xi)b'') \le \xi \varphi^1(a, b') + (1 - \xi)\varphi^1(a, b'')$$
for all a in A, and all b', b'' in B. For a geometric interpretation of these definitions, plot φ^1 against a. Select any two points on this curve and connect them with a line; then, if φ^1 is concave in a, the line connecting these two points lies beneath the curve. And if such lines for all possible pairs of points lie beneath this curve, then the curve is concave in a. The definition of concavity is illustrated in Figure 8.4.

An equivalent interpretation can be given to the definition of convexity except that now the lines must lie above the curve. The condition defining convexity is illustrated in Figure 8.5

of a, φ^1 decreases at a decreasing rate or increases at an increasing rate as b increases from 0 to 1.

If these assumptions are satisfied, and if φ^1 and φ^2 are continuous functions, then a pure-strategy pair (a^*, b^*) exists that satisfies (8.1).[17] Furthermore, if

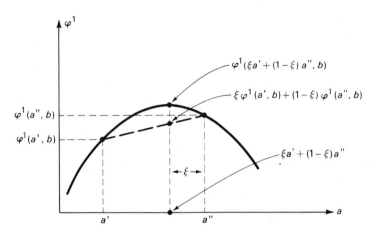

FIGURE 8.4
A concave function

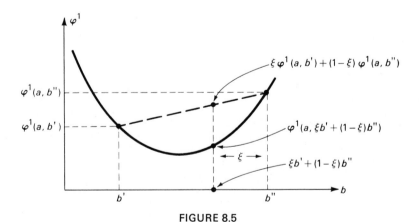

FIGURE 8.5
A convex function

[17]The proof of this theorem exists in various forms but it is generally attributed to H. F. Bohnenblust, S. Karlin, and L. S. Shapley, "Games with Continuous, Convex Pay-Off," in H.W. Kuhn and A. W. Tucker, eds., *Contributions to the Theory of Games*, vol. 1, Annals of Mathematics Studies, no. 24 (Princeton, N.J.: Princeton University Press, 1950), pp. 181–192; see also Owen, *Game Theory*, pp. 78–81; and Burger, *Introduction to the Theory of Games*, pp. 75–76.

the game is symmetric, $a^* = b^*$, and the decision makers possess identical minimax pure strategies.

This is one of the most powerful theorems proved for infinite games. It does not initially appear to have much practical application because it is difficult to interpret substantively the condition of concavity-convexity. It turns out, however, that some of our later assumptions about candidates and elections satisfy the conditions of this theorem. (See Chapters 11 and 12.) Hence, we can use it and thereby invest it with substantive significance.

Before we conclude our discussion of infinite zero-sum games, let us consider briefly one final possibility—namely, that φ^1 and φ^2 are not continuous. A typical example of such a game is the *game of timing*, in which A and B are the possible times at which the two decision makers take a specific action, and in which each decision maker prefers to take that action as late as possible, provided he does so before his opponent acts. For example, the game could be a duel in which the duelists walk toward each other, each holding a pistol with one bullet. Suppose the guns are sufficiently noisy that each duelist knows when the other has fired and missed, and let $P(a)$ denote the probability that if the first duelist fires at time a, he kills his opponent (and receives the payoff$+1$), while $P(b)$ is the probability that the second decision maker is successful if he fires at time b. Since the guns are noisy, if one duelist fires and misses, his opponent can wait until they meet: to miss is to lose. Thus, if $a < b$, the first duelist's probability of winning $+1$ is $P(a)$ and his probability of "winning" -1 is $1 - P(a)$. That is, if $a < b$,

$$\varphi^1(a, b) = P(a)(1) + [1 - P(a)](-1) = 2P(a) - 1.$$

Similarly, if $a > b$,

$$\varphi^1(a, b) = 1 - 2P(b).$$

And if $a = b$, we let $\varphi^1(a, b) = 0$. Summarizing,

$$\varphi^1(a, b) = \begin{cases} 2P(a) - 1 & \text{if } a < b, \\ 0 & \text{if } a = b, \\ 1 - 2P(b) & \text{if } a > b. \end{cases}$$

Assuming now that P is a linear function of time, the payoff function φ^1 is not necessarily continuous at $a = b$. Thus, let $P(a) = a$ and $P(b) = b$. Then, if $b = \frac{1}{3}$, φ^1 increases from -1 to $-\frac{1}{3}$ as a increases from 0 towards $\frac{1}{3}$. At $a = \frac{1}{3}$, however, $a = b$, so that φ^1 suddenly becomes equal to 0. Hence, φ^1 is discontinuous at $a = b$.

Although φ^1 is not everywhere continuous, this game has a solution. Observe that the game is symmetric, in which case we know that if an equilibrium strategy pair, (a^*, b^*), exists, $\varphi^1(a^*, b) \geq 0 \geq \varphi^1(a, b^*)$, and $a^* = b^*$. If we let $a^* = b^* = \frac{1}{2}$, we get

$$\varphi^1(a^*, b) = \begin{cases} 0 & \text{if } a^* < b, \\ 0 & \text{if } a^* = b, \\ > 0 & \text{if } a^* > b, \end{cases}$$

and

$$\varphi^1(a, b^*) = \begin{cases} < 0 & \text{if } a < b^*, \\ 0 & \text{if } a = b^*, \\ 0 & \text{if } a > b^*. \end{cases}$$

Hence, $\varphi^1(\frac{1}{2}, \frac{1}{2})$ satisfies (8.2) so that $(\frac{1}{2}, \frac{1}{2})$ is an equilibrium-strategy pair.

Not all infinite zero-sum games with discontinuous payoffs possess such nice properties as this example. In fact, many of them fail even to have mixed-strategy solutions in the conventional sense. Consequently, an alternative solution concept has been proposed—ϵ-optimal strategies. A strategy $p^*(a)$ is said to be ϵ-optimal if, for a given $\epsilon > 0$, it guarantees player 1 at least $v - \epsilon$, and $q^*(b)$ is said to be ϵ-optimal if it limits player 1 to at most $v + \epsilon$, where v is the value of the game. Hence, $v - \epsilon \leq \varphi^1(p^*, q^*) \leq v + \epsilon$. (Of course, if p^* and q^* are ϵ-optimal for all $\epsilon \geq 0$, they are optimal in the conventional sense.) We do not review the various theorems pertaining to such strategies, however, because of their mathematical complexity and because they have not yet been applied to politics.[18] We simply point to their existence as a warning to those who might assume that every zero-sum game has a conventional solution.

5. Nonzero-sum, finite, noncooperative games

Most of the powerful theorems of two-person theory concern zero-sum games. It is difficult to find, for example, a simpler and more persuasive notion than the idea of a solution to finite games with pure-strategy equilibrium pairs. Probably this solution is the exact sense of what people strive to achieve in the real world. And the minimax theorem, which extends solutions from games with pure-strategy pairs to games with mixed-strategy equilibrium pairs, is mathematically elegant even though it may be behaviorally dubious. Even in the realm of infinite games, zero-sum theory reveals solutions at least for continuous games on the unit square, if not for discontinuous games or for games with a countable infinity of strategies.

As we turn now to nonzero-sum games, we leave behind the relative power and simplicity of zero-sum theory. The situation of nonzero-sum games is more difficult to analyze because the relationships between the two players can be more varied than in the zero-sum case, thereby rendering generalization more difficult. A single relationship characterizes all zero-sum games: absolutely divergent interests. In nonzero-sum games, however, the players have some commonality of interests in that they both prefer to avoid certain admissible outcomes. An extreme instance of commonality is illustrated in Figure 8.6—an instance in which an increase in the payoff to one player involves an increase for the other. Hence both players have exactly the same

---

[18]For a review of these theorems, see Burger, *Introduction to the Theory of Games*, pp. 131–155.

goal and there is no divergence of interest.[19] A less extreme case—falling somewhere between perfect commonality of interests and the zero-sum condition—is illustrated in Figure 8.7, where φ^1, and φ^2 cannot both be maximized simultaneously but where some cooperation is possible.

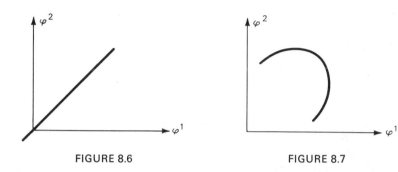

FIGURE 8.6   FIGURE 8.7

Nonzero-sum and zero-sum games differ also in the strategic role of pregame communication. In zero-sum games a rational decision maker communicates with his opponent only to deceive him but never to reveal the strategy he will choose. For many classes of nonzero-sum games, however, the decision makers seek to coordinate their choice of strategies so as to maximize both φ^1 and φ^2. Moreover, many of the strategic maneuvers that we wish to examine in nonzero-sum games, such as threats, commitments, and promises, involve the manipulation of information. In this section, however, we eliminate the possibility of pregame communication and restrict ourselves to the noncooperative case.

To explore some of the complexities of nonzero-sum, finite, noncooperative games, recall the definition of an equilibrium: restating expressions (8.1a) and (8.1b), (p^*, q^*) is an equilibrium if

$$\varphi^1(p^*, q^*) \geq \varphi^1(p, q^*),$$
$$\varphi^2(p^*, q^*) \geq \varphi^2(p^*, q).$$

[Note that we can no longer combine these two inequalities into a single expression such as (8.2) since it is no longer the case that $\varphi^1 = -\varphi^2$.] That is, once at (p^*, q^*), neither player has any incentive to alter his choice of a strategy unilaterally.

The most general result about equilibrium strategies for finite, nonzero-sum, noncooperative, two-person games is that every such game possesses at least one equilibrium pair.[20]

---

[19]Figures 8.6 and 8.7 should be compared with Figure 8.1, where every increase for φ^i is matched by an exactly opposite decrease for φ^j.

[20]J. F. Nash, "Noncooperative Games," *Annals of Mathematics*, vol. 54 (1951), pp. 286–295.

It might seem, then, that the mathematics of finite nonzero-sum games do not differ greatly from the mathematics of finite zero-sum games. But to see how equilibria for nonzero-sum games differ from those for zero-sum games consider the simple example in Figure 8.8, often referred to as the "Battle of the Sexes." (Note that in each cell of this figure the first entry is φ^1 and the second is φ^2.)

	b_1	b_2
a_1	3, 2	0, 0
a_2	0, 0	2, 3

FIGURE 8.8
Battle of the Sexes

This game has two equlibria, (a_1, b_1) and (a_2, b_2). Recall now that if a zero-sum game possesses two or more equilibrium-strategy pairs, the players are indifferent among all pairs. In Figure 8.8, however, the players are not indifferent between (a_1, b_1) and (a_2, b_2): the first player prefers (a_1, b_1) while the second prefers (a_2, b_2). Furthermore, recall that in a zero-sum game, two strategies involved in distinct equilibrium pairs are interchangeable. That is, in zero-sum games, if (a^*, b^*) and (a', b') are equilibrium pairs, then (a^*, b') and (a', b^*) are equilibrium pairs also, where both players are indifferent among all four possible pairs. In Figure 8. 8, however, strategies are not interchangeable: (a_1, b_2) and (a_2, b_1) are not equilibrium pairs.

The implication of the Battle of the Sexes now is this: equilibrium-strategy pairs cannot always be regarded as solutions to nonzero-sum, noncooperative games. Because the players are not indifferent between (a_1, b_1) and (a_2, b_2) and because equilibrium strategies are not interchangeable, the existence of equilibrium-strategy pairs does not terminate necessarily the "he thinks" regress. For example, player 1 can think thus: "Since player 2 prefers (a_2, b_2) to (a_1, b_1), he will choose b_2—in which case I should choose a_2. But if I think that he will choose b_2 because he prefers (a_2, b_2) to (a_1, b_1), he may think that I will chose a_1 because I prefer (a_1, b_1) to (a_2, b_2)," and so on.[21]

Since the pure-strategy equilibria of the Battle of the Sexes do not constitute a solution, we turn to another possibility (that further highlights the differences in the strategic imperatives of zero-sum and nonzero-sum games) : mixed strategies. Observe that the security levels of a_1, a_2, b_1, and b_2 are all 0. By randomization, however, both players can increase their security levels. Specifically, if the first player adopts the maximin strategy $(\frac{2}{5}, \frac{3}{5})$—if he plays a_1 with a probability of $\frac{2}{5}$ and if he plays a_2 with a probability of $\frac{3}{5}$—his security level

[21]This analysis of the Battle of the Sexes is taken largely from Luce and Raiffa, *Games and Decisions,* pp. 91–92.

is $\frac{6}{5}$ rather than 0. Similarly, the second decision maker can adopt the minimax strategy $(\frac{3}{5}, \frac{2}{5})$ and increase his security level to $\frac{6}{5}$.

Unfortunately, randomized strategies do not lead to a solution any more than pure strategies do. The first player can calculate his opponent's minimax strategy in order to find some strategy that increases his expected payoff above $\frac{6}{5}$. Specifically, the strategy a_1, if played against $[(\frac{3}{5})b_1, (\frac{2}{5})b_2]$ yields the first player the expected payoff of $(\frac{3}{5} \cdot 3) + (\frac{2}{5} \cdot 0) = \frac{9}{5} > \frac{6}{5}$. Stated differently, the minimax and maximin strategies for this nonzero-sum game are not—in contrast to zero-sum games—in equilibrium.

Our inability to find a solution to the game presented in Figure 8.8 results partly from the fact that there are two noninterchangeable equilibrium outcomes. But the difference between nonzero-sum and zero-sum games is even more complex. For example, an equilibrium pair in a nonzero-sum game can be an outcome that ranks low on both players' preference orderings. The classic example of this possibility is the so-called "Prisoners' Dilemma" which we illustrate in Figure 8.9.

	b_1	b_2
a_1	$-2, \quad -2$	$-20, \quad -1$
a_2	$-1, \quad -20$	$-10, \quad -10$

FIGURE 8.9.
The Prisoners' Dilemma

This game derives its name from the following story: Suppose two suspects are locked up in separate cells so that they cannot communicate. Let a_2 and b_2 denote confessing to a crime they are accused of committing jointly, and let a_1 and b_1 denote not confessing. If both prisoners confess, each gets a 10-year sentence. If neither confesses, both receive 2 years on some lesser charge. If one confesses but the other does not, the district attorney can convict both; but, as is typically the case, the one who confesses gets the lighter sentence—say 1 year —while the unrepentant suspect gets the maximum sentence—20 years.

Observe that, regardless of which strategy the second player selects, the first player's best strategy is to confess—a_2—rather than not to confess—a_1. If b_1 is selected, a_2 yields -1 while a_1 yields -2; and if b_2 is selected, a_2 yields -10 while a_1 yields -20. Thus, a_2 is always preferred to a_1. And for identical reasons b_2 is preferred to b_1. Hence, if each player is ignorant of what the other will do, there seems to be no choice but for both to confess, and receive a 10-year sentence. Stated differently, the strategy pair (a_2, b_2) is the equilibrium because neither prisoner has an incentive to change his strategy unilaterally and subject himself to a 20-year sentence. Note, however, that the strategy pair (a_1, b_1) yields an outcome that is strictly preferred to the equilibrium outcome by *both* prisoners. But this strategy pair is not an equilibrium, since each prisoner has an incentive to confess unilaterally and reduce his sentence from 2 years to 1. An awareness of this incentive and a dread of a 20-year sentence compels both prisoners towards (a_2, b_2)—which is the district attorney's intent when he locks them up in separate cells.

The Prisoners' Dilemma, then, can be said to have a solution—if not a happy one for the prisoners. In subsequent chapters we examine this dilemma in a different context—the context of public policy and public goods.[22] For the moment, however, let us see how we can generalize the solution of a Prisoners' Dilemma game to other nonzero-sum, finite, noncooperative games.

First, recall that every finite, nonzero-sum, noncooperative game has at least one equilibrium pair in either pure or mixed strategies.[23] Given that at least one such pair always exists, we seek to describe those games for which it is reasonable to suppose that equilibrium pairs are solutions. Since these descriptions are stated in terms of properties of equilibrium-strategy pairs, suppose that (p^*, q^*) and (p', q') are two such pairs (if the game has only one equilibrium $p^* = p'$, $q^* = q'$). These strategy pairs are *equivalent* if

$$\varphi^1(p^*, q^*) = \varphi^1(p', q') \qquad \text{and} \qquad \varphi^2(p^*, q^*) = \varphi^2(p', q').$$

That is, two pairs are equivalent if both players are indifferent as to which equilibrium prevails. Additionally, (p^*, q^*) and (p', q') are *interchangeable* if (p^*, q') and (p', q^*) are also in equilibrium. Finally, a strategy pair (p_0, q_0) is *jointly admissible* if, for any other strategy pair (p, q),

$$\varphi^1(p_0, q_0) > \varphi^1(p, q) \qquad \text{or} \qquad \varphi^2(p_0, q_0) > \varphi^2(p, q).$$

Hence, a strategy pair is jointly admissible if it is preferred to any other pair by at least one of the decision makers. (Note that a jointly admissible pair need not be an equilibrium.)

With these definitions we can offer two solutions:

1. The *Nash solution* exists if all equilibrium pairs are interchangeable. The solution is then the payoffs corresponding to the set of equilibrium pairs. The Prisoners' Dilemma is an example of a game with a Nash solution—the solution being the payoffs corresponding to the outcome (a_2, b_2). The Battle of the Sexes, however, does not possess a Nash solution, since the two equilibrium-strategy pairs are not interchangeable. (Parenthetically, we note that if a game has a unique equilibrium pair, it is interchangeable with itself. Hence, every non-

---

[22]In addition to its theoretical importance in the theory of public goods, this game and the story attached to it have attracted much popular political commentary: the prisoners' dilemma can easily be interpreted as the dilemma of an arms race or the dilemma of surprise attack. See, for example, Thomas C. Schelling, *The Strategy of Conflict* (New York: Oxford, 1963); Anatol Rapoport, *Strategy and Conscience* (New York: Harper & Row, 1964).

[23]See note 20, page 221.

cooperative game with a unique pair of equilibrium strategies—such as the Prisoners' Dilemma—has a Nash solution.)

2. *A solution in the strict sense* exists if

   (i)   at least one equilibrium pair is jointly admissible,

  (ii) all jointly admissible equilibrium pairs are both interchangeable and equivalent.[24]

This is a somewhat different and less demanding notion than the Nash solution because the requirement of interchangeability is limited to jointly admissible equilibrium pairs, not to all equilibrium pairs. Nevertheless, a Prisoners' Dilemma game is not solvable in the strict sense. The equilibrium pair, (a_2, b_2), is not jointly admissible because neither player prefers it to any other:

$$\varphi^1(a_2, b_2) < \varphi^1(b_1, a_1) \quad and \quad \varphi^2(a_2, b_2) < \varphi^2(a_1, b_1).$$

The Battle of the Sexes is also not solvable in the strict sense because, as we have already seen, its equilibrium pairs are neither interchangeable nor equivalent. Luce and Raiffa offer the following example of a game that has a solution in the strict sense:

	b_1	b_2
a_1	1, 1	0, 0
a_2	0, 0	2, 2

FIGURE 8.10

Note that both (a_1, b_1) and (a_2, b_2) are equilibrium pairs; but only (a_2, b_2) is jointly admissible because both decision makers prefer it to (a_1, b_1).

The Nash solution and the strict solution purport to justify the choice by rational decision makers of equilibria as outcomes in different kinds of games. The Nash solution serves as a justification for supposing that two rational decision makers converge to the equilibrium of a noncooperative game if, for example, this equilibrium is unique. The Prisoners' Dilemma is thus solvable in the Nash sense but not in the strict sense. The strict-solution concept is designed to justify the selection of equilibrium pairs that, from the perspective of each player, have much the same properties as a solution to a zero-sum game (i.e., equilibrium pairs in zero-sum games are also interchangeable and equivalent, and there are no other strategy pairs that are strictly preferred to them by both players). Thus, the game in Figure 8.10 is solvable in the strict sense but not in the Nash sense.

[24]Luce and Raiffa, *Games and Decisions,* pp. 106–108.

Many games, however, possess equilibria that satisfy neither the Nash nor strict criteria, yet offer some justification for asserting that certain equilibrium-strategy pairs are solutions. Consider, for example, the following game:

$$a_i = i, \quad i = 0, 1, \ldots, 30;$$
$$b_j = j, \quad j = 0, 1, \ldots, 30;$$

$$\varphi^1(a_i, b_j) = \begin{cases} -\$30 & \text{if } i + j \neq 30, \\ -\$i & \text{if } i + j = 30; \end{cases}$$

$$\varphi^2(a_i, b_j) = \begin{cases} -\$30 & \text{if } i + j \neq 30, \\ -\$j & \text{if } i + j = 30. \end{cases}$$

Here, without communicating, the players must each choose a number between 0 and 30. If the numbers sum to 30, each player looses an amount equal to the number he has chosen. If, however, the numbers do not sum to 30, both lose $30. This game possesses thirty-one equilibrium pairs—all of those pairs (a_i, b_j) in which $i + j = 30$. It is readily seen, however, that these pairs are not equivalent [e.g., $\varphi^1(a_0, b_{30}) \neq \varphi^1(a_{30}, b_0)$] and that they are not interchangeable [e.g., (a_{15}, b_{15}) and (a_{10}, b_{20}) are equilibrium pairs but (a_{15}, b_{20}) and (a_{10}, b_{15}) are not]. This game, then, is not solvable in either the Nash or the strict sense.

We seek solutions, however, in order to identify the choices that rational decision makers make, and in this spirit, Thomas Schelling offers a solution to games similar to the one we have just illustrated.[25] The essential feature of this game is that, while it is in each player's interest to minimize his loss, it is also in the interest of both to coordinate their strategies. Explicit coordination is, of course, prohibited by the assumption that the game is noncooperative. But, as Schelling points out, this assumption does not prohibit tacit coordination. Specifically, for many noncooperative games in which coordination is in the interest of both decision makers, particular equilibrium pairs are more prominent than others, and, therefore, they are more likely to be choosen. Their prominence, moreover, does not arise simply from the mathematical structure of the game but also from the particular cultural backgrounds of the decision-makers. Suppose, for example, that the game we are examining is derived from the following situation: Two citizens together must fund some public project at a cost of thirty dollars. If they cannot agree implicitly on a relative tax burden that efficiently funds the project, they must both forfeit an amount equal to the cost of the project. If this is all the information each decision maker possesses, it seems reasonable to suppose that the equilibrium (a_{15}, b_{15}) will prevail—if only because of the centrality of this pair. To see how a well-established cultural norm might affect a solution, however, consider the following two situations:

(i)   both decision makers are well socialized into accepting the standard that people should share equally in the cost of public projects;

[25]Schelling, *The Strategy of Conflict.*

(ii)   both decision makers are well socialized into accepting the standard that people should share the cost of public projects in accordance with their wealth.

Suppose that the wealth of the first decision maker is $10,000 and the wealth of the second decision maker is $20,000. Clearly, if the situation conforms to (i), the equilibrium pair (a_{15}, b_{15}) is prominent, while if the situation conforms to (ii), (a_{10}, b_{20}) is prominent. Since prominence is a function of culture, we require a knowledge of the decision makers' backgrounds to predict their strategies for some kinds of noncooperative games.

To identify generally the kind of game in which such knowledge is necessary, we must ascertain exactly what it is that this knowledge can tell us. Recall that the potential problem confronting a player in a game is the regress of "he thinks that I think . . . . " This regress can begin with an initial guess as to which strategy an opponent will choose, or it can begin with an initial guess as to the probability that the opponent will choose a particular strategy. Only equilibrium pairs can terminate this regress. Before Schelling's notion of a solution can be applied, we must know whether or not the equilibrium arrived at by the players is a function of their initial guesses. Clearly, for games in which the equilibrium is unique the answer is no. If a game possesses several equilibrium pairs but if these pairs are all equivalent and interchangeable (as they are in zero-sum games and in noncooperative games with a strong solution), our answer again is no—because coordination is unnecessary and because the decision makers are indifferent among the equilibrium outcomes. For all other games, however, our answer is yes. In the coordination game we have just considered, for example, the initial guess that the opponent will choose b_{15} yields the equilibrium (a_{15}, b_{15}) whereas an initial guess that the opponent will choose b_{20} yields (a_{10}, b_{20}).

The important feature of coordination games that Schelling recognizes, however, is that *any* initial guess immediately terminates the "he thinks that I think" regress for both decision makers. For example, if 1 thinks that 2 will choose b_{15}, 1 chooses a_{15}. If player 1 now asks whether or not his choice of a_{15} will change 2's choice, the answer is no. Hence, if $p_1(b_j)$ is the first decision maker's guess as to the probability that 2 will choose b_j and if $p_2(a_i)$ is the second decision maker's guess as to the probability that 1 will choose a_i, the first decision maker selects the a_i that maximizes

$$E(a_i) = \sum_j p_1(b_j)\varphi^1(a_i, b_j)$$

and the second decision maker maximizes

$$E(b_j) = \sum_i p_2(a_i)\varphi^2(b_j, a_i).$$

For the coordination game we have been examining, it is clear that if the first decision maker thinks that his opponent will most likely select b_k, then he should choose a_{30-k}. And if player 2 think that player 1 will choose a_{30-k}, he should choose b_k. Of course, the problem that Schelling points up is that nothing in the mathematical structure of the game generates $P_1(b_j)$ and $P_2(a_i)$, so we must consider factors such as the sociocultural contexts of games to predict and understand these probabilities. Nevertheless, once they are estimated, we can calculate the players' choices.

We have, then, at least three solution concepts for noncooperative games, each designed to handle a different class of games. The Nash solution is concerned with games that possess interchangeable but not equivalent equilibrium pairs. The strong solution treats games with interchangeable, equivalent, and jointly admissible equilibrium pairs. Schelling's solution is unlike the first two in that it is not derived strictly from the mathematical properties of games, but it is appropriate for games with jointly admissible equilibrium pairs that are not interchangeable.

It is evident, nevertheless, that decision makers possess some incentive to communicate even if they are confronted with a game that possesses one of these three solutions—if only to reduce risk. Moreover, the desire to communicate is even more compelling for games such as the Battle of the Sexes in which these solution concepts are inadequate. It seems, then, that before we can understand these games fully, we must relax the condition of noncooperation. For the sake of a complete survey, however, we first review briefly the case of infinite, noncooperative games.

6. Nonzero-sum, infinite, noncooperative games

We again assume that each player's set of strategies is the unit interval $[0, 1]$. Paralleling the result for infinite zero-sum games, we know that if mixed strategies are admissible and if φ^1 and φ^2 are continuous, then there exists at least one equilibrium pair of strategies.[26] This is reminiscent of finite noncooperative games, each of which also possesses at least one such equilibrium pair. Nevertheless, we encounter considerable difficulty defining solutions for infinite games; and so we may safely assume that knowing that an equilibrium exists for infinite games with continuous payoffs does not tell us very much about the choices of decision makers.

Perhaps the strongest theorem we have is that if, in addition to being continuous, $\varphi^1(a, b)$ is concave in a and $\varphi^2(a, b)$ is concave in b, then at least one pure strategy equilibrium exists. Furthermore, if $\varphi^1(a, b)$ is also convex in b and if $\varphi^2(a, b)$ is convex in a, the equilibrium is a unique pair.[27] The feature of uniqueness permits us to establish the existence of at least one kind of a solution. Specifically, we know that if a unique equilibrium exists, the conditions of

[26]Burger, *Introduction to the Theory of Games*, pp. 37–41.

[27]For proofs of these results, see H. Nikaido and K. Isoda, "Note on Noncooperative Convex Games," *Pacific Journal of Mathematics*, vol. 5 (1955), pp. 807–815; and J.B. Rosen, "Existence and Uniqueness of Equilibrium Points for Concave *N*-Person Games," *Econometrica*, vol. 33 (1965), pp. 520–534.

Nash's solution are satisfied. Hence, every continuous, concave-convex, non-cooperative game possesses a Nash solution.

7, 8. Nonzero-sum, cooperative games

The final class of games we must consider are those in which cooperation—implicit or explicit communication—is allowed (we combine finite and infinite games into a single discussion, distinguishing only when it is useful to do so). Note that cooperation has a broad interpretation: it includes any form of implicit or explicit communication. Hence, it can range from observing an opponent's facial expressions as he contemplates his alternatives to ascertaining directly from him the strategy he will choose. Thus, since some degree of communication can be assumed to occur in most real games, cooperative nonzero-sum games are more likely to be substantively relevent than their noncooperative counterparts. This, in part, accounts for social scientists' interest in cooperative games, even though mathematicians seem preoccupied with noncooperative ones.

Unfortunately, in spite of the superior social relevance of cooperative games, the theory of noncooperative games is by far the more adequate. While, as we showed in the previous section, several solutions for noncooperative games have been proposed, still these solutions are formulated within the parsimonious framework of a few definitions. Further, each of these solution concepts pertains to a distinct class of games, where the elements of each class are readily described by the mathematical features of a game. No such framework has yet been devised, however, for cooperative nonzero-sum games. The ease with which decision makers can communicate, the means of communication, and the actual content of messages all are essential features of the game, and, typically, they themselves are strategically variable. Consequently, while we know a great deal about the properties of particular cooperative games, we are far from establishing general theoretical principles. Specifically, solution concepts are mostly *ad hoc,* proliferating to the extent that more than one solution can be said to exist for almost any cooperative game—we might even say that the problem with the "theory" of cooperative games is that too many definitions of solutions exist.

We will examine several of these solution concepts in detail later. First, however, we demonstrate that an ability to communicate alters fundamentally one property of a nonzero-sum game. In Figure 8.11 we represent graphically the game of the Battle of the Sexes (see Fig. 8.8), where the vertical axis is the payoff to the first player and the horizontal axis is the payoff to the second player. If the players are not permitted to communicate and if they limit their domain of choice to pure strategies, the admissible outcomes are denoted in Figure 8.11 by the three large dots. If, however, their domain of strategic alternatives is expanded to the set of mixed strategies, the set of admissible outcomes becomes the entire shaded region of Figure 8.11.[28] Suppose now that the players are permitted to communicate and thus to coordinate their strategies. What then is the set of admissible outcomes? Clearly, the players can choose to play as if they could not communicate, so the original set of admissible outcomes (the shaded region) is still admissible. Additionally, however, if they coordinate successfully, the players can eliminate the mutually disadvantageous outcome $(0, 0)$ by choosing the joint strategy (a_1, b_1) with a probability of ξ and the joint strategy (a_2, b_2) with a probability of $(1 - \xi)$. Graphically, coordination permits the decision makers to choose any point in Figure 8.11 that lies on a straight line between the points (a_1, b_1) and (a_2, b_2). That is, shifting from the noncooperative to the cooperative version of the Battle of the Sexes expands the admissible set of payoffs to the shaded region in Figure 8.12. [It is readily demonstrated that the points below and to the left of the line from (a_1, b_1) to (a_2, b_2) which are not in the original set of outcomes are also admissible with a suitable choice of strategies.]

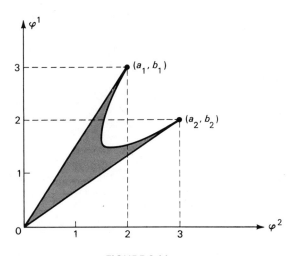

FIGURE 8.11
Noncooperative Battle of the Sexes

Permitting cooperation thus expands the set of admissible outcomes. This set is readily identified geometrically for any game. Locate the payoffs from the choice of pure strategies in a coordinate system, and connect the points necessary to form a convex figure that includes the outcomes from all possible choices of pure strategies. The set of admissible outcomes for the cooperative version of the game is now all points on and within the figure. For example, for the game

[28]See Luce and Raiffa, *Games and Decisions*, pp. 92–93.

	b_1	b_2	b_3
a_1	5, 4	2, 5	− 1, 4
a_2	3, 1	5, 8	7, 4
a_3	5, 2	2, 10	2, 7

the set of admissible payoffs is the shaded area of Figure 8.13.

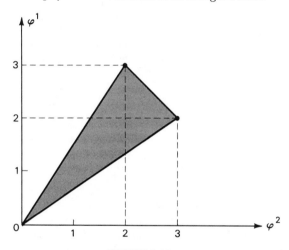

FIGURE 8.12.
Cooperative Battle of the Sexes

Having established the set of admissible outcomes, we can now begin speculating about solutions to cooperative games. Initially, we ignore such maneuvers as threats and commitments; and we assume the normative stance of seeking those admissible outcomes two rational players *should* select. First, we require that the players consider only Pareto-optimal outcomes. If an outcome is not Pareto-optimal, the payoff of at least one of the players can be increased without diminishing the payoff of the other. In Figure 8.13, the Pareto-optimal outcomes are all points on the two lines ac and ce. Within these restrictions, we look at the players' security levels, which we denote by φ_*^1 and φ_*^2. The payoff φ_*^1 is the amount the first player can guarantee himself even if he acts as if he were playing a noncooperative game. For the game illustrated in Figure 8.13, $\varphi_*^1 = 3$ and $\varphi_*^2 = 5$, since the first player receives at least 3 if he adopts a_2 (whereas he might receive −1 with a_1 and 2 with a_3) and the second receives at least 5 with b_2 (whereas he might receive 1 with b_1 and 4 with b_3). Finally, we require that no player cooperate in achieving an outcome that yields him a payoff less than what he can guarantee himself without cooper-

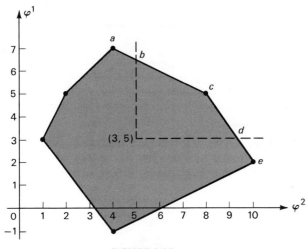

FIGURE 8.13

ating. For example, only outcomes lying on and above the line from point $(3, 5)$ to point d are considered admissible for the first player, while his counterpart contemplates only outcomes on and to the right of the line from point $(3, 5)$ to point b.

If we- combine the requirement of achieving security levels with that of Pareto optimality, we limit the admissible outcomes to those lying on the two lines bc and cd. These outcomes, termed the *negotiation set*, are offered by von Neumann and Morgenstern as the solution to the cooperative game. This definition of a solution clearly possesses some intuitively desirable properties, the most important being this: if the decision makers are not, in their deliberations, at some point in the negotiation set, incentives to shift towards such a point clearly exist for at least one and perhaps both of them.

But while the negotiation set is a general definition of a solution from the perspective of some simlep behavioral heuristics, it is not wholly satisfactory: the negotiation set typically contains more than one outcome—in Figure 8.13 it contains an uncountable infinity of outcomes—and many of these are substantively quite distinct. For example, in Figure 8.14 the negotiation set is the line ab, which includes outcomes in which one of the decision makers gets everything and the other gets nothing.

Assume that we wish to formulate a definition of a solution that is more restrictive. Specifically, assume that we want a function, g, which, given the set of all admissible outcomes, R, and the players' security levels, φ_*^1 and φ_*^2, selects a particular point, $(\bar{\varphi}^1, \bar{\varphi}^2)$, as the solution. That is,

$$g[R, \varphi_*^1, \varphi_*^2] = (\bar{\varphi}^1, \bar{\varphi}^2).$$

We must begin, of course, by specifying the properties that g must satisfy. First, in conjunction with what we already know about utility numbers, it is reasonable to require that g yield the same solution regardless of the scales used to measure φ^1 and φ^2. That is, if we let

$$\varphi^1{}_0 = r\varphi^1 \pm s,$$

$$\varphi^2{}_0 = t\varphi^2 \pm v,$$

where r and s and t and v are positive constants, then the solution to the transformed game should be $r\bar{\varphi}^1 + s$ and $t\bar{\varphi}^2 + v$. In order that g select a point in the negotiation set, we require, second, that

$$\bar{\varphi}^1 \geq \varphi_*{}^1 \quad \text{and} \quad \bar{\varphi}^2 \geq \varphi_*{}^2$$

(i.e., neither player accepts a solution that yields him a payoff less than his security level) and third, that $(\bar{\varphi}^1, \bar{\varphi}^2)$ be Pareto-optimal.

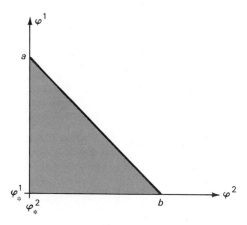

FIGURE 8.14

In the search for a function g, Nash adds two additional conditions.[29] The fourth condition he imposes is a version of *independence from irrelevant alternatives*.[30] In Nash's form this is the requirement that if R is augmented by an additional outcome, say $(\varphi^{1\prime}, \varphi^{2\prime})$, and if $g[R, \varphi_*{}^1, \varphi_*{}^2] = (\bar{\varphi}^1, \bar{\varphi}^2)$, then the solution to the augmented game is either $(\bar{\varphi}^1, \bar{\varphi}^2)$ or $(\varphi^{1\prime}, \varphi^{2\prime})$. That is, if we add an additional possibility to a game, either the solution is unchanged or it is this new possibility. The justification of this condition is, as in the case of voting, that one does not wish the solution of the larger game to be affected by the irrelevant outcomes in the smaller game.

Nash's final condition is simply a condition of *symmetry*. A nonzero-sum game

[29]J. F. Nash, "The Bargaining Problem," *Econometrica,* vol. 18 (1950), pp. 155–162. For a general discussion of Nash's solution, see Luce and Raiffa, *Games and Decisions,* p. 6, and Owen, *Game Theory,* pp. 140–147.

[30]See Chapter 4.

is said to be symmetric if for every (φ^1, φ^2) in R, (φ^2, φ^1) is also in R. Thus, if an outcome exists in which the first player's payoff is 5 and his counterpart's is -2, then, if the game is symmetric, there is an admissible outcome where the first player's payoff is -2 and the second's payoff is 5. The condition of symmetry is: if a game is symmetric, then $\bar{\varphi}^1 = \bar{\varphi}^2$.

We now state Nash's powerful theorem: *only one* function g satisfies these five conditions. That function can be characterized as follows:

$$(\bar{\varphi}^1 - \varphi_*{}^1)(\bar{\varphi}^2 - \varphi_*{}^2) \geq (\varphi^1 - \varphi_*{}^1)(\varphi^2 - \varphi_*{}^2)$$

for all $(\varphi^1, \varphi^2) \in R$ such that $\varphi^1 \geq \varphi_*{}^1$, $\varphi^2 \geq \varphi_*{}^2$. To state this result differently, suppose that we normalize both decision-makers' payoff functions so that $\varphi_*{}^1 = 0$ and $\varphi_*{}^2 = 0$. The function g is characterized then by

$$\bar{\varphi}^1 \bar{\varphi}^2 \geq \varphi^1 \varphi^2$$

for all $(\varphi^1, \varphi^2) \in R$, $\varphi^1 \geq 0$, $\varphi^2 \geq 0$. That is, the Nash solution to the two-person cooperative game is that pair (φ^1, φ^2) in the negotiation set such that the product of φ^1 and φ^2 is at a maximum.

For an example, suppose that two people must decide how to divide \$100 (let $\varphi_*{}^1$ and $\varphi_*{}^2 = 0$). Assume that the first person's utility is linear with money, i.e., $\varphi^1 = x$ where x is the amount of money the first person receives. Assume that the second person's utility function is

$$\varphi^2 = \log\left(\frac{100 + y}{100}\right)$$

Graphically, then, we have:

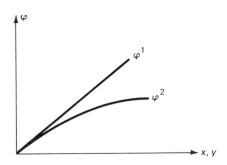

In the real world, such utility functions might occur if person 2 were poor and hence happier to get the first bit of money than to get the last and if person 1 were rich and hence no happier to get a small amount than a large one.

The Nash solution to this game is obtained now by maximizing

$$\varphi^1 \varphi^2 = x \log\left(\frac{100 + y}{100}\right)$$

subject to $x + y = 100$. By substituting $y = 100 - x$ into the expression above, this is equivalent to maximizing

$$x \log\left(\frac{200 - x}{100}\right).$$

It is readily shown that the solution to this problem is approximately

$$\bar{\varphi}^1 = \$54.40, \qquad \bar{\varphi}^2 = \$45.60,$$

so that the first person receives more money than the second.

This disproportionate division may seem counterintuitive to some: why not more money for the second person who is poor, or why not a simple 50–50 split? The answer, of course, lies partly in the particular values we assume for φ^1 and φ^2. But is also lies in the five conditions that Nash imposes on g. To evaluate, then, the significance of g so constructed, we pose the following question: if a bargainer believes that it is "fair" for the second person to receive either more money than the first or exactly the same amount, might this bargainer accept one of these outcomes which are "irrational" in terms of the Nash solution? It seems that our answer must be *yes*. We are then forced to the position of expecting rational persons to behave irrationally. We cannot accept this paradox, and so we reexamine Nash's conditions.

There is no way to derive all of Nash's conditions from the assumption of utility maximization and from the structure of cooperative games. Specifically, the condition of independence from irrelevant alternatives and the condition of symmetry are *ad hoc*; they are imposed on g simply because they appear to be reasonable and not because they are implied by the axiom of individual rationality. There is no reason to suppose that we cannot formulate other equally reasonable constraints on g that yield entirely different solutions to our example. And if these constraints are consistent with the axioms of choice, then we have several "rational" solutions to one game.

Observe, however, that we have now come to a curious point in our analysis of individual choice. In Chapters 2 and 3 we proceed implicitly on the assumption that a person's choices could be modeled with a delineation of alternatives, outcomes, probabilities, and utility numbers, and we illustrate the formulational models of choice and predictions about choice. In this chapter, however, we encounter situations (i.e., the "he thinks I think" regress) in which it may be unreasonable to suppose that a decision maker acts as if he assigned probabilities to outcomes. Seeking, then, to ascertain whether or not the assumption of utility maximization is sufficient for explaining the choices in these situations of a rational decision maker, we focus on the concept of a solution to a game. By using ideas such as equilibrium pairs and minimax strategies, we are reasonably successful in explaining these choices within the limited structure of utility maximization for certain classes of games. Now, however, we find a solution that appears to necessitate the assumption of something more than we were willing previously to admit; and so we are led to ask whether or not this solution is acceptable, and whether or not it must be rejected because it is *ad hoc*.

Our prejudice is to reject. We prefer not to move outside the limits of our present framework of utility theory. Unfortunately (and not for lack of trying), no one has yet succeeded in formulating a general solution concept for cooperative games—other than that of the negotiation set—that imposes only the assumption of utility maximization. This failure has several profound implications. It suggests that for many choice environments the concept of a rational decision is undefined or that our set of axioms must somehow be augmented. Thus, we meet again, even in the more structured situation of two-person theory, the absence of a general equilibrium that appeared in our analysis of n-person theory. We discovered there that the only way to generate equilibrium is to introduce more assumptions and institutional detail and to include other features of the decision makers or their environments. This is the tack we take here.

In this spirit we can interpret Nash's analysis as one admissible increment to our description of cooperative games. But just as there are an infinite number of payoff matrices that correspond to cooperative games, there may be many alternatives to Nash's formulation. Some of these alternatives may also yield the Nash solution, while others may serve to explain a simple 50–50 split in the payoffs. Unless their logic is internally inconsistent, however, none of these alternatives can be judged, a priori, as better or worse than another. Rather, each must be judged as more or less appropriate for specific choice environments. Hence, the acceptance of one description as against others is an empirical task.

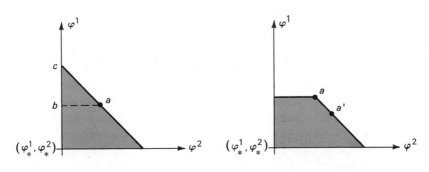

FIGURE 8.15

Regardless of how we define our task, however, if we find it necessary to go beyond the assumption of utility maximization and the simple description of a game in terms of its payoffs, there are likely to be objections and alternative suggestions as to how we should proceed. In order to examine the complexities of cooperative games in greater detail so that we might anticipate some of these objections and suggestions, let us examine the response to the condition of independence from irrelevant alternatives and the condition of symmetry. Our examination proceeds from a particular perspective. We ask:

How might a neutral observer resolve a cooperative game? If we conclude that such an observer might not abide by these *ad hoc* conditions, then we can conclude that another description of the game is necessary.

First, consider the two games illustrated in Figure 8.15, (a) and (b). Except for the outcomes inside the triangle *abc*, and on its edges *ac* and *bc*, the game in (a) is identical with the game illustrated in (b). The Nash solution to both games, moreover, is the point *a*. The reason that both games share one solution is that the outcomes in *abc* are irrelevant alternatives—they do not contain the solution to the game in (a), and so, if we eliminate them, the solution is unchanged in (b). The question, however, is whether or not both games should (normatively) share the same solution. If we were the bargainers, would we tend toward some other outcomes, say *a'*, in the second game? Luce and Raiffa defend the condition of independence for this example by arguing that, given the security levels of both decision makers, outcomes in the triangle *abc* are "merely empty dreams" for the first decision maker.[31] Nevertheless, because this example receives so much attention in the literature with respect to the condition of independence, there is ample reason to believe that two rational bargainers might be affected by the elimination of the outcomes in *abc*.

A more compelling criticism of Nash's solution exists. This criticism concerns, primarily, the condition of symmetry and the observation that Nash's solution ignores the threat capabilities of the decision makers. Consider the following game that Luce and Raiffa examine (see Figure 8.16):

	b_1	b_2
a_3	1, 4	-1, -4
a_2	-4, -1	4, 1

Noncooperatively, with pure strategies, the security level of each player is -1 (i.e., using a_1 and b_1). With mixed strategies this security level can be raised to zero [specifically, if $p = (\frac{4}{5}, \frac{1}{5})$ and $q = (\frac{1}{2}, \frac{1}{2})$]. Cooperatively, since the game satisfies Nash's definition of symmetry, the Nash solution is the point a—the point of equal division. If, however, in the bargaining, the second player threatens to play the pure strategy b_1, and if the threat is successful in driving the first player to a_1, then the second player receives 4. If the threat fails and the first player chooses a_2, the worse the second player can receive is -1. At the same time the first player does not posses an equivalent threat. If 1 says he will play his preferred strategy, a_2, then 2 can hurt 1 badly by playing b_1. On the other hand, if 2 says he will play his preferred strategy, b_1, then 1 cannot hurt 2 badly. Hence, the players' threat capabilities are not

[31]*Games and Decisions*, pp. 132–134.

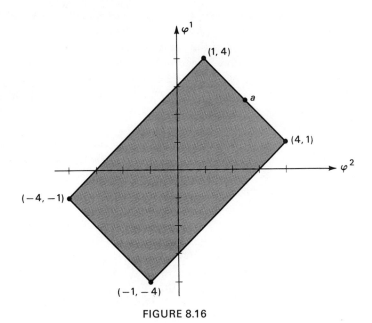

FIGURE 8.16

symmetric even though their payoffs are—a fact which the Nash solution fails to accommodate.

To accommodate the players' threat potentials, Nash offers a scheme that consists essentially of redefining $\varphi_*{}^1$ and $\varphi_*{}^2$ to include threats. But there is no reason to suppose, of course, that Nash's modified solution concept describes the choices of rational decision-makers any more than does his original solution concept. Numerous objections to it are raised, and several alternative schemes are proposed. Raiffa and Braithwaite, for example, propose solution concepts based on schemes for rendering interpersonal comparisons of utility, while Schelling elaborates on the basic concept of a threat by introducing the notions of promises and randomized threats.[32]

Given the inadequacy of the theory, we might, of course, continue to construct examples of cooperative games and to examine the variety of strategic possibilities they present.[33] Such an enterprise is clearly worthwhile, if only because it reveals the variety of interpersonal relations and illustrates some of this variety. The construction of examples must, however, be approached from

[32]For an exposition of Raiffa and Braithwaite's schemes, see Luce and Raiffa, *Games and Decisions*, pp. 145–150. The original references are H. Raiffa, "Arbitration Schemes for Generalized Two-Person Games," in Kuhn and Tucker, eds., *Contributions to the Theory of Games,* vol. 1, pp. 361–387; and R.B. Braithwaite, *Theory of Games as a Tool for the Moral Philosopher* (Cambridge: Cambridge University Press, 1955); Schelling, *The Strategy of Conflict*, pp. 175–203.

[33]An exhaustive examination of all 2×2 games has been conducted by Anatol Rapoport and Melvin Guyer, "A Taxonomy of 2×2 Games," *General Systems*, vol. 11 (1966), pp. 203–214.

the proper perspective. Political scientists too often take examples (as well as the theorems of game theory) as fully operating models of real political processes. Thus, we read such sentences as "let China be the first decision maker with strategies a_1 and a_2, and let. . . . " But it is absurd to believe that any complex process can be so simply modeled, just as it is absurd to suppose that the design of an efficicient gas turbine resides somewhere as a deduction from the basic laws of thermodynamics. Examples are valuable because they sensitize us to theoretical possibilities and because they reveal the necessity for extending our understanding of how people in different sociocultural contexts and decision-making tasks process information, learn, and invent new strategies. But such examples are rarely satisfactory models of real situations.

For example, we show in the next chapter that the Prisoners' Dilemma illustrates the problem of efficiently allocating public goods with a decentralized market mechanism—but this game cannot be taken as an adequate abstract model of such exchange processes in general. Rather, game theory should be regarded as simply an attempt to ascertain the logical consequences of an axiomatic structure that is imbedded in a set of conditions of particular interest to social scientists, while the theorems, conjectures, and other insights from this theory are assumed to perform the same role in the construction of models of political processes that the laws of thermodynamics perform in, say, the analysis of the performance of gas turbine engines. Game theory (more generally, decision theory) provides both the theoretical primitives—the vocabulary—of the sentences that constitute our models and the theorems that establish the logical truth or falsity of these sentences; beyond that, however, it cannot go.

SUGGESTIONS FOR FURTHER READING

Two very readable introductions to the theory of two-person games are ANATOL RAPOPORT, *Two-Person Game Theory* (Ann Arbor: University of Michigan Press, 1966) and MORTON D. DAVIS, *Game Theory* (New York: Basic Books, 1970). A slightly more technical review is to be found in Chapters 3, 4, 5, and 6 of R. DUNCAN LUCE and HOWARD RAIFFA, *Games and Decisions* (New York: Wiley, 1957). A collection of nontechnical essays that introduces the student to applications of two-person theory is MARTIN SHUBIK, ed., *Game Theory and Related Approaches to Social Behavior* (New York: Wiley, 1964). For the more mathematically advanced student GUILLERMO OWEN, *Game Theory* (Philadelphia: Saunders, 1968), presents a careful review of the major concepts and the theorems of two-person and *n*-person game theory, while many of the theorems pertaining to infinite games are analyzed in considerable detail in EWALD BURGER, *Introduction to the Theory of Games* (Englewood Cliffs, N. J.: Prentice-Hall, Inc., 1963). Some of the main collections of papers on the mathematics of game theory are listed under the Suggestions for Chapter 5. Two texts that give the beginning student a "feel" for two-person game theory and that substantively illustrate different types of games are THOMAS C. SCHELLING, *The Strategy of Conflict* (Cambridge, Mass.: Harvard University Press, 1960), and J. D. WILLIAMS, *The Compleat Strategyst* (New York: McGraw-Hill, 1954).

9

Markets, Pareto Optimality, and Externalities

Thus far in this book we have examined a number of diverse topics which, because each seeks to identify the logical implications of the postulate of rational choice, form a theoretically integrated subject. Each of these topics provides insights into the processes of politics—including participation, disequilibrium in social outcomes, bargaining, and coalition formation. But while an abstract analysis provides us with these insights, it is but the preface to an adequate understanding of politics. To secure this understanding we must examine some of the substantive content of people's wants. Specifically, we must examine and classify the properties of the things people value, because these properties help account for the occurrence and form of interdependent choice—and, therefore, for the occurrence and form of participation, disequilibrium, bargains, and coalitions processes—and because they determine (and are determined by) the institutions people establish and maintain in order to satisfy their needs.

We begin with a review of the essential features of the fundamental medium of economic activity—markets. We then review the characterization of Pareto-optimal allocations of private goods, demonstrating the classical result of welfare economics that perfectly competitive markets allocate private goods Pareto-optimally. Thus we provide a setting for the analysis of allocations of public goods, the main activity of politics and government.

CONSUMER CHOICE IN MARKETS

Markets consist of two classes of actors—consumers and producers—so that the description of the ideal type, the perfectly competitive market, consists of as-

240

sumptions about each of these classes. A perfectly competitive market is defined by four conditions.[1] First, all consumers are indistinguishable in the sense that a producer simply sells to the highest bidder, and the products of firms are homogeneous in the sense that brand labels, trademarks, and advertising advantages do not exist. Second, consumers and firms possess perfect information about the prices of commodites. Also, consumers are able to ascertain their benefits from alternative patterns of consumption, and all firms are equally aware of the possibilities for converting one resource into another. Third, firms and consumers can freely enter or leave the market. That is, if a demand for some commodity becomes apparent, firms can readily convert or be formed to meet this demand. Finally, there are a great many consumers and producers, which is to say that a firm alters its production and a consumer alters his consumption in the belief that their actions go unnoticed by others.

Although a complete discussion of markets necessarily entails an analysis of the behavior of consumers and firms, we simplify the exposition by focusing primarily on the behavior of consumers. Turning, then, to the formal description of consumers, suppose the market consists of goods $i = 1, 2, \ldots, n$, and let x_i^m denote the amount of good i that individual $m = 1, 2, \ldots, M$ consumes. Hence, the vector

$$x^m = (x_1^m, x_2^m, \ldots, x_n^m)$$

summarizes a person's overall pattern of consumption.[2] To analyze choice in markets we assume also that each consumer possesses a (perhaps distinct) utility function, U^m. And since the particular choices that interest us here are choices of patterns of consumption, we assume that U^m is defined over x^m. Thus, we write $U^m(x^m)$.

A consumer's task, now, is to select a pattern of consumption that maximizes his utility. In markets he so maximizes by purchasing goods at fixed prices subject to a budget constraint. That is, we suppose that each consumer, m, is endowed initially with a budget, say B^m dollars, that all consumers are confronted with the same price vector $p = (p_1, p_2, \ldots, p_n)$, and that, individually, no consumer can affect p. The consumer then proceeds to maximize his utility by purchasing x_1^m units of the first good at a total cost of $p_1 x_1^m$ dollars, x_2^m units of the second good at a total cost of $p_2 x_2^m$ dollars, and so on until he exhausts his budget, B^m. (To insure that his budget is exhausted and to

---

[1]Our description is taken essentially from James M. Henderson and Richard E. Quandt, *Microeconomic Theory* (New York: McGraw-Hill, 1958), pp. 87–88.

[2]This is not to assume, of course, that the concepts of a *good* and of *consumption*, and that the measure of consumption, x_i^m, are clear and unambiguous. Accustomed as we are to thinking about markets as mechanisms for the exchange of things such as bread, butter, guns, money, and so on, these concepts are rarely scrutinized closely. But if we also are concerned with less tangible things such as public order, security, envy, fire protection, health, and knowledge, their meaning is less clear. For the present, however, we sidestep these definitional problems, and content ourselves with the following (imprecise and imperfect) definition of consumption: individual m is said to consume good i if variations in x_i^m affect his welfare.

account for savings we can let $x_1{}^m$ denote the amount of the budget that the consumer saves.) Hence, his purchases are constrained so that

$$\sum_{i=1}^{n} p_i x_i{}^m - B^m = 0. \tag{9.1}$$

Thus, the consumer's budget constraint is that while making purchases that increase his utility, he cannot exceed the purchasing power of his initial endowment. We say, then, that the consumer maximizes $U^m(x^m)$ subject to (9.1).

Of course, we cannot compute the particular pattern of consumption that maximizes this utility directly unless we know the prices of all goods, the consumer's budget, and the exact functional form of $U^m(x^m)$. But we can characterize the nature of this maximum by solving for the necessary conditions for the maximization of utility in a competitive market. One means of ascertaining the maximum of some function, say $f(x)$, is to differentiate $f(x)$ with respect to x, set the result of this operation equal to zero, and solve for x. Thus, in order to characterize a consumer's choices, we should differentiate $U^m(x^m)$ with respect to each $x_i{}^m$ and solve appropriate equations. Here, however, we seek to maximize utility while seeking simultaneously to satisfy a constraint, expression (9.1). To perform this slightly more difficult operation we multiply (9.1) by a constant, λ, and subtract the result from $U^m(x^m)$, obtaining

$$U^m(x^m) - \lambda(p_1 x_1{}^m + p_2 x_2{}^m + \ldots + p_n x_n{}^m - B^m). \tag{9.2}$$

It is readily shown that, if we differentiate (9.2) with respect to each $x_i{}^m$ and then set the resultant n expressions—one for each good—equal to zero, we obtain the conditions necessary for a constrained maximum.[3] Hence, differentiating (9.2) with respect to $x_1{}^m$, we get

[3]This is the method of *Lagrangian multipliers*. Within the space of this chapter we cannot provide a complete discussion of this technique, but we can show its application with a simple example. Suppose we wish to cut a stick that is r units long into four pieces. Suppose also that we intend to nail these pieces together and form a rectangle that encompasses the greatest possible area. The question is: how long should we cut each piece? Since we propose to construct a rectangle, we know that the pieces must be either a or b units in length, where two pieces are a units in length and the remaining two are b units in length. Our constraint then is that $2a + 2b = r$ or $2a + 2b - r = 0$. The area of a rectangle with sides a, b equals a times b or ab. Thus, we seek to maximize ab subject to $2a + 2b - r = 0$. We set up the Lagrangian expression,

$$ab - \lambda(2a + 2b - r).$$

Differentiating this expression first with respect to a and then with respect to b and setting the resultant two equations equal to zero,

$$b - 2\lambda = 0 \quad \text{and} \quad a - 2\lambda = 0$$

or, equivalently, $\lambda = b/2 = a/2$. Thus, the condition for a maximum is $b = a$, which is to say that area is maximized by constructing a square. (Setting the first derivative of a function equal to zero provides a necessary but not a sufficient condition for a maximum; it also provides a necessary condition for a minimum. Thus, we must be careful that we have solved for a minimum area. For this example, however, it is readily seen that we have found a maximum.)

$$\frac{\partial U^m}{\partial x_i{}^m} - \lambda p_i = 0, \qquad\qquad i = 1, 2, \ldots, n,$$

or[4]

$$\lambda = \frac{\partial U^m}{\partial x_i{}^m} / p_i, \qquad\qquad i = 1, 2, \ldots, n. \qquad (9.3)$$

Consider now any two commodities, say i and j. Since, at the maximum, (9.3) must hold for these two commodities, we get

$$\frac{\dfrac{\partial U^m}{\partial x_i{}^m}}{p_i} = \frac{\dfrac{\partial U^m}{\partial x_j{}^m}}{p_j}, \qquad i, j = 1, 2, \ldots, n,$$

or, equivalently,

$$\frac{\dfrac{\partial U^m}{\partial x_i{}^m}}{\dfrac{\partial U^m}{\partial x_j{}^m}} = \frac{p_i}{p_j}, \qquad i, j = 1, 2, \ldots, n, \qquad (9.4)$$

which is to say that the consumer is maximizing his utility subject to his budget constraint if the ratio of his marginal utilities for any two goods equals the ratio of the prices of these goods.

If (9.4) is not satisfied, a consumer could exchange one good for the other at prevailing prices and further increase his utility. For example, if $p_i = 2$ and $p_j = 1$, but $\partial U^m/\partial x_i{}^m = 3$ and $\partial U^m/\partial x_j{}^m = 1$, equation (9.4) is not satisfied: $\frac{3}{1} \neq \frac{2}{1}$. Since good i is twice as expensive as good j, the consumer can exchange one unit of j for one-half unit of i. With this exchange the consumer loses one utile from giving up one unit of j, but he gains three-halves utiles from securing one-half unit of i. Thus, he achieves a net gain of one-half utile, which is to say that prior to the exchange he is not maximizing his utility.

Observe, finally, that since every consumer is confronted with the identical price vector, p, expression (9.5) must hold for all consumers if they are all individually maximizing their utilities. That is,[5]

[4]The constant λ has a simple interpretation. Suppose good 1 is money. Since money can be traded for money in the ratio 1:1, $p_1 = 1$. Thus, from (9.3), $\lambda = \partial U^m/\partial x_1{}^m$, which is to say that λ is the consumer's marginal utility for money.

[5]In a similar fashion we can characterize the equilibrium attained by firms in a perfectly competitive market. Firms are, of course, the producers of goods, but we assume, first, that each firm's production is constrained by prevailing technology. We summarize the state of technology by a production-possibilities function, which characterizes a single firm, say the kth firm, by

$$f^k(x_1{}^k, x_2{}^k, \ldots, x_n{}^k) = 0.$$

To illustrate this function, suppose that there are two goods ($n = 2$) and that for every unit of the first good the firm consumes, the firm can produce 3 units of the second good. Thus, $3x_2 = -x_1$ (the minus sign for x_1 indicates that x_1 is an input) or, equivalently, $f(x_1, x_2) = 3x_2 + x_1 = 0$. Assuming now that firms maximize net profits, we represent the kth firm's net profits, P^k, by

$$\frac{\frac{\partial U^1}{\partial x_i{}^1}}{\frac{\partial U^1}{\partial x_j{}^1}} = \frac{\frac{\partial U^2}{\partial x_i{}^2}}{\frac{\partial U^2}{\partial x_j{}^2}} = \cdots = \frac{\frac{\partial U^M}{\partial x_i{}^M}}{\frac{\partial U^M}{\partial x_j{}^M}} = \frac{p_i}{p_j}, \qquad i,j = 1, 2, \ldots, n. \qquad (9.5)$$

PARETO OPTIMALITY AND PRIVATE GOODS

Expression (9.5) states that if, for *every* consumer, the ratio of marginial utilities of every pair of goods equals the ratio of prices of those goods, the market is in equilibrium—no consumer seeks to make additional purchases or wishes to trade one good for another. We want, however, to do more than simply characterize a market equilibrium mathematically; we want to show that, in the one simple sense of Pareto optimality, the market can also be fair or efficient. That is, we want to know whether, in altering an allocation of

$$P^k = \sum_{i=1}^{n} p_i x_i{}^k,$$

where a term on the right side is positive if it represents the price of x units of an output, and is negative if it represents the price of x units of an input. The firm's profit is thus the gross price of its outputs less the gross price of its inputs. Each firm's task then is to maximize P^k subject to the constraints of technology. The procedure for characterizing this maximum is equivalent to the procedure for characterizing a consumer's maximum. Thus, we obtain as the necessary conditions for the maximization of net profits in a competitive market

$$\frac{\frac{\partial f^1}{\partial x_i{}^1}}{\frac{\partial f^1}{\partial x_j{}^1}} = \frac{\frac{\partial f^2}{\partial x_i{}^2}}{\frac{\partial f^2}{\partial x_j{}^2}} = \cdots = \frac{p_i}{p_j}, \qquad i,j = 1, 2, \ldots, n,$$

which is to say that, for all firms, the ratio of the marginal rates of productivities of any two goods must equal the ratio of their prices. To illustrate this condition suppose that $p_i = 2$ and $p_j = 1$, but that $\partial f^k / \partial x_i{}^k = 1$ and $\partial f^k / \partial x_j{}^k = 3$, i.e., the condition is not satisfied. Thus, the kth firm can purchase one additional unit of i for 2 dollars, produce three additional units of j, and sell all these three units for 3 dollars. The firm then secures a net profit of 1 dollar, which is to say that the firm cannot be at a maximum if it does not engage in this production.

Observe now that we can combine the expression above with expression (9.5), both of which contain the term p_i/p_j. We find then that utility maximization by consumers and profit maximization by firms in a competitive market implies that

$$\frac{\frac{\partial U^m}{\partial x_i{}^m}}{\frac{\partial U^m}{\partial x_j{}^m}} = \frac{\frac{\partial f^k}{\partial x_i{}^k}}{\frac{\partial f^k}{\partial x_j{}^k}} \qquad \text{for all } i, j, k, \text{ and } m.$$

This expression means that if a competitive market is in equilibrium, the ratio of marginal utilities of any pair of goods for any consumer equals the ratio of marginal productivities of the same pair for any firm. (Parenthetically, we note that this equality is often expressed in a somewhat different form. Specifically, if we sum the production functions of all firms and obtain the market production possibilities function

$$F(X_1, X_2, \ldots, X_n) = \sum_k f^k = 0,$$

and assume that each firm maximizes its profit subject to this market function, we obtain as the condition describing a competitive market equilibrium,

$$\frac{\frac{\partial U^m}{\partial x_i{}^m}}{\frac{\partial U^m}{\partial x_j{}^m}} = \frac{\frac{\partial F}{\partial X_i}}{\frac{\partial F}{\partial X_j}} \qquad \text{for all } i, j, \text{ and } m.$$

where X_i and X_j denote the total market production of goods i and j.)

goods that satisfies (9.5), we can increase the utility of one consumer only by decreasing the utility of someone else.

To analyze this problem we must first develop a formal characterization of Pareto-optimal allocations. The construction of such a characterization requires, however, that we know something about the properties of the goods people consume. Specifically, we must know something about the relationship between the total supply of each good, denoted by X_i, and the amount each person consumes of that good, $x_i{}^m$. The first type of good we consider is a *private good*, which is defined by the assumption that it is allocated according to the relation,

$$X_i = \sum_{m=1}^{M} x_i{}^m. \tag{9.6}$$

That is, the total supply of a private good equals the amount consumed by the first consumer plus the amount consumed by the second consumer, and so on.

Later we consider the characteristics of private goods in greater detail. It is sufficient to note here that their essential characteristic is that people can possess property rights to them. If one person consumes a loaf of bread—a standard example of a private good—another person cannot consume that loaf also. The only means for the second person to consume this particular loaf is to purchase the property right to it before it is eaten. Consequently, if the economy consists of two consumers and if each consumer possesses one loaf, the total supply of bread must be two loaves.

To outline the means by which Pareto-optimal allocations of private goods are characterized, suppose that a particular non-Pareto-optimal allocation exists. Thus, people's patterns of consumption can be altered [subject to (9.6)] such that the utility of at least one consumer, say m, is increased while no other consumer's utility is decreased. Let us then maximize $U^m(x^m)$ subject to (9.6) and

$$U^h(x^h) = \text{a constant}, \qquad \text{for all } h \neq m,$$

which is to say that we hold the utility of all other consumers constant. After performing this operation, we know that we are at a Pareto-optimal allocation—there cannot be any slack in the economy that might increase someone else's utility, since this slack could have been used to increase consumer m's utility. Using the method of Lagrangian multipliers, then, we obtain as the condition for a Pareto-optimal allocation of private goods:[6]

$$\frac{\dfrac{\partial U^m}{\partial x_i{}^m}}{\dfrac{\partial U^m}{\partial x_j{}^m}} = \frac{p_i}{p_j} \qquad \text{for all } i, j, \text{ and } m. \tag{9.7}$$

Observe now that expression (9.7)—the condition for a Pareto-optimal

[6]Outlining the derivation of (9.7), the Lagrangian expression is

allocation of private goods—is identical to expression (9.5)—the equilibrium condition of competitive markets.[7] This means that competitive markets provide Pareto-optimal allocations of private goods [i.e., goods that satisfy expression (9.6)]. That is, if individual consumers act as if they could not affect the prices of goods, if they maximize their utilities without regard for the choices of others, and if the goods they consume are private goods, then they arrive, as if by some "invisible hand," at a Pareto-optimal equilibrium.

This, then, is the classical justification for market activity: the perfectly competitive market for private goods renders allocations that are desirable in the sense that these allocations cannot be altered to improve one person's welfare without diminishing the welfare of others.

PARETO OPTIMALITY AND PUBLIC GOODS

Admittedly, however, the notion of Pareto optimality is an incomplete standard for evaluating the performance of any allocative mechanism. Allocations in which resources are divided equally throughout the population, for example, as well as allocations in which resources are concentrated in the hands of a

$$
U^m(x^m) - \sum_{h \ne m} \lambda_h [U^h(x^h) - a_h] - \sum_{i=1}^{n} \beta_i \left(\sum_{k=1}^{M} x_i^k - X_i \right),
$$

where the first summation is the $M - 1$ conditions that the utility of each consumer other than m is a constant, and the second summation is the n constraints that specify that each good i is a private good. Differentiating now with respect to individual m's consumption of goods i and j, x_i^m and x_j^m, we obtain

$$
\frac{\partial U^m}{\partial x_i^m} - \beta_i = 0; \qquad \frac{\partial U^m}{\partial x_j^m} - \beta_j = 0 \qquad \text{for all } i, j,
$$

or simply

$$
\frac{\partial U^m}{\partial x_i^m} \bigg/ \frac{\partial U^m}{\partial x_j^m} = \frac{\beta_i}{\beta_j} \qquad \text{for all } i, j. \tag{i}
$$

Differentiating with respect to the second set of variables—consumer h's consumption of goods i and j—we obtain

$$
\lambda_h \frac{\partial U^h}{\partial x_i^h} - \beta_i = 0; \quad \lambda_h \frac{\partial U^h}{\partial x_j^h} - \beta_j = 0 \qquad \text{for all } i, j, h,
$$

which, upon the elimination of λ_h, becomes

$$
\frac{\partial U^h}{\partial x_i^h} \bigg/ \frac{\partial U^h}{\partial x_j^h} = \frac{\beta_i}{\beta_j} \qquad \text{for all } i, j, h. \tag{ii}
$$

Observe now that (i) and (ii) are identical except that (i) refers only to consumer m and (ii) refers to consumer $h \ne m$. Together, then, they are identical to expression (9.7) insofar as they require that, for any two consumers and any two goods, the ratio of the marginal utilities of the goods for one consumer must equal the ratio of the marginal utilities of the goods for the other consumer. Note, however, that in (9.7) we have the ratio of marginal utilities equal to a ratio of prices; whereas here we have the ratio of marginal utilities equal to the ratio β_i/β_j. It is readily confirmed, however, that β_i and β_j are the prices of goods i and j, which completes our derivation of (9.7). For a more detailed discussion see Oscar Lange, "The Foundations of Welfare Economics," *Econometrica*, vol. 10 (1942), pp. 215–228, and James Quirk and Rubin Saposnik, *Introduction to General Equilibrium Theory and Welfare Economics* (New York: McGraw-Hill, 1968), pp. 124–147.

[7]If we include firms in the analysis, the condition for Pareto-optimal allocations of private goods is identical to the condition for a market equilibrium that we present in footnote 5.

few while the many are left to poverty and starvation, can be Pareto-optimal. Consequently, while everyone might agree that valued resources should not be wasted or thrown away—which is all that the notion of Pareto optimality is a test for—not everyone would be willing to say that the market for private goods is fair in some sense simply because it is efficient. Some surely would resist market allocations—even Pareto-optimal ones—in order to satisfy some moral principle that goes beyond this notion and classifies certain efficient allocations as desirable and others as undesirable. We wish to point out, however, that, if the goods in the market are public rather than private, the market is not even able to allocate resources in a Pareto-optimal fashion. That is, we turn now to consider situations in which, theoretically at least, market allocations can be altered somehow so as to increase some people's welfare without diminishing the welfare of others.

We begin with Paul A. Samuelson's two essays "The Pure Theory of Public Expenditure" and "A Diagrammatic Exposition of a Theory of Public Expenditure."[8] In these essays Samuelson examines the performance of markets as a mechanism for allocating goods other than private goods. Specifically, while markets yield Pareto-optimal allocations if the goods being exchanged are private, these decentralized mechanisms generally fail to yield Pareto-optimal allocations if the goods being exchanged are public.

To understand Samuelson's analysis and to explore the research it has stimulated, recall that private goods are those which are allocated according to expression (9.6). Public goods—the polar opposite to private ones—are goods "which are enjoyed in common in the sense that each individual's consumption of such a good leads to no subtraction from any other individual's consumption of that good," so that the total supply of the good, X_i, is allocated according to the relation[9]

$$X_i = x_i^1 = x_i^2 = \ldots = x_i^M. \tag{9.8}$$

We refer to goods that satisfy (9.8) as *pure public goods*. Some oft-cited examples are national defense and lighthouses. Clearly, if the Congress and the Defense Department decide to defend the country from nuclear attack by purchasing an ICBM force, our homes are protected as well as theirs. Hence, congressmen and soldiers are not the sole consumers of the defense goods they purchase. Nor are the taxpayers who approve of ICBM's. Moreover, it is unlikely that our presence in the country diminishes the protection supplied to others or that our homes are less well protected; everyone consumes equal quantities of the good without diminishing the amount consumed by others. Similarly, if some-

---

[8]*Review of Economics and Statistics*, vols. 36 and 37 (1954 and 1955), pp. 387–390 and 350–356. For a relatively nontechnical discussion and elaboration of our analysis, see James M. Buchanan, *The Demand and Supply of Public Goods* (Skokie, Ill.: Rand McNally, 1968).

[9]*Ibid.* Subsequently we argue that Samuelson's verbal definition and his formal definition of a public good—expression (9.8)—are inconsistent. Presently, however, we ignore any such inconsistency.

one erects a lighthouse near a treacherous shoal, anyone sailing near this shoal also consumes the warning of the lighthouse without diminishing the quality or quantity of the warning available to others.

To further illustrate the difference between public and private goods, consider a relatively simple but general example of a public good—an orderly, nonviolent society. To some it may seem absurd to reduce to a mere commodity so important a thing as public order. Peace and public safety, it may be said, are inherent in the nature of the community. They occur because it exists. To speak, therefore, of buying them is to speak as if one could buy the community, a turn of speech that appears to be lese majesty. We recognize, of course, that the community is not for sale. And yet there are very real senses in which one can say that public safety has a cost and a price. With one policeman, we may not have peace; with 100, we may. What makes the difference? Clearly, 99 policemen, whose cost is therefore a kind of marginal price of public safety. Or again: with income distributed in such a way that half of the society feels cheated, public safety may not exist even for the satisfied half. Yet with the proportion of dissatisfied reduced to say, one percent, life may be safe for everyone. What makes the difference is the redistribution. From the point of view of the originally satisfied, what they lose in the redistribution may be interpreted also as the marginal price of public safety.

Although, as we therefore insist, public as well as private goods are both commodities that might be bought and sold, the economic similarity ends there. And we here are much more concerned with the differences between them than we are with the similarity. For a private good, the seller furnishes a unit of the good to a buyer who is distinguished by the fact that he pays for exactly that unit. Short of madness, the seller does not give a unit to anyone other than a buyer in the sense just defined (as one who has contracted and paid for the good). In particular, when the orchardist sells a bushel of apples to one hungry man, he does not in celebration of the sale give bushels of apples away to all the onlookers who may be themselves hungry and therefore potential buyers. For a public good, however, the seller does almost that. He offers the good to a class of buyers who are defined in part by the good itself. And, if the good is produced and sold, every member of the class of consumers receives it whether or not he is in fact a buyer or indeed whether or not he needs or wants the good.

Consider, for contrast, an attorney who has several clients. For one he writes a will, for another he searches a title, for another he negotiates a settlement, and so on. His total production is the sum of the work done for each of his clients. Consider, on the other hand, apoliceman on a beat. He produces peace, and his total production is used up on the first resident of the block. If there are additional residents, they get this same amount of peace and there is no increment in the amount of peace produced. Furthermore, the additional residents cannot be kept from enjoying the peace produced for the first.

To see the difficulty associated with allocating goods such as national defense, lighthouses, and public safety in a decentralized market, we present the conditions for Pareto optimality with respect to public goods. Assume that for the n goods which people consume, the first r goods are private ones and all remaining $n - r$ goods are public (if the only private good is money, $r = 1$). Thus, if $i \leq r$, x_i^m represents person m's consumption of the private good i, whereas if $i \geq r + 1$, it represents his consumption of the public good i. With this notation, the public-good analogue to expression (9.7) is

$$\sum_{m=1}^{M} \frac{\partial U^m / \partial x_i^m}{\partial U^m / \partial x_j^m} = \frac{p_i}{p_j} , \qquad i \geq r + 1, j \leq r. \tag{9.9}$$

Observe now that expression (9.9)—the condition for a Pareto-optimal allocation of a public good—is not equivalent to expression (9.5)—the condition describing the equilibrium of consumers in a competitive market. Specifically, instead of a simple ratio of marginal utilities for a single consumer, the left side of expression (9.9) involves a summation of these ratios across all consumers. Hence, a perfectly competitive market for public goods generally fails to achieve Pareto optimality.

The explanation for this failure can be inferred directly from expressions (9.5) and (9.9). First, we know that one person's consumption of a public good *necessarily* entails an equivalent consumption of that good by everyone else. It is reasonable to expect, then, that the condition for Pareto-optimal allocations of public goods will accommodate the fact that, because variation in one person's consumption of a public good entails variations in others' consumption of that good, variation in one consumer's welfare leads to variations in the welfare of other consumers as well. By stating this condition in terms of the sum of ratios of marginal utilities across all consumers, this is exactly what expression (9.9) accomplishes.[10]

[10]To emphasize and illustrate the difference between (9.7) and (9.9) in characterizing optimal allocations, consider the social welfare function that is formed by *arbitrarily* weighting and summing individual utility functions thus:

$$SW = \sum_{m=1}^{M} \alpha_m U^m(x_1^m, x_2^m),$$

where the first good is a private good and the second is a public good. To characterize the allocation now that maximizes social welfare, we must impose the following $M + 2$ constraints:

$$\sum_{m=1}^{M} x_1^m - X_1 = 0,$$

$$\begin{bmatrix} x_2^1 - X_2 = 0 \\ x_2^2 - X_2 = 0 \\ \vdots \\ x_2^M - X_2 = 0 \end{bmatrix}$$

$$X_2 - \bar{X}_2 \leq 0.$$

The first constraint is expression (9.6) and it states that good 1 is a private good. The set of bracketed constraints is simply a restatement of expression (9.8)—one constraint for each consumer—and it states that good 2 is a pure public good. The last constraint states that, since we are considering an economy without production, there must be some upper limit, $\bar{X}_2$, on the amount of the public good, X_2, that each person can consume. Forming the Lagrangian expression now for the calculation of a constrained maximum,

PUBLIC GOODS AND THE PRISONERS' DILEMMA

Despite the impressive mathematics that can be used to demonstrate the inefficiency of perfectly competitive markets for public goods, a simple counterexample to efficiency perhaps best reveals the private incentives of consumers that lead them from any Pareto-optimal outcome. Consider a market for a single public good that is produced only if one or more consumers choose to buy it. Even if a vast majority want the good, each single person in that majority can reason thus: "If the good is produced, I will get it even if I do not pay for it. Since others want it, they can be relied upon to pay for it. I need not do so." If everyone reasons this way, then the good is not produced. So in a society composed entirely of reasonable people of this sort, there are no public goods supplied. We have thus an instance of the Prisoners' Dilemma, although here those impaled on the dilemma are those who want, but cannot get, a public good.

In a very simple way, the situation can be visualized thus: Suppose there is a society of two people, for each of whom the benefit from a public good is one unit of money, while the cost of production is one and one-half units. Each of the two persons has two possible courses of action, a_1, to produce, or a_2, not to

$$\sum_{m=1}^{M} \alpha_m U^m(x_1{}^m, x_2{}^m) - \lambda \left[\sum_{m=1}^{M} x_1{}^m - X_1\right] - \sum_{m=1}^{M} \beta_m(x_2{}^m - X_2) - \gamma(X_2 - \bar{X}_2),$$

where λ, β_1, β_2, . . ., β_M, and γ are the Lagrangian multipliers for the $M + 2$ constraints. Differentiating now with respect to the three classes of variables in the analysis, $x_1{}^m, x_2{}^m$, and X_2, and setting each derivative equal to zero,

$$\alpha_m \frac{\partial U^m}{\partial x_1{}^m} - \lambda = 0, \qquad m = 1, 2, \ldots, M;$$

$$\alpha_m \frac{\partial U^m}{\partial x_2{}^m} - \beta_m = 0, \qquad m = 1, 2, \ldots, M;$$

$$\sum_{m=1}^{M} \beta_m - \gamma = 0.$$

The last two conditions can be combined so as to eliminate the β_m's by summing the second condition across m and, in accordance with the third condition, setting the result equal to γ. Thus, the conditions for the maximization of social welfare are

$$\alpha_m \frac{\partial U^m}{\partial x_1{}^m} - \lambda = 0, \qquad m = 1, 2, \ldots, M;$$

$$\sum_{m=1}^{M} \alpha_m \frac{\partial U^m}{\partial x_2{}^m} - \gamma = 0.$$

Observe now that the first condition—the condition that pertains to the private good—requires only that each consumer adjusts his consumption until his marginal utility for the private good times his weight equals some constant (which, with further analysis, can be shown to be equal to the price of the good). The second condition—the one that pertains to the public good—requires, however, that the consumers somehow coordinate their consumption until the weighted sum of their marginal utilities equals some constant (again, the price of the good). Thus, for private goods, maximization of social welfare does not require coordination, whereas for public goods the coordination of individual consumption patterns is essential.

produce, and the total situation is summarized by Figure 9.1.[11] In each cell of the figure we denote the net benefit to each person of the joint actions. In the upper lefthand corner, where they join to produce, each person gets the benefit of one unit, while each pays half the cost (or three-fourths of a unit), thereby leaving each a net benefit of one-fourth unit. In the upper right hand corner, where 1 produces and 2 does not, 1 gets a negative benefit of one-half unit, which is the net benefit to him of one unit of gross benefit less the cost of one and one-half units. In that cell, however, 2 gets the full unit of benefit with no cost. The situation is simply reversed in the lower lefthand cell. Finally, in the lower right cell, where neither produces, there is neither cost nor benefit for either one, so we record zero.

PERSON 2

	a_1 PRODUCE	a_1 NOT PRODUCE
a_1: PRODUCE	$\frac{1}{4}, \frac{1}{4}$	$-\frac{1}{2}, 1$
a_2: NOT PRODUCE	$1, -\frac{1}{2}$	$0, 0$

PERSON 1

FIGURE 9.1

The central feature of this table is that neither has a private incentive to produce, even though, if they do jointly produce, they both gain. Let person 1 compare his alternatives, a_1 and a_2, under two assumptions: that person 2 performs a_1 or a_2.

If person 2 performs a_1, then for person 1, a_2 is better than a_1,

$$\text{i.e.,} \quad 1 > \frac{1}{4}.$$

If person 2 performs a_2, then for person 1, a_2 is better than a_1,

$$\text{i.e.,} \quad 0 > \frac{1}{2}.$$

So under either of the possible circumstances, it is better for person 1 to choose a_2 or not to produce. Since this situation is completely symmetric, the same holds true for person 2. Hence, if they look just to their own interests, no one has an

[11] For further examples of the analysis of public goods with Prisoners' Dilemma type games which elaborate on our discussion, see Russell Hardin, "Collective Action as an Agreeable n-Prisoners' Dilemma," *Behavioral Science*, vol. 16 (September 1971), pp. 436–441; James M. Buchanan, "Cooperation and Conflict in Public Goods Interaction," *Western Economic Journal* (October 1956), pp. 416–424; Charles J. Goetz, "Group Size and the Voluntary Provision of Public Goods" (Blacksburg, VPI, Working Paper no. 24); Clem Tisdell, "Some Bounds Upon the Pareto Optimality of Group Behavior," *Kyklos*, vol. 19 (1966), pp. 81–105; and William H. Riker, "Public Safety as a Public Good," in Eugene V. Rostow, ed., *Is Law Dead?* (New York: Simon and Schuster, 1971), pp. 370–385.

incentive to produce a public good, which in this case we suppose is a public benefit. One interpretation of the difference between expressions (9.7) and (9.9), then, is that to achieve Pareto-optimal allocations of public goods in perfectly competitive markets, people must choose irrationally.

BARGAINING

The Prisoners' Dilemma in Figure 9.1 illustrates the forces operating in a market for public goods—where consumers, lacking incentives for taking account of the effects on others of their decisions, rationally adopt strategies that yield non-Pareto-optimal outcomes. Suppose, however, that consumers are compelled to accommodate these effects in their decisions. Specifically, suppose that consumers are allowed to bargain and that any agreements they reach are binding. While we know from our review of the theory of two-person cooperative games that the analysis of such games entails several difficulties, we know also that it is rational for players to seek an outcome on the negotiation set (a subset of Pareto-optimal outcomes). Hence, we can assume that markets in which constraints on bargaining are not imposed but in which agreements are binding are more likely to satisfy expression (9.9)—are more likely to achieve Pareto-optimal allocations of public goods—than are perfectly competitive markets. To show this and to illustrate further the application and meaning of expression (9.9), we offer an example of a two-person cooperative game.[12]

First, we assume that the economy consists of two goods, the first a private and the second a public good. Player 1, then, seeks to maximize $U^1(x_1{}^1, y)$, while player 2 seeks to maximize $U^2(x_1{}^2, y)$, where y denotes the supply of the public good. Second, we assume that player 1, but not player 2, determines the magnitude of y, so that 1's level of consumption of y determines the level of consumption for both. Thus, 1 and 2 might be neighbors and y might denote the amount of soot released into the air from 1's furnace —both persons' homes are dirtied by the soot but only 1 controls the amount. Finally, we assume that the players cannot exceed their respective budgets, B^1 and B^2. Since it is player 1 that purchases y, his budget constraint is

$$p_1x_1{}^1 + p_2y = B^1,$$

while 2's constraint is

$$p_1x_1{}^2 = B^2,$$

since he can purchase only the private good—good 1.

Suppose now that the players fail to bargain, that 1 ignores the effects of his consumption on 2, and that 2 simply adjusts to the constraint that he must consume whatever amount of the public good 1 chooses. Let $\bar{x}^m$ and $\bar{y}$ denote the

---

[12]At this point our analysis parallels the model of bargaining presented in Otto A. Davis and Andrew B. Whinston, "Some Notes on Equating Private and Social Cost," *The Southern Economic Journal*, vol. 32 (1965), pp. 113–126.

equilibrium amounts of the goods consumed. There is no reason to assume, now, that this is a Pareto-optimal equilibrium. If player 2 benefits from the public good, he might be willing to pay 1 to increase $\bar{y}$, while if 2 is harmed by $\bar{y}$, he might be willing to pay 1 to decrease $\bar{y}$. And if either transaction increases the welfare of both players, the market equilibrium before the transaction is not Pareto-optimal.

To see how bargaining can yield Pareto-optimal allocations, assume that player 2's welfare is decreased by $\bar{y}$, and let him offer 1 the amount T for every unit decrease in $\bar{y}$ (assuming, of course, that 2 does not offer more than his budget allows). Thus, if player 1 alters his consumption from $\bar{y}$ to y and if $y < \bar{y}$, he receives a payment of $T(\bar{y} - y)$ from 2. Assume that this offer is accepted. Player 2 now must maximize

$$U^2(x_1^2, y)$$

subject to

$$p_1 x_1^2 = B^2 - T(\bar{y} - y).$$

Observe that an amount $T(\bar{y} - y)$ must be subtracted from B^2, since player 2 relinquishes this amount to get player 1 to alter his consumption.

Similarly, player 1's task is to maximize

$$U^1(x_1^1, y)$$

subject to

$$p_1 x_1^1 + p_2 y = B^1 + T(\bar{y} - y)$$

—that is, the payment from 2, $T(\bar{y} - y)$, is added to his initial budget, B^1.

With respect to the public good, player 1's maximum occurs when[13]

$$\frac{1}{\lambda_1} \frac{\partial U^1}{\partial y} - (p_2 + T) = 0. \tag{9.10}$$

That is, if (9.10) is satisfied, player 1 accepts 2's offer of $T(\bar{y} - y)$ and reduces his consumption from $\bar{y}$ to y (and, consequently, increases his consumption of good 1).

Turning to player 2—the person affected by player 1's consumption—we assume that by bargaining, 2 can affect the amount of the public good he consumes. That is, by varying T he affects 1's consumption of the public good, thereby affecting his consumption of this good. Again we can derive the usual conditions for utility maximization, but the relevant condition concerns player 2's evaluation of y. Specifically, consider

$$\frac{1}{\lambda_2} \frac{\partial U^2}{\partial y} + T = 0. \tag{9.11}$$

---

[13]Using the method of Lagrangian multipliers, the expression we seek to maximize is
$$U(x_1^1, y) - \lambda_1 [p_1 x_1^1 + p_2 y - B^1 - T(\bar{y} - y)].$$
Differentiating with respect to y, we obtain
$$\frac{\partial U}{\partial y} - \lambda_1(p_2 + T).$$
Setting this expression equal to zero and dividing by λ_1 yields equation (9.10).

If equation (9.11) holds, we know that player 1 is selecting an amount of the public good that maximizes the utility of player 2.[14] Alternatively, if inequality holds instead of equality, player 2 should attempt to make a new offer, T', which would either raise or lower 1's consumption of y.

Suppose now that expressions (9.10) and (9.11) is satisfied so that both players have maximized their utility with respect to y and do not wish to bargain further; i.e., suppose that an equilibrium is attained. We can show that this equilibrium is Pareto-optimal. First, we can substitute expression (9.11) into (9.10) by eliminating T, and obtain

$$\frac{1}{\lambda_1} \frac{\partial U^1}{\partial y} + \frac{1}{\lambda_2} \frac{\partial U^2}{\partial y} = p_2. \tag{9.12}$$

We can also eliminate λ_1 and λ_2, noting that if both players have maximized their utility with respect to the private good, then, from expression (9.3), the constants λ_1 and λ_2 must satisfy

$$\lambda_1 = \frac{\partial U^1}{\partial x_1{}^1} \Big/ p_1 \quad \text{for player 1,}$$

$$\lambda_2 = \frac{\partial U^2}{\partial x_1{}^2} \Big/ p_1 \quad \text{for player 2.}$$

Thus, expression (9.12) becomes

$$\frac{\dfrac{\partial U^1}{\partial y}}{\dfrac{\partial U^1}{\partial x_1{}^1}} + \frac{\dfrac{\partial U^2}{\partial y}}{\dfrac{\partial U^2}{\partial x_1{}^2}} = \frac{p_2}{p_1}. \tag{9.13}$$

Observe now that this expression and the condition describing Pareto-optimal allocations of public goods—expression (9.9)—are identical. Hence, a Pareto-optimal allocation is the solution to this bargaining game.

Can we assume, then, that bargaining is the solution to the inefficiencies of the market? And should we predict that the presence of public goods is sufficient reason for people to abandon markets in favor of more direct bargaining mechanisms? While we discuss this question in greater detail later, for the present our answer is, unfortunately, no. First, most situations of relevance to politics concern large numbers of people. And if the number of people who must bargain to achieve a Pareto-optimal allocation is large, bargaining is an impractical alternative. Bargaining requires coordination and information, and as the size of a group increases, coordination becomes increasingly difficult and information becomes increasingly costly. The town meeting, for example,

[14]Again, the Lagrangian expression is
$$U^2(x_1{}^2, y) - \lambda_2[p_1 x_1{}^2 - B^2 + T(\bar{y} - y)].$$
Differentiating with respect to y, we obtain
$$\frac{\partial U^2}{\partial y} + \lambda_2 T.$$
Setting this expression equal to zero and dividing by λ_2 yields equation (9.11).

might be interpreted as a form of bargaining in a community, where the meeting serves as a mechanism for rendering decisions about the supply of goods such as schools, roads, tax rates, and a memorial on the village green. Clearly, however, this mechanism is an impractical device for serving the needs of a community of even moderate size.

A second and more compelling consideration renders bargaining an impractical allocative mechanism in politics. Recall that in our example we let bargaining assume a very special form, namely that both players bargain in good faith. We assume that, after player 1 agrees to alter his consumption of good 1, he does in fact do so, and that after player 2 proposes to pay 1 at the rate T, he carries out this promise. We have not, however, explained why bargaining proceeds in good faith. Clearly, if player 1 benefits from the public good, he prefers to increase his consumption once again after he fools 2 into paying him $T(\bar{y} - y)$. Similarly, if 1 reduces his consumption from $\bar{y}$ to y, player 2 prefers to renege on the payment of $T(\bar{y} - y)$. That is, each player, as in a Prisoners' Dilemma, has an incentive to renege on his bargain.

We cannot state unconditionally that, with the opportunity to bargain, people avoid this dilemma since their decisions depend as much upon personality as upon the logic of the previous analysis. We can suggest, however, one factor that critically affects the likelihood that bargaining will proceed in good faith and will lead to a Pareto-optimal outcome—the number of people, M, who consume the public good. In Chapter 3 we said that typically the efficacy of individual decisions is inversely related to their scope. For public goods, scope equals M, so that we may take efficacy as being inversely related to M. Suppose now that M is small (in our example, $M = 2$ and efficacy is maximized because players 1 and 2 are the sole consumers of the public good). It then follows that the adverse effects on others of a bargain that is not kept are significant, in which case sanctions such as fines and an unwillingness to bargain later with an offender are likely to be employed. Also, if M is small, the offender is readily identified, so that these sanctions can be directly and immediately applied. Thus, a Pareto-optimal outcome is likely to be attained because people are not likely to renege on their bargains.

Conversely, if M is large, efficacy is small, so that nonoptimal outcomes are more likely to prevail. That is, each person can reason thus:

(i)   if the public good is provided, I derive the greatest net benefit by not contributing to the overall cost of supplying the good;

(ii) if I do not contribute to this cost by either bargaining in bad faith or by failing to reveal my preferences correctly, my actions will go largely unnoticed because I do not have an appreciable affect on the outcome;

(iii) I should disguise my true preferences, then, and not bargain in good faith.

Thus, as M increases, the private incentives to renege on a bargaining agreement typically increase, which is to say that the whole of society reverts to Prisoners' Dilemma.

The reader should be able to recognize quickly that this argument is identical with our review of Olson's ideas on participation in Chapter 3. Olson's remarks on collectivities—that the benefits of collective action are not a sufficient condition for such action—are a clever adaptation and extension of the analysis that we review here and they demonstrate its generality. That is, if we substitute latent groups for decentralized markets, collective interest for public goods, and the failure of a group to form for nonoptimal allocations, then we transform the previous analysis into Olson's.

EXTERNALITIES

Close adherence to Samuelson's definition of public goods is not desirable, however, because it confines us to a less-than-complete development of the theory he suggests. Samuelson's sharp distinction between public and private goods compels us to restrict unnecessarily the concepts of consumption and of goods. In particular, we note that most goods that people consume cannot be characterized as either purely private or purely public.

As we proceed, then, to formulate more general definitions, we note that the previous analysis is an analysis of externalities—interdependencies of social action—although the externalities assume an extreme form. We examine, therefore, the concept of externalities in its full generality and in its relationship to public and private goods.

As before, assume that a person has a utility function $U^m(O)$, that is defined over the set of outcomes, O, and that the person selects alternatives from the set of all acts available to him, A, so as to maximize his utility. Presumably, a person affects the occurrence of outcomes by his choice of an alternative. In markets, for example, a person's alternatives consist of different purchases and the outcomes consist of allocations of goods. In elections the elements of A include voting for a candidate or abstaining, and the outcomes can denote either a victorious candidate or a public policy. In general for all choice contexts we say that O is functionally related to A, or that $O = g(A)$. The function $g(A)$ links alternatives to outcomes: it summarizes the knowledge necessary to utter such sentences as "if the person chooses $a \in A$, then, *ceteris paribus,* the outcome in O that occurs is. . . " for decision making under certainty, or for decision making with uncertainty "if the person chooses $a \in A$, then, *ceteris paribus,* the outcome . . . occurs with a probability of . . . ."

With this simple notation we can define externality. An externality is the effect of one person's choice on the relationship between outcomes and the choices of another person. That is, an externality exists if at least one person in addition to our subject can alter the function $g(A)$ with his choices, i.e., if the *ceteris paribus* conditions of the previous paragraph include the choices of others.[15]

[15]Our definition of externalities is somewhat incomplete in the sense that it presupposes that people care about the effects of others' choices on them. Consider, for example, a change in a

It is the analysis of such effects, how they come to be, and what consequences for choice are implied by them that constitutes the analysis of externalities, market imperfections, public goods, and public policy. We illustrate, then, the intent and the application of this definition of externalities.

Consider first the analysis from Chapter 3 of a citizen's calculus of voting. In that analysis each citizen acts as if his decision contributed to the determination of the candidates' fortunes. While each citizen's subjective evaluation of his contribution is likely to overstate an objective calculation of it, the citizen doubtless has some effect, given our typically uncertain guesses about the outcomes of elections. And if the citizen's choice has some effect, his decision to vote or to abstain exhibits externalities. The particular externality is this: if the citizen abstains, the functional relationship, g, between A and O for another citizen states in part: "candidate 1 wins with probability p if you vote for him," whereas if the citizen votes for candidate 1, the other citizen's g is: "candidate 1 wins with probability p' if you vote for him." Presumably, $p' > p$, which is to say that g is changed and an externality exists.

The externality in this example is, of course, relatively minor, given the objectively small difference between p' and p. Consequently, we assume in Chapter 3 that each citizen acts as if he believed that his decision does not affect the choices of others.[16] For a more apparent instance of an externality, then, suppose that, in the selection of a victorious candidate, one citizen is a dictator and he alone selects a victor. Clearly, then, the dictator's decision exhibits externalities: it affects $g(A)$ for all "citizens" in that it determines whether or not $g(A)$ reads "candidate 1 for all $a \in A$," or "candidate 2 for all $a \in A$," and so on. (Conversely, other citizens' decisions on electoral politics in this case do not exhibit externalities, since their decisions, by assumption, cannot affect the outcome of the "election.")

For another example, consider one of our earlier illustrations of a public good, namely the soot that erupts from the chimney of a householder who heats his home with an inefficient coal-burning furnace. Assume that this soot eventually finds its way into homes and lungs in the neighborhood. Clearly, the homeowner gains utility from heating his house, but just as obviously, the quality of his neighbors' lives are affected by his actions. Thus, heating one's house with an inefficient furnace exhibits externalities. (On the other hand, if our household were to use a fuel that was so efficient that it was entirely consumed in combustion, no externality could occur.)

Observe that, in this example of soot, a rather special kind of externality

---

person's functional relationship between outcomes and acts so that for a particular $a \in A$, the probability that O' occurs decreases while the probability that O'' occurs increases. Clearly, now, it makes little sense to talk about the existence of an externality if the person is absolutely indifferent between O' and O''. Recognizing such possibilities, then, we assume hereafter that people are not so indifferent. For a more elaborate treatment of the definition of externalities, particularly as it pertains to economic theory, see James M. Buchanan and Wm. Craig Stubblebine, "Externality," *Economics,* vol. 29 (1962), pp. 371–384.

[16]See the discussion of interdependent choices in Chapter 8.

exists—one that decreases everyone else's utility. Thus, we say that the external-ity is an *external diseconomy*. Not all externalities, however, are diseconomies. For example, the homeowner might paint his house and thereby contribute to the beautification of the neighborhood. In this case, we say that the externality is an *external economy* since everyone's utility is increased. (Parenthetically, we note that a person's acts can exhibit both external economies and diseconomies simultaneously. Painting one's house contributes to the satisfaction of those residing in the neighborhood, but if it tends to raise the market value of the nearby houses, it increases the cost of someone who seeks to purchase one of them. For such a person, then, painting a house might exhibit external dis-economies. Or, for a more concrete example, consider the act of voting. If someone votes for the candidate we prefer—thereby increasing the probability that this candidate wins—then for us his act exhibits an external economy; but for opponents of this candidate the vote for him is a diseconomy, since it tends to decrease their anticipated utility.)

This example should not be taken to imply the common fallacy that only public goods and not private goods exhibit externalities. On the contrary suppose that a person increases his consumption of a private good from x_1^m to $5x_1^m$. The total amount everyone else can consume of this good diminishes from $X_1 - x_1^m$ to $X_1 - 5x_1^m$. Thus, externalities are present in the sense that the person's increased consumption makes it impossible for others to consume an amount $X_1 - x_1^m$.

If we conclude, then, that both private and public goods exhibit externalities, we must ask why we propose a definition of externalities in the first place. We see from our discussion that externalities are a pervasive feature of all social processes; our definition of external effects might easily serve as a definition of such processes. What then is the value of such an all-encompassing idea? One answer is that different kinds of goods exhibit different kinds of externalities and that these differences help account for the allocations rendered by a social choice mechanism such as a market.

Consider first the relationship between the externality associated with an individual's consumption of a private good and the number of consumers in an economy. If the economy consists of but a few consumers, the difference between $X_1 - x_1^m$ and $X_1 - 5x_1^m$ (and therefore the relevant externality) can be substantial. If we have two consumers and ten apples and if one person increases his consumption from one to five apples, the difference between five and nine apples is not likely to go unnoticed by the other consumer. If, however, the num-ber of consumers is large so that X_1 is likely to be substantially greater than ten, the relative difference between $X_1 - x_1^m$ and $X_1 - 5x_1^m$ is reduced. Finally, if we assume that there are an almost infinite number of consumers so that we can make the additional mathematical assumption that x_1^m/X_1 and $5x_1^m/X_1$ are nearly equal to zero for all reasonable values of x_1^m, the difference vanishes. That is, as M increases, the externality associated with the variations in an individual's consumption of a private good can reasonably be assumed to decrease in significance. Observe now that if variations in one person's consumption can significantly affect the supply of a good to others, these variations are likely to yield some change in the price of the good; but if the supply to others cannot be so changed, a single consumer cannot affect prices. Consequently, the assumption in models of perfectly competitive markets that no individual can vary his pattern of consumption so significantly as to affect prices is equivalent to the assumption that he cannot significantly affect the supply to others of a good and, therefore, that his consumption exhibits no externalities. That is, with private goods we can impose reasonable assumptions about the admissible relative variation in a consumer's choices and thereby eliminate externalities.

With public goods, however, no such assumption is possible. Regardless of the number of consumers, if individual m chooses to consume $x_1{}^m$ of a public good, individual k must consume $x_i{}^k = x_i{}^m$ of the good also. That is, no increase in the number of consumers diminishes the magnitude of the externality that k experiences from m's consumption.

It is clear, then, that there are significant differences in the nature and implications of externalities. This should not be a surprising conclusion. The subject of previous chapters can readily be interpreted to be externalities because an analysis of externalities is but an analysis of the interdependence of individual choices. And given the variety of forms of such interdependence— a variety that is perhaps best revealed by two-person games—it follows that the externalities that goods exhibit should vary greatly in form also. But while we sought earlier to understand this variety theoretically and abstractly, we can begin here to understand it in terms of the particular kinds of goods people exchange, consume, and produce—and thereby lend further substantive significance to an abstract, theoretical analysis. In the next section, then, we examine goods in greater detail, and we find that expressions (9.6) and (9.8) do not exhaust the range of possible types of goods and, therefore, the possible forms of externalities.

JOINTNESS OF SUPPLY AND EXCLUDABILITY

The formal definition of a pure public good and the one that Samuelson relies on—expression (9.8)—states that all persons in the relevant class consume identical quantities of the good. The verbal preface to this definition, however, states only that one person's consumption does not diminish the supply available to others. Observe that these two statements—the verbal and the formal— are not equivalent. Consider, for example, a park that is large enough not to be overcrowded, so that the admission of people to the park does not diminish the enjoyment (consumption) of those previously or subsequently admitted to it. Thus, parks are not strictly private goods in the sense of expression (9.6) because supply is not limited. We cannot say, however, that the park is a public good, since some people may want to go to the park while others may prefer a baseball game. That is, while a large park may satisfy our verbal definition in the sense that one person's attendance does not diminish the pleasure of another, the requirement of equal consumption stated by expression (9.8) is not satisfied because not everyone uses the park with equal intensity. We have, then, an example of a good that fails to fit neatly into either of our previously defined categories of goods.

To establish the relationship between public and private goods and goods such as recreation areas, we introduce the concept of *jointness of supply*.[17] We say that a good exhibits jointness of supply if, when X_i units of the good are made available to one person, these X_i units can simultaneously be consumed by others. Hence, pure public goods and large recreation areas both exhibit jointness of supply. The difference between them is that people are not required to consume the same amount of recreation but they are required to consume the same amount of a pure public good like public order or national defense. With this definition of jointness of supply, several additional instances can be offered as examples. Ignoring for the present such problems as the saturation of facilities, consider public education and those people who do not have high school diplomas. In this instance, public education exhibits jointness of supply in the sense that once school facilities are made available to a community, a person can consume the education that is being consumed simultaneously by others. For those people who have satisfied a statutory age requirement, however, education is not a pure public good, since they can freely choose to participate in alternative activities. Similarly, a free public road satisfies our definition of a jointly supplied good in that once such a road is constructed for the use of one person, it can be used by others. Roads, however, are not a pure public good, since people can choose alternative routes or modes of transportation. That is, consumption of a road does not conform necessarily to expression (9.8).

We have, then, at least two types of jointly supplied goods: those for which a person can choose the amount he consumes and those for which he cannot.

Before our typology of goods is complete, however, and before we can develop a means for characterizing the kind of externality we should associate with a good, we must note a second dimension in the character of jointly supplied goods. Specifically, we must distinguish between jointly supplied goods that are subject to *exclusion* and those that are not. In our examples of education and roads we use the word "free"—thereby eliminating tuition and tolls. The use of schools and of roads, however, is not always free; people can be excluded from consuming these goods by a price mechanism and by the legal system that legitimizes this price. In the examples of national defense and lighthouses, on the other hand, no one can be excluded from consuming them, although indivi-

[17]J. G. Head, "Public Goods and Public Policy," *Public Finance*, vol. 17, no. 3 (1962), pp. 197–219. See also E. J. Mishan, "The Relationship between Joint Products, Collective Goods, and External Effects," *Journal of Political Economy*, vol. 77 (1969), pp. 329–348.

dual shares in financing and maintaining them may differ. Thus, defense systems and lighthouses are not subject to exclusion.

TABLE 9.1

A Typology of Jointly Supplied Goods

	PERSON IS ABLE TO CHOOSE AMOUNT OF CONSUMPTION		PERSON IS UNABLE TO CHOOSE AMOUNT OF CONSUMPTION	
	UTILITY INCREASED BY CONSUMPTION	UTILITY DECREASED BY CONSUMPTION	UTILITY INCREASED BY CONSUMPTION	UTILITY DECREASED BY CONSUMPTION
PERSONS CAN BE EXCLUDED FROM CONSUMPTION	Recreation area Roads Cable television (1)	Polluted beaches (2)	Fire departments Civil liberties (3)	Infectious disease The military draft (4)
PERSONS CANNOT BE EXCLUDED FROM CONSUMPTION	Lighthouses Socialized medicine Knowledge (5)	Excess sunshine Airport noise (6)	Public order National defense Pollution control Flood control (7)	Air pollution Floods (8)

We can now differentiate among jointly supplied goods, first, according to whether or not a person is able to choose the amount he consumes and, second, according to whether or not a person can be excluded from using the good. If we add to this whether or not the person increases or decreases his utility by consuming the good we obtain Table 9.1.

We illustrate the cells of this table with a few substantive examples. Samuelson's pure public good is in cells (7) and (8) because everyone, without the possibility of any exclusion, must consume such a good in equal quantities. A public good that everybody wishes to consume is in cell (7), while a public good (bad?) that everyone wishes to avoid is in cell (8). Roads and recreation areas and polluted beaches, on the other hand, are diagonally opposite in the upper left cells—cells (1) and (2)—because they are subject to exclusion and because consumers can choose whether or not and how much of such a good to consume. The lower left cells show a third possibility: nonexcludable goods in which free choice is possible—goods, for example, which governments supply and which, legally, must be equally available to everyone. Socialized medicine, as in England, is an example, because it is universally available but citizens have the option of purchasing medical care privately if they so choose. Airport noise—located in cell (6)—is such that a person cannot be excluded from consuming it, but, theoretically at least, a person can move away from an airport if he so wishes. A third and less tangible example of the lower left cells is accumulated human knowledge. Assuming that all knowledge is ultimately equally available to anyone who wishes to acquire it, we can regard it as a nonexcludable jointly supplied good. Knowledge might serve as an example of cell (6) as well as of cell (5) if, for example, a cancer patient does not wish to question his physician about the extent of his illness for fear of what the physician might reveal.

Our final possibility—in the upper right cells (3) and (4)—consists of goods that are, in principle at least, excludable. Nevertheless, people are unable to choose the amount they consume, e.g., fire protection. Such protection is an excludable commodity, since firemen can choose to protect some buildings and not others. In principle, however, the quality of fire protection in a community is maximized if everyone is equally protected, in which case people are required to consume equally the benefits that a fire department supplies. Similarly, the protection of civil liberties supplied by the judicial structure is an excludable good, but the spirit, if not always the application of the legal tradition, requires that everyone consume an equal amount. Finally, while individual persons are unable to choose whether or not to "consume" an infectious disease, still some can be exluded in the sense that state and local health regulations can require that the available (but limited) supply of inoculants be distributed among a select group, such as children and pregnant women.

Clearly, many goods, as well as some of our examples, fail to correspond neatly to one cell or another, and we examine such mixed goods in the next section. First, however, we use the typology of Table 9.1 to explore the types of externalities associated with various goods and to demonstrate that frequently the externality can be controlled.

Consider a public good—a good that conforms to either cell (7) or cell (8). Reviewing again the character of the externality associated with such a good, assume that person m consumes an amount $x_1{}^m$ of the good. For everyone else, then, the functional relationship between the set of alternative acts, A, and the set of possible outcomes, O, must require that every alternative yield an outcome in which $x_1{}^k = x_1{}^m$. And if the person increases his consumption to $5x_1{}^m$, then this functional relationship, $g(A)$, must change so that, for all $a \in A$, $x_1{}^k = 5x_1{}^m$.

The externalities associated with goods in cells (5) and (6) conform to a similar characterization—the single difference being that a person no longer has to consume the good. Thus, if person m supplies himself with the amount $x_1{}^m$ of such a good, we do not require that $g(A)$ invariably yield $x_1{}^k = x_1{}^m$ for anyone else. Rather, we assume that there exists at least one alternative in A such that $x_1{}^k < x_1{}^m$. The externality, however, is this: prior to person m's consumption, some other person must pay for or otherwise secure the good, whereas if m supplies the good himself, others are no longer required to pay for the amount that m supplies.

The externalities associated with both types of nonexcludable goods generally cannot be accommodated by a decentralized allocative mechanism such as the market. In the case of cell (6), market failure is of little importance, since people can simply choose not to consume a good that decreases their utility. For the case of beneficial nonexcludable goods, however, a person has little incentive to provide the good for himself and everyone else, since the cost of provision typically (although not necessarily) outweighs private benefits. And if the good is somehow supplied, everyone has an incentive to avoid paying the costs of supply. Hence, goods such as public order, defense, flood control, lighthouses, and socialized medicine are provided typically through collective action, usually governmental action.

Public goods that people regard as undesirable—cell (8)—offer little justification for collective action if we assume that people produce only desirable goods. Public bads exist, however, because (like floods) they arise from nature or because (like air pollution) they are by-products of the consumption or production of other commodities. The particular difficulty in accommodating the externalities of public *bads* in markets is that some public *good* such as flood or pollution control must be supplied. That is, an optimal decrease in the supply of goods in cell (8) typically requires that some organized collective effort optimally produce a good in cell (7).

The questions of public policy associated with nonexcludable goods are generally of two sorts: how to organize collective action, and how to distribute its benefits and costs. The first question involves such diverse things as the design of a constitution for society, the choice of a spokesman for a neighborhood action committee, the decision to establish a regulatory agency, or a choice between federal and state authority. The second question typically concerns the selection of a tax mechanism (and a tax rate) such as proportional or progressive income taxes, real estate taxes, bond issues, and lotteries. If however, we are concerned with the allocation of excludable jointly supplied goods, [goods in cells (1), (2), (3), and (4)], at least one additional question must be considered: should private decisions be collectivized in the first place, or can a market mechanism operate efficiently? We raise this question in order to illuminate the essential property of excludable goods, namely, that they can exhibit the same kind of externalities as nonexcludable goods, or they can act very much like private goods. Consider, for example, recreation areas. First, we might have collective *qua* governmental supply of such areas with the proviso that no one can be excluded from enjoying them. Alternatively, a private concern might develop these areas and, with an entrance fee, exclude people from consumption. With collective supply, then, recreation areas exhibit the same externalities as lighthouses and socialized medicine, whereas with private supply, they appear to be private goods.

This example, however, should not be interpreted to mean that privately supplied excludable goods are like private ones, or that publicly supplied excludable goods act like nonexcludable ones. The fact that people can be excluded from a good means simply that they can be charged a price directly for consuming the good. Hence, a government, as well as a private enterprise, can charge admission to a park, can finance the construction and maintenance of a road with tolls, and can meter the consumption of water and charge people in proportion to the amount consumed. Alternatively, private enterprise might find it profitable to permit an excludable good to exhibit the properties of a nonexcludable good. Thus, by charging advertisers rather than an audience, radio broadcasting and network television permit anyone to consume a program. While radio and television sets are private goods, in any society where they are so widely distributed, the efforts of networks to satisfy the audiences' news and entertainment tastes must be regarded as nonexcludable goods.

Whether or not an excludable good should be supplied by a centralized or by a decentralized mechanism cannot, of course, be answered without a detailed analysis of the costs and benefits of alternatives. And an essential part of such an analysis concerns the choice of a description of a good. Table 9.1 is a typology of ideal types, and few goods can be classified unambiguously into one of the cells of this table. Moreover, most goods—even those we normally consider to be private—exhibit the properties of several cells of Table 9.1 simultaneously. To understand the problems associated with ascertaining the properties of a good we consider mixed goods.

MIXED GOODS

Samuelson's definition of a public good—expression (9.8)—is quite restrictive in the sense that goods satisfying this definition represent an extreme or polar case. Expression (9.8) states that all people consume identical quantities of the good, but it is difficult to imagine such a consumable item. Consider the example of national defense. Among other things, our defense policy seeks, by the threat of retaliation, to protect every city in the United States equally from attack by missiles. In this sense, defense satisfies Samuelson's definition. But if we examine more closely the mechanics of this defense, we find that there is a radar warning network across Canada but not across Mexico and the Gulf of Mexico. Consequently, the southern half of the United States is probably less well protected from an air attack than the northern half. And this fact has meaning as long as an attack from Cuba is a possibility. Thus, the consumption of national defense does not conform to expression (9.8).

Perhaps we have imagined a highly peculiar circumstance to demonstrate the ambiguity of national defense with respect to cell (7) of our typology of goods. It may well be that it satisfies the *intent* of this category of a jointly supplied good. But if we overstate the case, it is only because we initially select this good as a classic example of this category. If we look at other goods in Table 9.1, such as public recreation areas and roads, these are certainly not purely jointly supplied, because not everyone may be able to consume them freely once they are supplied to one person—not everyone has equal access to a recreation area or to a road. And even if the ability to consume were uni-

formly distributed, these goods still could not satisfy fully the intent of our definition because their use is subject to saturation. No matter how large a recreation area is, it is nevertheless finite and thereby subject to overcrowding so
that, as additional people are admitted to a park, the enjoyment of those
already admitted diminishes—as visitors to Yosemite National Park will
readily testify. Similarly, a traffic jam minimizes the usefulness of a road. Thus,
recreation areas and roads are jointly supplied goods which nonetheless exhibit
some of the properties of private goods.[18]

A second possibility that complicates the classification of goods is that some
goods can exhibit excludability and nonexcludability simultaneously. For
example, we classified a recreation area as an excludable good because an admission charge can be levied for its use. Consider, however, people who do not
directly consume a park by attending it, but who, nevertheless, value its existence. That is, parks are similar to hospitals; while we hope never to consume
the excludable resources of a hospital directly, we indirectly value it because,
if needed, it is available. Similarly, people may simply value the opportunity
(but not the actuality) of partaking in recreation, and they cannot be excluded
from valuing the opportunity alone. Thus, recreation areas (and hospitals)
exhibit both excludable and nonexcludable properties.[19]

A third way in which typologies such as Table 9.1 oversimplify reality is
illustrated by pollution. If a factory dirties a nearby stream and pours smoke
from its chimneys, those who live along the stream and near the factory suffer
this pollution. But families who are more distant are less affected, which is to
say that they suffer less from the pollution. Thus, the factory's externality has
only a localized (or neighborhood) effect. For a second illustration consider
aircraft noise. Again, as we move away from an airport, the externalities of noise
diminish so that, like pollution, the externalities are localized. In both of these
examples, then, the requirement of equal consumption by everyone is not
satisfied. Rather, the amount of noise or pollution inflicted on outsiders diminishes as the distance from the source of annoyance increases.

These instances of imperfect jointly supplied goods suggests letting the
amount a person consumes be some function of the number of people who
also consume the good, so as to account for the diminishing supply observed
in the cases of recreation areas and roads. Or, for the cases of pollution and
noise, the amount a person consumes can be a function of geographical location.
Nevertheless, despite these attempts to represent analytically the consumption
of real jointly supplied goods, our examples demonstrate the limitations of
Table 9.1. This should not be interpreted to mean that the definition of private

[18]See Julius Margolis, "Comments on the Pure Theory of Public Expenditure," *Review of
Economics and Statistics,* vol. 37 (November 1955), pp. 347–349.

[19]This possibility is discussed more fully in Burton A. Weisbrod, "Collective-Consumption
Services of Individual—Consumption Goods," *Quarterly Journal of Economics,* vol. 78 (1964),
pp. 471–477.

goods is any less restrictive. Specifically, we can conclude that there is no such thing as a perfectly private good.

Suppose that a person purchases an automobile and his neighbors are envious of this purchase. Or suppose that someone wins a state lottery and his friends rejoice in his good fortune. In both instances the utilities of people other than the owner of the automobile and the winner of the lottery are affected. Thus, these people also consume the automobile and the lottery, so that the automobile and the prize are jointly supplied goods as against private goods. Similarly, the parent rejoices in the child's accomplishments, and the envious are discomfited by the happiness of others. Thus, to the extent that others join with the primary "consumer," all of these goods are not strictly private but are jointly supplied.

More concrete instances of such externalities and ones which are more nearly relevant to the study of politics arise from the notion of *merit goods*. Musgrave uses this concept to describe goods that are excludable and subject to market allocation but that some regard as appropriate for regulation to increase or decrease production or to redistribute market allocations.[20] One example of a merit good is medical care. Clearly, we might interpret medical care as a purely private good (ignoring such things as communicable diseases) and require each person to purchase only as much care as he privately wishes, up to his budget constraint. Such a decision, however, renders the care which the poor consume inferior to that which the rest of society consumes, and we may wish to alter this allocation with public programs. That is, medical care is jointly supplied in the sense that we derive a negative benefit from the inferior consumption of others. Another example of a merit good is housing. Again, if we derive a diseconomy from inferior housing accommodations for the poor, we might seek an adjustment of the market allocation by seeking public subsidies for low-income housing.

Much legislation concerning civil rights, medical care, and so on can be attributed partly to the interpretation of these privileges as merit goods. Doubtless, one factor in the passage of such bills is the satisfaction of an interest —politicians' desire to obtain the electoral support of groups directly benefited by the legislation. But another factor arises from the feature of merit goods— politicians' desire to obtain the support of the persons who derive a positive private reward from seeing the welfare of others increased.

Our examples also illustrate an important property of goods: their classification as private, public, merit, and so on is a function of value judgments about them as well as of their inherent characteristics. That is, we say that air pollution is inherently a jointly supplied good, but housing for the poor is also jointly supplied because some people regard inadequate housing as ethically bad even though they themselves live in an attractive suburb. That is, they consume the inadequate housing of others because they suffer some utility loss

[20]Richard A. Musgrave, *The Theory of Public Finance* (New York: McGraw-Hill, 1959).

from their perception of the relative welfare of others. Thus in an age when it is taught that what a man gets depends only on himself or God, then poverty, hunger, and sickness are merely private. But in an age when it is taught that no man is an island, the condition of a man is a jointly supplied good. Thus, whether goods are public or private, excludable or nonexcludable, and whether market allocations are Pareto optimal or not depends very much on theology and political philosophy.

To summarize, we raise four questions that must be answered either explicitly or implicitly in order to allocate goods.

1. What are the properties of the good in question? In particular, what are the externalities associated with it?
2. Do these externalities render a market allocation unsatisfactory? In particular, is collective or governmental action desired?
3. If collective action is to be taken, how is it to be organized?
4. How are the benefits and costs of collective action distributed?

We cannot, of course, answer these questions in detail. They suggest, nevertheless, that we should reevaluate markets as a means for allocating jointly supplied goods and that we must ascertain the mechanics of collective action that accommodate those externalities that markets cannot accommodate.

MARKETS RECONSIDERED

This chapter began with a brief review of the abstract description of perfectly competitive markets and with an outline of the analysis that shows that such markets provide Pareto-optimal allocations if the goods exchanged are private.[21] But if the goods are public or if they are some other type of nonexcludable jointly supplied good, the allocations of unregulated and decentralized exchange are not Pareto-optimal. Moreover, a detailed analysis of types of goods

[21]A more extensive discussion of some of the topics covered in this section is contained in Gordon Tullock, *Private Wants, Public Means* (New York: Basic Books, 1970). See also James M. Buchanan, "Policy and Pigovian Markets," *Economica*, vol. 29 (1962); R. H. Coase, "The Problem of Social Cost," *Journal of Law and Economics*, vol. 3 (1960); R. Turvey, "On Divergences between Social Cost and Private Cost," *Economica*, vol. 30 (1963); E. J. Mishan, "Reflections on Recent Developments in the Concept of External Effects," *Canadian Journal of Economics and Political Science*, vol. 31 (1965); Stanislaw Wellisz, "On External Diseconomies and the Government Assisted Invisible Hand," *Economica*, vol. 31 (1964). Even a casual examination of this literature reveals a complex and, frequently, highly technical set of issues surrounding market allocations of nonprivate goods. For a particularly good academic exchange that highlights some of these issues see the following (all in *The Journal of Law and Economics*): James M. Buchanan, "Public Goods in Theory and Practice: A Note on the Minasian-Samuelson Discussion" (1967); Jora R. Minasian, "Television Pricing and the Theory of Public Goods" (1964); "Public Goods in Theory and Practice Revisited" (1967); Paul A. Samuelson, "Public Goods and Subscription TV: Correction of the Record" (1964), and "Pitfalls in the Analysis of Public Goods" (1967). Relevant to this debate is Samuelson's essay "Aspects of Public Expenditure Theories," *Review of Economics and Statistics* (1958).

reveals that jointness of supply and nonexcludability are common features of goods. Thus, we might conclude that the market is a totally unsatisfactory channel for exchange and demand that markets be abolished.

Such a demand, however, presupposes first that society is unanimous in its assessment of the properties of goods. But in our discussion of mixed goods we find that the properties of goods are very much a function of beliefs about which people are seldom unanimous—theology and political philosophy. Similarly, we find that many goods, such as recreation areas, exhibit both excludability and nonexcludability simultaneously, and there may be little agreement as to the feature of a good that should be weighed most heavily in deciding on the method of allocating it.

Nevertheless, even if some agreement about the property of a good is found and even if markets fail to yield a Pareto-optimal allocation of this good, we should not suppose that another mechanism exists that can produce a more unanimously desired outcome. The advantage of markets is that they minimize organizational costs because the only organizations that exist are firms and households. Alternative mechanisms, however, typically involve some bureaucratic device, which is necessarily more costly than the market. Hence, even if governments could render a theoretically feasible Pareto-optimal allocation and markets could not, the costs of collective action may cancel any of the anticipated benefits of supplanting unrestrained trade. Thus, we might not desire government involvement, for example, if we believe that the cost of maintaining a government bureaucracy is excessive.

One additional kind of cost deserves special emphasis. In markets consumers incur some cost in ascertaining the price, availability, and quality of goods; firms incur a cost in ascertaining the demand for goods and the potential size of new markets. If collective action is taken, these same costs exist. But whereas the competitive market operates to extinguish firms that gather information inefficiently or incorrectly, there is no reason to suppose without careful analysis that a similar process operates inside governmental bureaucracies.[22] And if a collectivity such as an administrative or regulatory agency fails to gather information about preferences as efficiently and correctly as consumers and firms, we cannot assert that the collective allocation is more desirable than a non-Pareto-optimal market allocation.

This cost deserves special emphasis. Suppose, for example, that collective action takes an extreme form, namely, dictatorship. Generally we do not prefer this alternative, fearing that the dictator will satisfy only his preferences and that his preferences will differ greatly from ours. Suppose, however, that

---

[22]For an economic analysis of governmental bureaucracy—including legislative bureaucracies—see William A. Niskanen, *Bureaucracy and Representative Government* (Chicago: Aldine-Atherton, 1971). See also J. Tinbergen, *Economic Policy: Principles and Design* (Amsterdam: North-Holland, 1956). While this book as well as subsequent research by Tinbergen and others is not concerned primarily with modeling political institutions, it does initiate inquiry into the interface between economics and politics in the area of the planning and evaluation of economic policy.

a dictator is benevolent, which means that he wishes at least to select some "generally acceptable" Pareto-optimal allocation of nonexcludable goods. Perhaps we might substitute "government agency" for dictator in our example and assume that the members of the agency perceive their obligation to be one of supplying Pareto-optimal allocations where there are none. From our bargaining example, the agency or dictator might seek to regulate the bargaining by establishing the rate, T, that player 2 must pay player 1 for a reduction in his consumption of the public good, and then enforcing this reduction. To do this or to optimally regulate the production of any good, however, an allocation must be induced which satisfies expression (9), which is to say that the agency and the dictator must know the marginal utilities of both persons. For a two-person situation this might not be an unreasonable requirement— certainly there are ways to attempt to insure that the players bargain in good faith, i.e., that they reveal their true preferences. But in larger societies, the Prisoners' Dilemma reasserts itself: people possess strong incentives to disguise their true preferences from the agency or from the dictator. Pareto optimality is achieved if each person shares in the cost of producing a public good, for example, according to his marginal evaluation for that good. But again each person may assume that his contribution is infinitesimal and that a slight reduction in supply (if any) caused by his failure to share in the cost of production is small compared to the benefit of not incurring this share of the cost. Thus, each person has some incentive to lie—to hide his true preferences from the dictator or agency. The dictator and the agency, then, are confronted with consumers who act as they acted in a decentralized market.

Collectivization, moreover, can generate private incentives that render efficient allocations unattainable. Suppose, for example, that a decision is taken to supply publically some good that, while exhibiting jointness, is an excludable good. Assume, however, that if the good is produced publically, exclusion is not enforced, and that the production of this good is financed by some tax structure. Clearly, now, every person has an incentive to minimize his direct costs. And if taxes are established through political mechanism such as elections, people can seek either to shift the burden of taxation onto others or simply to minimize tax rates overall. But if people benefit from consumption of the good, each person should seek to expand production or at least to maximize his consumption. Collectivization of this sort succeeds, then, in separating peoples' decisions about consumption from their decisions about costs. Decisions about costs are rendered at the polls, whereas decisions about consumption are made at other times. And this separation can have disastrous consequences for the efficient provision of goods. James Buchanan suggests, for example, that the inefficiencies of the British national health service are exactly of this sort.[23] People are generally unwilling to expand medical facilities by levying taxes on themselves, but they act as if medical care were a free public good.

---

[23]"The Inconsistencies of the National Health Service," *Occasional Paper* 7, Institute of Economic Affairs, London (November 1965).

The result, Buchanan contends, is a decrease in the quality of medical care available to everyone.

Another justification for preferring markets as a mechanism for allocating jointly supplied goods—even nonexcludable ones—is that these goods can be the natural by-product of market activity. Air and water pollution are frequently cited as undesirable nonexcludable by-products of the production of private goods, whereas clean air and clean water are cited as goods that the market fails to produce optimally. Not all jointly supplied by-products of market activity, however, are undesirable. Consider, for example, the by-product of technological progress. Clearly, firms invest considerable resources in the search for new products or better goods. And while the payoffs from this research are consumed directly through the consumption of private goods, this research also facilitates the operations of collectivities. Hence, cities can light dark and potentially dangerous streets because it was profitable to invent and to mass-produce the electric light, and people can freely consume television and radio broadcasts because it is profitable for stations to rent their facilities to advertisers. For another example, consider the contributions of industry to local educational institutions. Obviously a firm benefits from such contributions in terms of goodwill, of the availability of trained personnel, of the satisfaction derived from performing a public service, and of making the community more attractive to potential employees. And clearly, the costs of these contributions can be passed on to the consumers of the firm's goods. Nevertheless, the presence of a college or of a university in a community is generally regarded by residents with pride, and everyone can freely consume this pride whether or not he purchases the firm's product. Similarly, if the firm's contribution helps defray tuition costs, all students benefit and may even be permitted to attend college without charge.

Finally, we must note the possibilities for markets of nonexcludable jointly supplied goods—markets that exist because the externalities associated with these goods are localized. Some communities are less polluted than others. The quality of public education, hospitals, recreation facilities, and police protection are unequally distributed among communities. If we regard a community as a package of such jointly supplied goods, we can interpret a person's residence as a decision to consume a particular package.[24] Thus, choices of residence constitute a market in which people distribute themselves according to their tastes and their budget constraints. Of course, it is absurd to assert that such a market is perfectly competitive and that Pareto-optimal allocations are necessarily achieved. But we cannot also assert that some alternative mechanism renders a more efficient result. Suppose, for example, that a highly polluted community with poor public education is improved in both respects

---

[24]Charles Tiebout, "The Pure Theory of Local Expenditure," *Journal of Political Economy,* vol. 64 (October 1956), pp. 416–424; Wallace E. Oates, "The Effects of Property Taxes and Local Public Spending on Property Values: An Empirical Study of Tax Capitalization and the Tiebout Hypothesis," *Journal of Political Economy,* vol. 77 (1969), pp. 957–971.

with public funds. It is not unreasonable to suppose that the effect of such activities is to increase the demand for and thereby the costs of housing. Housing then becomes a more expensive good for those in the community. For some of the poor, the disutility of this increase may well exceed the benefits they derive from clean air and better schools. Thus, these activities cannot be said to have yielded a more efficient allocation than that of the market.

*   *   *

Despite these several justifications for leaving market allocations unchanged, it is probably rare in the affairs of men to find alternatives stated so simply as the choice between a competitive market and some abstract form of collective action. Rather, we find the forces of markets—forces illustrated by the Prisoners' Dilemma—acting everywhere to subvert collective choices while collective action everywhere subverts the choices of markets. Hence, in revealing preferences about this nexus of forces, men must answer the questions posed in the previous section in subtler ways. We turn in the next chapter, then, to a framework for the understanding of these preferences and answers.

SUGGESTIONS FOR FURTHER READINGS

The concept of externalities, the properties of goods, and efficient means for allocating goods are most widely studied by economists. Consequently, most of the literature pertaining to the topics reviewed in this chapter appears in economic journals. An excellent collection of recent essays that begins with a most comprehensive and readable essay by PETER O. STEINER, "The Public Sector and the Public Interest," is ROBERT H. HAVEMAN and JULIUS MARGOLIS, *The Analysis and Evaluation of Public Expenditures* (Chicago: Markham, 1970). Another good collection of essays that focuses primarily on questions of public finance—questions that we largely ignore in this book—is JAMES M. BUCHANAN and ROBERT D. TOLLISON, *Theory of Public Choice* (Ann Arbor: University of Michigan Press, 1971). Two general and largely expository works are JAMES M. BUCHANAN, *The Demand and Supply of Public Goods* (Skokie, Ill.: Rand McNally, 1968), and GORDEN TULLOCK, *Private Wants, Public Means* (New York: Basic Books, 1970). Finally, a concise elementary introduction to the basics of microeconomic theory is presented in GEORGE J. STIGLER, *The Theory of Price* (New York: Macmillan, 1966).

10

Regulation and Public Policy

We turn now to the study of regulation, a special element of the process of politics. As we indicated in the first chapter, not all of politics is decision making in the conventional sense. It is also necessary that a setting of decision making be provided for and that decisions, once made, be carried out. These latter activities are the substance of regulation. They also are a kind of decision making, but at a step removed—for they are decision making about decision making.

Regulation as a general topic has not often been studied. Particular kinds of regulation, such as the market, criminal law, and so on, have been studied in detail, and especially there is a long tradition of laissez-faire ideology, in which regulation of the market is denounced—but we do not count this literature just because it is concerned with the particular, rather than with social processes as a whole. And with all this attention to the particular, the general process of regulation, of which the market and criminal law are integral, meshed parts, has not been examined theoretically.

We attribute this lacuna largely to the fact that the various kinds of regulation have each had their professional experts whose concentration has precluded a general approach to the larger area of regulation generally. Economists, the theorists of exchange, typically concentrate on the self-equilibrating features provided by the market and tend therefore to regard other methods of regulation as interference. Having identified the true harmony of the unseen hand, they overlook the situations (e.g., the maintenance of competition) for which it is not appropriate. Similarly, political scientists and lawyers, who have probably seldom appreciated the remarkable ability of the market for private goods to arrive at Pareto-optimal outcomes, tend to

272

think in terms of legal imperatives to accomplish goals (e.g., minimum wages to help the poor) even where a market mechanism would probably be more efficient and more "equitable."

What is needed, we believe, for a full appreciation of the political process is an approach that transcends the narrow emphasis of either the student of economics or the student of jurisprudence. What we propose, therefore, is to set forth here heuristically (rather than formally) the beginning of a theory of regulation which has as components the two fields just mentioned. In particular, we offer an explanation of (1) how the individual decides whether or not to support regulation and what kind of regulation he prefers, and (2) how variations in the cost of imposing regulation affect the individual calculus.

THE CONTEXT OF REGULATION

To define regulation we must first examine the context in which it occurs. This means that we must look again at individual decision making (as in Chapter 3) but now include in our notation and conceptualization the effect of the influence of other decision makers on individual choice. The choices people make about regulation depend not only on their own private concerns but also on their interdependencies with others occasioned by the externalities of jointly supplied goods.

We assume first a society of n rational decision makers. Each decision maker, i, $i = 1, 2, \ldots, n$, is faced with a set of m alternatives, $A = \{a_1, a_2, \ldots, a_m\}$, and to simplify discussion we assume that all decision makers are confronted with an identical set of alternatives. The choice of alternatives determines an outcome in $O = \{O_1, O_2, \ldots, O_r, \ldots\}$; and each decision maker has preferences over the set O such that a utility function, $U_i(O)$, can be defined. The outcome in O that actually occurs is a function of the choices of particular alternatives selected by the several decision makers. That is, there is a function, G, that operates to produce outcomes from the set of the actual choices of alternatives by all decision makers. Thus, there is a set $\mathscr{A}$ that consists of all the possible sets of particular choices, $\mathscr{A} = \{(a_{j1}, a_{j2}, \ldots, a_{jn})\}$, where each a_{ji} is thus a choice of an alternative a_{j1} by person 1, a choice of another a_{j2} by person 2, and so on. We write: $G(\mathscr{A}) \longrightarrow O$ to summarize the fact that the set $\mathscr{A}$ of choices by individuals is transformed by some rule G into an outcome. More generally, we write $G(\mathscr{A}/S) \longrightarrow O$, by which we mean that, given a particular state of the world, the choice of alternatives by the choosers leads, according to the function G, to a particular outcome. And if states of nature are known probabilistically, then we write

$$G\left[\mathscr{A}/p(S)\right] \longrightarrow P(O), \qquad (10.1)$$

where p and P are probability functions.

Thus, the effect of a given choice on the occurrence of outcomes is not completely certain. To illustrate, let the choosers, i, be nations in a coalition-forming situation, S—for example, a diplomatic showdown on an international exchange mechanism. The nations have various weights, and each distribution of weight is a different situation, S. Before the event occurs, we do not know exactly which distribution pertains. Hence we indicate the existence of distributions probabilistically, $p(S_1)$, $p(S_2)$, and so on. The various outcomes in the set O are the possible ultimate decisions on a set of exchange rates (including, of course, a decision not to decide). For each nation, i, there is a set of possible actions from which i chooses, such as insisting unilaterally on a particular system, joining a coalition to insist on another system, and so on. The function, G, is then the rule that connects the several choices by nations with the outcome set, O. Ahead of time, the connections among $\mathscr{A}$ and O are known only probabilistically. Thus G might be a long list of sentences connecting choices with outcomes, and one such sentence on the list might be: "Any group of nations having international trade of an amount x may agree to use a particular national currency to settle accounts among themselves." Which one of many sentences like this actually governs the connection between $\mathscr{A}$ and O depends partly on the content of O and partly on chance.

Considering now the calculus for the individual decision maker, we can use the function G to define another function, g, which tells us what the individual person can expect given the choices of other choosers:

$$g[A/(a_{j1}, a_{j2}, \ldots, a_{ji-1}, a_{ji+1}, \ldots, a_{jn}), p(S)] \to \bar{P}(O), \quad (10.2)$$

where $\bar{P}(O)$ is a subset of the larger set $P(O)$. That is, given $p(S)$ and the choices of $n-1$ other decision makers, g defines the density function over outcomes for particular choices by i of an alternative from A.

The function g permits a calculation for the chooser of an expected value for each alternative $a_j \in A$, thus:

$$E^i[a_{ji}/(a_{j1}, a_{j2}, \ldots, a_{ji-1}, a_{ji+1}, \ldots, a_{jn})] \quad (10.3)$$

$$= E^i\{g[a_{ji}/(a_{ji}, a_{j2}, \ldots, a_{ji-1}, a_{ji+1}, \ldots, a_{jn}, p(S))]\}$$

$$= \sum_r U_{ij}(O_r)\bar{P}_i(O_r),$$

where $U_{ij}(O_r)$ is person i's utility for outcome O_r, given that he adopts alternative a_j.

We cannot assume, of course, that the decision maker simply selects the alternative that maximizes $E^i[a_{ji}/(a_{j1}, \ldots)]$. This expected utility is always conditional on the choices of others. And since the best alternative given one set of choices by others is, typically, not the best given another set, an individual decision maker must vary his own choices as others vary.

In analyzing the individual calculus as it varies with the choices by others, we differentiate two kinds of cases. The first conforms to the analysis of Chapter 3. That is, for other persons, k, the decision maker knows the probability, q_k, that k will adopt a particular alternative, a_{jk}. Knowing $q_k(a_{jk})$, it is a straightforward problem to calculate the expected value of $E^i(a_{ji})$ according to (10.3). A rational decision maker then selects that alternative which maximizes $E^i(a_{ji})$, receiving an expected utility of

$$\max_j E^i(a_{ji}).$$

We say that this maximum expected utility is the value of the decision maker's environment to him.

The second case conforms to the perspective of game theory. That is, we do not assume necessarily that the decision maker can estimate the probabilities $q_k(a_{jk})$ because he may be trapped in the regress of "he thinks I think that ..." If there is only one other person ($n=2$), the decision maker's choice is governed by the perspective of Chapter 8. And as we know from the analysis of that chapter, we cannot always know the choice by the other person, and hence we cannot always say what expected utility a decision maker receives. For zero-sum games we might substitute the value of the game, v_i, for $\max_j E^i(a_{ji})$, and

for bargaining games we might substitute i's security level for his maximum expected utility. If the bargaining involves coalitions, we might use the Shapley value. In many real world applications, however, the Shapley value is not meaningful, and so we may be unable to specify unambiguously the value to the decision maker of his environment for choice.

Disregarding the possible indeterminacy of the value of the context of choice, we summarize the problem of the individual decision maker as that of evaluating his position in the context, and we observe that the context includes at least the following:

(1) the set, A, of alternatives available to the decision maker and others,
(2) the set of outcomes and the utilities that the individual decision makers associate with them,
(3) the probabilities of states of nature,
(4) the function, G;

and, besides these features which can be clearly known to the decision maker, also at least the following features which may not be entirely clear:

(5) the probabilities, g, of choices by others, and
(6) differences in perception of A, O, $p(S)$, and G—that is, differences in the degree and kind of information in the world.

The context of choice consists, we say, of items (1)–(6).

Changing any one of the elements of the context of course changes the value of the context for the decision maker. To indicate some of the range of variation we comment on the ways that these elements of the context can change and be changed. The set of alternatives, A, can be expanded and contracted by nature or by conscious manipulation. To revert to our previous example of a diplomatic confrontation on exchange mechanisms, A might be expanded by the invention of some kind of international currency or it might be contracted by an agreement among the main trading nations not to settle in gold. Variations in O are, of course, initially dependent on variations in A; but $U_i(O)$ may vary by reason of changes in the judgment and socialization of decision makers. Thus, national leaders might vary their utilities for settlement with gold upon realizing that major beneficiaries of gold settlements are the main gold producers, especially South Africa and the Soviet Union. Again, a generation of admonitions by academic economists who view gold settlements as trivial may gradually induce a similar view in men of affairs. Variations in G may also be produced either by nature or by conscious manipulation. Suppose a sentence in G relates the size of a coalition supporting a method of exchange to an outcome consisting of the realization of that method in practice. But the appropriate size may be varied by technological variation that alters, for example, the number and strength of nations that are physically able to make a customs-union-currency bloc effective. Or nations may consciously agree to permit blocs only of a given size. The probabilities of states of nature, $p(S)$, are, of course, partly a function of knowledge, so that better knowledge of economics may significantly alter the nature of a diplomatic confrontation. Similarly, increase in knowledge of the goals, incentives, and so on of other national rulers may alter the decision maker's probability estimates, q, about, e.g., whether or not other actors in the confrontation will support or oppose him. To summarize, then, the context of choice is remarkably complex, and this complexity is highly significant for the behavior of regulators.

REGULATION DEFINED

The individual decision maker is always faced with two kinds of questions. One is immediate and is concerned with obtaining the maximum expected utility from a given context. This we call the question of action. The other is instrumental and is concerned with the possibility of varying the context under which the question of action is raised. This we call the question of regulation.

Questions of Action

The form of this question is : "Assuming that the social context of choice is fixed, what alternative should a rational decision maker choose to maximize expected utility?" This is the decision-theoretic question of individual maximization, the focus of Chapters 1 through 8.

Questions of Regulation

Of course, the decision maker is not necessarily faced with the world as it is right now, because the world can be made to be different. So he may be faced with possible future states of the world in which, for example, the set of alter-

natives has been increased or decreased, information and technology have been varied, and the function G has been altered. Then the question for the decision maker is: "In which one of the possible states of the world should the rational decision maker prefer to do his choosing on questions of action?" We may state this question more completely: assuming that the present context of social choice consists of a set of alternatives, A, a set of outcomes, O, a function relating them, G, and a utility, $U_i(O)$ which is the utility of the chooser i over the set of outcomes given a choice of $a_j \in A$, and assuming that there may exist distinctly different sets A^* and O^*, a different function G^*, and different utilities $U_{ij}^*(O^*)$, then in which context, $[A, O, G, U_{ij}(O)]$ or $[A^*, O^*, G^*, U_{ij}^*(O^*)]$, does the decision maker prefer to make his choice of an alternative a_j? The rule of preference may be stated precisely, allowing A always to be associated with $[A, O, G, U_{ij}(O)]$ and A^* always to be associated with $[A^*, O^*, G^*, U_{ij}^*,(O^*)]$: if max $E^i(a_{ji}^*) >$ max $E^i(a_{ji})$, then the chooser prefers A^*, and
      j j
so on. If the situation is gamelike, then v_i and v_i^* are substituted for max $E^i(a_{ji})$
                                                                                      j
and max $E^i(a_{ji}^*)$.
     j

The question of regulation can, of course, be asked with many variations of context in mind. If there may potentially be many sets of alternatives, outcomes, technologies, information, and so on, then the regulatory question can be asked about each possible combination in relation to the present context of choice. Much of human inventiveness is devoted to devising new combinations and thereby forcing continual reconsideration of questions of regulation.

Having distinguished these questions, we can easily define the notion of regulation, for it is no more than a change in the social context of choice in response to a question of regulation. Suppose the decision maker finds that his utility from choosing from (A^*, O^*, G^*, U^*) is greater than his utility from choosing from (A, O, G, U). Then he should, of course, take steps to change the context. And the act of regulation is precisely such a change.

Apparent Inconsistencies in Answers to the Questions of Action and Regulation

Questions of action are typically asked at the time a consumer chooses a market basket of commodities, at the time a producer chooses a mix and level of production, at the time a motorist chooses whether or not to obey a traffic ordinance, at the time a wife decides to bring a divorce action against her husband, and so on. The regulatory question, on the other hand, is typically asked at a time when the chooser must decide on the conditions under which he will subsequently decide questions of action—as typically, during elections, some voting in legislatures, and most voting in constitutional conventions.

Both kinds of questions involve decision-making tasks; but they differ in context as well as occasion. The regulatory question always occurs in a context of summation or anticipated summation. The action question asks only: "Do you want this object or outcome now?" But the regulatory question requires the respondent to think about what happens when everybody is deciding the same kind of question. It asks about the ground rules of decision, so it forces the respondent to consider what happens when others go through the same problems of choice as himself on action questions.

Given these differences of occasion and context, there is no reason to suppose that the answers to questions of action and regulation must be consistent. That is, in response to a question of action a person might choose an alternative that grants him some object, while in response to a question of regulation he might choose an alternative that denies him the same object. One of the commonest errors made by interpreters of social behavior is to assume that decision makers are confused because they choose apparently inconsistently in the two circumstances. Economists, especially, are prone to attribute confusion when, in answer to an action question, people choose more of commodity c_1 than of commodity c_2 and then, in answer to a regulatory question, inconsistently choose a route that leads to more of c_2 than c_1. Usually there is a higher rationale that reconciles this apparent inconsistency, as the following examples illustrate:

(a) With respect to the production of alcoholic beverages, a person may answer the question of action with implied approval of the business of taverns and at the same time answer the regulatory question with direct disapproval. There need not be an inconsistency between these answers, however. One does not need to be an abstainer to favor prohibition. One might decide, when offered a drink, to accept it in order, perhaps, to maintain easy social relations, while at the same time preferring never to be offered a drink. Such a person might believe that he himself is able to consume moderately but that many others are likely to be immoderate, given the opportunity. Such a person might further believe that so many evils are occasioned by immoderate consumption of alcohol (e.g., automobile accidents, nonsupport of families) that he is willing to forego his mild pleasure in consumption in order to avoid the pain to him of others' consumption (e.g., higher automobile insurance, higher welfare costs, and so on). Such a set of attitudes is perfectly consistent, and apparently many Americans held them in the period just before the passage of the Eighteenth Amendment and before they knew how difficult enforcement would be. The appearance of inconsistency is occasioned merely by the fact that the revelation of preference on personal consumption does not also reveal the full schedule of preferences on public policy. In answering the question of action, the decision maker does not consider the external costs imposed by others' answers to their questions of action. But in answering the questions of regulation, these externalities must be considered. And this difference is what occasions the apparent inconsistency.[1]

---

[1]See the discussion of externalities in Chapter 9. This particular example is alluded to in James M. Buchanan, "Individual Choice in Voting and the Market," *Journal of Political Economy*, vol. 62 (1954), pp. 334–343.

(b)   With respect to attendance at union meetings, the following paradox is noted: a person may regularly decide not to attend—an answer to an action question—thus implying that he thinks the meetings unimportant, and at the same time he may vote to impose a fine on nonattendance—an answer to the regulatory question—thus implying that he thinks the meetings are important.[2] There is no necessary inconsistency between the two positions, however. When answering the action question, the decision maker must assume that the world is as it is now. When answering the regulatory question, however, he may assume that he can—by his very answer itself—make the world over into what he would like it to be. The action question merely asks: "Do you want to go to the union meeting this evening?" and thereby reveals a portion of his preferences on his union and on his use of time. The regulatory question asks: "Do you want the kind of union in which very few people not including yourself go to union meetings?" and thereby reveals another and entirely different portion of his schedule of preferences. It is, of course, quite possible that a member might wish to have well-attended union meetings and be willing to be one of those attending and yet be unwilling to attend a poorly attended meeting.

(c)   With respect to personal expenditures on equipment to minimize air pollution from automobile exhaust, a person may answer the action question, which is posed when he decides whether or not to purchase an available device, by refusing to purchase and thus apparently displaying an indifference to air pollution. At the same time, he may answer the regulatory question, which is posed in a referendum on making such devices mandatory, by voting for the proposal and thus apparently displaying concern about air pollution. The reconciliation of these positions is obvious: When purchase is optional, a particular citizen may be unwilling to spend the money because his expenditure reduces by very little the pollution of the air he breathes. But if purchase is mandatory, then the expenditure of everybody has the effect of significantly reducing pollution for the particular citizen and thus giving him a gain in utility of at least as much as the cost of the device. Thus, if he decides only for himself, the device is not worth its cost; but if he decides for everybody, the device is worth its cost. The device does not change but the context of the question does.

The foregoing examples, wherein perhaps a majority of the relevant population is involved in apparent but unreal contradictions, underline the difference between action questions and regulatory questions. Since the portions of respondents' schedules of preferences tapped by each question are different, there is no reason to expect exactly the same results from them.

Furthermore, there is no reason to suppose that the one question produces answers that are more or less "correct" than another. The action questions are typically answered by behavior, e.g., by refusing to purchase an exhaust controlling device. The regulatory questions, on the other hand, are typically

---

[2]Mancur Olson, *The Logic of Collective Action* (Cambridge, Mass.: Harvard University Press, 1965), p. 86.

answered by expressions of opinion as in elections and referenda. And in the current enthusiasm of social scientists for behavioral evidence, it is sometimes asserted that evidence from these behavioral situations, such as the market, is "harder" than the opinion evidence from elections and votes. But voting is behavior also, and the portion of the schedule of preferences tapped by asking the regulatory question is just as real as the portion tapped with the action question. One simply accepts these apparent inconsistencies while seeking a theoretical reconciliation.

Regulation Defined Again

The distinction thus detailed between questions of action and questions of regulation permits us now to define the process of regulation in a few words. Regulation, we say, is the process of revising the range of alternatives, A, outcomes, O, the state of technology, G, patterns of socialization implied in individual utility functions, information, and so on, that are to be open to decision makers when they answer questions of action. Some writers call this same process constitution-making, for it has to do with the framework of day-to-day decisions. We prefer the term regulation, however, because in common usage constitutions seem limited to "broad" frameworks, while we want to include all framework whether broad or detailed.

THE OCCASION FOR REGULATION

Regulation involves answering by each individual the question of whether it is desired that decisions on action occur in one social context rather than another. The main reason for altering the original context is that as it stands it implies costly externalities for the regulators. Hence the bulk of a theory of regulation is a theory of external costs, the beginning of which we outlined in Chapter 9. In that place we defined external effects as actions by person(s) h that affect the relationship between actions and outcomes for person i. Now we wish to show that such effects are a necessary ingredient of every act of regulation.

Suppose, by way of example, it is proposed to exclude the alternative a_0 from A for all decision makers, or equivalently that costs are imposed (fines) or technology, socialization, and so on are changed so that no one seriously considers the selection of a_0. For this proposal to be serious, it must be that some persons profit more from a_0 than from any other alternative—given what actions they expect others to choose—otherwise a_0 would never be used and there would be no need to exclude it. The regulators themselves (or most of them) may also on occasion find a_0 maximally advantageous.

A proposal to exclude a_0, therefore, involves rejection of a course of action that, for each potential regulator considered alone, is typically worthwhile. In order to justify the elimination of a privately advantageous alternative, it must be the case that some cost is incurred if others also use that alternative. To speak more precisely, let

E_1 denote the potential regulator's expected utility for a_0 if no one else or nearly no one else chooses a_0;

E_2 denote the potential regulator's expected utility for a_0 if nearly everyone else chooses a_0; and

E' denote the potential regulator's expected utility from choosing the best alternative if a_0 is eliminated, transformed, or rendered different by changes in O, G, or $U(O)$.[3]

Suppose now that $E_1 > E_2$, which is very roughly what we mean by saying that an external cost exists. The external cost itself is $E_1 - E_2$. Presumably, then, the potential regulator prefers the elimination or alteration of a_0 if the benefits from choosing a_0 alone, E_1, less the external costs of others choosing a_0, $(E_1 - E_2)$, are less than the expected utility of having eliminated or altered a_0, E'. More succinctly, the potential regulator prefers the regulation if

$$E' > E_1 - (E_1 - E_2) = E_2. \qquad (10.4)$$

Of course, this inequation does not tell the whole story. Under any circumstances, it costs something to eliminate or change an alternative. Many times citizens initially prefer regulation, not realizing that, if their preference is made a general rule, a costly bureaucracy will be necessary to ensure that the banished alternative is not used. Maximum limits on prices and wages are an excellent example. Most regulators when adopting such regulation see only the benefits of stable prices and overlook the cost of policing. And, if the policing is effective, its cost is considerable, with the bureaucracy of sheriffs, investigators, bureau chiefs, judges, jailers, and so on. There is a mechanical cost of enforcement in any regulation, and this price tends to increase rapidly as the prohibited alternative is initially attractive to more people.

In addition to the mechanical cost, however, there is a more subtle cost involved in the externalities from substitute alternatives. Suppose an alternative a_0 is eliminated or transformed. The matter does not rest there, because some other alternative, a^*, is adopted. And this alternative also may exhibit externalities. For example, the alternative of a free market in housing was eliminated a generation ago in New York City and the alternative of regulated rents was substituted. Ultimately the externalities of the substitute were revealed to be the deterioration and abandonment of dwellings.

These two kinds of costs, the cost of enforcement and the cost of the externali-

---

[3]We recognize that the notion of "nearly everyone" is quite vague and that it would be desirable to use instead a marginal analysis (i.e., to speak for example, of the gain to the regulator if one more person is excluded from choosing a_0); but the introduction of a more accurate method would excessively complicate what we here intend as only an heuristic analysis.

ties of the substitute, must also be taken into account in our interpretation of E'. For this discussion, let a_0 be an eliminated or changed alternative and suppose that in its place a^* is adopted. Furthermore, let

E_3 denote the potential regulator's expected utiltity for a^* if no one else or almost no one else chooses a^*;

E_4 denote the potential regulator's expected utility for a^* if nearly everyone else chooses a^*; and

C' denote the potential regulator's share of the costs of policing the elimination or change of a_0.

We can now reexpress the value of E', the regulator's utility from a^*, assuming a_0 is eliminated or changed:

$$E' = E_3 - (E_3 - E_4) - C',$$

where $(E_3 - E_4)$ is, as before, an external cost. Hence, rewriting (10.4), we have the following rule: the potential regulator prefers the regulation if

$$E_3 - (E_3 - E_4) - C' > E_1 - (E_1 - E_2). \qquad (10.5)$$

Stated more heuristically, the regulator prefers regulation if

(i)	$(-)+$	(ii)	$-$	C'	$>$	(iii)	$(-)+$	(iv)	(10.6)
utility to chooser from his use of the substituted alternative, a^*		(dis) utility to chooser from others' use of the substituted alternative, a^*		cost to chooser of policing the elimination of the original alternative, a_0		utility to chooser from his use of the eliminated alternative, a_0		(dis) utility to chooser from others' use of the eliminated alternative, a_0	

Of course (10.5) and (10.6) reduce to

$$E_4 - C' > E_2,$$

which inequality, with its emphasis on the effect of others' action, dramatically displays the role of externalities in a judgment on regulation. Leaving aside the cost of policing, if externalities are costs, one prefers that alternative in which the action of others has the least impact on oneself. If externalities are benefits, however, one prefers that alternative in which the impact of the action of others is greatest. We turn now to some concrete examples of the effect of external costs in the judgment on regulation.

EXTERNAL COSTS AND REGULATION: SOME ILLUSTRATIONS

Perhaps the most universal regulation in human society is the prohibition of murder. This taboo may often be interpreted simply as human revulsion against an obscenity. But on deeper examination it turns out to be an attempt by politically relevant persons to minimize an external cost. If the prohibition were in fact merely a taboo on killing humans, then all homicide would be prohibited. But in very few societies is *all* killing of other persons defined as murder. It is usually permitted—even applauded—to kill in warfare. And in an overpopulated world, abortion has become customary and legal and infanticide may soon be so. Killing in self-defense is almost always tolerated. Often, also, murder is permitted for revenge—although this may be simply a cheap way of enforcing the prohibition of murder. Sometimes it is permitted to kill people if they are only marginally members of society, e.g., slaves, outlaws, members of minority races, low caste persons, and so on. In the modern world it has been praiseworthy to exploit and starve members of primitive cultures (e.g., American Indians and Australian aborigines) and even to hunt them down for sport. And finally, accidental homicide—extremely common in our mechanical civilization—is usually excused if the negligence is not too gross. The fact that all these exceptions are made and that not all killing of humans is defined as murder, i.e., as a legally punishable act, indicates that the regulation of murder is not a prohibition of killing generally but simply a prohibition of a special kind of killing.

From these exceptions it is easy to see that the definition and prohibition of murder involves controlling external costs for a politically relevant group, because just that killing is prohibited that can be controlled by the group. The relevant group is the lawmakers, whom we define broadly as the people who accept a body of law and by their acceptance give it authority, i.e., the tribe, the nation, the citizen-body. They prohibit killing among themselves and any other group they can control (e.g., among slaves and sojourners). But they do not prohibit killing outside the group, as in warfare or as of outlaws. Nor do they in areas of overpopulation prohibit abortion, which is the killing of unborn but potential members of the group. The threat of violent death to these outsiders generates no external cost to insiders so long as the direction of the threat is clear. Hence the threat and perpetration of these kinds of killing is not prohibited.

The killing that is prohibited is that which generates fear of violent death inside the society, which is a controllable external cost. Such killing is only a tiny fraction of the killing that occurs in the world, but the external costs it produces are so great that some philosophers (e.g., Hobbes, Spinoza, Schopenhauer, and others) have built their whole explanation of the existence of government around them. For Hobbes, the worst thing that could happen to men was to suffer continual fear and danger of violent death. He argued that in order to avoid this misery of anarchy men would sign away almost their entire liberty of action. Note that Hobbes emphasized not just the fear of death, a normal event that cannot be regulated, but the fear of violent death, especially that kind of death we define as murder, e.g., killing in disputes between members of the same law-accepting group, killing in robberies, killing in accidents due to gross negligence, and, worst of all, killing in riots and other civil disturbances. This is the kind of violent death Hobbes had in mind, and the depth of his concern indicates something about the magnitude of the external costs. These include not only the violent death itself, which is suffered by relatively few, but also the fear of violent death, which, in an anarchic world, is suffered by everyone all of the time.

Not all philosophers of politics have been as impressed as was Hobbes by the external costs of murder. We do not know whether or not he was correct in attributing the origin of government to attempts to control these costs. But we believe that his assertion and the widespread acceptance of it testifies to the extreme magnitude of these costs and, to a lesser degree, to their controllability. Beyond philosophers, ordinary citizens are, when reminded of it by hints of anarchy, almost as impressed by these costs as was Hobbes. Most repressive regimes in recent history have justified themselves to their citizens as necessary to prevent violence (e.g., revolution). And even in the relatively liberal United States of the late 1960's "law and order" became suddenly successful as electoral propaganda, largely, we assume, because of the wave of riots and crime in the mid-1960's.

Low External Costs

When external costs are high and controllable, alternatives involving them are often eliminated. This is true even when the direct utility of the prohibited action is negligible, as may well be the case with murder. On the other hand, when external costs are zero, no prohibitions occur, and this absence is even more noticeable when external effects are positive, i.e., when they are benefits rather than cost.

To examine some situations in which it is reasonable to suppose that external effects are negligible or positive, consider sumptuary laws. At present, we do not try to regulate personal budgets for clothes, food, housing, and so on, provided the objects purchased are legally for sale. In earlier times, however, some such alternatives have been forbidden, apparently because it was believed that a display of finery and wealth by rich but nonaristocratic persons upset the social structure. In terms of a proposed sumptuary law, we may restate (10.6) for an aristocrat:

$$\text{(i)} \quad + \quad \text{(ii)} \quad - \quad C' \quad > \quad \text{(iii)} \quad + \quad \text{(iv)}$$

(i)	(ii)	C'	(iii)	(iv)
utility from exclusive display	utility from elimination of competition in display	cost of enforcement of law	utility from competitive display	(dis)utility from competition in display

In our present society, where most people have probably never heard of sumptuary laws, we can ignore the cost term. Even if there were agitation for sumptuary laws, it is doubtful if most such agitators would remember to include the cost of enforcement in the initial calculation. (When alcoholic beverages were prohibited, most agitators became aware of the costs involved only after the prohibition became nearly nationwide, which was three generations after agitation began.)

For our imaginary aristocrat, it is probably the case that (iii), which is, for example, a best-dressed person's satisfaction in his clothes in a competitive market of display, is larger than (i), which is the satisfaction he would get if the supply of fine tailors were reduced. Term (iv) is, of course, the external cost, if it exists, of others' free choice of fine clothes, automobiles, houses, and so on, and represents the actor's jealousy over his bourgeois neighbor's Ferrari. Term (ii) is the absence of such jealousy, when the bourgeois' Ferrari is prohibited by law. Presumably (ii) is about zero for our imaginary aristocrat, while (iv) is negative because the aristocrat resents and is threatened by the presumptions of the nouveau riche. For our aristocrat to favor sumptuary laws, it would have to happen that: (ii) > (iii) − (i) − (iv), which can be expected to occur if the external costs to him of the behavior of the nouveau riche is great enough.

But few people have seriously attacked conspicuous consumption since Veblen invented the term. The populism he represented was probably the last serious opposition to material display. Since there is no agitation for sumptuary laws, evidently (ii) is not large enough to satisfy the requirement. This is, of course, merely another way of saying that (iv) is small, that there really are no external costs in matters of material display. Of course, our argument is somewhat circular: the absence of agitation indicates that external costs are low; and low external costs are the explanation of nonregulation. Since these features of the world reinforce each other in a kind of field effect, one should not be surprised at the circularity. Certainly, most observers would agree with us, we believe, that conspicuous display has very little external cost in our society. And, if this is true, it is, by our previous argument, a sufficient condition for the absence of sumptuary laws.

When Costs Are Benefits

To this point our discussion of regulation has focused on changing the context of choice so as to eliminate the selection of some alternative that exhibits external costs. An equivalent (but oftentimes not so regarded) situation is that in which the regulation is intended to make some alternative more available and more widely chosen. We can, of course, interpret such regulation as equivalent to the elimination of an alternative. That is, previously we focus on regulation as changing people's choices from $a_0 \rightarrow a^*$. Thus, regulation is changing the status quo. But once at a^*, we can interpret the regulation as defending the new status quo—i.e., making sure we do not revert from a^* to a_0. Such situations occur typically if the external effects of the status quo are positive.

Private charity, for example, is believed to bring utility, not disutility, to people other than the almsgiver. Thus, almost always and everywhere true charity is encouraged in law and religion. Lately, in the United States, some tax evasion masquerading as charity has been restricted; but so profound is our respect for charity that we allow a vast amount of tax evasion in the form of spurious charity simply in order to encourage some genuine charity. That is, we regulate in favor of charity, in favor of a choice context that yields positive external benefits, fearing that without the regulation, people's choices will exhibit less charity. Occasionally courts overthrow extremely absurd wills, such as some of those that endow named animals; on the whole, however, any charity at all is allowed and encouraged. Even if the cumulative effects of such charity are disastrous, as in the case of bequests to religious foundations in the middle ages, bequests that set the scene for the Reformation, still the charity is not regarded as having a social cost. Indeed, no sooner were the church lands confiscated in England than the whole process of testamentary endowment started over again. In our society, vast amounts of capital are in various charitable trusts: churches, universities, foundations, hospitals, almshouses, and so on. Yet, except for the occasional radical, such trusts are never criticized, even when they are devoted to such obviously useless purposes as the display of a button collection or agitation for a thirteen-month calendar.

From the point of view of a decision maker considering whether or not to permit charity, the calculus (omitting cost) is:

(i)	+	(ii)	>	(iii)	+	(iv)
utility to actor from giving charity alone		utility to actor from others' charity		utility to actor from spending on himself		utility to actor from others' spending on themselves

If we suppose that (iii) is greater than (i)[4] then to justify charity it must be that (ii) > (iv) + (iii) − (i). And this is often the case. Charity is believed to provide an external benefit (ii), first and most directly, to the recipient of the gift. And this externality is indeed always present, even when the gift is foolish. The keeper of the button collection benefits from the charity of the donor, even if the rest of society is hurt. Secondarily and more significantly, charity is supposed to provide an external benefit (ii) to everybody in the sense that everyone besides the donor and the recipient is relieved of costs they would otherwise be forced to bear. This second benefit, of course, exists only if the object of the charity is in fact something or someone that society would support (or would

---

[4]At least one form of regulation, however, seeks to set (i) greater than (iii). Specifically, we are socialized to obtain private benefits from giving charity. The regulation here is varying individual utility functions.

like to support) in the absence of the gift. The conventional objects of charity —the poor, the sick, the infirm, students, priests, scholars, and so on—would probably be supported in the absence of charity, though perhaps not as lavishly as they are now. Hence, for these gifts the secondary external benefit also exists. In the case of the unconventional charities, which are on the whole few, society probably would not support them in the absence of the gift. Consequently, such things as button collections are probably net external costs because they divert resources to wasteful (that is, socially unwanted) purposes. Such external costs have seldom been noticed. So charity generally has been consistently encouraged, never prohibited.

This contrast of extremes, the treatment of murder and the treatment of charity, emphasizes the role of external effects in regulation. When external effects of alternatives are large and negative, efforts are made to control them by forbidding the use of the alternative. When external effects are wholly positive (or believed to be so), no prohibitions occur and regulation seeks to insure the selection of alternatives that exhibit the positive externalities. All alternatives are permitted, even encouraged. That is, the regulation is reversed from prohibiting an action to establishing incentives to encourage it.

Borderline External Costs

If, as we argue, a necessary condition for the prohibition of alternatives is the existence of certain kinds of external costs, then one would expect that the main controversies over regulation would occur:

(1) where, for a proportion of regulators necessary for decision, external costs of an alternative proposed to be changed are only slightly larger than the external costs of substitute alternatives, or

(2) where, for a proportion of regulators necessary for decision, the cost of imposing prohibitions are themselves close in size to the difference between the external costs of the alternative proposed to be prohibited and the external costs of its substitute.

In either case, the net gain from eliminating alternatives is small, so that the case for prohibition cannot be made effectively.

It is easy to find examples of controversies arising in these circumstances. Consider the maze of prohibitions involved in regulation of sexual life in Western society. The current trend is toward the abandonment of many of these prohibitions. Yet there was a time when they were imposed and warmly advocated, presumably because of great savings in external costs.

In most places of the world, including even the West, until recent years, the main problem of human kind has been to maintain control of the environment by producing enough people to operate a civilized society. Even in the eighteenth and nineteenth centuries, when the current population explosion began— presumably because of slightly improved technology in agriculture, medicine, and sanitation—there was an apparently insatiable demand for people to fill the factories in European and American cities and the fertile empty land of the Americas. During all these eons of the shortage of people, one main cultural ideal in the West was that of the strong nuclear family organized to produce as many children as possible. Most of the governmental and religious regulation of sexual behavior had to do with prohibiting activities believed to weaken the family. Thus sexual activities outside the marriage bed, such as adultery or homosexuality, were both sins and punishable offenses. Even things believed to encourage these extramarital activities (such as pornography or any public displays of sexuality as on the stage) were sometimes forbidden. Also of course, birth control was forbidden as a direct threat to reproduction and as an encouragement of extramarital sexuality. Naturally, divorce, which is the most direct threat of all to the stability of the family, was rendered almost impossible. All these things were forbidden because, by presumably weakening the family, they occasioned severe external costs for the rest of the people in an under-populated world. To a society that values children highly, every divorce, indeed every act of extramarital sexuality, is a threat not just in the lives of those directly involved but also in the lives of every one of those who might benefit from the work of the unborn children of a failed marriage.

In the last two or three generations the economic and social value of children has declined as urbanization has been completed and overpopulation has become the main specter haunting the world. Coincidentally, the dangers of divorce and other offenses against the integrity of the family have seemed less threatening. One by one the ideologies supporting these prohibitions have been attacked, so that now birth control is almost universal in the West, religious opposition notwithstanding; divorce is in many places freely permitted; pornography and public displays of sexuality are common; and even homosexuality, the most profound threat of all to reproduction, is often tolerated.

The coincidence in time of the decline of need for children and the decline of prohibitory regulation of sexual behavior (either in the form of laws or of normative socialization) is certainly no accident. Each act of indifference to the enforcment of the old rules indicates a calculation by the majority of decision makers to the effect that external costs are minimal. And such a calculation is possible only if children are no longer so important socially. It is perhaps hard to say which has declined, the costs associated with the formerly prohibited sexual behavior or the benefits from sexuality confined to the marriage bed. But whether one or both have declined, the effect is that the difference between them is small, which means that one should expect great controversy over regulatory prohibitions.

And great controversy is precisely what we have. In every area into which birth control has penetrated there has been a controversy about it, a controversy that probably is the main dispute over modernization in the Roman Catholic church. Regulation of divorce, policy toward abortion, censorship, policing of homosexuality, and the like are the occasion for intense local controversy in every Western country. Surely all this controversy, continuing at a fairly high level for two generations now, must be occasioned by a change in the evaluation of external costs.

In the regulation of sexual life, the contemporary dispute probably arises because there is doubt that what is gained, namely "normal" sexuality, is worth much more to society generally than the things prohibited, e.g., adultery, pornography, abortion, birth control, divorce, and so on. By contrast, in the "noble experiment" of two generations ago in the United States, the prohibition of the production and sale of alcoholic beverages, the dispute arose because the costs of enforcement were so large relative to the savings in external costs. Even though drinking alcoholic beverages is an essentially private act, it cannot be doubted that addiction to alcohol had (and has) large external costs. These include the cost of maintenance of alcoholics and their dependents and the cost of crimes committed by angry or careless drunks (e.g., with guns and automobiles). Nor can it be doubted that Prohibition reduced these costs. One has only to observe the vast increases in alcoholism during the generation since repeal to be aware, as were those who voted for Prohibition, of the vast external costs to be saved. What we now know that all the voters for the Maine laws, local options, and the Eighteenth Amendment did not know is the very high cost of enforcement. The effect of the amendment was to put up a tariff to protect organized crime from the competition of legitimate business. The impetus that Prohibition gave to the Mafia extends the terrible costs of that noble experiment right up to the present day. This was truly a case where the costs of enforcement were vastly greater than any possible savings in external costs. Quite reasonably, therefore, Prohibition was abandoned after a short effort at enforcement.

THE RELATIVITY OF EXTERNAL COSTS

The occasion for regulation is, as we show by a detailed analysis of examples, the existence of external costs sufficiently large for a relevant majority of decision makers that they are willing to change or eliminate an alternative. Controversy arises, of course, whenever these external costs are small. Equally obviously, controversy arises whenever the external effects are costs for some and benefits for others. Thus, the regulation of farm prices became an accepted part of public policy in the United States in the 1930's when a large and politically important class (i.e., large-scale farmers) favored it. Now that class is less numerous and less politically relevant and the class of opponents (i.e. consumers) is more politically conscious. One can therefore expect intense controversy in the future over farm price controls.

As this example indicates, the external costs that serve as a base for regulation are a function of the social context. Indeed, as we show in the previous chapter, the very existence of such costs is a matter of perception. Nearly every social act involves an externality. What one man does limits or expands or varies the options open to another man. Truly, "no man is an island." Externalities are therefore inherent in almost every act. Whether or not they are interpreted as costs or benefits, however, depends on the ideology and interests and social circumstances of the regulators.

In that sense, externalities are wholly relative to culture. Although the kind of killing defined as murder has almost always been perceived as a cost, and charity has almost always been perceived as a benefit, in other examples of regulation that we have just discussed the popular judgment on the significance of the action has changed over time. Conspicuous consumption has sometimes been regarded as an external cost, sometimes not. Many kinds of sexual behavior formerly thought to involve extremely large external costs and therefore to deserve harsh punishment are now thought to be hardly worth prohibiting. In each case the acts have not changed, but the ideology and social circumstances have. Once upon a time, the fancy dress of the rich bourgeois confused him with the aristocrat and was therefore a cost to aristocratic rulers. So they forbade the display. But aristocrats no longer rule, and fancy dress, while it may occasion the resentment of poor populists like Veblen, does not apparently threaten the order of the now democratic polity.

It is easy to see, then, that the recognition of, indeed the intrinsic nature of, external costs typically is a matter of ideology. So also, therefore, is regulation, which depends on the perception of external costs. We offer one final example. In most of the world until quite recently, the main kind of farming was for subsistence, where the farmer raised his own food and fibers and bought and sold only a few objects in the market. Recently this has been displaced by its opposite, market agriculture, where the farmer raises one main crop, sells it on the market, and buys his food and clothing with the proceeds. In a world of subsistence agriculture, what a man plants and grows is entirely his own business and no one else's. If in such a world a man grows eleven acres of wheat one year and twenty-three acres the next, in both cases to feed his own animals, it cannot possibly concern his neighbors or the government. But change the scene to market agriculture, in which the government fixes prices by controlling the acreage devoted to a kind of produce. Now the extra twelve acres of wheat are relevant to everyone else, regardless of whether or not the product ever enters the market. So the Supreme Court of the United States affirmed in the case of *Wickard* v. *Filburn* (1942), where Mr. Justice Jackson said for a *unanimous* court:

> Even if appellee's [Filburn's] activity be local and though it may not be regarded as commerce, it may still, whatever its nature, be reached by Congress [i.e., subjected to regulatory prohibitions]. . . . The effect of the consumption of home-grown wheat on interstate commerce is due to the fact that it constitutes the most variable factor in the disappearance of the wheat crop. Consumption on the farm where grown appears to vary in an amount greater than 20 per cent of average production. . . . That the appellee's own contribution . . . may be

trivial [i.e., twelve extra acres in this case] . . . is not enough to remove him from the scope of federal regulation where, as here, his contribution taken together with that of many others similarly situated is far from trivial. . . . This record leaves us in no doubt that Congress may properly have considered that wheat consumed on the farm where grown, if wholly outside the scheme of regulation, would have a substantial effect in defeating and obstructing its purpose to stimulate trade therein at increased prices. . . . (317 U.S. 111, 125–129)

Thus, an action that had been for untold ages a purely private act with no observable external effects that could not be accommodated by a decentralized market, became, with a change to market agriculture and a new ideology as enunciated above, an action with significant externalities. So it has been ordered by the Supreme Court that a relevant externality exists, even though, up to a few years before, no such externality would have been perceived even by the most astute political scientist or economist. Quite clearly externalities, like beauty, are in the eye of the beholder. But this fact does not, of course, in any way detract from their reality.

THE MORAL CONFLICT OVER REGULATION

We are here trying to examine heuristically a calculus for regulation that explains, *inter alia,* why and when it occurs. But in the life of the world, the main issue is not, of course, why it occurs but whether or not it should occur. Our analysis cannot answer this practical question, but it can explain why it arises with such intensity.

In our view, regulation occurs if, for each member of a decisive set of decision makers, sentence (10.6) holds. (By "decisive set" we mean whatever group can of itself impose a regulation. In a democracy, this is a majority of some sort. In an autocracy, it is the autocrat.) The value of a choice context in which some particular, suitably attractive, alternative exists is composed of direct benefits from the alternative's use by decision makers and the indirect effects on the decision makers from its use by other people. Typically, for most decisions leading to regulation, the biggest effects are external ones. Hence in a judgment on regulation, the main feature is a comparison of the external effects of two actions and the costs of changing from one to another.

But, as we are trying now to show, the size of external effects is relative to ideology. Whether or not a person perceives an external cost is largely determined by his intellectual equipment. Consider the ideological difference in support for municipal zoning. There is no doubt that land use occasions considerable externalities, both costs and benefits. For the residents of a quiet street, a gas station on the corner, though convenient, may be a real nuisance in terms of noise, odors, and so on. Conversely, for the residents of a growing suburban neighborhood the location of a school in the neighborhood is probably an external benefit—despite the fact that it is a congregating point for hordes of children—if only because the school makes the resident's houses more saleable to young families. Attempts to segregate kinds of uses so that certain areas are exclusively residential and others exclusively commercial are clearly attempts to minimize external costs. In popular usage in the United States, however, municipal zoning has centered mostly on classification of residential areas themselves. The externality protected against is the cost to the more prosperous of having the less prosperous live near them. When the houses of the rich and poor are intermingled, probably the greatest cost to the more prosperous is the fact that in school and neighborhood their children are exposed to the moral values of the less prosperous. Whether or not such a cost exists is, clearly, a matter of ideology. A class conscious and conservative middle-class person is, of course, highly likely to perceive threats in the presence of poor neighbors. More liberal persons are likely to be willing to allow land to find its most efficient use in the market regardless of neighbors. Thus, whether or not one perceives externalities in housing patterns depends largely on one's temperament and ideology.

Conservatives, who see in every change some threat to themselves, are likely to perceive externalities everywhere. Hence follows a kind of organic state and mercantilist political ideology in which massive and detailed regulation is appropriate.

Radicals, who see externalities in the very existence of the present order, are also likely to perceive externalities everywhere. Hence from that perception follows notions of the planned economy and the ideology of socialism.

Liberals are likely to see a greater externality in the regulation to prevent an externality than in the prevented externality itself. The current apostle of liberalism, Milton Friedman, states the matter succinctly:[5]

> the use of government to overcome neighborhood effects [i.e., external effects] itself has an extremely important neighborhood effect which is unrelated to the particular occasion for government action. Every act of government intervention limits the area of individual freedom directly and threatens the preservation of freedom indirectly. . . .

In the battle of ideologies each ideological position involves a viewpoint on external effects and, indeed, one could write a history of political philosophy in terms of such a set of viewpoints. The concrete battles over particular regulations are thus expressions of the differing perceptions of what constitutes external costs. Each act of regulation and each decision to regulate or not to regulate thus represents a momentary triumph for some philosophical position. These positions are fundamental affirmations of morality, hence they are not objectively demonstrable truth; but they are, possibly for that reason, all the more deeply held emotionally. This is the reason that the dispute over particular regulations is always so intense.

[5]Milton Friedman, *Capitalism and Freedom* (Chicago: University of Chicago Press, 1962), p. 32.

THE COSTS OF REGULATION

Up to this point we have discussed the individual calculus about regulation as if its main component were the estimate of external effects and external costs. But the very act of regulation itself costs something in enforcement, and that cost should be included in the calculus. To regulate is to prohibit or change some action, some use of an available alternative. Regulated actions are, by assumption, always feasible and always attractive to some people—if they were not, there would be no point to regulating them. Since regulated actions are, therefore, feasible and attractive, some enforcement effort is necessarily required to prohibit or change them effectively. Such effort is costly, and so regulation itself is always costly.

It may well be that the cost of enforcement, rather than the cost of an externality, is the marginal element in a decision on whether or not to regulate. Recalling sentence (10.5) the condition for regulation, that

$$E_3 - [E_3 - E_4] - C' > E_1 - [E_1 - E_2],$$

or simply

$$E_4 - C' > E_2,$$

suppose that, without regard for the mechanisms by which a regulation is imposed, a decisive set of citizens prefers to alter the status quo: that is, for all members of a decisive set,

$$E_4 > E_2.$$

It might then appear reasonable to decide in favor of regulation. But suppose further that

$$E_4 - C' < E_2.$$

Then the marginal element in the decision is the cost of regulation, C'. Since calculations like this doubtless occur in the real world, it seems important to study the influences on the magnitude of the pro rata cost of enforcement, C'; to this task we now turn.

The magnitude of C' is dependent at least on:

(1) The effectiveness of the device for changing the context of choice. By "effectiveness" we mean whether or not the device is technically workable.

(2) The tractability of the subject matter of regulation. By "tractability" we mean whether or not the alternatives, outcomes, patterns of socialization, information, and so on over which the device is applied are inherently subject to modification.

In the former case, a device may fail simply because it is poorly constructed. In the latter case, it may fail, however well-designed, because no device could be successful in the circumstances. We turn now to the analysis of these two parameters of enforcement cost, considering the former first because it is the simpler to understand.

EFFECTIVENESS

To say that a device for changing a choice context is not effective is to say that $P(O_r)$, the probability distribution on the outcome set, is "almost" the same when the device is used (i.e., regulation) as when it is not used. It may well be that, while the act of regulation significantly changes the choices of people, it does not change the outcomes that occur. Suppose it is desired to make men good, and a regulation (e.g., a law or moral suasion) is therefore adopted requiring attendance at a particular church. Such a regulation may quite effectively alter choices over the set A by forcing people to go to church, without in any way changing $P(O_r)$, which in this case is the moral climate of society. Rather such a regulation is probably no more than a boondoggle for the agents of the regulators (that is, for the governmental bureaucracy) who carry out the regulation. However effective in form, it is not effective in its content.

Such inconsequential regulation doubtless does occur, though it is probably less frequent than is often alleged. Most commonly it occurs when a regulatory device is continued in use after the original circumstances for which the device was adopted have disappeared. Consider the device of dog licensing, which probably once was very useful but which now is at best a highly inefficient excise tax. It was originally intended, doubtless, to minimize the incidence of rabies and of dog packs by identifying owners so that they could be held responsible for their animals. Possibly at one time licensing helped to achieve both goals; but in changing circumstances its effectiveness for these goals apparently declined, and alternative devices have been emphasized. Rabies is controlled by almost universal vaccination and the message about the importance of vaccination has reached nearly every dog owner. Dog packs are controlled by leash laws under which all free-roaming dogs are subject to impounding regardless of whether or not they are licensed. In short, licensing turned out to be less efficient than these other devices in the sense that they can and do sometimes work without licensing whereas licensing by itself cannot be imagined to be effective. Yet licensing remains a not inconsiderable function of local government. Probably several thousand people in the United States are mainly engaged in operating licensing systems; and many thousands more —clerks and police—are partially employed at peak seasons. How can one explain the persistence of a device which accomplishes almost nothing and yet is costly to the citizen regulators?

One answer is that the system is, on the one hand, advantageous (in a sense) and relatively costless for local politicians and, on the other hand, inexpensive for all citizen regulators and differentially borne by them. The advantage to local politicians is that it provides a small but discernible amount of patronage, typically for persons who are otherwise nearly unemployable, so that it can even be justified as a kind of dole. Furthermore, since usually the licensing personnel probably collect slightly more in fees than they are paid in salaries, they may be immediately profitable for local government—however much they are a wasteful charge on the whole society. Since, therefore, politicians are able to give patronage to unemployables without appearing to use tax monies for the largess, they have some incentive to do so, an incentive which may or may not be blocked by a contrary incentive to offer effective government. On the other hand, citizens have almost no incentive to notice the charge on them, especially if the bureaucracy is discreet. Here discretion means keeping the fee low and not attempting to enforce the regulation on an owner who objects. Thus, each owner pays what he is willing to pay; and all citizens, owners and nonowners alike, on whom the waste is a charge, individually bear so little of this charge that, typically, they do not notice it. In this way the set of regulators (i.e., citizens) is gulled into continuing to impose a system of regulation that is wholly irrational in terms of its ostensible goals.

How frequent are such paradoxical occurrences where rational regulators impose a regulation that does not alter outcomes but nevertheless costs something to impose? Our impression is that these paradoxes are relatively rare. There are, however, symptoms that may indicate the contrary: (1) the fact that regulation is sometimes, even often, counterproductive; and (2) the fact that most bureaucracies are permeated with boondoggles. But actually these symptoms indicate quite different situations from that of an inconsequential regulation.

It is true that many regulations do not accomplish what is intended of them and are therefore counterproductive. This is quite different, however, from having no significant effect at all. Counterproductive regulation usually indicates that the subject matter of regulation is intractable rather than that the regulation is simply irrelevant. We defer discussion of counterproductive regulation until a later section.

It is also true that most bureaucracies are permeated with boondoggles, all of which can always be elegantly justified, but which remain boondoggles nevertheless because the work really does not need to be done. This waste is, however, usually associated with action programs rather than enforcement programs. Military officials, with great ingenuity, develop pointless weapons and meaningless training programs simply in order to justify a large officer corps. Welfare officials develop elaborate qualifications for alms so that administration requires a horde of social workers. But because this wasteful work does not purport to change social outcomes it is not easy to measure. Regulation does, however, purport to change; and so, when it does not, its failure is particularly glaring.

This is why we think that totally irrelevant regulation is relatively rare. It seems likely that most wholly ineffective regulation survives because it escapes notice, because the goals of the boondogglers are so modest that their waste is itself modest. In any event it seems likely that inefficient devices for regulation are—unlike subjects intractable to regulation—relatively easy to spot and hence to minimize in their effect. We turn therefore to the more interesting and difficult case of attempting to regulate what can and cannot be regulated.

TRACTABILITY

As we begin to investigate the inherent regulatability of a class of events, we immediately observe that whether or not these events can be modified at an acceptable cost depends profoundly upon whether or not the people affected by regulation prefer a regulated or unregulated choice context. Presumably, of course, those who consciously seek to regulate—to alter the choice context, and to change and eliminate alternatives—prefer some other context or alternatives to the status quo. Typically, however, the regulation to be undertaken affects more than the decisive set of regulators. Some who are not in the decisive set, e.g., landlords when the regulation is rent control, are not in favor of the regulation, but their behavior is nevertheless affected. How they respond to regulation depends, we believe, on how the regulation affects their behavior. We see two general categories of effect and hence of response:

(I)   There is a direct benefit to the regulated from the regulation because they are encouraged to choose substitute alternatives that are better for them than are the alternatives they would choose in the absence of regulation.

(II) There is a direct cost to a significant (but not decisive) portion of the regulated because they are required to choose substitute alternatives that are worse for them than are the alternatives they would choose in the absence of regulation.

Category I: Direct Benefits

This first category is best typified by the game of Prisoners' Dilemma, which has the property that what people will do by themselves leads to an outcome less advantageous for them than what they would get if they were regulated. Fundamentally, therefore, regulation is welcomed by the people regulated and consequently is relatively less costly than it would be if they did not welcome it. Regulation typically removes the dilemma, either by forbidding individual action or by subsidizing collusion, and this allows the situation to stabilize at a new—and better—outcome. The regulation (forbidding or subsidizing) may initially be expensive; but once the alternative leading to the worse outcome is effectively removed, the new equilibrium has its own motivational support and is itself difficult to abandon.

Examples of Prisoners' Dilemmas

As we point out in Chapter 9, social life is pockmarked with situations that can be construed as Prisoners' Dilemmas because of the pervasiveness (and indeed the generality of the concept) of public goods. The chief argument advanced for the adoption of world government is the assertion that war and the preparation for war have become such dilemmas. Suppose that the contestants are the United States and the Soviet Union and that the alternatives for each are to use or not to use thermonuclear weapons. Actions of use are initially attractive, for they can result in winning the draw on the opponent; but if the opponent is not utterly destroyed, the eventual outcome is surely destruction for both. Less dramatically, the alternatives may be interpreted as engaging in or not engaging in an arms race. By reason of the dilemma, each individually prefers more to arm than not to arm. But the resultant arms race is costly and dangerous. The argument for world government then is that some police force must be applied to eliminate the preferred but undesirable actions so that an equilibrium occurs at the more desirable ones.

Similarly, one may interpret Hobbes' justification of civil society as an argument from the Prisoners' Dilemma. In a state of nature, he argued, one has the alternatives of warring with each other man or not so warring, and this game exists for each possible pair of persons. The natural payoff structure is such that the dilemma exists, or so he supposed; and, since he also supposed men are utility maximizers, it follows that a state of nature is a war of every man against every man. The way out of the dilemma, Hobbes then argued, is a social contract by which civil government is authorized to prohibit private wars by force. Thus civil society arrives at a new and happier equilibrium, a state of public peace.

Hobbes was probably wrong in supposing that all of life in a state of nature is a Prisoners' Dilemma. There are many other possible situations—most of which doubtless occur. Rapoport and Guyer examined all 2×2 matrices possible for two-person games when for each player each outcome offers a different amount, $\{a, b, c, d\}$, where $a > b > c > d$. Ignoring rotations, there are 78 such matrices.[6] Only one is the Prisoners' Dilemma:

PERSON 2

		ACTION β_1	ACTION β_2
PERSON 1	ACTION α_1	b, b	d, a
	ACTION α_2	a, d	c, c

Many others, however, offer an advantageous equilibrium; for example,

[6]Anatol Rapoport and Melvin Guyer, "A Taxonomy of 2×2 Games," *General Systems,* vol. 11 (1966), pp. 203–214.

Person 2

		ACTION β_1	ACTION β_2
Person 1	ACTION α_1	a, a	b, c
	ACTION α_2	c, b	d, d

Since $a > c$ and $b > d$, person 1 prefers α_1; and person 2 prefers β_1; and the resultant equilibrium in the upper left cell pays both players the best they can get. This kind of situation appears, with some variations, in buying and selling (indeed in most of economic life), sexual relations where cooperation in a love affair leads to the best outcome for both man and woman, and, generally, in all productive activities where it is rational to choose an action that leads to the best result for both.

Although Hobbes overlooked all the myriad situations where utility maximization leads to a desired equilibrium, still he was right that, in many of the affairs with which government is especially concerned, one finds Prisoners' Dilemmas. The production of public goods is usually such a dilemma. As we show in Chapter 9, the problem in the production of such goods—which must usually be decided upon socially, not individually—is that each decision maker in the society has, individually a motive not to produce, even if everybody would be better off if the good were produced. Each person sees his own payoffs, in a game against other people, as if they were part of a Prisoners' Dilemma.[7] If, finally, one observes that the public goods to be produced include such things as public peace (e.g., not engaging in a riot or not committing an assault), then it is apparent that much of what is conventionally called regulation is the production of a public good.

Breaking out of Prisoners' Dilemmas

The strategy of resolving Prisoners' Dilemmas is to eliminate, in one way or another, the action that leads to the jointly undesirable result. Either of two devices can be used:

(1)   to punish players for the use of initially preferred alternatives, α_2 or β_2. If an amount k, where $k > a - b$ and $k > c - d$, is subtracted from the entries for player 1 in row 2 and for player 2 in column 2, then one gets a new matrix:

[7]In Olson, *The Logic of Collective Action*, it is argued that public goods are underproduced. They will be spontaneously produced in adequate quantity only if the benefit to some individual is greater than the total cost. This is the analogue of our requirement for regulation that (i) > (iii). (See our Chapter 3.)

PERSON 2

		ACTION β_1	ACTION β_2
PERSON 1	ACTION α_1	b, b	$d, a - k$
	ACTION α_2	$a - k, d$	$c - k, c - k$

where, as previously, $a > b > c > d$. Since $b > a - k$ and $d > c - k$, the players individually prefer α_1 and β_1 so that the outcome of the revised matrix is the upper left cell, which is a new and preferable equilibrium.

(2) to reward players for the use of the initially less desirable alternatives, α_1 and β_1. If k is added to the values for 1 in row 1 and for 2 in column 1, one gets:

PERSON 2

		ACTION β_1	ACTION β_2
PERSON 1	ACTION α_1	$b + k, b + k$	$d + k, a$
	ACTION α_2	$a, d + k$	c, c

Since $b + k > a$ and $d + k > c$, players again individually prefer α_1 and β_1, and again the outcome is in equilibrium in the upper left cell.

These methods are mathematically equivalent but behaviorally different. One is the stick, the other the carrot. To punish, to subtract k in row and column 2, is to dissuade players from using socially undesirable alternatives by making them fear retribution. This is what we do by the apparatus of civil law, police, courts, and prisons to discourage violations of public order. On the other hand, to reward, to add k in row and column 1, is to persuade users to eschew the socially undesirable alternative by making the socially desired one more attractive to the individual. This is what we do when we promote public order by making the structure of society more attractive to potential violaters, that is, by creating jobs for potential rioters, by rehabilitation and parole systems for ordinary criminals, and so on.

The instrumental means of breaking the dilemma and of imposing a charge or subsidy in the structure of the matrix is, of course, the joint action of people. Political entrepreneurs form groups or public policies to provide public goods.[8]

[8]Richard E. Wagner, "Pressure Groups and Political Entrepreneurs: A Review Article," in Gordon Tullock, ed., *Papers on Non-Market Decision Making* (Charlottesville: Thomas Jefferson Center for Political Economy, University Press of Virginia, 1966), pp. 162–170; and Norman Frohlich, Joe A. Oppenheimer, and Oran R. Young, *Political Leadership and Collective Goods*, (Princeton, N. J.: Princeton University Press, 1971).

And this provides an easy way to calculate costs. How much advantage can an entrepreneur get for himself by organizing society to provide a public good? If he can get some advantage, then it is probably socially worthwhile for those impaled on it to break the Prisoners' Dilemma. It may well be that all regulation to break Prisoners' Dilemmas is profitable both to the regulated and to society generally.

We use the Prisoners' Dilemma to illustrate the circumstance in which there are direct benefits from regulation to the regulated persons. We note, however, that it is not the only kind of situation to possess this property. So we offer as a final example an entirely different game with an entirely different kind of initial equilibrium which nevertheless has the same property of rendering regulation welcome—the game of Chicken. Two drivers of automobiles on a single-lane road race toward each other, and the one who turns off first, thereby avoiding a head-on crash, loses. A matrix for this game is:

PERSON 2

		TURN (β_1)	NOT TURN (β_2)
	TURN (α_1)	b, b	c, a
PERSON 1			
	NOT TURN (α_2)	a, c	d, d

where $a > b > c > d$. This game does not have a pure-strategy equilibrium in the sense of the equilibrium of Prisoners' Dilemma, where a particular row is clearly preferred regardless of what column is chosen. In Chicken there is a weaker kind of equilibrium: given a choice of a particular column (row), then there is a preferred row (column). The lower left and upper right cells both satisfy this equilibrium concept, so, furthermore, the equilibrium is not unique. Nevertheless it is a kind of equilibrium because, once in it, no one has an incentive to leave. Chicken is not an attractive game, either for the players or for the larger society. Its name, when it appears in international politics, is "brinkmanship." People in the larger society have a motive for breaking up the initial equilibrium, if it is at either (α_2, β_1) or (α_1, β_2). The difficulty of doing so, however, is evidenced by the number of drivers who seem to be perpetually engaged in playing this game. Nevertheless, regulation is profitable for both drivers here, and hence one may expect them to welcome it.

To conclude our discussion of category I: probably most of the regulation that is successful occurs in the kinds of situations found in this category, where those most affected by regulation benefit from it. Probably in these instances the cost, in terms of the tractability of the subject matter, is not excessive.

Category II: Direct Costs

Regulation in this category is doubtless more costly since, by definition, it is not advantageous to the participants, who therefore constantly seek to return to the initial equilibrium—which is precisely what regulation forbids. The cost of regulation is, then, the cost of constant vigilance in enforcement. Comparing this category with the previous one, regulation in both requires breaking an initial equilibrium; but in the previous one, the direct benefits to the regulated lead them to support the new equilibrium induced by regulation, while here such support is missing.

The most obvious and historically most important kind of regulation in this category is direct regulation of prices. Such regulation typically involves no effort to rearrange the underlying situation of demand and supply. It merely imposes a price change by fiat. Since, however, price causally depends on supply and demand, if these latter are not changed simultaneously with price, then traders have an intense motive to reject the regulated price in favor of the "natural" price. Given the intensity of the motive, therefore, one can expect many evasions and much difficulty in enforcement.

Owing to this difficulty, there are relatively few instances of direct price regulation in our society, perhaps because we are unwilling to punish vast numbers of people for economic crimes. When we do undertake such regulation it is usually where either the buyers or the sellers are few and hence easily kept track of. Thus, for example, prices in utilities and the transportation industry are much regulated. Neither of these is a particularly good example of the cost of regulation, however, because the procedure for continuous review of price means that the price is usually set near to what it would be in the absence of regulation. (When it is not so set, customers experience disastrous declines in service, as in the variations in the supply of natural gas owing to the bad judgment of the Federal Power Commission.) One direct price regulation which is, however, both effective and generally unrelated to conditions of supply and demand is the regulation of apartment house rents. By an examination of that regulation, we can perhaps appreciate some of the intractability to regulation that is disadvantageous to some of the persons regulated.

In the United States, rents were regulated almost universally during and shortly after World War II. The regulation broke down once the sacrifices of wartime were no longer believed necessary, simply because so many landlords and so many tenants were eager or willing to settle at far higher prices than the law allowed. No police force, however large, could possibly have controlled the violations. In New York City, however, where there were relatively few landlords, it was still physically possible to maintain regulation. Furthermore, it was politically expedient to fix rents at a very low level, far below what they would have been in a free market. Since effective policing was possible, rents were in fact usually maintained at the fixed level, except for new buildings and except for allowances for improvements in quality. Naturally, however, with prices fixed and successfully enforced at some distance from the free market price, something had to give. What gave was maintenance. Without genuine profits, landlords interpreted depreciation and maintenance reserves as profit and took them out of the enterprises. Consequently, as buildings decayed, funds were not available for repair and replacement. Indeed, many buildings were simply abandoned after being allowed to decay to the point that repair was infeasible. Naturally, regulatory bodies sought to control this process, and the city acquired a horde of inspectors to enforce building codes. But violations were beyond the ability of control, and so the housing supply in New York has been wearing out for thirty years without adequate replacement, until now some believe that the slums of the city are beyond repair and human control.

The disaster of housing in that city, almost totally the product of a generation of rent control, reveals the essential nature of regulation in this category: if, as sometimes happens, buyers or sellers are sufficiently few to admit direct regulation of prices, still the visible costs of enforcement are only a small portion of the true cost. The true cost also includes the waste generated from the dislocation of the market, in this case the deterioration and disappearance of housing. The waste arises because some participants have a strong motive to return to the condition prior to regulation. In the course of doing so, they occasion unanticipated consequences which compensate them for the departure from the free market price. Furthermore, unanticipated consequences are themselves costly, possibly as costly as the external effects that justified the regulation in the first place. Hence the net effect of regulation may well be negative for most members of the decision-making set.

Given the counterproductivity of regulation in this category, the question is often raised of why it occurs at all. There appear to be two kinds of answers: that the regulators simply err or that the regulators deliberately take advantage of the rest of society. We cannot, of course, inquire into the intent of others; still we believe it likely that most such regulation is consciously self-serving.

The former explanation envisions regulators of the intractable as not realizing the consequences of their action. From this picture of foolish innocence one infers that, when the error is revealed, regulators hasten to repair the damage. Typically, however, nothing like that ever happens. Beneficiaries of price control are invariably its champions no matter how much waste it generates in the whole society. It appears, in fact, that costly regulation of the intractable remains in force because the regulators (i.e., citizens) who impose it have a special political advantage that allows them to do so. Thus, rent control in New York City benefits all apartment dwellers but especially those older, middle-class, settled citizens who have lived in the same apartment a long time. Of course, the poor benefit immediately, but in the long run it is their homes and neighborhoods that are turned into slums or abandoned firetraps. The advantage of the middle-class apartment dwellers is not only that they are a major voting bloc but furthermore that by their rhetoric they have obscured the connection between rent control and the uniquely appalling nature of New York City slums. Thereby they have in a sense manipulated the poor, who would be far better off with subsidized rents in a free market for housing.

Something of the same manipulation has occurred with minimum wages, which are a direct regulation of prices for all those jobs that would, in the absence of price fixing, be paid less than the minimum. These minima, insofar as they have been effective at all, have had at least two consequences: (1) they have deprived marginally employable people of jobs, e.g., adolescents, blacks, old people, and so on, and (2) they have encouraged substitution of machines and skilled labor for unskilled labor. Both these effects encourage the unemployment of marginal workers. This consequence is sometimes said to have been unanticipated and unrecognized by those who advocate minimum wages. Yet the main lobbyists for increasing minimum wages continue regularly to be labor leaders, who represent mostly skilled workers and almost never represent the marginally employable. Since many of these leaders are highly sophisticated economically, it is difficult to believe they simply err. Rather it seems likely that they use the rhetoric of helping the marginally employable in order to hurt those very persons for the advantage of middle-class unionists. Historically, at least, such was clearly the case. When the minimum wage law was passed in 1938, one of the main rationales to collect support for it was that it would slow the flight of the textile industry from New England to the South. This is, of course, simply to say that minimum wage laws were intended to deprive marginal Southern labor of the chance to work in mills that remained in New England employing fairly skilled labor.

These two examples suggest some of the reasons for the persistence of costly regulation of the intractable. However much waste it generates, some people nevertheless gain from it. If the gainers are in some way pivotal in the political system and if those who are especially hurt by the waste are politically weak (i.e., the very poor and uneducated who do not vote much), then it is sometimes possible to perpetuate price regulation for a very long time.

REGULATION AS RULE SELECTION

We conclude this chapter with the observation that systematic and detailed social science is indispensable for effectively making public policy. The decision on whether or not to regulate, and indeed on the kind of regulation, includes, as we show in this chapter, the decision maker's judgments about

(1) the direct benefit to himself from his and the society's use of various alternatives,
(2) the external effects, positive or negative, on himself from the society's use of various alternatives,
(3) the objective costs of enforcing the use of various alternatives.

Calculations, even rough estimates, of these costs can be made only if one carries through analyses of a kind for which we have laid a foundation in this book. We would like to conclude with numerous examples of such calculations illustrating various considerations involved in practical problems. Unfortunately, very little social science has hitherto been directed toward such calculations, largely because no appropriate theory, outside of economics, has existed. Such a theory is starting to develop, however, and we can therefore offer at least one example which, even though it is imprecise, does indicate the direction, if not the distance, social science can take public policy-making.

Our illustration is the analysis by Buchanan and Tullock of the problem facing constitution-writers and constitution-acceptors about the kind of majority that ought to be required for the society as a whole to take action.[9] If there are n people, there are at least n possible rules: that one person decides for the whole, that two persons decide for the whole, . . ., and that n persons decide for the whole. When the rule of one is used, each person does as he chooses. The rule of two means that, if any pair agree, they can do as they like. The rule of n is the rule of unanimity. Of course, the most common rules are: the rule of one, which is in effect an agreement not to make *social* decisions in some area of action, say, household management; the rule of two, which we use for marriage, commercial transactions, and the like; and the rule of $(n + 1)/2$, which we use in assemblies, referenda, and so on. Many other rules are in occasional use: for various special decisions assemblies use $\frac{3}{5}n$, $\frac{2}{3}n$, $\frac{3}{4}n$, and so on; the Supreme Court decides whether or not to hear a case if $\frac{2(n+1)}{5}$ agree; and so on.

Each of these rules is a kind of constitutional regulation. Specifically, the choice of a rule is the choice of a function G. Majority rule, for example, defines G so that if a bare majority of persons vote for a_1 over a_2, the outcome "a_1 wins" occurs. Two-thirds rule, however, yields a different function G, a function that does not transform a bare majority into the outcome "a_1 wins." The question Buchanan and Tullock pose is: which rule, i.e. which function G, should the individual prefer in a given set of circumstances? Ignoring enforcement costs, which are probably trivial for this type of regulation, they offer the following method of calculating the answer: Arrange the possible rules from one to n on a scale, as on the horizontal axis of the graph in Figure 10.1. Let k be any particular rule, $k = 1, 2, . . ., n$. The benefit of a rule is to make a decision with the least possible trouble. Hence, in general, the smaller is k, the larger the benefit. We may present this as a cost—the cost of organization to make a decision—where the cost is zero when $k = 1$ and it is

[9]James Buchanan and Gordon Tullock, *The Calculus of Consent* (Ann Arbor: University of Michigan Press, 1961). For subsequent elaborations of this analysis see Douglas Rae, "Decision-Rules and Individual Values in Constitutional Choice," *American Political Science Review*, vol. 63 (March 1969), pp. 40–56; Michael Taylor, "Proof of a Theorem on Majority Rule," *Behavioral Science*, vol. 14 (1969), pp. 228–231; Richard B. Curtis, "Decision-Rules and Collective Values in Constitutional Choice"; Wade W. Badger, "Political Individualism, Positional Preferences, and Optimal Decision Rules"; Norman J. Schofield, "Is Majority Rule Special"; and Charles R. Plott, "Individual Choice of a Political-Economic Process," all in Richard G. Niemi and Herbert F. Weisberg, *Probability Models of Collective Decision-Making* (Columbus: Charles E. Merrill, 1972).

highest when $k = n$, as in curve A in Figure 10.1. The external effects are the costs of being left out of a decision. If one is included in a coalition required for a decision, then one's interests are protected. Hence, the larger the required majority, the greater one's chance of being included in a winning coalition and the lower the cost of the external effect. So when $k = 1$, the cost is highest and, when $k = n$, the cost is lowest, as in curve B in Figure 10.1.

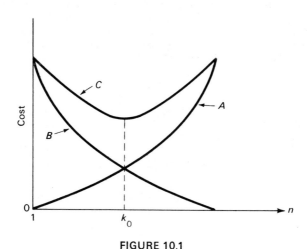

FIGURE 10.1

One can complete the cost-benefit analysis by summing the two kinds of cost, as in curve C of Figure 10.1, and then by minimizing the total cost, as at k_0 in Figure 10.1. The rule, k_0, may be interpreted as that rule having the greatest benefit relative to cost for the individual. The constitution-writer ought, therefore, to calculate roughly such curves as these for the potential acceptors and select that k_0 which will render his constitution acceptable to a decisive set, whatever that may be, of the acceptors.

As an illustration of the kind of analyses of public policy that we believe a well-developed social science can lead to, the foregoing has the merit of being brief and clear. Unfortunately it does not in its present form admit of direct numerical analysis, nor does it concern a subject of much practical importance. We offer it, therefore, merely as a hint of what may be done to exploit cost-benefit analysis of public policy using the concepts of utility maximization, equilibrium outcomes, external costs, and so on. In any event, we emphasize that rational judgment of public policy necessarily involves analyses of direct benefits, external effects, and costs of enforcement. Since these are the content of a practical science of politics, we are simply emphasizing that social science is a *sine qua non* of effective public policy.

SUGGESTIONS FOR FURTHER READING

The subject of regulation has not been approached in quite the same way as it is here. A more formal theory somewhat similar in spirit is found in GARY S. BECKER, "A Theory of Social Interaction" (unpublished paper, 1969), a general essay of which a particular example is GARY S. BECKER, "Crime and Punishment: An Economic Approach," *Journal of Political Economy*, vol. 76 (1968), pp. 169–217. Other works dealing with regulation as a problem of political economy are WILLIAM and JOYCE MITCHELL, *Political Analysis and Public Policy* (Skokie, Ill.: Rand McNally, 1967); ROBERT DAHL and CHARLES LINDBLOM, *Politics, Economics and Welfare* (New York: Harper, 1953); and, in a quite different vein, WILLIAM NISKANEN, *Bureaucracy and Representative Government* (New York: Aldine-Atherton, 1971).

11

Electoral Competition: Assumptions

In the previous chapter we presented a framework for explaining people's desires to have their choices, as well as the choices of others, regulated through collective action. This framework is incomplete, however, because we leave the mechanisms of collective choice unspecified. First, decisions to regulate presuppose the existence of mechanisms that render and enforce these decisions. Thus, the explanation and prediction of these decisions require an analysis of these mechanisms. Second, as we indicated in the last section of the previous chapter, the decision to regulate is itself a choice among alternative mechanisms. Since choice thus entails the evaluation of alternatives, an understanding of people's choices requires description of the allocations rendered by each mechanism and of the individual's evaluation of these allocations. In Chapter 9 we briefly examined competitive markets as one of these mechanisms; in this chapter and the next we analyze an alternative to markets—democratic elections.

Our approach to the study of elections, an approach inaugurated by Downs' *An Economic Theory of Democracy*, falls under the general rubric of "spatial models of party competition." We conceptualize the electoral mechanism in terms of spatial competition wherein candidates affect citizens' choices by offering proposed policies and manipulating the presentation of these policies to the citizens. With several alternative sets of assumptions, we ascertain the public policies candidates advocate.

CITIZENS

A theory that seeks to explain the policies that parties and candidates advocate must, logically, begin by considering the way in which citizens respond to the candidates' strategies and governmental outputs. A theory of voting behavior or, more generally, of electoral participation is, therefore, central to spatial analysis. We can disregard voters only by assuming that parties and candidates "waltz annually before a blind audience": that the electorate is not attentive and responsive to the maneuvers of the candidates.

Our discussion of a citizen's electoral calculus begins with the simplest possibility—an election in which only two candidates compete and in which citizens can either vote or abstain. Thus, we assume that a citizen's set of alternatives, A, consists of three elements: a_1, to vote for candidate 1, a_2, to vote for candidate 2, and a_0, to abstain. Similarly, the outcome set, O, consists of three elements: O_1, candidate 1 wins; O_2, candidate 2 wins; and O_{12}, the candidates tie. Recall, however, from Chapter 3 that a delineation of alternatives and outcomes is not sufficient for describing a person's decision-making calculus. Specifically, we must know the probabilities of events, given that a particular alternative is selected, and the citizen's evaluation of the outcomes in O.

To develop this calculus we conceptualize each citizen's choices and actions as the result of a two-stage sequential decision process. We assume, first, that the citizen evaluates both candidates and identifies a preferred candidate, and second, that he decides whether to vote or to abstain. We order the decision process in this fashion because the choice between voting and abstaining depends upon the citizen's comparative evaluation of the candidates, and because we wish to exploit the calculus of voting that we discussed in Chapter 3. Turning then to the first stage, we require assumptions concerning how citizens evaluate candidates, and, specifically, how such evaluations relate to the candidates' strategies.

THE REPRESENTATION OF A CITIZEN'S PREFERENCES AND PERCEPTIONS

A citizen's evaluation, typically, is not clear-cut. Initially we might assume that an outcome, say O_1, represents a policy such as "x dollars for public education," which means that, if candidate 1 wins, he seeks to appropriate x dollars for education. Alternatively, O_1 might denote "legislation requiring railroads to continue commuter service," which is to say that candidate 1 seeks to regulate the competitive market (which, presumably, will fail to provide such service). Downs, going a bit further toward generality in outcomes, substitutes ideology for a specific issue, and he assumes that citizens compare the candidates' ideological closeness to themselves. Unfortunately, each of these characterizations of outcomes is inadequate. We know that in most elections citizens' responses to candidates cannot be characterized as necessarily ideological or pertaining to a single well-defined dimension.[1] Some elections may concern the determination of a single policy, but policies typically are concerned with several dimensions. For example, the policy of funding public education concerns the means for raising revenues (e.g., income taxes, real estate taxes, lotteries), the absolute level of expenditures, the details of the budget, and so on. Moreover, candidates who are identified with specific proposals on an issue typically are evaluated also by such criteria as image and partisan identification. Thus, citizens' preferences cannot be ordered unambiguously on a single continuum, in which case spatial models must allow for more than one dimension of conflict and taste.

While a truly general model cannot be unidimensional, we do not know what issues are likely to arise on a public problem nor what criteria citizens in fact use to evaluate them. Issues such as war, education, busing, unemployment, inflation, and civil rights play some role in determining people's choices in, e.g., presidential elections, but citizens also employ the criteria of partisan identification and candidate image—if only because the complexity of modern society guarantees the inability of even the most educated citizens to obtain a thorough knowledge and understanding of governmental policy. Unfortunately, empirical evidence fails to specify a citizen's cognitive and evaluative processes sufficiently; we do not even know the relative roles of issues and partisan identification in citizens' voting decisions.[2] Consequently, we consider two alternative formulations of a citizen's evaluations, each of which permits us to incorporate concerns such as partisan identification and the images of candidates into a spatial analysis. First, with a multidimensional model, we

[1]V. O. Key, *Public Opinion and American Democracy* (New York: Knopf, 1963), chap. 7; Philip E. Converse, "The Nature of Belief Systems in Mass Publics," in David E. Apter, ed., *Ideology and Discontent* (New York: Free Press, 1964), pp. 206–261; "The Problem of Party Distances in Models of Voting Change," in M. Kent Jennings and L. Harmon Zeigler, eds., *The Electoral Process* (Englewood Cliffs, N. J.: Prentice-Hall, Inc., 1966), pp. 175–207; Donald E. Stokes, "Spatial Models of Party Competition," *American Political Science Review*, vol. 57 (1963), pp. 368–377.

[2]The relative importance of issues as against image and partisan bias as causal determinants of voting behavior remains an open question. Analyses of cross-sectional survey data demonstrate the predictive dominance of partisan identification. V. O. Key concludes, however, in *The Responsible Electorate* (Cambridge, Mass.: Harvard University Press, 1966), that policy is critical for many voters in the sense that voters tend to migrate toward that party the image of which fits best with their preferences. Arthur S. Goldberg, moreover, demonstrates "that there is a rational component to party identification rooted in group norms" (p. 21) with the suggestion that these norms are not unrelated to issues in "Social Determinism and Rationality as Bases of Party Identification," *American Political Science Review*, vol. 63 (1969), pp. 5–25. Thus, even evidence from aggregated survey research tends to show that issues are important. If one were to look directly at the voting decision of individuals, it would probably turn out that issues are of overwhelming importance. In a pioneering study of a three-way senatorial race in New York, William C. Stratmann finds that it is possible to predict the voting decisions of college freshmen in 93 percent of the cases, wholly from their preference structures and the candidates' positions. For this group of voters at least, partisan attachment seems subordinate to issue preference. See William C. Stratmann, "A Concept of Voter Rationality" (Ph.D. dissertation, University of Rochester, 1971).

allow one of the dimensions to represent partisan identification, another to represent the attractiveness of the candidates' images, and still others to represent policy. The advantage of this formulation is that we are not required to assume that candidates, parties, and public officials manipulate only governmental policy to win elections. They can also manipulate their own appearance. One disadvantage of this approach, however, is that partisan identification and image may not be represented readily in spatial terms because they defy meaningful spatial conceptualization in the sense they cannot be spread out in a dimension. A second formulation, then, is to let the dimensions denote only those policies that are readily conceptualized spatially and then, by some means, to add biases to a citizen's preferences. The manner in which these biases are introduced is discussed in detail later. In the analysis that follows immediately we restrict the discussion to citizens who evaluate candidates by criteria which we are willing to represent in spatial terms.

Disregarding nonspatial considerations, then, we seek a conceptualization of a citizen's ideal candidate. Assuming that such a candidate consists of a position on each of many dimensions, we represent a position by a number, x, on the scale identified with each dimension. The symbol x_i, then, indicates the position that a citizen most prefers with respect to the dimension i. The citizen's preferred positions for all n dimensions can be denoted by a vector:[3]

$$x = \begin{Bmatrix} x_1 \\ x_2 \\ \cdot \\ \cdot \\ \cdot \\ x_n \end{Bmatrix} \qquad (11.1)$$

The positions that a citizen prefers, however, are only a partial identification of the variables relevant for describing his calculus of voting. The act of voting implies a choice among candidates; consequently, a representation of the alternative candidates is also required. And, since these choices involve a comparison between the citizen's preferred positions and each candidate, the representation of the candidates must be similar in form to expression (11.1). That is, since we characterize the citizen's preferences as a vector and since a citizen's choice involves a comparison between these preferences and position he perceives for each candidate, we must also characterize each candidate's positions as a vector. Thus, the vector

$$\theta_j = \begin{Bmatrix} \theta_{j1} \\ \theta_{j2} \\ \cdot \\ \cdot \\ \theta_{jn} \end{Bmatrix} \qquad (11.2)$$

[3]This approach is not sensitive to the number of relevant dimensions or to their labels, but every element of x must be assigned some value. That is, to represent a citizen's calculus, we assume that citizens act as if they estimated a preferred position for every dimension.

denotes the citizen's estimate of candidate j's position on each dimension. Although we represent the voter's perception of the positions of each candidate as a vector, we cannot assume that we know how citizens form estimates of θ_j. Downs offers several suggestions, such as that they estimate a candidate's position on the basis of past performance or perhaps on the previous reliability of his utterances. But, like Downs, we cannot specify which suggestion is more satisfactory. Again the insufficiency of existing psychological theory must be recognized: the cognitive and evaluative processes of voters are not sufficiently understood to permit us to identify the psychological mechanisms by which citizens form estimates of θ_j.

Even though the behavioral questions pertaining to θ_j remain unanswered, the analysis can proceed only if we specify precisely some mathematical properties of this vector. So we assume that the citizen behaves as if he estimated a preferred position for each candidate on every dimension. A second and related assumption is that θ_j is not stochastic, which is to say that the citizen knows precisely the positions of the candidate. Clearly, such a state of perfect information is not typical of reality, and so in a later section we weaken this assumption and consider strategies in which the candidates can vary the degree of certainty of their positions.

CITIZENS' EVALUATION OF CANDIDATES

The vectors x and θ_j summarize a citizen's preferences, the alternatives presented to him, and the possible outcomes. The citizen's alternatives are: vote for candidate 1, vote for candidate 2, and abstain. The outcomes are: candidate 1 wins, in which case the social choice is the vector θ_1, and candidate 2 wins, in which case the social choice is the vector θ_2 (ties can be disregarded if we assume that they are broken with the toss of a fair coin). To ascertain a citizen's choice, however, we must know at least his evaluation of these outcomes. So we denote the utility a citizen associates with θ_j, given that he most prefers x, by $U(x, \theta_j)$.

We do not know how citizens construct such utility functions, but we can offer a somewhat abstract interpretation of $U(x, \theta_j)$ in terms of the concept of regulation. Suppose that in the market, citizens seek to maximize their utility by trading goods $y_1, y_2, \ldots$, subject to their budget constraints. For even the most abstract world, however, it is clear that individual budget constraints and market prices are both determined to a significant extent by the activities of government, even by such simple activities as the imposition of taxes. Similarly, the enjoyment a person derives from consuming a market good is, typically, in part a function of governmental activity. A person can buy a car; but the utility he associates with the car is partly a function of the quality of the roads on which he drives. Private choices in markets are questions of action, while the collective choice of a particular θ_j is a question of regulation; and θ_j

partly determines a person's private choices, as well as the utility he associates with these choices. We can interpret $U(x, \theta_j)$, then, as the utility a citizen derives from his private choices, given that θ_j is the vector denoting the policies of the government and x is the vector of policies that allows the citizen the greatest satisfaction from private choices.

Of course, this interpretation is designed simply to demonstrate the possibility of linking theoretically models of market choice and models of collective choice proceed. It is suggestive only. But even if we accept such a suggestion (or perhaps some other suggestion) we must know a great deal more about $U(x, \theta_j)$ in order to proceed. In earlier chapters, we review introductory theoretical concepts such as participation, the paradox of voting, and solutions with only the basic axioms of utility theory. At this point, however, we seek to analyze a more specific political process—elections. Hence, simply denoting utility symbolically is not sufficient; some specific mathematical properties for U must be assumed. Unfortunately, specification of these properties is difficult, not only because the set of mathematical expressions admissible on the basis of *a priori* judgments is infinite, but also because available empirical evidence about the way citizens behave in elections fails to restrict this set. A partial solution to this problem is afforded by deriving theorems when only a general rather than a specific mathematical form for U is assumed.

We restrict the set of admissible forms by requiring that they satisfy two intuitive properties. First, if $\theta_j = x$, the utility the citizen associates with candidate j's position should be at some maximum value, say λ, since the candidate's position and the citizen's preference are identical for all dimensions. Second, and consonant with this requirement, if $x \neq \theta_j$ (i.e., if at least one element, x_i, of x is not equal to the corresponding element, θ_{ji}, in θ_j), $U(x, \theta_j)$ should be less than λ. Summarizing,

$$\begin{array}{ll} \text{(i)} & \text{if } \theta_j = x, \text{ then } U(x, \theta_j) = \lambda; \\ \text{(ii)} & \text{if } \theta_j \neq x, \text{ then } U(x, \theta_j) < \lambda. \end{array} \qquad (11.3)$$

These properties are simple and reasonable. Unfortunately, many different mathematical formulations of U satisfy (11.3). We therefore adopt the procedure of suggesting several alternative restrictions on these formulations. The justification for this procedure is that, when a science is in its infancy as political science is, it is desirable to try a variety of assumptions to see which ones work out best.

ASSUMPTIONS ABOUT UTILITY: CONCAVITY

One assumption concerning U that satisfies both conditions in (11.3) is:

A1: $U(x, \theta_j)$ *is concave in* θ_j.

This assumption satisfies (11.3) by the fact that, when the peak of a concave curve is set at $\theta = x$, it is downward-sloping from x, so that all other points on the curve are below the maximum.

That A1 is satisfied means: (1) that for any issue, as we consider positions further to the left, say, of x, the citizen's utility declines, and (2) that utility decreases at an increasing rate as x and θ_j become more disparate. In Figure 11.1 we illustrate a unidimensional concave utility function for a given individually preferred position, x.[4]

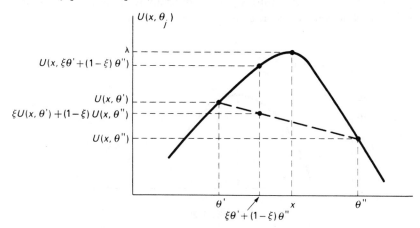

FIGURE 11.1
Concave utility function

ASSUMPTIONS ABOUT UTILITY: THE QUADRATIC FORM

To illustrate further the meaning of assumption A1 let us consider an important class of concave functions. This class—referred to as the inverse of the quadratic form—imposes some additional restrictions. Nevertheless, the quadratic form plays a central role in the development of spatial models, and if the restrictions implied by it are accepted, several general theorems can be derived.

---

[4]Recall from the discussion of concave payoff functions in Chapter 8 that a curve is strictly concave if, for any two points on it, a straight line connecting them lies wholly below the curve and intersects it only at the connected points. Algebraically, this fact can be expressed by requiring that, for any pair of points, $U(x, \theta')$ and $U(x, \theta'')$, on the curve (see Figure 11.1):

$$U(x, \zeta\theta' + (1 - \zeta)\theta'')' \geq \zeta U(x, \theta') + (1-\zeta)U(x, \theta'')$$

where $1 \leq \zeta \leq 0$. We can see the equivalence of the geometric and algebraic definitions by observing that, if the algebraic inequality were reversed, the line connecting the two points would be everywhere above the curve and the curve itself would be turned upside down, or convex.

We begin by considering the following expression which is illustrated in Figure 11.2:

$$\lambda - a(x_1 - \theta_{j1})^2. \tag{11.4}$$

The term $(x_1 - \theta_{j1})^2$ is the squared distance between the citizen's preferred position and candidate j's position on issue 1. Observe that if $a > 0$, $\lambda - a(x_1 - \theta_{j1})^2$ decreases as x_1 and θ_{j1} become more disparate, and that if $x_1 = \theta_{j1}$, $\lambda - a(x_1 - \theta_{j1})^2 = \lambda$. Thus, expression (11.3) satisfies the two conditions in (11.3) that utility functions must satisfy. Additionally, it is readily verified that (11.4) is concave, so that it satisfies assumption A1.

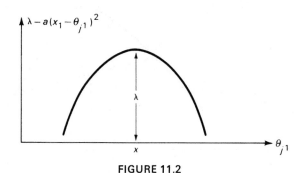

FIGURE 11.2

Expression (11.4) is not totally satisfactory, since it may be that the number of dimensions or issues, n, exceeds one. Suppose, therefore, that if n is two, we sum two such terms. Thus, another possible specification for the citizen's utility function is

$$\lambda - a_1(x_1 - \theta_{j1})^2 - a_2(x_2 - \theta_{j2})^2. \tag{11.5}$$

This expression satisfies the first condition in (11.3): if $x_k = \theta_{jk}$, for $k = 1, 2$, the expression reduces to λ. Thus, if (11.5) represents a citizen's utility function, his utility equals λ whenever $x = \theta_j$. This expression, moreover, satisfies the second necessary condition in (11.3): if a_1 and $a_2 > 0$, $U(x, \theta_j) < \lambda$ whenever $\theta_j \neq x$. Thus, another reasonable assumption about individual utility functions is that they are represented by expression (11.5). In Figure 11.3 we graph such a function.

If the election involves more than two issues we might continue adding the necessary terms to (11.5). But this expression ignores one possibility—that the utility a citizen associates with a candidate's position on one issue is a function of the candidate's positions on other issues. So we add to (11.5) the interaction term $2a_{12}(x_1 - \theta_{j1})(x_2 - \theta_{j2})$ to account for this possibility (where the "2" appearing before a_{12} is included as a convenience and does not affect the analysis since a_{12} is an arbitrary constant). Thus (11.5) becomes

$$\lambda - a_1(x_1 - \theta_{j1})^2 - a_2(x_2 - \theta_{j2})^2 - 2a_{12}(x_1 - \theta_{j1})(x_2 - \theta_{j2}). \tag{11.6}$$

If we graph expression (11.6) it resembles Figure 11.3—the graph of (11.5)—except that now it is rotated either to the right or left (depending on the magnitudes of a_1, a_2, and a_{12}).

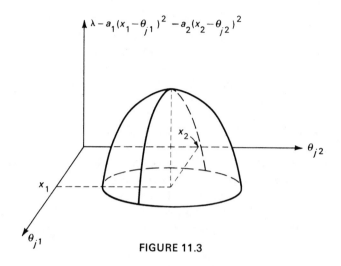

FIGURE 11.3

For $n > 2$, expression (11.6) is easily generalized to (letting $a_{mk} = a_{km}$)

$$\lambda - \sum_{m=1}^{n} \sum_{k=1}^{n} a_{mk}(x_m - \theta_{jm})(x_k - \theta_{jk}) \qquad (11.7)$$

which is frequently written as $\lambda - \| x - \theta_j \|_A^2$. Thus, expression (11.7) represents the weighted sum (where the weights are the a_{mk}'s) of squared distances (the terms for which $k = m$) plus the interaction terms between each pair of dimensions ($k \neq m$). One admissible assumption about U then is that

A2: $U(x, \theta_j) = \lambda - \| x - \theta_j \|_A^2.$

To interpret more precisely now the weights in (11.7), we return to the case of $n = 2$—expression (11.6). If a_2 and a_{12} equal zero, we say that only issue 1 is salient for the citizen, and expression (11.6) reduces to (11.4). Consider a second example: assume that both dimensions are measured in terms of dollars spent on a program, so that θ_j reads "candidate j wishes to spend θ_{j1} dollars on the first program, and θ_{j2} dollars on the second program." Assume, furthermore, that there are two candidates, $j = 1, 2$, and that the candidates have the following perceived platforms:

$$\theta_1 = \begin{Bmatrix} \$1 \\ \$1 \end{Bmatrix}, \qquad \theta_2 = \begin{Bmatrix} \$3 \\ 0 \end{Bmatrix},$$

and that the citizen prefers spending no money, i.e.,

$$x = \begin{Bmatrix} 0 \\ 0 \end{Bmatrix}.$$

Substituting these vectors into (11.5) [or, equivalently, into (11.6), since to simplify the example we let $a_{12} = 0$],

$$U(x, \theta_1) = \lambda - a_1(0 - 1)^2 - a_2(0 - 1)^2 = \lambda - a_1 - a_2,$$

$$U(x, \theta_2) = \lambda - a_1(0 - 3)^2 - a_2(0 - 0)^2 = \lambda - 9a_1.$$

Although the first candidate proposes to spend \$2 and the second candidate proposes to spend \$3, it may still be possible that the utilities associated with both candidates are identical if $a_1 + a_2 = 9a_1$, or, equivalently, if $a_2 = 8a_1$. Thus, because of the unequal weighting of the issues, the utilities a citizen associates with the two candidates' positions can be equal even though the candidates adopt dissimilar programs.

With this simple example in mind, one might be tempted to conclude that whenever $a_k < a_m$, issue k is "more salient" than issue. m. Unfortunately, this inference is not generally true. In the example just set forth the scales of both dimensions are represented by a common measure, dollars, whereas, in general, campaign issues have no common scale for measurement. The units for each dimension are wholly arbitrary, and this fact creates some difficulty. If, in the previous example, the second dimension is measured in cents, then

$$\theta_1 = \begin{Bmatrix} \$1 \\ 100¢ \end{Bmatrix} \quad \text{and} \quad \theta_2 = \begin{Bmatrix} \$3 \\ 0 \end{Bmatrix}$$

and the necessary condition for equality of utility becomes $a_2 = 0.0008a_1$. Thus, when both dimensions are measured in dollars, equality of utility requires that $a_2 > a_1$, but when the second dimension is measured in cents, equality requires that $a_2 < a_1$.

This example reveals an important fact about the a's—their relative magnitudes are dependent on the units of measurement that are applied to each dimension. Unfortunately we do not know much about the a's and the influences on them. We do not know the scales that measure all conceivable dimensions, nor do we know the relative importance citizens attach to each dimension, nor the prior identification of salient issues—and all of these unknowns affect the values of the a's. Consequently, to avoid the criticism that it is difficult, if not impossible, to estimate these weights in any real campaign, no proof of a theorem should require knowing the values of the weights. In general, it seems desirable to limit ourselves to theorems that are insensitive to the magnitudes of the a's.

ASSUMPTIONS ABOUT UTILITY: QUASI-CONCAVITY

If we let U be the inverse of the quadratic form instead of simply assuming that U is concave, however, we must recognize that the assumption implies an important restriction on utility functions. Specifically, if we adopt A2, then U is symmetric. Thus, a citizen's preferences cannot be skewed either to the right or to the left; he cannot prefer "moderate" positions first and, say, "liberal" positions second and "conservative" positions last. If he prefers moderate positions, then he must be indifferent between conservative and liberal positions.[5] While it might be reasonable to assume that utility functions are symmetric, the assumption of concavity is more difficult to accept. There is, of course, some rationale for assuming that utility functions are concave, other than to satisfy one's curiosity about the implications of A1 and A2. Concavity is a means for representing the utility functions of citizens who are concerned about and discriminate among all admissible policies. It is quite possible, however, that citizens are not invariably concerned and are not always able to discriminate. Especially it is possible that the further θ_j gets from x, the more the alternative policies become a blur.

Assumptions A1 and A2 imply marginally decreasing utility as x and θ_j become more disparate. Indeed, the further θ_j gets from x, the more swiftly U decreases. That is, A1 and A2 require that the slowest rate of decrease in U occurs when θ_j is near x and that, as the distance between θ_j and x increases, this rate increases. It may be, however, that the rate of change in utility is also slow when θ_j is distant from x. This might happen when the citizen becomes increasingly indifferent among policies that are far from x. The utility function of such a citizen could be represented by the curve drawn in Figure 11.4.

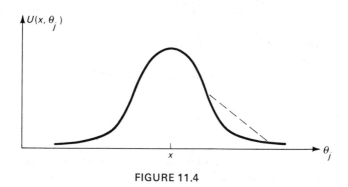

FIGURE 11.4

We can provide for such possibilities and still retain a sufficiently structured model by assuming that

A3: $U(x, \theta_j) = \phi(\lambda - \| x - \theta_j \|_A^2)$

where ϕ is any continuous monotonically increasing function of its argument, in this case, expression (11.7). More conveniently, we can summarize A3 by saying that U is *quasi-concave*. To explain the notion of quasi-concavity

[5]We refer to this situation as *radial* symmetry, i.e., $U(0, \theta_j) = U(0, -\theta_j)$.

and thus to draw out the implications of A3, we point out that the curve illustrated in Figure 11.4 is not *concave,* since a line connecting two points on it (the dotted line in this figure) can lie wholly above the curve. Nevertheless, this curve does exhibit one general characteristic: it is always decreasing (has a negative slope) everywhere to the right of x and is increasing (has a positive slope) everywhere to the left of x. Hence we say this curve is *quasi-concave.* For more than one dimension, the description of quasi-concavity is more complex, and so we relegate a formal definition to a footnote.[6] Instead, we present in Figure 11.5 a utility function in two dimensions that satisfies A3.

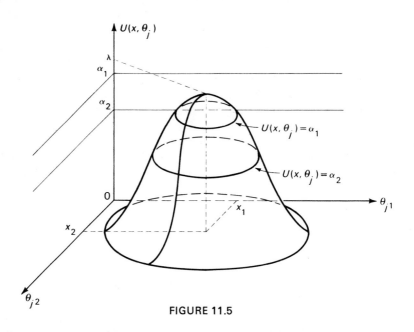

FIGURE 11.5

With this illustration we can demonstrate graphically the meaning of quasi-concavity in this special case in such a way that the general meaning of A3 is also suggested. First, suppose we pass a plane parallel to the θ_{j1} and θ_{j2} axes which intersects the $U(x, \theta_j)$ axis at α_1 (see Figure 11.5). This plane also intersects the utility function, and the curve which constitutes this intersection is called an *indifference contour* [represented in Figure 11.5 by the elliptical

---

[6]To define quasi-concavity, we set $U(x, \theta_j)$ to equal a constant, say α, and we assume that x is fixed. Next we define the set S_α as all values of θ_j that satisfy $U(x, \theta_j) \geq \alpha$. That is,

$$S_\alpha = \{\theta_j : U(x, \theta_j) \geq \alpha\}.$$

Suppose that S_α is a convex set for all possible values of α (i.e., for all α between 0 and λ). Consider two specific values of α, say α_1 and α_2 such that $\alpha_1 > \alpha_2$, and construct the sets S_{α_1} and S_{α_2}. If S_{α_1} is totally contained in S_{α_2} (written $S_{\alpha_2} \subset S_{\alpha_2}$) and if this is true for all α_1 and α_2, provided only that $\alpha_1 > \alpha_2$, then the utility function $U(x, \theta_j)$ is said to be quasi-concave.

curve $U(x, \theta_j) = \alpha_1$]. This curve is similar to those found on topographical maps, except that now it represents points of constant utility instead of points of constant altitude. If U satisfies A3, the indifference contour is an ellipse, and, for a value of α, say α_2, which is smaller than α_1, there is a larger elliptical indifference contour which circumscribes the contour for $U(x, \theta_j) = \alpha_1$. By passing many planes through U, we obtain a set of indifference contours. If a set of these contours is projected onto the $(\theta_{j1}, \theta_{j2})$ plane and if U satisfies A3, we obtain a set of ellipses which are concentric about x and which all possess the same major and minor axes.[7] In Figure 11.6 we illustrate such a set of contours.

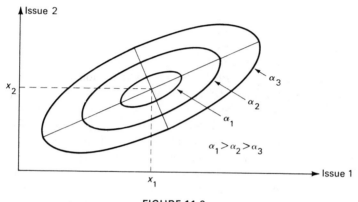

FIGURE 11.6

A COMPARISON OF ASSUMPTIONS ABOUT UTILITY

Reviewing now the several alternative assumptions about a citizen's utility function, we consider essentially two restrictions on this function: concavity and symmetry. The three assumptions about the form of U and their relationship to these two restrictions are summarized in Table 11.1 (where a check means that the assumption implies the restriction). Assumption A2 is clearly stronger than either A1 and A3, and if a theorem is proved with A1 or A3, this theorem holds also for A2—but the converse is not true.

One additional consideration, however, makes the application of A1 appear less restrictive than either A2 or A3. In the theorems we review later, we do not require with A1 that all citizens' utility functions be identical in shape. While all are expected to be concave, their declivity and their skewness may be quite different. But if either A2 or A3 is used, then we also require that, while citizens may prefer different policies, the functional forms of their utility functions are identical. This is equivalent to requiring that all citizens weight

[7]Assumption A2 also implies this statement.

TABLE 11.1

RESTRICTION

		SYMMETRY	CONCAVITY
	A1		✓
ASSUMPTIONS	A2	✓	✓
	A3	✓	

the issues in an identical fashion (i.e., all citizens share a common matrix of the weights a_{mk}). Consider, for example, the issue of school desegregation. The application of either assumption A2 or A3 allows some citizens to desire segregated schools and other citizens integrated ones. The requirement that the weights be common to all citizens implies, however, that everyone assigns the same degree of relative importance to the issue of schools vis-à-vis, say, foreign policy. Thus the model with A2 and A3 does not allow some citizens to care, while others do not care whether or not schools are integrated.[8]

To interpret the meaning of this restriction on weights, we portray it for the case of two issues in Figure 11.7. Recall that if $n = 2$ and if either A2 or A3 is assumed, a person's indifference contours are a set of ellipses. The restriction of common weights requires that the rotation of the major and the minor axes of the elliptical contours of each citizen's utility function are the same for all citizens. This common orientation for three citizens is illustrated in Figure 11.7.

An equivalent way of portraying this restriction is to assume that distance in a coordinate system is a measure of utility loss. Thus the further away a position is from a citizen's idea, the greater the loss the citizen associates with it. With this interpretation, if two citizens exhibit different patterns of weighting the issues, we cannot arrange the alternatives in the coordinate space in the same way for both citizens. Thus, two such citizens might locate the policies A, B, C, D, and E as in Figure 11.8

[8]This is clearly a highly restrictive assumption but one relaxation of it is generally permitted. We can assume that there exists some average level of concern for each issue, and if individual variations are permitted, these variations are represented as deviations from this average. This relaxation provides a tractable assumption if the patterns of individual variations in level of relative concern do not correlate with preference. Note that this relaxation does not conflict with the proposition that a citizen is more likely to react intensely about an issue if he prefers an extreme rather than a moderate position. If the proposition is correct, then relatively large and positive deviations from average concern are associated with citizens who prefer either extreme on an issue; so there may be a zero correlation, although intensity and preference are not really independent. On this relaxation see Otto A. Davis and Melvin J. Hinich, "Some Results Related to a Mathematical Model of Policy Formation in a Democratic Society," in J. Bernd, ed., *Mathematical Applications in Political Science*, vol. 3 (Charlottesville: University Press of Virginia, 1967), and, "On the Power and Importance of the Mean Preference in a Mathematical Model of Democratic Choice," *Public Choice*, vol. 5 (1968), pp. 59–72.

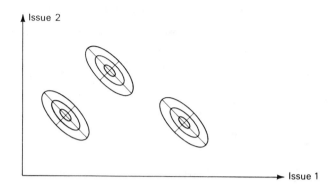

FIGURE 11.7

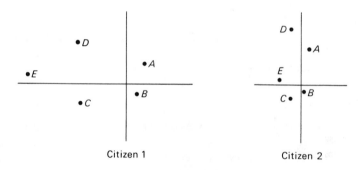

FIGURE 11.8

Such possibilities are considered by Converse and Stokes.[9] On the basis of empirical evidence in France and Finland, Converse concludes that " . . . there are bothersome differences among voters in the shapes of party spaces [issue coordinate systems] . . . and consequently in the patterns of distances perceived to exist."[10] Similarly, Stokes suggests that "we may . . . have as many perceived spaces as there are perceiving actors."[11]

Clearly, then, the assumption of a common pattern of weighting the issues is an important restriction, in which case we must reformulate Table 11.1 so that it indicates the presence of this restriction in the *application* of assumptions A2 and A3. Thus, we get Table 11.2.

[9]Converse, "The Nature of Belief Systems in Mass Publics"; Stokes, "Spatial Models of Party Competition."

[10]*Op. cit.*, p. 202.

[11]*Op. cit.*, p. 375.

TABLE 11.2

RESTRICTION

		SYMMETRY	CONCAVITY	COMMON PATTERN OF WEIGHTS
	A1		✓	
ASSUMPTIONS	A2	✓	✓	✓
	A3	✓		✓

The assumptions listed in Table 11.2 constitute only a description of preference and candidate choice, however, and as such they describe but the first stage of the citizen's two-stage sequential decision process. The second stage is the choice between voting for a candidate or abstaining, to the analysis of which choice we now turn.

THE CITIZEN'S CALCULUS OF PARTICIPATION

We begin by assuming that if $U(x, \theta_i) < U(x, \theta_j)$, the citizen never votes for candidate i.[12] One calculus that employs this assumption is

B1: *All citizens vote.*

For an electorate in which as many as 83 percent of all eligible citizens vote (e.g., the 1960 presidential election), and in which most nonvoting can be attributed to illness or to registration systems, this assumption is not unduly restrictive.[13] Electoral outcomes, however, are determined frequently by variations in turnout. Consequently, spatial analysis requires a theory about why people decide to vote or not to vote as well as a theory about how people choose among candidates. In Chapter 3 we posit that the decision to vote involves a comparison of the relative expected utility from voting and adstaining. Only if the expected utility of voting is greater than that of abstaining is it rational to vote. The analysis of this calculation reveals that for two-candidate contests the differential expected utility of voting, R, equals

[12]We are now considering elections between two candidates; for such elections it is readily shown that, if citizens choose deterministically, they either abstain or vote for their most preferred candidate (see note 31, Chapter 12). Hence, the intent of this assumption is simply to postpone consideration of a calculus of voting that allows probabilistic choice between candidates. In effect this assumption also limits consideration to the case of two candidates because it prohibits the voter from voting on the basis of candidates' chances of winning—one of the main strategies in a three or more candidate election. That is, $U(x, \theta_i) < U(x, \theta_j)$ does not preclude voting for i if, for example, $U(x, \theta_k) < U(x, \theta_i)$ and i is more likely than j to beat k.

[13]William G. Andrews, "American Voting Participation," *The Western Political Quarterly*, vol. 19 (1966), pp. 639–652.

$$R = PB + D - C, \qquad (11.8)$$

where

P = the citizen's subjectively estimated probability that his vote materially affects the outcome,

B = the absolute value of the citizen's subjective differential utility between the candidates,

D = the private utility a citizen derives from participating in the electoral process (U^+),

C = the cost of voting (U^-).

In Chapter 3 we analyze this equation to show that it applies to participation in general and that it must include the PB term. Now we use this equation to indicate the relevant factors in a citizen's decision to vote and to justify the relationships we posit between a citizen's decision and the candidates' strategies.

Indifference

For expression (11.8) the definition of B indicates that it is dependent on the candidates' strategies. We can represent this dependence by the variables employed in a spatial model. Specifically, from the definitions of B and $U(x, \theta_j)$,

$$B = |U(x, \theta_1) - U(x, \theta_2)|,$$

where $|\quad|$ means "absolute value of." Thus, B (and therefore R) decreases as the utilities associated with both candidates become less disparate. Typically this means that the more similar the candidates are, the less benefit the voter gets from voting for one of them. Additionally, if we assume that factors other than P, B, D, and C have only random effects on a citizen's expected utility calculation, then the citizen's probability of voting decreases as the difference, B, between the utilities which he associates with the candidates become less distinct. Terming this relationship between voting and the candidates' strategies "abstention because of indifference," we can assume that

B2: *Citizens abstain because of indifference.*

One obvious kind of indifference, which probably occurs only rarely, is that in which the citizen is absolutely indifferent between the candidates on every issue, even though the candidates may not be identical. Another obvious and related kind is that in which the candidates are perceived as identical on every issue. More commonly, the indifference of assumption B2 subsumes what is commonly referred to as cross-pressures.[14] For example, if the election

---

[14]The notion of abstention by reason of indifference or cross-pressures was first introduced by Paul F. Lazarsfeld, Bernard Berelson, and Hazel Gaudet, *The People's Choice* (New York: Columbia University Press, 1948), and Berelson, Lazarsfeld, and William N. McPhee, *Voting*

consists of two issues and if the citizen prefers candidate 1 on the first issue and candidate 2 on the second issue, then, with appropriate assumption about the relative saliency of each issue, we have $U(x, \theta_1) = U(x, \theta_2)$. Thereby B is made to equal zero and the citizen's probability of voting is reduced.

Alienation

Pool, Abelson, and Popkin suggest, however, that the candidates' strategies affect participation by other means:

> Non-voting is not necessarily a function of cross-pressure.... There are apparently some as yet undefined intervening variables.... We can say with confidence that the simple theory that postulates non-voting as the outcome of cross-pressure can no longer be maintained.[15]

Close scrutiny of the terms in equation (11.8) suggests the origin of these intervening variables. Specifically, assumption B2 ignores the possible effects the candidates' strategies might have on D; consequently we need an assumption that relates the candidates' strategies to D. Of course, the basic size of D is probably determined largely by long-term socialization (e.g., learning or long-term reinforcement by often-repeated voting and often-repeated non-voting). There are probably many potential short-term effects on D, however, that do arise from candidates' strategies. We can include them in a spatial analysis by assuming that D decreases as the utility the citizen associates with his *most preferred candidate* decreases. Stated differently, if one's most preferred candidate supports policies very different from what one would like, then the private incentive to vote (D) diminishes. We illustrate this assumption for the case of a single dimension in Figure 11.9, in which the vertical axis measures the citizen's probability of voting for candidate 1 and the horizontal axis measures x.[16]

This hypothesis appears to capture the essential notion behind the concept of alienation, which has been empirically related closely to abstention. V. O. Key, for example, observes that "many persons with opinions of high intensity (i.e., who are not indifferent or cross-pressured) are not high participators, they may not even vote."[17] (For example, with some justification in the spring

---

(Chicago: University of Chicago Press, 1954), where it was applied to, e.g., rural Catholics, who because of their Catholicism preferred Democrats and because of their rural life preferred Republicans and who, out of the indecisiveness thus induced, exhibited below-average turnout.

[15] Ithiel de Sola Pool, Robert P. Abelson, and Samuel L. Popkin, *Candidates, Issues and Strategies* (Cambridge, Mass.: M. I. T. Press, 1964), p. 76.

[16] Note that, for $x > (\theta_1 + \theta_2)/2$, the probability of voting for candidate 1 equals zero. This illustration, then, supposes that $U(x, \theta_i)$ is symmetric. If $U(x, \theta_i)$ is symmetric, and if $x > (\theta_1 + \theta_2)/2$, then, $U(x, \theta_1) < U(x, \theta_2)$. A zero probability of voting for candidate 1, then, follows from our present assumption that citizens never vote for a candidate unless he is preferred in spatial terms to all other candidates.

[17] *Public Opinion and American Democracy* (New York: Knopf, 1963), p. 231.

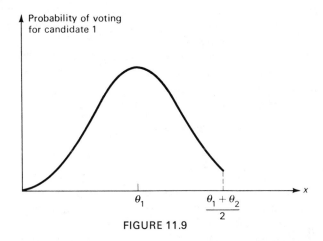

FIGURE 11.9

of 1964, Goldwater argued for his candidacy with the assertion that many persons on the far right, who had never previously voted, would vote for him. Unfortunately for Goldwater there were not as many such people as he believed.) Key's explanation of the nonvoting by the politically intense suggests our hypothesis: "pockets of people with intense opinions are evidently dominated by such feelings of futility and ineffectiveness that they do not exert themselves politically and often fail to vote."[18] If the citizen believes, therefore, that the political system is unresponsive to his demands, that candidates neither advocate nor are likely to adopt satisfactory policies, then this "frustration . . . may lead to demoralization and loss of faith in the political process."[19] Furthermore, this frustration, leading to a reduction in D, is not simply a function of socialization factors. While Levin's alienated voter is the product of long-term discontent and continued neglect, evidence indicates that alienation also can be attributed to the shorter-term strategic maneuvers of the parties.[20] Torgersen, for example, observes that the Conservative party of Norway has, since the war, attempted to attract the increasing numbers of white-collar workers by stressing reformist and welfare-state policies.[21] This change of strategy has meant a certain alienation from the business elements in the party, and a very hostile attitude between 'Libertus,' . . . and the Conservative headquarters."[22] Similarly, in the United States in 1964, the shift in campaign contributions

[18]*Ibid.*, p. 232.

[19]Angus Campbell, "The Passive Citizen," *Acta Sociologica*, vol. 6 (1962), pp. 9–21.

[20]Murray B. Levin, *The Alienated Voter* (New York: Holt, Rinehart and Winston, 1960).

[21]Ulf Torgersen, "The Trend Towards Political Consensus: The Case of Norway," *Acta Sociologica*, vol. 6 (1962), pp. 159–172. For a confirmation of the existence of these short-term alienation effects in France see Howard Rosenthal and S. Sen, "Electoral Participation in the French Fifth Republic: The FY Vote," *American Political Science Review* (forthcoming).

[22]*Ibid.*, p. 161.

and the sudden increase in contributors who had never previously participated financially in a campaign probably reflected a short-term change in D because Goldwater came closer to satisfying previously alienated rightist voters than had other Republican candidates.

Thus, one reasonable assumption about abstentions is that D (and, therefore, a citizen's probability of voting) decreases as the utility associated with the preferred candidate decreases. Terming this effect "alienation," we can employ the following assumption in a spatial analysis:

B3: *Citizens abstain because of alienation.*[23]

Alienation and Indifference Combined

One additional assumption about nonvoting that is suggested by B2 and B3 is that citizens abstain because of both indifference and alienation. Unfortunately, the attempt to combine rigorously these two hypotheses directly has not yet led to any tractable model.[24] Instead, a slightly different approach can be taken. In formulating assumptions B1, B2, and B3, we translate some empirical hypotheses about individual choice directly into mathematical terms —using a theoretical calculus [expression (11.8)] to justify the assumptions. Then, as we show in the next chapter, theorems about the strategies candidates adopt can be deduced directly from these assumptions. An alternative approach to the development of theory, however, is possible. Instead of deducing a theorem, we begin with one. Typically, we find in some other discipline a theorem that, because of its generality, we can translate to suit the problem at hand. In this case the problem is the identification of optimal strategies for candidates. Together with this translation we must also provide assumptions—in this case assumptions about individual choice—which are reasonable in the sense that they are consistent with acceptable behavioral heuristics and which satisfy the conditions of the theorem. Thus, instead of beginning with a precise assumption about individual choice such as B1, B2, or B3, we begin with a theorem and then seek to satisfy the conditions of this theorem with the most general and plausible assumptions possible.

In the next chapter we translate spatial analysis into game-theoretic terms, and we use several theorems from the theory of games to prove some results about candidates' optimal strategies. Before we can do this, however, we must present the conditions that permit the use of such theorems, and these conditions

---

[23]Alienation appears to be the primary cause of nonvoting considered by Anthony Downs, *An Economic Theory of Democracy.* Gerald Garvey ["The Theory of Party Equilibrium," *American Political Science Review*, vol. 60 (1966), pp. 29–38] seeks to consider both B2 and B3 simultaneously.

[24]The exception to this observation is Richard McKelvey, "Some Extensions and Modifications of a Spatial Model of Party Competition" (Unpublished Ph. D. dissertation, University of Rochester, 1972). Unfortunately, those results pertaining to the combination of B2 and B3 came to our attention too late to be incorporated in this text.

turn out to be a kind of combination of B2 and B3. To show this, we first let $h^1[U(x, \theta_1), U(x, \theta_2)]$ denote the probability that a citizen votes for candidate 1 if candidate 1 is at θ_1, if candidate 2 is at θ_2, and if the citizens most preferred position is x. Similarly, let $h^2[U(x, \theta_2), U(x, \theta_1)]$ denote this citizen's probability of voting for candidate 2. The conditions that render some of the theorems of game theory relevant to spatial analysis are assumptions about the relationship of h^1 and h^2 to $U(x, \theta_1)$ and $U(x, \theta_2)$. These conditions are selected because they permit us to state relationships that conform to the two behavioral heuristics we present in Chapter 3, namely:

(a)   the probability that a citizen votes for a candidate increases as the utility he associates with this candidate's strategy increases;

(b)   the probability that a citizen votes for a candidate decreases or at best remains constant as the utility he associates with the opponent's strategy increases.

Our first condition is simply a restatement of heuristic (a):

(i) h^1 increases as $U(x, \theta_1)$ increases and h^2 increases as $U(x, \theta_2)$ increases,

whereas the second condition is a restatement of (b):

(ii) h^1 decreases or remains unchanged as $U(x, \theta_2)$ increases, and h^2 decreases or remains unchanged as $U(x, \theta_2)$ increases.

Finally, we add the following assumption:

(iii) h^1 is concave in $U(x, \theta_1)$ and convex in $U(x, \theta_2)$, and h^2 is concave in $U(x, \theta_2)$ and convex in $U(x, \theta_1)$.[25]

The implications of these three conditions taken together are not intuitively obvious. It can be shown, however, that they define a class of admissible formulations of the citizen's calculus of voting which are similar to but not identical with B2 and B3. To see this, let us consider three admissible formulations, the first of which corresponds approximately to assumption B2:

$$h^1 = a[U(x, \theta_1)],$$
$$h^2 = a[U(x, \theta_2)],$$
(11.9)

where a is a positive constant. (Formulation (11.9) does not, of course, automatically satisfy (iii). Assumption (iii) is satisfied if $U(x, \theta_j)$ is concave in θ_j. Thus, we use this formulation, as well as those that follow, only with assumption A1 and A2). Like B3, a citizen's probability of voting for his prefer-

---

[25]For a similar formulation of a citizen's calculus that does not impose convexity or concavity but that imposes *separability* [i.e., $h^1 - h^2$, the citizen's bias for candidate 1, can be written as $f(\theta_1) - f(\theta_2)$], see Melvin J. Hinich and Peter C. Ordeshook, "Transitive Social Preference and Majority Rule Equilibrium with Separable Probabilistic Choice Functions" (forthcoming).

red candidate, say θ_1, as well as his overall probability of voting, $h^1 + h^2$, increases as the utility the citizen associates with his preferred candidate's strategy, $U(x, \theta_1)$ increases. Unlike B3, however, $h^1 + h^2$ increases as the utility of the less preferred candidate's strategy increases. This feature of (11.9) is a consequence of the fact, that while $U(x, \theta_2) < U(x, \theta_1)$—$\theta_1$ is preferred to θ_2—the citizen retains a positive probability of voting for θ_2. We illustrate (11.9) in Figure 11.10 so that it can be compared with Figure 11.9—the figure that corresponds to assumption B3.

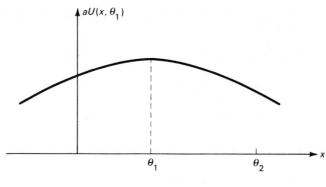

FIGURE 11.10

We cannot express a preference for either the formulation of alienation in expression (11.9) or the formulation represented by B3 without some empirical evidence. Unfortunately, this evidence is not now available. It is plausible, moreover, that neither formulation is right or wrong, but rather that they are more or less applicable in varying situations. Assumption B3 seems appropriate for studying elections in which measurement is precise and in which only known spatial considerations are relevant or in which the known spatial considerations are highly salient. This is because B3 supposes that citizens vote only for the most preferred candidates and that preference is totally determined by spatial location. Expression (11.9), on the other hand, may be more applicable for analyzing elections in which nonspatial considerations affect citizen's choices, or where our measurement of spatial considerations is imprecise. Thus, under (11.9) a citizen can vote for candidate 2 although, spatially, he prefers θ_1 to θ_2.

To see one immediate application of the distinction between B2 and (11.9) recall our earlier statement that factors such as partisan identification and candidate image can be incorporated into a spatial model in two ways. The first way is to assume that such factors can each be represented by a dimension, in which case the spatial values of x, θ_1, and θ_2 are sufficient to determine a citizen's preference for θ_1 or θ_2. This approach is implied by assumption

B3 (as well as B1 and B2), since citizens never vote for a candidate that is not preferred spatially. A second way to incorporate factors such as partisan identification, however, is to assume that they are not spatial dimensions, that citizens' preferences are determined by these factors as well as by spatial values, and that these factors have a random component. Hence, as in (11.9), a citizen has a nonzero probability of voting for candidate 2 although $U(x, \theta_1)$ $> U(x, \theta_2)$—although the utility associated with candidate 1's spatial position is greater than the utility associated with candidate 2's spatial position —because the positive aspects of the second candidate's image, say, might outweigh an inferior spatial position.

The approach one selects—whether one chooses a model embodying B3 or one embodying (11.9)—is, of course, a function of methodological convenience and, in the absence of any compelling empirical justifications, of the power of the theorems we can prove. To further illustrate, however, the flexibility of (i)–(iii) we present a second admissible formulation that corresponds closely to abstention because of indifference, assumption B2:

$$h^1 = \begin{cases} b[U(x, \theta_1) - U(x, \theta_2)] & \text{if } U(x, \theta_1) \geq U(x, \theta_2), \\ 0 & \text{otherwise}; \end{cases}$$

$$h^2 = \begin{cases} b[U(x, \theta_2) - U(x, \theta_1)] & \text{if } U(x, \theta_2) \geq U(x, \theta_1), \\ 0 & \text{otherwise}; \end{cases} \qquad (11.10)$$

where b is a positive constant.[26] The citizen's overall probability of voting, then, is either h^1 or h^2, depending on which candidate he prefers. Thus, as required by the indifference hypothesis, the citizen's probability of voting decreases as the difference between $U(x, \theta_1)$ and $U(x, \theta_2)$ decreases.

Out final example is the combination of (11.9) and (11.10):

$$h^1 = \begin{cases} \xi a U(x, \theta_1) + (1 - \xi)b[U(x, \theta_1) - U(x, \theta_2)] & \text{if } U(x, \theta_1) > U(x, \theta_2), \\ \xi a U(x, \theta_1) & \text{otherwise}; \end{cases}$$

$$h^2 = \begin{cases} \xi a U(x, \theta_2) + (1 - \xi)b[U(x, \theta_2) - U(x, \theta_1)] & \text{if } U(x, \theta_2) > U(x, \theta_1), \\ \xi a U(x, \theta_2) & \text{otherwise}; \end{cases}$$

$$(11.11)$$

where $\theta < \xi < 1$. Thus, by varying ξ between θ and 1, we can vary the relative importance of alienation and indifference. If ξ is close to θ, indifference predominates, and if ξ is close to 1, alienation predominates.

We could continue constructing admissible formulations of h^1 and h^2— perhaps by imagining some relationship between θ_1 and θ_2 and a citizen's

[26]This formulation requires that condition (i) be altered slightly to (i'): h^1 increases as $U(x, \theta_1)$ increases provided that θ_1 is preferred to θ_2, otherwise $h^1 = 0$, and h^2 increases as $U(x, \theta_2)$ increases, provided that θ_2 is preferred to θ_1, otherwise $h^2 = 0$. Either (i) or (i') can be used in the analysis of candidates that maximize plurality. If, however, candidates maximize votes, (i) must be used. For a more detailed discussion of (i') see Hinich, Ledyard, and Ordeshook, "A Theory of Electoral Equilibrium: A Spatial Analysis Based on the Theory of Games," *Journal of Politics* (1972).

calculus of voting unlike alienation or indifference, or perhaps by devising some alternative formulations for these two hypotheses. Keeping in mind, of course, that we are not somehow simply adding B2 and B3 algebraically, let us summarize all such formulations by the assumption:

B4: *Citizens abstain because of alienation or indifference.*

THE DISTRIBUTION OF PREFERENCES

Our review of assumptions about a citizen's decision is complete, but we cannot yet analyze an election. It is necessary also to make assumptions about the electorate as a whole and about the candidates. For one thing, we must find a more convenient summary of the preferences of citizens. We can obtain such a summary by using the fact that the vector represented by expression (11.1) is not simply a collection of numbers: it also defines a multidimensional coordinate system. Thus, the vector x, which represents a citizen's preference, identifies that citizen with some point in an n-dimensional coordinate system, where the citizen's preference on the ith issue is measured along the ith axis of the coordinate system.

Assuming now that the preferred positions of all citizens are ascertained, we calculate the probability that a citizen, selected randomly from the electorate, prefers on dimension x_i a particular position, say x_{i_0}, by counting citizens preferring x_{i_0} and dividing this number by the total number of citizens. When this calculation is performed for all particular positions, we plot a density of preferences, $f(x)$, that characterizes the population in the sense that it is a summary statement of the preferred positions of all citizens. Figure 11.11 is a unidimensional example of such a density function.[27]

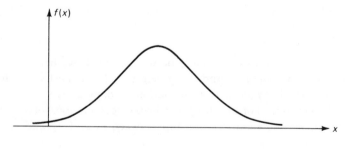

FIGURE 11.11

[27]Observe that Figure 11.11 represents $f(x)$ as a continuous density function rather than a discrete function. This representation follows from two assumptions: (1) that the electorate is large, so that a discrete distribution can be approximated by a continuous density; (2) that each dimension is continuous, which is to say that each element of x can assume an infinity of values.

Clearly, however, our ability to ascertain and then to order individual preferences along a set of dimensions common to all citizens—which is necessary to summarize preferences by a density—presupposes a great deal about the conceptualization and the measurement of attitudes. It is one thing to assume, as we have already done, that the elements of one citizen's vector of preferences, x, can be assigned numbers. But it is another and very much more difficult thing to suppose that all citizens' preferences can be assigned numbers simultaneously and meaningfully within a common multidimensional space. Nevertheless, this is exactly what we do assume, which is to say that we wave away all the hard and innumerable difficulties confronting researchers who study the real world. We recognize that it is not easy to ascertain the preferences of an electorate and that the theory about techniques such as multidimensional scaling is rudimentary. Model building would never occur, however, if we waited for the gathering of data to become wholly adequate; so we proceed with the bold assumption that $f(x)$ can be arrived at.

If it be granted, then, that the preferences of an electorate can be characterized by a density, we must in turn consider what assumption we can make about the form of these densities (other than to assume that they satisfy the usual set of probability assumptions). Surely, one admissible assumption is to assume nothing. That is, we can seek theorems which do not require any knowledge of the form of the electorate's density of preferences. The statements of these theorems can be interpreted as descriptions of general properties of electoral competition (given, of course, certain assumptions about citizens' decision rules). Hence, the simplest assumption about $f(x)$ is that

C1: $f(x)$ *is a density.*

More powerful theorems can be derived, however, if we consider specific forms of $f(x)$. One restriction on the form of $f(x)$ is the requirement of symmetry, which is to say that every citizen is balanced by some other citizen who prefers a diametrically opposed position.[28] Symmetry, therefore, conforms to situations in which, say, the preferences for and against some policy are equally balanced numerically.

A second type of restriction on $f(x)$ concerns the number of modes in the distribution of opinion. First, we can assume that $f(x)$ is a unimodal density,

---

This latter assumption apparently ignores Stokes' observation that many dimensions are discrete and that some are dichotomous—which Stokes, terms "valence issues." [Stokes, "Spatial Models of Party Competition."] Conceptually, however, discrete dimensions present no serious additional problems for spatial analysis. Most of our conclusions apply to discrete as well as continuous dimensions. Continuity is assumed so that we can apply the continuous calculus and because it is difficult to mix continuous and discrete dimensions in one model. For a discussion of a discrete vs. continuous conceptualization of spatial competition see Brian L. Meek, "The Formulation of Models of Party Competition," *British Journal of Political Science*, vol. 2, (1972), pp. 116–120.

[28]By symmetry we refer to *radial* symmetry. Thus, if the mean of $f(x)$ equals zero, and if $f(x)$ is radially symmetric, $f(x) = f(-x)$. The point of balance then is the multivariate median of $f(x)$.

i.e., that citizens' preferences tend to cluster about some common point. Thus, unimodal distributions, such as the one illustrated in Figure 11.11, describe situations in which there exists some degree of consensus among the electorate as to what policies are preferred.[29] An alternative assumption to unimodality is bimodality. We illustrate in Figure 11.12 a bimodal distribution, and it is clear from this illustration that such distributions are an important contrast to the unimodal case. Where unimodality indicates some minimal consensus, bimodal densities describe situations in which citizens' preferences are polarized on one or more issues.

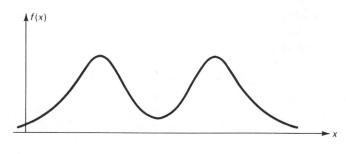

FIGURE 11.12

Combining the restrictions of symmetry and unimodality or bimodality, we have two alternative assumptions about the form of $f(x)$:[30]

C2: $f(x)$ is a symmetric unimodal density.

C3: $f(x)$ is a symmetric bimodal density.

[29]Our interpretation of consensus is at best imprecise since consensus should depend on the variance of $f(x)$ as well as the number of modes. On this point, see Robert Axelrod, *Conflict of Interest* (Chicago: Markham, 1970).

[30]These assumptions are not, of course, an exhaustive categorization of the possible features of $f(x)$. Using modality and symmetry as properties for categorization, we would have

I. nonsymmetric unimodal,
II. nonsymmetric bimodal,
III. nonsymmetric multimodal,
IV. symmetric unimodal,
V. symmetric bimodal,
VI. symmetric multimodal.

Not all these cases are convenient or useful, however, so we include all six of them in C1, we identify IV with C2 and V with C3, and we simply ignore I–III and VI as too complex for detailed analysis. We note, however, that some of the results reported in this chapter require only that $f(x)$ be symmetric (i.e., VI can be assumed), and we identify these cases as they occur. [Parenthetically, we note that sometimes even more restrictive assumptions are necessary; e.g., we must assume that $f(x)$ is the normal density function in addition to being unimodal and symmetric. In lieu of adding such restrictive detail to our discussion in Chapter 12, however, we simply refer the reader to the original sources of the theorems that we review.]

THE CANDIDATES

Assumption sets A, B, and C characterize our theoretical electorate. But social choices are the policy package advocated by a victorious candidate. Thus, we also require assumptions about candidates and the candidates' incentives in planning strategy.

We begin our description of candidates by recalling that we characterized candidate j by a vector, θ_j, where each element, θ_{ji}, of this vector is the citizen's estimate of the policy candidate j advocates on an issue i. For the present, we also assume that this vector is not stochastic—we postpone a discussion of uncertainty and risk. We do, however, introduce one additional assumption about θ_j: that all citizens make identical estimates of θ_j. Thus, we ignore such problems as cognitive balance, imperfect information, and the candidates' attempts to have different citizens believe different things about them. Our procedure is analogous to that of the literary critic who assumes that a sentence or a word means the same to all readers when in fact he knows it does not. His justification is that words have "dictionary meanings" on which all can agree. And this is our justification also. Of course, we recognize that citizens make "rational" decisions (i.e., decisions consistent with an observer's prejudices) by their failure to perceive the disadvantages of an already preferred candidate.[31] If, for example, a voter favors the passage of strong civil rights measures and his preferred candidate does not, he may, nevertheless, perceive this candidate as favoring such measures. The voter, moreover, may guard against disruptive information by erecting a perceptual screen to filter out dissonant messages. Party identification is known to bias citizens' perceptions of candidates' platforms, and highly salient issues often perform an equivalent function.

Such psychological possibilities reveal an additional assumption of spatial analysis: that the candidates have perfect spatial mobility. That is, there is no restriction on the spatial location, θ_j, that a candidate may choose for his platform. Later, we consider the consequences of spatial restrictions, but since we seek with the basic model to ascertain the strategies candidates prefer to adopt, we assume that candidates are free to adopt any position. Obviously, this assumption does not typically characterize the real world. The voters' perceptual distortion and their imperfect information, for example, often frustrate a candidate's campaign objectives. Thus, citizens in a secure Democratic constituency favoring liberal labor legislation may remain unconvinced that a Republican candidate is pro-labor—even though the Republican is in fact more pro-labor than the Democrat. In such a case the Republican is not

---

[31]See, for example, Donald E. Stokes, "Some Dynamic Elements of Contests for the Presidency," *American Political Science Review*, vol. 60 (1966), pp. 19–28; Berelson, Lazarsfeld, and McPhee, *Voting*, chap. 10; and Michael J. Shapiro, "Rational Political Man: A Synthesis of Economic and Social Psychological Perspectives," *American Political Science Review*, vol. 63 (1969), pp. 1106–1119.

free to adopt any position, simply because the voters' biases will not permit him to do so. Similarly, in a multidimensional world candidates often find it impossible to alter their positions on one issue without altering their positions on other issues.

With the assumption of perfect spatial mobility we ignore even more, however, than considerations about voters' perceptions. We are also led to ignore the institution of political parties—we associate θ_j with a candidate, not a whole party. We do this because we cannot treat parties as homogeneous entities which propose specific platforms. Rather, we treat party leaders and activists as one element of a candidate's environment. That is, as a candidate manipulates strategies to secure votes, we assume that he must also gauge these strategies to secure the support (e.g., endorsements, finances, and the like) of his party. As a consequence of the candidate's need to get the support of particular people (i.e., party leaders), his freedom to move about on all dimensions of an issue space is severely restricted because he must locate himself in a way that satisfies these particular people rather than the electorate as a whole. If the nominators' preferences are not representative of the whole electorate's preferences—and often they are not—then the nominators may prefer a candidate who satisfies these preferences to one who stands a better chance of winning.[32] Clearly political parties restrict spatial mobility, and our assumption of perfect mobility leads us to ignore them, at least for the moment in developing this model. This means that we also ignore other spatial restrictions. For example, a candidate may be unwilling to advocate some policy for fear of alienating vital support from within his party, from political activists in general, or from special interest groups that might otherwise support his campaign. We are even forced to ignore the fact that candidates themselves obviously possess preferences and that typically these preferences are reflected in the strategies they adopt publicly.

To ignore all these features of political life by assuming perfect spatial mobility may seem to throw out too much vital detail. To make a model is, however, to simplify by emphasizing basic characteristics. That spatial mobility is basic is apparent both from the model and from such examples as the fact that President Nixon in the course of several weeks abandoned two major policies deeply held by him and his party, namely exclusion of mainland China from the U.N. and a belief in a free market for wages.

The Candidates' Objectives

Assumptions concerning the vector θ_j, however, do not complete our

---

[32]See Peter H. Aranson and Peter C. Ordeshook, "Spatial Strategies for Sequential Elections," and James S. Coleman, "The Positions of Political Parties in Elections," both in Richard G. Niemi and Herbert F. Weisberg, eds., *Probability Models of Collective Decision-Making*; and James S. Coleman, "Internal Processes Governing Party Positions In Elections," *Public Choice*, vol. 11 (1971), pp. 35–60.

description of candidates. We must also specify the candidates' objectives. To specify which strategies are "best" we must identify the candidates' motives, because "best" is—as in any decision theory—relative to the goals and motives of the decision makers, who here are the candidates.

Briefly, we assume that the goal of candidates and of parties is to win elections. While the primary motivations of candidates may in fact be to affect governmental policies or to satisfy private and idiosyncratic objectives (such as status, money, and power), spatial analysis requires that winning be at least an instrumental goal for all candidates. Moreover, since we are concerned with democratic elections, we assume that some relative tabulation of votes determines who wins and who loses and, therefore, that votes or some measure on votes are the arguments of the candidates' strategic considerations. Thus, while the outcome for citizens is conceptualized as a policy vector, the relevant outcome for a candidate is the distribution of votes among candidates. (One might be tempted to think of the candidates' outcomes as policy also, were it not that candidates so often change policy on very important and salient dimensions, as President Nixon did on China and wages. Given such startling changes we can begin with the assumption that it is the office, not the policy, that counts for candidates.)

In addition to conceptualizing what we mean by a relevant outcome for a candidate, we must also postulate each candidate's evaluations of these outcomes. That is, we must postulate a utility function over the set of all possible distributions of votes. Unfortunately, the goal of winning does not specify what form this function should take because winning can be interpreted in several ways. First, winning typically means in two-party contests that the candidate secures more votes than his opponent. But in multiparty systems with proportional representation, winning can mean such things as achieving some minimal representation in a legislature, securing seats sufficient for inclusion in a coalition government, or securing a majority of seats.

The literature of spatial analysis generally simplifies this universe of possibilities by focusing on two objective functions. The first, which is appropriate for two-candidate contests, asserts that a candidate's utility increases as his plurality increases. Stated as an assumption:[33]

D1: *Candidates maximize plurality.*

One alternative assumption, which is probably most relevant in multiparty

---

[33]William H. Riker in *The Theory of Political Coalitions* (New Haven: Yale University Press, 1962) suggests an alternative assumption. Specifically, if candidates seek minimal winning coalitions, then a candidate's utility increases as plurality increases to one vote, and decreases thereafter. We note, however, that if two candidates compete, the election is a zero-sum game, in which case the maximization of plurality and the formation of minimal winning coalitions lead to identical results—the selection of minimax strategies. The criterion of minimal winning coalitions yields different results only if the position of one candidate is fixed, so that his opponent adjusts his position to suit his objectives with the opponent's strategy a fixed parameter of his calculus.

systems, is that a candidate's utility increases as his total vote increases, irrespective of the votes received by his opponents. Although multiparty contests are not considered in the basic spatial model, we analyze two-candidate contests with vote-maximizing candidates as an initial step to some multiparty generalizations. Furthermore, we employ this two-candidate analysis to consider situations in which candidates maximize resources, such as campaign finances as well as plurality. In one interpretation of spatial theorems, if the word "finances" is substituted for "votes," and "contributing finances" for "voting," then the strategic imperatives of candidates who maximize votes and of those who maximize finances are equivalent. Thus, we can assume that:

D2: *Candidates maximize votes.*

Assumptions D1 and D2 do not, of course, exhaust all realistic or interesting possibilities. We might assume, for example, that candidates maximize their proportion of the vote, the probability of winning, or the probability of securing a fixed percentage of the vote. Maximizing one's proportion of the vote seems a natural objective for candidates in electoral systems with proportional representation. Assuming that candidates maximize the probability of winning in two-candidate contests is clearly an alternative to the assumption that candidates maximize plurality. Thus, it would be valuable to ascertain the conditions under which these two assumptions are or are not equivalent.[34] Finally, the assumption that candidates maximize the probability of attaining a certain fixed percentage of the vote seems reasonable in local elections that historically are dominated by one party. Each candidate knows with near certainty who will win and who will lose. Perhaps, however, if each candidate is seeking nomination to some higher office in the future, his goal is simply to make a good showing by doing as well as or better than he or his party did in the previous election. Unfortunately, these alternative objectives have not yet been subject to as extensive an analysis as D1 and D2. Consequently, our review of spatial theory must focus on plurality and vote maximization.

*   *   *

This completes our review of assumptions. Their various combinations do not exhaust all existing models of spatial competition, but they exhibit the "flavor" of this theoretical approach to the study of elections. Moreover, while these assumptions do not begin to encompass the full complexity of electoral politics, the results obtained with them provide the foundation for more elaborate analyses of elections. For future reference, then, in Table 11.3. we summarize the assumptions.

[34]This kind of inquiry is initiated in Peter H. Aranson, Melvin J. Hinich, and Peter C. Ordeshook, "Equivalent and Non-Equivalent Objectives for Candidates in Electoral Competition," (forthcoming). See also Bruno Frey and Lawrence J. Lau, "Towards a Mathematical Model of Government Behavior," *Zeitschrift fur Nationalokonomie*, vol. 28 (1968), pp. 355–380 and "Ideology, Public Approval, and Government Behavior," *Public Choice*, vol. 10 (1971), pp. 21–40.

TABLE 11.3

Summary of Assumptions

On $U(x, \theta_i)$:

A1: U is concave.
A2: U is given by expression (11.7).
A3: U is a monotonic, increasing function of expression (11.7).

On a citizen's calculus:

B1: All citizens vote.
B2: Citizens abstain because of indifference.
B3: Citizens abstain because of alienation.
B4: Citizens abstain because of indifference or alienation.

On $f(x)$.

C1: $f(x)$ is a density.
C2: $f(x)$ is a symmetric unimodal density.
C3: $f(x)$ is a symmetric bimodal density.

On the candidates' objectives:

D1: Candidates maximize plurality.
D2: Candidates maximize votes.

SUGGESTIONS FOR FURTHER READING

The seminal work on spatial analyses of electoral competition is ANTHONY DOWNS' *An Economic Theory of Democracy* (New York: Harper and Row, 1957). Essentially all subsequent research and exposition appears in the form of articles published in professional journals. Since we mention most of those articles in our review of spatial analysis, we simply refer the student to those references.

12

Electoral Competition: Analysis

THE MEANING OF EQUILIBRIUM SPATIAL STRATEGIES

The purpose of a spatial analysis of electoral competition is to discover the positions that two maximizing candidates adopt. In particular, such an analysis aims at discovering whether or not there exists a pair of strategies that the candidates move toward and, once arrived, stay at. Such strategies are called an equilibrium-strategy pair and are denoted by $(\theta_1{}^*, \theta_2{}^*)$. An equilibrium pair has the property that the candidates are attracted to it (1) because the strategy $\theta_j{}^*$ guarantees candidate j some minimal plurality and no other strategy guarantees the candidate more in the face of all contingencies and (2) because candidate j's plurality decreases or at best remains unchanged if he shifts from an equilibrium strategy while his opponent remains at one. Given this property of equilibrium pairs, to conduct a spatial analysis means, if the candidates maximize plurality and if the election is symmetric, to ascertain whether or not a spatial position exists that at least ties and perhaps defeats all alternative spatial positions in a majority vote.[1]

This statement of the goal of spatial analysis reveals a correspondence

[1]By symmetric we mean that (1) all candidates choose from an identical set of strategies and (2) citizens are unbiased in the sense that their decisions to vote or abstain and their choice of candidates are functions only of the candidates' spatial strategies. Thus, if we assume that partisan identification—an obvious source of bias—is not given a spatial representation, the election generally will not be symmetric. If the election is symmetric and if $\varphi^j(\theta_1, \theta_2)$ denotes candidate j's expected plurality, then $\varphi^j(\theta_1, \theta_2) = 0$ for all $\theta_1 = \theta_2$. Thus, the maximum security level of any strategy is zero, in which case it follows that an equilibrium spatial strategy for a symmetric election cannot guarantee more than the expectation of a tie to a candidate.

between spatial analysis and the analysis of the paradox of voting. In its most fundamental form, if the candidates maximize plurality, an equilibrium spatial strategy makes its user a Condorcet winner. Hence to ascertain sufficient conditions for the existence of an electoral equilibrium is equivalent to ascertaining sufficient conditions for avoiding the disequilibrium implied by Arrow's theorem (see Chapter 4).

This correspondence suggests another: between spatial analysis and the analysis of n-person games. In Chapter 5 we suggest that the disequilibrium of the paradox illustrates n-person games without a core—that is, games without imputations (associated with majority coalitions) that are stable against all alternative imputations. Thus, a spatial model is a variant of an n-person game in which the players are citizens and in which an equilibrium strategy is a strategy of forming a majority coalition with an imputation in the core.

This correspondence between spatial analysis and n-person games is not, however, perfect. Markets too are modeled as n-person games. If the correspondence between elections and n-person games were perfect, then there would be no theoretical difference between a market and an election. But there is a difference. The n-person market game is a cooperative game in the sense that each player (consumer or firm) is free to bargain with every other player so as to seek the best coalition and imputation (exchange) for himself. The mechanics of the electoral process, however, transform the n-person game into a two person noncooperative game in which the players become the candidates. The n-person market game supposes that the citizens seek to form coalitions and thereby establish prices of commodities by bargaining among themselves; but in elections citizens bargain with candidates as their intermediaries, where each candidate seeks to form a winning coalition of citizens. Thus, by assuming that the candidates are the motivating actors in forming coalitions we transform an n-person game into a two-person game. Furthermore, if both candidates maximize plurality, the game is zero-sum; if both candidates maximize votes, the game is nonzero-sum and noncooperative. Thus, the correspondence is really one between spatial analysis and the theory of two-person zero-sum or nonzero-sum noncooperative games.

With the development of this correspondence it is tempting now to assume that, if the candidates maximize plurality, equilibrium spatial strategies, Condorcet winners, and minimax solutions to zero-sum games are equivalent; and if the candidates maximize votes it is tempting to assume that equilibrium spatial strategies and, say, Nash solutions to nonzero-sum, noncooperative games are equivalent. This equivalence, unfortunately, does not follow. To see that it does not, we must consider the three kinds of strategies that candidates can adopt—and, therefore, the three kinds of equilibria that can exist in the game-theoretic description of electoral competition. These three kinds of strategies are: pure, risky, and mixed. A pure strategy is a specific allocation (e.g., level of supply of a public good) that is proposed by a candidate. Thus, in terms of the definitions we offer in Chapter 11, a pure strategy is a vector

θ_j. A risky strategy is a probability distribution $P(\theta)$, over some subset of pure strategies, which the candidate "tells" the voter he will use to choose a policy if elected. Thus, a candidate can appear not to take any specific stand on an issue and, instead, disguise in ambiguity the policy he will adopt if elected. The voter then knows that, on issue i, the candidate's position is θ_{ji} with probability $P(\theta_{ji})$, θ'_{ji} with $P(\theta'_{ji})$, and so on. Mixed strategies, like risky strategies, involve probabilities, but in the mixed-strategy case the probabilities concern only the mechanism by which some pure strategy is selected prior to the balloting. The decision to adopt a mixed strategy means that the candidate publically adopts a pure strategy which is selected probabilistically before the balloting. Thus, if the candidates choose to use mixed strategies, they eventually present citizens with a choice between pure strategies.

The assumption that candidates employ mixed strategies, however, is untenable. While candidates might prefer to adopt a strategy involving risk, the inclusion of mixed strategies as an alternative means—to apply the theory of games properly—that candidates reveal their pure strategies simultaneously and that neither candidate can alter his strategy once it is revealed (i.e., the payoffs are realized immediately). Obviously, however, candidates in the real world attempt to adjust their strategies if they are inferior to those of an opponent. We cannot imagine a candidate adopting a mixed strategy which results in the selection of a pure strategy inferior to his opponent's pure strategy without attempting to alter his position if he has time to do so before the election. And such inferior choices are entirely possible in the theory of games.[2] Thus, only pure strategies or risky strategies are relevant to the study of elections.

Disregarding risky strategies for the present, we know, then, that if the candidates maximize plurality and if the election is symmetric, the search for equilibrium spatial strategies is equivalent to (1) the search for Condorcet winners and (2) the search for pure minimax solutions in the game-theoretic representation of election competition. That is, if we let $\varphi^j(\theta_1, \theta_2)$ denote candidate j's plurality and if the pair of spatial strategies $(\theta_1{}^*, \theta_2{}^*)$ satisfies the definition of a minimax solution in pure strategies, i.e., if

$$\varphi^1(\theta_1{}^*, \theta_2) \geq \varphi^1(\theta_1{}^*, \theta_2{}^*) \geq \varphi^1(\theta^1, \theta_2{}^*)$$

for all θ_1, θ_2, then $(\theta_1{}^*, \theta_2{}^*)$ is an equilibrium spatial strategy pair. Further, if the election is symmetric so that we can let $\theta_1{}^* = \theta_2{}^*$, $\theta_1{}^*$ is a Condorcet winner. [If the candidates maximize votes and if $V^j(\theta_1, \theta_2)$ denotes candidate j's vote, equilibrium spatial strategies satisfy

$$V^1(\theta_1{}^*, \theta_2{}^*) \geq V^1(\theta_1, \theta_2{}^*),$$
$$V^2(\theta_1{}^*, \theta_2{}^*) \geq V^2(\theta_1{}^*, \theta_2),$$

[2]For a criticism of the application of conventional game theory to politics because of this feature of mixed minimax strategies, see Thomas C. Schelling, *The Strategy of Conflict* (New York: Oxford, 1963).

which is to say that if $(\theta_1{}^*, \theta_2{}^*)$ is unique, it is a Nash solution to the corresponding noncooperative game.]

Recall now that, in Chapter 4, we noted that there are alternative sets of conditions for a majority-rule winner: those in which the set of alternative motions is finite and those in which this set is infinite and uncountable.[3] Similarly in Chapter 8 we distinguished between finite and infinite games. In developing correspondences between spatial analysis, the analysis of the paradox, and the theory of games, then, we must choose between a finite and an infinite (and uncountable) representation of spatial strategies. We choose in Chapter 11 the infinite representation. Consequently, those conditions relating to infinite alternative motions as well as the theorems pertaining to infinite, rather than finite, games are the ones that are relevant to the analysis of elections that we review here.

Their particular relevance is this: We know that majority-rule winners do not always exist, nor do two-person, noncooperative, infinite games necessarily possess pure-strategy solutions. Consequently, equilibrium spatial strategies do not always exist. There is, however, at least one condition (Plott's) for the existence of a majority-rule winner in a multidimensional world; and, in Chapter 8, we observed that constraints can be imposed on the payoff functions of the players of a two-person, noncooperative, infinite game that guarantee the existence of an equilibrium in pure strategies. Thus, it is possible to formulate general sufficient conditions for the existence of spatial equilibria. Some of these conditions can be interpreted as equivalent to or extensions of Plott's analysis—typically, these conditions include assumptions similar to Plott's, such as symmetric distributions of preference and utility functions that satisfy A2 or A3. Other conditions are designed to satisfy certain constraints on the candidates' payoff functions—constraints such as continuity, convexity, and concavity. To the review of these conditions we now turn.

ANALYSIS OF THE BASIC MODEL

In Chapter 11 we reviewed three alternative assumptions about utility functions, four alternative assumptions about participation, three alternative assumptions about preference densities, and two alternative assumptions about the candidates' motives. Thus, we have a total of seventy-two possible combinations of assumptions. Clearly, this is not acceptably parsimonious. The situation is not, however, as muddled as it appears since several combinations can be incorporated under general theorems. Nevertheless, not all combinations have

---

[3]Recall that uncountable means that alternatives cannot be indexed by the integers. Thus, the set of all positive integers is infinite but countable, whereas an interval of real numbers (e.g., all numbers between 0 and 1) is both infinite and uncountable. Thus, if the range of admissible alternatives is an interval (or intervals if the issue space is multidimensional) on a line (as in Figures 12.1 through 12.4), the set of alternatives is uncountably infinite.

been examined, and to identify those about which we know something we present Table 12.1 (where a check means that the particular combination of assumptions has been analyzed and has been accounted for by some theorem or by a reasonable conjecture).[4]

TABLE 12.1

		A1				A2				A3			
		B1	B2	B3	B4	B1	B2	B3	B4	B1	B2	B3	B4
C1	D1	√	√	√	√	√	√	√	√	√	√	√	
	D2	√	√	√	√			√					
C2	D1	√	√	√	√	√	√	√	√	√	√	√	√
	D2	√		√	√		√	√	√	√		√	
C3	D1	√	√	√	√	√	√	√	√	√		√	
	D2	√		√	√	√		√	√	√		√	

Table 12.1 clearly reveals the opportunities for further analysis—16 combinations are not checked. And, as we reveal soon, information about some of the 56 combinations that are checked consists of conjectures and not rigorously proved theorems. Those cases that are explored, however, provide an understanding of the forces operative in the electoral processes, and they therefore deserve exposition here.

Several methods for reviewing these forces are possible, such as considering each combination separately. With 56 cases to analyze, however, that would be tedious. A more logical and fruitful approach is afforded by observing that, basically, we are concerned with solutions in every case, by which we mean equilibrium outcomes and whether or not they exist. If we restrict ourselves

[4]The specific sources of our results are Otto A. Davis, Melvin J. Hinich, and Peter C. Ordeshook, "An Expository Development of a Mathematical Model of the Electoral Process," *American Political Science Review*, vol. 64 (1970), pp. 426–428 (this essay extensively references several earlier essays); Melvin J. Hinich and Peter C. Ordeshook, "Plurality Maximization vs. Vote Maximization: A Spatial Analysis with Variable Participation," *American Political Science Review*, vol. 64 (1970), pp. 772–791; Richard McKelvey, "Some Extensions and Modifications of a Spatial Model of Party Competition" (Unpublished Ph. D. dissertation, University of Rochester, 1972); Melvin J. Hinich, John O. Ledyard, and Peter C. Ordeshook, "A Theory of Electoral Equilibrium: A Spatial Analysis Based on the Theory of Games" *Journal of Politics* (1972); and "Electoral Equilibrium and Majority Rule," *Journal of Economic Theory* (1972). See also Gerald Garvey, "The Theory of Party Equilibrium," *American Political Science Review*, vol. 60 (1966) pp. 29–38; Gordon Tullock, *Toward a Mathematics of Politics* (Ann Arbor: University of Michigan Press, 1967); David E. Chapman, "Models of the Working of a Two-Party Electoral System," *Papers on Non-Market Decision-Making*, vol. 3 (1967), and *Public Choice*, vol. 4 (1968).

initially to symmetric elections, the theorems and conjectures of spatial analysis lead to four classes of solutions. These classes are:

(i)   in general no equilibrium exists,
(ii) an equilibrium exists such that the candidates converge but the point of convergence cannot be generally specified,
(iii) an equilibrium exists such that the candidates converge to the median or mean of $f(x)$,
(iv) an equilibrium exists but the candidates may or may not converge—depending on the saliency of the issues.

In the next few pages we review these cases. As a guide to this review we offer in Table 12.2 a survey of the distribution of these cases.

TABLE 12.2

		A1				A2				A3			
		B1	B2	B3	B4	B1	B2	B3	B4	B1	B2	B3	B4
C1	D1	(i)	(i)ᵃ	(i)ᵃ	(ii)	(i)	(i)ᵃ	(i)ᵃ	(ii)	(i)	(i)ᵃ	(i)ᵃ	
	D2	(i)ᵃ	(i)ᵃ	(i)ᵃ	(ii)			(ii)					
C2	D1	(i)ᵃ	(i)ᵃ	(i)ᵃ	(iii)	(iii)	(iii)	(iii)	(iii)	(iii)	(iii)	(iii)	(iii)ᵃ
	D2	(i)ᵃ	(i)ᵃ	(i)ᵃ	(ii)	(iii)		(iv)	(ii)	(iii)		(iv)	
C3	D1	(i)ᵃ	(i)ᵃ	(i)ᵃ	(iii)	(iii)	(iii)	(iv)ᵃ	(iii)	(iii)		(iv)ᵃ	
	D2	(i)ᵃ	(i)ᵃ	(i)ᵃ	(ii)	(iii)		(iv)ᵃ	(ii)	(iii)		(iv)ᵃ	

ᵃ: conjecture.

Case (i)

Excluding those combinations of assumptions that include B4, we either know or conjecture that an equilibrium-strategy pair does not generally exist if utility functions are not symmetric (A1) or if $f(x)$ is not symmetric (C1). For the general multidimensional case, we know from the analyses of Black and Plott as well as from several counterexamples to equilibrium that if all citizens vote and if only A1 and C1 are imposed, the existence of a Condorcet winner—and, therefore, a spatial equilibrium—cannot be guaranteed. And since neither the formulation of citizens abstaining because of indifference (B2) nor the formulation of citizens abstaining because of alienation (B3) appears to alter the compelling logic of these counterexamples and of Black and Plott's analyses, we conjecture that the exchange of either B2 or B3 for B1 does not generate an equilibrium if it did not previously exist.[5]

[5]Of course, if the number of issues equals one, and if all citizens vote (B1), then, from Black's

The fact than an equilibrium does not exist might seem to imply that we are unable to specify what candidates should or would do. But this absence of equilibrium conforms to situations in which a frequently observed regularity occurs—the formation of a coalition of minorities to defeat an incumbent candidate. Downs observes that the incumbent frequently is strategically disadvantaged because he must select his strategy before his opponent does.[6] Since the incumbent's strategy is known beforehand (e.g., his strategy is the package of policies he advocates during his tenure in office), his opponent can defeat him by advocating positions that appeal to a minority on each issue, but which, when summed across all issues, yield a majority. Thus, if an incumbent alienates some minority of the electorate on each issue by his position, and if the minorities on every issue are sufficiently numerous and distinct, his opponent can select positions that cause minorities to coalesce into a majority.

It is easily verified now that a successful coalition-of-minorities strategy exists whenever an equilibrium under majority rule fails to exist. First, recall the correspondence between equilibrium spatial strategies and the core of an n-person game. Specifically, if an equilibrium strategy exists, the corresponding n-person game has a core; and if an equilibrium strategy does not exist, the game has no core. Second, if a game does not have a core, a majority coalition of players (citizens) cannot be found that is stable against all other coalitions. Hence, if an equilibrium spatial strategy does not exist, a candidate can propose or advocate some package of policies (i.e., an imputation) that forms a coalition of citizens that defeats (dominates) the imputation of his opponent's coalition.

Extending the application of n-person game theory, we know also that the V-solution for games without cores consists typically of many imputations, which is to say that many alternative, but equally successful, coalition-of-minorities strategies exist simultaneously. And because we are unable in Chapter 5 to predict the imputation in the V-solution that eventually prevails, we conclude that the coalition-of-minorities strategy that prevails cannot be predicted unless we examine additional features of the environment. That is, if equilibrium spatial strategies do not exist, factors such as the candidates' policy preferences and historical circumstance are relevant for ascertaining the positions candidates select.

Case (ii)

In lieu of relegating the study of elections to the realm of psychopathology and historical circumstance, however, we can impose additional restrictions on one or more of the assumptions. The first restriction is the assumption that each citizen's calculus conforms to B4. This assumption, in conjunction with

---

single-peakedness condition, the median preference is an equilibrium. It is possible, therefore, that the substitution of B2 or B3 for the assumption that all citizens vote (B1) does not upset the existence of an equilibrium, although it may no longer be the median.

[6]Anthony Downs, *An Economic Theory of Democracy* (New York: Harper, 1957), pp. 55–62.

the assumption that utility functions are concave, yields electoral equilibria if the candidates maximize plurality or if they maximize votes. We introduced this result in Chapter 4 but postponed a detailed discussion of it because the requisite theoretical tools were not adequately developed. We can, however, outline a proof now. Recall that the search for an equilibrium spatial strategy is equivalent to ascertaining whether or not a pure-strategy equilibrium exists for the equivalent noncooperative game (which is zero-sum if the candidates maximize plurality and nonzero-sum if the candidates maximize votes). In Chapter 8 we reviewed an important theorem about such games: if the players' payoff functions are continuous, and are concave in one player's (candidate's) strategy and convex in the other player's (candidate's) strategy, both players possess unique pure equilibrium strategies. These continuity, convexity, and concavity requirements are satisfied by the conditions that B4 summarizes.[7]

Even though B4 is itself a somewhat restrictive condition, this fact alone should not lead us to suppose that disequilibrium is a pervasive feature of electoral competition. Indeed, B4 often leads to an equilibrium without the imposition of other, quite restrictive assumptions. We summarize here those requirements that are not imposed in order to bring about an equilibrium with B4. First, the electorate's distribution of preferences can be unimodal, bimodal, or multimodal as well as symmetric or nonsymmetric. Second, citizens are not required to weight the relative saliencies of the issues in an identical fashion (e.g., they need not share a common matrix of the weights a_{mk} if utility functions satisfy A2). Some citizens can care most about farm subsidies, some about civil rights, some about labor policy, and some can care about two or more of these issues simultaneously. Third, it is not necessary to suppose that candidates possess perfect spatial mobility. For example, even if one or both of the candidates' strategies are restricted so that one candidate must adopt "conservative" positions, a pure-strategy equilibrium exists.

---

[7]We outline the proof for plurality-maximizing candidates as an illustration. If $h^1[U(x, \theta_1), U(x, \theta_2)]$ is a citizen's probability of voting for candidate 1 and if $h^2[U(x, \theta_2), U(x, \theta_1)]$ is his probability of voting for candidate 2, and if each citizen has one vote, candidate 1's expected plurality is

$$\varphi^1(\theta_1, \theta_2) = \sum \{h^1[U(x, \theta_1), U(x, \theta_2)] - h^2[U(x, \theta_2), U(x, \theta_1)]\}$$

where the sum is taken over the set of all citizens. We now use the following general results about concave (convex) functions:

(a) if $r(x)$ is concave (convex) in x, $-r(x)$ is convex (concave) in x;
(b) if $r_i(x)$ is concave (convex) in x for all i, then $\sum_i r_i(x)$ is concave (convex) in x;
(c) if $t(x)$ is concave (convex) in x, and if $r[t(x)]$ is concave (convex) in t, then r is concave (convex) in x.

From condition (iii) of B4, h^2 is concave in $U(x, \theta_2)$ and convex in $U(x, \theta_1)$, so that from (a), $-h^2$ is concave in $U(x, \theta_1)$ and convex in $U(x, \theta_2)$. From the assumption that h^1 is concave in $U(x, \theta_1)$ and convex in $U(x, \theta_2)$ and from (b), it follows that $h^1 - h^2$ is concave in $U(x, \theta_1)$ and convex in $U(x, \theta_2)$. Again from (b), then, $\sum [h^1 - h^2]$ is concave in $U(x, \theta_1)$, and convex in $U(x, \theta_2)$. Finally, from the assumption that U is a concave utility function, it follows from (c) that $\varphi^1(\theta_1, \theta_2) = \sum [h^1 - h^2]$ is concave in θ_1 and convex in θ_2. It is also readily shown that conditions (i) and (ii) of B4 guarantee that φ^1 is continuous. Hence, φ^1 is a continuous, concave-convex payoff function, and the conclusion that a unique pure minimax strategy exists follows from the game-theoretic result.

Finally, it is not entirely necessary to assume that citizens are unbiased. Thus, without upsetting the spatial analogy, we can assume that partisan identification and personality do not have a spatial component and that these considerations can override spatial preference. Only with the absence of such bias, however, can we guarantee that the candidates converge to the same spatial strategy (assuming, of course, that constraints on strategies do not prohibit convergence) and that the equilibrium does indeed conform to case (ii). To see how bias can preclude convergence, suppose that a single issue characterizes preferences, and that citizens with preferences to the left of the median preference are biased in favor of candidate 1 while citizens with preferences to the right of this median are biased in favor of candidate 2. It is reasonable now to anticipate an equilibrium, (θ_1^*, θ_2^*), in which $\theta_1^* < \theta_2^*$. That is, the candidates are not likely to campaign for those citizens that they cannot attract—regardless of their spatial strategies. Instead, they maximize plurality by attempting to satisfy those citizens that they can attract, thereby maximizing the turnout of voters likely to support them.

If we wish to ascertain the policies that electoral competition induces, however, we must know more than that an equilibrium exists: we must also ascertain its location. But the location is not identified by the analysis we review here; far too many variables, such as the nature of citizens' biases and the distribution of preferences, are unspecified. We can, of course, seek a general method—a numerical procedure—with which the location of equilibria can be found. That is, if we ascertain the distribution of preferences, the form of citizens' utility functions, the citizens' decision rules, and, if they exist, the constraints on the candidates' strategies, we might then use our procedure to calculate the location of the equilibrium. (Parenthetically, note that this approach parallels the analysis of two-person, zero-sum, finite games. In that analysis, the minimax theorem establishes the existence of an equilibrium strategy pair, but, given the admissible variety of forms of such games, it does not identify the equilibrium. Instead, from the correspondence between these games and linear programming, we know that the Simplex method for solving linear programming problems can be interpreted as a numerical procedure for calculating minimax strategies.) The relevance of the analysis that we review here is that, first, it identifies the theoretical variables that must be measured to locate equilibria and, second, it tells us that what we are attempting to calculate exists. A second approach—the one that we pursue here—is to impose some general restrictions on the distribution of preferences, $f(x)$, and to consider alternative assumptions about utility functions.

Case (iii)

Recall that, in Chapter 4, Plott's condition for the existence of a majority-rule winner identifies that winner as the multivariate mean preference of citizens. This result is not unanticipated, since the mean is the point of symmetry for his conditions—$f(x)$ is symmetric about it and citizens that ideally prefer diametrically opposed positions with respect to the mean weight the relative saliencies of the issues identically. Paralleling this analysis, perhaps the best-known spatial theorem about the strategies of candidates that maximize plurality is that if $f(x)$ is a *symmetric unimodal* density (C2), the candidates converge to the mean preference on every issue (i.e., the multivariate mean is a unique equilibrium). The fame of this theorem is doubtless due to its simplicity and its intuitive appeal. It asserts that the candidates select strategies at the point where citizens' preferences are most densely distributed, and it also implies that if some minimal consensus exists within the electorate, the candidates' platforms become indistinguishable. The theorem, moreover, is valid if all citizens vote (B1), if citizens abstain because of indifference (B2), alienation (B3), or alienation and indifference (B4).[8, 9]

[8]If citizens abstain because of alienation, a slightly stronger assumption about $f(x)$ must be imposed to guarantee convergence—namely, all conditional distributions of preference must be unimodal (e.g., the normal density). Also, note from Table 12.2 that if B4 is assumed and if utility functions satisfy A3 but not A2, no general theorems exist. Nevertheless, one reasonable conjecture is that if $f(x)$ is symmetric and unimodal, the mean is the equilibrium under the conditions imposed by B4 and A3.

[9]We can briefly review the proof of this assertion for the case of one issue and for abstention because of alienation (B3) if we omit some tedious mathematical details. We select this proof as an example because it demonstrates a mode of analysis that differs from the one used in the discussion of case (ii). In that case we carefully select our assumptions about a citizen's calculus so as to use a result proved elsewhere in the theory of games. The proof, then, consists of showing that the conditions embodied by B4 satisfy the conditions of the result we propose to use. Here, however, we do not use any such theorem; rather, we deduce the conclusion that the mean is the equilibrium directly from the assumptions. First, let $g(x - \theta_j)$ denote the probability that citizens vote if they prefer x and the spatial location of candidate j is θ_j. Also, without loss of generality let $\theta_1 \leq \theta_2$. Finally, suppose that utility functions are symmetric, so that if $x < (\theta_1 + \theta_2)/2$—if x is to the left of the midpoint between the candidates' strategies—the citizen prefers θ_1, and if $x > (\theta_1 + \theta_2)/2$, he prefers θ_2. Thus, the expected vote for candidate 1 is represented as

$$\int_{-\infty}^{(\theta_1 + \theta_2)/2} f(x)g(x - \theta_1) \, dx;$$

i.e., we "add up" the number of citizens who prefer θ_1 times their respective probabilities of voting. Similarly, candidate 2's expected vote is

$$\int_{(\theta_1 + \theta_2)/2}^{\infty} f(x)g(x - \theta_2) \, dx,$$

so that candidate 1's expected plurality, φ^1, is expressed as

$$\varphi^1(\theta_1, \theta_2) = \int_{-\infty}^{(\theta_1+\theta_2)/2} f(x)g(x - \theta_1) \, dx - \int_{(\theta_1+\theta_2)/2}^{\infty} f(x)g(x - \theta_2) \, dx.$$

If we calculate the rate at which φ^1 changes as θ_1 changes, we can ascertain whether candidate 1 should shift his strategy. Denoting this rate by φ_0^1, we know that if $\varphi_0^1 > 0$, candidate 1 increases his expected plurality by shifting to the right and should do so. If $\varphi_0^1 < 0$, the candidate should shift to the left. From the previous expression the rate of change can be found to be equal to

$$\varphi_0^1(\theta_1, \theta_2) = \int_{-\infty}^{(\theta_1+\theta_2)/2} f'(x)g(x - \theta_1) \, dx,$$

where $f'(x)$ is the slope of $f(x)$ [i.e., the rate of change of $f(x)$ as x increases]. Suppose that can-

Certainly it is not surprising to find that two plurality maximizing candidates converge if $f(x)$ is a symmetric *unimodal* density. If this were the only accomplishment of spatial analysis, then perhaps it would draw the criticism that the obvious is proved by complex mathematics. Justifiably, we require nonobvious inferences about reality from our formalizations. And in the search for such inferences we find, among other things, that candidates converge to the mean under conditions for which some persons might anticipate divergent strategies. Specifically, we might believe that whenever preferences are distributed *bimodally*, the candidates would be wise to adopt strategies near or at the modes of $f(x)$. Contrary to this proposition, however, conditions exist under which plurality-maximizing candidates converge to the mean of a symmetric bimodal distribution.

One such condition can be derived directly from Plott's analysis, namely: if all citizens vote, the mean is the equilibrium for all symmetric distributions. A more interesting condition for the mean to be the equilibrium, when preferences are distributed symmetrically and bimodally, consists of the assumptions that citizens abstain because of indifference (B2), that their utility functions are concave and symmetric (A2), and that the candidates maximize plurality (D1). Thus, if we interpret abstention because of indifference as the citizens' punishment of candidates for their failure to provide programs that are sufficiently distinct, somewhat paradoxically we find that even though the citizens do so punish, the candidates nevertheless refuse to distinguish themselves. [This conclusion seems to contradict Downs' analysis of spatial strategies with bimodal distributions of preferences. Downs asserts that candidates adopt strategies near the modes of $f(x)$ because they fear that converging to the mean costs them the support of citizens who prefer positions near or at these modes.[10] Downs, however, apparently has in mind a cause of nonvoting that is more nearly akin to alienation (B3) than to indifference.]

Candidates and parties, nevertheless, do differ significantly on many issues. Should the existence of these differences, then, be interpreted as a refutation

---

didate 2 adopts the mean, which we set equal to 0 for convenience. Thus, $\theta_2=0$, and $\varphi_0{}^1$ becomes

$$\varphi_0{}^1(\theta_1, 0) = \int_{-\infty}^{\theta_1/2} f'(x) g(x - \theta_1) \, dx.$$

Observe now that $g(x - \theta_1)$ is a probability number, in which case it never assumes negative values. Also, since $\theta_1 < \theta_2 = 0$, $\theta_1/2 < 0$. Thus, our expression involves values of $f'(x)$ only for $x < 0$. Note, however, that if $f(x)$ is a symmetric unimodal density with mean 0, $f'(x) > 0$ for all $x < 0$. Thus, $f'(x) g(x - \theta_1) > 0$ for all $x < 0$. Hence $\varphi_0{}^1 > 0$ for all $\theta_1/2 < 0$, which is to say that candidate 1 increases his expected plurality by shifting towards candidate 2. But $f(x)$ and citizens' utility functions are symmetric, so that if both candidates are near the mean of $f(x)$, their expected pluralities are nearly identical, i.e., nearly zero. Thus, as candidate 1 converges towards candidate 2 who is at the mean, his expected plurality increases to zero, which is to say that if he is not at the mean and if his opponent is, he receives a negative expected plurality. Thus, the mean is better than all alternative strategies, in which case both candidates converge to the mean.

[10]Downs, *An Economic Theory of Democracy*, pp. 119–121.

of the results we consider here? Obviously, the validity of the theory can be reasserted by attributing the failure of candidates to adopt similar policies in real campaigns to the violation of the assumptions of the model, such as imperfect information or spatial mobility. Or again, it may be said in excuse that a candidate can find it necessary to advocate policies distant from the mean in order to win the nomination of his party, and later find himself committed to these policies in the campaign. Or, it may be said that candidates possess ideological prejudices which they may be unwilling or unable to forego. Finally, it may be said simply that candidates err. These attempts to resolve an apparent disparity between theory and empirical evidence, nevertheless, are not entirely necessary: conditions can be found in spatial analysis for which the candidates should provide distinct alternatives.

Case (iv)

Before we discuss these conditions, however, we must introduce one additional concept: the *sensitivity of voting* to variations in strategy.[11] In defining this concept we restrict ourselves to the assumption that citizens abstain because of alienation (B3). The intuitive idea of sensitivity is that a citizen's probability of voting is sensitive to variations in his preferred candidate's strategy if, when the preferred candidate moves from platform θ_j to θ_j', where $\theta_j' \neq \theta_j = x$, the citizen's probability of voting decreases. And the more rapidly a citizen's probability of voting decreases as candidate j's strategy shifts from x, the greater is the citizen's sensitivity.[12] Hence, we say that the sensitivity of turnout is lowest if all citizens vote, and that it is greatest if only those citizens who are perfectly satisfied (i.e., $x = \theta_j$) vote.

With this definition in mind we find at least two situations in which distinct spatial strategies are adopted by two candidates. This first situation involves candidates who maximize plurality (D1). Although we are unable to state a rigorous theorem, examination of several general cases suggests that if the sensitivity of turnout is sufficiently high, if $f(x)$ is bimodal (C3), if citizens abstain because of alienation (B3), and if utility functions are symmetric (A2 or A3), then the candidates adopt divergent strategies—strategies that lie between the mean and the modes of $f(x)$.[13] Hence, in partial agreement with Downs' proposition, distinct strategies are induced by alienation and by bimodal densities.

[11]This concept is discussed more extensively in Melvin J. Hinich and Peter C. Ordeshook, "Plurality Maximization vs. Vote Maximization."

[12]Somewhat imprecisely we also refer to this measure as the *saliency* of an issue; i.e., the greater the saliency of an issue, the more rapidly a citizen's probability of voting decreases as the disparity between the citizen's preference and the candidate's strategy on that issue increases.

[13]Admittedly, "sufficiently high" is an ambiguous condition. This condition, however, cannot be formulated precisely because it depends on many parameters of the citizens' decision rules and $f(x)$. The exact use of this condition, together with some examples, is presented in Peter C. Ordeshook, "Theory of the Electoral Process" (unpublished Ph. D. dissertation, Rochester, 1969).

Nevertheless, we must add two qualifications to this proposition. The first is that if sensitivity is not sufficiently high, the candidates converge to the mean. Thus, bimodal densities of preference and abstention because of alienation are not sufficient conditions for distinct strategies (e.g., if sensitivity is minimized so that all citizens vote, the candidates converge). The second qualification is that an equilibrium may exist only if the candidates' strategies are restricted so that neither candidate can "jump over" his opponent's position on an issue. One interpretation of this observation is afforded by recalling that party activists and special interests may provide such constraints on strategic maneuverability. Considering then that bimodal densities characterize preferences on many issues, the restrictions that activists and special interests impose on candidates may be regarded as stabilizing. By not permitting the candidates to cross each other, these groups not only keep the candidates from converging but they also insure that equilibria exist. Interest groups, therefore, while perhaps introducing "divisive" forces into the electoral arena, simultaneously insure a degree of stability in this nonconvergent competition.

A second situation in which distinct strategies may be adopted involves candidates who maximize votes (D2). If preferences are distributed unimodally (C2), if citizens abstain because of alienation (B3), if utility functions are symmetric (A2 or A3), and if the sensitivity of turnout is at some *intermediate* value, then vote maximizing candidates do not converge.[14] Thus, unimodal preference densities are not sufficient for convergence.

Observe, however, that this result is qualified by the condition that sensitivity assumes intermediate values. This qualification is necessary because if sensitivity is either high or low, the candidates do converge. Consequently, vote maximization is not a sufficient condition for distinct alternatives. And while words such as "intermediate," "high," and "low" are imprecise, we can formulate this qualification as an empirical hypothesis. Specifically, the relationship between sensitivity or saliency and the distance candidates diverge from each other is of the form of an inverted "U"—distance increases and then decreases as sensitivity increases.[15]

---

[14]This surprising conclusion results from the fact that the incentives for convergence are greater if the candidates maximize plurality than if they maximize votes. To show this, we compare for the two kinds of maximization the gain of, say, candidate 1 as he shifts θ_1 toward θ_2. Before the shift, 1 gets V_1 votes, and (ignoring the votes lost through alienation) afterward he gets $V_1 + \varepsilon$, where ε is (approximately) the number of votes lost by 2. Candidate 2 ends up with $V_2 - \varepsilon$. Under vote maximization, candidate 1's net gain is ε, but under plurality maximization his new plurality less his old plurality is

$$[(V_1 + \varepsilon) - (V_2 - \varepsilon)] - (V_1 - V_2) = 2\varepsilon.$$

Thus the gain—and hence the incentive to converge—under plurality maximization is double the gain under vote maximization. If the smaller gain is wiped out, as it is in the case of intermediate sensitivity, by the loss of alienated voters to the left of θ_1 who cease to vote as θ_1 is moved to the right, then the incentive to converge is also eliminated and candidates diverge.

[15]At this point we must resolve an apparent inconsistency in the results on convergence. In the discussion of case (iv) we state that, if citizens abstain because of alienation (B3), conditions exist under which plurality and vote-maximizing candidates do not converge. In our

This completes our review of the major theorems of spatial analysis that concern the existence of equilibrium. With this review we can now explore several general interpretations of and inferences from these results. Moreover, we can consider several results that are not readily summarized in Table 12.2. We consider these additions first.

review of case (ii), however, we state that if each citizen's calculus of voting conforms to B4, the candidates converge for all $f(x)$. The apparent inconsistency is this: In Chapter 11 we assert that B4 is consistent with the alienation hypothesis. Clearly, then, before we can confidently render any substantive conclusions about spatial analysis, we must answer the question: Why with one formulation of alienation do the candidates converge while with another formulation they diverge?

The answer, of course, is that the two formulations are quite different. To see this, assume that $f(x)$ is an extreme case of a bimodal density—citizens prefer either 0 or 1—that $\theta_1 < \theta_2$, and that alienation corresponds to B3. This density is depicted in Figure 12.1 by two vertical bars at 0 and 1, and we also graph in this figure two functions denoting a citizen's probability of voting for candidate 1—one function for θ_1' and the other for θ_1''. Recall now from our discussion of B3 in Chapter 11 that a citizen votes for a candidate only if the candidate's spatial location is preferred. Hence, assuming B3, candidate 1's electoral support comes only from those citizens at 0: he receives no support from citizens at 1. Suppose now that candidate 1 shifts to the right from θ_1' to θ_1''. This move does not secure any additional support at 1 since these citizens continue to prefer θ_2. Moreover, because each citizen's calculus conforms to B3, the probability that citizens at 0 vote decreases as θ_1 shifts from θ_1' to θ_1''. This decrease is a loss for candidate 1 since; if these citizens vote, they vote for him. The candidate, then, prefers θ_1' to θ_1''—he prefers the strategy which is closer to the mode 0.

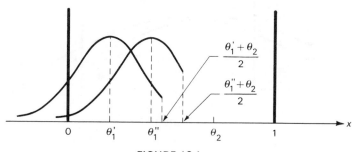

FIGURE 12.1

If B4 is assumed, however, every citizen has some probability of voting for candidate 1 even if θ_2 is preferred to θ_1. Hence, candidate 1 secures some support from citizens at 1 as well as from citizens at 0. What we wish to show now is that if alienation conforms to B4, candidate 1's gains exceed his losses as he shifts from θ_1' to θ_1''. Recall that with B4, a citizen's probability of voting for candidate 1, h^1, increases concavely as $U(x, \theta_1)$ increases, and, therefore, is a concave function of θ_1. In Figure 12.2 we graph two concave curves for h^1—one for θ_1' and the other for θ_1''—and we also redraw the two vertical bars which represent $f(x)$. Observe now that as candidate 1 shifts from θ_1' to θ_1'', he loses support among citizens at 0, since their probability of voting for candidate 1 decreases; but candidate 1 gains support among citizens preferring 1, since their probability of voting for him increases. His losses are measured by $d_0' - d_0''$ and his gains by $d_1'' - d_1'$ [assuming that $f(x)$ is symmetric]. It is readily seen now that since h^1 is concave, $d_1'' - d_1' > d_0' - d_0''$, which is to say that candidate 1's gains

EXPLOITATION OF AN OPPONENT'S WEAKNESS

Thus far we assume that each candidate selects a spatial strategy in the expectation that his opponent will try to defeat him. That is, if a winning strategy for the opponent exists, he will adopt it. We further assume that the first candidate responds with his best strategy. These assumptions together imply that if an equilibrium-strategy pair exists, candidates will adopt it. Earlier we discuss the way a candidate might, when no such pair exists, take advantage of an opponent's weakness by implementing a coalition of minorities strategy. Now let us suppose that an equilibrium does exist, but that one candidate, either because of imperfect information or imperfect spatial mobility, fails to adopt it. For example, suppose that one candidate adopts a strategy that can be defeated in a majority vote. The question to be considered is: What strategy should his opponent adopt that best takes advantage of the situation?

To answer this question suppose, first, that all citizens vote and that the election is unidimensional. It is obvious now that if a candidate maximizes either votes or plurality he should adopt a position near his opponent but closer to the median of $f(x)$ than his opponent's strategy. We illustrate in

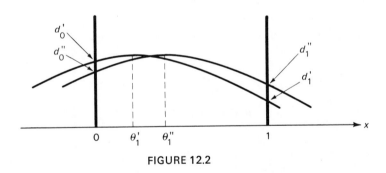

FIGURE 12.2

among citizens at 1 exceed his losses among citizens at 0. Hence, unlike the analysis with B3, candidate 1 does not prefer the strategy that is closer to the mode 0.

The essential difference between B3 and the formulation of alienation that is consistent with B4, then, is that with B4, h^1 is concave in θ_1 and is greater than zero for all x. Since h^1 is greater than zero for all x, a candidate secures some support from citizens at every point on an issue. And since h^1 is a concave function, he can maximize his net support by a central rather than an extreme position.

The appropriateness of this formulation of alienation as against the formulation implied by B3 cannot, of course, be ascertained abstractly. As we note earlier, B3 seems more appropriate if all criteria that citizens use to evaluate candidates are given a spatial interpretation, whereas B4 seems more appropriate if criteria such as partisan identification, image, and error are external considerations. An important general lesson is learned however: alienation *per se* does not imply distinct spatial strategies.

Figure 12.3 a strategy, θ_2, that is readily defeated in a majority vote and a strategy θ_1 that best takes advantage of candidate 2's error. This illustration conforms to Tullock's observation that if all citizens vote, "an extremist candidate can pull a vote-maximizing [and a plurality-maximizing] opponent far off toward the extremist's desires."[16]

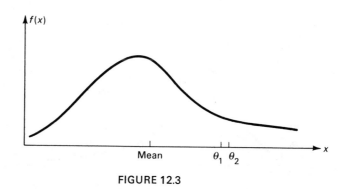

FIGURE 12.3

This conclusion is not generally true, however, if citizens are permitted to abstain. To see this, assume that $f(x)$ is symmetric and unimodal, that citizens abstain because of alienation, and that the candidates maximize plurality. Under these different conditions it is apparent that, were the candidates to adopt platforms like those in Figure 12.3, candidate 1's plurality over 2 need not be at its maximum. Candidate 1 might increase his plurality by moving θ_1 toward the mean. He would thereby lose some voters whose ideal is between θ_1 and θ_2; but he would gain some of the alienated nonvoters to his left who would become voters as he moved closer to the mean. Given appropriate probabilities of voting, it is possible that the votes gained as θ_1 moves leftward exceed those that are lost, especially since there are more voters to his left than his right.

If, with a particular selection of probabilities of voting, we now plot the value of θ_1 that maximizes candidate 1's plurality against candidate 2's strategy, we obtain a function such as the one illustrated in Figure 12.4, where the origin is the mean of $f(x)$. Thus, as candidate 2 shifts away from the mean of $f(x)$, candidate 1 initially "follows" him because each move of 1 to keep up with 2 increases 1's plurality. But when θ_2 gets farther than distance p from the mean, candidate 1 shifts back toward the mean.[17] With each step back toward the mean candidate 1 picks up alienated voters (who might otherwise abstain)

[16]Gordon Tullock, *Toward a Mathematics of Politics*, p. 52.

[17]Melvin J. Hinich and Peter C. Ordeshook, "Abstention and Equilibrium in the Electoral Process," *Public Choice*, vol. 8 (Fall 1968), 97–98.

and thereby increases his plurality. Hence, if citizens abstain because of alienation, an extremist candidate *cannot* pull an opponent arbitrarily far from the mean.[18] Adoption of the mean, then, maximizes plurality either when the candidates are closely matched or when one candidate advocates extreme policies.

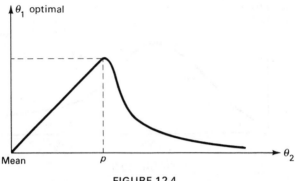

FIGURE 12.4

The content of this result is that, if his opponent is far from the mean, the candidate should not adopt a strategy that is also far from the mean. The internal logic is that, if he does adopt a strategy far from the mean, he succeeds only in greatly decreasing the probability that citizens near the mean, who comprise the bulk of the electorate, vote. This logic and the resultant description of a candidate who wishes to take advantage of his opponent's vulnerability are not without analogues in the real world. It is generally assumed, for example, that Senator Goldwater alienated many segments of the electorate in the United States in 1964 by taking an "extreme" position, and his percentage of the vote suggests this. Assume that President Johnson was not simply attempting to win, but to build a consensus and win by a landslide (i.e., maximize plurality). The combination of Goldwater's strategy and Johnson's goal explains the logic of a consensus strategy, which consists of advocating the mean preferences of the electorate. By becoming estranged from the bulk of the electorate, Goldwater permitted Johnson to maximize his plurality by appealing to that bulk of the electorate near the mean. If Goldwater's policies had not been so radical, and if Johnson still sought to maximize his plurality, it seems safe to say that Johnson would have been drawn, during the campaign, toward Goldwater's positions.

[18]The maximum distance a plurality-maximizing candidate diverges, p, is a function of the sensitivity of turnout to variations in strategy: the greater the sensitivity, the smaller is p.

VARIATIONS IN SALIENCY AND IN THE COST OF VOTING

In our discussion of case (iv) we point out the relation of the concept of the sensitivity of turnout to variations in strategy. Specifically we argue that, for suitable conditions, different levels of sensitivity yield different electoral outcomes. This dependence can be interpreted in terms of the notion of the weights that we introduce in our discussion of utility functions, where we observe that the magnitudes of these weights are functions of the scales used to index the dimensions. Because of that functional relation, we profess a desire to prove theorems that are independent of the magnitudes of the a's. Unfortunately, this cannot always be accomplished, and it is exactly the outcomes that are dependent on sensitivity that are not independent of the magnitudes of these weights. But while such a dependence may appear to be an unfortunate property of the spatial model, one interpretation of sensitivity yields several interesting and important extensions of this analysis.

The main problem with the notion of sensitivity as we have previously used it is that the measure of sensitivity varies according to issues. To demonstrate this we first point out that, if the number of issues exceeds one, sensitivity is a multidimensional concept. Hence, sensitivity can be high on one issue and low on another. Particularly, if the weight associated with one issue exceeds the weight associated with another, then sensitivity is high on the first and low on the second. Consequently (recalling that we assume that citizens abstain from voting because of alienation), as the distance between x and θ_j increases one unit on both issues, the decrease in the probability of voting can be attributed more to the first (or highly sensitive, heavily weighted) issue than to the second. Our difficulty now is that if we seek to compare levels of sensitivity, we must contend with the possibility that each dimension is measured on a different scale. And if the meaning of the words "high" and "low" in comparing sensitivity is dependent on these scales, sensitivity is not strictly comparable.

To facilitate our use of the notion of sensitivity, therefore, we seek a different and more general measure of sensitivity. Briefly, we standardize the measure of sensitivity in terms of the variance of $f(x)$ on each dimension.[19] Denoting the standard deviation of $f(x)$ on issue i by σ_i, the intuitive idea behind sensitivity is that it is high [low] on issue i if the probability of voting for θ_j decreases rapidly [slowly] as we move, say, σ_i units from θ_j on issue i.

This interpretation permits sensitivity to be meaningfully compared among issues. It also permits us to interpret sensitivity as a measure of the *saliency* of an issue. The notion of saliency, as we understand its use in empirical studies

[19]Also, we normalize all weight to equal one by transforming the scales used to index each dimension. The variances of $f(x)$ are then measured in the transformed space. See Hinich and Ordeshook, "Plurality Maximization vs. Vote-Maximization." The operation of standardizing measures of sensitivity is analogous to the procedure of standardizing regression coefficients and comparing beta weights.

of voting, is that the greater the saliency of an issue, the greater the impact the candidates' strategies with respect to that issue have on citizens' decisions. The difficulty with this idea—one that is typically ignored in research on attitudes and voting—is that, like sensitivity, saliency is dependent on the scales used to index issues. How, for example, are we to interpret a statement such as "issue 1 is more salient than issue 2"? Probably in current usage this means that a candidate who satisfies a citizen's preference on issue 1 but not on issue 2 is more likely to be supported by him than is a candidate who satisfies him on issue 2 but not on issue 1. If this is indeed what saliency means, then clearly the measures of distance affect relative saliency. Since these measures are functions of the units we select to index each issue, comparisions of saliency are rendered difficult. Such comparisons are difficult because of exactly the same considerations we encountered when we sought to compare sensitivity. Nevertheless, we can apply an identical procedure of normalization so as to render comparisons of saliency meaningful. Moreover, if we select the decision to vote as the criterion for ascertaining saliency, then saliency and sensitivity become synonymous concepts. That is, the greater the saliency of an issue, the more rapidly a citizen's probability of voting decreases as x and θ_j become more disparate (as measured in the standardized issue space).

These manipulations permit us to utter some intuitively satisfying propositions. For example, we can say that the divisive effects of bimodal distributions of preference increase as saliency increases. This is a proposition that observers of politics often assert; yet so far as we know it has never been proved.[20] It is, therefore, quite satisfying to find it as a deduction from spatial theory. If candidates maximize plurality (D1), if citizens abstain because of alienation (B3), and if preferences are distributed bimodally on an issue, the candidates offer more distinct alternatives as the saliency of that issue increases. That is, the greater the saliency of an issue, the closer the candidates' strategies approach the modes of $f(x)$. Thus, the asserted relation among saliency, bimodal distributions, and divisiveness follows logically from a spatial analysis.

Clearly, the concept of saliency can be substituted for that of sensitivity of turnout to variations in strategy. In lieu of simply restating these results we can formulate some second-level propositions by considering a factor that affects saliency and sensitivity—the cost of voting, Obviously, legal rules can alter electoral outcomes by selectively raising or lowering the cost of voting through such devices as poll taxes and residency requirements. Consider, however, the implications of uniform variations in the cost of voting, where a uniform variation is one that affects all citizens equally in terms of the functional relationships between their probabilities of voting and the candidates' strategies. We wish to compare the effects of uniform variations in the cost of

[20]For a more extensive discussion of intensity, saliency, and divisiveness see Robert A. Dahl, *A Preface to Democratic Theory* (Chicago: University of Chicago Press, 1956), chap. 4; and Douglas W. Rae and Michael J. Taylor, *The Analysis of Political Cleavages* (New Haven: Yale University Press, 1970).

voting on electoral outcomes for systems in which candidates maximize plurality as against systems in which candidates maximize votes.

We approach this query by examining the relationship between this cost and the citizen's utility of voting. If cost increases, this utility decreases, *ceteris paribus*, so that the citizen's probability of voting decreases. From this, it follows that the sensitivity of turnout increases as cost increases.[21] Recall now from our discussion of case (iii), where the spatial equilibrium is the mean, that if $f(x)$ is a symmetric unimodal density and if candidates maximize plurality, the candidates converge to the mean regardless of the level of sensitivity (or saliency). Thus, for these conditions electoral outcomes are unaltered if the cost of voting is varied uniformly throughout the electorate. But, from our discussion of case (iv) we now know that such variations affect outcomes if the candidates maximize votes or if the candidates maximize plurality and $f(x)$ is a bimodal density.

Uniform variations in the cost of voting, then affect the electoral strategies of candidates who maximize plurality if $f(x)$ is a bimodal density, but not if it is a unimodal density; such variations affect outcomes in the case of both densities if the candidates maximize votes. Thus, in this sense we can say that the policies rendered by elections in which candidates maximize votes are characterized by a greater sensitivity to variations in the cost of voting than are the policies rendered by elections in which candidates maximize plurality.

THE DOCTRINE OF RESPONSIBLE PARTIES

The comparison of political systems, however, is typically not concerned with an analysis of the effects of variations in the cost of voting. A much more important kind of comparison of political systems concerns the doctrine of responsible party government. The major components of this doctrine are: (1) parties and candidates should respond to the variegated opinions of the electorate by advocating clear and distinct programs, and (2) once elected, the internal discipline of parties should guarantee the implementation of those programs to which the electorate has given its consent. In this section we propose to examine one part of the first component of this doctrine, namely, whether or not *distinct* electoral choices are in fact available. Later we examine a second part of this component—the availability of *clear* choices—when we discuss strategies involving risk and uncertainty.

Ranney asserts that proposals for a responsible party system are predicated on the "appeal . . . [of] a people committed to the desirability of unlimited

---

[21]If R is the utility of voting, let $R = U + \varepsilon$, where U is the deterministic component of R, and ε is a random variable. Assuming that U decreases as the cost of voting, C, increases, the disparity between x and θ_j necessary to set U equal to zero decreases. And since it is this critical distance that determines sensitivity, i.e., since the more rapidly U decreases the greater the sensitivity, it follows that sensitivity increases as C increases.

majority rule."[22] Thus if Ranney and the advocates of party responsibility are correct, the necessary and sufficient conditions for responsible party government include competitive elections and candidates who are able to implement their programs once these programs are approved by a majority of voters.

It is clear that the assumptions and theorems of spatial analysis constitute a description of one prerequisite for majority rule—namely, a constitutional structure providing for the election of candidates who advocate policies approved by half or more of those voting. Moreover, spatial models satisfy Ranney's "unlimited" condition. That is, spatial models that assume complete information and perfect spatial mobility can be taken as an idealized description of unlimited majority rule. While, of course, spatial analysis and its results are insufficient for resolving all controversy about a political system, they are relevant to an analysis of the requirement that the parties and the candidates offer the electorate clear choices among different policies. Furthermore, they demonstrate that unlimited majority rule is not a sufficient condition for the existence of such choices.

To see this in its starkest form, we consider first the results concerning abstention because of indifference (B2). Restating this assumption: If a citizen perceives the candidates to be offering distinct policies in the sense that the utility he associates with one candidate is substantially greater than the utility he associates with the alternative candidate, the citizen votes for the candidate whose policies yield the greater utility. But to the extent that these policies are not distinct (in terms of the differences in utility derived from them) the citizen punishes both candidates by abstaining. Thus, it appears, that the candidates possess clear incentives for attempting to provide distinct programs. A review of Table 12.2 reveals, however, that these incentives are not implied by assumption B2: distinct spatial strategies are not selected by the candidates. Rather, if $f(x)$ is symmetric, the candidates converge to the mean. And somewhat surprisingly, we find that convergence does not require that $f(x)$ be a unimodal density; if utility functions satisfy A2, the candidates converge to the mean of a symmetric *bimodal* density.

This convergence, moreover, is not the artifact of one (perhaps empirically incorrect) assumption about nonvoting—the assumption that citizens abstain because of indifference. If citizens abstain because of indifference and alienation (B4) or if all citizens vote (B1), distinct strategies again are not selected. Thus, for these assumptions at least, the mean is a powerful attraction to candidates in perfectly competitive elections. That is, unlimited majority rule is not a sufficient condition for distinct electoral choices.

The conclusion that candidates fail to provide distinct programs if $f(x)$ is unimodal is not unanticipated. Presumably, proponents of the doctrine of responsible parties do not envision the necessity for distinct choices in all cir-

---

[22]Austin Ranney, *The Doctrine of Responsible Party Government* (Urbana: The University of Illinois Press, 1954), p. 160.

cumstances. Woodrow Wilson's critique of parties in the United States is that the voter is "[un]able to vote for a definite line of policy with regard to the great questions of the day."[23] And if citizens' preferences are distributed uni-modally on an issue—a situation corresponding to some minimal consensus of opinion—perhaps we might not categorize the issue as "great." Nevertheless, convergence with assumptions B1, B2, and B4 does not require that $f(x)$ be unimodal: with these assumptions the candidates converge if $f(x)$ is bimodal. And, presumably, many issues on which preferences are bimodally distributed are exactly those categorized as "great." They should, therefore, induce distinct programs. Apparently, then, the forces uncovered by spatial analysis and the forces the proponents of the doctrine of responsible parties seek to instill in electoral processes do not coincide.

To this point spatial analysis demonstrates that the provision of distinct elec-toral choices may require the candidates and the parties to behave irration-ally, i.e., nonoptimally. Additionally, spatial analysis illustrates the fact that initial guesses as to the necessary and sufficient conditions for some event (here, that unlimited majority rule yields responsible parties) are frequently disproved, or, at least, are rendered more precise by the rigorous formal analysis of positive political theory. Specifically, if proper assumptions in addition to unlimited majority rule are made, we can discern forces in our model that foster distinct electoral choices. First, we note from Table 12.2 and our discussion of case (iv) that if citizens abstain because of alienation (B3) and if saliency is sufficiently great, the candidates diverge towards the modes of $f(x)$. Thus, abstentions caused by alienation rather than indifference yield distinct choices on "the great issues of the day."

This result can be given an interesting interpretation by recalling the voter's calculus developed in Chapter 3 and represented in Chapter 11 by equation (11.8). In introducing the concepts of alienation and indifference, we associate indifference with B (the differential utility between candidates) and alienation with D (the utility from socialization to vote). That is, variations in indifference correspond to variations in B, and variations in alienation correspond to varia-tions in D. Assume now that if the citizen is perfectly satisfied by some can-didate's position, D is maximized —say max $D = D_0$. Clearly, if D_0 is small or zero relative to the remaining terms in (11.8), D cannot vary greatly, which is to say that if D_0 is small, any variation in D produces only a small variation in R, the net reward from voting. In this circumstance, the candidates' strategies affect R primarily through B (i.e., the primary relationship between the deci-sion to vote and B2, the hypothesis that citizens abstain because of indifference). And since the candidates generally converge if we assume B2, the implication is that an electorate that consists of citizens with a low sense of citizen duty yields parties and candidates that fail to provide distinct choices because the

---

[23]Woodrow Wilson, "Leaderless Government," an address before the Virginia Bar Associ-ation, August 4, 1897, in I. R. S. Baker and W. E. Dodd, eds., *The Public Papers of Woodrow Wilson: College and State* (New York: Harper, 1925), p. 355.

spatial equilibrium is the mean position on issues. Conversely, if D_0 is relatively large so that B3—abstention from alienation—is the more nearly relevant assumption, distinct programs are offered (if, of course, preferences are distributed bimodally and if the saliency of the issue is sufficiently great). Making a leap from the theory to the world, then, responsible parties are possible if the sense of citizen duty is high in the populace generally, but that they are not possible if the sense of citizen duty is relatively low. Thus an alert electorate whose response to unsatisfactory candidates is to abstain, which, in the classical theory, responsible parties are supposed to create, is itself a precondition of responsible parties.

Thus far, however, we assume that candidates maximize plurality, which is a valid assumption for single-member district systems in which the candidates require a plurality to win. But, from Table 12.2, we see that another means for obtaining distinct choices in spatial theory is to assume that the candidates maximize votes.[24] This in turn suggests that constitutional structure affects the propensity of parties to provide distinct policy choices. Specifically, plurality maximization is the appropriate assumption for single-member district systems in which the candidate with a positive plurality wins. If we have multimember districts and proportional representation, however, and if more than two parties compete, the criterion of vote maximization is more satisfactory assumption than plurality maximization. The inference, then, is that, *certeris paribus*, responsible parties *qua* parties that provide distinct choices are more prevalent in multimember districts than in single-member districts. (Perhaps it is the correspondence between distinct strategies, vote maximization and multi-member district systems with proportional representation that accounts for the preoccupation with such systems by proponents of the doctrine of responsible parties.)

Discussion of such systems cannot be conducted properly, however, without consideration of the coalition processes of legislatures. Postponing this discussion, we consider a second means by which our results on vote maximization can be rendered relevant to the discussion of responsible party government. We explore how governments with single-member districts can exhibit some of the characteristics of systems in which candidates maximize votes.

THE JOINT MAXIMIZATION OF RESOURCES

Candidates do not simply look at the preferences of all citizens on all issues, calculate an equilibrium strategy if such a strategy exists, and adopt it. Rather,

---

[24]Of course, the patterns of these differences may not correspond to those sought by proponents of the doctrine of responsible parties. In addition to diverging on issues for which preferences are distributed bimodally, vote-maximizing candidates may also diverge if $f(x)$ is unimodal. Some divergence, however, may be desirable, in which case it is desirable to have candidates that maximize votes or behave as if they maximized votes.

they bargain, cajole, and compromise as they progress through the maze of individual and conflicting demands present in a plural society. Similarly, citizens do not simply vote or abstain in elections: voting is only one form of electoral participation. Citizens contribute finances, ring doorbells, provide endorsements, or, frequently, nominate a candidate. Thus, candidates must weight some citizens' preferences more heavily than others when formulating campaign strategy. Consequently, the strategies candidates actually adopt reflect the unequal importance of citizens.

Considering a simple example, assume that:

(1)   The electorate consists of two groups which are differentiated by the resources their members are able to contribute to a campaign, the many poor and the few rich.

(2)   Members of the first group, the poor, either vote or abstain.

(3)   Each member of the second group, the rich, may, in addition to voting, contribute a commodity, say A, to his most preferred candidate's campaign.

(4)   A member of the second group contributes A if his expected utility from voting is sufficiently great.

(5)   Each candidate values the commodity A, and each candidate seeks, *inter alia,* to maximize his supply of it.

(6)   The candidates seek, *inter alia,* to maximize their plurality of votes.

(7)   The preferences of both groups of citizens are distributed symmetrically and unimodally with identical means.

Ceteris paribus, because the candidates are, by (6), plurality maximizers, they tend to *converge* to the mean preference of the first group, the poor. But, since the candidates are, by (5), commodity maximizers with respect to A, they perhaps tend to *diverge* from the mean preference of the rich, as explained in footnote 14 of this chapter. Thus, to get elected they should converge, but to get contributions they should diverge, a thoroughly paradoxical situation. Clearly, the candidates' campaigns are simplified if the strategies that they adopt with respect to each group are independent: each group may be concerned with a different subset of issues, or each group may be unaware of the policies that a candidate advocates to the other group. Frequently, however, the concerns of the poor and the rich overlap and information cannot readily be controlled. The strategic imperatives for the two groups conflict.

One approach to this conflict is to adopt some simplified decision rule such as selecting a strategy that compromises the optimal strategies for the two groups. The question is, however: What weight should a candidate assign to the demands of each group? Should a candidate adopt a position near the mean of the poor or near the optimal strategy with respect to the rich? To answer such questions candidates must ascertain the relative value of A, which is to say that they must ascertain the rate at which A can be converted into votes. For example, a candidate may be willing to forego a safe spatial position on an issue in order to obtain finances sufficient for a campaign to change his spatial location on, or vary the saliency of, some other issue.

Unfortunately, virtually no systematic knowledge exists either about the production possibilities of campaign resources or about how candidates calculate these possibilities.[25] In lieu of such knowledge we propose a hypothesis: the greater the degree of competition the more value a candidate assigns to such resources as finances, endorsements, and the support of activists. The logic of this hypothesis is that as competition increases, a candidate needs more resources to implement an effective campaign. For example, a candidate might attempt to convince the electorate that his opponent supports some unpopular policy. The greater the threat that such attempts pose, the more resources a candidate requires to counteract it. Thus, in terms of our illustration, the greater the degree of competition the greater the weight a candidate assigns to the strategic imperatives of the second group. Consequently, as competition increases, the distance each candidate's strategy diverges from the mean increases.

This conclusion clearly contradicts the assertion that competition fosters middle-of-the-road candidates. But it provides one explanation for Warren E. Miller's observation that "party differences *within* [a congressional] district are heightened when electoral competition is keen and are reduced under single party domination of congressional electoral politics," and that "evenly balanced two-party competition . . . is associated with the reduction if not the total absence of direct representation of constituency policy preferences."[26] Thus, two candidates may not converge even if the citizens' preferences are distributed unimodally—the candidates may be maximizing valuable resources other than plurality, and this maximization can warrant strategies that diverge from the mean preference.

Thus, two candidates who maximize plurality may behave as if they maximized votes on issues that are salient to activists. And, in this manner, forces that proponents of the doctrine of responsible party government deem appropriate are generated. Nevertheless, distinct alternatives are only one element of this doctrine. A second important element is the requirement that these alternatives be clear. We turn now to an examination of the expectation of clarity.

[25]The notable exception is Gerald Kramer, "A Decision-Theoretic Analysis of a Problem in Political Campaigning," in J. L. Bernd, ed., *Mathematical Applications in Political Science,* vol. 2 (Dallas: SMU Press, 1966), pp. 137–160. For an application of Kramer's analysis see John C. Blydenburgh, "A Controlled Experiment to Measure the Effects of Personal Contact Campaigning," *Midwest Journal of Political Science,* vol. 15 (1971), pp. 365–381.

[26]"Majority Rule and the Representative System of Government," in E. Allardtand and Y. Littunen, eds., *Cleavages, Ideologies and Party Systems: Contributions to Comparative Political Sociology* (Helsinki: Transactions of the Westermarch Society, 1964), pp. 359, 376. Similarly, Morris Fiorina has shown that within marginal districts congressional candidates are further apart than are candidates from safe districts: Fiorina: "Representatives and Their Constituencies: A Decision-Theoretic Analysis" (unpublished Ph. D. dissertation, University of Rochester, 1972).

STRATEGIES INVOLVING RISK

To this point in our discussion the vector θ_j is a collection of precise and well-defined numbers. That is, citizens fail to perceive any ambiguity in the candidates' positions and act as if they know exactly the policies a candidate will adopt once elected. Doubtless, this assumption is not very restrictive in the case of such "issues" as partisan identification because a candidate's party typically is designated on the ballot. Nevertheless, it is often true that on many policy dimensions the policies candidates are likely to adopt if elected either are not readily ascertained or are inherently unknowable. Indeed, the candidates' positions are lotteries in which θ_j is represented by stochastic terms. Strategies involving such probabilistic considerations are termed risky strategies.

The importance of risky strategies to spatial analysis is suggested by Downs' proposition that "Ambiguity . . . increases the number of voters to whom a party may appeal . . . . Thus political rationality leads parties in a two-party system to becloud their policies in a fog of ambiguity."[27] If Downs is correct, a spatial analysis which assumes that θ_j possesses no stochastic elements neglects an imporant clue for understanding of the candidates' strategic environment. We examine Downs' proposition, then, more carefully in order to ascertain the conditions under which a candidate prefers a risky strategy to a certain strategy.

One counterexample to Downs' proposition is readily established. In a two-candidate contest where citizens have quadratic utility functions (A2), assume that the first candidate's strategy is θ_1, where θ_1 possesses no stochastic terms, and that the second candidate selects the strategy $\theta_2 = \theta_1 + \epsilon$, where ε is a vector of random variables. Thus, citizens must choose between a riskless strategy, θ_1, and a risky strategy, θ_2. If we now substitute θ_1 and θ_2 into expression (11.7)—the general form for a quadratic utility function—and calculate expected values, the expected utility a citizen associates with θ_1 is simply $U(x, \theta_1)$, whereas the expected utility associated with θ_2 becomes $U(x, \theta_1) - \sigma$, where σ is a positive number. Thus, every citizen prefers θ_1 to θ_2. This means that the strategy θ_2 is defeated by θ_1 in a majority vote.

Of course, this result does not imply that an equilibrium exists and, if one does exist, that it consists of pure (riskless) strategies. Some risky alternative other than θ_2 may defeat θ_1: if this is true for every certain strategy, then no equilibrium exists. A certain strategy can be defeated by a risky alternative and, as we have just established, a risky alternative is defeated by a certain strategy. Shepsle shows, however, that, for at least one set of conditions in which utility functions are concave, an equilibrium exists and it consists of a single certain strategy.[28] If all citizens vote and if competition is unidimensional, the median of $f(x)$ defeats all risky strategies.

[27]*An Economic Theory of Democracy*, p. 136.
[28]Kenneth Shepsle, "Parties, Voters, and the Risk Environment: A Mathematical Treatment

Thus, if citizens have concave utility functions—which is to say if they are risk-averse—Downs' proposition does not apply. Both candidates converge to the median [which is equivalent to the mean if $f(x)$ is symmetric] and neither candidate possesses any incentive to render his position ambiguous.

Concave utility functions, however, need not characterize citizens' preferences. They represent the preferences of citizens whose rate of change of dissatisfaction increases as policies become more distant from a most preferred policy. Other citizens, however, may regard all such unsatisfactory policies as approximately equally distasteful, in which case we represent their preferences by assumption A3—quasi-concave utility functions. And citizens with utility functions that can be characterized by A3 but not by A1 or A2 (concave) are said to be risk-acceptant over some interval of the strategy space.[29] Returning then to Downs' proposition, Shepsle shows that if "almost all" voters are risk-acceptant in some interval containing the median of $f(x)$, a risky strategy over this interval defeats the certain strategy at the median.[30] Thus, Downs' proposition about the vulnerability of the median to a risky strategy is correct for at least one condition.

Reconsidering the doctrine of responsible party government, then, we find that unlimited majority rule can provide unambiguous positions. But we find also that this is not a necessary feature of elections, since a risky strategy might defeat a riskless strategy if utility functions are not concave. In conjunction with our discussion of the previous section, then, we conclude that the requirement that candidates present the electorate with clear and distinct choices may require the candidates to act contrary to their goal of winning elections. And if so, then the ideal of responsible party government is unobtainable in a world of rational actors.

MULTIPARTY SYSTEMS AND COALITION FORMATION

Our discussion of risky strategies, as well as our discussion of the controversy over responsible parties, assumes that only two candidates compete. Clearly,

---

of Electoral Competition Under Uncertainty," in Niemi and Weisberg, *Probability Models of Collective Decision-Making*, and "Uncertainty and Electoral Competition: The Search for Equilibria" (paper presented at the MSSB Advanced Research Seminar in Mathematical Theory of Collective Decisions, Hilton Head, S. C., August 1971). See also Shepsle, "The Strategy of Ambiguity: Uncertainty in Electoral Competition," *American Political Science Review* (forthcoming).

[29]See our discussion of risk-averse and risk-acceptant utility functions in Chapter 3.

[30]"Parties, Voters, and the Risk Environment." An interesting footnote to the analysis of risky strategies is that while an equilibrium may exist if we permit only certain (riskless) strategies, the inclusion of risky strategies may upset this equilibrium entirely and yield complete disequilibrium. Shepsle conjectures that if "almost all" voters are risk-acceptant, an equilibrium in risky strategies exists. (In a private communication, however, Shepsle indicates that he now believes this conjecture to be incompletely specified. Clearly, then, a great deal of additional research must be undertaken before risky strategies can be adequately understood.)

many important features of electoral competition are thereby ignored. If more than two candidates compete, we must reconsider both citizens' decision rules for choosing candidates and their rules for choosing to participate. Furthermore, we must analyze anew the candidates' strategic considerations. Finally, we must explore the possibility that candidates or their parties form coalitions either during the election or after it in legislatures.

Turning first to citizens' decisions, we observe that, in a two-candidate election with majority rule, if a citizen votes, his choice is a relatively simple one: he votes for the candidate whose policies he prefers. This decision rule follows logically from the postulate of rationality and is insensitive to the electoral viabilities of the candidates.[31] In multiparty systems, however, the postulate of rationality may dictate that some citizens vote for their second (or third, etc.) choice. To see this, consider, first, systems in which candidates must have a plurality to win (i.e., single-member district systems). Certainly, a citizen desires to have his most preferred candidate win. But what if this candidate is hopelessly behind his opponents and has virtually no chance of being elected? Should the citizen, if he votes, vote for the almost certain loser? The answer to this question usually is no. The postulate of rationality dictates that citizens vote to maximize expected utility, and only in two-candidate contests does this decision-rule unequivocally imply voting for the most preferred candidate.[32] If three candidates compete, for example, and if the citizen's most preferred

---

[31]Let P_{ij} denote the probability that candidate i wins if the citizen votes for candidate j, where $i, j = 0$, 1, or 2, where $i = 0$ denotes "candidates 1 and 2 tie," and where $j = 0$ denotes "the citizen abstains." Also, let U_i denote the utility the citizen associates with outcome i. The expected utility of voting for candidate 1 is

$$E(a_1) = P_{01}U_0 + P_{11}U_1 + P_{21}U_2.$$

If $U_0 = (U_1 + U_2)/2$—if the utility of a tie equals the average of the utilities associated with the candidates involved in the tie—and if $P_{01} = 1 - P_{11} - P_{21}$, then we have

$$E(a_1) = (1 - P_{11} - P_{21})\left(\frac{U_1 + U_2}{2}\right) + P_{11}U_1 + P_{21}U_2$$

$$= \left(\frac{U_1 + U_2}{2}\right) + P_{11}\left(\frac{2U_1 - U_1 - U_2}{2}\right) - P_{21}\left(\frac{U_1 + U_2 - 2U_2}{2}\right)$$

$$= \left(\frac{U_1 + U_2}{2}\right) + (P_{11} - P_{21})\left(\frac{U_1 - U_2}{2}\right).$$

Similarly, for $E(a_2)$ we get

$$E(a_2) = \left(\frac{U_1 + U_2}{2}\right) + (P_{12} - P_{22})\left(\frac{U_1 - U_2}{2}\right).$$

If the citizen votes, he votes for candidate 1 if and only if $E(a_1) > E(a_2)$, which, with suitable cancellations and algebraic manipulations, can be restated as

$$(P_{11} + P_{22} - P_{12} - P_{21})\left(\frac{U_1 - U_2}{2}\right) > 0.$$

Clearly, now, $P_{11} > P_{12}$, because, if the citizen shifts from voting for candidate 2 to voting for candidate 1, the probability that candidate 1 wins increases (assuming, of course, that negative bandwagon effects do not exist). Similarly, $P_{22} > P_{21}$. Thus, $(P_{11} + P_{22} - P_{12} - P_{21}) > 0$, in which case $E(a_1)$ is greater than $E(a_2)$ if and only if $(U_1 - U_2)/2 > 0$—if and only if $U_1 > U_2$. Consequently, the citizen never votes for candidate 1 if he prefers candidate 2—if he votes, he votes only for the candidate he prefers.

[32]See note 14, Chapter 3, page 64, for the debate between Casstevens and Kramer.

candidate has no chance of attaining a positive plurality, the citizen maximizes his expected utility by voting for his second choice because this act diminishes the chances of the candidate he least prefers. While such considerations can be modeled and explored, they are not readily incorporated into a tractable spatial model.[33] Hence, little is known about the candidates' strategic incentives if such considerations are relevant.

A spatial analysis of multicandidate elections is rendered difficult, moreover, by a second feature of multiparty politics—coalitions. If parties form coalitions in legislatures and if citizens are aware of such possbilities, a vote does not simply increase the probability that a candidate is elected. A vote also changes

[33]See Robin Farquharson, *Theory of Voting* (New Haven: Yale University Press, 1969), and Gerald Kramer, "Sophisticated Voting over Multidimensional Choice Spaces" (paper presented at MSSB conference, Hilton Head, S. C., 1971) for the analysis of a different but related problem in the theory of voting that might provide a means of modeling multicandidate elections spatially. Farquharson distinguishes between sincere and sophisticated voting. Reviewing this distinction, which is set forth in Chapter 4, with sincere voting a citizen ignores the effect that his choice might have on the choices of others and he simply votes for his most preferred alternative. This is the assumption we make, for example, in the analysis of voting in Chapter 3, and which is a reasonable assumption for large electorates. With sophisticated voting, however, a citizen assumes that his choice can affect the choices of others (therefore, it is more likely to occur in smaller voting bodies). That is, the citizen assumes that all choices are interdependent, so that voting is an n-person (perhaps noncooperative) game. To illustrate the distinction between sincere and sophisticated voting, assume that the electorate consists of three citizens, that one of three alternative motions must be selected, and that the citizens' preferences over these motions yield the standard example of the paradox of voting under majority rule, i.e.,

		Preference
	1	$a_1 \rightarrow a_2 \rightarrow a_3$
Citizen	*2*	$a_3 \rightarrow a_1 \rightarrow a_2$
	3	$a_2 \rightarrow a_3 \rightarrow a_1$

so that a_1 defeats a_2, a_2 defeats a_3, and a_3 defeats a_1 in a majority vote. Assume now that the voting procedure places a_1 against a_2 and the winner against a_3. If all citizens vote sincerely, a_1 defeats a_2 and a_3 defeats a_1, so a_3 is the social choice. Suppose, however, that citizen 1 chooses a_2 over a_1; a_2 then is the social choice. Thus, by disguising his true preference, citizen 1 can bring about a more favored outcome, a_2 rather than a_3. Of course, citizens 2 and 3 can anticipate 1's deception, in which case voting becomes a three-person noncooperative game that may or may not possess pure minimax strategy solutions; i.e., the minimax choice for a citizen might be to vote sincerely, to vote for a second or third choice, or to choose randomly. Farquharson analyzes such situations for three alternatives and for six common voting procedures—including plurality voting. Kramer extends Farquharson's analysis and develops a sufficient condition for the existence of a majority-rule equilibrium in a multidimensional issue space. Kramer assumes that all citizens vote and that voting is sophisticated. His equilibrium condition is (1) utility functions are separable so that if $U(\theta)$ is the utility the citizen associates with θ, $U(\theta) = u(\theta_1) + u(\theta_2) + \ldots + u(\theta_n)$, where θ_i denotes the position of the alternative on issue i, and (2) votes are taken separately on each issue so that θ' defeats θ'' if and only if θ' defeats θ'' for all i.

the probability that the candidate and his party are included in some legislative coalition. Thus, the effect of a citizen's vote on policy is determined both by the electoral mechanism and by the nature of coalition processes. Clearly, then, a citizen's voting calculus is, in its abstract form, complex.

We can attempt to simplify this calculus by assuming that citizens act as if they believed that legislative coalition processes conform to our models of coalition formation. For example, we can assume that citizens vote in accordance with the proposition that minimal winning coalitions form. Such assumptions are worth pursuing, since totally unanticipated conclusions—conclusions that lead us to question some of our preconceived notions about voting in multiparty systems—can be derived from them. For example, if citizens believe that minimal winning coalitions form in legislatures and if the election is closely contested by three candidates, citizens should vote for their *least* preferred candidate.[34]

Whether or not citizens behave as if they made the difficult calculations implied by coalition politics is an unanswered empirical question.[35] It is likely that citizens employ simplified decision rules, but the nature of such rules also awaits empirical determination.

Difficult as it is to understand citizens' behavior in multiparty politics, it is equally difficult to understand candidates' behavior. Nevertheless, if some simplifying assumptions are imposed, we can understand some features of the candidates' spatial strategies. Suppose, for example, that the candidates maximize votes (D2), that competition is unidimensional, that abstention is caused by alienation (B3), and that if a citizen votes, he votes sincerely—i.e., he votes for his preferred candidate. For such conditions, Downs asserts that "parties in a multiparty system try to remain as ideologically distinct from each other as possible."[36] From the result, however, that two vote-maximizing candidates seek to converge to the mean if $f(x)$ is a symmetric unimodal density and if saliency is either high or low, it is reasonable to conjecture that candidates in a multiparty system seek to converge to spatial positions near the mean for similar conditions. If this is correct, Downs' proposition is not general. This result, moreover, corresponds to some intuitive notions: If saliency is low, the issue can be regarded as relatively unimportant, in which case the candidates simply seek safe positions, and the safest position is the mean. Second, if saliency is high, the issue can be regarded as critical, in which case each candidate seeks to adopt the mean while driving all opponents from it. Thus, if saliency is low, a rather noncompetitive convergence occurs, and if saliency is high, a highly competitive fight near the mean results.

[34]Peter H. Aranson, "Political Participation in Alternative Election Systems" (paper presented at the American Political Science Association Convention, Chicago, 1971). See also Richard J. Trilling, "Coalition Government, Political Parties, and the Rational Voter" (unpublished Ph. D. dissertation, University of Wisconsin, 1970).

[35]Howard Rosenthal, "A Study of the Effects of Coalitions on Voting Behavior" (Carnegie-Mellon University, GSIA, 1970).

[36]*An Economic Theory of Democracy*, pp. 115, 126–127.

Of course, such factors as misperception and the molasses-like variability of parameters in real elections typically preclude the absolute convergence of candidates in a multiparty system. Thus, some differences among all candidates and parties are likely to exist. Certainly a candidate can attempt to convince an electorate that he, and not some opponent, is at the mean; and such attempts are likely to be successful for some voters. Nevertheless, some forces for non-convergence can be culled directly from spatial analysis. For example, if saliency is at some intermediate value for the case we examine above, the candidates do not converge. Tullock, moreover, demonstrates that the number of issues is an important factor in determining whether or not vote-maximizing candidates converge.[37] We know that such candidates converge to the mean if $f(x)$ is unidimensional, if all citizens vote, and if they vote sincerely. Tullock, however, considers an election in which three candidates compete and assumes that the electorate's preferences are characterized by *two* issues and a symmetric density. He then shows that, rather than converging to the mean, the equilibrium is one in which the three candidates locate themselves symmetrically about but not at the mean. Given, then, this dependence of the location of equilibria on saliency and on the number of issues, it is evident that much difficult research remains before we can begin to answer even some simple questions about competition in multiparty systems.

The difficulties inherent in the conduct of this research are compounded, moreover, by the fact that elections often constitute only the first stage in the selection of a government. A second stage is the formation of coalitions in legislatures. Earlier we observe that the possibility that a government is a coalition of parties complicates a voter's decision, and we suggest that at least one feature of coalitions—their tendency towards minimal winning size—can be used by citizens to narrow the range of potential coalitions. Similarly, the modifications of the size principle that we review in Chapter 7 might also be used by citizens to simplify choice.

These modifications were not proposed, however, to explain citizens' choices but rather to explain the actions of parties; and as such they represent an extension of spatial analysis. First, the modifications of the minimal-winning-size hypothesis that Axelrod and De Swaan propose are stated in spatial terms.[38] Briefly, they hypothesize that parties negotiate only with spatially adjacent parties and that the resultant government coalition tends to minimize the total spatial distance among its members. The logic of the first part of this hypothesis is that, in addition to simply winning, parties seek to win something in the form of policy outputs. But in forming a coalition, parties must compromise their

[37] *Toward a Mathematics of Politics,* p. 55.

[38] Robert Axelrod, *Conflict of Interest* (Chicago: Markham, 1970); Abraham De Swaan, "An Empirical Model of Coalition-Formation as an N-Person Game of Policy Distance Minimization," in Sven Groennings, E. W. Kelley, and Michael Leiserson, eds., *The Study of Coalition Behavior* (New York: Holt, Rinehart and Winston, 1970), pp. 424–444. See also Howard Rosenthal, "Voting and Coalition Models in Election Simulation," in W. Coplin, ed., *Simulations and the Study of Politics* (Chicago: Markham, 1968).

programs, and the greater the spatial distance between two parties the more each must compromise in order to form a coalition. Thus, to minimize the amount of compromise, i.e., to maximize the value of a coalition, parties prefer to negotiate with spatially adjacent parties. The second part of this hypothesis is a logical extension of the first part, with the additional observation that the smaller the total distance among the members of a coalition the more stable is that coalition. Spatial distance and, therefore, diversity of policy positions increase the possibility that the coalition is easily disrupted. Hence, coalitions of minimal distance are more durable than less spatially compact coalitions.

Clearly, the logic of this hypothesis has much in common with that of the proposition that minimal winning coalitions occur: both are concerned with the maximization of payoffs in terms of policy. Despite this similarity, there is one important difference. Specifically, the criterion of minimal spatial distance (connected coalitions) can yield coalitions larger than minimal size, and the minimal-winning-size criterion can yield disconnected coalitions. For example, the closest available party may be larger than necessary to form a winning coalition, whereas a more distant party may be just large enough. Of course, if we believe that both criteria influence coalition-formation processes, we might attempt a synthesis thus: among the set of connected coalitions the one of smallest size forms, or among the set of minimal winning coalitions the one that minimizes total spatial distance forms. Any such synthesis (as well as the modification of the size principle) is, however, entirely *ad hoc*—so that, while it might account for coalitions in one society, there is no reason to suppose that it accounts for coalitions in another.

It may be possible, though, to deduce some generalizations from a spatial perspective. For example, assuming (1) that every coalition can be denoted by a spatial position, (2) that the spatial position of a coalition is a function of the sizes and spatial positions of its members, and (3) that a preferred spatial position (e.g., the electoral equilibrium) and a utility function can be ascribed to each party, then we can deduce the utility each party associates with each coalition. That is, if s_j denotes the number of seats and θ_j the spatial position of party j, then

$$\theta_S = F(s_j, \theta_j, j \in S),$$

where θ_S is the spatial position of coalition S.[39] We can then associate with each coalition the imputation,

[39]For example, the function F might simply take θ_S as the convex combination of the θ_j's, $j \in S$. I.e.,

$$\theta_S = \sum_{j \in S} \lambda_j \theta_j, \qquad 0 \leq \lambda_j \leq 1, \quad \sum_{j \in S} \lambda_j = 1,$$

where the weight assigned to each party in S, λ_j, is the relative size of party j to the coalition S, i.e.,

$$\lambda_i = \frac{s_j}{\sum_{S} s_j}.$$

Other functions can, of course, be imagined, and we offer this one only as an illustration.

$$[U(\theta_1, \theta_S), \ U(\theta_2, \theta_S), \ \ldots, \ U(\theta_n, \theta_S)],$$

where $U(\theta_j, \theta_S)$ denotes the utility party j associates with coalition S. Finally, if coalitions are interpreted as alternatives, parties as weighted voters (where their weights are the numbers of seats they control), and if party j votes for coalition S over S' if $U(\theta_j, \theta_S) > U(\theta_j, \theta_{S'})$, we can ascertain whether or not a majority winner exists. If it exists, then that coalition is the one that we predict will form. If no majority winner exists—if an intransitivity exists—then we can at best narrow the prediction to a subset of coalitions.

To our knowledge, no one has yet approached coalition formation from this perspective, and so we do not know if these predictions conform to the minimal-size hypothesis, to the modifications of this hypothesis, or to some synthesis. There is, however, some reason for believing that this is a fruitful approach. Specifically, we note that

(1) as the number of parties increases, the number of possible winning coalitions increases, *ceteris paribus:*

(2) as factionalism increases, the number of possible winning coalitions increases, *ceteris paribus.*[40]

Calculations of the probability that a majority winner exists (see Chapter 4) indicate that this probability decreases as the number of alternatives increases. Consequently, one implication of (1) and (2) is that a coalition that can defeat all alternative coalitions in a majority vote is less likely to exist as the number of parties increases or as factionalism increases. Finally, the stability of a coalition government should be greatest whenever it represents a coalition that is a majority winner in the legislature because no other coalition can upset it, in which case stability should correlate negatively with the number of parties and the level of factionalism in the legislature. This is the conclusion that Taylor and Herman strongly support empirically.[41]

WELFARE CONSIDERATIONS

Elections, like markets, aggregate individual preferences into a social choice. The advantage of markets is that if certain assumptions are satisfied, the allocations made by them are Pareto-optimal and are secured with minimal organizational cost. Since political mechanisms such as elections are used, however, to supplant or to modify market allocations, it is appropriate to conclude

[40]By factionalism we mean, roughly, the disparity in the distribution of seats among the parties. Thus, if factionalism is minimized, i.e., if one party controls all of the seats, only one winning "coalition" exists. If factionalism is maximized, i.e., if all parties control the same number of seats, a maximum number of winning coalitions exist.

[41]Michael Taylor and V. M. Herman, "Party Systems and Government Stability," *American Political Science Review*, vol. 65 (March 1971), pp. 28–37.

our review of spatial theory by investigating the social-welfare properties of competitive elections.

The simplest and most basic comparison of markets and elections consists of ascertaining whether or not elections yield Pareto-optimal outcomes. This comparison can be conducted if we take spatial models as our descriptions of perfectly competitive elections and if we let either candidate's equilibrium strategy be the outcome of the election.[42] While not all possible combinations of assumptions have been analyzed, the general finding thus far is that such elections are efficient in the sense that the outcomes corresponding to competitive equilibria are Pareto-optimal.[43] Hence, in their abstract descriptions, markets do not seem to possess an inherent advantage over elections.

To arrive at this conclusion, however, it is necessary to ignore the possibility that pure or risky minimax strategies do not exist, and also to impose the unrealistic assumption that candidates employ mixed strategies if such strategies are minimax. Suppose instead that candidates adjust their strategies sequentially whenever a pure or risky strategy equilibrium does not exist, so that, while the adjustment process is terminated only because campaigns cannot endure forever, each candidate is always identified with some pure or risky strategy. The question now is: Must a candidate select a Pareto-optimal strategy to defeat his opponent if this opponent selects a Pareto-optimal strategy? To answer this question we reconstruct Figure 4.5, which in Chapter 4 demonstrates the absence of a majority-rule equilibrium in a multidimensional world. In Figure 12.5 we assume two issues and three voters, denoting the voters' most preferred positions by x_1, x_2, and x_3, respectively. Additionally, we illustrate some indifference contours for each voter, which, for simplicity, are concentric circles so that the set of Pareto-optimal strategies is composed of the triangle connecting x_1, x_2, and x_3 and all the interior points of this triangle. Assume now that the first candidate adopts some Pareto-optimal strategy, say θ^*. Obviously, since no majority-rule equilibrium exists, some other strategy defeats θ^* —say θ^{**}. But the position θ^{***} also defeats θ^*, which is to say that θ^* is defeated by a non-Pareto-optimal strategy. And if the second candidate adopts θ^{***}, the social choice provided by the election is not op-

---

[42]Hence, if this equilibrium is a pure strategy, the outcome is this strategy; if the equilibrium is a risky strategy, the outcome can be interpreted to be either this risk or the particular pure strategy the victorious candidate adopts after the election. If neither a pure nor a risky equilibrium strategy exists, suppose, for a complete argument, that a mixed minimax strategy does exist. The outcome, then, is the particular pure strategy the victorious candidate adopts prior to the balloting according to the minimax criterion.

[43]Martin Shubik, "A Two Party System, General Equilibrium and the Voter's Paradox," *Zeitschrift fur Nationalokonomie,* vol. 28 (1968), pp. 341–354; and Peter C. Ordeshook, "Pareto Optimality in Electoral Competition," *American Political Science Review,* vol. 65 (1971), pp. 1141–1145. In "Voting, or a Price System in a Competitive Market Structure," *American Political Science Review,* vol. 64 (March 1970), pp. 179–181, Shubik attempts to construct a situation in which a market is efficient but an election is not. It is readily shown, however (see Ordeshook, "Pareto Optimality in Electoral Competition," above), that Shubik's analysis entails a confusion between risky and mixed strategies and that Pareto-optimal outcomes prevail in his example.

timal. Thus, we cannot guarantee that the election yields a Pareto-optimal outcome.

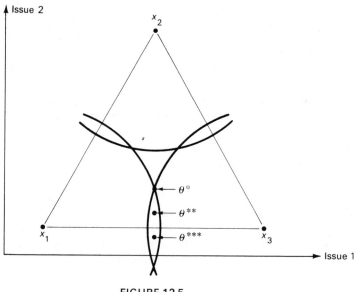

FIGURE 12.5

Having thus qualified our conclusion that competitive elections are efficient, we note one potential advantage of elections over markets: although electoral outcomes are Pareto-optimal for certain only if a pure or a risky strategy equilibrium exists, elections are not limited, as are markets, to the allocation of goods of a particular type. As we point out in Chapter 9, markets generally fail to account efficiently for the externalities associated with public goods. But if an equilibrium exists, the competitive election yields Pareto-optimal allocations of public goods.

This conclusion may, of course, appear unwarranted. In models of perfectly competitive elections the candidates know the electorate's preferences, whereas the definition of perfectly competitive markets does not impose the condition that firms know the tastes of every consumer. Rather, Pareto-optimality is attained in markets by a Darwinian process: inefficient firms are displaced by efficient ones, so that in the long run or on the average the market is Pareto-optimal. The assumption of perfect information, then, appears to give elections an advantage over markets—an advantage that is not likely to exist in the real world.[44] Nevertheless, an election can also be regarded as a Darwinian process, a process in which inefficient candidates are displaced in the long

[44]See, for example, Howard R. Bowen, "The Interpretation of Voting in the Allocation of Economic Resources," *Quarterly Journal of Economics*, vol. 58 (November 1943), pp. 27–48.

run or on the average by those who adopt equilibrium strategies.[45] Such an interpretation might seem to be tortured for, say, presidential elections—elections normally consisting of two or three candidates competing every four years—where averages are of little statistical significance. But even for such contests candidates are selected by a "survival of the fittest" process. Typically, candidates must rise through the party hierarchy, win several election contests for lesser offices, secure the support of numerous activists and professionals, and survive several primary elections and convention battles. Additionally, the early stages of a campaign consist of pretesting alternative promises and ascertaining the strategy that yields the most favored response. This is not to suggest that elections invariably provide Pareto-optimal social choices (any more than real markets for private goods provide such choices) because we neglect such factors as the inability of citizens to learn much about public policies, the inability of candidates to know the preferences of citizens, and the inability of candidates to implement programs once elected. The argument is simply that an ideal description of electoral competition can be constructed which is no less acceptable than the description of perfectly competitive markets and in which the forces for Pareto-optimal allocations are evident.

Summarizing the comparison of perfectly competitive markets and elections, the advantage of such markets is that they provide Pareto-optimal allocations of private goods while they minimize the requirements on information; perfectly competitive elections, while perhaps imposing greater information requirements, can provide Pareto-optimal allocations of public as well as private goods.

Recall from Chapter 9, however, that the criterion of efficiency provided by the notion of Pareto-optimality is a weak criterion of fairness since it includes many allocations that are not fair by more complex standards. That is, a market can be efficient while reinforcing an initial distribution of resources in which wealth and well-being are concentrated in the hands of a few. Similarly, an election can be efficient while being used by a majority to expropriate the wealth of a minority or to deny a minority its civil liberties. It is an interesting exercise, then, to evaluate competitive elections by some criterion in addition to that of Pareto optimality.

Of course, any policy can be justified with a value judgment that places a positive value on that policy alone. Consider, however, a more general situation in which the society is governed by an omniscient and beneficent dictator faced with the task of selecting the "best" policies for his country. The dictator should realize that in any nontrivial situation there is no possibility of satisfying everyone, so he must select some scheme for evaluating the relative importance of the society's citizens—some scheme for making interpersonal comparisons of utility. Suppose that the dictator decides to admit such comparisons as legitimate and meaningful, and to weight everyone equally. These

[45]See William H. Riker, *The Theory of Political Coalitions,* chap. 1.

judgments imply that the dictator assumes that all citizens' utility functions are identical in form and that the best policies are those which maximize the total utility of the society. If it is the case now that citizens' utility functions are concave and symmetric (A2) and $f(x)$ is symmetric, then the beneficent dictator accomplishes his objective by selecting a position identical to the average desires of the population, so he selects the mean.[46] Hence, competitive conditions that cause the candidates of two parties to converge to the mean result in the electoral process producing the kind of result that a beneficent dictator would choose.

The beneficent dictator's preference for the mean is, in fact, more pervasive than this example suggests. Instead of weighting each citizen identically, assume that a citizen who prefers the position x is assigned the weight $w(x)$. Assume that $w(x)$ is not necessarily equal to $w(x')$ if $x \neq x'$, but let the function $w(x)$ be symmetric about the mean of $f(x)$ so that $w(x) = w(-x)$ if the mean is zero. Two general forms of the weighting function, $w(x)$, then, are of interest here. First, the beneficent dictator might assign more importance to those in the "middle" than to those who hold extreme positions; in this instance $w(x)$ is said to be *unimodal*. Second, the dictator might weight "liberals" and "conservatives" more heavily than "moderates"; in this instance $w(x)$ is *not unimodal*. With these assumptions the dictator's preferences are presented in Table 12.3.[47]

TABLE 12.3

Dictator's Preference

$f(x)$	A2 (CONCAVE UTILITY FUNCTIONS)		A3 (QUASI-CONCAVE UTILITY FUNCTIONS)	
	$w(x)$ UNIMODAL	OTHERWISE	$w(x)$ UNIMODAL	OTHERWISE
SYMMETRIC UNIMODAL	Mean	Mean	Mean	No general solution
SYMMETRIC BIMODAL	Mean	Mean	No general solution	No general solution

[46]Otto A. Davis and M. J. Hinich, "A Mathematical Model of Policy Formation in a Democratic Society," in J. S. Bernd, ed., *Mathematical Applications in Political Science*, vol. 2, pp. 175–208.

[47]Melvin J. Hinich and Peter C. Ordeshook, "Social Welfare and Electoral Competition in Democratic Societies," *Public Choice*, vol. 11 (Fall 1971), pp. 73–87. Also relevant are the essays by Frank DeMeyer and Charles R. Plott, "A Welfare Function Using 'Relative Intensity' of

Thus, *if the citizens' utility functions are concave and symmetric* (*A2*), *the dictator selects the mean for all symmetric* $f(x)$ *and* $w(x)$. Alternatively, if utility functions are both marginally increasing and marginally decreasing as well as symmetric (A3), no general solution exists [unless $f(x)$ and $w(x)$ are both unimodal]. The social-welfare "optimality" of the mean, therefore, is sensitive to the form of the citizens' utility functions, as well as their density of preferences. The point here, however, is that in a variety of situations—including bimodal densities with a variety of ethical assumptions arbitrarily assigned—including weighting citizens at the mean less heavily than those at the extremes—the mean appears to be a desirable point. Returning, then, to the controversy surrounding the doctrine of responsible parties, we find that, contrary to this doctrine, forces that cause candidates to converge toward the mean, rather than recognizing differences in opinion, are not necessarily "bad" and, in the majority of the cases above, are positively "good" if one is willing to accept the assumptions.

Preference," *Quarterly Journal of Economics*, vol. 85 (February 1971), pp. 179–186; and John C. Harsanyi, "Cardinal Welfare, Individualistic Ethics, and Interpersonal Comparisons of Utility," *Journal of Political Economy*, vol. 63 (1955), pp. 309–321.

Index of Names

377

Index of Subjects